FRENCH-ENGLISH COMMERCIAL DICTIONARY
ENGLISH-FRENCH INDEX

For
Michèle and Gérard Larrousse
Olivia and Juan Miguel
Aurelio Cid Acedo
Rémy Paindavoine
Richard Johnson
Barbara Wright
Susan Bowie
James Fife
Samson Hu
Marius
and
June

French-English
COMMERCIAL DICTIONARY
English-French Index

GEORGES LANNOIS

MAX PARRISH & CO. LTD.
LONDON

MAX PARRISH & CO. LTD.
2 PORTMAN STREET
LONDON W.1

Printed in Great Britain by
R. & R. Clark, Ltd., Edinburgh

CONTENTS

LIST OF ABBREVIATIONS

adj	adjective	n	noun
adv	adverb	o.s.	oneself
Amer.	American	Pej.	Pejorative
Belg.	Belgium, Belgian *Belgique, Belge*	Pers.	Person *Personne*
Can.	Canada, Canadian *Canada, Canadien*	pl.	plural *pluriel*
cin.	cinema	pr.	pronoun *pronom*
Coll.	Colloquial		
conj.	conjunction *conjonction*	pref.	prefix *préfixe*
f	feminine *féminin*	pres. part.	present participle
Fam.	*Familier*	qqch.	*quelque chose*
Fig.	Figurative(ly)	qqun	*quelqu'un*
Fr.	France, French *France, Français*	Rail.	Railways
		sing.	singular *singulier*
G.B.	Great Britain *Grande-Bretagne*	sl.	slang
inf.	infinitive *infinitif*	St. Ex.	Stock Exchange
		sth.	something
inv.	invariable	Swi.	Switzerland, Swiss *Suisse*
lat.	latin		
Leg.	Legal *Légal*	Tech.	Technical *Technique*
lit.	literally *littéralement*	tel.	telephone
		vb	verb *verbe*
loc.	locution		
m	masculine		

. . . . . indicates that the word is part of a compound one and cannot be used on its own.

à *prép*	1	at, in
— la douzaine	2	by the dozen
— Londres	3	in London
— l'usine	4	ex works
— quai	5	at docks
abaisser *vb*	6	to lower, to reduce; to bring down (a figure)
abandonner *vb*	7	to give up, to drop (idea); relinquish (option)
abattement *m*	8	abatement
— à la base	9	personal allowance
abîmé *adj*	10	spoiled, damaged
abîmer *vb*	11	to spoil, ruin
s'—	12	to go bad, to get spoiled
abonné *n*	13	subscriber (to papers, the telephone); consumer (of gas, etc.)
abonnement *m*	14	subscription; season ticket
souscrire un —	15	to take out a subscription
abonner *vb*	16	to get a subscription for (s.o.)
s'—	17	to subscribe (to a paper, *à un journal*), to become a subscriber (to *à*)
abordable *adj*	18	[price] reasonable
aboutir *vb*	19	to lead to, to end at
faire — qqch.	20	to bring sth. to a successful issue
leurs démarches n'ont pas abouti	21	their efforts were unsuccessful
n'— à rien	22	to come to nothing
ne pas —	23	to fail; to fall through
aboutissement *m*	24	outcome, result
abroger *vb*	25	to abrogate, repeal; to rescind, revoke
absence *f*	26	absence
— motivée	27	excused —
en l'— de	28	in the — of
abus *m*	29	1 abuse
	30	2 misuse
— de confiance	31	breach of trust
accaparement *m*	32	cornering, buying up
accaparer *vb*	33	to corner, to buy up, to hoard; to monopolize
accapareur *m*	34	monopolist
accélérer *vb*	35	to speed up, to expedite

1

accent *m*	1	accent
mettre l'— sur	2	to stress
accentuer *vb*	3	to stress; to accentuate (a change or fashion)
acceptation *f*	4	acceptance
— à découvert	5	uncovered —
— conditionnelle	6	qualified —
— de cautionnement	7	collateral —
— de complaisance	8	accommodation —
— en blanc	9	blank —
— partielle	10	partial —
— sans réserves	11	general —
compte d'—	12	— account
débiteurs par —	13	liabilities of customer
délai d'—	14	term of —
envoyer à l'—	15	to send out for
faute d'—	16	in default of, for lack of
munir de l'—	17	to accept
présenter à l'—	18	to present for —
refus d'—	19	non acceptance, refusal to accept
revêtir de l'—	20	to accept
soigner l'—	21	to procure —
accommodement *m*	22	arrangement; compromise
accommoder *vb*	23	to accommodate, to adjust
s'— de	24	to make shift with
accompagnement *m*	25	accompaniment
feuille d'—	26	covering letter
accord *m*	27	agreement
d'—!	28	O.K.!, Fair enough!
d'— avec	29	in — with
d'un commun —	30	by common/mutual consent
l'— s'est fait sur tous les points	31	— was reached on all points
mettre d'—	32	to reconcile (two points of view)
n'être pas d'—	33	to disagree
tomber d'—	34	to agree on sth.
accoster *vb*	35	to come alongside
accréditer *vb*	36	to accredit; to confirm
s'—	37	to gain credence
accréditeur *m*	38	guarantor
accréditif *adj*	39	credit
— rotatif	40	revolving —

2

— rotatif cumulatif	1	cumulative revolving —
accroissement *m*	2	increase, rise; growth
— de la production	3	increase of production
taux d'—	4	rate of increase/of growth
accueil *m*	5	reception, welcome
faire bon — à une traite	6	to honour/meet a draft
acculer *vb*	7	to corner; to bring to bay
accusé *m* **de réception**	8	acknowledgment (of a letter, payment, etc.)
accuser *vb*	9	to indicate
— une perte/hausse/ baisse	10	to show a loss/rise/fall
achalandage *m*	11	custom, trade; goodwill
achat *m*	12	purchase
— à découvert [en Bourse]	13	bull —
— à terme	14	— on credit
— à terme ferme	15	— for settlement during specified periods
— au comptant	16	cash —
— ferme	17	firm —
—s de placement	18	buying for investment purposes
— sur échantillon	19	— against sample
contrat d'—	20	purchasing contract
faire des	21	to go shopping
note d'—	22	bought note
pouvoir d'—	23	purchasing power
prix d'—	24	— price
acheminement *m*	25	progression; [mail] handling; [goods] forwarding, routing
acheminer *vb*	26	to handle (mail)
acheter *vb*	27	to buy
— à la baisse	28	— on a fall
— à la hausse	29	— on a rise
— à tempérament	30	— by instalments
— à terme	31	— forward; — for the settlement
— (au) comptant	32	— for cash
— ferme	33	— firm
— qqun.	34	to bribe s.o.
acheteur, —se *n*	35	buyer
au gré de l'—	36	at —'s option
marché des —s	37	—s' market

position —	1	bull position
accompte m	2	instalment, deposit, down-payment, cash down
donner un —	3	to pay (a sum) on account
verser un —	4	to pay a deposit
acquéreur m	5	purchaser, buyer
acquérir vb	6	to acquire, buy; to obtain, get
— de l'influence	7	to gain influence
acquêts n.m.pl.	8	dowry, property acquired in common
acquis adj	9	acquired, secured
bien mal —	10	ill-gotten goods
mal —	11	ill-gotten
tenir pour —	12	to take for granted
acquisition f	13	acquisition, purchase
faire l'— de	14	to purchase, acquire
une nouvelle —	15	a new asset (to a firm, etc.)
acquit m	16	receipt, discharge
— -à-caution	17	bond/transhipment note
— de douane	18	custom house receipt
— de transit	19	transit bond
pour —	20	paid/received with thanks
acquittement m	21	1 [Lég.] acquittal
	22	2 discharge, payment
acquitter vb	23	1 [Lég.] to acquit
	24	2 to pay, discharge
— une dette	25	to pay (off) a debt
— une facture	26	to receipt an invoice
acre m [=4,840 sq. yards]	27	acre
acte m	28	deed
— constitutif	29	— of partnership
— de cautionnement	30	surety bond
— de cession	31	— of conveyance/of transfer
— de décès	32	death certificate
— de naissance	33	birth certificate
— de protêt	34	— of protest
— de vente	35	sale contract
— judiciaire	36	writ
— sous seing privé	37	— under private seal
donner — de	38	to acknowledge officially
faire — d'héritier	39	to claim the estate
rédiger un —	40	to draw up a document
actif m	41	assets

4

— et passif	1	— and liabilities
— immobilisé	2	fixed —
—s donnés en garantie	3	— pledged as collateral
à son —	4	to his credit
côté de l'—	5	— side
passer à l'—	6	to put to the credit side
action *f*	7	share
— à la souche	8	unissued —
— au porteur	9	bearer —
— à vote plural	10	— with plural voting rights
— bénéficiaire	11	participating —
— de numéraire	12	cash —
— de préférence	13	preferred —
— de priorité cumulative	14	cumulative preference —
— différée	15	deferred —
— entièrement libérée	16	fully paid —
— gratuite	17	bonus —
— minière	18	mining —
— nominative	19	registered —
— ordinaire	20	ordinary —
— privilégiée	21	preference —
— privilégiée participante	22	participating preferred —
— sans montant nominal	23	— without par value, no par value —
— souscrite	24	— applied for/subscribed
— statutaire	25	qualifying —
à raison d'une nouvelle — pour	26	in the proportion of one new — for two old ones/ for every two ones
capital —s	27	— capital/equity value
certificat d'—	28	— certificate
compagnie par —s	29	joint-stock company
cours des —s	30	— prices
émettre des —s	31	to issue —s
émission d'—s	32	issue of —s
indice des —s	33	— index
libération des —s	34	paying up of —s
lot d'—s	35	block of —s/stock
marché des —s	36	stock market
rachat d'—s	37	redemption of —s
racheter des —s	38	to redeem —s
répartir des —s	39	to allot —s
répartition d'—s	40	allotment of —s
société par —s	41	joint-stock company
souscripteur à des —s	42	subscriber/applicant for—s

action *f*	1	action; operation
intenter une — en justice	2	to take legal action
rayon d'—	3	coverage
— revendicatoire	4	action for recovery
actionnaire *n. m/f*	5	shareholder
assemblée des —s	6	general meeting of —s
registre des —s	7	— register of activity
actuaire *m*	8	actuary
actualité *f*	9	current events/news
perdre son —	10	to become stale
actuel, —le *adj*	11	present
prix —s	12	current prices
additif *m*	13	additional clause, rider
additif, —ve *adj*	14	additive
addition *n*	15	addition, sum; [restaurant] bill, [Amér.] check
additionnel, —le *adj*	16	extra, additional
clause —le	17	rider
additionner *vb*	18	to add up; to mix (with, *de*)
adhésion *f*	19	agreement, support
donner son — à	20	to agree on, to give one's approval to
adjoindre *vb*	21	to adjoin, associate, add
adjoint *adj*	22	assistant, associate; deputy;
directeur —	23	assistant manager
adjudication *f*	24	1 tender
	25	2 giving out of a contract, disposal by auction
— au plus bas soumissionnaire	26	allocation to the lowest tender(er)
l'— aura lieu le . . .	27	the allotment will take place on . . .
(vente) par —	28	(sale) by tender
adjuger *vb*	29	to adjudicate; [auction] to knock down
Une fois ! deux fois ! adjugé !	30	Going ! going ! gone !
admettre *vb*	31	to admit; to concede, grant
en admettant que . . .	32	even if . . .
il est généralement admis que . . .	33	it is generally accepted that . . .
n'— aucun retard	34	to admit no delay
administrateur *m*	35	administrator, manager; trustee; director
— délégué	36	managing director

administration *f*	1	management
— communale	2	municipal administration
Conseil d'—	3	board of directors
entrer dans l'—	4	to enter the civil service
administrer *vb*	5	to manage, to govern (country)
adopter *vb*	6	to adopt; to take up (an attitude)
— une ligne de conduite	7	to take a line
— une résolution	8	to pass/carry a resolution
adresse *f*	9	address
— commerciale	10	business —
— complète	11	full —
— privée	12	private —
— télégraphique	13	telegraphic —
à l'— indiquée	14	to the stated —
bureau d'—s	15	inquiry office
changement d'—	16	change of —
liste d'—s	17	mailing list
livre d'—s	18	directory
parti sans laisser d'—	19	left; no forwarding —
prendre le nom et l'—	20	to take name and —
adresser *vb*	21	to address (a letter); to send
— la parole à	22	to speak to
Nous vous adressons sous ce pli	23	We enclose herewith
s'— à	24	to speak to
aérien, -ne *adj*	25	aerial
lettre de voiture —ne	26	airway bill
ligne —ne	27	airline
métro —	28	elevated railway
pont —	29	airlift
service —	30	air service
aéro- *pref*	31	aero-
—drome *m*	32	airfield, aerodrome
—dynamique *adj*	33	—dynamic
—dynamique *n.f.*	34	—dynamics
—gare *f*	35	airline terminal
—nautique *f*	36	—nautics
—nautique *adj*	37	—nautical
—nef *m*	38	aircraft
—plane *m*	39	airplane
—port *m*	40	airport
affaire *f*	41	business
accroissement des —s	42	increase of —

— à terme	1	time bargain
—s à la gomme	2	bogus transactions
—s à prime	3	option dealings
—s courantes	4	current matters
avoir — à	5	to deal with
avoir — avec	6	to have to transact with
chiffre d'—s	7	turnover
essor des —s	8	development of —
être dans les —s	9	to be in —
homme d'—s	10	-man
Il connaît son —	11	He knows his —
le Ministère des Affaires étrangères	12	the Foreign Office
les —s ralentissent	13	— declines
les —s reprennent	14	— is picking up
les —s sont à peu près nulles	15	there is almost nothing to do in —
les —s vont bien	16	— is thriving
les —s vont mal	17	trade is bad
pour —s	18	on —
ralentissement des —s	19	decline of —
relations d'—s	20	— relations; -dealings
se retirer des —s	21	to retire from —
voyage d'—s	22	— trip
affectation f	23	1 earmarking, appropriation (of a sum)
	24	2 assignment (of person)
— hypothécaire	25	mortgage charge
affecter vb	26	to earmark, assign; to appropriate (a sum)
affermer vb	27	to take on lease; to lease; to farm out (taxes)
affermage m	28	leasing
affichage m	29	(bill-)posting, billsticking
tableau d'—	30	notice-board, [Amér.] bulletin board
affiche f	31	bill, poster
annoncer par voie d'—s	32	to placard, bill, post up
colonne d'—s	33	advertising pillar
afficher vb	34	to post up, bill
— les prix	35	to make up prices
Défense d'—	36	Stick no bills
s'—	37	to make a show of o.s.
affluer vb	38	to flow, run (towards, to, into, vers, à, dans)

affranchi *adj*	1	stamped, prepaid
affranchir *vb*	2	to stamp, to frank (a letter), to prepay
affranchissement *m*	3	postage; stamping, franking
affrètement *m*	4	chartering, freighting
— aller retour	5	round trip charter
— au voyage	6	voyage charter
contrat d'—	7	chartering agreement
affréter *vb*	8	to charter, freight
affréteur *m*	9	charterer
afin que *conj*	10	so that, in order that
agence *f*	11	agency
— de placement	12	employment —
— de publicité	13	advertising —
— de renseignements	14	inquiry —
— de voyage(s)	15	travel —
— en douane	16	customs —
— immobilière	17	real estate office
— maritime	18	shipper
supprimer une —	19	to discontinue an —
agenda *m*	20	engagement book, date book, (pocket) diary
agent *n*	21	agent
— consulaire	22	consular —
— d'affaires	23	business —
— d'assurances	24	insurance —
— de change	25	stockbroker
— de douane	26	— for customs
— en douane	27	customs —, custom house broker
— exclusif	28	sole —
aggraver *vb*	29	to worsen
— les impôts	30	to increase taxes
agio *m*	31	exchange premium
les —s	32	discount charges
agiotage *m*	33	gambling, speculation
agioter *vb*	34	to job; to gamble, speculate, play the market
agioteur *m*	35	gambler, speculator
agiter *vb*	36	to stir, disturb
— une question	37	to debate a point
agrafe *f*	38	hook, clasp, staple
agrafer *vb*	39	to hook (on), to staple
agrafeuse *f*	40	stapler
agraire *adj*	41	agrarian

réforme —	1	land reform
agrandir *vb*	2	to enlarge, to increase
s'—	3	to grow, expand, become larger
agréé *adj*	4	recognized, chartered, accepted
comptable — [Can.]	5	chartered accountant
agréer *vb*	6	to agree to, to accept
Veuillez —, . . ., (l'expression) de mes salutations distinguées.	7	Yours sincerely,
agricole *adj*	8	agricultural
exposition —	9	— show/exhibition
industrie —	10	farming
région —	11	— district
aide 1. *n.f.* 2. *n.m.*	12	1 aid, help; relief
	13	2 helper, assistant, junior clerk
— -comptable	14	assistant accountant
à l'— de	15	with (the help of)
aider *vb*	16	to help, assist
s'— *or* s'entrai —	17	to help one another
aiguiller *vb*	18	to switch, shunt
— sur [Fig.]	19	to switch on to
aire *f*	20	area, space, surface
ajournement *m*	21	postponement, adjournment; [Lég.] summons
ajourner *vb*	22	to adjourn, postpone
ajouter *vb*	23	to add
— foi à	24	to give credence to
ajustement *m*	25	adjustment
ajuster *vb*	26	to adjust, to fit (clothes)
ajusteur *m*	27	fitter
alibi *m*	28	alibi
fournir un —	29	to produce an —
plaider l'—	30	to plea an —
prouver son —	31	to establish an —
aliénation *f*	32	alienation, transfer
aliéner *vb*	33	to alienate, transfer
alimentation *f*	34	1 feeding
	35	2 grocery trade; food, grocery
	36	3 supplies; feed
un magasin d'—	37	a food store
alimenter *vb*	38	to feed, supply

10

— un fonds	1	to maintain a fund
aliquote *n.m.* and *adj*	2	aliquot, being a factor of another number
parties —s	3	aliquot parts
allègement *m*	4	alleviation
— des impôts	5	— of taxation
alléger *vb*	6	to lighten ; to alleviate
alléguer *vb*	7	to allege, adduce, give (a reason)
allocation *f*	8	allocation ; assignment ; allowance ; allotment
— de chômage	9	unemployment benefit, dole
— de naissance	10	birth allowance
— familiale	11	family allowance
allouer *vb*	12	to allocate, allow, award, grant
aloi *m*	13	1 quality
	14	2 taste
de bon —	15	sterling, genuine
de mauvais —	16	dubious
alphabétique *adj*	17	alphabetical
dans l'ordre —	18	in — order
altérer *vb*	19	to impair, adulterate
s'—	20	to deteriorate, go bad
alternance *f*	21	alternation
alternatif, -ve *adj*	22	alternate, alternating, alternative
alternativement *adv*	23	by turns, alternately
amalgamer *vb*	24	to merge, consolidate
amarrer *vb*	25	[bateau] to moor
	26	[à quai] to berth
	27	[canot] to secure
amasser *vb*	28	to accumulate, hoard
s'—	29	to pile up
amélioration *f*	30	improvement
susceptible d'—	31	that can be improved
aménagement *m*	32	arrangement ; equipment, fitting
aménager *vb*	33	to fit up ; to adjust
amende *f*	34	fine
infliger une —	35	to fine
amendement *m*	36	1 improvement
	37	2 amendment
amiable *adj*	38	friendly, conciliatory
arrangement à l'—	39	amicable settlement

11

vente à l'—	1	private sale
amoindrir *vb*	2	to diminish, lessen; to depreciate
s'—	3	to grow less
amoindrissement *m*	4	decrease, lessening
amortir *vb*	5	to pay off, to amortize; to sink; to redeem
amortissable *adj*	6	redeemable
amortissement *m*	7	1 redemption, amortization; repayment
	8	2 [Banque] writing-off
— d'un emprunt	9	redemption of a loan
— d'une dette	10	discharge of a debt
— pour usure	11	depreciation for wear and tear
— sur les bâtiments	12	writing off, depreciation of premises
caisse/fonds d'—	13	sinking fund
plan d'—	14	terms of redemption
ampliation *f* [Lég.]	15	certified copy
ancienneté *f*	16	seniority
ancrage *m*	17	anchorage, anchoring
animé *adj*	18	animated; lively
marché —	19	brisk market
rue —e	20	busy street
année *f*	21	year
— bissextile	22	leap —
— budgétaire/financière	23	financial —
— civile	24	Calendar —
— de base	25	base —
l'— scolaire	26	the school —, the academic session
ouvert toute l'—	27	open all the — round
pendant toute l'—	28	throughout the —
annexe *f*	29	enclosure; annex; supplement, addition; appendix; rider
annexé *adj*	30	herewith, enclosed, annexed
annexer *vb*	31	to annex; [brochure] to append; [dans une lettre] to enclose
annonce *f*	32	announcement, notification; ad(vertisement)
insérer/mettre une —	33	to insert an ad
les petites —s	34	classified ads

annoncier *m*	1	advertising agent; advertiser
annuel, —le *adj*	2	yearly, annual
annuité *f*	3	annuity
— à vie	4	life —
— différée	5	deferred —
annulation *f*	6	cancellation, voidance (of a contract)
annuler *vb*	7	to annul, cancel; to make void
anonyme *adj*	8	anonymous, nameless
société —	9	limited company
antécédents *n.m.pl.*	10	background
antichrèse *f*	11	assignment of the revenue of real estate given in security of a debt
anticipatif, -ve *adj*	12	anticipative, in advance
paiement —	13	prepayment
remboursement —	14	accelerated redemption
anticipation *f*	15	anticipation
par —	16	in —, in advance
anticiper *vb*	17	to anticipate; to forestall
— sur ses revenus	18	to spend one's income in advance
aperçu *m*	19	rough estimate, general outline
apériteur *m*	20	leading underwriter
aplanir *vb*	21	to level; to smooth (down); to iron out (difficulties)
apocryphe *adj*	22	[documents] spurious; of doubtful authenticity
appareil *m*	23	apparatus; machine; device, system
— administratif	24	administrative machinery
— de levage	25	lifting appliance
—s à gaz	26	gas-fittings
appareillage *m*	27	1 equipment, outfit
	28	2 sailing
appartenance *f*	29	(party) affiliation
appartenir *vb*	30	to belong; to concern
à qui il appartiendra/de droit	31	to whom it may concern
il vous appartiendra de . . .	32	it will be your concern to . . .
appel *m*	33	call
— de fonds	34	calling, —

— téléphonique	1	telephone —
Cour d'—	2	Court of Appeal, [Amér.] Appelate Court
faire — à	3	to — on, to — in, to have recourse to
faire un — de fonds de . . .	4	to make a — of
interjeter un —	5	to lodge an appeal
verser un — de fonds de . . .	6	to pay a — of . . .
appendice m	7	appendix (*pl.*: -ices, -ixes), subsidiary material (added at the end of a book)
application f	8	1 applying
	9	2 care, attention
	10	3 enforcement
en — de	11	in pursuance of
mettre en —	12	to implement, [Lég.] to enforce
appliquer vb	13	to apply, to carry out
s' —(à)	14	1 to do one's very best
	15	2 to be applicable (to)
appoint m	16	balance, odd money
faire l'—	17	1 to be applicable to
	18	2 to make up the odd money
appointements n.m.pl.	19	salary
toucher ses —	20	to draw one's —
appointer vb	21	to pay a salary to
apport m	22	contribution, share, assets brought into business
— en nature	23	assets in kind brought in
— en société	24	assets transferred to company
apposer vb	25	to affix (a seal), to append (one's signature)
— les scellés	26	to put . . . under seal
apprentissage m	27	apprenticeship
contrat d'—	28	articles of —
être en —	29	to be apprenticed
approbation f	30	approval, approbation
appropriation f	31	appropriation; [défendue] embezzlement
approprier vb	32	to fit, adapt
s'—	33	to usurp, appropriate
approuvé m **de compte**	34	reconcilement
retourner l'— dûment signé	35	to return the signed —

approuver *vb*	*1*	to approve (of), endorse; to agreee with
J'approuve sa manière d'agir	*2*	I approve of his attitude
approvisionnement *m*	*3*	1 supplying
	4	2 supply, supplies, stock
approvisionner *vb*	*5*	to supply (with, *en*), to stock
s'—	*6*	to get in supplies (of, *en*)
appui *m*	*7*	support
à l'— de	*8*	in — of
point d'—	*9*	fulcrum
sans —	*10*	unprotected
apte *adj*	*11*	qualified, fit; [Lég.] capable (of, *à*)
apurer *vb*	*12*	to wipe out (a debit balance), to check and close (an account)
arbitrage *m* (des litiges)	*13*	arbitration
soumettre à un —	*14*	to refer to —
trancher par —	*15*	to settle by —
arbitragiste *m*	*16*	dealer (on the Stock Exchange)
arbitral *adj*	*17*	(of) arbitration
sentence —e	*18*	— award
tribunal —	*19*	court of —
arbitre *m*	*20*	arbitrator
arbre *m*	*21*	tree
— généalogique	*22*	family —
archives *n.f.pl.*	*23*	archives, records; record office
are *m* [=100 sq. metres]	*24*	are
argent *m*	*25*	1 silver
	26	2 money
	27	3 currency
— à bon marché	*28*	cheap money
— à vue	*29*	call money, money at call
— comptant/liquide	*30*	(spot) cash
— de poche	*31*	pocket money
— en barres	*32*	bar silver
— en caisse	*33*	cash in hand
— liquide	*34*	ready money
— monnayé	*35*	specie
gagner de l'—	*36*	to make money
loyer de l'—	*37*	price of money
marché de l'—	*38*	money market
payable en — français	*39*	payable in French currency

15

placer de l'—	1	to invest —/funds
taux de l'—	2	price of money
armateur *m*	3	ship-owner
armement *m*	4	commissioning, fitting out
mettre un navire en —	5	to put a ship in commission
armer *vb*	6	[navire] to commission, to man and supply
arpentage *m*	7	land-surveying
arpenter *vb*	8	to survey (land)
arpenteur *m*	9	surveyor
arrangement *m*	10	agreement, arrangement; adjustment; terms
— à l'amiable	11	amicable settlement
— avec les créanciers	12	composition with the creditors
arriver à un —	13	to compromise
arranger *vb*	14	1 to set in order, arrange
	15	2 to repair, fix
s'—	16	1 to manage
	17	2 to come to terms; to compound with (one's creditors)
arrérages *n.m.pl.*	18	arrears
arrêt *m*	19	stop(page); seizure, impounding
— de paiement	20	stoppage of payment
— par défaut [Lég.]	21	judgement by default
faire — sur (des marchandises)	22	to attach, seize (goods)
arrêter *vb*	23	to stop; to settle (an account)
— un compte (au . . .)	24	to make up/close an account (on . . .)
— le paiement d'un chèque	25	to stop a cheque
arrhes *n.f.pl.*	26	deposit, earnest; [provision] retainer
arrière-saison *f*	27	late season; late fall
arriéré *n.m.* and *adj*	28	1 in arrears, outstanding, overdue
	29	2 backward
	30	3 balance
régler l'—	31	to pay off arrears, to make up back payments, to settle the balance
arrimage *m*	32	stowage
arrimer *vb*	33	to stow (cargo); to trim (ship)

arrivage *m*	1	arrival
nouvel —	2	new consignment, fresh —
arriver *vb*	3	1 to happen, to take place
	4	2 to come, arrive
— à	5	to manage, succeed in
— à bon port	6	to arrive safely
arrondir *vb*	7	to round off
— au franc supérieur	8	— to the next higher franc
— en moins	9	— downwards to
— en plus	10	— upwards to
arrondissement *m*	11	(postal) district
article *m*	12	article; item; clause (of a contract); entry
— collectif	13	combined/compound entry
— de dépense	14	item of expense
— de réclame	15	leading line; loss leader
— de série	16	mass produced article
— de virement	17	transfer entry
— rectificatif	18	correcting entry
—s de bureau	19	stationery
—s de consommation	20	commodities
—s de voyage	21	travel requisites
— six de la loi	22	section six of the Act
en vertu de l'—	23	in pursuance/by virtue of section . . .
pointer des —s	24	to check off items
radier un —	25	to strike out an item
tenir un —	26	to keep/carry/stock an article
assainir *vb*	27	to make healthier; to reform
assainissement *m*	28	reform
— monétaire	29	re-establishment of currency, financial rehabilitation
assemblée *f*	30	meeting
convoquer une —	31	to call a —
tenir une — générale	32	to hold a general —
assentiment *m*	33	assent, consent
donner son —	34	to approve
asseoir *vb*	35	to establish (a tax)
assermenté *adj*	36	sworn (in)
fonctionnaire/traducteur —	37	— official/translator
assermenter *vb*	38	to swear in

17

assiette *f*	1	basis
— des impôts	2	— of assessment
l'— au beurre	3	[Coll.] the plums
assignation *f*	4	1 assignment, allotment
	5	2 [Lég.] writ, subpoena
remettre une —	6	to serve a writ on
assigner *vb*	7	1 to set (limits to, *à*) ; to earmark (a sum) ; to ascribe (to, *à*) ; to vest (property)
	8	2 to appoint, to fix (time, etc.)
	9	3 [Lég.] to issue a writ against, to subpoena
assister *vb*	10	1 to help, to assist
	11	2 to attend
— à la réunion	12	to attend the meeting
association *f*	13	association
— des banques	14	bankers' —
— ouvrière	15	labour —
— patronale	16	employers' —
— sans but lucratif (A.S.B.L.)	17	non-profit-making —
associé *n.m.* and *adj*	18	partner ; associated, in partnership
— commanditaire	19	sleeping partner
—gérant	20	managing partner
associer *vb*	21	to join, unite, associate
s'—	22	1 to go into partnership with
	23	2 to share, to have a part in
assortiment *m*	24	match(ing) ; assortment, range
assortir *vb*	25	to match, pair (with, *à*), to suit
assouplir *vb*	26	to make flexible, supple
le règlement a été assoupli	27	Regulations have been eased
assujetti *adj*	28	subject (to, *à*)
— à l'impôt	29	liable for tax
assumer *vb*	30	to undertake, assume
n'— aucune responsabilité	31	to take no responsibility
assurable *adj*	32	insurable
assurance *f*	33	[vie] assurance ; insurance
agent d'—s	34	insurance broker
— à capital différé	35	endowment insurance

— au premier risque	1	first loss assurance
— au tiers	2	third-party insurance
— automobile	3	motor car insurance
— avec participation aux bénéfices	4	profit sharing/participating insurance
— contre la grêle	5	hail-storm insurance
— contre la maladie	6	sickness insurance
— contre la maladie et l'invalidité	7	sickness and disablement insurance
— contre le bris des vitres	8	plate glass insurance
— contre le chômage	9	unemployment insurance
— contre les accidents	10	accident insurance
— contre les accidents du travail	11	employers' liability insurance
— contre les risques de guerre	12	war risk insurance
— contre le vol	13	burglary/theft insurance
— contre l'incendie	14	fire insurance
— contre tous les risques	15	all risks insurance
— contre tous risques d'auto	16	comprehensive motor car insurance
— de cautionnement	17	guarantee insurance
— de responsabilité civile	18	public liability/third party insurance
— des bagages	19	luggage insurance
— dotale	20	dowry insurance
— du bétail	21	livestock insurance
— du fret	22	freight insurance
— en cas de décès	23	whole life assurance
— en cas de vie	24	endowment assurance
— fluviale/maritime	25	marine insurance
— mixte	26	pension and life assurance schemes
— omnium [Belg.]	27	comprehensive motor car insurance
— pour le compte de qui il appartiendra	28	insurance for account of whom it may concern
— pour une somme supérieure à la valeur	29	overinsurance
—s sociales	30	social insurance
— supplémentaire	31	additional insurance
— sur la vie	32	life assurance
— sur marchandises	33	cargo insurance
— sur navire	34	hull insurance
certificat d'—	35	insurance certificate

19

contracter une —	1	to take out an insurance
contrat d'—	2	insurance contract
courtier d'—	3	insurance broker
fonds d'—	4	insurance fund
police d'—	5	insurance policy
preneur d'—	6	policy taker
prime d'—	7	insurance premium
valeur d'—	8	insurance value
assuré *n.m.* and *adj*	9	1 insured, insurant
	10	2 sure, firm
	11	3 assured, confident
assurer *vb*	12	1 to assure (s.o. of sth.)
	13	2 to insure, to cover a risk
s'—	14	1 to make certain, to make sure (of, *de*)
	15	2 to insure o.s.
s'— contre l'incendie	16	to get insured against fire
s'— contre la vie	17	to have one's life insured
assureur *m*	18	insurer, underwriter
— conseil	19	insurance consultant
atelier *m*	20	workshop
atermoiement *m*	21	arrangement (for deferred payment)
atermoyer *vb*	22	to defer payment
attaché (commercial) *m*	23	(commercial) attaché
attacher *vb*	24	to attach
coupon attaché	25	with/cum coupon
attenant *adj*	26	adjoining
atteindre *vb*	27	1 to reach 2 to hit
atteinte *f*	28	1 reach
	29	2 infringement (of, *à*)
hors d'—	30	beyond reach
porter — à	31	to harm, to do injury, to be detrimental to
attendre *vb*	32	to wait
en attendant votre réponse	33	awaiting your reply
s'— à	34	to expect
attendu que	35	inasmuch as
attendus *n.m.pl.*	36	the reasons adduced
attente *f*	37	expectation, wait(ing)
contre toute —	38	contrary to all expectations
dans l'— de (votre réponse)	39	awaiting (your reply)
liste d'—	40	waiting list
salle d'—	41	waiting room

20

attention *f*	*1*	attention
à l'— de M. X	*2*	for the — of Mr. X
attirer l'—de qqun sur qqch.	*3*	to call s.o.'s — to sth.
atténuer *vb*	*4*	to subdue, soften; to tone down; [Fam.] to soft-pedal
attestation *f*	*5*	certificate, testimonial
— du titre	*6*	warranty of title
— sous serment	*7*	affidavit
attester *vb*	*8*	to certify; to bear witness to; to call to witness
attirer *vb*	*9*	to draw, attract
— des capitaux	*10*	to attract capital
s'— des ennuis	*11*	to get into trouble
attitré *adj*	*12*	recognized, appointed
fournisseur — de (la Cour)	*13*	by appointment to (the Court)
attribution *f*	*14*	1 allotment, assignment
	15	2 *pl.* functions; powers; terms of reference
aubette *f* [Belg.]	*16*	newstand
audition *f*	*17*	audition, hearing
faire passer une —	*18*	to give an audition
augmentation *f*	*19*	increase, rise; [Amér.] raise; enlargement
accuser une —	*20*	to show a rise
— de valeur	*21*	increase in value
subir une —	*22*	to undergo/experience a rise
augmenter *vb*	*23*	to increase, put up
— les prix (de 10%)	*24*	to increase/put up prices (by 10%)
édition augmentée	*25*	enlarged edition
les prix augmentent	*26*	prices are going up/rising
aujourd'hui *adv*	*27*	today; nowadays
d'— en huit	*28*	this day week
aurifère *adj*	*29*	gold
terrain —	*30*	-field
valeur —	*31*	-share
auspices *n.m.pl.*	*32*	auspices
sous les — de . . .	*33*	sponsored by . . .
authentifier *vb*	*34*	to make valid, to legalize
authentique *adj*	*35*	genuine; positive
automation *f*	*36*	automation
automatique *adj*	*37*	automatic

distributeur —	1	vending/slot machine
automobilisme *m*	2	motoring
autorail *m*	3	railcar
autorisation *f*	4	authorization; permission, permit, licence, [Lég.] warranty
— d'exportation	5	export permit
— d'importation	6	import permit
— maritale	7	husband's authorization
— préalable	8	prior authorization
autorisé *adj*	9	authorized, authoritative
de source —e	10	authoritatively
milieux —s	11	influential circles
signatures —es	12	signatories
autoriser *vb*	13	to authorize, permit, allow, empower; to justify; to warrant
autorité *f*	14	authority, power
les —s (locales)	15	the (local) authorities
aval *m*	16	endorsement (on a bill)
— de banque	17	bank guaranty
commission pour —	18	commission for bank guaranty
donneur d'—	19	guarantor, backer
signé pour —	20	guaranteed
avaliser *vb*	21	to back, endorse, guarantee
avaliseur *m*, **avaliste** *m*	22	guarantor
avance *f*	23	advance (payment)
à l'—, d'—, par —	24	in —
— à découvert	25	unsecured —
— garantie	26	secured —
— gratuite	27	— free of interest
—s de caisse	28	cash —s
—s en clearing	29	clearing —s
— sur marchandises	30	— on/against goods
— sur nantissement	31	— against securities
— sur titres	32	— on/against securities
consentir des —s	33	to make —s
en —	34	early, before time
avancement *m*	35	progress, advancing, advancement; promotion
avancer *vb*	36	1 to advance
	37	2 to be promoted
avantage *m*	38	advantage
à son —	39	to one's profit

avoir — à faire qqch.	1	to find it profitable to do sth.
avoir l'— (sur)	2	to have the edge (on)
Nous avons l'— de vous faire savoir	3	We have pleasure to inform/of informing you . . .
avant-bourse *adv*	4	before hours
avant-port *m*	5	outer harbour
avant-projet *m*	6	pilot project; draught, preliminary plan
avarie *f*	7	damage, injury (to engine, ship)
avarié *adj*	8	damaged
— par l'eau de mer	9	sea-water —
— par l'étalage	10	shop-spoiled
avenant *m*	11	endorsement, amendment, additional clause
avenu *adj*	12	. . . .
(considérer comme) nul et non- —	13	(to consider) null and void
avers *m*	14	obverse, face side
avilir *vb*	15	to depreciate
avilissement *m*	16	depreciation
avion *m*	17	(air)plane
par —	18	air mail
prendre l'—	19	to fly
avis *m*	20	advice
— de convocation	21	notice of meeting
— de disposition	22	— of draft
— d'embarquement	23	— of shipment
— d'encaissement	24	collection —
—de réception	25	acknowledgement of receipt
— de répartition	26	letter of allotment
— de retour de souscription	27	letter of regret
— de virement (au bénéficiaire)	28	notification of crediting (to the recipient)
être d'—	29	to be of the opinion
jusqu'à nouvel —	30	until further — /notice
sans — préalable	31	without notice
sauf — contraire	32	unless advised to the contrary
aviser *vb*	33	to inform, to notify, to advise
s'—	34	to take upon o.s.

23

avocat *m*	*1*	lawyer, barrister; advocate
— conseil	*2*	consulting barrister, counsel
consulter un —	*3*	to take legal advice
avoir *m*	*4*	1 credit (side)
	5	2 property, possessions
— bloqué	*6*	blocked/frozen assets
— en caisse	*7*	cash in hand
tout mon —	*8*	all I possess
ayant(s) droit *m* (*pl*)	*9*	beneficiary; interested party; rightful claimant
bac *m*	*10*	1 ferry(boat)
	11	2 vat, tank
— à fiches	*12*	file basket
bâche *f*	*13*	tarpaulin, canvas cover
bagage *m*	*14*	1 luggage, [Amér.] baggage
	15	2 background, knowledge
bulletin de —	*16*	luggage ticket
excédent de —	*17*	excess luggage
bail *m, pl* : **baux**	*18*	lease
— à ferme	*19*	rural/farming —
— à loyer	*20*	house —, letting —
— assuré	*21*	fixity of tenure
— emphytéotique	*22*	long —, 99 year —
résiller/renouveler un —	*23*	to cancel/renew a —
bailleur *m*	*24*	lessor
— de fonds	*25*	money lender; sleeping partner
— et preneur	*26*	— and lessee
baisse *f*	*27*	fall, decline, drop
acheter en —	*28*	to buy on a falling market
— des prix	*29*	fall of prices
être à la —	*30*	to go for a fall
(être) en —	*31*	(to be) falling/down
mouvement de baisse	*32*	downward movement
opération à la baisse	*33*	bear operation
tendance à la —	*34*	downward tendency
baisser *vb*	*35*	to drop, sag, fall
— de ... à ...	*36*	to drop from ... to ...
faire —	*37*	to lower; to bear, to force down
balance *f*	*38*	balance
— commerciale active	*39*	favourable — of trade

— commerciale/du commerce	1	trade —/— of trade
— commerciale passive	2	adverse — of trade
— de caisse	3	cash —
— déficitaire	4	adverse —
— des comptes et des payements	5	— of payments
— de vérification	6	trial —
— d'un compte	7	— of an account
— flattée	8	cooked —
balancer *vb*	9	to balance
— les livres	10	— the books
— un compte	11	— an account
balle *f*	12	bale (of cotton, wool, etc.)
mettre en —	13	to —
banane *f*	14	banana
régime de —	15	stalk of —s
banc *m*	16	bank, shoal (of sand), school (of fish), bed (of oysters)
bancaire *adj*	17	banking
bande *f*	18	[papier] wrapper, strip
	19	[terrain] strip, belt
— fiscale	20	revenue band
sous —	21	in a wrapper, by bookpost
banque *f*	22	bank
—:.....	23	— account:.....
— à charte [Can.]	24	chartered —; national —
— agricole	25	rural —
— de circulation/d'émission	26	issuing —
— de commerce	27	merchant/commercial —
— de compensation	28	clearing —
— de crédit	29	credit —
— de dépôt	30	deposit —
— de recouvrement	31	collecting agency
— d'escompte	32	discount —
— des Règlements Internationaux (BRI)	33	— of International Settlements (BIS)
— d'Etat	34	State —
— de virements	35	transfer —
— d'outre-mer	36	overseas —
— foncière	37	land —
— hypothécaire	38	mortgage —
consortium de —	39	banking syndicate
guichets de la —	40	— counters

la — [système]	1	banking
ruée sur les guichets de la —	2	run on a —
situation de la —	3	statement of affairs
verser à la —	4	to pay into the —
banqueroute *f*	5	bankruptcy
— frauduleuse	6	fraudulent —
— simple	7	—
faire —	8	to go bankrupt
banqueroutier *m*	9	(fraudulent) bankrupt
banquier *m*	10	banker
banquier, -ère *adj*	11	banking
baraterie *f*	12	barratry
barême *m*	13	schedule; tariff, price list; printed tables (of charges, fares), scale (of salaries); ready reckoner
— graphique	14	graph
baril *m*	15	[en métal] drum, barrel
	16	[en bois] keg, cask
mettre en —	17	to barrel
barre *f*	18	[or] ingot
barrement *m*	19	[chèque] crossing
barrer *vb*	20	to cross (out), strike out
barrières *f.pl.* **douanières**	21	customs barriers, tariff walls
barrique *f*	22	large barrel, hogshead
bas *m*	23	1 bottom, foot (of the page)
	24	2 stocking
— de laine	25	nest-egg
base *f*	26	basis
de —	27	basic
jeter les —s de	28	to lay the foundations
prix de —	29	—/base price
sur la — de	30	on the — of
sur une — solide	31	on a lasting/sound —
baser *vb*	32	to found, base (on, *sur*)
bassin *m*	33	1 dock, basin
	34	2 [récipient] reservoir, tank
	35	3 [gisement] layer, bed, field
— à flot	36	wet dock
— à marée	37	tidal dock
— de radoub	38	dry dock
— flottant	39	floating dock
— houiller	40	coal field

entrer au —	1	to dock
faire passer un navire au —	2	to dock a ship
bateau *m*	3	boat
— -citerne	4	tanker
— de pêche	5	fishing —
— de sauvetage	6	life- —
— -feu/-phare	7	lightship
— mouche	8	sightseeing —
— pilote	9	pilot —
— -pompe	10	fire —
bâtiment *m*	11	building
entrepreneur en —	12	— contractor
bâtir *vb*	13	to build
terrain à —	14	building site/plot
battre *vb*	15	to beat
— monnaie	16	to mint, to coin money
— un pavillon	17	to fly a flag
bazar *m*	18	general store
bénéfice *m*	19	profit
avec part aux —s	20	with share in the —s
— brut	21	gross —
— d'exploitation	22	working —s
— net	23	net/clear —
— non distribué	24	undistributed/unappropriated —
— reporté	25	balance brought forward from
— sur le change	26	exchange —s
diminution du —	27	shrinking of —s
le — du doute	28	the benefit of the doubt
prise de —s	29	— taking
réaliser de gros —s	30	to make big —s
répartition de —	31	appropriation of —s
bénéficiaire *n.m.* and *adj*	32	beneficiary; payee (of a cheque)
marge —	33	margin of profit
solde —	34	profit/credit balance
solde — non réparti	35	undivided —s
bénéficier *vb*	36	to profit (by, *de*)
faire — qqun d'une réduction	37	to allow s.o. a discount
besoin *m*	38	need
avoir — de	39	to —, to have — of
au —/en cas de —	40	if necessary; when required

pourvoir à un —	1	to meet the requirements/ a want
bétail *m, pl* : **bestiaux**	2	cattle, livestock
gros/menu —	3	large/small livestock
biais *m*	4	1 bias, slant
	5	2 shift, expedient
trouver un —	6	to find a round-about method (of doing . . .)
biens *n.m.pl.*	7	property
— corporels	8	tangible —
— de production	9	producer —
— d'investissement	10	capital —
— et avoirs	11	— and assets
— -fonds	12	landed —, personal estate
— immeubles	13	real estate, —
— incorporels	14	intangible —
— meubles/mobiliers	15	movables, chattels, personal —
bière *f*	16	beer
— à la pression/au tonneau	17	draught —
— blonde	18	lager
biffer *vb*	19	to strike out, cross out
— les mentions inutiles	20	strike out if not applicable/ what is not wanted
bilan *m*	21	balance sheet
analyse de —	22	statement analysis
article de —	23	— item
— consolidé	24	consolidated —
— déficitaire	25	— showing a loss
— de fin d'année	26	annual —
— flatté/maquillé	27	cooked —
camoufler le —	28	to fake the —
déposer son —	29	to file one's petition
dresser le —	30	to draw up the —
établissement du —	31	drawing up of a —
extrait de —	32	extract from a —
porter au —	33	to put into the —
truquer/maquiller le —	34	to cook/fake the —
bille *f*	35	ball
roulement à —s	36	— bearing
stylo à —	37	— -point pen
billet *m*	38	ticket
— à ordre	39	promissory note
— au porteur	40	bill payable to bearer

— à vue	1	bill payable at sight
— circulaire	2	tourist —
— (d')aller-retour	3	return/round-trip —
— de banque	4	bank note
— de complaisance	5	accommodation bill
— d'entrée	6	admission —/card
— de faveur	7	complimentary —, free —
— de loterie	8	lottery —
— de quai	9	platform —
— de santé	10	bill of health
— simple	11	single (—)
billion *m*	12	[G.B.] one thousand million
	13	[Amér.] billion
bimensuel, -le *adj*	14	fortnightly, twice a month
bimestriel, -le *adj*	15	every two months
biscuiterie *f*	16	biscuit company/trade
bissextile *adj*	17	. . . .
année —	18	leap year
blanc *adj*	19	blank
chèque en —	20	— cheque
endossé en —	21	— endorsed
blanc-seing *m, pl*: **des**	22	blank signature
blancs-seings		
bloc *m*	23	block
— -notes	24	writing-pad
en —	25	together, as a group
faire — (avec/contre)	26	to work as a unit (with/against)
blocus *m*	27	[par mer] blockade
	28	[par terre] siege
forcer le —	29	to run the blockade
bloquer *vb*	30	to block, to stop (a cheque), to tie up, to freeze (a bank account, s.o.'s credit)
bois *m*	31	wood; lumber
abattre le —	32	to cut timber
— de chauffage	33	firewood
— de pâte	34	pulpwood
de/en —	35	wooden
boisseau *m*	36	bushel
au —	37	by the —
boîte *f*	38	box
— à suggestions	39	suggestion —
— aux lettres	40	letter/mail —
— en fer blanc	41	tin, can

— postale	1	postal —, post office —
bon *m*	2	note, coupon, order; bond, bill
— au porteur	3	bearer bond
— de caisse	4	cash voucher
— d'épargne	5	savings certificate
— de poste	6	postal order
— du Trésor	7	Treasury bond
— nominatif	8	registered bond
donner le — à tirer	9	to pass for press
bon, -ne *adj*	10	good
à — marché/à — compte	11	cheap(ly)
— pour	12	— for
— pour aval	13	guaranteed
— rendement	14	— yield
de —ne foi	15	in — faith
être dans la —ne voie	16	to be on the right track
un — nombre de	17	quite a number of
une —ne distance	18	quite a distance
boni *m*	19	1 balance in hand, surplus, over
	20	2 bonus
bonification *f*	21	allowance, rebate, bonus; improvement; [en Bourse] backwardation
— d'intérêt	22	compounding interest
bonifier *vb*	23	1 to allow (s.o. a discount)
	24	2 to improve
— des intérêts sur . . . au taux de . . .	25	to allow an interest on . . . at the rate of . . .
se —	26	to improve, become better
bord *m*	27	edge, side; board
au — de la ruine	28	on the brink/verge of disaster
jeter par-dessus —	29	to throw overboard
livre de —	30	log book
monter à —	31	to go on board
bordereau *m*	32	memorandum, list, slip, statement; consignment note
— d'achat	33	bought note
— de caisse	34	cash statement
— de chargement	35	cargo list
— de crédit/débit	36	credit/debit note
— de paye	37	wages docket
— de salaires	38	pay roll
— des espèces	39	specification

bouton   switch

— de vente	1	sold note
— de versement	2	credit/paying in slip
— numérique	3	[shares] specification of numbers
botte *f*	4	bunch, bundle; bale
botteler *vb*	5	to tie in bunches, bundles; to bale
bouche *f*	6	mouth, (tube) entrance
— d'incendie	7	fire hydrant
Bourse *f*	8	(Stock) exchange
après/avant —	9	after/before hours
— de commerce	10	produce —
— des grains	11	corn —
— des valeurs	12	Stock —
— du Travail	13	labour Exchange
— maritime	14	Baltic —
bulletin de la —	15	— gazette
chômage de la —	16	bank holiday
clôture de la —	17	closing of the Stock —
en —, à la —	18	on the Stock —
boursicoter *vb*	19	to dabble on the market
boursicoteur, boursicotier *m*	20	dabbler (on the market)
boursier, —ère *n.* and *adj*	21	Stock exchange (operator)
milieux —s	22	— circles
boutique *f*	23	small shop, store
parler —	24	to talk shop
tenir —	25	to run a shop
boycotter *vb*	26	to boycott
B.P. [= Boîte postale]	27	P.O. Box [= Post Office Box]
brader *vb*	28	to sell off
braderie *f*	29	(annual) sale on the pavement; (yearly) jumble sale
branche *f*	30	line, section (of business, enterprise, teaching)
brasser *vb*	31	to brew (beer)
— des affaires	32	to handle a lot of business
brasserie *f*	33	brewery; beer-making
brasseur *m*	34	brewer
— d'affaires	35	tycoon
brevet *m*	36	certificate, diploma, licence; patent
bureau des —s	37	patent office
demande de —	38	application for a patent

prendre un —	*1*	to take out a patent
titulaire d'un —	*2*	patentee
breveté *adj*	*3*	patented, certified, licensed; qualified
breveter *vb*	*4*	to patent, to issue a patent
bricolage *m*	*5*	do - it - yourself; pottering (about)
briqueterie *f*	*6*	brick works
bris *m*	*7*	breaking; [Lég.] wilful damage
— de clôture	*8*	breach of close
briseur *m* **de grève**	*9*	blackleg, scab
brocanteur *m*	*10*	junk dealer
broché *adj*	*11*	paper-backed
brocher *vb*	*12*	to stitch
brocheuse *f*	*13*	stapler; stitcher
brochure *f*	*14*	1 brochure, pamphlet
	15	2 stitching
broder *vb*	*16*	to embroider
brouillard *m*	*17*	1 fog 2 day-book
brouillon *m*	*18*	rough draft
broutilles *n.f.pl.*	*19*	odds and ends, bits and pieces; trash
brûler *vb*	*20*	[café] to roast
	21	[récoltes] to parch up, to wilt
— les étapes	*22*	to make rapid strides/progress
— ses vaisseaux	*23*	to burn one's bridges
brut *adj*	*24*	[matière] raw, unrefined
	25	[pétrole] crude
	26	[or] nugget
	27	[diamant] uncut, rough
	28	[bois] lumber
	29	[bénéfice, poids] gross
bruyère *f*	*30*	[pipe] French briar
budget *m*	*31*	budget
approuver un —	*32*	to pass a —
boucler le — [Coll.]	*33*	to make both ends meet, to manage
— complémentaire	*34*	supplementary —
— de famine	*35*	starvation —
— de fonctionnement	*36*	operational —
— des dépenses	*37*	estimates
— familial	*38*	family —
— ordinaire	*39*	ordinary —

discussion du —	1	—debate
exposé du —	2	— speech
inscrire au —	3	to — for
budgétaire *adj*	4	budgetary
déficit —	5	— deficit
dépenses —s	6	budget expenditure
exercice —	7	fiscal year
prévisions —s	8	budget estimate(s)
bulletin *m*	9	bulletin, form, ticket; report; certificate
— de consigne	10	(deposit) ticket
— de paie	11	pay slip
— de souscription	12	application form
— de versement	13	paying-in slip
— de vote	14	ballot
— d'expédition [Post office]	15	dispatch note
—météorologique	16	weather report
bureau *m*	17	office
— d'enregistrement	18	registration —
— de l'état civil	19	registry —
— de placement	20	employment/staff agency
— de poste	21	Post —
— de publicité	22	advertising agency
— de renseignements	23	inquiry/information —
— de tabac	24	tobacconist
— des hypothèques	25	mortgage registry
— du contentieux	26	legal department
— du Timbre	27	stamp —
— principal	28	head —
employés de —	29	— staff/clerks
fournitures de —	30	stationery
heures de —	31	business/— hours
Les théâtres jouent à —x fermés	32	The theatres are all booked up
nos —x seront fermés du ... au ...	33	our — will be closed from ... to ...
travail de —	34	— work
travailler dans un —	35	to work in an —
bureaucratie *f*	36	bureaucracy; red tape
but *m*	37	aim, target, mark
dans le — de	38	with a view to
être loin du —	39	to be far off the mark
le — d'une société	40	the objects of a company
butin *m*	41	spoils *n.pl*, loot

cabine *f*	1	cabin
— téléphonique	2	telephone call box, (phone) booth
câble *m*	3	cable
expédier un —	4	to send a —
câbler *vb*	5	1 to cable
	6	2 [Elect.] to wire (up)
cabotage *m*	7	1 coasting trade, coastwise shipping
	8	2 inland/coastal traffic
faire du — (sur la côte)	9	to coast (along the coast)
caboteur *m*	10	coaster
cachet *m*	11	1 seal, ring
	12	2 fee (of an artist)
apposer un — sur	13	to seal (a document)
— de la poste	14	postmark
cadastral *adj*	15	cadastral [pertaining to an office or register or survey of landed property]
extrait —	16	land registry certificate
plan —	17	— plan
cadastre *m*	18	1 land titles register
	19	2 land survey
bureau du —	20	Land Registry Office
registre du —	21	land register
cadastrer *vb*	22	to enter into the land register
cadenas *m*	23	padlock
— à chiffres	24	combination —
cadence *f*	25	speed, output
— accélérée	26	increased speed, speeded-up (production)
cadre *m*	27	1 frame, framework; scope; bounds, limits
	28	2 staff; executive
dans le — de l'accord	29	within the framework of the agreement
dans le — de ses attributions	30	within its terms of reference
dépasser le — de	31	to be beyond the scope of
les —s	32	the management
cadrer *vb*	33	to agree (with), to tally; to fit
cagnotte *f*	34	kitty, pool
cahier *m*	35	notebook, writing book, copy book; section (of a book)

— des charges	1	specifications
caisse f	2	cash
alimenter une —	3	to supply a fund
argent en —	4	— on hand
— d'amortissement	5	sinking fund
— d'épargne	6	savings bank
— de retraite	7	pension/provident fund
— des dépôts et consignations	8	Deposit and Consignment office
— de secours	9	relief fund; sick benefit fund
— enregistreuse	10	— register
— et banque	11	— in hand and at bankers'
consolider la —	12	to strengthen the funds
faire la —	13	to balance/make up the —
inspection de la —	14	— check
payable à nos —s	15	payable at our counters
payer à la —	16	to pay at the desk
solde en —	17	— balance in hand
tenir la —	18	to keep the —
caisse f	19	case
— à claire-voie	20	crate
— doublée de fer-blanc	21	tin-lined —
caissier m	22	cashier
— principal	23	head/chief —
caissière f	24	(lady) cashier
calcul m	25	calculation, reckoning, computation
— différentiel et intégral	26	calculus
— mental	27	mental arithmetic, to reckon in one's head
faux —	28	miscalculation
règle f à —s	29	slide rule
calculateur, -rice n	30	[Pers.] calculator; schemer
	31	[machine] computer
calculateur, -rice adj	32	calculating
calculer vb	33	1 to calculate, reckon, compute
	34	2 to reckon, to be sparing
	35	3 to plan, scheme
machine à —	36	calculating machine
calculé en DM	37	expressed in DM
cale f	38	hold (of a ship)
buée de —	39	ship's sweat
— sèche/flottante	40	dry/floating dock

fond de —	1	bilge
odeur de —	2	ship's odour
passager de —	3	stowaway
vider les —s	4	to empty the —
calepin m	5	notebook
calorifère m	6	heating system
calorifuger vb	7	to insulate
calque m	8	tracing
faire un —	9	to make a —
papier —	10	— paper
calquer vb	11	to trace, copy
cambial adj	12	exchange
droit —	13	— law
cambiste m	14	(exchange) dealer
cambriolage m	15	burglary, house-breaking
cambrioler vb	16	to break into (a building), to burglarize
cambrioleur m	17	burglar
camelot m	18	huckster, seller (of cheap goods), hawker, pedlar
camelote f	19	junk, trash
camion m	20	lorry
camionnage m	21	cartage (and hauling); cartage/freight charges
camionnette f	22	(delivery) van, [Amér.] light truck
camionneur m	23	lorry-driver; [bétail] teamster
Syndicat des —s	24	[Amér.] Teamster(s') Union
camoufler vb	25	to fake (a balance sheet)
canal m	26	1 canal
	27	2 channel, means
— de navigation	28	ship canal
canaliser vb	29	1 to canalize, guide in a single direction
	30	2 to ship, to pipe oil by pipe line
	31	3 to channel (people, orders, etc.)
candidature f	32	candidature, candidacy
poser sa — (à un poste)	33	to apply (for a position), to stand as a candidate
caoutchouc m	34	rubber
plantation de —	35	— estate/plantation
caoutchoutier, -ère adj	36	rubber
société caoutchoutière	37	— company

valeur caoutchoutière	1	— share
capacité *f*	2	capacity
— [Lég.]	3	(legal) competency
— d'achat	4	purchasing power
— de charge	5	[ship] loading/carrying —
— de travail	6	[worker] fitness for work
—s excédentaires	7	excess —, surplus of (productive) —
ce bidon a une — d'un gallon	8	this can holds one gallon
capitaine *m*	9	captain, master
— de port	10	harbour master
copie du —	11	captain's copy
capital *m, pl*: **—aux**	12	capital
afflux de capitaux	13	inflow of —
apport de —	14	— produced
approvisionnement en —	15	supply of —
augmentation de/du —	16	increase of —
besoins en capitaux	17	— requirements
— acceptant les risques	18	risk (-bearing) —
— appelé	19	called up —
— circulant/mobile	20	floating —
— d'apport	21	initial —
— de réserve	22	contingent fund ; reserve —
— en espèces/en numéraire	23	cash —
— engagé	24	invested —
— en quête d'emploi	25	— seeking investment
— entièrement versé	26	fully paid up —
— et intérêt	27	principal and interest
— immobilisé	28	locked up —
— improductif	29	idle/dead —
— libéré de 40%	30	— of which 40% are paid up
— nominal	31	nominal —
— non appelé	32	uncalled —
— obligations	33	debenture —
— social/nominal	34	— stock, share —, registered —; equity value
— souscrit	35	subscribed —
— versé	36	paid up —
compte de —	37	— account
diminution de —	38	reduction of —
entamer son —	39	to break into one's —
fuite de capitaux	40	flight of —
manque de capitaux	41	want of —

marché des capitaux	1	— market
mouvement des capitaux	2	movement of —
pénurie de capitaux	3	scarcity of —
placement de —	4	investment of —
prélèvement sur le —	5	— levy
rapatriement de capitaux	6	repatriation of —
reflux de capitaux	7	outflow of —
capitaliser *vb*	8	to capitalize, to save (money)
carburant *m*	9	fuel
carence *f*	10	insolvency; deficiency
carène *f*	11	keel, hull (of a ship)
cargaison *f*	12	cargo
— en vrac	13	bulk —
— mixte	14	general —
embarquer la —	15	to board the —
cargo *m*	16	cargo boat, freighter; tramp (steamer)
carnet *m*	17	(note)book
— à souches	18	counterfoil —
— de banque	19	bank —
— de bord	20	log —
— d'échéances	21	bill diary
— de chèques	22	cheque —
— de commandes	23	order —
— de dépôt	24	deposit —
— de passages en douane	25	customs pass —
— de recettes	26	receipt —
carreau *m*	27	1 checks
	28	2 floor
— des halles	29	market square
— d'une mine	30	pit head
une étoffe à —x	31	a checked cloth
cartable *m* **du navire**	32	ship's bag
carte *f*	33	card
abattre ses —s	34	to show one's hand
— d'abonnement	35	season ticket
— d'achat/de crédit	36	credit —
— d'identité	37	identity —
— des vins	38	wine list
— de visite	39	visiting —
— -lettre	40	letter —
— marine	41	chart
— postale (avec réponse payée)	42	(reply paid) post —
— routière	43	route map, road map

—s sur table	1	aboveboard
cartel *m*	2	cartel, trust; monopoly
carton *m*	3	1 cardboard
	4	2 cardboard box
— à chapeau	5	hatbox
cas *m*	6	case
en — d'alarme	7	at a time of emergency
le — échéant	8	should the occasion arise, if need be, in case of need, if necessary
un — de force majeure	9	a — of absolute necessity
case *f*	10	1 small house
	11	2 (mail) box, pigeonhole, section (of shelf)
	12	3 space, blank square (on a paper)
caser *vb*	13	to store away; to place
casier *m*	14	1 set of pigeon-holes
	15	2 [Lég.] record
— à bouteilles	16	bottle rack
— à homards	17	lobster pot
— judiciaire	18	police record
—s d'une malle	19	trays of a trunk
cassable *adj*	20	breakable
casse *f*	21	breakage
casser *vb*	22	to break, crush
— un testament	23	to break a will
cassette *f*	24	case, casket
— à bijoux	25	jewel case
catalogue *m*	26	catalogue, price-list
Demandez notre —	27	Write for our catalogue
cataloguer *vb*	28	to catalogue, list
catégorie *f*	29	category, class
catégorique *adj*	30	categorical
un refus —	31	a flat refusal
caténaire *adj*	32	connected (in a series)
réaction —	33	chain reaction
causalité *f*	34	causality
principe de —	35	law of cause and effect
cause *f*	36	1 cause, reason, interest, motive
	37	2 case, action, lawsuit
avoir gain de —	38	to win a case
faire — commune avec qqun	39	to stand by s.o., to make common — with s.o.

mettre qqun en —	1	to implicate s.o.
pour — de santé	2	for reasons of health
caution *f*	3	surety
bonne et valable —	4	good and valid security
—	5	deposit (on a bottle)
— de banque	6	bank guarantee
— solvable	7	good surety
—s pour compte de tiers	8	guarantees given for account of others
— solidaire	9	joint security
être — de qqun	10	to vouch for s.o., to stand — for s.o.
fournir —	11	to give security
fournir une —	12	to find a —
s'adresser aux —s	13	to apply to one's sureties
se porter — pour qqun	14	to go bail for s.o.
sujet à —	15	unreliable
cautionnement *m*	16	deposit, surety bond, guaranty
— accessoire	17	collateral security
— en actions	18	deposit in shares
— en numéraire	19	security in cash
— personnel	20	personal security
cavalerie *f*	21	accommodation bill
cédant *m*	22	transferor, grantor, assignor
céder *vb*	23	to cede, to yield
— des actions	24	to transfer shares
— un droit	25	to cede a right
— (un fonds de commerce)	26	to sell
commerce à —	27	business (offered) for sale
cédule *f*	28	schedule (of taxes) ; [Lég.] notification
centime *m* [1/100 of a franc]	29	centime
centimètre, (cm) *m* [1/100 of a metre]	30	centimetre
central *adj*	31	central ; chief, principal ; head
chauffage —	32	central heating
centre *m*	33	centre
— commercial	34	shopping centre
— de villégiature	35	holiday resort
certain *m*	36	fixed (rate of) exchange
donner le —	37	to quote in home currency
certain *adj*	38	certain
indice —	39	sure indication
un fait —	40	a positive fact

certificat *m*	*1*	certificate
— d'action(s)	*2*	share —
— d'analyse	*3*	— of analysis
— d'aptitude profession-nelle	*4*	— of proficiency, of compe-tency
— d'assurance	*5*	insurance —
— de bonne conduite	*6*	good-conduct —
— (d'employeurs)	*7*	testimonial
— de navigabilité	*8*	— of seaworthiness
— d'entrepôt	*9*	warehouse warrant
— de jauge/de tonnage	*10*	— of measurement
— de trésorerie	*11*	Treasury bond
— d'expédition postale	*12*	— of mailing
certificateur *m*	*13*	guarantor, countersurety
certifier *vb*	*14*	to certify, to warrant, to vouch (for) ; to witness (a signature)
copie certifiée conforme	*15*	certified true copy
cessation *f*	*16*	ceasing
— de payement	*17*	stoppage/suspension of payments
cesser *vb*	*18*	to cease, stop
— le travail	*19*	to stop work(ing)
— ses payements/de payer	*20*	to stop payment
Le commerce avec l'étran-ger n'a cessé de s'amé-liorer	*21*	Foreign trade has improved steadily
cessible *adj*	*22*	transferable
cession *f*	*23*	transfer ; assignment
acte de —	*24*	deed of transfer
— de biens	*25*	cession of property to
— d'une créance	*26*	assignment of debts to
cessionnaire *m*	*27*	transferee, assignee
chaîne *f*	*28*	chain
la — de montage	*29*	assembly line
réaction en —	*30*	— reaction
travail à la —	*31*	flow production
chambre *f*	*32*	room
Chambre de compensa-tion	*33*	Clearing House
Chambre des Notaires	*34*	Board of Notaries
la — des machines	*35*	engine —
retenir une —	*36*	to reserve a —
champ *m*	*37*	field

avoir le — libre	1	to have a clear —
— d'activité	2	— of operation, sphere of action
— d'application	3	applicability
— d'expérience	4	—
chancelier *m*	5	chancellor; secretary
grand —	6	Lord Chancellor
change *m*	7	exchange
agent de —	8	stockbroker
bureau de —	9	foreign — office
— contraire	10	unfavourable —
donner le — à qqun	11	to fob s.o. off, to lead s.o. astray
lettre de —	12	bill of —
le cours du —	13	the rate of —
marché des —s à terme	14	forward — market
pair du —	15	par of —
première de —	16	first of —
changement *m*	17	change, shift, alteration
apporter un — (à)	18	to make a change (in), to alter sth.
— de direction/propriétaire	19	under new management
— de domicile	20	change of domicile
chanter *vb*	21	to sing
faire — (qqun)	22	to blackmail
chantier *m*	23	works, work area
— de construction (navale)	24	shipyard
le temps des —s [Can.]	25	logging season
mettre en —	26	1 to start work on
	27	2 to lay down, steer (ship) further away
(ouvrage) en —	28	(job) on the stocks
chapeau *m*	29	hat
droit de —	30	primage
charbon *m*	31	coal
— de soute	32	bunker, —s
—s domestiques	33	house —
faire le —	34	to —, to bunker
charbonner *vb*	35	1 to char, burn 2 to coal
charbonnier *m*	36	[Pers.] coal dealer, coal man, coaler
	37	[bateau] coaler, coal ship, boat
charcuterie *f*	38	delicatessen, pork-butcher's shop

charge *f*	*1*	1 burden, load; cargo
	2	2 care, charge, position; office; duty
	3	3 utilities and extras; expense
à — (du locataire)	*4*	payable (by the tenant)
avoir — d'âmes	*5*	to be responsible for others
—s fixes	*6*	standing charges
—s sociales	*7*	social charges
Elle est à ma —	*8*	She's in my care; I am supporting her
être à la — de (la firme)	*9*	to be chargeable to/to be borne by (the firm)
(frais) à notre —	*10*	(expenses) at our expense
Le loyer est de £50 plus les —s	*11*	The rent is £50 plus the utilities
personnes à —	*12*	dependent persons
revenir à la —	*13*	to try again
sans —s de famille	*14*	without encumbrances
chargé *adj*	*15*	1 loaded (with, *de*)
	16	2 entrusted (with, *de*)
chargé d'affaires *n.m.*	*17*	chargé d'affaires, envoy
chargement *m*	*18*	load, cargo; lading, loading
frais de —	*19*	loading expenses
charger *vb*	*20*	1 to load
	21	2 to give a responsibility to, to entrust
— en vrac	*22*	to ship in bulk
charpentier *m*	*23*	carpenter; [de navire] shipwright
charrier *vb*	*24*	to carry (down), transport
charroi *m*	*25*	cartage
charte *f*	*26*	charter
— -partie	*27*	— -party
chauffage *m*	*28*	heating
— automatique	*29*	stoker
— central	*30*	central —
chef *m*	*31*	head
— d'accusation	*32*	count of indictment
— de bureau	*33*	—/chief clerk
— de file	*34*	leader
— de gare	*35*	stationmaster
— d'équipe	*36*	foreman
— de rayon	*37*	floor-walker
— de service	*38*	— of department

— de train	1	train conductor
— de vente	2	sales manager
— d'exploitation	3	works manager
— de contentieux	4	solicitor
— du personnel	5	staff manager, personnel officer
— -lieu	6	county seat, chief town
de mon propre —	7	on my own authority, off my own bat
ingénieur en —	8	chief engineer
chemise f	9	folder, jacket (for filing)
chemiserie f	10	trade in/manufacturing of shirts; haberdashery
chemisier m	11	shirtmaker; haberdasher
cheptel m	12	(live-)stock
chèque m	13	cheque
— au porteur	14	bearer —
— barré	15	crossed —
— en blanc	16	blank —
— endossé	17	endorsed —
— en duplicata	18	duplicate —
— refusé	19	rejected —
— sans provision	20	— without sufficient funds; dud —; R.D. [=refer to drawer]
carnet de —s	21	— book
encaisser/toucher un —	22	to cash a —
endosser un —	23	to endorse a —
faire un —	24	to write a —
payer par —	25	to pay by —
refuser le payement d'un —	26	to dishonour a —
tirer un — sur la banque X	27	to draw a — on X bank
cher, -ère adj	28	dear
indemnité de vie chère	29	cost-of-living bonus
un peu —	30	pricy
cherté f	31	dearness, high prices
— de la vie	32	high cost of living
chevalier m **d'industrie**	33	swindler
chiffre m	34	figure
— d'affaires	35	turnover
—s arabes	36	Arabic numerals
chiffré adj	37	1 calculated, worked out
	38	2 [message] in cipher
	39	3 [linge] marked in cipher
en —	40	in cipher

mot —	1	code —
chiffrer *vb*	2	¹ to calculate
	3	² to number (pages) ; to en-code (a message), to reckon
Nos dépenses se chiffrent à . . .	4	Our expenses add up to . . .
chirographaire *adj*	5	[Lég.] depending on a simple contract ; unsecured
créance —	6	unsecured debt
créancier —	7	unsecured creditor
obligation —	8	simple debenture/contract
choc *m*	9	impact
phrase de —	10	slogan, punch line
choix *m*	11	choice
(article) de —	12	selected, —
au —	13	at —, by —
au — de l'acheteur	14	at buyer's option
de tout premier —	15	first class, of the best qua-lity
faire un — parmi	16	to select from
grand — de . . .	17	large assortment/range of...
questions au —	18	optional questions
deux francs au —	19	all priced at two francs
chômage *m*	20	unemployment
allocation de —	21	— benefit, [Fam.] dole
assurance- —	22	— insurance
— d'une usine	23	shutting down of a works
être en —	24	to be out of work
chômer *vb*	25	[gens] to be idle, out of work
	26	[usine] to be at a standstill, to stand idle
. . . ne chôme pas	27	. . . is kept busy
chômeur *m*	28	unemployed worker
— complet	29	wholly unemployed
— partiel	30	temporarily unemployed
les —s	31	the unemployed
chronique *f*	32	chronicle
la — financière	33	the financial news
chute *f*	34	downfall, decline, heavy fall (of prices)
ci-après *adv*	35	thereafter, further on
ci-contre *adv*	36	opposite, see opposite page ; annexed

45

ci-dessous *adv*	1	see below, hereunder
ci-dessus *adv*	2	see above, above(-mentioned)
ci-inclus, ci-joint *adv* & *adj*	3	herewith, enclosed
Ci-joint copie de votre lettre	4	Herewith copy of your letter
les pièces ci-jointes	5	the documents enclosed herewith
Veuillez trouver ci-joint . . .	6	Enclosed please find . . .
circonstance *f*	7	circumstance
—s aggravantes	8	aggravating —s
—s atténuantes	9	extenuating —s
—s indépendantes de notre volonté	10	—s outside/beyond our control
concours de —s	11	sequence of events
mesure de —	12	emergency measure
orateur de —	13	guest speaker
par suite de —s imprévues	14	owing to unexpected —s
pour la —	15	for the occasion
circonstancié *adj*	16	detailed
circulaire *n.f.*	17	circular
envoyer des —s	18	to send out —s
circulaire *adj*	19	circular
billet —	20	tourist ticket
circulation *f*	21	circulation
— des devises	22	currency dealings
— des valeurs mobilières	23	transactions in securities
— interdite	24	no thoroughfare
libre — des travailleurs/de la main-d'œuvre	25	free movement of labour
mettre en —	26	to put in —
circuler *vb*	27	to circulate
Ce train ne circule pas le dimanche	28	This train does not run on Sundays
faire circuler (une lettre)	29	to pass around (a letter)
faire circuler une nouvelle	30	to spread a piece of news
citation *f*	31	[Lég.] summons
— des témoins	32	subpoena of witnesses
cité *f*	33	city
avoir droit de —[of custom, etc.]	34	to be acceptable
— ouvrière	35	low rent development (for workmen)
citer *vb* (en justice)	36	to summon

citerne f	1	cistern, tank
navire/bateau —	2	tanker
civil adj	3	civil
état —	4	marital status
classe f	5	class
de grande —	6	top quality, first —
la — ouvrière	7	the working —
voyager en première (classe)	8	to travel first —
classé adj	9	filed, classified
une affaire —e	10	a closed case
classement m	11	filing
— des fiches	12	— of cards
— par fiches	13	cardindex system
— par ordre alphabétique	14	— in alphabetical order
— par ordre chronologique	15	in order of date, chronologically
— par ordre numérique	16	— in numerical order
classer vb	17	to file
— par ordre de grandeur	18	to arrange in order of size/ by size
— une affaire	19	to shelve a question
classeur m	20	file, filing cabinet
classification f	21	classification f
clause f	22	clause
— additionnelle	23	rider
— commissoire	24	commissoria lex
— compromissoire	25	arbitration —
— de sauvegarde/de résiliation	26	escape —
— résolutoire	27	avoidance —
clearing m	28	clearing
par la voie du —	29	through —
clef, clé f	30	key
mettre sous —	31	to put under lock and —
poste- —	32	— job
client m	33	customer
— [d'une banque, d'un avocat]	34	client
— de passage	35	chance/casual —
clientèle f	36	custom, customers, connection; goodwill
— (d'un médecin, d'un avocat)	37	practice
la — diminue	38	custom is dropping off

47

clore *vb*	1	to close
— les débats	2	[Lég.] to end the hearings of a trial
— un compte	3	— (out) an account
clos *m*	4	vineyard
clos *adj*	5	closed
à huis —	6	in camera, behind — doors
clôture *f*	7	closing
— annuelle des livres	8	annual balancing of the books
— de la Bourse	9	close of the Exchange
— d'un compte	10	— of an account
en — [en Bourse]	11	at the close
être ferme en —	12	to close firm
clôturer *vb*	13	to bring to an end, wind up, close
cocher *vb*	14	to notch, nick
code *m*	15	code
— de la route	16	traffic regulations
— chiffré	17	cipher
— civil	18	Civil —
— de commerce	19	commercial law
— télégraphique	20	telegraphic —
— maritime	21	navigation laws
écrire en —	22	to send a —d message
codicile *m* [Lég.]	23	rider
coeffecent *m*	24	ratio
— de liquidité	25	liquidity —
— de pondération	26	weighted —
— de sûreté/sécurité	27	safety factor
— de trésorerie	28	cash —
coéquation *f*	29	proportional assessment
coffre(-fort) *m*	30	safe, strong box
avoir accès aux coffres-forts	31	to have access to safes
contrat de location de —	32	safe deposit agreement
galerie de coffres-forts	33	safe deposit, vaults
location de —	34	safe hiring
cogestion *f*	35	joint management
colis *m*	36	parcel
— avec valeur déclarée	37	insured/registered —
(envoyer par) — postal	38	(to send by) — post
collaborateur, —rice *n*	39	collaborator; colleague, associate, [d'un journal] contributor

collatéral *adj*	*1*	collateral
collège *m*	*2*	1 secondary school
	3	2 examining board
collègue *n.m/f*	*4*	colleague, fellow member
Monsieur et cher —	*5*	My dear Mr. Johnson
colleur *m* **d'affiches**	*6*	bill sticker
collusion *f*	*7*	[Lég.] collusion
colocataire *n.m/f*	*8*	cotenant
colonne *f*	*9*	column
— créditrice	*10*	credit —
— débitrice	*11*	debit —
— du libellé	*12*	description/particulars —
— du montant	*13*	amount —
un en-tête de —	*14*	headline
colportage *m*	*15*	hawking, peddling
colporter *vb*	*16*	to hawk, peddle; [nouvelles] to spread
colporteur *m*	*17*	hawker, peddler
combinaison *f*	*18*	combination, arrangement, grouping
— de couleurs	*19*	colour scheme
combine *f*	*20*	[Fam.] racket
combiné *n.m.*	*21*	French telephone, hand phone
combler *vb*	*22*	to fill, make up; to overload
— un déficit	*23*	to make up a shortage
— une lacune	*24*	to fill a gap
comité *m*	*25*	committee
— consultatif	*26*	advisory — /board
— d'accueil	*27*	reception —
— de direction	*28*	board of management
en petit —	*29*	an informal gathering
commande *f*	*30*	order
bulletin de —	*31*	— form
carnet de —s	*32*	— book
— postale	*33*	mail —
—s en carnet/en cours	*34*	—s on hand, backlog of —s
exécuter une —	*35*	to execute/fulfil an —
faire une —	*36*	to place an —
passer une —	*37*	to give an —
sourire de —	*38*	forced smile —
sur —	*39*	(made) to —
commanditaire *m*	*40*	sponsor, backer, sleeping-partner
commandite *f*	*41*	1 limited partnership

49

	1 *2*	(part of) capital invested by sleeping partner(s)
société en —	*2*	sleeping / limited partnership
commanditer *vb*	*3*	to finance, back
commerçable *adj*	*4*	negotiable
commerçant *m*	*5*	dealer, trader, merchant; tradesman
commerçant *adj*	*6*	commercial, business
bon —	*7*	keen trader
nation —e	*8*	mercantile nation
quartier —	*9*	business district/quarter
rue —e	*10*	shopping street
commerce *m*	*11*	trade
— de cabotage	*12*	coasting/coastal —
— d'échange	*13*	barter
effets de —	*14*	— bills
être dans le —	*15*	to be in business
faire le — de	*16*	to deal in
faire le — de gros/de détail	*17*	to wholesale/retail
fonds de —	*18*	business; goodwill
le — de détail	*19*	retail —
le — de gros	*20*	wholesale —
le — extérieur	*21*	foreign —
le — d'exportation	*22*	export —
le — d'importation	*23*	import —
le — d'outre-mer	*24*	overseas —
le — intérieur	*25*	home —
le régistre du Commerce	*26*	— register
le — transitaire	*27*	transit —
office du — extérieur	*28*	foreign — agency
ouvrir un —	*29*	to start a —
société de —	*30*	commercial firm, business
tribunal de —	*31*	commercial court
un — de (voitures)	*32*	a (car) business
commettant *m*	*33*	principal [chief participant in a transaction]
commis *m*	*34*	clerk
— (à la vente)	*35*	salesman, (shop-)assistant
— (aux écritures)	*36*	—
— de banque	*37*	bank —
— voyageur	*38*	commercial traveller, (travelling) salesman
Grand — de l'Etat	*39*	high official

commissaire *m*	1	commissioner, commissary
—	2	[ship] purser
— de police	3	police commissioner
— -priseur	4	auctioneer; appraiser, valuer
commission *f*	5	commission, committee, board
— d'arbitrage	6	arbitration committee
— d'assurance-chômage	7	Unemployment Insurance Commission
— d'enquête	8	board of enquiry
— d'examen	9	board of examiners
— du budget	10	Budget Committee
commission *f*	11	commission, percentage
prélever une —	12	to charge a commission
toucher une —	13	to get a commission
travailler à la —	14	to work on commission
une — de 4%	15	a 4 per cent commission
commissionnaire *m*	16	agent, factor
— en douane	17	customs agent
— expéditeur	18	shipping/forwarding agent
commun *adj*	19	common
compte —	20	joint account
des intérêts —s	21	— interests
d'un — accord	22	with one accord
communauté *f*	23	order, society, corporation
— de biens	24	co-ownership
communication *f*	25	communication
— téléphonique	26	telephone call
donner — de qqch à qqun	27	to inform s.o. of sth.
entrer en — avec qqun	28	to get in touch with s.o.
être en — avec qqun	29	to be in touch with s.o.
mettre en —	30	to connect
communiqué *m*	31	communiqué, official report, press release
communiquer *vb*	32	to communicate, to pass on, to impart; to join
chambres qui communi-quent	33	connecting rooms
compagnie *f* (Cie)	34	company (Co.)
— d'aviation	35	airline —
comparaison *f*	36	comparison
établir une — entre deux choses	37	to draw a parallel between two things
comparaître *vb*	38	to appear

— en justice	1	— before a court
être appelé à —	2	to be summoned to appear
comparution f	3	[Lég.] appearance
non- —	4	default
compensation f	5	compensation
caisse de —	6	equalization fund
Chambre de —	7	clearing-house
en — de	8	to compensate for
jour de —	9	contango day
offrir une — (pour)	10	to make up (for)
compétence f	11	1 competency
	12	2 jurisdiction
Ce n'est pas de ma —	13	It's not within my competence
compétent adj	14	competent; efficient
compétitif, -ve adj	15	competitive
complaisance f	16	compliance, kindness
effet/billet de —	17	accommodation bill, [Fam.] kite
complet, -ète adj	18	full
salle complète	19	— house
un four —	20	a flop
comporter vb	21	to allow; to include, to admit of
composé n.m. & adj	22	1 compound
	23	2 composed (of, de)
— chimique	24	chemical compound
intérêts —s	25	accrued/compound interest
composer vb	26	to compose
— avec ses créanciers	27	to settle with one's creditors
— un numéro	28	to dial a number
se composant de	29	being composed of
se — de	30	to consist of
composition f [Lég.]	31	agreement, settlement
entrer en — avec qqun	32	to reach an agreement with s.o.
comprendre vb	33	1 to understand
	34	2 to include
— à demi-mot	35	to take a hint
faire —	36	to hint at
faire — à qqun	37	to make it clear to s.o.
se faire bien —	38	to make o.s. clear
comprimer vb	39	to check, to restrain; to compress
compris adj	40	included

non —	1	not —
tout (est) —	2	everything (is) —
... y —(e)(s)	3	including ...
compromissoire *adj*	4	arbitral
clause —	5	arbitration clause
comptabiliser *vb*	6	to record, to enter (in)
comptabilité *f*	7	1 bookkeeping, accounting
	8	2 accounts; accounting department
— en partie double	9	double-entry bookkeeping
— en partie simple	10	single-entry bookkeeping
la — d'une compagnie	11	the accounts of a firm
tenir la — d'une maison	12	to keep the books of a firm
comptable *n.m. & adj*	13	1 accountant, bookkeeper
	14	2 responsible, accountable (for, *de*)
expert- —	15	chartered accountant
machine —	16	accounting machine
période —	17	accounting period
pièce —	18	voucher
valeur —	19	book value
comptant *n.m., adj & adv*	20	cash
affaires au —	21	— transactions
argent —, du —	22	ready money
au —	23	for —
cours du —	24	— price
payer —	25	to pay (in) —
vendre/acheter au —	26	to sell/buy for —
vente au —	27	— sale
compte *m*	28	account
à bon —	29	cheap
(acheter) pour le — de	30	(to buy) on s.o.'s behalf
— à demi	31	joint —
— à recevoir	32	receivables
— commun	33	joint —
— chèques postaux (CCP)	34	postal cheque —
— courant	35	current —
— courant postal	36	Post Office current —
— de frais	37	disbursement —
— d'exploitation	38	trading —
— en participation	39	joint —
— particulier	40	private —
—s d'ordre	41	contingent —s; contra-items
demander — à qqun	42	to bring s.o. to — (for sth.)

extrait de votre — chez nous	1	statement/abstract of your — with us
faire le — de	2	to reckon up, add up
faire les —s	3	to settle up
livre de —s	4	— book
ne tenir aucun — de	5	to ignore
pour le — de qui il appartiendra	6	for — of whom it may concern
pour son propre —	7	for one's own —
relevé de —	8	statement of —
rendre — de	9	to report on
solder un —	10	to balance an —
tenir ses —s	11	to keep one's —s
tout — fait	12	everything considered
trouver son — à	13	to find it advantageous to
un — rond	14	in round numbers
compte rendu m	15	report, account; review
compter vb	16	1 to reckon, count; to number; to number among
	17	2 to charge; [trop cher] to overcharge
	18	3 to expect, to intend
	19	4 to count, rely (on, sur); to imagine; to depend (upon, sur)
à — du 13 mars	20	as from March 13
— pour (deux, etc.)	21	to count as (two, etc.)
dépenser sans —	22	to squander
sans —	23	exclusive of
sans — que	24	without mentioning that
comptoir m	25	1 counter; bar
	26	2 branch, agency [usual. overseas]
	27	3 bank
— d'escompte	28	discount bank
compulser vb	29	to examine (papers)
concerner vb	30	to concern; to affect; to relate to
Ça ne nous concerne pas	31	That's no business of ours
Cela concerne vos intérêts	32	It affects your interests
en ce qui concerne	33	with regard to
en ce qui me concerne	34	as far as I am concerned
concerter vb	35	to plan, arrange (plan)
se —	36	to plan together, consult

concession *f*	1	grant (of land); homestead; concession
faire une —	2	to make a concession, to stretch a point
concessionnaire *m*	3	1 concessionnaire [holder of official concession]; licence-holder
	4	2 grantee (of land)
concevoir *vb*	5	to devise (a plan), to conceive; to imagine; to draft; to word
le télégramme était ainsi conçu	6	the telegram was worded/ running as follows
concluant *adj*	7	conclusive
peu —	8	inconclusive
conclure *vb*	9	1 to conclude
	10	2 to end, finish (a transaction)
	11	3 to decide, give an opinion
en —	12	to infer/deduce one thing from another
on vous demande de —	13	your comment is required
conclusion *f*	14	conclusion; termination; [Lég.] motion, plea
déposer des —s [Lég.]	15	to raise a point of law
en arriver à une —	16	to arrive at/come to a conclusion
en tirer ses propres —s	17	to draw one's own conclusions
tirer une —	18	to draw a conclusion, to make an inference
concordat *m*	19	composition
accorder le —	20	to accept the —
— de 50%	21	a — of 10s. in the £
— préventif (à la faillite)	22	scheme of — [between debtor and creditors]
homologuer le —	23	to sanction the —
projet de —	24	draft —
concordataire *adj* [Lég.]	25	of bankrupt who has made a composition with his creditors
procédure —	26	composition proceedings
proposition —	27	proposal for a composition
concorder *vb*	28	to tally, agree (with, *avec*)
concours *m*	29	1 assistance, help

	1	2 examination
	2	3 match, show, competition
	3	4 concourse (of circumstances)
— d'admission	4	entrance examination
— d'étalages	5	window-dressing competition
hors —	6	1 not for competition
	7	2 in a class by itself
offrir/prêter son —	8	to help, collaborate
concurrence f	9	competition
— déloyale	10	unfair —; dumping
faire — à	11	to compete with
concurrencer vb	12	to compete with
concurrent m	13	1 competitor, rival
	14	2 candidate
concurrentiel, -le adj	15	competitive
condamner vb	16	to forbid
— la vente de qqch.	17	— the sale of sth.
condition f	18	condition
—s de payement	19	terms of payment
Faites vos —s	20	Name your terms
(marchandises) à —	21	(goods) on sale or return, on approval
poser des —s à (qqun)	22	to impose —s (on s.o.)
sans —	23	unconditionally
sous —	24	conditionally
conditionner vb	25	1 to condition (silk, wool, etc.); to season (wood)
	26	2 to prepare goods for market
condoléances n.f.pl.	27	condolence, sympathy
lettre de —	28	letter of condolence
exprimer/offrir/présenter à qqun ses —	29	to offer one's sympathy to s.o.
conducteur, -rice n & adj	30	1 engineer; driver
	31	2 conducting, driving
— de bestiaux	32	drover
— des ponts et chaussées	33	public works engineer
— de(s) travaux	34	works foreman
— d'une machine	35	machine-minder
confection f	36	1 construction
	37	2 ready-made clothes
la — d'une machine	38	the construction of a machine
maison de —	39	1 dress-making firm

	1	2 ready-made shop
un complet de —	2	a ready-made suit
confectionner *vb*	3	to make (up) (dress); to construct (machine); to manufacture (clothing)
confectionneur, -se *n*	4	outfitter
conférence *f*	5	lecture, talk, conference
— de presse	6	press conference
— sur un pied d'(entière) égalité	7	a round-table —
faire une —	8	to give a lecture
confiance *f*	9	trust
abus de —	10	breach of —; embezzlement
avoir — en qqun	11	to — s.o.'s word
digne de —	12	trustworthy
faire — à qqun	13	to — s.o.
firme/homme de —	14	reliable firm/person
poser la question de —	15	to ask for a vote of confidence
poste de —	16	position of —
confiner *vb*	17	1 to border
	18	2 to imprison, confine
confirmation *f*	19	confirmation; ratification
dans l'attente de votre —	20	awaiting your confirmation
confiscation *f*	21	confiscation, appropriation
confiserie *f*	22	confectionery trade; confectionery shop
confisquer *vb*	23	to take away; [Lég.] to seize, confiscate, appropriate, attach
conflit *m*	24	conflict
entrer en — avec	25	to — with
être en — (avec)	26	to clash (with)
(opinions) en —	27	conflicting (opinions)
conforme *adj*	28	identical
— à	29	corresponding (to), consistent (with); identical (with), true (to)
— au contrat/à la loi	30	in accordance with the contract/the law
copie —	31	certified true copy
conformément (à) *adv*	32	in accordance (with), according to
conformer *vb*	33	to adapt; to shape; to conform

se — à	1	to comply with
se — aux instructions	2	to obey orders, to toe the line
conformité *f*	3	conformity, similarity (with, *avec*)
en — de	4	in accordance with
congé *m*	5	leave
— de maladie	6	sick —, — of absence
—s payés	7	holidays with pay
donner — à (un ouvrier)	8	to dismiss, lay off (a workman)
donner son — à	9	to give notice to
prendre — de	10	take — of
congédiement *m*	11	dismissal
congédier *vb*	12	[domestique] to dismiss, discharge
	13	[ouvrier] to lay off
	14	[équipage] to pay off
	15	[visiteur importun] to send away
conjecture *f*	16	conjecture, surmise, guess
conjoint *adj*	17	joint
commission —e	18	— committee
légataires —s	19	co-legatees
conjointement *adv*	20	jointly
— et solidairement [Lég.]	21	— and severally
conjoncture *f*	22 1	conjuncture, (combination of) circumstances
	23 2	present situation
	24 3	[statistiques] contingency; probability, possibility of happening
des —s difficiles	25	hard times, predicament
haute —	26	boom
connaissance *f*	27	knowledge
avoir — de qqch.	28	to know/to be aware of sth.
avoir une parfaite — de la langue	29	to have a perfect command of the language
— [Lég.]	30	cognizance
être en pays de —	31	to be on familiar ground
(faire qqch.) en — de cause	32	(to do sth.) knowingly, with full — of the facts
prendre — de qqch.	33	to learn sth.
connaissement *m*	34	bill of lading (B/L)

rédiger un —	1	to make out a —
suivant —	2	as per —
connu adj	3	known
bien —	4	well- —
— sous le nom de	5	going by the name of
conseil m	6	(piece of) advice
— d'administration	7	board of directors
— de l'Europe	8	Council of Europe
— des ministres	9	Cabinet
— des prud'hommes	10	conciliation board [court of conciliation in disputes between employer and employee]
— du Trésor [Can.]	11	Treasury Board
— municipal	12	municipal/town council
faire qqch. sur le — de qqun	13	to do sth. on the — of s.o.
ingénieur- —	14	consulting engineer
consentement m	15	assent, consent
du — de tous	16	by general consent
consentir vb	17	to agree, consent
— un prêt	18	to grant a loan
Ils consentent à ce que nous le fassions	19	They consent to our doing it
conservateur n.m.	20	keeper, guardian
— des hypothèques	21	registrar of mortgages
conservatoire adj	22	of conservation
l'apposition des scellés est une mesure —	23	the affixing of seals is a measure —
considération f	24	consideration
Agréez, (Monsieur le Directeur), l'assurance de ma — distinguée.	25	Yours truly,
en — de	26	in recognition of
considérer vb	27	1 to consider, examine
	28	2 to esteem; to respect
considérant que . . . [Lég.]	29	whereas . . .
Il faut — que	30	It must be borne in mind that
consignataire m	31	1 consignee 2 [Lég.] trustee
consignateur m	32	consignor; shipper
consignation f	33	[marchandises] consignment
	34	[argent] deposit
consigne f	35	1 orders, instructions
	36	2 left-luggage office

consigner *vb*
- *1* 1 to deposit (a sum)
- *2* 2 to put one's luggage in the cloakroom
- *3* 3 to invoice temporarily items given on loan
- *4* 4 to mention, record (a fact, answer, etc. in a report)
- *5* 5 to stop (goods) at the customs

consolidation *f*
- *6* funding (of floating debt); [construction] bracing

consolidé *adj*
- *7* consolidated; strengthened
- les fonds —s *8* consols

consommation *f*
- *9* 1 consumption, use
- *10* 2 [au café] drink
- *11* 3 accomplishment; [marriage] consummation

- — intérieure/locale *12* home consumption
- — mondiale *13* world consumption
- denrées/biens de — *14* consumer goods
- la — de l'électricité *15* power consumption

consortium *m*
- *16* consortium, alliance, association

constat *m*
- *17* report
- dresser un — *18* to draw up a —

constatation *f*
- *19* ascertainment, [Lég.] verification; investigation; proof; inquiry

constater *vb*
- *20* 1 to establish
- *21* 2 to certify, record
- *22* 3 to verify; to find, ascertain

constituer *vb*
- *23* to form, constitute, set up; to make up

- — une commission *24* to set up a committee
- — une rente à qqun *25* to settle an annuity on s.o.
- — une société *26* to form a company

constitutif, -ve *adj*
- *27* constituent
- acte — *28* deed of partnership
- titres —s *29* title deeds

constitution *f*
- *30* 1 forming, formation
- *31* 2 incorporation (of a company)
- *32* 3 constitution (of a country)

constructeur *m*
- *33* 1 manufacturer [builder]
- *34* 2 [entrepreneur] contractor;

construction *f*	1	building
autorisation de —	2	— licence
bois de —	3	timber
— de logements	4	housing project
— de routes	5	road-making
— mécanique	6	mechanical engineering
— navale	7	ship-
matériaux de —	8	— materials
société de —	9	— company
voiture de — britannique	10	British-built car
consul *m*	11	consul
— général	12	general —
le — de Grande-Bretagne à . . .	13	the British — in . . .
consulaire *adj*	14	consular
consultatif, -ve *adj*	15	advisory
à titre —	16	in an — capacity
commission —	17	— committee
consultation *f*	18	consultation, [d'avocat] advice, opinion
heures de —	19	office hours
contenance *f*	20	[bouteille] capacity
	21	[champ] area
contenant *n.m. & adj*	22	1 container 2 containing
contentieux *m*	23	law department; solicitor's office
service du —	24	legal department
contentieux *adj*	25	[Lég.] contentious
contenu *m*	26	contents
contestable *adj*	27	debatable, questionable
contestation *f*	28	dispute
en — avec	29	at variance with
sans —	30	without opposition, unquestionably
contester *vb*	31	to contest; to dispute
une créance contestée	32	a questionable claim
contingent *m*	33	quota
— d'importation	34	import —
contingentement *m*	35	quota system
contingenter *vb*	36	to fix quotas for (imports, etc.); to allocate, to distribute (goods) according to a quota
contractant *adj*	37	contracting
les parties —es	38	the — parties

contracter *vb*	*1*	to contract
— des dettes	*2*	to — debts
— une assurance	*3*	to take out a policy
— une obligation (envers)	*4*	to make oneself liable (to)
contractuel, -le *adj*	*5*	on/by contract
contradiction *f*	*6*	contradiction
en — avec	*7*	inconsistent with
contradictoire *adj*	*8*	contradictory
conférence —	*9*	debate, forum
examen — [Lég.]	*10*	cross-examination
contrainte *f*	*11*	1 [Lég.] warrant, distraint
	12	2 pressure
agir par —	*13*	to act on pressure
— par corps	*14*	arrest
contraire *n.m. & adj*	*15*	opposite, contrary
au —	*16*	on the contrary
au — de	*17*	unlike
— au règlement	*18*	contrary to regulations
dans le cas —	*19*	if not
être d'un avis —	*20*	to be of the opposite opinion
sauf avis —	*21*	unless you hear otherwise/ to the contrary
contrat *m*	*22*	contract
— d'assurance	*23*	insurance policy
— de mariage	*24*	marriage settlement
— de vente	*25*	bill of sale
passer un — avec qqun	*26*	to conclude an agreement with s.o.
résilier un —	*27*	to cancel, annul a —
rupture de —	*28*	breach of —
contravention *f*	*29*	(police) offence, minor infraction
contre *n.m., prép & adv*	*30*	against
ci- —	*31*	on the opposite page
— toute attente	*32*	contrary to all expectations
le pour et le —	*33*	the pros and cons
livraison — remboursement	*34*	C.O.D.
contre-coup *m*	*35*	rebound; repercussion, consequence
contredire *vb*	*36*	1 to contradict
	37	2 to be inconsistent with, contrary to
contredit *adv*	*38*	contradictorily

sans —	1	without doubt, unquestionably
contre-écriture *f*	2	contra entry
contrefaçon *f*	3	[fait] forging, counterfeiting
	4	[l'objet] forgery, counterfeit, (fraudulent) imitation, faked article, sham
Méfiez-vous des —s	5	Beware of imitations
contrefaire *vb*	6	[signature] to forge
	7	[argent] to counterfeit
	8	[page, image] to copy
	9	[maladie] to simulate, sham
contrefait *adj*	10	counterfeit, forged; [pièce de monnaie] spurious
contre-partie *f*	11	counterpart
contre-passer *vb*	12	1 to return, to endorse back (bill to drawer)
	13	2 to reverse, transfer (entry, item)
contre-pied *m*	14	contrary, opposite
prendre le — (d'une opinion) [adv	15	to take the opposite side (of an opinion)
contre remboursement	16	C.O.D.
contreseing *m*	17	counter-signature
contresignataire *m*	18	person who signs a document already signed by s.o. else
contresigner *vb*	19	to countersign; to ratify, to confirm
contretemps *m*	20	inconvenience
(agir) à —	21	(to act) untimely, at the wrong moment
contre-valeur *f*	22	counterpart, equivalent
contribuable *n.m. & adj*	23	ratepayer, taxpayer
le rôle des —s	24	register of taxpayers
contribuer *vb*	25	to contribute
— à une dépense	26	to help pay an expense
— au succès d'une entreprise	27	to contribute to the success of an undertaking
contribution *f*	28	1 contribution; share
	29	2 tax, rate; excise; duty
apporter une précieuse —	30	to give invaluable assistance
—s directes	31	direct taxes
—s foncières	32	rates
—s indirectes	33	indirect taxes

63

payer une —	1	to pay a tax
contrôle *m*	2	control
— des changes	3	exchange —
— [marque officielle sur l'or, etc.]	4	(official) stamp, imprinted mark, hallmark
— postal	5	postal inspection
le contrôle des billets [au cinéma]	6	the taking of tickets
numéro de —	7	check number
passer au —	8	to go through a check point
contrôler *vb*	9	to control, verify, check, inspect
— l'or/les bijoux	10	to stamp/hallmark gold/jewels
contrôleur *m*	11	1 controller, inspector
	12	2 supervisor
	13	3 ticket collector
— des contributions [Belg.]	14	inspector of taxes
— du Trésor	15	comptroller of the Treasury
convenable *adj*	16	decent, proper
recevoir un salaire —	17	to be paid a suitable wage
convenir *vb*	18	1 to agree (upon)
	19	2 to admit, recognize
	20	3 to be right, proper, advisable to
	21	4 to suit, fit
convention *f*	22	convention
— verbale	23	verbal agreement
les —s d'un accord	24	the clauses/terms of an agreement
les —s sociales	25	social —s
sauf — contraire	26	unless otherwise agreed
conversation *f*	27	conversation
amener la — sur qqch.	28	to steer/bring the — around [sth.
— téléphonique	29	telephone call
conversion *f*	30	change, conversion
échelle de —	31	conversion table
convertissable *adj*	32	convertible
conviction *f*	33	conviction, firm belief
pièce à —	34	exhibit
convocation *f*	35	summons; convening
recevoir une —	36	to receive notice of meeting; to receive a letter fixing an appointment

convoquer *vb*	1	to convene (meeting) ; to invite s.o. to an interview ; to summon ; to call (shareholders, etc.) together
copie *f*	2	copy
— conforme	3	certified true —
dessin d'après —	4	reproduction (from a picture)
copropriétaire *m/f*	5	co-proprietor, joint owner
copropriété *f*	6	co-property, joint ownership
coquet, -te *adj*	7	generous ; fairly large
somme —te	8	tidy sum
corbeille *f*	9	1 basket
	10	2 [à la Bourse] Floor
cordonnerie *f*	11	[atelier] shoemaker's (shop)
	12	[profession] shoemaking
cornet *m* [tél]	13	(telephone) receiver
corporel, -le *adj*	14	tangible (property)
corps *m*	15	body, matter, main part
étoffe/vin avec du —	16	cloth/wine with body
perdu — et biens	17	lost with all hands
correcteur, -rice	18	proof-reader
correction *f*	19	correction
sauf —	20	subject to —
corrélation *f*	21	correlation
mettre en —	22	to correlate with
correspondance *f*	23	correspondence
— d'idées	24	thinking alike
dépouiller/ouvrir sa —	25	to open one's mail
être en — avec qqun	26	to be writing to s.o.
correspondance *f* [train]	27	connection
billet de —	28	transfer ticket
trains en —	29	trains which make connection
correspondancier, -ère *n*	30	one who writes letters or looks after the mail
correspondant *m*	31	correspondent
— à l'étranger	32	foreign —
correspondre *vb*	33	1 to agree, tally
	34	2 adjoin
	35	3 to correspond (by letter) with s.o.
deux chambres qui correspondent	36	adjoining rooms

La théorie ne correspond pas aux faits	1	The theory does not agree with the facts
corroborant *adj*	2	corroborating, confirming
corroborer *vb*	3	to corroborate, confirm
cosignataire *m*	4	one who signs with others on the same document
cotation *f*	5	quoting (of prices)
cote *f*	6	quotation
— des prix	7	share-list
faible/forte —	8	long/short odds
coté *adj*	9	quoted, marked
bien —	10	in high esteem
point — [sur une carte]	11	landmark
valeurs (non) —es	12	(un)listed securities
coter *vb*	13	to quote, rate, give a quotation on
coterie *f*	14	guild
cotisation *f*	15	contribution, share; membership fee [tion
verser une —	16	to send in one's subscrip-
cotiser (se) *vb*	17	[Fam.] to pass the hat (to buy a gift for s.o.); to take up a collection
couchette *f*	18	[train] berth
	19	[bateau] bunk
coup *m*	20	blow; shot; move
passer un — de fil	21	to give s.o. a (phone) call
tomber sous le — d'une loi	22	to come under (the provisions of) a law
coupe-fil *m*	23	pass
coupon *m*	24	1 remnant, cutting [of yard goods]
	25	2 coupon; ticket
— de dividende	26	dividend-warrant
— détaché/ex —	27	ex dividend
— échu	28	due coupon
— périmé	29	lapsed coupon
— -réponse (international)	30	(international) reply coupon
—s d'étoffe	31	oddments; remnants
encaisser des —s	32	to cash coupons
coupure *f*	33	1 [de journal] clipping, cutting
	34	2 [billet de banque] denomination
	35	3 fractional share

cour *f*	1	Court
— d'appel	2	— of appeal
courant *adj*	3	current
compte —	4	— account
dépenses —es	5	— expenses
être de vente —e	6	to have a ready sale
le mois —	7	the — month
le prix —	8	present price, list price
monnaie —e	9	legal tender
courant *n.m. & adv*	10	movement
dans le — de (la semaine)	11	in the course of (the week)
être au —	12	1 to know
	13	2 to be well-informed
mettre qqun au — de	14	1 to inform s.o. about
	15	2 [Fam.] to keep s.o. posted on/up to date
se tenir au — des événements	16	to keep up with the times
tenir qqun au —	17	to keep s.o. informed
courbe *f*	18	curve, graph
courrier *m*	19	mail
— maritime	20	sea —
— mondain	21	social column
— surface	22	surface —
dépouiller le —	23	to open the —
faire son —	24	to write one's letters
le — du matin, le premier —	25	the first post
par retour du —	26	by return (—)
cours *m*	27	1 course, length
	28	2 course, class
— d'application	29	demonstration course
— du soir	30	evening class
— spécialisé	31	honours course
en — de route	32	on the way
le programme des —	33	curriculum
les — d'eau	34	rivers
suivre des —	35	to take classes
voyage au long —	36	ocean trip, lengthy voyage
cours *m*	37	rate
— acheteur	38	buying —
— à terme	39	forward —
— à vue	40	demand —
— de clôture	41	closing —
— d'émission	42	issue price
— de déport	43	backwardation —

— de report	1	contango —
— de souscription	2	subscription price
— d'ouverture	3	opening price
— du comptant	4	spot —
— du marché	5	market price
— faits/pratiqués	6	business/bargains done
— officiel	7	official —
dernier/premier —	8	closing/opening price
idées qui n'ont plus —	9	outdated ideas
pièce qui n'a plus —	10	coin which is no longer legal tender
coursier, -ère	11	errand-boy, messenger
court *adj & adv*	12	short
(emprunt) à — terme	13	-dated (loan)
être à — de personnel/de main-d'œuvre	14	to be — -handed
être à — de qqch.	15	1 to be — 2 to run — of sth.
pris de —	16	taken unawares
courtage *m*	17	commission, brokerage, brokerage fee
coût *m*	18	cost
indice du — de la vie	19	— of living index
coûtant *adj*	20	cost, costing
au prix —	21	at cost price
coûteux, -se *adj*	22	expensive
peu —	23	in-
coutumier, -ère *adj*	24	usual, customary
droit —	25	common law
couture *f*	26	needlework
maison de —	27	dressmaking establishment
couvert *n.m. & adj*	28	1 cover charge
	29	2 to be covered
à —	30	in a safe place ; under cover
mettre sa fortune à —	31	to safeguard one's fortune
sous le — de	32	under the pretence of
couverture *f*	33	cover, covering
coefficient de —	34	cover ratio
commande sans —	35	order without security/cover
lettre de —	36	covering letter
sous — d' (amitié)	37	under the cover of (friendship)
couvrir *vb*	38	to cover
— une distance	39	— a distance
— une perte	40	to meet/make good a loss

créance *f*	1	1 belief, trust
	2	2 debt, claim
— active	3	outstanding debt
ajouter — à qqch.	4	to have faith in sth.
avoir — sur qqun	5	to have a claim on s.o.
— chirographaire	6	unsecured debt
— douteuse	7	doubtful debt
— exigible	8	debt due
— garantie	9	secured debt
— hypothécaire	10	mortgage
— litigieuse	11	contested claim
— passive	12	debt
—s gelées	13	frozen credits
— véreuse	14	bad debt
lettres de —	15	credentials
créancier, -ère *n*	16	creditor
commission des —s	17	board of —s
— gagiste	18	pledgee
— nanti	19	secured —
créateur, -rice *n*. & *adj*	20	1 founder 2 creative
création *f*	21	creation, foundation, setting-up
crédit *m*	22	credit
à —	23	on —
— à découvert/en blanc	24	blank —
— de/en réserve	25	stand-by —
— foncier	26	loan society
— immobilier	27	— on real property
— mobilier	28	— on personal property
— subsidiaire/dos à dos	29	back to back —
octroi de —	30	granting of —s
restriction du —	31	— squeeze
voter des —s	32	to vote supplies
créditer *vb*	33	to credit s.o. (with, *de*)
créditeur *n.m.* & *adj*	34	1 creditor 2 credit
compte —	35	credit account
solde —	36	credit balance
créer *vb*	37	to create; to found, start (a business, etc.)
se — une clientèle	38	to build up a connection
creux, -se *adj*	39	hollow
heures creuses	40	slack hours
cri *m*	41	cry
le dernier —	42	the latest style
crible *n*	43	sieve, sifter

passer au —	1		to sift, screen
criée *f*	2		auction
vente à la —	3		public —
crieur, -se *n*	4		hawker
un — de journaux	5		newsboy
crise *f*	6		crisis
— économique	7		depression
— politique	8		political —
critique *adj*	9		critical, crucial
situation —	10		emergency
croulant *adj*	11		crumbling; ramshackle
cubage *m*	12		cubic content/volume
cuir *m*	13		leather
— repoussé	14		tooled —
culture *f*	15	1	farming, cultivation
	16	2	culture
— générale	17		background
cumul *m*	18		cumulation, continuation
— de fonctions	19		pluralism
cuprifère *adj*	20		copper-bearing
valeur —	21		copper share
curatelle *f*	22		trusteeship, guardianship
curateur, -rice *n*	23		trustee, guardian
dactylo(graphe) *n.m/f*	24		typist
dactylographie *f*	25		typing, typewriting
dactylographier *vb*	26		to type(write)
date *f*	27		date
— postale	28		— as postmark
de vieille/longue —	29		longstanding
en — du 15 courant	30		—d the 15th inst.
être le premier en —	31		to come first
portant la — du 12 mai 1966	32		—d May 12, 1966
sans —	33		undated
dater *vb*	34	1	to date
	35	2	to date (from, *de*)
à — de ce jour	36		from now on
— de loin	37		to go far back
dateur *m*	38		date-marker
davantage *adv*	39		more, longer
bien —	40		much more
de *prép & explétif*	41		from, of, by, with
à la fin — mars	42		in late March

70

à partir —	1	from
au bout —	2	at the end of, after
dans un délai —	3	within
— la part —	4	from
deux — plus	5	two more
semaine — quarante heures	6	forty-hour week
débâcle f	7	disaster, downfall, collapse
déballage m	8	unpacking; display (of goods)
déballer vb	9	to unpack; [marchand ambulant] to spread out one's goods
débarcadère m	10	landing stage
débardeur m	11	stevedore
débarquement m	12	[marchandises] unloading
	13	[passagers] disembarkation, landing
débarquer vb	14	to unload (freight)
débat m	15	dispute, debate
soulever un —	16	to raise a question
suivre les débats	17	to follow the hearings of a trial
débattre vb	18	to discuss, to debate
se —	19	to struggle
débaucher vb	20	1 to seduce away from work
	21	2 to lay off workers
débit m	22	1 shop, retail store
	23	2 cutting up (of wood)
	24	3 output, delivery
	25	4 retailing (of goods)
article d'un bon —	26	fast-moving article
avoir un — facile	27	to have a fluent delivery
— de tabac	28	tobacconist's (shop)
le — d'un fleuve	29	the rate of flow of a river
débit m	30	debit
porter une somme au — de qqun	31	to — s.o. with a sum
débitant m	32	retailer
débiter vb	33	1 to saw up, to cut up (stone, wood)
	34	2 to produce, turn out, yield
	35	3 to sell; to retail
	36	4 to debit (s.o. with an amount)

débiteur, -rice *n. & adj*	1	1 debtor 2 debit
compte —	2	debit account
— saisi	3	distrainee
— solidaire	4	joint debtor
solde —	5	debit balance
débouché *m*	6	outlet, market, opening
chercher de nouveaux —s	7	to look for new outlets
débours *n.m.pl.*	8	disbursements, expenses
débourser *vb*	9	to pay, to disburse
sans rien —, sans — un sou	10	without spending a penny
débris *n.m.pl.*	11	remains, fragments
— de métal	12	scraps
— d'un naufrage	13	wreckage
débrouiller *vb*	14	to disentangle, to straighten out (s.o.'s accounts)
décacheter *vb*	15	to unseal
décalage *m*	16	shifting, staggering; discrepancy
décaler *vb*	17	to set back/forward
décalitre *m*	18	decalitre [= about 10 quarts]
décharge *f*	19	1 receipt; exoneration
	20	2 [Lég.] release, acquittal
	21	3 dumping ground
témoin à —	22	witness for the defence
décharger *vb*	23	to unload; to release
failli déchargé	24	discharged bankrupt
failli non déchargé	25	undischarged bankrupt
déchéance *f*	26	loss (of rights)
action en — de brevet	27	action for forfeiture of patent
— de propriété littéraire	28	lapse of rights in literary matter
— de titres	29	forfeiture of shares
— d'une police (d'assurance)	30	expiration of a policy
déchet *m*	31	waste, refuse
déchu *adj*	32	deprived of one's shares or rights; fallen
décider *vb*	33	1 to decide (sth.)
	34	2 to decide (to, *de*)
se —	35	to arrive at a decision; to make up one's mind
décimal *adj*	36	decimal
fraction —e	37	— fraction
le système —	38	the — system

décisif, -ve *adj*	1	decisive, crucial; conclusive
décision *f*	2	decision
— arbitrale	3	arbitrator's award
forcer une —	4	to bring matters to a head
réserver une —	5	to delay a —
revenir sur une —	6	to change one's mind, to think better of it
déclaration *f*	7	1 declaration
	8	2 affidavit
	9	3 notification
— de revenu	10	income-tax return
— en douane	11	customs' declaration
— sous serment	12	affidavit
faire sa — d'impôts	13	to return one's income to
faire une —	14	to make a statement
la — des droits de l'homme	15	the bill of human rights
déclarer *vb*	16	to declare
— ses intentions	17	to make one's intentions known
se — [incendie, guerre, etc.]	18	to break out
se — pour/contre un candidat	19	to come out for/against a candidate
déclassé *adj*	20	[bateau] obsolete
	21	[article] struck off the records
déclasser *vb*	22	to transfer from one class to another; to move to a lower class or category
décliner *vb*	23	to refuse, decline, turn down (an offer, an invitation, responsibility)
décommander *vb*	24	to countermand, cancel
décompte *m*	25	detail (of account); breakdown
découvert *n.m. & adj*	26	overdraft, overdraught; overdrawn
achat à —	27	bull purchase
acheteur à —	28	bull purchaser
à —	29	without cover, uncovered
compte —	30	overdrawn account
crédit à —	31	unsecured/blank credit
vendre à —	32	1 to bear the market
	33	2 to sell short
découvrir *vb*	34	to discover

— du pétrole	1	to strike oil
— une faute	2	to detect an error
décréter *vb*	3	to decree; [Lég.] to issue (a writ against)
décroître *vb*	4	to drop, decrease, diminish
dédire (se) *vb*	5	to go back (on statement), to retract
dédit *m*	6	1 forfeit, penalty (for breaking contract, etc.)
	7	2 retraction, withdrawal
dédommagement *m*	8	indemnity, compensation
une somme en — de qqch.	9	a sum as/in compensation for sth.
dédommager *vb*	10	1 to indemnify (for, *de*)
	11	2 to compensate, recoup
— qqun d'une perte	12	to make good a loss
se faire — par qqun	13	to recover from s.o.
dédouanage *m*, **dédouane-ment** *m*	14	clearance (of goods)
dédouaner *vb*	15	to clear through the customs; to take (goods) out of bond
dédoublement *m*	16	division into two; splitting (in two)
dédoubler *vb*	17	to divide in(to) two
déduction *f*	18	deduction
sans —	19	strictly net
sous — de 10%	20	less 10%
déduire *vb*	21	1 to deduct
	22	2 to deduce, infer
à — de (votre traitement)	23	to be deducted from (your salary)
— 5%	24	to take off, allow 5%
— ses frais (de)	25	to deduct one's expenses (from)
défalquer *vb*	26	to deduct; [Lég.] to recoup
défaut *m*	27	1 lack, absence of; failure
	28	2 defect, fault; wrong
à — de	29	for want of, in place of; failing
— de payement	30	non-payment, failure to pay
" — de provision "	31	" no funds "
faire —	32	to be lacking
faire — [Lég.]	33	to default, to fail to appear (in court)

prendre qqun en —	1	to catch s.o. napping/in the wrong
sans —	2	flawless, faultless, without a blemish
défectueux, -se *adj*	3	faulty, defective
défectuosité *f*	4	flaw, defect
défendeur *m* [Lég.]	5	defendant
défendre *vb*	6	1 to defend
		2 to forbid, prohibit
se —	7	to deny
se — (d'une prétention)	8	to disclaim
défense *f*	9	1 defence 2 prohibition
— d'afficher	10	stick/post no bills
la — [Lég.]	11	counsel (for the defence)
défenseur *m* [Lég.]	12	counsel for the defence
déficit *m*	13	deficit
combler le —	14	to make up the —
être en —	15	to show a —
déficitaire *adj*	16	showing a deficit/a debit balance
définitif, -ve *adj & adv*	17	final, definitive
à titre —	18	permanently
en définitive	19	in short ; after all, finally
définitivement *adv*	20	finally ; positively
déflation *f*	21	deflation
défraîchi *adj*	22	shop-soiled, shop-worn
défricher *vb*	23	to reclaim (land)
dégagé *adj*	24	free ; redeemed
dégagement *m*	25	release (from a promise) ; clearing (of road)
dégager *vb*	26	1 to redeem, clear (mortgage)
	27	2 to release (pledged) securities
	28	3 to bring out ; to come out
— l'idée essentielle	29	to bring out the important idea
se —	30	to free oneself
dégats *n.m.pl.*	31	damage
— matériels	32	property —
évaluer les —	33	to estimate the —
degré *m*	34	degree
— de liquidité	35	liquidity ratio
par —s	36	by —s, gradually
dégrèvement *m*	37	[taxes] reduction ; decrease

dégrever *vb*	*1*	1 to reduce (tax); to reduce the rates on (a building)
	2	2 to disencumber (estate); to clear off the mortgage on (a house)
dégringolade *f*	*3*	downfall, collapse
dégringoler *vb*	*4*	[entreprise] to go downhill
	5	[prix] to drop fast
délai *m*	*6*	delay, notice, time, speed
à court —	*7*	at short notice
dans le — prescrit, dans les —s voulus	*8*	within the required time
dans les meilleurs —s	*9*	with all possible speed
dans un — de (deux mois)	*10*	within (two months)
— de livraison	*11*	time of delivery
— de payement	*12*	term of payment
dernier —	*13*	deadline
délaissement *m* [Lég.]	*14*	renunciation (of right); abandonment (of ship to insurer)
délaisser *vb* [Lég.]	*15*	to relinquish, forgo (right); to abandon (ship to insurer)
délégation *f*	*16*	[pouvoir] delegation
	17	[personnes] delegation, delegacy
	18	[dette] assignment [s.o.
(agir) par —	*19*	(to act) on the authority of
délégué *m*	*20*	delegate
déléguer *vb*	*21*	to delegate, hand over (powers); to delegate (people)
délester *vb*	*22*	[navire] to unballast; to lighten
délibération *f*	*23*	deliberation
régistre des —s	*24*	minute-book
délicat *adj*	*25*	delicate; difficult
procédé peu —	*26*	unscrupulous behaviour
délictueux, -se *adj*	*27*	punishable, unlawful
acte/fait —	*28*	(minor indictable) offence, misdemeanour
délier *vb*	*29*	to release
— qqun d'un serment	*30*	— s.o. from an oath
délimitation *f*	*31*	fixing (of boundaries); defining (of powers)

délimiter *vb*	1	to fix (boundaries) ; to define (powers)
délinquant *m*	2	delinquent
— primaire	3	first offender
délit *m*	4	crime, offence, mislead, trespass, misdemeanour
être pris en flagrant —	5	to be caught in the act
délivrer *vb*	6	to issue (a certificate, tickets)
demande *f*	7	demand, request ; inquiry
— de renseignements	8	inquiry
— en divorce	9	action for divorce
" —s d'emploi "	10	" situations wanted "
faire sa —	11	to send in a request, to apply
l'offre et la —	12	supply and demand
sur —	13	on application, on request
demander *vb*	14	to ask (for)
Ça demande du temps	15	It requires time
Combien demandez-vous pour . . . ?	16	How much do you charge for . . . ?
— des dommages-intérêts	17	to claim damages
On vous demande au téléphone	18	You are wanted on the 'phone
demandeur *m* [Lég.]	19	plaintiff
démarche *f*	20	step, errand ; proceeding
faire une — auprès de qqun	21	to go and see s.o. (about, *au sujet de*)
Nous avons fait les —s nécessaires	22	We took the necessary steps
démarcheur *m*	23	canvasser
démarquer *vb*	24	to mark down (the prices)
démarrage *m*	25	start ; unmooring (of a ship)
démarrer *vb*	26	1 to start ; to leave ; [Fam.] to get under way
	27	2 to unmoor (ship) ; to cast off (the mooring lines of a ship)
avoir du mal à —	28	to have difficulty in getting under way
démêlé *m*	29	difficulty ; quarrel
avoir des —s avec	30	to argue, to have unpleasant dealings with
déménagement *m*	31	removal, moving
déménageur *m*	32	(furniture) mover

démentir *vb*	1	to refute, contradict; to belie
— un témoin	2	to refute a witness
démettre *vb* [Lég.]	3	to dismiss (a case)
se —	4	to resign
se — de ses fonctions	5	to resign one's position
démission *f*	6	resignation
donner sa —	7	to resign
remettre sa —	8	to tender one's —
démissionner *vb*	9	to resign
démonétiser *vb*	10	to call in, withdraw from circulation
démonstrateur, -rice *n*	11	demonstrator
démonstration *f*	12	demonstration
— sans engagement	13	free demonstration
faire une —	14	to give a —, to demonstrate
démontable *adj*	15	collapsible
déni *m*	16	refusal, denial
— de justice	17	miscarriage of justice
denier *m*	18	1 small coin; farthing
	19	2 money, funds
de ses propres —s	20	out of his own pocket
les —s publics	21	public funds
dénier *vb*	22	to disclaim (responsibility)
dénombrer *vb*	23	to enumerate, count
dénomination *f*	24	denomination, name
dénoncer *vb* [Lég.]	25	terminate (an agreement)
dénonciation *f* [Lég.]	26	notice of termination (of an agreement, partnership, treaty)
denrée *f*	27	commodity, produce
—s alimentaires	28	foodstuffs
dentelure *f*	29	[feuille] serrations
	30	[timbre, vignette] perforations
dépannage *m*	31	fixing, repairs, repairing
équipe de —	32	wrecking crew
dépanner *vb*	33	1 to make emergency repairs
	34	2 [Fig.] to get (s.o.) out of difficulty
dépareillé *adj*	35	unmatched
exemplaire —	36	odd number (magazine, etc.)
dépassement *m*	37	overdraft
départir *vb*	38	to allot, give out
se —	39	to leave; to renounce, abandon, give up

dépêche *f*	*1*	note, dispatch, notice (sent by the PTT)
dépendance *f*	*2*	1 [pays] dependency
	3	2 subordination, dependence
	4	3 *n.f.pl.* annexes, outbuildings, appendages (to)
dépens *n.m.pl.*	*5*	costs, expense
dépense *f*	*6*	expense, expenditure
— à vide	*7*	wasted energy
faires des —s	*8*	to incur expenses
recettes et —s	*9*	receipts and expenditure(s)
déperdition *f*	*10*	wastage; loss; diminution
dépérir *vb*	*11*	to go downhill, to go to pot
déplacement *m*	*12*	removal, shifting; travelling, commuting
— de 2.000 tonnes	*13*	displacement of 2,000 tons
frais de —	*14*	travelling expenses
déplacer *vb*	*15*	1 to move, shift; [bateau] to have a displacement of
	16	2 to transfer (a clerk)
dépliant *m*	*17*	(printed) folder
déport *m*	*18*	premium
le report ou le —	*29*	discount or —
déportation *f*	*20*	deportation
déporté *n.m.* & *adj*	*21*	1 convict
	22	2 deported (person), deportee
déporter *vb*	*23*	to deport
déposant *n.m.*	*24*	1 depositor
	25	2 [Lég.] witness, deponent
déposé *adj*	*26*	entered; registered
marque —e	*27*	registered trade mark
déposer *vb*	*28*	1 to deposit (money)
	29	2 to introduce (a bill)
	30	3 to lodge (a complaint)
	31	4 to register (a trade mark)
	32	5 to testify, to give evidence
	33	to go bankrupt
— son bilan		
— une caution	*34*	to deposit a security (in cash)
dépositaire *m*	*35*	1 agent 2 [Lég.] trustee
déposition *f* [Lég]	*36*	deposition, testimony (of a witness), sworn statement

déposséder *vb*	1	to dispossess; to oust
dépôt *m*	2	1 deposit (of a sum)
	3	2 depot, warehouse; [Lég.] jail
	4	3 deposition; registering (of a trade mark)
— à vue	5	demand deposit
— de la préfecture de	6	central police station
— des machines [Rail.]	7	engine shed
— en numéraire	8	cash deposit
— légal (d'un livre)	9	copyright privilege (of a trade mark)
— libre en garde	10	safe custody
en —	11	on deposit
faire un — en banque	12	to make a deposit at the bank
marchandises en —	13	goods in bond
dépouillement *m*	14	[de ses biens] despoiling
— du scrutin	15	counting of the ballots
dépouiller *vb*	16	1 to deprive (s.o. of his rights)
	17	2 to count (the ballots)
	18	3 to open (the mail)
dépréciation *f*	19	depreciation, fall in value
déprécier *vb*	20	to depreciate, to lower the value of; to underrate; to fall in value
se —	21	to fall in value
déprimé *adj*	22	[marché, etc.] depressed
députer *vb*	23	to depute, delegate
déréglé *adj*	24	out of order; irregular
dernier, -ère *adj*	25	last
au — étage	26	on the top floor
en — lieu	27	finally
la dernière mode	28	the latest fashion
mettre la dernière main à un ouvrage	29	to give the finishing touches to a work
dernièrement *adv*	30	recently, lately
tout —	31	only recently
dérogation *f*	32	derogation, impairment (of law)
déroger *vb*	33	to depart from (the law), not to conform to (a condition); to derogate (from, *à*)

dérouter *vb*	1	to deroute (a ship, train, etc.)
dès *prép* & *çonj*	2	from, since; as early as
— à présent	3	from now on, henceforth
— son arrivée	4	as soon as he arrives
— son retour	5	immediately on his return
désarmer *vb*	6	to put (ship) out of commission, to lay up (ship)
désarrimer *vb*	7	to unstow (cargo)
désavantager *vb*	8	to put at a disadvantage
désaveu *m*	9	disowning
désavouer *vb*	10	to disown; to disavow, repudiate
déscellé *adj*	11	unsealed
desceller *vb*	12	to unseal
description *f*	13	[de brevet] specification
(article) conforme à la —	14	(item) as represented
désignation *f*	15	1 description, designation (of goods)
	16	2 nomination (of s.o. to a post)
désigner *vb*	17	1 to describe, to mark (goods)
	18	2 to nominate (s.o. to a post)
	19	3 to be qualified, marked out (for a job)
désintéressé *adj*	20	1 impartial, disinterested
	21	2 having no interests at stake, not interested, no longer concerned
désintéressement *m*	22	paying (of creditors)
désintéresser *vb*	23	1 to buy out (partner, shareholder, etc.)
	24	2 to pay off (creditors)
se —	25	to give up one's interests (in, *de*); to lose one's interest (in, *de*)
désistement *m*	26	withdrawal
désister (se) *vb*	27	to withdraw (from a committee, one's candidature)
desservir *vb*	28	1 [faire un service de communication] to serve
	29	2 [nuire] to be detrimental (to one's interests)
dessinateur, -rice *n*	30	drawer; illustrator; draughtsman; designer
destinataire *m*	31	[lettre] addressee, " TO "

81

	1	[chèque, mandat] payee
	2	[caisse, valise] consignee
destination *f*	3	destination
arriver à sa —	4	to arrive at one's —
(bateau, train) à — de	5	(ship, train) bound for, for
(colis, lettre) à — de	6	(parcel, letter) addressed to
se diriger vers telle —	7	to set out for a certain —
destituer *vb*	8	to discharge, dismiss (from a position), to remove (official) from office
destitution *f*	9	dismissal, removal
détaché *adj*	10	separate, detached
pièces —es	11	spare parts
détacher *vb*	12	to take out/off; to separate, detach [line
— suivant le pointillé	13	Tear out along the dotted
détail *m*	14	detail
C'est un —	15	It's a mere —
entrer dans les —s	16	to go into —s
le — d'un compte	17	the items of an account
tous les —s	18	full particulars
détail *m*	19	retail
marchand au —	20	— dealer
prix de —	21	— price
vendre au —	22	to sell —
détaillant *n & adj*	23	retailer, retail (dealer)
détaillé *adj*	24	in detail, detailed
détailler *vb*	25	1 to cut up
	26	2 to retail
	27	3 to give the details
détaxe *f*	28	reduction or abatement of tax
détaxer *vb*	29	to reduce or abate tax
détenir *vb*	30	to retain, possess (power); to hold (a position)
détenteur, -rice *n*	31	holder; owner (of copyright, etc.)
— de titres	32	stockholder
déterminer *vb*	33	1 to determine; to fix
	34	2 to cause, to bring (sth.) about
détournement *m* [Lég.]	35	1 misappropriation (of funds), embezzlement
	36	2 abduction (of a minor)
détourner *vb*	37	1 [Lég.] to embezzle, misappropriate (funds)

	1	2 [Lég.] to abduct (a minor)
détriment m	2	detriment, disadvantage
dette f	3	debt
avoir des —s	4	to be in —
— consolidée	5	funded —
—s actives	6	book- —s ranking as assets
—s passives	7	liabilities
— véreuse	8	bad —
faire des —s	9	to run into —
deux adj	10	two
tous les — du mois	11	every second of the month
tous les — mois	12	every second month
devanture f	13	store window, front (of store)
développement m	14	development; growth
devis m	15	estimate
devise f	16	1 motto; slogan
	17	2 currency
avoir m en —s	18	currency assets
—s à terme	19	forward exchange
—s (traitées) au comptant	20	spot exchange
devoir vb	21	1 to owe 2 to be supposed to
dévolu adj [Lég.]	22	passed by transmission or succession
diagramme m	23	diagram, graph
diamantaire n.m & adj	24	1 diamond-cutter 2 diamond
différé adj	25	deferred
action —e	26	— share
annuité —e	27	— annuity
différence f	28	difference, disparity; discrepancy
à la — de . . .	29	unlike . . ., contrary to . . .
à la — que . . .	30	except that . . .
différend m	31	difference, dispute, disagreement
avoir un — avec	32	to be at variance with
régler un —	33	to settle a dispute
différentiel, -le adj	34	[calcul] differential
	35	[tarif] discriminatory, discriminating
différer vb	36	1 to defer, postpone, put off
	37	2 to differ
difficulté f	38	difficulty
être en — avec qqun	39	to be at odds with s.o.
faire des —s	40	to raise objections
se heurter à une —	41	to run up against a —

surmonter une —	1	to overcome a —
digne *adj*	2	worthy
— de foi	3	credible, trust- —
être — de	4	to be — of, to deserve to be
dilapider *vb*	5	to waste, squander
diligence *f*	6	speed, haste
en toute —	7	with all possible dispatch
faire —	8	to hurry
faire preuve de —	9	to be speedy
diminuer *vb*	10	to cut down, diminish, decrease, shorten, lessen, lower, reduce
direct *m*	11	[train] through
directeur *m*	12	head, manager, director
— -gérant	13	managing director
direction *f*	14	direction, management
discrédit *m*	15	discredit
discréditer *vb*	16	to discredit
discrétion *f*	17	discretion
à —	18	unlimited, [Fam.] on tap
à la — de	19	at the — of
discriminer *vb*	20	to discriminate
disculper *vb*	21	to clear, exonerate
discussion *f*	22	discussion, debate; [prise de bec] argument
discuter *vb*	23	to discuss, to debate
— un débiteur	24	to inquire into the assets of a debtor
disette *f*	25	lack, scarcity, want
disjoindre *vb*	26	to dissociate, to separate
dispensé *adj*	27	exempted; excused
— du timbrage	28	post free
disponibilité *f*	29	availability
—s	30	liquid assets, available funds
disponible *adj*	31	available
— (à volonté)	32	on tap
disposer *vb*	33 1	to arrange, fix, lay out
	34 2	to have at one's disposal/ control
	35 3	to use; to transfer legally
— de ses biens en faveur de qqun	36	to make over one's property to s.o.
disposition *f*	37 1	arrangement, preparation
	38 2	disposal

	1	3 aptitude, natural capacity (for)
	2	4 clause
	3	5 arrangement, design, lay-out, order
les —s de la loi	*4*	the provisions of the act
prendre ses —s	*5*	to arrange to
dissentiment *m*	*6*	dissent, disagreement
distance *f*	*7*	distance
table des —s	*8*	mileage chart
distribuer *vb*	*9*	1 to issue, hand out
	10	2 to deliver (the mail)
distributeur, -rice *n.m.* & *adj*	*11*	distributor
— automatique	*12*	slot/vending machine
distribution *f*	*13*	distribution, delivery (of mail)
En cas de non- —, prière de retourner à l'expéditeur	*14*	If undelivered, please return to sender
divers *adj*	*15*	various
frais —	*16*	sundry/miscellaneous expenses
dividende *m*	*17*	dividend
avec —	*18*	cum —
— brut/net	*19*	gross/net —
— final	*20*	final —
— provisoire	*21*	interim —
ex —	*22*	ex —
toucher un —	*23*	to receive a —
diviser *vb*	*24*	to divide
diviseur *m*	*25*	divisor
division *f*	*26*	1 division, dividing
	27	2 class, division; branch, department
	28	3 discord, dissension
divorcer *vb*	*29*	to divorce
Elle a divorcé d'avec son troisième mari	*30*	She divorced her third husband
dizaine *f*	*31*	tens; ten or so
colonne des —s	*32*	tens column
il y a une —d'années	*33*	about ten years ago
dock *m*	*34*	[bassin] dock
	35	[hangar] warehouse
docker *m*	*36*	docker, stevedore
document *m*	*37*	document

—s d'expédition	1	shipping —s
fournir des —s à l'appui (d'une affirmation)	2	to — a statement
doit *m* **et avoir** *m*	3	*See :* le passif et l'actif
domaine *m*	4	1 estate, domain, property
	5	2 field, sphere, line
domicile *m*	6	[Lég.] domicile
élire —	7	to come to live
livraison à —	8	free delivery, We deliver
livrer à —	9	to deliver
sans — fixe	10	with no fixed abode
domicilé *adj*	11	domiciled, living, residing (at, à)
domicilier *vb*	12	to domicile (bill at banker's)
se —	13	to reside, to take up residence
dommage *m*	14	damage, harm, wrong, injury ; loss
demander des —s et inté-rêts	15	to sue for damages
— causé à un tiers	16	injury to a third party
—s indirects	17	consequential damages
donné *adj*	18	given
étant —	19	knowing
étant — que	20	considering that, [Lég.] in-asmuch as
données *n.f.pl.*	21	data
donner *vb*	22	to give
— lieu à	23	— rise to
— raison à	24	to side with
donneur, -se *n*	25	giver
— à la grosse aventure	26	underwriter
— d'aval	27	backer, guarantor
dorénavant *adv*	28	in future, from now on
dos *m*	29	back, reverse
voir au —	30	see the reverse side
dossier *m*	31	record, file
dot *f*	32	dowry, marriage settlement
constituer une —	33	to provide for a dowry
doter *vb*	34	[sa fille] to give a dowry to
	35	[hôpital, bibliothèque, etc.] to endow
	36	[usine, armée] to equip
douane *f*	37	customs ; customs house
déclaration de la —	38	customs declaration

droit de —	1	customs duty
employé des —s	2	revenue officer
faire passer en —	3	to clear through customs
franc de —	4	duty paid
marchandises en —	5	bonded goods
passer la —	6	to go through customs
payer la —	7	to pay customs duty
remboursement des droits de —	8	drawback
visite de la —	9	customs examination
douanier, -ère n. & adj	10	1 customs officer
	11	2 customs
barrières douanières	12	tariff-walls
politique douanière	13	customs policy
tarif —	14	customs tariff
double n.m. & adj	15	double
augmenter du —	16	to —
— emploi	17	duplication
en —	18	in two, twofold, in duplicate
payer (le) —	19	to pay twice as much
plus du —	20	more than —
doute m	21	doubt
(accorder) le bénéfice du —	22	(to give) the benefit of the —
douzaine f	23	dozen, about twelve
à la —	24	by the dozen
d'ici une — d'années	25	about twelve years from now
treize à la —	26	a baker's dozen
droit m	27	1 right
	28	2 law
	29	3 fee, duty, dues
à bon —	30	with good reason
A qui de —	31	To whom it may concern
avoir des —s sur	32	to have rights over
avoir — à	33	to have a right to
de —	34	by right
— cambial	35	exchange law
— coutumier	36	common law
— d'aînesse	37	birthright
— de chapeau	38	primage
— de douane	39	customs duty
— écrit	40	statute law
— de gage/de suite	41	lien

— d'inscription	1	registration fee
— de passage	2	usage, right of way
— de reproduction	3	copyright
— de rétention [Lég.]	4	lien
—s acquis [Lég.]	5	vested interests
—s civils	6	civil rights
—s d'auteur	7	royalties
—s de port	8	harbour dues
— des sociétés	9	company law
—s de succession	10	death/estate duties
— de timbre	11	stamp duty
être dans son —	12	to be within one's rights
être en — de	13	to be entitled to
faire — à	14	to accede to (a request)
faire son —	15	to study law
par voies de —	16	by legal process
" tous —s réservés "	17	" all rights reserved "
dû, due *n.m. & adj*	18	1 due; share
	19	2 due, owing
cette somme est due	20	this is owing
donner à chacun son dû	21	to give each his due
payer son dû	22	to pay one's share/debt
dûment *adv*	23	duly, properly, in due form
duplicata *m*	24	(second) copy; duplicate
duplicateur *m*	25	duplicator, duplicating machine

eau *f*	26	water
— douce	27	fresh —
— dure	28	hard —
faire — [bateau]	29	to leak
ébauche *f*	30	outline, sketch; rough draft
écarté *adj*	31	[idée, objection] brushed aside
	32	[candidat] eliminated, ruled out, excluded
	33	[manuscrit] rejected, ruled out
	34	[endroit] remote, isolated
écarter *vb*	35	1 to separate
	36	2 to brush aside, to eliminate, to rule out, to exclude
s' — de	37	to stray from, deviate from

88

échafauder *vb*	1	to build a scaffold; [Fig.] to plan, construct, build up
échange *m*	2	exchange, interchange; commerce, trade
faire un —	3	to barter, swap
échanger *vb*	4	to exchange, to trade, to swap
échantillon *m*	5	sample
à titre d' —s	6	as a —
cahier d' —s	7	— book
collection d' —	8	range of —s
conforme à l' —	9	up to —
d'après l' —	10	from —
— gratuit	11	free —
— sans valeur	12	—
salle d' —	13	show-room
échantillonnage *m*	14	sampling
échantillonner *vb*	15	to prepare/make samples (of sth.)
échappatoire *f*	16	way out, loophole
échéance *f*	17	(date of) maturity
à l' —	18	when due
à trois mois d' —	19	at three months from date
payable à l' —	20	payable at —
(prêt) à longue/courte —	21	long/short term (loan)
venir à l' —	22	to fall due
échéancier *m*	23	bill diary
échéant *adj*	24	payable, falling due
les cas —	25	should the occasion arise, if necessary, if needs be
échelle *f*	26	scale
— de conversion	27	conversion table
sur une grande —	28	on a large —
échelon *m*	29	step
d' — en —	30	— by —
par —s	31	by degrees
échelonné *adj*	32	graduated, spread
intérêts —s	33	graduated interests
payement par versements —s	34	deferred payment
échelonner *vb*	35	to spread (out), graduate, stagger (holidays)
— des payements sur 3 ans	36	to spread payments out over a period of 3 years
s' —	37	to be spread out

échevin *m*	*1*	alderman
échoir *vb*	*2*	1 to fall (to s.o., *à qqun*)
	3	2 to fall, to mature, to become due
intérêts échus	*4*	interest due, outstanding interest
échouer *vb*	*5*	1 to run aground; to be stranded; to hit a rock; to be wrecked
	6	2 [Fam.] to go on the rocks; to fail
faire — un navire [sur le rivage]	*7*	to beach a ship
faire — un navire [sur un écueil]	*8*	to wreck a ship (on the rocks)
éclaircir *vb*	*9*	to clear up (a question, mis-understanding, mystery); to explain, clarify (an idea, a point)
éclaircissement *m*	*10*	explanation; explanatory note
économat *m*	*11*	[charge] treasurership
	12	[bureau] treasurer's office
économie *f*	*13*	economy
avec —	*14*	thriftily
— d'entreprise	*15*	business economics
—s	*16*	savings, [Fam.] nest-egg
faire des —s	*17*	to save (up)
réaliser une — de . . .	*18*	to save
écorner *vb*	*19*	to make a (large) dent in (fortune, etc.)
écossais *m*	*20*	[tissu] plaid, tartan
écot *m*	*21*	quota, share [placing
écoulement *m*	*22*	[de marchandises] flow, sale,
écouler *vb*	*23*	to sell, dispose of
s' —	*24*	[temps] to elapse
	25	[marchandises] to sell
écrit *n.m.*	*26*	writing, written
coucher par —	*27*	to put in writing
par —	*28*	in writing
écriture *f*	*29*	(hand-)writing; entry
commis aux —s	*30*	accounting clerk
les —s	*31*	the accounts
tenir les —s	*32*	to keep the accounts
écru *adj*	*33*	unbleached; raw
écueil *m*	*34*	[Fig.] snag; stumbling block

édition *f*	1	1	edition, issue, publication
	2	2	book trade
effet *m*	3	1	effect 2 bill
à cet —	4		to this end, for that purpose
— à renouvellement	5		revolving draft
— à vue	6		sight draft
—s mobiliers	7		goods and chattels
faire l' —de	8		to strike as, to give the impression of
prendre —	9		to take effect
sans —	10		ineffective
efficacité *f*	11		efficacy, efficiency; competence, capability
effondrement *m*	12		collapse, collapsing, slump (in prices)
effondrer (s') *vb*	13		to slump, drop
efforcer (s') *vb*	14		to endeavour, make every effort (to, *de*)
effraction *f*	15		house-breaking
égaler *vb*	16	1	to equal
	17	2	to put on a par
égaliser *vb*	18		to equalize, even; to level (up); to screen (coal)
égide *f*	19		protection, shield
sous l' — de	20		under the sponsorship of
élaborer *vb*	21		to work out, prepare, draft
élastique *adj*	22		elastic; [règlement, etc.] which can be stretched
élection *f*	23		election
— complémentaire	24		by- —
électrique *adj*	25		electric, electrical
centrale —	26		power station
élever (s') *vb*	27		to increase, rise, amount to
La population s'élève à ... habitants	28		The population numbers ...
émaner *vb*	29		[pouvoir] to originate (with, in, *de*)
émarger *vb*	30	1	to sign in the margin
	31	2	to get benefit, salary, subsidy (from the state)
Il émarge au budget	32		He's on the pay-roll; he's on the dole
emballage *m*	33		packing (material)
— maritime	34		seaworthy
frais de port et d' —	35		— and shipping charges

papier d' —	1	brown paper
spécification d' —	2	packing list
emballer vb	3	to pack
embarcadère m	4	landing-stage
embarcation f	5	boat; small craft
embargo m	6	embargo
mettre l' — sur un navire	7	to lay an — on a ship
embarquement m	8	[de marchandises] shipment; shipping, loading
	9	[de personnes] embarkation
port d' —	10	loading port
embarquer vb	11	to take on board
poids embarqué	12	shipping weight
s' —	13	to go on board; to go aboard
embaucher vb	14	to engage, take on (staff); to hire
embaucheur m	15	labour contractor
embranchement m	16	[point de jonction] fork
	17	[voie de garage] siding
	18	[division] branching off
émetteur, -rice adj	19	issuer (of banknotes)
émettre vb	20	[opinion] to express
	21	[emprunt] to float
	22	[radio] to transmit
	23	[actions, billets de banque] to issue
actions émises	24	issued shares
émigration f	25	emigration
émigré m	26	emigrant
émigrer vb	27	to emigrate
émissaire m	28	emissary, envoy, delegate
émission f	29	[actions, billets de banque, timbres] issue
	30	[prêt] floating [cast
	31	[radio] transmission, broad-
emmagasinage m	32	warehousing, storing up
emmagasiner vb	33	to store up
émoluments n.m.pl.	34	perquisite, emoluments, fee, pay, remuneration, salary
empaquetage m	35	packing, packaging
empaqueter vb	36	to wrap up, to package, to pack (up)
empêchement m	37	impediment, hindrance
emphytéose f	38	long lease

emphytéote *m*	*1*	holder of a long lease
emphytéotique *adj*	*2*	[bail] long lease, ninety-nine year lease
emplacement *m*	*3*	location, site; space
emploi *m*	*4*	1 use
	5	2 job, occupation, employment
— du temps	*6*	timetable, schedule
mode d'—	*7*	directions for use
offres d'—	*8*	situations vacant, 'want' ads
plein —	*9*	full employment
employé *m*	*10*	employee, clerk
employer *vb*	*11*	to employ (staff); to use (a sum)
employeur *m*	*12*	employer
empocher *vb*	*13*	to pocket, [faire un profit net de] to net
empreinte *f*	*14*	print, impression
—s digitales	*15*	fingerprints
emprunt *m*	*16*	loan
accorder un —	*17*	to grant a —
à titre d'—	*18*	as a —, on —
contracter un —	*19*	to raise a —
d'—	*20*	assumed, feigned
émettre un —	*21*	to float a —
— à primes	*22*	premium —
— sur titres	*23*	— on stock
emprunter *vb*	*24*	[argent] to borrow (from, *à*; on, *sur*)
	25	[nom] to assume
	26	[itinéraire] to go along
emprunteur *m*	*27*	borrower
encaisse *f*	*28*	cash in hand
encaissement *m*	*29*	collection
à l'—	*30*	for —
donner un chèque à l'—	*31*	to pay in (a cheque)
encaisser *vb*	*32*	to collect (funds), to receive (accounts), to cash (a cheque)
encaisseur *m*	*33*	collector
encan *m*	*34*	public auction
enchère *f*	*35*	bid, bidding
— au rabais	*36*	Dutch auction
folle —	*37*	irresponsible bid that cannot be made good

vente aux —s	1	sale by auction, auction sale
enchérir *vb*	2	[faire une offre] to bid for
	3	[prix] to rise
— sur qqun	4	to outbid s.o.
enchérissement *m*	5	1 increase, rise (in price)
	6	2 bidder
encoche *f*	7	notch
encocher *vb*	8	to notch, nick
encolure *f*	9	size (of shirts), neckline (of dress)
encombrement *m*	10	obstruction; measurements
encombrer *vb*	11	[marché] to glut, overstock (with, *de*)
	12	[circulation] to block (up), to jam
s'—	13	to burden o.s. (with, *de*)
encourir *vb*	14	[frais] to incur
encre *f*	15	ink
— de Chine	16	India —
— d'impression	17	printer's —
— sympathique	18	invisible —
endéans *prép* [Belg.]	19	in, within
endetter *vb*	20	to get s.o. into debt
s'—	21	to run into debt
endiguer *vb*	22	to dike, dam up; [Fig.] to check, stem
endommager *vb*	23	to damage, to suffer damage
endos *m*	24	endorsement (on cheque)
endosser *vb*	25	to endorse (a cheque), [Fig.] to assume, take on (responsibility)
endosseur *m*	26	endorser
énergie *f*	27	energy
— hydraulique	28	water power
enfreindre *vb*	29	to infringe, break
engagé *adj*	30	pawned; [argot Amér.] in hock
engagement *m*	31	1 engagement, promise, commitment
	32	2 hiring, appointment (of staff)
remplir ses —s	33	to fulfil one's commitments
engager *vb*	34	1 to commit, promise, pledge; to bind

	1	2 to engage, take on (staff) ; to hire
	2	3 to begin, start
	3	4 to urge (s.o. to do sth.)
s'—	4	to commit o.s., to promise
engendrer vb	5	to give birth to ; to bring about
enjeu m	6	stake [in betting or gambling]
enlever vb	7	to remove, take away, carry off
s'—	8	1 to come off
	9	2 to sell well
énoncé m	10	wording ; statement
énoncer vb	11	to set forth, state (facts, problem, etc.)
s'—	12	to be stated
enquérir (s') vb	13	to ask, inquire (about, de)
enquête f	14	investigation, inquiry
l'inspecteur chargé de l'—	15	the inspector in charge of the case
procéder à/faire une —	16	to hold an inquest
enquêter vb	17	to investigate, to inquire (into a matter, sur une affaire)
enregistrement m	18	1 registration 2 recording
bureau de l'—	19	registry office
— sur bande	20	tape recording
frais d'—	21	registration fee
enregistrer vb	22	to register, record ; to check (luggage)
enregistreur, -se n. & adj	23	1 registrar ; recorder ; [Belg.] tape recorder
	24	2 recording
caisse enregistreuse	25	cash-register
ensabler (s') vb	26	[navire] to run aground, to strand
enseigne f	27	sign
— au néon	28	— advertisement
— lumineuse	29	electric —
entamer vb	30	to start
— des négotiations	31	— negotiations
— son capital	32	to break into one's capital
en-tête m	33	head(ing)
papier à —	34	letterhead
entrecroiser (s') vb	35	to interlace, intersect
entrée f	36	entry, entrance, admission

droit d'—	1	admission fee
— interdite	2	No Admittance
— principale	3	main entrance
entremise *f*	4	intervention
par l'— de	5	through (the agency/ courtesy of)
entrepont *m*	6	steerage
entreposage *m*	7	warehousing, bonding, storage
entreposer *vb*	8	to store, bond
entrepôt *m*	9	warehouse
à prendre en —	10	ex —
certificat d'—	11	— warrant
en — /à l'—	12	in bond, bonded
— en douane	13	bonded —
entrepreneur *m*	14	contractor, builder, [de pompes funèbres] undertaker
entreprise *f*	15	venture, undertaking, business
Conseil d'—	16	works council
— familiale	17	family concern
entrer *vb*	18	to enter
défense d'—	19	No Admittance
— des marchandises en fraude	20	to smuggle in goods
— en vigueur	21	to come into force
entretenir *vb*	22	to maintain, keep (up)
bien entretenu	23	in good repair
— de bonnes relations avec	24	to be on good terms with
s'— (de)	25	to talk, converse (about)
entretien *m*	26	1 upkeep, maintenance, support
	27	2 talk, conversation
avoir un — avec	28	to have an interview with
frais d'—	29	maintenance charges
entrevue *f*	30	interview; appointment
enveloppe *f*	31	envelope
— à fenêtre	32	window —
mettre sous —	33	to slip into an —
envers *prép*	34	to, towards, with regard to
Ils ont agi honnêtement — nous	35	They have been straight with us
envers *m*	36	reverse (side)

à l'—	1	upside down; inside out
envi *m*	2	....
à l'—	3	in emulation
envisager *vb*	4	to consider, contemplate, anticipate
envoi *m*	5	1 dispatch, shipping, sending, forwarding
	6	2 consignment, parcel
— d'argent/de fonds	7	remittance
— en possession [Lég.]	8	occupancy
envoyer *vb*	9	to dispatch, send
— sa démission	10	to send in one's resignation
épargne *f*	11	saving, thrift, economy; savings
caisse d'—	12	savings bank
livret de caisse d'—	13	savings bank book
épave *f*	14	wreck
—s flottantes	15	flotsam
—s rejetées	16	jetsam
épicerie *f*	17	grocery store, grocery trade
éplucher *vb*	18	to go over (bills, etc.) minutely
épreuve *f*	19	1 test; examination
	20	2 trial, ordeal; hardships
	21	3 proof
corriger les —s	22	to proof read
épuisé *adj*	23	[mine] worked out
	24	[livre] out of print
	25	[article] out of stock, unavailable; sold out
épuiser *vb*	26	to exhaust; to use up
s'—	27	to wear out, to run out
épure *f*	28	1 working drawing
	29	2 finished design
épurer *vb*	30	to purify, to filter, to refine
équipage *m*	31	crew
maître d'—	32	boatswain
équipe *f*	33	team, crew, working party; shift
chef d'—	34	foreman
— de nuit	35	night shift
équipement *m*	36	equipment, outfit
équiper *vb*	37	to equip, fit out
équitable *adj*	38	fair, just
équité *f*	39	equity

ériger *vb*	1	to erect; to set up, establish
— en principe	2	to lay down as a principle
erreur *f*	3	slip, error, mistake
induire qqun en —	4	to mislead s.o., to fob s.o. off
par —	5	in error, by mistake
sauf —	6	if we are not mistaken
sauf — ou omission	7	errors and omissions excepted
escale *f*	8	1 call 2 port of call
faire — à Marseille	9	to put in at Marseilles
vol sans —	10	nonstop flight
escalier *m*	11	stairs; staircase
— de secours	12	fire escape
— roulant/mécanique	13	escalator
escamoter *vb*	14	[dérober subtilement] to pinch, to whisk away, to spirit away/off
	15	[éviter, éluder] to skip (a question)
escient *m*	16	cognizance
à bon —	17	purposely, knowingly
escompte *m*	18	discount, rebate
courtier d'—	19	discount broker
— au comptant	20	cash discount
faire un — de 2%	21	to allow a 2% discount
taux d'—	22	discount rate, the Bank rate
escompter *vb*	23	1 to discount
	24	2 to anticipate; to bank upon (a success)
escroc *m*	25	swindler, sharper, crook
escroquer *vb*	26	to swindle (out of, *à*)
escroquerie *f*	27	swindle
espacement *m*	28	interval, space; spacing (out)
espacer *vb*	29	to space, separate
espèce *f*	30	1 kind, sort
	31	2 cash, specie
	32	3 case
avoir en —s	33	cash assets
cas d'—	34	special case, specific case
dividende en —s	35	cash dividend
en l'—	36	in this case
payer en —s (sonnantes)	37	to pay in (hard) cash
essai *m*	38	trial, test; attempt

à l'—, à titre d'—	1	on a trial basis; on approval
essayage m	2	fitting, try-on (of clothes)
essence f	3	1 essence
	4	2 [Amér.] gas(oline), [G.B.] petrol
	5	3 variety, kind, species (of tree)
poste d'—	6	filling-station
essor m	7	soaring; expansion
prendre un grand —	8	to make great strides
essuyer vb	9	to suffer (a setback), to meet with (a refusal)
estampillage m	10	stamping (of weights, shares, etc.)
estampille f	11	label, stamp, (trade-)mark; imprinted mark, official mark
estampiller vb	12	to stamp, mark, make a mark or impression on
estarie f (jours d')	13	lay-days
estimateur m	14	valuer, appraiser
estimation f	15	assessment, appraisal, valuation
estime f	16	1 esteem 2 guesswork
à l'—	17	at a guess; [marine] by dead reckoning
établi adj	18	established
solidement —	19	four-square
établir vb	20	1 to establish, to set up
	21	2 to strike (a balance)
	22	3 to prove, to make the trust of, to substantiate
	23	4 to make out, to draw up
venir s'—	24	to settle in, at; to move to
établissement m	25	1 establishment, setting up, founding
	26	2 drawing up, making out (of a document)
	27	3 settlement, firm, institution, trade centre
— du prix de revient	28	costing
frais d'—	29	initial expenses
les Etablissements Adam	30	Adam and Co.
étain m	31	tin, pewter

D*

étalage *m*	1	display (of goods) ; window-dressing ; stall
étalagiste *n.m/f*	2	(window-)dresser
étalon *m*	3	standard (of weights)
le mètre —	4	the — metre
l'— or	5	the gold —
étalonnage *m*, **étalonne-ment** *m*	6	standardization
étalonner *vb*	7	to standardize, calibrate
état *m*	8	state, condition ; statement ; status ; occupation ; state
électricien de son —	9	electrician by trade
en bon —	10	in good condition/order
en — d'ivresse	11	intoxicated
en tout — de cause	12	in any case
— civil [on form]	13	married or single
— de caisse	14	cash statement
— de frais [Lég.]	15	bill of costs
— des lieux	16	inventory of fixtures
— d'urgence	17	emergency
être hors d'— de	18	to be unfit for/incapable of
étayer *vb*	19	to stay, support, prop up, shore
éteindre *vb*	20	[dette] to pay off
	21	[droit] to abolish
éteint *adj*	22	[dette] paid off, [Fig.] dying
étiqueter *vb*	23	to label, [Amér.] to tag
étiquette *f*	24	label, sticker, [Amér.] tag
étoffe *f*	25	material, stuff, fabric
étoffer *vb*	26	to pad (out), fill in, stuff
étouffer *vb*	27	to choke
— une affaire	28	to hush up a case
étranger, -ère *n & adj*	29	1 foreigner, alien
	30	2 foreign
à l'—	31	abroad
— à la question	32	beside the point
le ministère des Affaires étrangères	33	[G.B.] the Foreign Office
	34	[Amér.] the State Department
étude *f*	35	1 study
	36	2 study hall ; office
à l'—	37	under study
bureau d' —s	38	research department
— de notaire/d'avocat	39	notary's/solicitor's office

étui *m*	1	case, box, cover
évaluation *f*	2	valuation, appraisal, assessment, estimation; estimate (of weight, etc.)
évaluer *vb*	3	to estimate, value, reckon, [propriété] to appraise, [dégâts] to assess
évasion *f*	4	escape, flight, evasion
— de capitaux	5	flight of capital
évidence *f*	6	obviousness; the facts
de toute —	7	surely; obviously
mettre en —	8	to show up
nier l'—	9	to fly in the face of facts
se rendre à l'—	10	to bow to facts [evict
évincer *vb*	11	to supplant; [Lég.] to oust,
évoluer *vb*	12	to develop, evolve, change; to move about
évolution *f*	13	evolution, change, development, trend
exact *adj*	14	1 accurate, right, exact, correct
	15	2 punctual
C'est (tout à fait) —	16	That's (quite) right
être — à payer (son loyer)	17	to be punctual in paying (one's rent)
le montant —	18	the correct/exact amount
excédent *m*	19	excess
en —	20	in —
— budgétaire	21	budget surplus
— de bagages	22	— luggage
exception *f*	23	exception
à l'— de	24	with the — of
faire — à une règle	25	to be an — to the rule
faire une — à	26	to make an — to
soulever une —	27	to take — to, to object to
exceptionnel, -le *adj*	28	exceptional, unusual
lois —s	29	emergency legislation
excès *m*	30	excess
à l'—	31	too (much)
commettre un — de pouvoir	32	to exceed one's powers
exclure *vb*	33	to exclude, shut out
exclusif, -ve *adj*	34	sole, exclusive
avoir la représentation exclusive de	35	to be sole agent(s) for

exclusivité *f*	1 exclusive rights
exécuter *vb*	2 [commande] to execute, carry out (an order)
	3 [travail] to do
	4 [débiteur] to distrain
exécuteur *m*	5 executor
exemplaire *n.m. & adj*	6 1 copy, issue
	7 2 exemplary, model
en double/triple —	8 in duplicate/triplicate
un — gratuit	9 a free copy
un — justificatif	10 a voucher copy
exemple *m*	11 example
par —	12 for instance/ —
prendre — sur	13 to model o.s. on
sans —	14 unprecedented
exempt *adj*	15 not liable to; free, exempt (from, *de*)
— du timbre	16 exempt from stamp duty
exempter *vb*	17 to dispense, excuse, exempt (from, *de*)
exercer *vb*	18 to exert (an influence); to practise (medicine)
exercice *m*	19 1 performance (of a duty)
	20 2 financial year
	21 past year
— écoulé	
exiger *vb*	22 to claim, demand
exigible *adj*	23 demandable
exil *m*	24 exile, banishment
exonérer *vb*	25 to exonerate, free, release, relieve, exempt (from, *de*)
expansion *f*	26 expansion
expédient *m*	27 makeshift; loophole
expédier *vb*	28 [marchandises] to dispatch, send, ship, forward
	29 [un indésirable] to send away; to get rid of
	30 [bâcler] to botch
	31 [Lég.: un contrat] to draw up
expéditeur *m*	32 [lettre] sender
	33 [marchandises] shipper, consigner, consignor
	34 [agent] forwarding agent
expéditif, -ve *adj*	35 speedy
expédition *f*	36 1 dispatch (of business)
	37 2 sending, forwarding

	1	3 [Lég.] copy (of document)
bordereau d'—	2	despatch note
déclaration d'—	3	manifest [=list of ship's cargo]
expéditionnaire *m*	4	1 shipper 2 shipping clerk
expérience *f*	5	1 experience; training
	6	2 test, trial, experiment
avoir l'— de	7	to experience in
faire une —	8	to make an experiment
par —	9	from experience
expérimenté *adj*	10	trained, experienced
expérimenter *vb*	11	to test, experiment with, try out, make experiments
expert *n.m.* & *adj*	12	expert; valuer; surveyor
— -comptable	13	chartered accountant
— répartiteur d'avaries	14	(average) adjuster
expertise *f*	15	1 valuation, appraisal
	16	2 (expert's) report
— d'avarie	17	damage survey
faire une —	18	to survey
rapport d'—	19	survey report
expertiser *vb*	20	to value; to survey
expirer *vb*	21	to expire, to be up, to run out
explicatif, -ve	22	explanatory
notice explicative	23	prefatory note
expliquer *vb*	24	to explain, account for
s'—	25	1 to justify o.s., to explain one's actions
	26	2 to understand; to account for
exploit *m* (d'huissier) [Lég.]	27	writ, summons
signifier un — à qqun	28	to serve a writ on s.o.
exploitant *m*	29	[agriculture] grower, farmer
	30	[mine] owner, operator
	31	[huissier-exploitant] process-server
exploitation *f*	32	working
bénéfice d'—	33	trading profit
capital d'—	34	— capital
— à outrance [du sol]	35	exhaustive cultivation
frais d'—	36	— expenses
exploiter *vb*	37	[personne] to use (s.o.)
	38	[mine] to work
	39	[sol] to till
exploiteur, -se *n*	40	[Péj.] exploiter

exportateur, -rice *n.* & *adj*	1	1 exporter 2 exporting
exportation *f*	2	export
commerce d'—	3	— trade
prime d'—	4	— bonus
exporter *vb*	5	to export
exposant *m*	6	[exposition] exhibitor
	7	[chiffre] exponent
exposé *n.m.* & *adj*	8	1 account, statement
	9	2 on show, displayed
exposer *vb*	10	1 to show, display
	11	2 to expound, set forth, explain
s'— (à)	12	to lay o.s. open (to) ; to expose o.s. (to)
exposition *f*	13	1 show, exhibition
	14	2 orientation, aspect (of a house)
— universelle	15	world exhibition
salle d'—	16	show room
express *n.m.* & *adj*	17	[train] express
	18	[lettre] special delivery
une lettre par —	19	express letter
expressément *adv*	20	specifically, precisely, explicitly
expropriation *f*	21	expropriation, [Lég.] purchase under compulsion
exproprier *vb*	22	to expropriate
expulser *vb*	23	[un locataire] to evict
	24	[du pays] to deport
expulsion *f*	25	expulsion, eviction, deportation
extension *f*	26	1 expansion
	27	2 growth, development
par —	28	in a wider sense
prendre de l'—	29	to expand ; to spread out
extincteur *m*	30	fire-extinguisher
extinction *f*	31	[contrat] termination
	32	[dette] paying off, wiping out
extorquer *vb*	33	to extort (from, *à*)
extra *n.m.* & *adj*	34	1 something extra
	35	2 first-rate
extraction *f*	36	[charbon] mining, [pétrole] production, [pierre] quarrying
extrait *m*	37	extract ; excerpt

— de compte	1	statement (of account)
— de naissance	2	birth certificate
extrajudiciaire *adj* [Lég.]	3	extrajudicial
extrinsèque *adj*	4	extrinsic; external
fabricant *m*	5	maker, manufacturer
fabrication *f*	6	1 making, manufacturing; production
	7	2 make
(de) — britannique	8	made in Great Britain
— en série	9	mass production
fabrique *f*	10	1 factory, works, mill
	11	2 vestry
conseil de —	12	vestry, fabric council
marque de —	13	trade mark
prix de —	14	maker's price
fabriquer *vb*	15	1 to make, manufacture
	16	2 to make up, invent, fabricate (a story)
face *f*	17	1 face, aspect
	18	2 [pièce de monnaie] obverse
en — de	19	facing, opposite, across from
faire — à des difficultés	20	to cope with difficulties
faire — (à ses engagements)	21	to meet (one's liabilities)
perdre/sauver la —	22	to lose/save face
facial *adj*	23	face
(acheter à la) valeur —e	24	(to buy at) — value
facilité *f*	25	facility
—s de payement	26	easy terms
façon *f*	27	1 [costume] making
	28	2 [facture, habileté professionnelle] workmanship
tailleur à —	29	jobbing tailor
fac-similé *m*	30	facsimile; exact copy, accurate reproduction
factage *m*	31	carriage (and delivery); delivery (of letters)
facteur *m*	32	1 factor 2 postman
faction *f*	33	1 faction, group
	34	2 guard duty
facture *f*	35	1 invoice, bill

	1	2 workmanship
acquitter une —	2	to receipt a bill
— consulaire	3	consular invoice
— de consignation	4	consignment invoice
faire/établir une —	5	to make out an invoice
prix de —	6	invoice price
selon/suivant —	7	as per invoice
facultatif, -ve *adj*	8	elective, optional
faculté *f*	9	right, power; privilege; option
faïence *f*	10	earthenware, crockery
failli *m*	11	bankrupt
— réhabilité	12	discharged —
faillite *f*	13	1 failure
	14	2 bankrupt, bankruptcy
être déclaré en —	15	to be declared bankrupt
faire —	16	to go bankrupt, to smash
la — d'une expérience	17	the failure of an experiment
masse de la —	18	bankrupt's estate
ouverture de la —	19	opening of bankruptcy proceedings
requête en déclaration de —	20	bankruptcy petition
faire *vb*	21	to make
— en sorte que . . .	22	to see to it that . . .
— fortune	23	— a fortune
— une faute	24	— a mistake
— un travail	25	to do a job
se — une idée de	26	to figure out
faire-part *m*	27	notification
— de décès	28	— of death
— de mariage	29	wedding card
le présent avis tient lieu de —	30	no cards
faisceau *m*	31	1 bundle 2 accumulation
un — de preuves	32	cumulative evidence
fait *m*	33	fact
possession de —	34	actual possession
falsification *f*	35	[signature, chèque] forgery
	36	[monnaie] counterfeit
	37	[faits] falsification
falsifier *vb*	38	[monnaie] to counterfeit
	39	[documents] to forge
	40	[faits] to falsify
	41	[nourriture] to adulterate

fascicule *m*	1	instalment, part, section (of publication)
faussaire *m*	2	forger
fausseté *f*	3	falseness, double dealing
faute *f*	4	1 fault, mistake, error
	5	2 lack, want
être en —	6	to be at fault
— de frappe	7	typing error
— de mieux	8	for want of sth. better
— de quoi	9	failing which
— de (temps)	10	for lack of (time)
— d'impression	11	misprint
— d'ortographe	12	spelling mistake
— grave	13	serious offence
rejeter la — sur	14	to throw the blame on
sans —	15	without fail
fautif, -ve *adj*	16	at fault; faulty, wrong
faux, -sse *n.m., adj & adv*	17	1 forgery
	18	2 false, erroneous, wrong, incorrect
	19	3 out of tune, off key
faux-monnayeur *m*	20	counterfeit
faveur *f*	21	favour
à la — de	22	under cover of
billet de —	23	complimentary ticket
en — de	24	in — of, for
être en — (auprès de)	25	to find — (with)
faire une — à qqun	26	to do s.o. a —
favoriser *vb*	27	1 to favour
	28	2 to help, facilitate; to promote
favoritisme *m*	29	favouritism; patronage; partiality
félicitation *f*	30	congratulation
Nos plus vives —s	31	Our heartiest —s
féliciter *vb*	32	to congratulate (on, *de*)
ferblanterie *f*	33	tinware
fermage *m*	34	farm rent
fermeture *f*	35	[magasin] shutting, closing
	36	[usine] closing down, shutdown, lockout
heure de la —	37	closing time
ferraille *f*	38	scrap iron
mettre à la —	39	to scrap
fête *f*	40	celebration, holiday

107

— légale	1	legal holiday
jour de —	2	holiday
la Fête-Dieu	3	Corpus Christi Day
la Fête du travail	4	Labour Day
feuille *f*	5	sheet
cahier à —s mobiles	6	loose-leaf notebook
— de chou	7	rag, pulp magazine
— d'émargement/de paie	8	payroll
— d'étain	9	tinfoil
— volante	10	loose —
fiasco *m*	11	failure, [Fam.] flop
fibre *f*	12	fibre; thread
fiche *f*	13	(index) card
fichier *m*	14	card index, index card box, index file
fidéicommis *m*	15	trust
acte de —	16	— deed
fidéicommissaire *m*	17	beneficiary of a trust
fiduciaire *adj*	18	fiduciary
contrat —	19	trust deed
monnaie —	20	paper money
société —	21	trust company
fiducie *f*	22	trust
figurer *vb*	23	to appear (on a list, etc.)
filet *m* (à provisions)	24	stringbag
filiale *f*	25	subsidiary company
filière *f*	26	[Fig.] channels
passer par la —	27	to go through (the usual) —
filigrane *m*	28	watermark
filon *m*	29	cushy job, [Fam.] plum
trouver le —	30	[Fig.] to strike oil
filouter *vb*	31	to rob
fin *f*	32	end
à seule — de	33	for the sole purpose of
à toutes —s utiles	34	for your information
— de non-recevoir [Lég.]	35	demurrer
— janvier	36	at the — of January
mener à bonne —	37	to bring to a successful issue
rendre une — de non-recevoir [Lég.]	38	to dismiss a case
tirer à sa —	39	to be coming to an —
finance *f*	40	finance
Ministère des Finances	41	[G.B.] Treasury
	42	[Amér.] Treasury (Dept.)

	1	[Can.] Department of Finance
moyennant —	2	for a consideration
financement *m*	3	financing
financer *vb*	4	to finance
financier, -ère *n.& adj.*	5	1 financier 2 financial
aide financière	6	financial assistance
marché —	7	money market
rubrique financière	8	financial column
finasser *vb*	9	to manœuvre
firme *f*	10	firm, concern
fisc *m*	11	[G.B.] Inland Revenue
	12	[Amér.] Internal Revenue
	13	[Can.] Department of Finance
les agents du —	14	revenue officials
fiscal *adj*	15	fiscal
charges —es	16	burden of taxation, tax burden
conseiller —	17	tax consultant
dette —e	18	tax liability
lois —es	19	taxation laws
privilèges fiscaux	20	tax privileges
fixation *f*	21	fixing
fixe *m*	22	fixed salary
fixe *adj*	23	fixed, regular; definite
sans domicile —	24	of no fixed abode
flagrant *adj*	25	flagrant
être pris en — délit	26	to be caught in the act
fléchir *vb*	27	[prix, cours] to decline, fall off
fléchissement *m*	28	decline
floralies *n.f.pl.*	29	Flower Show
florin *m*	30	[Pays-Bas] florin, guilder
flot *m*	31	wave
bassin à —	32	wet dock
être à —	33	to be afloat
mettre un navire à —	34	to launch a ship
remettre à —	35	to refloat
flottaison *f*	36	floating
ligne de —	37	water-line
flottant *adj*	38	floating
fluctuation *f*	39	fluctuation, ups and downs
fluvial *adj*	40	fluvial
port —	41	river harbour
flux *m*	42	flow, tide

109

— et reflux	1	ebb and flow
foi *f*	2	faith
de bonne —	3	sincere(ly), in good —
de mauvaise —	4	dishonest
digne de —	5	trustworthy
en — de quoi	6	in witness whereof
faire — de	7	to prove (the authenticity) of) sth.
qui fait —	8	authentic
foire *f*	9	fair
foncier, -ère *adj*	10	land(ed)
crédit —	11	— bank
impôt —	12	— /property tax
propriété foncière	13	real estate
fonction *f*	14 ¹	function, duty, official task
	15 ²	position, post
	16 ³	function, role, purpose
en — de	17	in terms of
entrer en —	18	to take up one's duties
faire — de	19	to serve/act as
rester en —	20	to remain in office
fonctionnaire *m*	21	civil servant
fonctionner *vb*	22	to work, function, operate
fondamental *adj*	23	basic
fondateur, -rice *n*	24	founder
fondation *f*	25 ¹	foundation (of a building)
	26 ²	endowment (of a hospital)
	27 ³	establishment (of an award, etc.)
fondé *n.m. & adj*	28	authorized (person)
— de pouvoir	29	proxy; director; first signature
fondement *m*	30	basis
sans —	31	without foundation, unfounded
force *f*	32	force, strength
un cas de — majeure	33	circumstances outside one's control; act of God
forcé *adj*	34	forced, compelled
emprunt —	35	compulsory loan
forfait *m*	36 ¹	outrage, crime
	37 ²	package deal; contract
acheter qqch. à —	38	to buy sth. outright
à —	39	for a lump sum
travail à —	40	work by contract

voyage à —	1	all-expense tour
forfaitaire *adj*	2	contractual
marché —	3	outright purchase
prix —	4	fixed price
forge *f*	5	blacksmith's workshop, forge
forgé *adj*	6	made (up)
fer —	7	wrought iron
forger *vb*	8	to forge (metal) ; to coin (a word) ; to forge (a signature) ; to counterfeit (coin, handwriting, bank-notes) ; to fabricate (document) ; to make up (story)
formalité *f*	9	formality
C'est une pure —	10	It's a mere matter of form
les —s administratives	11	red tape
format *m*	12	format, size
formation *f*	13	1 formation
	14	2 training, education
	15	3 make-up (of a train)
— de réserves	16	building up of reserves
— professionnelle	17	vocational training
(une nation) en voie de —	18	(a nation) in the making
forme *f*	19	form, shape
dans les —s	20	in order, in due form
en bonne —	21	in due form
en — de (cloche)	22	(bell)-shaped
pour la —	23	for form's sake
statistiques sous — de tableau	24	statistics in tabular form
vice de — [Lég.]	25	faulty drafting
formel, -le *adj*	26	explicit, strict, categorical
formellement *adv*	27	in set terms, absolutely, strictly
former *vb*	28	to form ; to train, educate
formule *f*	29	1 formula, concise statement (in words or symbols)
	30	2 form, document (to be filled in with information)
— de chèque	31	cheque form
— de politesse	32	complimentary close
— de télégramme	33	telegraphy form
— imprimée	34	printed form
formuler *vb*	35	to express, draw up, compose

— une plainte	1	to lodge a complaint
fort n.m., adj & adv	2	1 experienced, skilful, expert, clever
	3	2 considerable, large
	4	3 much, very, extremely, exceedingly
	5	4 strong point
le prix —	6	full price, catalogue price
une —e baisse (de prix)	7	big drop (in price)
une —e perte	8	heavy loss
une —e somme	9	a large sum of money
un tabac —	10	strong tobacco
une terre —e	11	heavy soil
fortuit adj	12	accidental, (by) chance, fortuitous
un cas — [Lég.]	13	an act of God
fortune f	14	fortune
avoir de la —	15	to be well off
état de —	16	financial status/position
fortuné adj	17	rich, wealthy, well off
fourgon m	18	luggage van
fourneau m	19	stove
haut- —	20	blast-furnace
fournir vb	21	to provide, supply
— aux besoins	22	to provide for the needs
— de l'argent	23	to supply the money
— un alibi	24	to produce an alibi
— qqch. à qqun	25	to supply s.o. with sth.
l'effort fourni par . . .	26	the effort put forth by . . .
(magasin) bien fourni	27	well-stocked (shop)
fournisseur m	28	supplier, purveyor; tradesman
— de la Cour	29	by appointment to H.M. the Queen/King
fourniture f	30	supply
—s de bureau	31	stationery, office requisites
—s scolaires	32	school supplies
fourreur m	33	furrier
fraction f	34	fraction, portion; fractional part
fractionner vb	35	to divide into fractions, to segment, to split (shares, etc.)
fragile adj	36	fragile, brittle
fragment m	37	fragment; chip; scrap; snatch
frais, fraîche adj	38	1 fresh 2 recent 3 cool

de fraîche date	1	recently
" peinture fraîche "	2	" wet paint "
frais *n.m.pl.*	3	expenses
à grands —	4	at great cost, expensively
à peu de —	5	inexpensively
couvrir ses —	6	to break even
faux —	7	petty —, sundries
—s courants	8	standing —
— d'affranchissement	9	postage
— d'arrimage	10	stowage
— de banque	11	bank charges
— de bureau	12	trade —
— de déplacement	13	travel —
— d'entretien (minimum)	14	(low) upkeep
— d'entrepôt	15	storage
— d'envoi	16	shipping charges
— de port et d'emballage	17	packing and shipping charges
— de représentation	18	expense account, entertainment allowance
— de scolarité	19	tuition fees
— de séjour	20	living —
— d'inscription	21	registration fee
— divers	22	sundry, miscellaneous —
— généraux	23	working —, overheads
sans —	24	free of charge
franc *m*	25	franc
franc, -he *adj*	26	1 clear, exempt, free (from, *de*)
	27	2 complete
— de port	28	postpaid ; carriage paid
huit jours —s [Lég.]	29	one clear week
franchise *f*	30	exemption
— postale	31	franking privilege
(lettre) en —	32	O.H.M.S.
(marchandises) en —	33	free of duty, duty free
franco *adv*	34	free of charge
frappe *f*	35	[monnaie] minting
	36	[estampille] stamp
	37	[dactylo] touch
faute de —	38	typing mistake
frapper *vb*	39	to mint (coins) ; to ice (champagne)
fraude *f*	40	fraud, deceit ; smuggling
(faire) passer en —	41	to smuggle in

113

la — fiscale	1	tax evasion
frauder *vb*	2	to smuggle; to defraud
fraudeur, -se *n*	3	cheat; smuggler
frauduleux, -se *adj*	4	fraudulent
frein *m*	5	1 bit, bridle 2 brake
mettre un — à qqch.	6	to check/curb sth.
frelater *vb*	7	to adulterate
fret *m*	8	freight
faux —	9	dead —
— à l'aller	10	outward —
— au long cours	11	ocean —
— proportionnel	12	pro rata —
prendre un navire à —	13	to charter a ship
taux du —	14	— rates
fréter *vb*	15	to charter
fréteur *m*	16	ship-owner
frigorifier *vb*	17	to freeze (food)
fur *m*	18	. . . .
au — et à mesure	19	(in proportion) as
fusion *f*	20	1 melting, smelting 2 merger
fusionner *vb*	21	to merge, combine
gabarit *m*	22	gauge, model
gage *m*	23	1 security given, pawn; collateral
	24	2 *m.pl.* wages
	25	3 sign, token
être aux —s de qqun	26	to be in s.o.'s pay
mettre en —	27	to pawn
gageure *f*	28	bet, wager
gagne-pain *m*	29	livelihood
C'est son —	30	That's his bread and butter
gagner *vb*	31	1 to gain
	32	2 to earn
	33	3 to win
— du terrain	34	to gain ground
— gros	35	to make a packet
— la partie	36	to win the game
— sa vie	37	to earn a living
Vous y —ez	38	You stand to gain
gain *m*	39	gain, profit
avoir — de cause	40	to win one's case
donner — de cause à qqun	41	to decide in s.o.'s favour
gala *m*	42	gala

habit de —	1	formal wear
gamme *f*	2	range, variety ; set ; gamut
gangster *m*	3	gangster
entreprise de —	4	racket
ganterie *f*	5	glove - shop, glove - trade ; glove - making ; glove - factory
garage *m*	6	garage
voie de —	7	shunting, siding
garant *n.m. & adj*	8	guarantor, warrantor
se porter — de	9	to vouch for
garantie *f*	10	guarantee ; warranty ; security ; surety
garantir *vb*	11	to guarantee ; to vouch for ; to warrant
créance garantie	12	secured debt
— une émission d'actions	13	to underwrite an issue of shares
garde *f*	14	guard
avoir la — de	15	to be in charge of
mettre en — contre	16	to caution against
page de —	17	flyleaf
prendre — de	18	to be careful not to
sous bonne —	19	well guarded
garde *m*	20	guard
— -champêtre *m*	21	rural police
— -chasse *m*	22	game-keeper
— -côte *m*	23	coast- ; coast-vessel
— -meuble *m*	24	furniture-repository
garder *vb*	25	to keep, retain
— à vue	26	to keep under close watch
— qqch. en bon état	27	to keep sth. in good repair
se — de	28	to be careful not to
gare *f*	29	(railway) station
chef *m* de —	30	— master
— de triage	31	marshalling yard
— maritime	32	harbour- —
— routière	33	road transport —
gaz *m*	34	gas
— en cylindre	35	bottled —
usine à —	36	— -works
geler *vb*	37	to freeze, immobilize
gêne *f*	38	1 embarrassment, constraint
	39	2 money difficulties
générique *m* [Cin.]	40	credit titles ; credits and cast

génie *m*	1	engineering
le — civil	2	civil —
genre *m*	3	type, kind ; species
géomètre *m*	4	geometer
— arpenteur	5	land-surveyor
gérance *f*	6	management, administration
gérant *m*	7	manager
directeur- —	8	managing director
gérer *vb*	9	to manage, conduct, run
mal —	10	to mismanage
gestion *f*	11	management, administration
gisement *m*	12	layer, bed, deposit
— pétrolifère	13	oil-field
—s houillers	14	coal-measures
global *adj*	15	rough, total, lump
gourde *f*	16	[monnaie haïtienne] gourd
grâce *f*	17	grace
de bonne —	18	willingly
de mauvaise —	19	reluctantly, unwillingly
— à	20	thanks to
jours de —	21	days of —
gracieux, -se *adj*	22	gracious
à titre —	23	free of charge
graisser *vb*	24	to grease, lubricate
— la patte à qqun	25	to grease/oil s.o.'s palm
gramme *m*	26	gram
grand *adj*	27	large, big
au — jour	28	in broad daylight
en —e partie	29	largely
— -livre	30	ledger
— -rue	31	main/high street
— -route	32	highway, main road
la Grande-Bretagne	33	(Great) Britain
grandeur *f*	34	size
— nature	35	life —
maquette — nature	36	mock up
graphique *n.m. & adj*	37	1 graph ; diagram 2 graphic
dessin —	38	industrial drawing
gratification *f*	39	gratuity ; bonus
gratis *adj*	40	free (of charge)
grattoir *m* (de bureau)	41	eraser (knife)
gratuit *adj*	42	1 free, gratuitous
	43	2 gratuitous, unfounded ; arbitrary
entrée —e	44	admission free

insulte —e	1	unprovoked insult
gratuité f	2	1 exemption from fee
	3	2 gratuitousness
graveur m	4	engraver, etcher
gré m	5	will, liking
à son —	6	to one's liking
au — de l'acheteur	7	at the option of the buyer
bon —, mal —, de — ou de force	8	willy-nilly
contre son —	9	against his wishes
de — à —	10	by mutual consent
de son plein —	11	willingly
savoir — à qqun de . . .	12	to be grateful to s.o. for . . .
greffe m [Lég.]	13	1 office of the clerk of the court [pany)
	14	2 registry (of joint-stock com-
greffier m	15	1 clerk (of the court)
	16	2 registrar
grève f	17	strike
briseur de —	18	blackleg, scab, — -breaker
être en —	19	to be on —
faire la —	20	to —
faire la — sur le tas	21	to stage a sitdown —
— de la faim	22	hunger —
— des cheminots	23	railway —
— illégale	24	wild-cat —
— perlée	25	go-slow —, slow-down —
— sur le tas	26	sitdown —
— symbolique	27	token —
piquet de —	28	— picket
se mettre en —	29	to go on —, walk out
grever vb	30	to burden (with, de)
gréviste m	31	striker [tion
grief m	32	complaint, grievance; objec-
griffe f	33	mark, stamp
— de pesage	34	weight stamp
gros, -se adj & adv	35	large, big; heavy
en —	36	1 wholesale 2 roughly
jouer —	37	to play for high stakes
le — lot	38	the jack-pot
un — bonnet	39	a big shot
grosse f	40	1 [Lég.] (enlarged) copy; probate
	41	2 gross, twelve dozen
grossiste m	42	wholesaler

grosso-modo *adv*	*1*	roughly
groupement *m*	*2*	1 grouping
	3	2 organization, association
grue *f*	*4*	crane
droit de —	*5*	cranage
gruger *vb*	*6*	to fleece
guichet *m*	*7*	[G.B.] position; till
	8	[Amér.] window
	9	[Can.] wicket
guichetier *m*	*10*	counter clerk
ha. (hectare)	*11*	hectare
haleine *f*	*12*	breath
un ouvrage de longue —	*13*	a long-term project
halle *f*	*14*	market; market-place
hangar *m*	*15*	shed
hausse *f*	*16*	rise; upward trend
en —	*17*	rising, going up
forte —	*18*	sharp rise
jouer/spéculer à la —	*19*	to bull; to stag
la — des prix	*20*	higher prices
hausser *vb*	*21*	to raise
haussier *m*	*22*	bull, stag
haut *adj*	*23*	tall, high, upper
la —e mer	*24*	the high seas
la marée est —e	*25*	the tide is in
haut(s)-fourneau(x) *m(pl)*	*26*	blast-furnace
hauturier, -ère *adj*	*27*	of the high seas
navigation hauturière	*28*	deep-sea shipping
hebdomadaire *n.m. & adj*	*29*	1 weekly paper/magazine
	30	2 weekly
bulletin —	*31*	weekly report
hectare *m*	*32*	hectare
hecto [=a Greek prefix meaning a hundred]	*33*	hecto
héligare *f*	*34*	helicopter terminal
héliport *m*	*35*	helicopter landing station, heliport
héritage *m*	*36*	inheritance, legacy
faire un —	*37*	to inherit, come into some property
part d'—	*38*	portion
répudier un —	*39*	to renounce a succession

hériter *vb*	1	to inherit
héritier, -ère *n*	2	heir, heiress
hétéroclite *adj*	3	odd, strange
assemblage —	4	an unusual collection of things, conglomeration
heure *f*	5	time
à l'— actuelle	6	at the present —
à une — convenable	7	at a reasonable hour
fixer une —	8	to set a —
— de l'Atlantique	9	Atlantic Time
— d'été	10	summer —
—s d'affluence	11	rush hours
—s de consultation [on the door of a doctor's or lawyer's office]	12	office hours
—s de pointe	13	peak hours
—s supplémentaires	14	over-time
toutes les —s	15	every hour, hourly
historique *m*	16	account
faire l'— d'une affaire	17	to retrace the development of a case
homicide *m*	18	homicide
— involontaire	19	manslaughter
— volontaire	20	murder
hommage *m*	21	homage, tribute, compliment; token
— de l'auteur/l'éditeur	22	compliments of the author/ publisher
présenter ses —s à qqun	23	to pay o.'s respects to s.o.
rendre — à qqun	24	to pay tribute to s.o.
homme *m*	25	man
droits de l' —	26	human rights
— d'affaires	27	business- —
— de confiance	28	reliable —
— de lettres	29	writer, author
— de paille	30	figure-head
— de peine	31	labourer, odd-job —
homologuer *vb*	32	to confirm officially; to agree, to approve (of); to ratify, to make valid
honorabilité *f*	33	good name, respectability
honoraires *n.m.pl.*	34	[docteur, professeur] fee(s), honorarium
	35	[avocat] retainer
	36	[homme d'église] stipend

— préalables	1	retainer
honorer *vb*	2	to honour; to meet (bill)
honorifique *adj*	3	honorific
distinction —	4	award, distinction
horaire *m*	5	schedule, time-table
horaire *adj*	6	hourly
horloge *f*	7	clock
— contrôleuse	8	automatic timekeeper
horloger *m*	9	clockmaker, watchmaker
hors *prép*	10	out (of)
— de doute	11	unquestionable, certain
— de la ville	12	outside the town
— de prix	13	exorbitant, extravagant
— ligne	14	exceptional, outstanding, remarkable
hors-la-loi *m*	15	outlaw
hôtelier, -ère *n.* & *adj*	16	1 hotel-keeper 2 hotel
l'industrie hôtelière	17	hotel industry
houille *f*	18	1 coal 2 source of energy
la — blanche	19	hydro-electric power, water-power
la — bleue	20	tide power
la — d'or	21	sun power
la — incolore	22	wind power
houillère *f*	23	coal-mine, coal-pit, colliery
huis *m*	24	door
à — clos	25	in camera, behind closed —s
huissier *m*	26	1 usher
	27	2 bailiff, writ server
	28	3 court bailiff/attendant
huit *n.m.* & *adj*	29	eight
dans les — jours	30	in a week
de demain en —	31	a week from tomorrow
il y a — jours	32	a week ago
huitaine *f*	33	about eight
remis à —	34	postponed for a week
hypothécaire *adj*	35	(on) mortgage
créancier —	36	mortgagee
contrat —	37	— deed
débiteur —	38	mortgagor
prêt —	39	loan on —
hypothèque *f*	40	mortgage
grevé d' —s [mière —	41	burdened with —
— de premier rang, pre-	42	first —

— de second rang	1	second —
libre/franc d'—	2	unmortgaged
mainlevée d'—	3	release of —
prêt sur —	4	— loan
purge d'—	5	redemption of —
purger une —	6	to pay off/redeem a —
hypothéquer *vb*	7	to mortgage

idem *adv*	8	idem, ditto
identité *f*	9	identity
carte d'—	10	— card
papiers d'—	11	identification
ignifuge *adj*	12	non-inflammable
île *f*	13	island, isle
les —s Anglo-Normandes	14	the Channel Islands
les —s Britanniques	15	the British Isles
illégal *adj*	16	illegal, unlawful
illégalité *f*	17	illegality, unlawfulness
illégitime *adj*	18	illegitimate, unlawful ; invalid
conclusion —	19	unjustified conclusion
illégitimité *f*	20	illegitimacy
illicite *adj*	21	illicit
illimité *adj*	22	unlimited, [congé] indefinite
imitation *f*	23	1 imitation, copy
	24	2 copying, imitating
immatriculation *f*	25	registration
immatriculer *vb*	26	to register
immeuble *n.m.* & *adj*	27	1 building ; premises
	28	2 real estate, (landed) property
biens —s	29	real estate
— à vendre	30	premises/property for sale
un — de dix étages	31	a ten-storey building
immobilier, -ère *adj*	32	immovable
agence immobilière	33	real estate agency
biens —s	34	real estate
immobilisation *f*	35	immobilization, tying up, locking up, [Lég.] conversion into real estate
—s	36	fixed assets
immobiliser *vb*	37	to lock up, tie up, immobilize ; [Lég.] to convert (personalty) into realty

impaire *n.m. & adj*	1	1 blunder 2 odd (number)
impayé *adj*	2	unpaid
impérieux, -se *adj*	3	[besoin] pressing, urgent
impliquer *vb*	4	1 to implicate 2 to imply
importance *f*	5	importance; size
avoir de l'—	6	to matter
être d'une — capitale	7	to be vital (to, *pour*)
sans grande —	8	not particularly important
sans —	9	immaterial
importateur, -rice *n &* *adj*	10	1 importer 2 importing
importation *f*	11	[fait] importation
	12	[marchandises] import
— en provenance de	13	imports from
importer *vb*	14	1 to import
	15	2 to matter, be important
imposable *adj*	16	taxable, rat(e)able, liable to taxation
imposé *adj*	17	fixed; taxed; prescribed; set
prix —	18	fixed price
imposer *vb*	19	1 to thrust, inflict (on, à)
	20	2 to tax
en — à	21	to impress
s'—	22	1 to be necessary
	23	2 to force on o.s. (a task)
imposition *f*	24	levying; taxation
impossibilité *f*	25	impossibility
être dans l'—de	26	to find it impossible to
impôt *m*	27	tax
assiette de l' —	28	basis of assessment
— de capitation [taxe par tête]	29	head —
— foncier	30	property/land —
—s cédulaires	31	schedule —es
— sur le revenu	32	income —
— sur les bénéfices	33	— on profits
— sur les sociétés	34	corporation —
lever des —s	35	to levy —es
impression *f*	36	1 impression
	37	2 point, printing
faire/donner une mauvaise —	38	to create a bad impression
faute d'—	39	misprint
imprévu *n.m. & adj*	40	1 (the) unexpected
	41	2 unforeseen

imprimé *n.m. & adj*	1	1 printed material; printed matter
	2	2 printed
imprimerie *f*	3	printing office; printing
imprimeur *m*	4	printer
imputable *adj*	5	1 imputable, attributable (to, *à*)
	6	2 that must be taken off/subtracted
frais —s sur un compte	7	expenses chargeable to an account
somme — sur un fonds de réserve	8	sum deducted/drawn from a reserve fund
imputer *vb*	9	1 to impute (to s.o., *à qqun*)
	10	2 to charge (to an account)
	11	3 to deduct; to draw; to subtract
inactif, -ve *adj*	12	[marché] dull, [personne, argent] idle
inaliénable *adj* [Lég.]	13	[droit, propriété, etc.] inalienable, untransferable, unassignable
inaliéné *adj* [Lég.]	14	unalienated
incapable *n.m. & adj*	15	incapable (of, *de*); inefficient, useless, incompetent, unable, unfit
un(e) — [Lég.]	16	incapable, a legally unfit/disqualified person
incarcération *f*	17	incarceration
incarcérer *vb*	18	to incarcerate
incassable *adj*	19	unbreakable
incendiaire *adj*	20	incendiary
incendie *m*	21	fire
— de forêt	22	forest —
— volontaire	23	arson
incendier *vb*	24	to set on fire
incertain *m*	25	indirect rate of exchange
donner l'—	26	to quote in foreign currency
incessamment *adv*	27	any time now
incessible *adj*	28	[droit] inalienable
	29	[objet] untransferable
incident *m*	30	incident; event
inclure *vb*	31	to enclose, include
inclus *adj*	32	included, enclosed
ci- —	33	enclosed herewith

E

inclusivement *adv*	1	inclusively
incomber *vb*	2	to be incumbent (on, *à*), to devolve (upon), to fall as a duty or responsibility
inconduite *f*	3	misconduct, misbehaviour
inconvénient *m*	4	inconvenience; objection; disadvantage, drawback
incorporer *vb*	5	to incorporate
incriminer *vb*	6	to incriminate
inculpation *f*	7	indictment, charge
sous l'—de	8	on a charge of
inculpé *m*	9	defendant, accused
inculpé *adj*	10	accused (of, *de*), charged (with, *de*)
inculper *vb*	11	to charge (with *de*), to accuse (of, *de*); to indict
indemne *adj*	12	undamaged, unhurt, without a scratch
indemnisation *f*	13	indemnification
indemniser *vb*	14	to indemnify; to recoup
indemnité *f*	15	1 indemnity, compensation, allowance
	16	2 emoluments
demande d'— de sinistre	17	claim
— de chômage	18	unemployment benefit
— de représentation	19	entertainment allowance
— de route/de déplacement	20	travelling allowance
— d'expropriation	21	compensation for expropriation
— parlementaire	22	M.P.'s salary
réclamer une —	23	to claim compensation
indésirable *n & adj*	24	undesirable
index *m*	25	index
faire l'— d'un livre	26	to — a book
indicateur *m*	27	[horaire] timetable
	28	[instrument] gauge
	29	[police] informer
indicatif *n.m. & adj*	30	1 signature tune
	31	2 indicative
à titre —	32	as a rough approximation, as an indication
indication *f*	33	direction, instruction, indication, information
indice *m*	34	1 sign, indication 2 index

l'— du coût de la vie	1	the cost-of-living index
indisponible *adj*	2	unavailable
indivis *adj* [Lég.]	3	undivided, joint
par —	4	jointly
induire *vb*	5	to lead
— en erreur	6	— astray
indûment *adv*	7	unduly, without permission
industrie *f*	8	industry, trade, manufacture
chevalier d'—	9	confidence man, swindler
industriel *m*	10	manufacturer, industrialist
industriel, -le *adj*	11	industrial
in extenso *adv*	12	in full, completely
infime *adj*	13	negligible, very small
inflation *f*	14	inflation
— contenue	15	pent-up —
information *f*	16	1 information, news
	17	2 [Lég.] investigation
aller aux —s	18	to make inquiries, to inquire
— de presse	19	press report
informer *vb*	20	to inform, notify
— contre qqun [Lég.]	21	to start proceedings against s.o.
s'—	22	to find out, inquire
infraction *f*	23	infraction, violation, infringement
— au règlement	24	breach of regulations
ingénieur *m*	25	engineer
— chimiste	26	chemical —
— civil	27	civil —
— -conseil	28	consulting —
— des mines	29	mining —
— -électricien	30	electrical —
— -mécanicien	31	mechanical —
ingérence *f*	32	interference
ingrat *adj*	33	ungrateful
un travail —	34	a thankless job; a tedious job
inhabile *adj* [Lég.]	35	legally unqualified
— à tester	36	incompetent to make a will
initiale *f*	37	initial
signer de ses —s	38	to —
initiative *f*	39	initiative
avoir de l'—	40	to be resourceful

injonction *f*	1	order, command, injunction; [Can.] court order
inonder *vb*	2	to flood; to glut (the market)
inopportun *adj*	3	inopportune, untimely
inoxydable *adj*	4	stainless
insaisissable *adj* [Lég.]	5	not distrainable, not seizable, unattachable
inscription *f*	6	1 inscription, lettering on coins and medals; notice
	7	2 [formalité] enrolment, registration
	8	3 entry (in a register)
droit d'—	9	entrance fee
feuille d'—	10	entry form
frais d'—	11	registration fee
inscrire *vb*	12	1 to inscribe; to enter (in a book), to write down
	13	2 to register; to record (in a register)
se faire —	14	to register, enrol, put down one's name
inscrit *adj*	15	inscribed, registered; recorded
insérer *vb*	16	to insert, to put in
prière d'—	17	for the favour of publication in your columns
insistance *f*	18	insistence
sur l'— de	19	pressed by
insister *vb*	20	to insist, to emphasize, to stress (the point)
insolvabilité *f*	21	insolvency
insolvable *adj*	22	insolvent
insonoriser *vb*	23	to sound-proof
insoumission *f*	24	insubordination
inspecter *vb*	25	to inspect, to examine (accounts)
— les lieux	26	to survey
inspecteur, -rice *n*	27	inspector, police inspector; surveyor
— (de grand magasin)	28	floor-walker
inspection *f*	29	inspection, inspecting; examining; survey
instable *adj*	30	unreliable, unstable
installation *f*	31	[d'un magistrat] induction, inducting

	1	[d'une machine] installation, fitting up
	2	[ensemble d'appareils] fittings, plant, equipment
	3	[de l'électricité] putting in
instamment *adv*	*4*	urgently, earnestly
instance *f*	*5*	1 instancy, solicitation
	6	2 [Lég.] suit, action, proceedings
acquitté en seconde —	*7*	acquitted on appeal
frais d'—	*8*	costs
Ils sont en — de divorce	*9*	Their divorce proceedings are taking place
tribunal de première —	*10*	County court
instituer *vb*	*11*	to found, to establish, to set up
— un héritier	*12*	to appoint an heir
institution *f*	*13*	institution, establishment, founding
instruction *f*	*14*	1 instruction, guidance, information
	15	2 [Lég.] investigation
avoir de l'—	*16*	to be educated
— judiciaire	*17*	preliminary examination (of a case)
—s permanentes	*18*	standing orders
juge d'—	*19*	examining magistrate
insu *m*	*20*	. . . .
à l'— de qqun	*21*	unknown to (s.o.)
à son —	*22*	without his knowledge
intégral *adj*	*23*	integral, complete, in full
intenter *vb*	*24*	to undertake (sth. against s.o.)
— un procès à	*25*	to take legal action against, to sue
intention *f*	*26*	intention, will, wish; [Lég.] intent
à l'— de	*27*	for, in honour of
avec — délictueuse [Lég.]	*28*	with malicious intent
sans —	*29*	unintentionally
intentionnellement *adv*	*30*	intentionally, deliberately
inter *m*	*31*	long-distance (telephone)
intercaler *vb*	*32*	to interpolate
interdiction *f*	*33*	1 prohibition, forbidding, interdiction

interrupteur m ~ switch

	1 *2*	[*Lég.*: — d'un prodigue] deprival of control over money
— légale	*2*	suspension of civil rights (on account of conviction)
interdit *adj* & *n.m.*	*3* *1*	prohibited, forbidden
	4 *2*	interdict
entrée —e	*5*	no admittance
— de séjour	*6*	ex-convict prohibited from entering a certain area
jeter l'— sur	*7*	to forbid ; to issue an interdict against
passage —	*8*	no thoroughfare
intéressé *n.m.*	*9*	the applicant, the person concerned
intéressé *adj*	*10* *1*	interested, showing interest
	11 *2*	mercenary, self-seeking ; on the make
	12 *3*	(personally) involved (in, *dans*)
intérêt *m*	*13* *1*	interest, concern, care anxiety
	14 *2*	advantage, benefit
	15 *3*	interest, sum, percentage
Il y aurait — à	*16*	It would be advisable to
Ils ont — à le faire	*17*	It is in their interest to do so
payer des —s	*18*	to pay interest
prendre de l'— à qqch.	*19*	to be interested in sth.
intérieur *n.m.* & *adj*	*20* *1*	home, inside, interior
	21 *2*	inner, inside
à l'—	*22*	indoors, inside
le ministre de l'—	*23*	[G.B.] the Home Secretary
	24	[Amér.] the Secretary of the Interior
intérim *m*	*25*	interim ; acting
par —	*26*	provisional
intermédiaire *n.m.* & *adj*	*27* *1*	middleman
	28 *2*	intermediary
par l'— de	*29*	through
interné *n.m.* & *adj*	*30* *1*	internee
	31 *2*	interned, confined
interner *vb*	*32*	to intern, confine
interview *f*	*33*	interview

solliciter une —	1	to ask for an —
interviewer *vb*	2	to interview (s.o.)
intimer *vb*	3	to command, decree; to notify; [Lég.] to summon to appear
intrinsèque *adj*	4	intrinsic, real, genuine, [valeur] specific
introduction *f*	5	introduction; bringing in, admission
lettre d'—	6	letter of introduction
introduire *vb*	7	to introduce; to bring in
— une mode	8	to start a fashion
introuvable *adj*	9	not/nowhere to be found, impossible to find
invalide *adj* [Lég.]	10	not valid, null and void
invalider *vb* [Lég.]	11	to nullify, invalidate (will), annul (marriage), quash (election)
— un député	12	to unseat an M.P.
invalidité *f*	13	invalidity
invendable *adj*	14	unsalable, unmarketable
invendu *n.m.* & *adj*	15	unsold (copies, etc.)
inventaire *m*	16	inventory, stock-taking
bénéfice d'— [Lég.]	17	right of heir to accept an estate without liability to debts beyond the assets descended
faire l'— (de)	18	to take stock (of)
par/sous bénéfice d'—	19	with reservations; conditionally
inventorier *vb*	20	to make a list of (goods, etc.); to take stock of
investir *vb*	21	to invest
investissement *m*	22	investment
invisible *adj*	23	invisible
importations/exportations —s	24	— imports/exports
issu *adj*	25	descended (from, *de*); born (of, *de*)
issue *f*	26	1 close, end, issue, conclusion
	27	2 outcome, result
	28	3 exit, outlet
à l'— de	29	at the end of
voie sans —	30	dead end

italique *n.m. & adj*	*1*	1 italics 2 italic (type)
mettre en —	*2*	to italicize
ivresse *f*	*3*	intoxication
en état d'— publique	*4*	drunk and disorderly
jauge *f*	*5*	tonnage
— brute	*6*	gross —
— nette	*7*	register(ed) —
jaugeage *m*	*8*	measurement
jauger *vb*	*9*	to measure ; to have a capacity of
jet *m*	*10*	throw(ing), cost(ing)
d'un seul —	*11*	in one sweep
— à la mer	*12*	jettison(ing)
un premier —	*13*	a first draught
jeter *vb*	*14*	to throw (away)
— l'ancre	*15*	to drop the anchor
— les fondements	*16*	to lay the foundations
jeton *m*	*17*	token, counter, tally
— de présence	*18*	attendance fee
jeu *m*	*19*	game, gamble
avoir beau —	*20*	to be in a good position
entrer en —	*21*	to come in the picture
être en —	*22*	to be at stake
mettre en —	*23*	to stake
joaillier, -ère *n*	*24*	jeweller
joindre *vb*	*25*	1 to join, connect
	26	2 to combine, mix
	27	3 to reach (a person)
	28	4 to enclose, place in envelope
— l'utile à l'agréable	*29*	to combine work with pleasure
joint *m*	*30*	junction ; joint
trouver le —	*31*	to find the best way, to hit upon the right plan
joint *adj & adv*	*32*	joined, enclosed
ci- —	*33*	enclosed herewith
pièce —e	*34*	enclosure
jouer *vb*	*35*	to play
— à la baisse	*36*	to bear, to speculate for a fall
— à la Bourse	*37*	— the stock market
— à la hausse	*38*	to bull, to speculate for a rise

— gros jeu	1	— for high stakes
— un tour à qqun	2	— a trick on s.o.
jour *m*	3	day
— de planche	4	lay —
— de semaine	5	week-
— férié	6	(bank) holiday
— ouvrable	7	working —
le — de l'an	8	New Year's Day
mettre à —	9	to bring up to date, to write up
par —	10	by —
journal *m*	11	1 newspaper 2 diary, book
— de bord	12	log book
— d'entreprise	13	house organ
— hebdomadaire	14	weekly paper
kiosque à journaux	15	newstand
tenir un —	16	to keep a diary
journalier, -ère *n*	17	(day) labourer, journeyman
judiciaire *adj*	18	judicial, legal
vente —	19	sale by order of the court
juge *m*	20	judge, justice
— de paix	21	justice of the peace
jugement *m* [Lég.]	22	trial; sentence, decision
— provisoire	23	decree nisi
mise en —	24	arraignment
passer en —	25	to be brought up for trial
prononcer un —	26	to pass sentence
rendre un — arbitral	27	to make an award
juger *vb* [Lég.]	28	to try
— un procès	29	— a case
juré *m*	30	juryman, juror
les —s	31	the jury
Messieurs les —s	32	gentlemen, members of the jury
jurer *vb*	33	to swear, to take an oath
Je jure de	34	I swear to
Je jure par	35	I swear by
Je jure que	36	I swear that
juridiction *f*	37	jurisdiction
juridique *adj*	38	juridical, legal
conseiller —	39	legal adviser
jurisprudence *f*	40	jurisprudence
justice *f*	41	justice
le ministère de la —	42	the Department of Justice
poursuivre en —	43	to bring an action against

E*

rendre — à qqun	1	to give s.o. credit
traduire en —	2	to hale into court
justificatif, -ve *adj*	3	justificative
pièce justificative	4	voucher; [Lég.] relevant paper
un numéro —	5	a voucher copy
justifier *vb*	6	to justify; to vindicate
se — (de)	7	to clear o.s. (of)
kilométrage *m*	8	mileage
krach, krack *m*	9	(financial) crash, smash
lacune *f*	10	deficiency, gap
lainage *m*	11	woollens, woollen goods
laine *f*	12	wool
le bas de —	13	nest-egg
laissé-pour-compte *m*	14	returned or rejected article
laissez-passer *m*	15	permit, pass
laminoir *m*	16	rolling mill
lampiste *m* [Coll.]	17	scapegoat
lancement *m*	18	launching
lancer *vb*	19	to launch; to issue
— un appel	20	to send out a call
— un ballon d'essai	21	to fly a kite
— une souscription	22	to start a fund; to launch a fund-raising campaign
— un mandat d'amener [Lég.]	23	to issue a warrant against s.o.
— un navire	24	to launch a ship
— un nouveau produit	25	to introduce a new product
larcin *m*	26	slip; lapse; larceny; pilferage
ledit, ladite *adj*	27	the aforesaid, the above-mentioned
légal *adj*	28	legal, statutory, lawful
légalisation *f*	29	legalization
légaliser *vb*	30	to legalize, make legal, certify (a signature)
légalité *f*	31	legality, lawfulness
rester dans la —	32	to keep within the law
légataire *m*	33	legatee
— particulier	34	specific —
— universel	35	residuary —

légation *f*	1	legation
légiférer *vb*	2	to legislate
législateur, -rice *n*	3	lawmaker, legislator
législatif, -ve *adj*	4	legislative
législation *f*	5	law, legislation
législature *f*	6	legislature
légiste *n.m.* & *adj*	7	legist
médecin- —	8	medico-legal expert, court pathologist
légitime *adj*	9	lawful, legitimate
— défense	10	self-defence
légitimer *vb*	11	[enfant] to legitimate
	12	[titre] to recognize, authorize
	13	[droit] to justify
légitimité *f*	14	lawfulness, legitimacy
legs [le] *m*	15	bequest, legacy
léguer *vb*	16	to bequeath, will, descend
lendemain *m*	17	next day
du jour au —	18	overnight
sans —	19	short-lived
léser *vb*	20	to injure, wrong, be detrimental to
la partie lésée	21	the injured party
lésiner *vb*	22	to be stingy, stint, dole (out)
lest *m*	23	ballast
jeter du —	24	1 to discharge —
	25	2 [Fig.] to make sacrifices (in order to achieve a purpose)
lester *vb*	26	to ballast, weigh
lettre *f*	27	letter
à la —	28	to the —
en-tête de —	29	— head
en toutes —s	30	in full
— avec valeur déclarée	31	— with value declared, insured —
— de change	32	bill of exchange
— de faire-part	33	announcement
— de recommandation	34	— of introduction
— de transport aérien	35	airway bill
— de voiture	36	consignment note
— majuscule	37	capital (—)
— morte	38	dead —
— recommandée	39	registered —
mettre une — à la poste	40	to post a —

levé *m*	1	plan, survey; charting, mapping
levé *adj*	2	up
au pied —	3	offhand, unexpectedly
voter à mains —es	4	to vote by a show of hands
levée *f*	5	1 removal 2 cancelling
la dernière — (des lettres)	6	the last (mail) collection
la — des impôts	7	levying taxes
lever *vb*	8	to lift, raise
— des impôts	9	to levy taxes
— l'ancre	10	to weigh anchor
— la séance	11	to adjourn the meeting
— le courrier	12	to collect the mail
— le pied	13	to abscond
— les scellés	14	to remove/break the seals
— une punition	15	to remit a punishment
— un plan	16	to draw a plan
— une saisie	17	to lift an embargo
lez, les *prép* [used only before name of town]	18	near
liasse *f*	19	wad, bundle
une — de billets	20	a wad
libellé *m*	21	phrasing, wording
libeller *vb*	22	[chèque] to make out
	23	[documents] to word
libéralisme *m*	24	liberalism
— économique	25	laissez-faire, laisser-faire
libération *f*	26	release, discharge, freeing
libéré *adj*	27	released, discharged; paid up (capital)
libérer *vb*	28	to free, release, discharge, to clear (debt)
se —	29	to free o.s.
se — d'une dette	30	to redeem a debt
se — d' (une obligation)	31	to disengage o.s. from (an obligation)
liberté *f*	32	freedom, liberty
mettre en — (sous caution)	33	to release (on bail)
librairie *f*	34	1 bookshop 2 book trade
libre *adj*	35	1 free, at liberty (to, *de*)
	36	2 disengaged, off duty
	37	3 clear; clean (bill)
	38	4 [sur une porte] vacant
" — " [taxi]	39	" for hire "

zone de — échange	1	free trade area
licence f	2	licence; permit [uate
licencié n.m. & adj	3	1 licensee; licentiate; grad-
	4	2 licensed; graduated
licenciement m	5	dismissal, lay-off (of workers)
licencier vb	6	[employé] to dismiss
	7	[ouvrier] to lay off
licite adj	8	licit, lawful
lié adj	9	connected; bound
opération —e	10	combined deal
lien m	11	link; tie, bond
lier vb	12	to bind, tie; to connect, link
Ce contrat vous lie	13	You are bound by this agreement
lieu m	14	place
donner — à	15	to give rise to
en haut —	16	high up, in high circles
en premier/second —	17	firstly/secondly
Il y a — de croire	18	We have every reason to think
sur les —x	19	on the spot, on the premises
tenir — de	20	to take the — of
limitation f	21	restriction; limit
limite f	22	limit; termination
dépasser une —	23	to exceed a limit
jusqu'au 31 décembre, dernière —	24	not later than December 31st
sans —s	25	unlimited
vitesse —	26	maximum speed
limitrophe adj	27	adjacent
lingerie f	28	linen goods; underwear
lingot m	29	ingot
de l'or en —s	30	bullion
liquidateur m	31	liquidator
liquidation f	32	winding up, liquidation; selling off, [en Bourse] account, clearance
chambre de —	33	(bankers') clearing-house
entrer en—	34	to go into liquidation
— totale	35	clearance sale
liquide adj	36	liquid
argent —	37	cash, ready money
liquider vb	38	1 to wind up, liquidate
	39	2 to pay in full, pay off, settle

	1	3 to clear, sell off
	2	4 to get rid of
liquidité *f*	*3*	liquidity
coefficient de —	*4*	— ratio
—s	*5*	liquid assets
liste *f*	*6*	list, roll; register; panel (of teachers, juries, etc.); roster
grossir la —	*7*	to swell the numbers
— de colisage	*8*	packing list
— de départs [navires]	*9*	sailing list
— de souscription	*10*	list of applications
— officielle de taux	*11*	schedule of charges
litige *m*	*12*	litigation, dispute, contest at law
cas en —	*13*	case at issue
le point en —	*14*	the point at issue
litigieux, -se *adj*	*15*	litigious
un point —	*16*	subject of dispute
litre *m*	*17*	litre, [Amér.] liter
livrable *adj*	*18*	deliverable
livraison *f*	*19*	1 delivery
	20	2 [livre] instalment, part; [magazine] copy, issue
bon de —	*21*	delivery order
comptant sans —	*22*	cash and carry
défaut de —	*23*	non-delivery
— à domicile	*24*	We deliver
— franco	*25*	free delivery
par —	*26*	in parts
payable à la —	*27*	payable on delivery
livre *m*	*28*	book
le grand —	*29*	ledger
— de bord	*30*	ship's log, log —
— de caisse	*31*	cash —
— de commandes	*32*	order —
— de paye	*33*	wages —
— des effets à payer/à recevoir	*34*	bills payable/receivable
— des entrées	*35*	purchase —
— des inventaires	*36*	stock —
tenue des —s	*37*	—keeping
livre f [lb. *or* £]	*38*	1 pound 2 pound (sterling)
mille —s de rente	*39*	private income of one thousand —s (a year)

se vend à la —	1	sold by the —
livret *m*	2	booklet, record book
— de banque	3	pass-book
— de caisse d'épargne	4	savings-bank book
livreur *m*	5	delivery man
locataire *n. m/f*	6	tenant, lodger; lessee
locatif, -ve *adj*	7	tenant, rental
réparations locatives	8	tenant repairs
location *f*	9	letting, hiring, tenancy
bureau de —	10	booking office
en —	11	for hire
— des places	12	reservation(s)
— des voitures	13	rent-a-car service
logement *m*	14	accommodation(s)
la crise du —	15	the housing shortage
loger *vb*	16	1 to stay; to live
	17	2 to accommodate, to house
loi *f*	18	law
abroger une —	19	to repeal a —
aux yeux de la —	20	in the eye of the —
avoir force de —	21	to be law
faire des —s	22	to legislate
faire la —	23	to lay down the —
homme de —	24	lawyer
hors-la- —	25	outlaw
les —s pénales	26	penal —s
— exceptionnelle	27	emergency legislation
Nul n'est censé ignorer la —	28	Ignorance of the — is no defence
projet de —	29	bill
long, -ue *adj*	30	long
capitaine au — cours	31	merchant marine captain, master mariner, sea captain
— cours	32	offshore navigation
papiers à —ue échéance	33	— -dated bills
longueur *f*	34	length
dans le sens de la —	35	— -wise
mesure de —	36	linear measure
traîner en —	37	to drag
lopin *m*	38	portion, small piece
— de terre	39	piece of land
lot *m*	40	1 portion, share
	41	2 lot, batch (of goods)
	42	3 prize

	1	4 premium
emprunt à —s	2	lottery loan
obligations à —s	3	premium bonds
le gros —	4	the highest prize, the jackpot
tirage à —s	5	prize-drawing
lotir *vb*	6	to share out, parcel out (land)
lotissement *m*	7	parcelling out; development (of building land)
louage *m*	8	hire, hiring
loué *adj*	9	reserved, engaged
louer *vb*	10	to let (out), rent, lease, hire (out)
— des places	11	to book/reserve seats
— (une maison) à qqun	12	to lease (a house) out to s.o.
prendre un appartement à —	13	to lease a flat
loup *m*	14	stag, premium hunter
loyer *m*	15	rent, rental
lucratif, -ve *adj*	16	lucrative, profitable
association sans but — (A.S.B.L.)	17	non-profit-making association
M. (Monsieur)	18	Mr (Mister)
plural: MM.	19	*pluriel*: Messrs
machine *f*	20	engine, machine
— à affranchir (le courrier)	21	franking machine
— à écrire	22	typewriter
— -outil	23	machine tool
madame *f*	24	Mrs
Madame la présidente	25	Madam Chairman
Mesdames (Mesdemoiselles) et Messieurs	26	Ladies and gentlemen
Mme Adam	27	Mrs Adam
mademoiselle (Mlle)	28	Miss [doit être suivi du nom de famille]
Mesdemoiselles Simon	29	the Misses Simon
magasin *m*	30	1 store, shop 2 warehouse
(avoir) en —	31	(to have) in stock
chaîne de —s	32	group of stores
les grands —s	33	department stores
marchandises en —	34	stock in hand

pris en —	1	ex store
magasinage *m*	2	storing, warehousing; [chemin de fer] demurrage
magasinier *m*	3	storekeeper, warehouse-man
magistrat *m*	4	magistrate, judge
magistrature *f*	5	magistracy, judgeship
entrer dans la —	6	to become a judge
la — assise	7	the Bench
la — debout	8	the body of public prosecutors; the law-officers of the State
magnat *m*	9	tycoon
main *f*	10	hand
(donner) de la — à la —	11	(to give) privately
faire — basse sur	12	to grab
fait à la —	13	— -made
prêter — forte	14	to give assistance/strong support
— -d'œuvre	15	labour, manpower
sous la —	16	within reach
mainlevée *f*	17	withdrawal
— de saisie	18	restoration of goods (taken in distraint)
mainmise *f*	19	seizure (of, *sur*); distraint (upon property)
maintenir *vb*	20	to maintain, keep, support, preserve
se —	21	to stay, continue
maison *f*	22	house, firm, establishment
— de prêt	23	money lender
— de rapport	24	tenement house, apartment house
maître *m* **chanteur**	25	blackmailer
majeur *adj*	26	1 of age 2 important
devenir —	27	to come of age
raison —e	28	chief reason
un cas de force —e	29	1 act of God
	30	2 a case of absolute necessity
majoration *f*	31	1 additional charge (on bill)
	32	2 increase (in price)
majorer *vb*	33	to make an additional charge (on bill); to raise, put up (the price of sth.)
— une facture de 5%	34	to put 5% on an invoice

majorité *f*	*1*	1 majority; coming of age, age of full legal responsibility
	2	2 majority, greater number
à sa —	*3*	when he comes of age
atteindre sa —	*4*	to come of age
majuscule *f*	*5*	capital (letter)
mal *n.m., adj & adv*	*6*	bad; badly; wrong; injury
bien — acquis	*7*	ill-gotten gains
faire du — à qqun	*8*	to harm s.o.
Nous avons du — à le croire	*9*	We find it difficult to believe that
pas — de	*10*	a fair amount, quite a few
malentendu *m*	*11*	misunderstanding
malversation *f*	*12*	malversation, fraud; misuse of public funds; embezzlement
manchette *f*	*13*	[journal] head-line
mandat *m*	*14*	1 mandate
	15	2 term, limited period
	16	3 [Lég.] proxy; power of attorney
	17	4 warrant
	18	5 money order, draft
fonctionnaire sans —	*19*	unauthorized official
lancer un —	*20*	to issue a warrant
— d'arrêt	*21*	warrant of arrest
— de comparution	*22*	summons to appear
— de perquisition	*23*	search warrant
— international	*24*	foreign money order
— (-poste)	*25*	money order
un — d'amener [Lég.]	*26*	warrant
mandataire *m*	*27*	representative, proxy; [Lég.] authorized agent, attorney; trustee
mander *vb*	*28*	1 to send news
	29	2 to call, summon [sels ...
On mande de Bruxelles ...	*30*	It is reported from Brus-
manifester *vb*	*31*	to show
— l'intention de	*32*	to express a desire to
mannequin *m*	*33*	1 model, mannequin
	34	2 dummy
manœuvre *m*	*35*	(unskilled) labourer, navvy
manœuvre *f*	*36*	1 manœuvre; handling; shunting

	1	2 manœuvring, scheme
manque *m*	2	lack, shortage
à la —	3	dull, incapable, incompetent, poor
" — " [sur une facture]	4	out of stock ; sold out
— de	5	for want of
manqué *adj*	6	abortive, unsuccessful, coming to nothing
manquer *vb*	7	1 to fail
	8	2 to be lacking
	9	3 to be missed ; to be missing
Il en manque un	10	There is one missing
— à sa parole	11	to break one's word
manteau *m*	12	coat
sous le —	13	sub rosa, in secret ; privately
manufacture *f*	14	manufacture, manufacturing
manutention *f*	15	handling
manutentionnaire *m*	16	handler
manutentionner *vb*	17	to handle
maquette *f*	18	model
— grandeur nature	19	mock up
maraîcher, -ère *n. & adj*	20	1 [G.B.] market-gardener, [Amér.] truck-gardener
	21	2 [G.B.] market-gardening (industry), [Amér.] truck-gardening
marasme *m*	22	stagnation (of business)
marc *m*	23	[poids ou monnaie] mark
au — le franc	24	pro rata, proportionally
marchand *m*	25	dealer
— ambulant	26	pedlar, hawker, vendor, vender
— de journaux	27	newsagent
— de poisson	28	fishmonger
— de tabac	29	tobacconist
— des quatre saisons	30	costermonger
— en détail	31	retailer
— en gros	32	wholesale —, wholesaler
— forain	33	booth keeper
marchand *adj*	34	marketable, trade
marine —e	35	mercantile marine, merchant service
navire —	36	merchant ship, merchantman

prix —	1	trade price
valeur —e	2	sale value
ville —e	3	trading city
marchandage *m*	4	haggling
marchander *vb*	5	1 to bargain, to haggle
	6	2 [lésiner] to grudge
marchandise *f*	7	goods, merchandise, wares
train de —s	8	freight train, goods train
marche *f*	9	movement, operation, running
faire — arrière	10	to back, move back, go in reverse
la — à suivre	11	the correct procedure
marché *m*	12	market
bon —	13	cheap
conclure un —	14	to strike a bargain
— inactif/sans ressort	15	dull —
meilleur —	16	cheaper
marcher *vb*	17	to work, operate; to run
Les affaires marchent	18	Business is good
marée *f*	19	tide
— descendante	20	ebb —
— montante	21	flood —
marge *f*	22	1 margin, blank space
	23	2 margin, cover
avoir de la —	24	to have time left (to do sth.)
en —	25	outside; on the fringe
— bénéficiaire	26	margin of profit
— de garantie	27	margin, cover
— de temps	28	leeway
— supplémentaire	29	further margin/cover
maritime *adj*	30	maritime, shipping
agent —	31	shipping-agent
assurance —	32	marine insurance
commerce —	33	sea-borne trade
courtier maritime	34	ship-broker
gare —	35	harbour station
maroquinerie *f*	36	leather goods
marque *f*	37	[fabrication] make
	38	[signe distinctif, griffe] mark, sign
	39	[goût, parfum] brand
— déposée	40	registered trade mark
un hôte de —	41	a distinguished visitor
marquer *vb*	42	to mark

142

masse *f*	1	1 mass, bulk 2 assets
en —	2	in the mass
— active	3	assets
— des biens (de la faillite)	4	(bankrupt's) total estate
— passive	5	liabilities
pas des —s [Belg.]	6	not in great numbers, crowds
matériau *m*	7	1 building material
	8	2 [Fig.] materials
matériel *m*	9	material, aid, equipment; [outils] implements
— roulant	10	rolling stock
matière *f*	11	matter; material; subject
—s premières	12	raw materials
table des —	13	contents
matricule *m*	14	number
numéro —	15	registration —, serial —
mazout *m*	16	fuel oil
méfait *m*	17	misdeed
mégarde *f*	18	. . . .
par —	19	unawares, inadvertently, through carelessness
mêler *vb*	20	to mix (up)
être mêlé à une affaire	21	to be mixed up in an affair/a case
se — (de)	22	1 to dabble (in)
	23	2 to interfere (with)
mémoire *n.f* & *m*	24	1 memory
	25	2 memorandum, paper
de —	26	from —
pour —	27	for the record
mémorandum *m*	28	memorandum; note-book
ménage *m*	29	household
articles de —	30	— utensils
ménagement *m*	31	caution, care
ménager *vb*	32	to husband, manage carefully, use economically; to take good care of
mener *vb*	33	to conduct, lead; to drive
— à bien	34	to bring to a successful issue/conclusion, to achieve
— une enquête	35	to conduct an investigation
mensualité *f*	36	monthly payment
payer par —s	37	to pay by monthly instalments

143

mensuel, -le *adj*	1	monthly
mensuellement *adv*	2	monthly, each month
mention *f*	3	mention ; reference
faire — de	4	to mention
mentionner *vb*	5	to mention ; to name (s.o.) ; to state
en mentionnant	6	stating
mentionné ci-dessus	7	above-mentioned
menu *adj*	8	small
—e monnaie	9	— change
par le —	10	in detail
menuiserie *f*	11	carpentry ; woodwork
mer *f*	12	sea
au bord de la —	13	by the —
en —	14	at —
en pleine —	15	out at —
jeter à la — [d'un navire]	16	to throw overboard
grosse —	17	heavy —
mercanti *m*	18	profiteer
mercantile *adj*	19	mercantile ; [Péj.] profiteering
mercerie *f*	20	small wares ; small-ware shop, haberdashery
mercier, -ère *n*	21	haberdasher
mercuriale *f*	22	official list of exchange prices, market price list
mère *f*	23	mother
la maison —	24	the head office
messager, -ère *n*	25	messenger ; carrier
messagerie *f*	26	carrying trade
—s maritimes	27	shipping service ; shipping line
service de —s	28	road haulage
métallurgie *f*	29	metallurgy
métallurgiste *m*	30	steelworker
métayer *m*	31	tenant farmer
métier *m*	32	trade, line, business
acteur de —	33	professional actor
de —	34	by trade
mètre *m*	35	metre, [Amér.] meter
métropole *f*	36	1 metropolis, capital city
	37	2 mother/home country
mettre *vb*	38	to put ; to set
— à l'épreuve	39	to test
— au point	40	to overhaul ; to clarify

— de côté	1	to put by, set aside, save
— en état	2	to repair
se — en frais	3	to go to great expense
meuble *m*	4	a piece of furniture
les —s	5	the furniture
meuble *adj*	6	movable
biens —s	7	chattels, personal estate, —s, — property
mévente *f*	8	slump, stagnation (of business)
mi *n.m. & adv*	9	mid, half, semi-
mieux *adv*	10	better, best
au —	11	at best
faute de —	12	for want of sth. better
Nous agirons au — de vos intérêts	13	We'll do what's best for you
un —, du —	14	a change for the better
milieu *m*	15	1 centre, middle
	16	2 milieu, environment, sphere, circle
dans les —x autorisés	17	in responsible quarters
tenir le — entre . . . et . . .	18	to be sth. between . . . and . . .
mille *n.m.*	19	mile
milliard *m*	20	[G.B.] milliard
	21	[Amér.] billion
milliardaire *m*	22	millionaire [étant donné la différence entre les francs et les livres ou les dollars]
millier *m*	23	(about one) thousand
million *m*	24	million
dix —s	25	ten —
un emprunt de dix —s	26	a ten — loan
millionnaire *m*	27	millionaire
minerai *m*	28	ore
mineral *n.m. & adj*	29	mineral
chimie —e	30	inorganic chemistry
mineur *n.m. & adj*	31	1 minor 2 under age
minime *adj*	32	small
ministère *m*	33	Ministry
le — de l'Air	34	Air —
le — de la Justice	35	Department of Justice
le — public	36	the (Department of the) Public Prosecutor
ministre *m*	37	minister

145

le Ministre des Finances	1	1 [G.B.] the Chancellor of the Exchequer
	2	2 [Amér.] the Secretary of the Treasury
minorité f	3	[Lég.] infancy
minoterie f	4	1 flour mill
		2 flour industry
minuscule f	5	small letter, lower case letter
minute f	6	1 minute
	7	2 original draft (of deed, judgment)
minuter vb	8	to record, enter (deed, etc.)
minuterie f	9	automatic time switch, motion work (of clock, meter)
mire f	10	sight
point de —	11	[Fig.] centre of attraction
mis à jour loc.	12	[account] up-to-date
mise f	13	1 putting, placing, setting
	14	2 stake; bid
— à exécution	15	carrying out
— à la retraite	16	pensioning (off)
— à pied	17	suspension
— à prix	18	upset price
— au point	19	overhauling; clarification; adjustment
— de fonds	20	putting up of money
— en chantier	21	laying down
— en demeure	22	injunction, summons
— en gage	23	pawning
— en jeu	24	use
— en liberté	25	release, releasing
— en marche	26	starting
— en œuvre	27	putting into action
— en vente	28	sale; offered for sale
— en vigueur	29	enforcement
miser vb	30	to bid (at auction); to stake (on, sur)
mission f	31	mission; assignment
mi-temps f	32	half-time
mitoyen, -ne adj	33	dividing (two properties)
mur —	34	party wall
mitraille f	35	grapeshot; [ferraille] scraps
mixte adj	36	mixed; joint
mobile n.m. & adj	37	1 motive [able]
	38	2 mobile, movable; change-

mobilier *m*	1	furniture
mobilier, -ère *adj*	2	movable, transferable
biens —s	3	chattels, personal property
valeurs mobilières	4	transferable property
mode *f*	5	fashion, style
à la —	6	fashionable, in style
magasin de —s	7	boutique, millinery
mode *m*	8	instructions, directions; method, mode
— d'emploi	9	directions for use
modèle *n.m. & adj*	10	1 model, pattern; copy
	11	2 exemplary, model
modification *f*	12	modification, alteration
modifier *vb*	13	to amend, modify, alter
modique *adj*	14	small, low
modiste *f*	15	milliner
mois *m*	16	month
. . . — de vue	17	. . . —'s sight
par —	18	—ly, on a —ly basis
(payer, louer) au —	19	(to pay, hire) by the —
toucher un treizième —	20	to get a bonus
une fois par —	21	once a —
moitié *f*	22	half
à — prix	23	at — the price
— —	24	fifty-fifty
monétaire *adj*	25	monetary, currency
monnaie *f*	26	1 (small) change
	27	2 currency; money
battre —	28	1 to mint
	29	2 to raise the wind
fausse —	30	counterfeit money
— qui a cours	31	current money, legal tender
une pièce de —	32	a coin
monnayer *vb*	33	1 to mint
	34	2 to exchange for money, to market
monopole *m*	35	monopoly
— de l'Etat	36	Government —
montage *m*	37	[machine] assembling
montant *n.m. & adj*	38	1 total, amount, sum
	39	2 rising, ascending; uphill
monter *vb*	40	to go up
— en flèche	41	to shoot up
se — (à)	42	to amount (to)
moratoire *n.m. & adj*	43	1 moratorium

	1	2 over-due, delayed
intérêts —s	2	interest in arrears
morceau *m*	3	bit, piece, cut, portion
les bas —x	4	the cheap cuts
morceler *vb*	5	to cut into pieces; to break up, to parcel out
mortalité *f*	6	death-rate
mort-né *adj*	7	still-born; [Fig.] abortive
mot *m*	8	word
au bas —	9	at the least
envoyer un —	10	to drop a line
— à —	11	— for —
— d'ordre	12	slogan, motto
motif *m*	13	1 motive, reason
	14	2 motif, theme, feature; pattern
motion *f*	15	motion, proposal
appuyer une —	16	to second a motion
déposer une —	17	to make a motion
motiver *vb*	18	to justify
mouillage *m*	19	[vin] watering
	20	[bateau] anchorage
mouiller *vb*	21	to wet
— l'ancre	22	to drop anchor
mousseline *f*	23	muslin
— de soie	24	chiffon
mousser *vb*	25	to foam
faire — qqun	26	to give s.o. a plug
faire — un article	27	to boost an article
mouvementé *adj*	28	[discussion] lively
	29	[vie] colourful, eventful
moyen, -ne *adj*	30	average, medium, ordinary
moyen *n.m.*	31	means, way
au — de	32	by means of
les grands —s	33	drastic actions
—s de transport	34	transportation
moyenne *n.f.*	35	average
au-dessus/au dessous de la —	36	above/below par
en —	37	on an —
multiplicateur *m*	38	multiplier
municipal *adj*	39	municipal
conseil —	40	town/city council
munir *vb*	41	to fit, equip, provide (with, *de*)

mur *m*	1	wall
mettre qqun au pied du —	2	to corner s.o.
mutation *f*	3	mutation
naissance *f*	4	birth
bulletin/extrait de —	5	— certificate
lieu de —	6	— place
Napoléon *n.m.* [gold coin worth 20 francs]	7	napoléon
nationaliser *vb*	8	to nationalize
nationalité *f*	9	nationality, citizenship
prendre la — britannique	10	to become a British citizen
naturalisation *f*	11	naturalization
naturaliser *vb*	12	to naturalize
se faire —	13	to get naturalized
nature *f*	14	1 nature
	15	2 kind, sort
	16	3 life
	17	4 goods
de — à	18	likely to
grandeur —	19	life-size
payer en —	20	to pay in kind
naturel, -le *adj*	21	natural
le gaz —	22	— gas
naufrage *m*	23	shipwreck
faire —	24	to be -ed
naval *adj*	25	naval
chantier de construction —e	26	shipbuilding yard
chantier —	27	shipyard
navette *f*	28	shuttle (line)
faire la — entre (Douvres et Calais)	29	to ply between (Dover and Calais)
navigant *adj*	30	sea-going; flying
navigation *f*	31	navigation
compagnie de —	32	steamship line, shipping company
— aérienne	33	air —
— au long cours	34	sailing across the seas
— de plaisance	35	yachting, boating
terme de —	36	nautical term
navire *m*	37	ship
le mouvement des —s	38	shipping news
— de commerce	39	merchantman

149

— de course	1	privateer
nécessaire *adj*	2	necessary; that which is necessary
faire le —	3	to take care of it
nécessité *f*	4	necessity
être dans la — de faire qqch.	5	to be compelled to do sth.
par —	6	of —
nécessiter *vb*	7	to require, call for, demand, need
négative *f*	8	negative
se maintenir sur la —	9	to adopt a — attitude
négligence *f*	10	carelessness
par —	11	through —
négliger *vb*	12	to neglect (to, *de*), to disregard, ignore
négoce *m*	13	trade, business
négociable *adj*	14	negotiable; transferable
négociant *m*	15	merchant, dealer
négociation *f*	16	[traité] negotiation
	17	[traite] transaction
négocier *vb*	18	to negotiate
net *adj*	19	1 net
	20	2 clean
	21	3 clear, distinct
bénéfice —	22	return
nettoyer *vb*	23	to clean
— à sec	24	to dryclean
niveau *m*	25	level
le — des salaires	26	the standard of wages
le — de vie	27	standard of living
nom *m*	28	name
— de famille	29	surname
— d'emprunt	30	assumed —
se faire un —	31	to achieve fame
sous le — de	32	under the — of
nombre *m*	33	number
— de	34	many
— entier	35	integer
— pair/impair	36	even/odd —
sans —	37	countless
nominatif, -ve *adj*	38	nominal
action nominative	39	registered share
nommé *adj*	40	called
le —	41	the said

nommément *adv*	1	by name; in so many words
nommer *vb*	2	1 to name, mention a name
	3	2 to appoint
se —	4	to be called
non-lieu *m*	5	no grounds for prosecution
rendre une ordonnance de —	6	to dismiss a charge
note *f*	7	1 note, memo
	8	2 bill, account
payer la —	9	to foot the bill
régler la —	10	to pay the bill
noter *vb*	11	to note, jot down, take note
bien noté	12	in good standing
mal noté	13	not in good standing
notice *f*	14	note
notice *f*	15	introduction, note
notification *f*	16	notice, intimation
notifier *vb*	17	to signify, make known, communicate
notion *f*	18	notion, idea
avoir des —s de	19	to have a smattering of
notoire *adj*	20	notorious, well-known
un fait —	21	a well-known fact
nouveauté *f*	22	1 novelty, innovation
	23	2 fancy articles, latest model
nuance *f*	24	shade of meaning, nuance
avoir le sens des —s	25	to have a feeling for subtlety
nuancer *vb*	26	to moderate, to qualify (statement)
nuire *vb*	27	to harm, do injury
nuisible *adj*	28	injurious, harmful, detrimental
nuit *f*	29	night
de —	30	by —
travailler la —	31	to work at —
nul, -le *adj & pr.*	32	no, not any, null, worthless, non-existent
— et non avenu	33	null and void
nullité *f*	34	1 nullity (of a deed)
	35	2 incapacity
entaché de — [Lég.]	36	null and void
numéraire *m*	37	(gold) coins; cash, specie, legal tender
numéro *m*	38	1 number
	39	2 issue (of a magazine)
faux —	40	wrong number

— d'immatriculation	1	registration number
— justificatif	2	voucher copy
numérotage *m*, **numéro-** tation *f*	3	numbering
numéroter *vb*	4	to number
objet *m*	5	1 object, article
	6	2 object, purpose
obligation *f*	7	1 obligation
	8	2 bond, debenture
être dans l' — de	9	to be/feel compelled to
—s à lots	10	premium bonds
remplir une —	11	to fulfil an obligation
obligatoire *adj*	12	compulsory
obligé *adj*	13	obliged, bound, compelled (to, *de*)
Nous vous sommes très —s	14	We are much obliged to you
obligeance *f*	15	kindness
avoir l'— de . . .	16	to be so kind as to . . .
obliger *vb*	17	1 to compel, force, enforce
	18	2 to please, oblige
Vous nous —iez beaucoup en le faisant	19	You would greatly oblige us by doing it
oblitération *f*	20	postmark; cancellation
oblitérer *vb*	21	to cancel, postmark
occasionner *vb*	22	to cause, bring about, be cause of, to produce
occupant *m*	23	occupant
le droit du premier —	24	the right of occupancy
occupation *f*	25	1 job, occupation, work, business
	26	2 occupancy, [locaux, etc.] tenure
— secondaire/supplé- mentaire	27	side-line
occuper *vb*	28	1 to employ
	29	2 [poste] to hold, to occupy
	30	3 [locaux, etc.] to reside, live in [keep busy
	31	4 to provide work for, to
Il s'occupe d'exportation	32	He is in the export business
s'— de	33	to take care of; to handle; to deal in

occurrence *f*	1	event, juncture
en l'—	2	in/under circumstances
octroi *m*	3	1 grant
	4	2 duty; toll dues
être soumis à l'—	5	to be liable to duty
octroyer *vb*	6	to grant, concede
s'—	7	to take [in many cases unduly]
oculaire *adj*	8	ocular
témoin —	9	eye-witness
œuf *m*	10	egg
étouffer dans l'—	11	to nip in the bud
œuvre *f*	12	work
à pied d'—	13	ready to start
la main-d'—	14	labour, manpower
les bonnes —s	15	charities
se mettre à l'—	16	to get to —
office *m*	17	1 office, duty
	18	2 Board, council
d'—	19	as a matter of course, automatically
exercer un —	20	to perform a function
— de la propriété industrielle	21	Patent Office
— de placement	22	labour exchange
officiel, -le *adj*	23	official, formal
un avis —	24	an official notice
officier *m*	25	officer
Officier ministériel	26	notary (public), solicitor
officieux, -se *adj*	27	unofficial
offrant *m*	28	bidder
le plus —	29	the highest —
offre *f*	30	offer; bid; tender
l'— et la demande	31	supply and demand
omission *f*	32	omission, oversight
once *f*	33	ounce (oz.)
onéreux, -se *adj*	34	expensive, heavy
onglet *m*	35	tab
dictionnaire à —s	36	thumb-indexed dictionary
opération *f*	37	dealing, transaction
— au comptant	38	cash transaction
opérer *vb*	39	to operate
— un changement	40	to bring about a change
opinion *f*	41	opinion
sondage d'—	42	public — poll, Gallup poll

opportunité *f*	1	seasonableness, opportuneness ; suitability
opposé *adj*	2	opposed to, contrary ; over against
diamétralement —	3	poles apart
opposition *f*	4	opposition
faire — à un jugement	5	to appeal against a judgement
faire — à un paiement	6	to stop a payment
— sur titre	7	attachment against securities
par — à qqch.	8	as opposed to sth.
une forte —	9	a considerable —
optant *m*	10	taker of an option
opticien *m*	11	optician
option *f*	12	choice, option
droit d'—	13	right of option
or *m*	14	gold
chercheur d'—	15	— -digger
étalon —	16	— standard
mine d'—	17	— mine
— en barres	18	ingot —
— massif	19	solid —
pièce d'—	20	— coin
prime sur l'—	21	— premium
valoir son pesant d'—	22	to be worth one's weight in —
or *conj*	23	Now,...; Well,...; But,...
ordinaire *adj*	24	1 common, ordinary, usual
	25	2 mediocre, cheap, second-rate
ordinateur *n.m.*	26	computer
ordonnance *f* [Lég.]	27	writ
ordre *m*	28	order
comptes d'—	29	contingent accounts ; contra-items
d'— de	30	on behalf of
l'— du jour	31	the agenda
payer à l'—de	32	to pay to the — of
orfèvre *m*	33	goldsmith
organe *m*	34	1 organ 2 medium ; voice
organisme *m*	35	organization, association, agency
orientation *f*	36	trend, orientation
— professionnelle	37	vocational guidance

orienter *vb*	1	to direct
une maison bien orientée	2	a house with a good exposure
origine *f*	3	origin
à l'—	4	—ally, in the beginning
être à l'— de	5	to initiate, originate, be responsible for
outillage *m*	6	equipment, collection of tools, apparatus
outiller *vb*	7	to tool up, equip
outrage *m* [Lég.]	8	contempt
— à la justice	9	— of court
outre *prép & adv*	10	1 apart from, in addition to
	11	2 further
en —	12	moreover
passer —	13	to ignore, overrule, override
outre-mer *adv*	14	overseas
outrepasser *vb*	15	to go beyond (one's rights) ; to exceed given orders
ouvert *adj*	16	open(ed) ; on
— toute l'année	17	open all the year round
(traduire) à livre —	18	(to translate) at sight
ouverture *f*	19	opening ; gap
heures d'—	20	opening hours
ouvrable *adj*	21	workable
jour —	22	working day
ouvreuse *f*	23	usher, attendant
ouvrier, -ère *n. & adj*	24	1 worker, labourer
	25	2 labour, working
la classe ouvrière	26	the working class
page *f*	27	page, folio
de la première à la dernière —	28	from cover to cover
pagination *f*	29	paging
paginer *vb*	30	to page
paie *f*	31	wages
jour de —	32	pay day
paiement, payement *m*	33	payment
effectuer un —	34	to make a —
paille *f*	35	1 straw ; chaff 2 flaw
panne *f*	36	engine trouble, breakdown, failure
avoir une — d'essence	37	to run out of petrol

Il y a eu une — d'électricité	1	The power was off
panneau *m*	2	panel
— réclame	3	advertisement hoarding
paperasserie *f*	4	paper work, red tape
papeterie *f*	5	1 stationery, stationer's
	6	2 paper mill; paper trade
papier *m*	7	paper
— à en-tête	8	letterhead
— à firme	9	headed note-
— à lettres	10	letter —, note —
— collant	11	gummed tape
— d'emballage	12	brown —
— de soie	13	tissue —
— de verre	14	sand-
— hygiénique	15	toilet —
— -monnaie	16	— money
— paraffiné	17	waxed —
— peint	18	wall —
— pelure	19	flimsy —
papillon *m*	20	notice, small poster; [Belg.] slip, narrow strip of paper
paquebot *m*	21	steamer, liner
paquet *m*	22	1 parcel, package
	23	2 batch, bundle, lot (of, *de*)
par *prép* & *adv*	24	by, through, on, in, per, from, out of, of
garder une lettre — devers soi	25	to keep a letter in one's possession
— avion	26	by air (mail)
— erreur	27	by mistake, in error
quatre livres — jour	28	four pounds a day
paragraphe *m*	29	paragraph
paraître *vb*	30	1 to appear; to come out
	31	2 to seem, to look
à ce qu'il paraît	32	so it would seem
faire —	33	to publish
vient de —	34	just out
parallèle *n.m/f*	35	parallel
établir un —	36	to draw a —
tracer une —	37	to draw a —
paraphe *m*	38	1 paraph, flourish (at the end of a signature)
	39	2 initials
apposer son —	40	to initial

parcours *m*	1	route, run, trip ; distance covered
— maritime	2	sea transit
parent *m*	3	relative, relation
le plus proche —	4	the next of kin
un proche —	5	a close relative
parenthèse *f*	6	parenthesis, bracket
entre —s	7	1 in brackets
	8	2 by the way, incidentally
parité *f*	9	parity
change à la —	10	exchange at par
— du change	11	equivalence of exchange
parjure *n.m.*	12	perjury
commettre un —	13	to commit —
parjure *n.m/f*	14	perjurer
parjure *adj*	15	perjured
un témoin —	16	a — witness
parjurer (se) *vb*	17	to perjure, break one's oath
parole *f*	18	word
de belles —s	19	wind
donner sa —	20	to give one's —
libérer sur —	21	to release on parole
manquer à sa —	22	to break one's —
prendre la —	23	to talk, speak, take the floor
ses propres —s	24	his/her own —s
tenir (sa) —	25	to keep one's —/promise
parquet *m*	26	1 [Lég.] public prosecutor's office
	27	2 [Bourse] ring
parrainage *m*	28	sponsorship
part *f*	29	part, share ; side ; interest
d'autre —	30	on the other hand
de la — de	31	from
de — et d'autre	32	on both sides
d'une —	33	on the one hand
faire la — de	34	to make allowance for
faire — de	35	to announce, inform
— aux bénéfices	36	share in the profits
prendre — à	37	to take part in, join
partage *m*	38	sharing, division
sans —	39	undivided
partance *f*	40	departure
en — pour . . .	41	bound for . . .
parti *m*	42	1 party ; side [choice
	43	2 course of action, decision,

	1	3 advantage
tirer le meilleur — de	*2*	to make the most of
tirer — de	*3*	to turn to account, to take advantage of
participation *f*	*4*	contribution; participation; share, interest (in, *à*); holding
compte en —	*5*	joint account
— aux bénéfices	*6*	profit-sharing
participer *vb*	*7*	to share (in, *à*); to take part (in, *à*)
particulier, -ère *n.m. & adj*	*8*	1 people, individual, (private) person
	9	2 peculiar, particular; special; personal, private
en —	*10*	privately
les intérêts —s	*11*	private interests
un cas —	*12*	a special case
un compte —	*13*	a personal account
une chambre particulière	*14*	a private room
partie *f*	*15*	1 part, lot, share
	16	2 line, occupation
	17	3 party
avoir affaire à forte —	*18*	to have s.o. to reckon with
Ce n'est pas ma —	*19*	It's not my line
en grande —	*20*	largely
en —	*21*	partly, in part
faire — de	*22*	to be a member of; to be part of
gagner la —	*23*	to win the game
— en cause	*24*	party to the case, party concerned
se porter — civile	*25*	to put in a claim for damages
partiel, -le	*26*	partial, in part
élection partielle	*27*	by-election
parution *f*	*28*	[livre, magazine] publication
parvenir *vb*	*29*	1 to reach
	30	2 to succeed (in, *à*)
passage *m*	*31*	passage, crossing, arcade, gangway
barrer le —	*32*	to block the way
droit de — [Lég.]	*33*	right of way
être de —	*34*	to be passing through
livrer —	*35*	to let through
— à niveau	*36*	railway crossing

— clouté	1	pedestrian/zebra crossing
— couvert	2	covered walk, [Amér.] breezeway
— souterrain	3	subway
passant *n.m. & adj*	4	1 passer-by
	5	2 frequented, busy
passation *f*	6	signing
— d'écriture	7	entering
passé *prép*	8	beyond, past, after
— cette date	9	after this date
passer *vb*	10	1 to leave out, omit; to over-look
	11	2 to pass; to go through
entrer en passant	12	to drop in
faire — un test à qqun	13	to give s.o. a test
— chez qqun	14	to call on s.o.
— outre	15	to overrule, override
— un accord	16	to conclude an agreement
— une commande	17	to place an order
soit dit en passant	18	be it said in passing
une fois en passant	19	once in a while
passible (de) *adj*	20	liable (to, for), subject (to)
— de droits	21	liable for duty
— d'impôts	22	liable for tax
passif *n.m. & adj*	23	1 liabilities 2 adverse, debit
— éventuel	24	contingent liability
— (non-)exigible	25	(non-)current liabilities
patente *f*	26	licence
— de santé	27	bill of health
payer —	28	to be licensed
pâtissier, -ère *n*	29	baker, pastry cook
patrimoine *m*	30	heritage
patron *m*	31	1 boss, employer, owner
	32	2 model, pattern
patronage *m*	33	1 support, patronage
	34	2 social club (for children)
patronal *adj*	35	pertaining to employers
syndicat —	36	employers' association
patronat *m*	37	management
pause *f*	38	break, pause, interval
faire les —s [Belg.]	39	to work shifts
faire une —	40	to stop, break off
pavillon *m*	41	1 detached house, building
	42	2 flag, colours
baisser —	43	to knuckle under

navire battant — britannique	1	ship flying the British flag
payable *adj*	2	payable
— à vue	3	— at sight
payant *adj*	4	paying; charged for
paye, paie *f*	5	wages, pay
jour de —	6	pay day
payement, paiement *m*	7	payment
— anticipatif	8	pre- — [settle
payer *vb*	9	to pay, to pay for (sth.), to
— de retour	10	to reciprocate, pay back
— rubis sur l'ongle	11	to pay on the nail
payeur *m*	12	payer; [banque] teller
mauvais —	13	defaulter
pays *m*	14	country
étoffe du —	15	homespun
vin du —	16	local wine
péage *m*	17	toll
bureau de —	18	— house
payer un droit de —	19	to pay —
pont à —	20	— bridge
route à —	21	— road
péager *m*	22	toll-keeper
peau *f*	23	1 skin
	24	2 [d'un grand animal] hide
— de porc	25	pigskin
— de vache	26	cowhide
pêcherie *f*	27	fishery
pécule *m*	28	savings
pécuniaire *adj*	29	pecuniary
peine *f*	30	penalty, punishment
la — capitale	31	capital punishment
purger une —	32	to serve a sentence
sous — de	33	under penalty of
pelleterie *f*	34	fur trade; furs
pénal *adj*	35	penal
pénalisation *f*	36	penalization
pénalité *f*	37	penalty
pencher *vb*	38	to lean; to incline
faire — la balance	39	to tip the scale
pendant *n.m.*	40	counterpart
pénitancier *m*	41	house of correction, penitentiary
pension *f*	42	pension, annuity, retiring allowance

— alimentaire	1	alimony
— de vieillesse	2	old-age pension
— viagère	3	life annuity
versements pour la —	4	superannuation contribution
pensionnaire n.m/f	5	boarder; paying guest
pensionner vb	6	to pension (off)
perce f	7	bore (of barrel)
en — [tonneau]	8	on tap
mettre en —	9	to broach
percepteur m	10	tax-collector, revenue officer
perception f	11	[impôts] collection
percevoir vb	12	to collect (taxes)
périmé adj	13	no longer valid, expired; outdated, [chèque] stale
périssable adj	14	perishable
permanence f	15	1 permanence, permanency
	16	2 [commissariat central] police station
	17	3 building, headquarters
en —	18	without interruption, permanently
permanent adj	19	lasting, permanent, unchanging
spectacle —	20	non-stop show
permis m	21	permit, licence; warrant
— de conduire	22	driver's licence
— de coupe (de bois)	23	timber licence
permis adj	24	permitted, lawful, permissible
permission f	25	permission; [armée] leave
permuter vb	26	to change over (by switching), to exchange
perpétuité f	27	perpetuity
à —	28	for ever
perquisition f	29	search
mandat de —	30	— warrant
perquisitionner vb	31	to search
personnel m	32	staff, personnel
le — navigant	33	sea-going personnel; flight personnel/crew
persuader vb	34	to persuade, convince
Nous sommes persuadés que . . .	35	We are convinced that . . .
perte f	36	loss
à —	37	at a —

passer aux —s et profits	1	to write off
— de temps	2	waste of time
— sèche	3	dead —
— totale	4	write-off, total —
pesage m, **pesée** f	5	weighing, weighing in
peser vb	6	to weigh (out)
— le pour et le contre	7	— the pros and cons
pétition f	8	petition
pétrole m	9	(mineral) oil, petroleum
— brut	10	crude oil
puits de —	11	oil well
trouver du —	12	to strike oil
pétrolier n.m.	13	(oil) tanker
pétrolier, -ère adj	14	oil
industrie pétrolière	15	— industry
valeurs pétrolières	16	— shares
pétrolifère adj	17	oil(-bearing)
champs —s	18	-fields
pharmacien, -ne n	19	pharmacist; (dispensing) chemist
photo f	20	photo
— -copie	21	-stat
prendre des —s	22	to take pictures
photographe m	23	photographer
photostat m	24	photostat, photostatic copy
pièce f	25	1 room
	26	2 play
	27	3 coin, piece
	28	4 part
	29	5 document, paper
	30	6 apiece
	31	7 bolt, roll (of fabric)
— de caisse	32	cash voucher
— de rechange	33	spare part
— d'étoffe	34	bolt of material, roll of fabric
— d'or	35	gold coin
— justificative	36	voucher
une livre —	37	one pound apiece
vendre à la —	38	to sell singly, in ones
pied m	39	foot (pl: foot ou feet)
à — d'œuvre	40	on site
au — levé	41	offhand
avoir/mesurer 10 —s de haut	42	to be ten — high/tall

mettre sur —	1	to set up
prendre —	2	to gain a —hold
récolte sur —	3	standing crops
pierreries *n.f.pl.*	4	precious stones, gems
pillage *m*	5	loot(ing), plunder(ing) ; spoliation
piller *vb*	6	to loot, plunder
pilon *m*	7	pestle ; rammer
mettre (un livre) au —	8	to destroy (an edition)
pilote *m*	9	pilot
— d'essai	10	test —
— professionnel	11	commercial —
piloter *vb*	12	[bateau] to pilot
	13	[avion] to fly
	14	[voiture] to steer
	15	[des gens en ville] to guide
pique-notes *n.m.inv.*	16	spike-file
pis aller *n.m.inv.*	17	makeshift
pistonner *vb*	18	to back s.o.
placard *m*	19	1 closet, cupboard ; recess
	20	2 poster, bill
	21	3 galley (proof)
place *f*	22	1 room, space
	23	2 position, job, post
	24	3 seat
	25	4 square
	26	5 town, place, spot ; market
placement *m*	27	1 investment 2 employment
bureau de —	28	employment agency
placer *vb*	29	1 to sell (goods)
	30	2 to place ; to set
	31	3 to invest
	32	4 to find a post, a situation for s.o.
être bien placé (pour en juger)	33	to be in a good position (to judge), to know best
plaider *vb*	34	1 to plead
	35	2 to present a case in court
plaideur *m*	36	suitor, litigant, petitioner
plaidoirie *f*	37	1 pleading, intercession
	38	2 pleading, presentation of a case in court, lawyer's speech
plaignant *m*	39	plaintiff
plainte *f*	40	complaint

— en diffamation	1	action for libel
porter —, déposer une — contre qqun	2	to lodge a — against s.o.
plan *m*	3	plan
à l'arrière- —	4	in the background
au premier —	5	in the foreground
gros —	6	close-up
laisser en —	7	to leave in the lurch
— d'ensemble	8	general —
— quinquennal	9	five-year —
planche *f*	10	board, plank
jours de —	11	lay days
planification *f*	12	planning
plantation *f*	13	[action] planting, [propriété] plantation
planter *vb*	14	to plant
planteur *m*	15	plantation-owner; grower
plastique *adj*	16	plastic
platine *m*	17	platinum
plein *adj*	18	full
de — gré	19	of one's free will
en —e mer	20	on the high sea(s)
— pouvoir	21	— power
pli *m*	22	1 letter
	23	2 envelope, cover
	24	3 fold, wrinkle
sous ce —	25	enclosed, herewith
sous — cacheté	26	in a sealed envelope
sous — recommandé	27	under registered cover
sous — séparé	28	under separate cover
pliage *m*	29	folding
plier *vb*	30	1 to fold (up); to bend
	31	2 to bow; to give way, to yield
Ne pas plier s.v.p.	32	Please do not bend
Prière de ne pas plier	33	Please do not fold
plomb *m*	34	lead, seal
sous — de douane	35	in bond, bonded
plombé *adj*	36	[marchandises] in bond, sealed
plomber *vb*	37	to seal with lead
pluralité *f* d'assurances	38	double insurance
plus *n.m.* & *adv*	39	plus; more
au —	40	at most
sans — attendre	41	without further delay

plus-value *f*	*1*	increase in value
pneu *m*	*2*	1 [G.B.] tyre, [Amér.] tire
	3	2 Paris express, special delivery letter [sent pneumatically]
pneumatique *m see* PNEU	*4*	
poids *m*	*5*	weight
les — et mesures	*6*	—s and measures
— à l'embarquement	*7*	shipping —
— à vide	*8*	— empty
— maximum admissible	*9*	maximum permissible —
— maximum autorisé	*10*	maximum licensed —
— net légal	*11*	net — without taring
— unitaire	*12*	unit —
vendre au —	*13*	to sell by the pound/by —
poinçon *m*	*14*	1 punch, instrument for piercing holes
	15	2 [argenterie, monnaie] stamp, mark
	16	3 [garantie] hall-mark
poinçonner *vb*	*17*	to punch, to stamp
point *m*	*18*	1 point, dot, mark
	19	2 point, degree
au — où en sont les choses	*20*	as matters stand
être au —	*21*	to be ready, adjusted
mettre au —	*22*	1 to develop, to perfect
	23	2 to clarify
venir à —	*24*	to come at the right moment
pointage *m*	*25*	1 checking
	26	2 clocking in/out
feuille de — (des ouvriers)	*27*	time sheet (of workers)
feuille de — (d'un navire)	*28*	out-turn report (of ship)
pointer *vb*	*29*	1 [liste] to check
	30	2 [à l'usine] to clock
— à l'arrivée	*31*	to clock in/on
— au départ	*32*	to clock out/off
pointure *f*	*33*	size, number (of shoes, gloves, etc.)
poire *f*	*34*	pear
couper la — en deux	*35*	to split the difference
poissonnier, -ère *n*	*36*	[G.B.] fishmonger, [Amér.] fish dealer
police *f*	*37*	1 police
	38	2 [assurance] policy

165

agent (de —)	1	policeman
polycopier *vb*	2	[G.B.] to stencil, duplicate
	3	[Amér.] to mimeograph
pont *m*	4	1 bridge 2 deck
faire le —	5	to throw one day in, to have a long week-end
Ponts & Chaussées	6	[G.B.] Department of civil engineering
	7	[Amér.] Roads Department
porcelaine *f*	8	china, chinaware
port *m*	9	port, harbour
avant- —	10	outer port
capitaine/maître de —	11	port warden
droits de —	12	port dues/charges
— d'attache	13	home port; port of registry
— de mer	14	seaport
— d'escale	15	port of call
— fluvial	16	inland port
port *m*	17	postal charge, postage, shipping charges; carriage
— payé, franc de —	18	postage paid, post paid
portatif, -ve *adj*	19	portable
porte *f*	20	door(way), gate(way), entrance
forcer une —	21	to break open a door
— cochère	22	carriage entrance
portefeuille *m*	23	1 wallet, billfold
	24	2 office, portfolio
	25	3 holding, stocks and shares, investment
commandes en —	26	orders in hand
porter *vb*	27	1 to carry, to take
	28	2 to bring, yield, bear
	29	3 to pass, put, enter, to carry out (balance)
	30	4 to bring up, raise, increase
dividende porté de 6 à 9%	31	dividend raised from 6 to 9%
— au grand livre	32	to post, transfer to a ledger
— intérêt	33	to bear interest
— témoignage	34	to bear witness
— une somme (à)	35	to pass an amount (to)
se — garant	36	to be/stand surety, to guarantee
porteur *m*	37	1 porter 2 bearer, holder

actions au —	1	bearer shares
chèque au —	2	cheque to bearer
donner ses valises au —	3	to give one's suitcases to the porter
(payable) au —	4	(payable) to bearer
portier *m*	5	porter, janitor, doorman
posséder *vb*	6	1 to own, possess, hold
	7	2 to know perfectly, be well up in, have a thorough knowledge of
Elle possède le français à fond	8	She has a perfect command of French
possesseur *m*	9	possessor, owner, proprietor, holder
possession *f*	10	possession; ownership, property
— vaut titre	11	possession is nine points of the law
possible *adj*	12	possible
dès que —	13	at your earliest convenience
faire (tout) son — (pour)	14	to do one's (very) best (for)
postal *adj*	15	post, postal
boîte —e	16	post office box
carte —e	17	post-card
colis —	18	parcel post
date —e	19	date as postmark
services postaux	20	postal services
postdater *vb*	21	to postdate
poste *f*	22	1 station
	23	2 post, job
	24	3 post office
	25	4 item; heading (of a balance sheet, etc.)
	26	5 [carriage or lorry] mail
bon de —	27	postal order
bureau de —	28	post office
Ministre des Postes	29	Postmaster General
— de douane	30	port of entry
— de secours	31	first-aid station
— d'essence	32	filling station
— restante	33	poste restante, to be called for
Postes, Télégraphes et Téléphones (PTT)	34	General Post Office (GPO)
postérieur *adj*	35	back; later, subsequent

postier / précaution

postier *m*	1	post-office employee
post-scriptum (P.S.) *m*	2	post-script
postuler *vb*	3	to apply (for a job)
pot-de-vin *m*	4	graft
poterie *f*	5	earthenware, pottery
pourboire *m*	6	tip
— compris	7	— included
pourcentage *m*	8	percentage
pourparlers *n.m.pl.*	9	talks, negotiations
poursuite *f*	10	[Lég.] action, lawsuit
engager-entamer des —s contre	11	to take legal action, to bring an action against
poursuivre *vb*	12	to sue, prosecute, process
pourvoi *m*	13	[Lég.] appeal
pourvoir *vb*	14	to provide (for, *à*)
se —	15	— o.s. (with, *de*)
se — (en cassation)	16	to appeal
pouvoir *n.m.*	17	1 power, means, influence
	18	2 authority
	19	3 proxy, power of attorney
avoir plein(s) —(s)	20	to have full powers
fondé de —	21	director, first signature
le parti au —	22	the party in power
le — d'achat	23	the purchasing power
—s	24	terms of reference
—s publics	25	public authorities
pratique *f*	26	practice, experience, habit
C'est la — de . . .	27	It is customary to . . .
mettre en —	28	to put in practice
(navire en) libre —	29	(ship in) pratique/free pratique
pratiquer *vb*	30	to practise, to put into practice
cours pratiqués [en Bourse]	31	bargains done
— un amortissement	32	to make a reserve for depreciation
se —	33	to rule ; to be made/done
préalable *adj*	34	previous, preceding, earlier, prior
au —	35	first, previously ; prior to
préavis *m*	36	(advance) notice
donner un — de six jours	37	to give six days' —
précaire *adj*	38	precarious, insecure, uncertain
précaution *f*	39	precaution ; care

168

avec —	1	carefully, with care, cautiously
précédent *n.m. & adj*	2	1 precedent
	3	2 former, preceding, previous
créer un —	4	to create a precedent
sans —	5	unprecedented, unheard of, without precedent
précieux, -se *adj*	6	precious, valuable, rare
pierres précieuses	7	gems
précis *n.m.*	8	abstract, summary
préciser *vb*	9	to specify, to define exactly, to indicate in precise detail
précité *adj*	10	above-mentioned
préconiser *vb*	11	to recommend, support, to advocate
préemption *f*	12	pre-emption [purchase by one person or group before opportunity is offered to others; right so to purchase]
préfabriqué *adj*	13	prefabricated
maison —e	14	prefab
préfecture *f*	15	1 prefecture, district (under a prefect)
	16	2 prefectship
— de police	17	police headquarters
préférence *f*	18	liking, partiality (for, *pour*), preference; prior claim
donner la — à	19	to give preference to
préférentiel, -le *adj*	20	preferential
tarif —	21	— tariff
préjudice *m*	22	injury, wrong, detriment, damage
porter — à	23	to prejudice, be prejudicial to
sans — de	24	without prejudice to
préjudiciable *adj*	25	prejudicial, harmful, detrimental (to, *à*)
prélèvement *m*	26	drawing; taking; appropriation; levy; charge
—s sur compte courant	27	drawings on current account
prélever *vb*	28	to draw; to take; to appropriate; to levy; to charge

169

dividende prélevé sur le capital	1	dividend paid out of capital
intérêts sur les sommes prélevées	2	interest on the amounts drawn
— une commission sur une opération	3	to charge a commission on a transaction
somme prélevée	4	sum taken from the reserve
premier, -ère *adj*	5	first
matières premières	6	raw materials
— cours [en Bourse]	7	opening prices
première *f* **de change**	8	first of exchange
Payez par cette —, la seconde ne l'étant pas	9	Pay this our —, second of the same tenor and date being unpaid
prémunir *vb*	10	to warn, to caution, to guard (against, *contre*)
se —	11	to provide (against, *contre*)
prendre *vb*	12	to take
la société prendra le passif à sa charge	13	the company will take over the liabilities
— à bord	14	— on board
— à sa charge	15	— upon s.o., to undertake
— charge	16	to load
— des renseignements	17	to make inquiries
— en charge (l'actif et le passif)	18	— over (assets and liabilities)
— en considération	19	— into consideration
— ferme	20	— firm
— fin	21	to end [a concern
— la direction d'une affaire	22	— over the management of
— l'engagement (de)	23	to undertake (to)
preneur *m*	24	1 taker, buyer, purchaser
	25	2 lessee, taker
le bailleur et le —	26	the lessor and the lessee
trouver —	27	to find a taker
preneur, -se *adj*	28	purchasing, buying
préparatifs *n.m.pl.*	29	preparations
prépondérant *adj*	30	preponderant
voix —e	31	casting vote
préposé *n.m.*	32	(man, woman, clerk, officer, official) in charge (of, *à*)
près *adv*	33	near(ly)
(compte) exact à un centime —	34	(account) correct to a penny

étudier qqch. de —	1	to study sth. closely
prescription [Lég.]	2	1 prescription
	3	2 limitation
	4	3 provision, stipulation, condition
délai de —	5	term of limitation
les —s de la loi	6	the provisions of an act
— acquisitoire	7	prescription [= uninterrupted possession over a long period]
prescrire *vb*	8	to prescribe, enjoin, order, command
délai prescrit	9	deadline
se — [Lég.]	10	to be barred by statute of limitations
présence *f*	11	presence
feuille de —	12	time sheet
jeton de —	13	attendance fee
présentation *f*	14	1 showing, production, presentation
	15	2 introduction
sur —	16	on presentation; on demand; at sight
présenter *vb*	17	1 to present, offer, show
	18	2 to introduce
Ce problème présente quelques difficultés	19	This problem presents some difficulties
Le cas ne s'est jamais présenté	20	The case/This never arose before
se —	21	to come up; to turn up
président *m*	22	president, chairman
Madame la Présidente	23	Madam Chairman
Monsieur le Président	24	Mr Chairman
Président-Directeur général	25	Chairman and Managing Director
présidentiel, -le *adj*	26	presidential; the President's ...
présider *vb*	27	1 to preside (at, over, *à*)
	28	2 to act as chairman, preside; to be in the chair, to chair
présomptif, -ve *adj*	29	presumed, presumptive, probable
héritier —	30	heir presumptive
présomption *f*	31	1 presumption, probability
	32	2 conceit

presse *f*	*1*	1 letterpress, press
	2	2 the press, newspapers
la — du matin	*3*	the morning papers
livre sous —	*4*	book in the press
service de —	*5*	press copies
pression *f*	*6*	pressure
faire — sur qqun	*7*	to put/bring/bear — on s.o.
la — du crédit	*8*	credit squeeze
sous la — des circons- tances	*9*	under the — of events
prestation *f*	*10*	1 loan, lending
	11	2 payment; contribution; ex- pense
	12	3 allowance, benefit
	13	4 taking of an oath
— de capitaux	*14*	lending of capital
— de serment	*15*	taking of an oath
—s en nature/en deniers	*16*	allowance in kind/in cash
—s sociales	*17*	social contributions
prêt *n.m.*	*18*	loan
consentir un — (à)	*19*	to grant a — (to)
— à court terme	*20*	short —
— à découvert	*21*	— on overdraft
— à long terme	*22*	long period —
— à terme	*23*	— at notice; time —
— garanti	*24*	secured —
— hypothécaire	*25*	mortgage
— sur nantissement	*26*	— on collateral
— sur titres	*27*	— on stock
prétendre *vb*	*28*	to claim, to maintain
prétention *f*	*29*	1 claim, pretension
	30	2 wish; will
prêter *vb*	*31*	1 to lend, loan
	32	2 to attribute, ascribe (to, *à*)
— au taux de 6%	*33*	to lend at the rate of 6%
— des titres en report	*34*	to lend stock on contango
prêteur *m*	*35*	lender
preuve *f*	*36*	proof, (piece of) evidence; token
faire la — d'une opération	*37*	to prove an operation
fournir des —s	*38*	to give evidence
— directe	*39*	direct evidence
— indirecte	*40*	circumstantial evidence
prévaloir *vb*	*41*	to prevail, predominate

se — de	1	to take advantage of, to avail o.s. of
prévarication *f*	2	breach of trust
prévariquer *vb*	3	to betray one's trust
prévenir *vb*	4	1 to forestall, anticipate
	5	2 to prevent
	6	3 to warn, notify, inform
Prévenez-nous longtemps à l'avance	7	Give us plenty of warning
prévention *f*	8	prejudice
préventivement *adv*	9	previously, preventively
prévenu *n.m.* [Lég.]	10	defendant
prévenu *adj*	11	1 warned, informed
	12	2 prejudiced
prévision *f*	13	1 conjecture; forecast
	14	2 reserve, provision
en — de	15	in anticipation of
— de caisse	16	cash requirement; cover for the day; floating
— pour créances douteuses	17	reserve for doubtful debts
—s budgétaires	18	(annual) estimate
prévoir *vb*	19	1 to foresee, forecast
	20	2 to provide, allow
prévu par les statuts	21	provided by the articles (of association)
prévoyance *f*	22	foresight, precaution
caisse de —	23	provident fund
fonds de —	24	reserve fund
— sociale	25	state insurance
prier *vb*	26	to pray, request
Nous vous prions de bien vouloir . . .	27	Please . . .
sans se faire —	28	willingly
prière *f*	29	prayer, request
— de . . .	30	please . . .
prime *f*	31	premium
complément de —	32	additional —
emprunt qui fait ¼% de —	33	loan which is ¼%
faire —	34	to be at a —
— à débattre	35	— to be arranged
— à la production	36	bounties on production
— de rapidité (inverse de surestaries)	37	dispatch money

— entière/intégrale	1	full —
— de remboursement	2	redemption —
— de renouvellement	3	renewal —
— unique	4	single —
salaire avec —	5	pay with bonus
primer *vb*	6	1 to rank before, to take priority over
	7	2 to award, give as prize
être primé par	8	to rank after
principe *m*	9	principle
en —	10	1 as a —
	11	2 as a rule
faire une pétition de —	12	to beg the question
par —	13	on —
priorité *f*	14	1 priority, preference
	15	2 [voiture] right of way
action de —	16	preference share
— à droite, à gauche	17	yield to oncoming traffic
prise *f*	18	taking
— à domicile	19	collection
— de bénéfice	20	profit —
priseur *m*	21	valuer
commissaire —	22	(official) appraiser, auctioneer
privé *adj*	23	private
capitaux —s	24	private investors
Conseil —	25	Privy Council
privilège *m*	26	privilege; right; lien; preferential claim; licence
— d'hypothèque	27	mortgage lien
prix *m*	28	price
à moitié —	29	at half —
à tout —	30	at all costs
à vil —	31	dirt cheap
baisse des —	32	fall in —s
C'est notre dernier —	33	It's our lowest —
hors de —	34	extravagant, exorbitant
le — de la vie	35	the cost of living
Nos — sont très étudiés	36	Our —s are the keenest
— actuel	37	current —
— au comptant	38	cash —
— concurrentiels	39	exposed —s
— convenu	40	— agreed on
— courant	41	list —
— d'achat	42	purchase —

— d'occasion	1	bargain —
— d'ouverture	2	opening —
— de clôture	3	closing —
— de départ	4	upset —
— de détail	5	retail —
— d'émission	6	issue —
— de fabrique	7	maker's —
— de faveur	8	special —
— de gros	9	wholesale —
— de revient	10	cost —; manufacturing —
— de souscription	11	pre-issue —
— de vente	12	selling —
— dérisoire	13	(ridiculously) low —
— du jour	14	current —
— du marché	15	market —
— du silence	16	hush money
— exorbitant	17	tall/exorbitant —
— fixe	18	standing —
— fort	19	full—, catalogue —
— imposé	20	fixed —
— initial	21	starting —
— marchand	22	trade/wholesale —
— marqué	23	catalogue —
— maximum	24	ceiling —
— modique	25	low —
— moins la remise	26	discount —
— moyen	27	average —
— sacrifiés	28	slashed —s
— surfaits	29	fancy —
si vous mettez le —	30	at a —
prix-courant *m*	31	price-list, catalogue
probant *adj*	32	convincing, conclusive
pièces —es	33	documentary evidence
procéder *vb*	34	1 to proceed (to, *à*)
	35	2 to proceed, arise, come (from, *de*)
— à une enquête	36	to initiate an enquiry
procédure *f*	37	procedure, proceedings; proceeding
la — civile	38	civil proceedings
procès *m*	39	case, lawsuit; trial
gagner un —	40	to win a case
intenter un — à	41	to take legal action against, to prosecute
subir un —	42	to be tried

175

procès-verbal *m*	1	report, minutes (of a meeting) ; [police] ticket
dresser — (contre)	2	to report
procuration *f*	3	agent ; proxy, procuration, power of attorney
agir par —	4	to act by proxy
procurer (se) *vb*	5	to procure, get, obtain
se — des fonds	6	to raise capital
procureur *m*	7	proxy ; attorney
le — général	8	public prosecutor
producteur *n.m. & adj*	9	1 producer 2 productive
productif, -ve *adj*	10	productive
production *f*	11	1 production, output
	12	2 produce
— en série	13	mass production
produire *vb*	14	to produce ; to yield
produit *m*	15	1 product, goods, article
	16	2 proceeds, yield
— de marque	17	branded goods
—s agricoles	18	farm produce
—s finis	19	finished goods
—s manufacturés	20	manufactured products
profession *f*	21	profession, business, trade
les —s libérales	22	the professions
sans —	23	no occupation
professionnel, —le	24	professional, vocational
formation —le	25	vocational training
orientation —le	26	vocational guidance
profit *m*	27	profit, gain, benefit, return
au — de	28	for, for the benefit of
mettre à —	29	to turn to account
tirer — de	30	to profit by
profitable *adj*	31	profitable, advantageous, beneficial, lucrative
profiter *vb*	32	to profit, gain (by, *de*), to derive benefit (from, *de*)
— d'une occasion	33	to take advantage of an opportunity
profiteur *m*	34	profiteer
programme *m*	35	programme, scheme, plan,
— d'études	36	curriculum, syllabus
progrès *n.m.inv.*	37	progress, headway, improvement
faire des — (sensibles)	38	to make (good/marked) progress

progressif, -ve *adj*	1	progressive, graduated
progression *f*	2	progression, progress
prohibitif, -ve *adj*	3	prohibitive, prohibitory
projet *m*	4	scheme, project, plan, design ; draft, draught
— de loi	5	bill [longation
prolongation *f*	6	extension, lengthening, pro-
prononcer *vb*	7	to pronounce
— un discours	8	to deliver a speech
se — (sur)	9	to express an opinion, to declare o.s.
proportion *f*	10	proportion, ration, percentage ; size
toute(s) —(s) gardée(s)	11	due allowance being made ; other things being equal
proportionnel, -le *adj*	12	proportional (to, *à*)
directement — (à)	13	in direct ratio (to)
inversement — (à)	14	in inverse ratio (to)
proportionner *vb*	15	to proportion, adjust
propos (à) *n.m., prép, adv, adj*	16	1 remark(s)
	17	2 design, purpose
à ce —	18	talking of this ; in this connection
à —	19	1 by the way ; that reminds me ; incidentally
	20	2 appropriate
à — de	21	about ; in connection with
juger à — de	22	to see fit to
proposer *vb*	23	to suggest, propose, offer ; to recommend
— un dividende	24	to recommend a dividend
se — (pour)	25	to volunteer (for)
proposition *f*	26	proposal, suggestion, proposition ; condition(s), terms
— de loi	27	bill
propre *adj*	28	own, proper
remis en mains —s	29	delivered personally
son — chef	30	one's own boss
proprement *adv*	31	properly ; reasonably well
— dit ⎫ à — parler ⎭	32	strictly speaking
propriétaire *m/f*	33	owner ; householder, landlady, landlord ; landowner

177

changement de —	1	new management
— foncier	2	ground landlord; land-owner
propriété *f*	3	1 property, ownership
	4	2 (real) estate; land owned
	5	3 property, characteristic attribute
les —s de la matière	6	the properties of matter
—s immobilières	7	real property
— foncière libre, pleine —	8	freehold
— industrielle	9	patent rights
— littéraire	10	copyright
titres de —	11	title-deeds
prorata *n.m.inv., adv & prép*	12	pro rata, proportion, share
au —	13	on a pro rata basis, in proportion
au — de	14	proportionately to, in proportion to
fixer au —	15	to prorate
une répartition au —	16	a pro rata distribution
proscription *f*	17	proscription; prohibition; abolition; denunciation
proscrire *vb*	18	to ban, to prohibit; to abolish; to reject
prospectus *m*	19	handbill, leaflet, small pamphlet
protection *f*	20	1 protection; patronage, influence
	21	2 risks covered by insurance policy, safety
— civile [assurance]	22	coverage
protectionnisme *m*	23	(doctrine of) protection, protectionism
protestation *f*	24	protest(ation)
protester *vb*	25	to protest (against, *contre*)
— de son innocence	26	— one's innocence
— une traite	27	— a bill (of exchange)
protêt *m*	28	protest
— faute de paiement/d'acception	29	— for non-payment/acceptance
provenance *f*	30	origin, source
en — de	31	from
provenir *vb*	32	to come, proceed (from), to arise [supply
provision *f*	33	1 stores, stock (in hand),

	1	2 provision, funds, [avocat] retaining fee; deposit, margin, sum, cover; reserve, security
chèque sans —	2	dud cheque
défaut de — [en banque]	3	no funds
faire des —s (de)	4	to stock up (on)
jugement exécutoire par — [Lég]	5	provisional judgement
par —	6	provisionally, temporarily
— insuffisante [en banque]	7	not sufficient funds (N.S.F.)
—s de bord	8	ship's stores
PTT (Postes, Télégraphes et Téléphones)	9	GPO (General Post Office)
public, publique adj	10	public
dette publique	11	national debt
la fonction publique	12	— service
réunion publique	13	— meeting
services publics	14	— utilities/services
vente publique	15	— sale
publication f	16	1 publication; periodical
	17	2 publishing
publicitaire adj	18	advertising
publicité f	19	publicity, ownership
faire de la —	20	to advertise
publier vb	21	to publish, edit
— l'inventaire détaillé du porte-feuille	22	to publish a detailed list of investments
puits m	23	[eau, pétrole] well, [mine] pit, shaft
creuser un —	24	to dig/drill a well
purge f	25	redemption; paying off
purger vb	26	to free, clear, to redeem, pay off (a mortgage)
quai m	27	[port] quay, pier, wharf
	28	[gare] platform, [Amér.] track
à (prendre sur) —	29	ex quay
à —	30	alongside the quay
— à —	31	wharf to wharf
qualifié adj	32	qualified; skilled (labourer)
qualité f	33	1 quality, grade
	34	2 capacity, qualification

179

	1 3 right to membership
avoir les —s requises (pour)	*2* to be fitted (for)
avoir — pour	*3* to be qualified to
en — de	*4* in the capacity of, as
(viande, vin) de première —	*5* quality, choice (meat, wine)
quantité *f*	*6* quantity, amount
avoir — de	*7* to have plenty of
en —	*8* in quantity
en —s industrielles	*9* in large quantities, in masses
par petites —s	*10* in small amounts
quantum *m*	*11* quantum, amount
quarantaine *f*	*12* about forty
quart *m*	*13* fourth part; quarter (of an hour)
quelconque *adj*	*14* 1 any, whatever, some (. . . or other)
	15 2 ordinary, mediocre, worthless
pour une raison —	*16* for some reason (or other)
question *f*	*17* 1 question, matter, problem, point
	18 2 question, query
la personne en —	*19* the person in question
la — est de savoir si . . .	*20* the question is whether . . .
mettre qqch. en —	*21* to question sth.
questionnaire *m*	*22* questionnaire
questionner *vb*	*23* to ask (s.o.) questions (about, *sur*)
quiconque *pr*	*24* whoever, whomever, whichever
quincaillerie *f*	*25* hardware
quincaillier *m*	*26* ironmonger, hardware dealer
quintal *m*	*27* quintal, a hundredweight
quintuple *n.m. & adj*	*28* fivefold
quintupler *vb*	*29* to increase fivefold
quinzaine *n.f.*	*30* about fifteen; two weeks
quittance *f*	*31* receipt
quote-part *f*	*32* share, quota
quotient *m*	*33* quotient
rabais *m*	*34* reduction, discount, rebate; allowance

180

au —	1	at a reduced price
faire un — sur	2	to allow a reduction on
six % de —	3	six % off
rabattre *vb*	4	to lower, reduce
raccourci *m*	5	short cut
en —	6	in abbreviated form
raccrocher *vb*	7	to hang up (the phone receiver)
Raccrochez, c'est une erreur	8	Sorry, wrong number
rachat *m*	9	repurchase, buying back, redemption
— de titres	10	buying in stock
valeur de — d'une police d'assurance	11	surrender value of an insurance policy
racheter *vb*	12 1	to buy back, repurchase, redeem
	13 2	to buy again
	14 3	to buy in against
— des titres	15	to buy in stock
— une créance	16	to buy off a claim
— une obligation	17	to redeem a debenture bond
— une police d'assurance	18	to surrender an insurance policy
radier *vb*	19	to strike off, cross out
radiodiffuser *vb*	20	to broadcast
radiogramme *m*	21 1	X-ray (photograph), radiograph
	22 2	radio message, radiogram
raffermir *vb*	23 1	to strengthen, to consolidate
	24 2	to harden (again)
raffinage *m*	25	refining
raffinerie *f*	26	refinery
raison *f*	27 1	reason, cause
	28 2	rate, ration
à — de	29	at the rate of
comme de —	30	justifiably, as one might expect
des —s suffisantes	31	adequate grounds
en — de	32	owing to, because of
en — directe/indirecte de	33	in direct/inverse ratio to
plus que de —	34	to excess
— sociale	35	(trade) name
rajouter *vb*	36	to add (more, again)

rajuster / rattraper

rajuster *vb*	1	to readjust, set right, modify
ramassis *m*	2	heap, jumble
ramener *vb*	3	1 to bring back
	4	2 to reduce
— qqch. à sa plus simple expression	5	to reduce sth. to its simplest expression
ramifier (se) *vb*	6	to branch out; to extend
rang *m*	7	1 [ligne] row, line, rank
	8	2 [position sociale] rank, status
par — d'ancienneté	9	by seniority
rapide *m*	10	express (train)
rappel *m*	11	1 recall, calling back
	12	2 reminder
	13	3 calling in (of)
lettre de —	14	reminder
— de cours [en Bourse]	15	marking of omitted bargain
rappeler *vb*	16	[au téléphone] to call back
— un prêt	17	to call in a loan
rapport *m*	18	1 yield, return, profit
	19	2 report, survey, statement, written account
	20	3 connection, relation(ship), bearing, link
de bon —	21	profitable
en — avec (son rang)	22	in keeping with (his status)
par — à	23	compared with, in comparison with
se mettre en — avec	24	to get in touch with
sous tous les —s	25	in all respects [(sth.)
rapporter *vb*	26	1 to bring back, to return
	27	2 to bring in; yield, bear, pay
	28	3 to report (facts)
	29	4 to revoke, repeal (a decree)
s'en — à	30	to rely on s.o., to go by s.o.'s opinion [gether
rapprochement *m*	31	1 reconciliation; bringing to-
	32	2 comparison
rareté *f*	33	1 scarcity, shortage
	34	2 curio, valuable object
ratifier *vb*	35	to confirm, approve, ratify
rationnement *m*	36	rationing
rattacher (se) *vb*	37	to be linked, related (to, à)
rattraper *vb*	38	to catch up with, to make up (for lost time)

se —	1	to make good, recoup o.s.
rature f	2	crossing out, erasure, deletion
raviser (se) vb	3	to think better of it, change one's mind
ravitailler vb	4	to supply
se — (en)	5	to take in (fresh) supplies (of)
rayer vb	6	to strike off/out, to cross off/out
rayon m	7	1 line, field of interest
	8	2 beam, ray
	9	3 department
	10	4 shelf space; set of shelves
Ce n'est pas mon —	11	That's not in my line
chef de —	12	floorwalker
dans un — de six milles	13	within six miles of
— d'action	14	radius
réaction f	15	reaction
avion à —	16	jet aircraft
— en chaîne	17	chain —
réadaptation f	18	1 readaptation
	19	2 rehabilitation
— professionnelle	20	occupation retraining
réalisable adj	21	feasible, [actif] liquid
réalisateur, -rice n	22	[cinéma] director, [télévision] producer
réalisation f	23	1 realization; achievement, accomplishment, fulfilment
	24	2 sell, selling
réaliser vb	25	1 to realize, understand
	26	2 to come true, realize
	27	3 to sell
réapprovisionner vb	28	to restock (with, en)
réassurance f	29	reinsurance, reassurance
réassurer vb	30	to reinsure, reassure
se —	31	to reinsure
rebours m	32	reverse, contrary
à —	33	against the grain; the wrong way; backwards
rebut m	34	waste, discard, refuse, rejects, throw-outs; [Poste] dead letter
mettre au —	35	to throw away, discard, scrap

183

récapitulatif, -ve *adj*	1	recapitulatory
récapitulation *f*	2	recapitulation, summing up
récapituler *vb*	3	to sum up, recapitulate; to summarize
receler *vb*	4	to receive stolen goods
receleur *m*	5	receiver of stolen goods, [Fam.] fence
recensement *m*	6	[population] census, [vote] counting
recenseur *m*	7	census-taker
récépissé *m*	8	acknowledgement (of receipt), receipt
— à l'expéditeur/au destinataire	9	railway consignment note
— de souscription	10	application receipt
réception *f*	11 1	receipt (of an order, letter, etc.)
	12 2	at-home; party, reception, social gathering
	13 3	reception, registration desk
	14 4	taking delivery (of goods)
réceptionniste *m/f*	15	desk clerk
recette *f*	16 1	receipt(s), takings, gains; revenue
	17 2	collection of debts/bills/duties
	18 3	Revenue office
la — brute	19	the gross receipts
les — fiscales	20	inland revenue
receveur *m*	21 1	collector
[rectes	22 2	[bus] conductor
— des contributions di-	23	tax collector
rechange *m*	24 1	replacement, spare, extra, in reserve
	25 2	re-exchange
payer le change et le —	26	to pay the exchange and the re-exchange
pièces de —	27	spare parts
recherche *f*	28 1	search, pursuit (for, after)
	29 2	research, investigation
	30 3	(studied) elegance, refinement, affectation
La — de la paternité est interdite [Code Napoléon, Art. 340]	31	Investigations into paternity are forbidden

recherché *adj*	*1*	in demand, sought after, choice
rechercher *vb*	*2*	to inquire into, search into, search for; to try to locate, track down defects/thieves
récidive *f* [Lég.]	*3*	second offence
récidiver *vb*	*4*	to repeat an offence, relapse into crime
récidiviste *m*	*5*	recidivist; second offender
réciprocité *f*	*6*	reciprocity; interchange
réciproque *adj* & *n.f.*	*7*	1 reciprocal, mutual
	8	2 converse, opposite, contrary
La — n'est pas vraie	*9*	The converse is not true
réclamant *m*	*10*	claimant
réclamation *f*	*11*	1 complaint, protest, objection
	12	2 claim; notice of claim; demand
réclame *f*	*13*	advertising, advertisement
article(s) de —	*14*	special offer; bargain(s) of the week
en —	*15*	reduced; [Amér.] on special
faire de la —	*16*	to advertise
— à éclipse	*17*	flashing sign
— lumineuse	*18*	illuminated sign
réclamer *vb*	*19*	1 to complain, protest
	20	2 to claim
	21	3 to beg, to call for (sth.)
	22	4 to demand, require (of s.o.)
se — de qqun	*23*	to appeal to s.o.; to quote s.o. as one's authority (for a statement)
récolte *f*	*24*	crop(s), harvest
— exceptionnelle	*25*	bumper crop
— sur pied	*26*	standing crops
recommandable *adj*	*27*	1 respectable, reputable
	28	2 advisable
recommandation *f*	*29*	1 recommendation (of a person)
	30	2 advice, injunction
	31	3 registration (of a letter)
lettre de —	*32*	letter of introduction

taxe de —	1	registration fee
recommander *vb*	2	1 to recommend, advise, speak favourably of
	3	2 to register (a letter)
se — à qqun	4	to seek s.o.'s help or protection
se — de qqun	5	to give s.o. as a reference
récompense *f*	6	reward
en — de	7	in return for
récompenser *vb*	8	to reward
— qqun de qqch.	9	— s.o. for sth.
reconnaissance *f*	10	recognition, acknowledgement
en — de	11	in recognition of
— de dette	12	I.O.U.
reconnaître *vb*	13	1 to recognize, to identify
	14	2 to concede, admit, acknowledge
reconstituer *vb*	15	1 to reconstitute, restore
	16	2 to reconstruct (a crime)
	17	3 to build up (reserves)
recours *m*	18	resort, appeal
avoir — à	19	to resort to
— en grâce	20	petition for pardon
recouvrable *adj*	21	recoverable
recouvrement *m*	22	1 recovery, collection
	23	2 overlap(ping)
la remise d'un effet en —	24	the remittance of a bill for collection
reçu *n.m.*	25	receipt
— de bord	26	mate's —
recul *m*	27	loss (of ground), recession
reculer *vb*	28	to move back, to put off (date, payment, marriage, etc.); [se retirer, renoncer] to back out
ne — devant aucun sacrifice	29	to spare no expense
récupérer *vb*	30	to recover, get back/again; to recuperate
récuser *vb*	31	to take exception to, to object to; to discard
se —	32	to decline, refuse
rédaction *f*	33	1 editorial staff; editorial office

	1	² drawing-up, drafting, writing
secrétaire de —	*2*	associate editor
redevable *adj*	*3*	indebted (for, to, *de*, *à*)
redevance *f*	*4*	dues, tax (on radio set), rental
rédiger *vb*	*5*	to draw up, write out
redoubler *vb*	*6*	to redouble (with, *de*), to increase
redressement *m*	*7*	upward movement, recovery
redresser *vb*	*8*	to correct, rectify, adjust
— un tort	*9*	to set wrong to rights
redû *m*	*10*	balance due
réduction *f*	*11*	discount; reduction, decrease; price cut, cutting
réduire *vb*	*12*	to reduce, lessen, diminish, decrease; to cut down (expenses)
être réduit à	*13*	to be driven to
réduit *adj*	*14*	reduced, cut
refaire *vb*	*15*	to do/make again
faire —	*16*	to have . . . done again
se —	*17*	to make good, recoup
réfection *f*	*18*	repair, restoration
route en —	*19*	road up
refiler *vb*	*20*	to palm off
refuser *vb*	*21*	[offre, invitation] to decline, turn down, [candidat] to fail
Les hôtels refusaient du monde	*22*	The hotels were booked solid
régie *f*	*23*	excise; excise office
droit de —	*24*	excise tax
en —	*25*	State-managed, under State supervision
régime *m*	*26*	system; rate
— de faveur	*27*	preference, preferential duty
— de transport	*28*	transport rate
régir *vb*	*29*	to manage, rule, govern
régistre *m*	*30*	register, book, record
— de présence	*31*	attendance book
— des actionnaires	*32*	share register
— des délibérations	*33*	minute book
— des procès-verbaux	*34*	minute book
— du Commerce	*35*	Trade Register; register of business names

G

187

règle *f*	*1*	1 rule 2 ruler
— absolue	*2*	hard and fast rule
— à calcul	*3*	slide rule
règlement *m*	*4*	1 rule, regulation; bylaw; statute; standing orders
	5	2 settlement, payment
— intérieur	*6*	rules of procedure
— judiciaire	*7*	rule of court
réglementaire *adj*	*8*	regular; regulation; prescribed, statutory
réglementairement *adv*	*9*	strictly speaking; according to the book; normally
réglementation *f*	*10*	1 regulation, control
	11	2 making of rules
réglementer *vb*	*12*	to regulate, to control
régler *vb*	*13*	to settle, pay
régression *f*	*14*	regression; throw-back; drop, decline, decrease
régulariser *vb*	*15*	to regularize, standardize, to put (sth.) in order, to clear up
régulier, -ère *adj*	*16*	regular, steady; [en ordre] correct, valid
réhabiliter *vb*	*17*	to rehabilitate
se —	*18*	to clear one's good name; to obtain one's discharge (after bankruptcy)
réintégrer *vb*	*19*	to reinstate (s.o. in former position)
— son domicile	*20*	to return home
rejet *m* [Lég.]	*21*	dismissal
rejeter *vb*	*22*	to reject, turn down
— un appel [Lég.]	*23*	to dismiss an appeal
relâche *f*	*24*	1 let up, respite
	25	2 port of call
— lundi soir	*26*	no performance Monday evening
relation *vb*	*27*	relation(ship), connection
avoir des —s	*28*	to have influential friends
être en —s (avec qqun)	*29*	to be in touch (with s.o.)
—s d'affaires	*30*	business relations
relayer *vb*	*31*	to relieve
se —	*32*	to work in shifts/relays
relevé *m*	*33*	1 (check) list, statement
	34	2 survey

— de compte	*1*	statement
relèvement *m*	*2*	[amélioration] recovery; improvement
	3	[augmentation] increase, rise (in, *de*), raising (of, *de*)
relever *vb*	*4* 1	[finances, etc.] to restore
	5 2	[prendre note] to pick up, note, list
	6 3	[rehausser] to enhance, set off
	7 4	[dépendre de, ressortir de] to come under, to be within the competence (of, *de*)
relieur *m*	*8*	bookbinder
reliquat *m*	*9*	remainder, balance; residue
remanier *vb*	*10*	to re-vamp, revise; to renovate
remarquer *vb*	*11*	to observe, notice
faire — qqch. à qqun	*12*	to point out sth. to s.o., to draw s.o.'s attention to sth.
remblayer *vb*	*13* 1	to fill (sunk part of ground)
	14 2	to bank up (road, railway line)
remboursable *adj*	*15*	repayable; redeemable
emprunt — sur demande / en espèces	*16*	loan repayable on demand / in cash
remboursement *m*	*17*	reimbursement, refund, repayment; redemption, redeeming; withdrawal (from Savings Bank)
livraison contre —	*18*	cash on delivery (C.O.D.)
rembourser *vb*	*19*	to reimburse, pay back, refund, repay
remercier *vb*	*20* 1	to thank
	21 2	to dismiss, discharge (from office or service)
réméré *m*	*22*	repurchase
vente à —	*23*	sale with option of —
remettre *vb*	*24* 1	to hand (over), deliver; [confier] to entrust
	25 2	[différer] to put off, postpone
— en état	*26*	to fix, repair

s'en — à qqun	1	to rely on s.o. (for sth.) ; to leave it to s.o.
remise *f*	2	1 shed
	3	2 reduction, discount, allowance
	4	3 delivery, presentation, handing (over)
	5	4 remittance ; bill, draft
	6	5 delay ; postponement, adjournment
	7	6 commission
	8	7 repair
— à domicile	9	We deliver
— en état	10	repairing, reconditioning
remonter *vb*	11	to go back, date back (to, *à*)
remorquer *vb*	12	to haul ; to row
remplaçant *m*	13	substitute, deputy, stand-in
remplacement *m*	14	replacement ; substitution
en — de	15	in place of, in lieu of
remplacer *vb*	16	to deputize, replace, substitute for
— un gréviste	17	to scab
remplir *vb*	18	[formulaire] to fill in, fill out
	19	[obligations] to fulfil
remporter *vb*	20	1 to take back
	21	2 to win (a prize)
rémunérateur, -rice *adj*	22	remunerative, affording due payment ; profitable
renchérir *vb*	23	to increase, go up, rise in price
— sur qqun	24	to outbid s.o.
rendement *m*	25	[personnel] efficiency
	26	[capital] return, profit, yield
	27	[machine] output, turn-out
	28	[terre] bear, produce, yield
	29	[port, bassin] capacity
rendez-vous *n.m.inv*	30	appointment, date, engagement
prendre —	31	to make an appointment
rendre *vb*	32	to return, give back, to restore ; to pay, yield
renflouer *vb*	33	to refloat (a ship), [Fig.] to rescue, salvage
renier *vb*	34	to disown (one's child)
renom *m*	35	renown, repute, fame

renommer *vb*	1	to re-elect, reappoint
renoncer *vb*	2	to give up, renounce, waive, relinquish, abandon, disclaim; to withdraw from; [solennellement] to swear off
— à un droit	3	to waive a right
— à une idée	4	to drop an idea
— à une prétention	5	to renounce a claim
y —	6	to give up, abandon
renonciataire *m* [Lég.]	7	beneficiary (of claim or right transferred and waived by s.o. entitled to it)
renonciateur, -rice *n*	8	person who waives a right
renonciation *f*	9	disclaimer, waiver, renunciation, act of relinquishing
renouvelable *adj*	10	renewable
renouveler *vb*	11	1 to renew, extend, to repeat (an order)
	12	2 to renovate
renouvellement *m*	13	renewal; revival
rénover *vb*	14	to renovate; to renew
renseignement *m*	15	(a piece of) information, particulars
demande de —s	16	inquiry
pour plus amples —s s'adresser à ...	17	for further particulars, apply to ...
prendre des —s (sur)	18	to make inquiries (about), to get information (on)
renseigner *vb*	19	to inform
se —	20	to inquire, find out
rente *f*	21	income, endowment
— foncière	22	ground rent
— sur l'Etat	23	government endowment
— viagère	24	life annuity, life endowment
— viagère réversible	25	reversionary/reversional annuity
vivre de ses —s	26	to live on one's income
rentier, -ère *n*	27	person in receipt of a private income or annuity; annuitant
rentrée *f*	28	1 return, reopening
	29	2 receipt
—s et sorties de caisse	30	cash receipts and payments
—s fiscales	31	revenue receipts

renvoi *m*	*1*	1 discharge, dismissal
	2	2 return, sending back
	3	2 marginal alteration, reference
croix de — (†)	*4*	reference
renvoyer *vb*	*5*	1 to discharge, dismiss
	6	2 to send back, return
	7	3 to refer
— à plus tard	*8*	to put off, postpone, adjourn
répandu *adj*	*9*	widespread, found in many places, prevalent; [idée, opinion] widely held, [magazine] with a wide circulation
réparable *adj*	*10*	repairable, mendable, that can be put right
réparation *f*	*11*	1 repair, repairing, mending
	12	2 redress, compensation; amends, reparation
atelier de —	*13*	repair shop
être en —	*14*	to be under repair
— légale	*15*	legal redress
réparer *vb*	*16*	[objet] to repair, fix, mend
	17	[dédommager] to make amends
répartir *vb*	*18*	to distribute, divide, share (out); to apportion, to allot (shares); [échelonner] to spread out
répartition *f*	*19*	distribution, sharing out, apportionment, allotment (of shares), assessment (of taxes)
(actions) à la —	*20*	(shares) on allotment
— du bénéfice	*21*	appropriation of the profit
— proportionnelle entre les intéressés	*22*	pro rata apportionment between the parties concerned [over
repasser *vb*	*23*	[compte] to go over, check
répercussion *f*	*24*	repercussion, consequence(s), influence
répercuter (se) *vb*	*25*	to have repercussions/consequences/an indirect effect

repère *m*	1	point of reference
répertoire *m*	2	index, list, repertory; register, [Fig.: bagage] stock-in-trade
— à onglets	3	thumb-index
— maritime	4	shipping directory
répéter *vb*	5	[Lég.] to claim back
replacer *vb*	6	to put back, replace; to reinvest
répondant *m*	7	surety, warrantor, sponsor
répondre *vb*	8	1 to answer, reply
	9	2 to meet, satisfy
	10	3 to answer, vouch (for, *de*)
— à une prime [en Bourse]	11	to declare an option
réponse *f*	12	reply, answer; response
des éléments de —	13	material for an answer
— des primes [en Bourse]	14	declaration of options
— payée (R.P.)	15	reply paid
report *m*	16	carrying (forward), amount/balance carried forward, brought forward; posting; contango
le — ou le déport	17	discount or premium
reporter *vb*	18	1 to put off, postpone (till, *à*)
	19	2 to bring forward, to carry over
reprendre *vb*	20	1 [Lég.] to resume possesson
	21	2 to look up, pick up, improve, recover
	22	3 to resume (negotiations),
	23	4 to take over (assets)
représentant *m*	24	agent, representative, [Fam.] rep
représentation *f*	25	1 agency 2 performance
représenter *vb*	26	1 to represent; to act as agent(s) for
	27	2 to represent, stand for, take the place of
	28	3 to perform, give (a show)
reprise *f*	29	1 taking back
	30	2 recovery, picking up (of business)
	31	3 revival (play); renewal, resumption (of negotiations)
	32	4 occasion, time

à plusieurs —s	1	repeatedly, several times
donner en — contre qqch.	2	to trade in on sth.
— des invendus	3	taking back of unsold goods
reproduction f	4	reproduction; duplicating, copy
droits de — réservés	5	copyright reserved
réputation f	6	reputation
jouir d'une bonne —	7	to enjoy a good —, to have a good name
réputé adj	8	renowned, of high repute; famous
requérir vb	9	to demand, to call for
requête f	10	request, petition
— des créanciers	11	petition in bankruptcy
requis adj	12	required, requisite
conditions —es	13	prerequisites
réquisition f	14	requisition
droit de —	15	[International & Amer. law] Eminent Domain
réquisitionner vb	16	to seize (for military use), to requisition, commandeer
réseau m	17	network
— routier/ferroviaire	18	road/railway system
réserve f	19	1 reserve
	20	2 reservation, exception, limitation
en —	21	in reserve
fonds de —	22	reserve fund
— d'or	23	gold reserve
sans —	24	unreservedly, without restrictions, fully
sous les —s d'usage	25	under usual reserves, under reserve
sous — de	26	subject to, contingent upon
sous — de modifications	27	subject to alteration
sous toute —	28	without guaranty
réserver vb	29	1 to reserve, put aside, lay by
	30	2 to reserve, book (seats)
se — (le droit de)	31	to reserve (the right to)
résident m	32	resident
résiliable adj	33	voidable
résiliation f	34	cancellation, annulment
résilier vb	35	to cancel, annul, void
résolution f	36	1 resolution, determination

	1 **2** [Lég.] cancellation
résolutoire *adj*	*2* cancelling
clause —	*3* — clause
résorber *vb*	*4* to remove, clear
— un déficit	*5* to wipe off/clear off a deficit
résoudre *vb*	*6* **1** to solve (a problem)
	7 **2** to resolve, decide (to, *de*)
	8 **3** to void, cancel (a contract)
se — (à)	*9* to accept [as a last resort]
	10 to resolve [however reluctantly]
responsabilité *f*	*11* responsibility, liability
avoir la — de	*12* to be responsible for
— civile	*13* civil liability
— (il)limitée	*14* (un)limited liability
sous sa propre —	*15* on one's own responsibility
responsable *adj*	*16* responsible, liable, answerable, accountable
être — des dommages	*17* to be liable for the damage
ressort *m*	*18* [aiguillon] motive, incentive
	19 [pouvoir]competence; [Lég.] jurisdiction
en dernier —	*20* **1** as a last resort
	21 **2** [Lég.] without appeal
ressortir *vb*	*22* **1** to be evident, appear
	23 **2** to be under the competence (of, *de* *)
	24 **3** to ensue, to result (from, *de*)
affaire qui ressortit à un tribunal civil	*25* case coming under a civil court
ressource *f*	*26* resource(fulness); means
restant *m*	*27* remainder, rest
restant *adj*	*28* remaining, left
poste —e	*29* [G.B.] poste restante, to be called for
	30 [Amér.] general delivery
reste *m*	*31* balance, remainder, rest
être en reste	*32* to be behindhand
les —s	*33* remains, leavings, left-overs
restriction *f*	*34* cutting down (of expenses)

* C'est la prép. à qu'il faudrait ici employer mais beaucoup d'écrivains s'écartent souvent de cet usage.

résultat *m*	1	result, outcome, issue, consequence; conclusion
sans —	2	of no avail, to no effect
retard *m*	3	delay
avoir une heure de —	4	to be an hour late
être en —	5	to be late, to be behind; to be in arrears
Il est en — pour son loyer	6	He is behind with his rent
mettre qqun en —	7	to make s.o. late
retardataire *n.* & *adj*	8	late, behind time, late-comer
retenue *f*	9	[sur un salaire] deduction
retirer *vb*	10	1 to withdraw, take back, pull out
	11	2 to derive (benefits)
se — des affaires	12	to retire from business
retoucher *vb*	13	to touch up, improve or repair
retour *m*	14	return
en —	15	in exchange, for
être de —	16	to be back
par — du courrier	17	by — mail
— [Lég.]	18	reversion
un — d'opinion	19	a reversal of opinion
rétractation *f*	20	retraction
rétracter *vb*	21	to withdraw, take back
se —	22	to retract, eat one's words
retrait *m*	23	withdrawal
retraite *f*	24	1 retirement, pension
	25	2 retreat, withdrawal
caisse de —	26	superannuation fund
en —	27	retired
mettre à la —	28	to pension off
prendre sa —	29	to retire
retraité *adj*	30	retired, pensioned off; superannuated
retrancher *vb*	31	to retrench, take off (from, *de*), to subtract, deduct
rétribuer *vb*	32	to pay, remunerate
rétribution *f*	33	remuneration, compensation
rétroactif, -ve *adj*	34	retroactive
rétrograde *adj*	35	retrograde, backward, going backwards, reversed
réunir *vb*	36	to join, convene, collect
— des fonds	37	to raise funds
révélation *f*	38	revelation, disclosure
revendication *f*	39	claim, demand

revendiquer *vb*	1	to claim, ask for, demand for sth. as one's due
revendre *vb*	2	to resell
revenir *vb*	3	1 to return, come back; to revert
	4	2 to cost, to amount (to, *à*), to come (to the same thing)
— sur une décision	5	to reconsider a decision
revenu *m*	6	income, revenue
impôt sur le —	7	income tax
— national	8	national revenue
—s de l'Etat	9	public revenue
reviser, réviser *vb*	10	to revise, [machine] to overhaul, service
révision *f*	11	1 revision
	12	2 [machine] overhauling, servicing
revoir *vb*	13	to review (o.'s notes), to look over, go over, see again
édition revue et corrigée	14	revised edition
révolu *adj*	15	finished, completed, over
révoquer *vb*	16	[destituer] to dismiss, [déclarer nul] to revoke, countermand
— en doute	17	to question
— un fonctionnaire	18	to dismiss an official
rigueur *f*	19	1 severity; sharpness
	20	2 exactness, rigour
à la —	21	at a pinch, if necessary
de —	22	compulsory, strictly enforced
risque *m*	23	risk
à vos —s et périls	24	at your own —
— locatif	25	tenant's third party —
ristourne *f*	26	rebate; return, refund
rivaliser *vb*	27	to compete with, to rival (in, *de*)
rodage *m*	28	breaking-in (of motor)
en —	29	[G.B.] running in, [Amér.] new car
rogner *vb*	30	[papier] to trim
rôle *m*	31	1 part, role 2 roster
à tour de —	32	by turns, in turn, in rotation

rompre *vb*	1	to break
— un marché	2	to call off a deal
rompu *adj*	3	well trained (in, *à*)
— aux affaires	4	experienced in business
rond *n.m. & adj*	5	1 ring, circle 2 round
en chiffres —s	6	in round figures
en —	7	in circles
— -de-cuir	8	pen-pusher
rossignol *m*	9	unsaleable goods, drug on the market; piece of junk
roulement *m*	10	1 roll, rolling, running
	11	2 rotation, taking turns (in duties)
	12	3 cash (in hand), assets; circulation (of money)
fonds de —	13	working capital; [valeurs réalisables] available assets
— à billes	14	ball bearing
— de fonds	15	cash circulation
routage *m*	16	routing
route *f*	17	way, road
en —	18	on the way
faire fausse —	19	to be on the wrong track
grand-route	20	highway
se mettre en —	21	to set out/off
routier, -ère *adj*	22	road
carte routière	23	— map
circulation routière	24	— traffic
transports —s	25	— transport
routier *m*	26	lorry-driver
R S V P (Répondez s'il vous plaît)	27	R S V P
rupture *f*	28	[relations, négociations] breaking off, [d'un contrat] annulment, breach
sacrifice *m*	29	sacrifice
ne reculer devant aucun —	30	to spare no expense
saisi *m* [Lég.]	31	distrainee
saisie *f* [Lég.]	32	seizure, distraint; attachment; foreclosure
saisir *vb*	33	1 to understand, grasp, catch, get

	1	2 [Lég.] to seize, distrain, to foreclose; to attach
	2	3 to refer (a matter to a court)
saisissable [Lég.] *adj*	3	distrainable, attachable
saisissant *m*	4	distrainer, distrainor
salaire *m*	5	wages, pay, salary
— indexé au coût de la vie	6	salary geared to the cost of living
salarié *adj*	7	paid (by the week), salaried, wage-earner
salle *f*	8	room
— d'attente	9	waiting —
— de cinéma	10	movie theatre
— de classe/de cours	11	class —
— de conférence/de concert	12	auditorium
— d'étude	13	study hall
— des coffres	14	strong- —
— (de théâtre)	15	house
salon *m*	16	1 room, shop
	17	2 show, exhibition
— de coiffure	18	barber shop
— de thé	19	tea room
— de l'automobile	20	motor show
salutation *f*	21	salutation, greeting
Agréez,..., mes —s distinguées	22	Yours faithfully,
Veuillez agréer, ..., (l'expression de) mes —s distinguées	23	Yours sincerely, *ou*: Yours truly,
sanction *f*	24	1 sanction, authorization, assent, approval
	25	2 sanction, penalty, measure
prendre des —s (contre)	26	to inflict punishment or hardship (on), to penalize, to take action (against)
— royale	27	royal assent
sanctionner *vb*	28	1 to sanction, to authorize, to approve
	29	2 to punish, to penalize
sans *prép*	30	without; but for; free (of, from); ... less
— garantie [à découvert]	31	unsecured
— profession	32	no occupation

199

— travail	1	out of work, unemployed
— valeur	2	worthless
santé *f*	3	health
Ministère de la — publique	4	Ministry of Health
patente de —	5	bill of —
satisfaction *f*	6	1 satisfaction, gratification
	7	2 amends, reparation
satisfaire *vb*	8	1 to satisfy; to give satisfaction to (s.o.)
	9	2 to fulfil, meet, answer
— à des conditions	10	to meet requirements
— à la demande	11	to meet the demand
sauf *prép*	12	except, barring; unless
— accidents	13	barring accidents
— avis/stipulation contraire	14	unless otherwise agreed
— correction	15	subject to correction
— erreur ou omission (S.E. ou O.)	16	errors & omissions excepted (E. & O. E.)
— imprévu	17	circumstances permitting
— mieux [en Bourse]	18	or better
sauvegarder *vb*	19	to protect, safeguard; to watch over
sceau *m*	20	seal
sceller *vb*	21	to seal (up)
scellés *n.pl.*	22	seal(s)
mettre les —	23	to put under —
schéma *m*	24	diagram; plan; synopsis
sciemment *adv*	25	purposely, knowingly
scierie *f*	26	saw/lumber mill
scinder *vb*	27	to divide, split up (into, *en*), to split (shares)
scission *f*	28	split
scolaire *adj*	29	academic, school
année —	30	academic/school year
fournitures —s	31	school supplies
matériel —	32	school equipment
scolarité *f*	33	school
frais de —	34	tuition fees
scrutin *m*	35	ballot, vote
séance *f*	36	1 meeting; session 2 show
lever la —	37	to close the meeting
— [cinéma]	38	performance
— publique	39	open meeting
sec, sèche *adj*	40	dry

cal sèche	1	— dock
navire à —	2	ship aground
nettoyage à sec	3	— cleaning
tenir au sec	4	keep in a — place
une perte sèche	5	a total loss
sécession f	6	secession
faire —	7	to secede
secrétaire n.m., n.m/f	8	1 [meuble] desk
	9	2 [Pers.] Secretary
— de	10	secretary to
secrétariat m	11	[fonction] secretaryship
	12	[bureau] secretary's office
secteur m	13	area, section, district
seing m	14	signature, seal
acte sous — privé	15	deed under private seal
semestre m	16	half-year, semester
semestriel, -le adj	17	semi-annual, half-yearly
sens m	18	1 meaning, sense
	19	2 direction, way
au — propre/figuré	20	in a literal/figurative sense
dans le — des aiguilles d'une montre	21	clockwise
en — inverse	22	in the opposite direction
sentence f	23	[Lég.] judgement, penalty
rendre une — arbitrale	24	to make an award
séquestrer vb [Lég.]	25	[des biens] to sequestrate [pending satisfaction of claims], [navire] to lay embargo upon, [personnes] to confine
série f	26	series, succession; line; [timbres] set
fin de —	27	remainder line
— complète	28	full set (of B/L, stamps, etc.)
voiture de —	29	car of standard model
serviette f	30	[porte-documents] portfolio
siège m	31	head office; registered office
— social	32	head office
signalement m	33	description
signaler vb	34	to indicate, point out
signature f	35	signature
apposer sa —	36	to sign
revêtu de sa —	37	bearing his —
— sociale	38	first —

signe *m*	*1*	sign, mark, [marque, témoignage] token
signet *m*	*2*	bookmark
signifier *vb*	*3*	1 to mean, signify
	4	2 to notify (sth. to s.o., *qqch. à qqun*)
silence *m*	*5*	silence
passer qqch. sous —	*6*	to omit (sth.)
simili- *prefixe*	*7*	imitation
— -cuir	*8*	leatherette
sinistre *n.m.*	*9*	disaster; loss; casualty; damage; accident; claim
sinistré *n* & *adj*	*10*	1 victim (of a disaster)
	11	2 damaged
situation *f*	*12*	1 place, location, situation; position
	13	2 position, job, post
	14	3 standing, status, rank
— financière	*15*	financial status
une — difficile	*16*	a predicament
situer *vb*	*17*	to locate; to situate
(magasin, etc.) bien situé	*18*	(shop, etc.) very central
slogan *m*	*19*	slogan [to stimulate public interest in commercial products]
smoking *n.m.*	*20*	[G.B.] dinner jacket, [Amér.] tuxedo
société *f*	*21*	society, association, firm, company
droit des —s	*22*	company law
— anonyme (S.A.)	*23*	limited company
— à responsabilité limitée (S.A.R.L.)	*24*	limited liability company
— de contrôle	*25*	holding company
— de financement	*26*	financing company
— de placement	*27*	investment company
(—) filiale	*28*	subsidiary company
— immobilière	*29*	building society
— par actions	*30*	joint stock company
— verbale en nom collectif	*31*	verbal partnership
soierie *f*	*32*	1 silks, silk fabric(s)
	33	2 silk trade
soin *m*	*34*	care
les —s médicaux	*35*	medical —

sol *m*	1	ground, soil
sous- — *m*	2	basement
solde *m*	3	clearance sale
" en—"	4	" to clear "
—s	5	sale
solde *m*	6	balance
pour — de tout compte	7	in full settlement
— créditeur	8	credit —
— débiteur/déficitaire	9	debit —
— de dividende	10	final dividend
solder *vb*	11	[compte] to settle
	12	[des rossignols] to clear, to undersell
se — (par)	13	to result (in), to show (loss, profit)
— un découvert	14	to pay off an overdraft
solidaire *adj*	15	1 joint and several
	16	2 liable, (jointly) responsible, answerable
créance —	17	joint and several debt
le mari est — des dettes de sa femme	18	the husband is responsible for the debts of his wife
obligation —	19	obligation binding on all parties
responsabilité conjointe et —	20	joint and several liability
solliciter *vb*	21	to beg, request
solvabilité *f*	22	solvency
solvable *adj*	23	solvent, responsible
sommation *f* [Lég.]	24	summons
somme *f*	25	sum
arrondir une —	26	to round off a —
— coquette	27	a tidy —
— due	28	amount due
— globale/forfaitaire	29	lump —
sommer *vb*	30	to call upon; to summon
— un débiteur de payer	31	to call upon a debtor to pay
sondage *m*	32	sounding
le — de l'opinion publique	33	the polling of public opinion
sortant *n.m. & adj*	34	outgoing, coming out; retiring
administrateur —	35	retiring director
le numéro —	36	the winning number
numéraire —	37	outgoing cash

sortie *f*	*1*	going out, coming out; exit, way out; export; payment; retirement
à l'entrée ou à la — du port	*2*	on entering or leaving port
des rentrées et des —s	*3*	receipts and payments
les entrées et les —s (des marchandises)	*4*	imports and exports (of goods)
— de capitaux	*5*	outflow of capital
souche *f*	*6*	[carnet] counterfoil
soudoyer *vb*	*7*	to bribe
soudure *f*	*8*	welding; joining
faire la —	*9*	to manage to cope (until new supplies or receipts come), to tide over
souffrance (en) *loc.*	*10*	pending; awaiting delivery; on demurrage
compte en —	*11*	overdue account
effets en —	*12*	bills held over
marchandises en —	*13*	unclaimed/undelivered goods
soumis *adj*	*14*	subject to
— à l'impôt	*15*	liable to tax, dutiable
soumission *f*	*16*	1 tender (for a contract)
	17	2 obedience; surrender
par (voie de) —	*18*	by tender
soumissionnaire *m*	*19*	tenderer, [Douanes] bonder
soumissionner *vb*	*20*	to tender (for)
source *f*	*21*	source
de — sûre	*22*	reliably, from a reliable —
— de revenu	*23*	— of income
tenir de bonne —	*24*	to have on good authority
sous-chef *m*	*25*	[bureau] deputy head clerk
souscripteur *m*	*26*	applicant, subscriber; underwriter, drawer (of a bill of exchange)
souscription *f*	*27*	1 subscription, subscribing
	28	2 signature; signing
	29	3 application (for shares, *à des actions*)
	30	4 fund; contribution, sum of money
à la —, en souscrivant	*31*	on application
lancer une —	*32*	to start a fund
— à une émission	*33*	subscription to an issue

souscrire *vb*	*1*	to subscribe
entièrement souscrit	*2*	fully subscribed
police souscrite à Londres	*3*	policy underwritten in London
— à une émission	*4*	— to an issue
— des actions	*5*	to apply for shares
— un acte	*6*	to sign a deed
— une lettre de change	*7*	to draw a bill of exchange
— un emprunt	*8*	— for a loan
— un risque maritime	*9*	to underwrite a marine risk
sous-directeur *m*	*10*	assistant-manager
sous-locataire *m*	*11*	subtenant
sous-location *f*	*12*	subletting
soussigné *adj*	*13*	undersigned
Je, —, certifie que . . .	*14*	I, the —, certify that . . .
sous-sol *m*	*15*	basement
sous-titre *m*	*16*	subtitle
soustraction *f*	*17*	subtraction
— frauduleuse	*18*	abstraction
soustraire *vb*	*19*	to subtract; [subtiliser] to remove, steal, purloin
se — (à)	*20*	to shirk, escape (from)
sous-traitant *m*	*21*	sub-contractor
sous-traiter *vb*	*22*	sub-contract
soute *f*	*23*	[navire] store-room
soutenir *vb*	*24*	1 [défendre] to defend, side with
	25	2 [aider] to help, support, provide for
	26	3 [appuyer] to prop (up), to support
	27	4 [affirmer] to maintain, claim
soutirer *vb*	*28*	[vin] to draw off
— de l'argent à qqun	*29*	to worm money out from s.o.
spécialiste *m*	*30*	specialist, expert (in, *de*)
spéculateur *m*	*31*	speculator
— à la baisse/hausse	*32*	bear/bull
spéculatif, -ve *adj*	*33*	speculative
valeurs spéculatives	*34*	— stocks
spéculation *f*	*35*	speculation, operations
— à la baisse/hausse	*36*	bear/bull operations
— mixte	*37*	spreading, straddling
spéculer *vb*	*38*	to speculate (in, *sur*)

— à la baisse	1	— on a fall, to take a bear position, to go a bear
— à la hausse	2	— on a rise, to take a bull position, to go a bull
stabilisation *f*	3	stabilization
— des prix	4	pegging
stabiliser *vb*	5	to stabilize, steady, [prix] to peg, fix at a stable level
stage *m*	6	probation period, term of probation, period of instruction, qualifying period
stagiaire *n.m/f*	7	trainee
stand *m*	8	stand, stall
standard *m*	9	1 [tél.] (office) switchboard
	10	2 level, standard; type
— de vie	11	standard of living
standardiser *vb*	12	to standardize
standardiste *m/f*	13	(switchboard) operator
station *f*	14	station; resort; place
— balnéaire	15	seaside resort
— de métro	16	tube station
— de sports d'hiver	17	winter sport resort
— thermale	18	watering place
— touristique	19	tourist centre
stationnaire *adj*	20	stationary
statistiques *n.m/f*	21	statistics
statuer *vb*	22	to resolve, decide
— sur un litige	23	to settle a dispute
statut *m*	24	statute
statutaire *adj*	25	statutory, appointed by the articles of association
statuts *n.m.pl.*	26	articles of association
sténographe *n.m/f*	27	shorthandwriter, stenographer
sténographie, sténo *f*	28	shorthand, stenography
sténographier *vb*	29	to take down in shorthand
stock *m*	30	stock
— en magasin	31	— in hand
subalterne *n. & adj*	32	inferior, subordinate
subdiviser *vb*	33	to subdivide, to split up (into, *en*)
subir *vb*	34	to experience, to suffer (loss), to undergo (change)
subordonné *n. & adj*	35	subordinate

subséquent *adj*	1	subsequent, succeeding
subsidiaire *adj*	2	subsidiary
substituer *vb*	3	to substitute (for, *à*)
— un héritage	4	to entail an estate
— un héritier	5	to appoint an heir in succession to another
substitut *m*	6	substitute; assistant deputy (to official)
subvenir *vb*	7	to supply, provide (for, *à*)
subvention *f*	8	subsidy, grant
subventionner *vb*	9	to subsidize
succession *f* [Lég.]	10	inheritance
droits de —	11	death duties
succursale *f*	12	branch
— de province	13	country branch
suite *f*	14	1 sequel; sequence, succession
	15	2 consequence, result
	16	3 perseverance
	17	4 suite, retinue, party
à la — de	18	as a result of, following
donner — à	19	to follow up
la — au prochain numéro	20	to be continued
le président et sa —	21	the President and his party
six heures de —	22	six hours on end
six jours de —	23	six days running
six trains de —	24	six trains in succession
suivre *vb*	25	to follow
lettre suit	26	letter to follow
Prière de faire —	27	Please forward
sujet, -te *adj*	28	prone, exposed (to, à)
— à caution	29	unreliable
suppléant *adj*	30	assistant, substitute
suppléer *vb*	31	1 to supplement, to complete, to make up
	32	2 to replace, be the stand-in of
supplément *m*	33	supplement, extra, additional sum
en —	34	additional, extra
supplémentaire *adj*	35	additional, extra, supplementary, further
faire des heures —s	36	to work overtime
supporter *vb*	37	[avoir la charge de] to bear (expenses)

suppression *f*	1	suppression, removing; cancelling, abolition, abolishment [continue
supprimer *vb*	2	to do away, abolish; to dis-
supputer *vb*	3	to reckon, to weigh (chances), to calculate
sûr *adj*	4	1 sure, certain, positive
	5	2 safe, secure
	6	3 reliable, trustworthy
surcharge *f*	7	1 alteration, correction
	8	2 overprint (on postage stamp)
	9	3 excess weight; extra load
surcharger *vb*	10	1 to alter, correct
	11	2 to overprint (stamp)
	12	3 to overload
surcroît *m*	13	excess, surplus
par/de —	14	in addition
— de travail	15	more work
surenchère *f*	16	higher bid
surenchérir *vb*	17	to outbid
surestarie *f*	18	(days of) demurrage
jours de —	19	extra lay days
surévaluer *vb*	20	to overestimate
surfait *adj*	21	overestimated, overrated
surimposer *vb*	22	to overtax
surmonter *vb*	23	to overcome (a difficulty)
surplus *m*	24	surplus, excess
surpoids *m*	25	overweight
surproduction *f*	26	overproduction
sursis *m*	27	respite, delay, [Lég.] stay, suspension of proceedings; reprieve
surtaxe *f*	28	[taxe supplémentaire sur un revenu] surtax, [supplément sur la valeur faciale d'un timbre] surcharge
surveillant *m*	29	watchman, supervisor
survenir *vb*	30	to happen, arrive (unexpectedly)
sus *adv*	31	extra
en —	32	in addition
susceptible *adj*	33	capable (of), liable (to)
susciter *vb*	34	to bring about, give rise to, create

susdit *n. & adj*	1	aforesaid, abovementioned
suspendre *vb*	2	[ses paiements] to stop
	3	[un jugement] to defer, stay
	4	[un fonctionnaire] to suspend
suspendu *adj*	5	suspended; interrupted; delayed, [Lég.] deferred
suspens (en) *adv*	6	pending, held over, in abeyance
suspension *f*	7	suspension, interruption
syndic *m*	8	syndic, trustee
— de faillite	9	trustee, assignee (in bankruptcy)
syndicat *m*	10	1 trade union; syndicate
	11	2 trusteeship
— industriel	12	pool
— patronal	13	employers' federation
table *f*	14	table
mettre des chiffres en forme de —	15	to tabulate
— des matières	16	contents
tabler *vb*	17	to count (on, *sur*)
tâche *f*	18	work, task, job, assignment
taille *f*	19	1 size; height
	20	2 waist
	21	3 cut, cutting
de — moyenne	22	of middle height, medium
être de — à	23	to be big enough, to be quite capable of
la — des diamants	24	diamond cutting
pierre de —	25	freestone
tailler *vb*	26	to cut
— en biseau	27	to bevel
talent *m*	28	[habilité; monnaie] talent
talon *m*	29	counterfoil, stub
tampon *m*	30	1 pad
	31	2 [cachet] rubber stamp
tant *adv & çonj*	32	so (much, many, long, well, etc.)
en — que président	33	in his capacity as a President
payer — pour la façon	34	to pay so much for the making of a garment
tant *m* **pour cent**	35	percentage
taper *vb*	36	1 [à la machine] to type

209

	1	² [emprunter de l'argent] to touch
tare *f*	*2*	[poids de l'emballage] tare
	3	[défectuosité] blemish, taint
— intégrale	*4*	lump tare
— proportionnelle	*5*	average tare
— réelle	*6*	actual tare
tarif *m*	*7*	rate
(billet) à plein —	*8*	full — ticket
— dégressif	*9*	decreasing tariff
— de recouvrement	*10*	collection tariff
— des abonnements	*11*	subscription —s
— des courtages	*12*	commission —s
— des imprimés	*13*	printed —
— douanier	*14*	customs tariff
— horaire	*15*	hourly —
— marchandises	*16*	freight —
— syndical	*17*	union —
tarifier *vb*	*18*	to tariff, fix the rate of
taux *m*	*19*	rate
— de capitalisation	*20*	yield (of a stock)
— de la natalité/des naissances	*21*	birth- —
— de (la) prime	*22*	premium
— de marque	*23*	mark up
— d'escompte	*24*	bank —
— des salaires	*25*	standard of wages
— du change	*26*	— of exchange
— forfaitaire	*27*	through —(s)
— uniforme	*28*	flat —
taxable *adj*	*29*	taxable, assessable
taxation *f*	*30*	taxation, assessment
taxe *f*	*31*	tax
— de séjour	*32*	non-resident —
— de transmission [Belg.]	*33*	purchase/sales —
— de vente { Taxe locale (T.L.); Taxe sur la valeur ajoutée (T.V.A.) }	*34*	purchase —
— forfaitaire	*35*	standard charge
taxer *vb*	*36*	to tax, assess
télégraphier *vb*	*37*	to wire, telegraph
télégraphique *adj*	*38*	telegraphic
téléphone *m*	*39*	telephone
annuaire du —	*40*	— book

coup de —	1	ring
— public	2	pay —
téléphonique adj	3	telephone
appel —	4	— call
cabine —	5	booth, call-box
téléscripteur m	6	telex
témoignage m	7	testimony, evidence; hearing (of witness)
en — d'amitié	8	as a token of o.'s friendship
faux —	9	perjury
témoigner vb	10	1 to testify, give evidence, attest
	11	2 to show
témoin m	12	witness
prendre à —	13	to call to —
suborner un —	14	to tamper with a —
— à charge	15	— for the prosecution
— à décharge	16	— for the defence
— oculaire	17	eye —
tempérament m	18	adjustment; instalment
acheter à —	19	to buy on the instalment plan
temporaire adj	20	temporary, provisional
temporiser vb	21	to temporize, procrastinate; [lambiner, lanterner] to stall
temps m	22	time
emploi du —	23	— table
en — utile	24	in due course
tenancier, -ère n	25	keeper, manager
teneur f	26	substance, tenor; [minerai] grade, percentage, amount
tenir vb	27	1 to hold, keep
	28	2 to care for
s'en — à	29	to limit o.s. to
— à jour	30	to keep up to date
— conseil	31	to hold a meeting
— les comptes	32	to keep accounts
— un article	33	to carry an article, to keep a line
— un magasin	34	to run a shop/store
tentative f	35	attempt
tenue f	36	1 keeping, holding
	37	2 behaviour
	38	3 dress

211

	1	4 firmness
bonne — (des valeurs pétrolières)	*2*	firmness (of oil shares)
— des livres	*3*	book-keeping
terme *m*	*4*	1 end, limit
	5	2 quarter, term, rent, date, time
	6	3 term, word
	7	4 credit, instalment(s)
	8	5 [en Bourse] account; settlement
à court/long —	*9*	short-/long-dated
avant —	*10*	prematurely
marché à —	*11*	1 forward transaction
	12	2 dealing for settlement, bargain for account
	13	3 options market
—s de métier	*14*	technical terms
terminer *vb*	*15*	to finish, end
se —	*16*	to end, terminate
terminus *m*	*17*	terminus, terminal
terrain *m*	*18*	ground
accidents de —	*19*	broken —
préparer le —	*20*	to pave the way (for)
tâter le —	*21*	to see how the land lies, to throw out feelers
— à bâtir	*22*	building/plot site
— vague	*23*	vacant plot
testament *m*	*24*	will
mourir sans —	*25*	to die intestate
faire son —	*26*	to make one's —
testimonial *adj* [Lég.]	*27*	deponed to by witness
preuve —e	*28*	proof by witnesses
textuellement *adv*	*29*	verbatim, word for word
théoriquement *adv*	*30*	in theory
thésauriser *vb*	*31*	to hoard
ticket *m*	*32*	ticket
— d'entrée	*33*	admission —
— de quai	*34*	platform —
tiers *n.m.*	*35*	third; third person, third-party
remise d'un — (sur le prix fort)	*36*	a third off (the list price)
timbrage *m*	*37*	stamping
timbre *m*	*38*	stamp

exempt du —	1	exempt from — duty
oblitérer un —	2	to frank/cancel a —
— à date	3	date —
— en caoutchouc	4	rubber —
— fiscal	5	Revenue —
— poste	6	postage —
— taxe	7	postage due —
timbré *adj*	8	stamped
papier —	9	— paper
timbrer *vb*	10	to stamp
tirage *m*	11	1 drawing, pulling
	12	2 printing, circulation
journal à gros —	13	paper with a wide circulation
— à part	14	offprint
— au sort	15	drawing lots
tiré *n.m.*	16	drawee
tirer *vb*	17	1 to pull, draw
	18	2 to fire, shoot
	19	3 to draw, derive, deduce
	20	4 to print, to run off
épreuve en bon à tirer	21	press-proof
se — d'affaire	22	to pull through
— à découvert	23	to overdraw
— à sa fin	24	to draw to an end
— à vue sur qqun	25	to draw on s.o. at sight
— au clair	26	to clarify
— au sort	27	to draw lots
— des conclusions	28	to draw conclusions
— en longueur	29	to drag out
— parti de	30	to make good use of, turn to account, make the most of
— un chèque sans provisions suffisantes	31	to overdraw
tireur *m*	32	drawer
tiroir-caisse *n.m.*	33	till
tissage *m*	34	weaving
tissu *m*	35	material; fabric
titre *m*	36	1 securities; certificate; script; bond
	37	2 title; heading; headline
	38	3 claim, right
	39	4 qualifications
	40	5 title deed, deed

	1 6	[minerai] standard; [monnaie] fineness
à juste —	*2*	rightfully
à — de	*3*	as, in the capacity of
à — gracieux	*4*	free of charge
à — onéreux	*5*	for a price/consideration
en —	*6*	regular, titular, holder (of an office)
monnaies au — légal	*7*	coins of legal fineness
souscrire à — irréductible	*8*	to apply as of right
souscrire à — réductible	*9*	to apply for excess shares
— d'action	*10*	share certificate
titulaire *m*	*11*	holder (of share, office, passport), occupant (of a post), incumbent
titulariser *vb*	*12*	to appoint as titular
tolérance *f*	*13*	tolerance; [poids ou dimension] allowance; margin, limit
par —	*14*	on sufferance
— permise (d'alcool, etc.)	*15*	quantity permitted
tomber *vb*	*16*	to fall, drop
— d'accord	*17*	to come to an agreement
tombola *f*	*18*	(charity) lottery
tonnage *m*	*19*	tonnage
tonne *f*	*20*	ton
Ce navire jauge 15.000 —s	*21*	This ship is 15,000 —s
— courte	*22*	short —
— forte	*23*	long —
— de jauge/d'arrimage	*24*	measurement —
— métrique	*25*	metric —
tonneau *m*	*26*	cask, barrel; keg
torréfier *vb*	*27*	to roast (coffee)
tort *m*	*28*	wrong, injury, damage, [Lég.] tort
faire — à	*29*	to wrong
total *n.m. & adj*	*30* 1	whole, full amount, total, full sum
	31 2	whole, complete; gross, aggregate, entire
au —	*32*	on the whole
faire le — de	*33*	to add, sum up
— global	*34*	grand total
totaliser *vb*	*35*	to totalize; to add up
totalité *f*	*36*	totality, whole, entirety

toucher *vb*	*1*	1 to touch, lay hands on
	2	2 to cash, draw, receive
	3	3 to concern, affect
en — un mot	*4*	to mention it (briefly), to touch on (upon)
Prière de ne pas —	*5*	Please do not touch
— ses appointements/son traitement	*6*	to draw one's salary
— un chèque	*7*	to cash a cheque
tour *m*	*8*	turn
à — de rôle	*9*	in turn, by roster
tournée *f*	*10*	tour, round
tournure *f*	*11*	to turn, course (of events)
attendre la — que prendront les événements	*12*	to await further developments
tout, toute, tous, toutes *adj*	*13*	1 whole, all, entire
	14	2 each, any
à tout prix	*15*	at all costs
toute affaire cessante	*16*	dropping everything else
Tout employé qui (désire) . . .	*17*	Any clerk who (wishes) ..
toute(s) proportion(s) gardée(s)	*18*	due allowance being made; other things being equal
tout *adv*	*19*	all, quite
tout *n.m.*	*20*	(the) whole, the main, important thing
en — ou en partie	*21*	wholly or partly
tout, tous, toutes *pr.*	*22*	all, anything, everything
à tout prendre	*23*	on the whole, on balance
tracé *m*	*24*	(proposed) line, lay-out, drawing
traducteur, -rice *n*	*25*	translator
traduction *f*	*26*	translation, rendering
— exacte	*27*	faithful translation
— inexacte	*28*	mistranslation
traduire *vb*	*29*	1 to translate
	30	2 [Lég.] to sue, prosecute
— de . . . en . . .	*31*	to translate from . . . into . . .
— en justice	*32*	to prosecute, hail into court
trafic *m*	*33*	1 trading, dealing
	34	2 illicit trading, illegal trade
	35	3 transport, movement, traffic
— ferroviaire	*36*	railway traffic
trafiquant *m*	*37*	trafficker

215

trafiquer *vb*	1	to traffic, to deal (against the law), to trade (illegally)
train *m*	2	1 speed, pace, rate (of movement)
	3	2 manner, way (of life) scale
	4	3 carriage; train
	5	4 course, way, process
chef de —	6	[G.B.] guard, [Amér.] conductor
(grand) — de vie	7	(high) standing, (grand) scale
prendre un —	8	to catch/take a train
— de banlieue	9	suburban train
— de marchandises	10	[G.B.] goods train, [Amér.] freight train
— de voyageurs	11	passenger train
— direct	12	through train
traite *f*	13	(banker's) draft; [lettre de change] bill (of exchange)
tirer une — sur	14	to draw a bill on
— à échéance	15	title draft
— de complaisance	16	accommodation bill; kite
— en l'air [Belg.]	17	kite, worthless bill
— (payable) à vue	18	draft (payable) at sight
— simple	19	clean bill
Un chèque est une — sur un banquier	20	A cheque is a draft on a banker
traité *m*	21	1 [convention] treaty
	22	2 [ouvrage] treatise, book
conclure un —	23	to sign a treaty [law
— de droit commercial	24	handbook of commercial
traitement *m*	25	1 treatment
	26	2 salary; stipend
— initial	27	starting salary
traiter *vb*	28	to negotiate, transact
traiteur *m*	29	caterer
trajet *m*	30	trip, distance, run
tranche *f* **d'actions**	31	block of shares
trancher *vb*	32	1 to settle, decide, solve
	33	2 to speak, to decide peremptorily, be positive
transaction *f*	34	1 transaction, dealings
	35	2 arrangement, compromise, settlement

transatlantique *m*	1	liner
la Compagnie générale —	2	the French Line
transborder *vb*	3	to tranship; to transfer
transcrire *vb*	4	to transcribe
transférer *vb*	5	to move, transfer, remove; to make over
transfert *m*	6	transfer
bénéficiaire d'un —	7	beneficiary of a —
droit de —	8	— duty [change
transformer *vb*	9	to transform, convert, alter,
transgresser *vb*	10	to transgress, break, to violate (a law); to trespass against, to infringe, contravene
transgresseur *m*	11	trespasser
transiger *vb*	12	to compromise
transitaire *n.m. & adj*	13	1 forwarding/shipping agent
	14	2 transit
pays —	15	transit country
transmettre *vb*	16	to transmit, convey, forward
transport *m*	17	transport, transportation, conveyance, carriage, freight, cartage, haulage
— fluvial	18	river transport
— routier	19	road transport
transport *m* [Lég.]	20	transfer, making over; assignment [of incorporeal property]
— d'une créance	21	transfer of a debt
transporter *vb*	22	1 to transport, carry, remove
	23	2 [Lég.] to make over, transfer; to assign (rights)
transposer *vb*	24	to transpose, change the order or position of
travail *m*	25	work
être au —	26	to be at —
heures de —	27	—ing hours
le Ministère du Travail	28	The Ministry of Labour
sans —	29	without a job, out of —, unemployed
— à forfait	30	job —
— à la chaîne	31	flow production
— à la pièce	32	piece —
— bâclé	33	slapdash —
— en série	34	mass production

— manuel	1	manual —
— soigné, beau —	2	fine —manship
pl. travaux	3	Works Ahead
— forcés	4	hard labour
— ménagés	5	house—
travailler vb	6 1	to work
	7 2	to stir up, to upset, to worry
— la terre	8	to till the land
— sans dételer	9	to work unremittingly
treizième adj	10	thirteenth
un — mois	11	bonus
Trésor m	12	Treasury
Bon du —	13	— Bill
trésorerie f	14	treasury
trésorier, -ère n	15	treasurer
tri m	16	[courrier] sorting
triage m	17	classification; selection; sorting (of mail)
gare de —	18	[G.B.] marshalling yard
	19	[Amér.] classification/freight yard
tribunal m	20	court, tribunal
comparaître devant un —	21	to appear in court, to go before a tribunal, to stand trial
— de Commerce	22	Commercial Court
— de police	23	Police court
trier vb	24	[courrier] to sort out
trié sur le volet	25	carefully selected, hand-picked
trieur, -se n	26	sorter
trimestre m	27	term, quarter
trimestriel, -le adj	28	quarterly
tripatouiller vb	29	to tamper with; to paw (over); [sabrer] to make drastic cuts in a text
triple n.m. & adj	30	triple, threefold; treble; three times (as much)
tripler vb	31	to triple, treble
triplicata m	32	triplicate
tripoter vb	33	[Péj.] to mess (about), [se mêler de] to dabble in, meddle with, [faire des opérations malhonnêtes] to tamper with

218

troc *m*	*1*	barter, swap
trombone *m*	*2*	paper clip
trompe-le-fisc *n.m.*	*3*	tax-avoidance device; tax-dodger
tronçon *m*	*4*	[route, voie ferrée] section
tronquer *vb*	*5*	[la version d'un film] to mutilate
troquer *vb*	*6*	to barter, swap
trousse *f*	*7*	case, kit
truc *m*	*8*	trick, knack, gimmick
trucage *m*	*9*	faking
truchement *m*	*10*	go-between, intermediary
par le — de	*11*	through, with the help of
T.S.V.P. (Tournez, s'il vous plaît)	*12*	P.T.O. (Please turn over)
tutelle *f*	*13*	protection, guardianship; [mandat] trusteeship
tuteur, -rice *n*	*14*	guardian
tuyau *m*	*15*	1 pipe, tube, hose
	16	2 tip, inside information
ultérieur *adj*	*17*	subsequent, later
séance reportée à une date —e	*18*	meeting postponed to a later date
ultimatum *m*	*19*	ultimatum
ultime *adj*	*20*	last, final
unanime *adj*	*21*	unanimous
unanimité *f*	*22*	unanimity
être élu à l'—	*23*	to be elected unanimously
unifier *vb*	*24*	to unify, streamline
union *f*	*25*	1 union, association; society
	26	2 unity, agreement
	27	3 marriage
l'Union postale universelle (U.P.U.)	*28*	Universal Postal Union (U.P.U.)
unique *adj*	*29*	only, single, sole, the only one
être fils —	*30*	to be an only son
rue à sens —	*31*	one-way street
unité *f*	*32*	1 unity, concord
	33	2 unit
— de longueur/poids	*34*	unit of length/weight
urbanisme *m*	*35*	town-planning
urgence *f*	*36*	need, urgency; emergency

H

convoquer d'—	1	to call an emergency meeting
en cas d'—, appeler ...	2	in case of emergency, call ...
état d'—	3	state of emergency
urne f	4	1 urn 2 ballot box
usage m	5	1 custom, practice
	6	2 use
	7	3 wear, usage
à l'— de	8	for, designed for
faire un bon — (de)	9	to last long, wear well
hors d'—	10	out of order
pour l'— externe	11	for external use only
usine f	12	plant, factory, works
à l'—	13	in the factory; ex works
usufruitier m	14	tenant for life
vacance f	15	1 *sing.*: vacancy
	16	2 *pl.*: holiday(s)
vacant adj	17	vacant, empty
place —e	18	vacancy
vacations n.f.pl.	19	(notary) fee
vain adj	20	vain, empty, futile, useless
de —es promesses	21	empty promises
de —s efforts	22	futile efforts
valable adj	23	valid
(billet) — un mois	24	(ticket) good for one month
des raisons —s	25	sound reasons
une excuse —	26	a — excuse
valeur f	27	1 value, worth
	28	2 stocks and shares, security
... de valeur	29	valuable
envoyer (une lettre) en — déclarée	30	to insure (a letter)
la — locative d'une maison	31	the rental value of a house
mettre en —	32	1 to show to advantage
	33	2 to develop (land)
objets de —	34	valuables
sans (aucune) —	35	of no value, trashy
— comptable	36	book value
— de rachat	37	surrender value
—s actives	38	assets
—s à revenu fixe	39	fixed yield securities
—s aurifères	40	gold shares

—s cuprifères	1	copper shares
—s de père de famille/de tout repos	2	gilt-edged securities, gilts
—s immobilières	3	real estate; fixed property
—s immobilisées	4	fixed assets
—s minières	5	mining shares
—s mobilières	6	transferable securities
—s passives	7	liabilities
—s pétrolières	8	oil shares
valider *vb*	9	to validate (a passport)
valoir *vb*	10	to be worth, equal
à —	11	on account
faire —	12	1 to use to advantage
	13	2 to claim (expenses)
vapeur *n*	14	1 *f*: steam
	15	2 *m*: steamer, steamboat, steamship
veilleur *m*	16	watchman, guard
— de nuit	17	night guard, watchman
vendable *adj*	18	saleable, marketable
vendange *f*	19	grape harvest
faire les —s	20	to pick the grapes
vendeur, -se *n*	21	salesman, saleswoman, shop-assistant
vendre *vb*	22	to sell
à —	23	for sale, to be sold
— à découvert	24	to bear the market; to sell short
— au détail	25	to retail
— aux enchères	26	— by auction
— en gros	27	to wholesale
vente *f*	28	sale
comptoir de —	29	overseas agency
en — chez/à ...	30	obtainable at, on — at
mettre en —	31	to put on —
salle des —s	32	auction room
— à crédit	33	credit —
— à découvert	34	bear/short —
— à forfait	35	outright —
— à l'amiable	36	private deal
— à la consommation	37	duty-paid/ex-bond —
— à réméré	38	— with option of repurchase
— à tempérament	39	hire purchase, instalment selling

— à terme	1	time-payment —; credit —; forward —, — for the account
— à terme ferme	2	— for future delivery during specified period
— au comptant	3	cash —
— aux enchères	4	auction —
— contre remboursement	5	C.O.D.
— de la main à la main	6	private/unrecorded —
— facile	7	ready/quick —
— ferme	8	firm —
— judiciaire	9	judicial/compulsory —
— par soumission	10	— by tender
— pour cause de départ	11	removal —
— pour cessation de commerce	12	winding up —
— réclame	13	bargain —
verdict *m*	14	verdict
rendre un —	15	to return a —
vérificateur *m*	16	auditor; inspector (of weights & measures)
vérification *f*	17	auditing (of accounts), checking
— par épreuves	18	spot check
vérifier *vb*	19	to verify, check, to audit; [s'assurer que] to make sure (that)
véritable *adj*	20	real, genuine
or —	21	real gold
vérité *f*	22	truth, fact
versement *m*	23	payment, instalment; deposit
en plusieurs —s	24	by instalments
un premier —	25	a down payment
verser *vb*	26	[argent] to deposit, pay (in)
On — cette somme à votre compte	27	This sum will be paid into your account
— un appel de fonds	28	to pay a call
— une cotisation	29	to subscribe
viager, -ère *adj*	30	limited to one's lifetime, for life
rente viagère	31	life annuity
vide *n.m. & adj*	32	1 vacuum; void
	33	2 empty, vacant
(bateau, camion revenant) à —	34	(ship/lorry returning) empty

une place —	1	a vacant seat
vie *f*	2	life
gagner sa —	3	to earn one's living
le coût de la —	4	the cost of living
vignette *f*	5	label
vigueur *f*	6	force, vigour
cesser d'être en —	7	to lapse
Cette loi est toujours en —	8	This law is still in force
entrer en —	9	to take effect, come into force
mettre une loi en —	10	to enforce a law
violation *f*	11	violation, infringement
violer *vb*	12	[loi, règlement] to break, infringe
	13	[domicile] to trespass
— un accord	14	to break an agreement
— un serment	15	to violate an oath
virement *m*	16	transfer, bank transfer
virer *vb*	17	to transfer (a sum)
virgule *f*	18	comma
six — cinq (6,5)	19	six point five (6·5)
viser *vb*	20	1 to aim (at)
	21	2 to direct, allude to
	22	3 to initial, countersign
— une facture	23	to initial or stamp an invoice (as authentication)
visite *f*	24	1 visit, call
	25	2 inspection, examination
la — des bagages	26	luggage inspection
passer une — médicale	27	to have a medical examination
vitesse	28	speed
par grande —	29	by fast passenger train, by express service
par petite —	30	by slow/goods train,[Amér.] slow train
vitrine *f*	31	shop window
vivres *n.m.pl.*	32	supplies, rations
couper les — à qqun	33	to starve s.o. out, to cut off s.o.'s supplies
vœu *m*	34	wish
Avec mes meilleurs —x	35	With my best —es
Nos —x vous accompagnent	36	We — you well
vogue *f*	37	fashion

être en —	1	to be popular, be in —
voie f	2	way
en — d'achèvement	3	nearing completion
les —s navigables	4	water — s
par la — des airs	5	by air
par — de terre	6	by land, overland
se livrer à des —s de fait	7	to use violence
— de chargement	8	goods siding
voirie f	9	1 garbage dump
	10	2 the Highways Department, department of public roads
voiture f	11	(motor-)car, carriage
voix f	12	1 voice 2 vote
avoir — prépondérable	13	to have the deciding vote
— prépondérante	14	casting vote
vol m	15	1 flight; flying time
	16	2 theft, robbery
— à la tire	17	pickpocketing
— à main armée	18	armed robbery
— sans escale	19	non-stop flight
volonté f	20	1 will
	21	2 desires, wishes
à —	22	at will, on tap
dernières —s	23	last wishes
volume m	24	1 volume, tone
	25	2 volume, bulk
vote m	26	vote; voting, ballot
droit de —	27	right of vote
passer au —	28	to vote on
— à main levée	29	a show of hands
voter vb	30	to vote
— une loi	31	to pass a law
vouloir vb	32	to wish, want
Veuillez ...	33	Please ...
Veuillez me faire savoir ...	34	Kindly let me know ...
voyage m	35	trip, journey
agence de —	36	travel agency
chèque de —	37	traveller's cheque
— d'affaires	38	business trip
être en —	39	to be away, be on a trip
voyageur m	40	traveller
commis —	41	travelling salesman
vrac m	42	loose
en —	43	in bulk

wagon *m*	*1*	wagon
— de marchandises	*2*	goods —, [Amér.] freight car
— de première classe	*3*	pullman
— -lit	*4*	sleeping-car
— -restaurant	*5*	dining-car

IMPERIAL WEIGHTS AND MEASURES

Linear Measure

12 inches	. . . .	1 foot
3 feet	. . . .	1 yard
22 yards	. . :	1 chain
10 chains (220 yards)	. .	1 furlong
8 furlongs (1,760 yards)	. .	1 mile

Weight (Avoirdupois)

16 ounces	. . . .	1 pound
14 pounds	. . . .	1 stone
8 stones (112 pounds)	. .	1 hundredweight
20 hundredweights (2,240 pounds)	. . . .	1 ton

METRIC WEIGHTS AND MEASURES

Linear Measure

10 millimetres .	. .	1 centimetre
100 centimetres	. .	1 metre
1,000 metres .	. .	1 kilometre

Weight

1,000 milligrams	. .	1 gram
1,000 grams .	. .	1 kilogram

IMPERIAL AND METRIC EQUIVALENTS

Linear Measure (Metric to Imperial)

1 centimetre .	. .	0·3937 inch
1 metre	. . .	39·37 inches
1 kilometre .	. .	0·621 mile

Linear Measure (Imperial to Metric)

1 inch .	. . .	2·54 centimetres
1 foot .	. . .	30·48 centimetres
1 yard .	. . .	0·914399 metre
1 mile .	. . .	1·609 kilometres

Weight (Avoirdupois) (Metric to Imperial)

1 gram	. . .	0·03527 ounce
1 kilogram	. . .	2·2046 pounds

Weight (Avoirdupois) (Imperial to Metric)

1 ounce	. . .	28·35 grams
1 pound	. . .	0·45359 kilogram
1 hundredweight .	. .	50·8 kilograms
1 ton .	. . .	1,016 kilograms

ENGLISH-FRENCH INDEX

Note : the figure before the hyphen refers to the page number, the italic figure after to the phrase number

advantage, 22-*38*; 128-*14*; 158-*1*
  take — of, 158-*3*; 173-*1*; 176-*33*
  use to —, 221-*12*
advantageous, 176-*31*
  find it — to, 54-*13*
adverse, 159-*23*
advertise, 179-*20*; 185-*16*
advertisement, 12-*32/34*; 185-*13*
advertiser, 13-*1*
advertising, 179-*18*; 185-*13*
  — agency, 33-*22*
  — agent, 13-*1*
  — pillar, 8-*33*
advice, 23-*20/32*; 59-*6*; 61-*18*; 185-*30*
  do something on legal —, 59-*13*
advisable, 128-*16*; 185-*28*
advise, 23-*33*; 186-*2*
  unless —d to the contrary, 23-*32*
advisory, 61-*15*
advocate, 24-*1*
advocate (*vb*), 169-*11*
aerial, 7-*25*
aero, 7-*31*
aerodynamic, 7-*33/34*
aeronautics, 7-*36/37*
affect (*vb*), 215-*3*
  it —s your interests, 54-*32*
affectation, 184-*30*
affidavit, 21-*7*; 73-*8*; 73-*12*
affiliation, 13-*29*
affix (*vb*) (a seal), 14-*25*
afloat, be —, 109-*33*
aforesaid, 132-*27*; 209-*1*
against, 62-*30*
age, of —, 139-*26*
agency, 9-*11/16*; 9-*19*; 154-*35*; 193-*25*
  collecting —, 25-*31*
  employment/staff —, 33-*20*; 176-*35*
agenda, 154-*31*; 176-*35*
agent, 9-*21/28*; 51-*16*; 79-*35*; 140-27
  customs —, 9-*26*; 51-*17*
  shipping/forwarding —, 51-*18*; 102-*34*
aggregate, 214-*31*
ago, 85-*33*
agrarian, 9-*41*   [119-*32*
agree, 34-*33*; 55-*28*; 59-*17*; 65-*33*;
  — to, 10-*6*
  — on/upon, 6-*20*; 64-*18*
  unless otherwise —d, 64-*26*
agreement, 2-27; 6-*19*; 16-*10*; 52-*31*;
    219-*26*
  animal —, 62-*7*
  break an —, 223-*14*
  clauses of —, 64-*24*
  come to an —, 214-*17*
  conclude an —, 62-*26*
  reach an —, 52-*32*
  social —, 64-*25*
  verbal —, 64-*23*
agricultural, 10-*8/11*
aground, ship —, 201-*2*
  run —, 90-*5*
aid, 10-*12*; 143-*9*
aim, 33-*37/39*; 223-20

aircraft, 7-*38*; 183-*16*
airfield, 7-*32*
airlift, 7-*29*
airline, 7-27
  — terminal, 7-*35*
airmail, 23-*18*; 156-*26*
Air ministry, 145-*34*
airplane, 7-*39*; 23-*17*
airport, 7-*40*
air service, 7-*30*
airway, — bill, 7-*26*; 133-*35*
alderman, 90-*1*
alibi, 10-*28/31*;
alien, 100-*29*
alienate, 10-*33*
alienation, 10-*32*
alimony, 161-*1*
aliquot, 11-*2/3*
all, 215-*13*; 215-*19/22*
allege, 11-*7*
alleviate, 11-*6*
alleviation, 11-*4*
  — of taxation, 11-*5*
alliance, 60-*16*
allocate, 11-*12*
allocation, 11-*8*
allot, 78-*38*; 192-*18*
allotment, 6-*27*; 18-*4*; 21-*14*; 192-*19*
  on — (shares), 192-*20*
allow, 30-*23/25*; 52-*21*; 74-*24*; 173-20
  — a discount, 98-*21*
allowance, 30-*21*; 124-*15*; 172-*12/17*;
    180-*34*; 190-*3*; 214-*13*
  due — being made, 177-*11*; 215-*18*
  make — for, 157-*34*
  personal —, 1-*9*
allude, 223-*21*
alphabetical, 11-*17/18*
alter, 147-*13*; 208-*10*; 217-*9*
alteration, 11-*21*; 147-*12*; 208-*7*
  marginal —, 192-*3*
alternate, 11-*22*
amend (*vb*), 147-*13*
amendment, 11-*37*; 23-*11*
amends, 192-*12*; 200-*7*
amortization, 12-*7*
amortize, 12-*5*
amount, 147-*38*; 180-*6*; 180-*11*; 211-*26*
  — due, 203-*28*
  fair —, 140-*10*
  in small —s, 180-*10*
amount (*vb*), 147-*42*
  — to, 91-*27*; 197-*4*
anchorage, 12-*17*; 148-*20*
animated, 12-*18*
annex, 12-*29/31*
annexes, 79-*4*
announce, 157-*35*
announcement, 12-*32*; 133-*33*
annual, 13-*2*; 62-*27*; 129-*11*; 194-*35*
annuitant, 191-27
annuity, 13-*3/5*; 160-*42*; 161-*3*; 191-*24*;
    222-*31*
annulment, 194-*34*; 198-*28*

anonymous, 13-*8*
answer, 193-*8/10*; 193-*12*; 200-*9*
answerable, 195-*16*; 203-*16*
anticipate, 13-*16*; 97-*4*; 98-*24*; 173-*4/19*
anticipation, 13-*15/16*
  in — of, 173-*15*
anticipative, 13-*12*
apiece, 162-*30*; 162-*37*
apparatus, 13-*23*; 155-*6*
appeal, 14-*5*; 168-*13*; 186-*18*
  court of —, 14-*2*
  without —, 195-*21*
appeal (*vb*), 168-*16*
  — against a judgement, 154-*5*
  — to s.o., 185-*23*
appear, 51-*38*; 108-*23*; 156-*30*; 195-*22*
  — before a court, 52-*1*
appearance (Leg.), 52-*3*
append, 12-*31*
  — a signature, 14-*25*
appendix, 12-*29*; 14-*7*
appliance, 13-*23/26*
applicable, be — to, 14-*15*, 14-*17*
applicability, 42-*3*
applicant, 128-*9*; 204-*26*
application, 77-*13*
  — (shares), 204-*29*; 204-*31*
  — receipt, 184-*10*
apply (*vb*), 14-*13*; 77-*11*
  — as of right, 214-*8*
  — for a job, 168-*3*
  — for excess shares, 214-*9*
  — to, 191-*17*
appoint, 18-*8*; 151-*3*
  — an heir, 127-*12*; 207-*5*
appointed, 21-*12*
appointment, 94-*32*; 96-*30*; 190-*30*
  by —, 21-*13*
  by — to H.R.H., 112-*29*
  make an —, 190-*31*
apportion, 192-*18*
apportionment, 192-*19*
appraisal, 99-*15*; 101-*2*; 103-*15*
appraise, 101-*3*
appraiser, 99-*14*; 174-*22*
apprenticeship, 14-*27/29*
appropriate, 177-*20*
appropriate (*vb*), 14-*33*; 57-*23*; 169-*28*
  — (a sum), 8-*26*
appropriation, 14-*31*; 57-*21*; 169-*26*
  — of the profit, 192-*21*
  — of a sum, 8-*23*
approval, 14-*30*; 199-*24*
  goods on —, 56-*21*
  on —, 99-*1*
approve, 15-*1/2*; 17-*34*; 119-*32*; 182-*35*; 199-*28*
aptitude, 85-*1*
arbitral, 53-*4*
arbitration, 15-*13/15*; 15-*17/19*
arbitrator, 15-*20*
  —'s award, 73-*3*
arbitrary, 116-*43*
arcade, 158-*31*

archives, 15-*23*
area, 10-*20*; 61-*21*; 201-*13*
argue (*vb*), 77-*30*
argument, 84-*22*
arise (*vb*) from, 175-*35*; 178-*32*
arithmetic, 35-*27*
arose, this never — before, 171-*20*
arraignment, 131-*24*
arrange (*vb*), 16-*14*; 54-*35*; 84-*33*; 85-*5*
arrangement, 2-*22*; 11-*32*; 16-*10*; 84-*37*; 85-*3*; 216-*35*
arrears, 16-*18*
  in —, 16-*28*; 196-*5*
arrest, 62-*14*
arrival, 17-*1*
arrive, 17-*4*
  as soon as he —s, 81-*4*
  — at one's destination, 82-*4*
  — safely, 17-*6*
  — unexpectedly, 208-*30*
arson, 123-*23*
article, 17-*12*; 17-*16*; 17-*26*; 152-*5*; 176-*15*
  —s of association, 206-*25/26*
  returned —, 132-*14*
ascending, 147-*39*
ascertain, 60-*22*
ascertainment, 60-*19*
ascribe (*vb*) to, 18-*7*; 172-*32*
ask (inquire), 95-*13*
  — for, 77-*14*; 197-*1*
  — for an interview, 129-*1*
  — questions, 180-*23*
aspect, 104-*14*; 105-*17*
assembly, — line, 41-*29*
assent, 17-*33*; 59-*15*; 199-*24*
  royal —, 199-*27*
assess, 101-*3*; 210-*36*
assessable, 210-*28*   [*29/30*
assessment, 99-*15*; 101-*2*; 192-*19*; 210-proportional —, 48-*29*
asset, a new —, 4-*15*
assets, 4-*41*; 14-*22/24*; 143-*1*; 143-*3*; 198-*12*; 220-*38*
  — pledged as collateral, 5-*3*
  — side, 5-*5*
  available —, 198-*13*
  blocked/frozen —, 24-*6*
  fixed —, 5-*2*; 121-*36*; 221-*4*
assign, (rights), 217-*23*
  — (a sum), 8-*26*
assignee, 41-*27*; 209-*9*
assignment, 18-*4*; 21-*14*; 41-*26*; 76-*18*; 146-*31*; 209-*18*; 217-*20*
  (of a person), 8-*24*
assignor, 40-*22*
assistance, 55-*29*
  give invaluable —, 63-*30*; 139-*14*
assistant, 6-*22*; 10-*13*; 207-*30*
  — accountant, 10-*14*
  — manager, 6-*23*; 205-*10*
associate (*vb*), 18-*21*
association, 18-*13/17*; 60-*16*; 118-*3*; 154-*35*; 219-*25*; 202-*21*

assortment, 18-*24*
assume (*vb*), 18-*30*; 93-*25*
— (responsibility), 94-*25*
assumed, 93-*20*
assurance, 18-*33*
assured, 20-*11*
attach (*vb*), 20-*24*; 199-*1*
attachable, 199-*3*
attaché (commercial), 20-*23*
attachment, 198-*32*
— against securities, 154-*7*
attempt (*vb*), 98-*38*; 211-*35*
attend (*vb*), 18-*11/12*
attendance book, 187-*31*
— fee, 130-*18*; 171-*13*
attendant, 155-*23*
attention, 14-*9*; 21-*1/3*
attest (*vb*), 211-*10*
attitude, adopt an —, 7-*6/7*
attorney, 140-*27*; 176-*7*
attract (*vb*), 21-*9/10*
attributable, 123-*5*
attribute, characteristic —, 178-*5*
attribute (*vb*), 172-*31*
auction, 70-*2*
— room, 221-*32*
— sale, 222-*4*
by — 221-*26*
disposal by —, 6-*25*
Dutch —, 93-*36*
public —, 70-*3*; 93-*34*
auctioneer, 51-*4*; 174-*22*
audit (*vb*), 222-*19*
auditing, 222-*17*
audition, 21-*17/18*
auditor, 222-*16*
auditorium, 199-*12*
auspices, 21-*32*
authentic, 110-*8*
author, 119-*29*
authoritatively, 22-*10*
authority, 22-*14/15*; 44-*7*; 168-*18*
have on good —, 204-*24*
on the — of, 76-*19*
authorization, 22-*4/13*; 199-*24*
authorize (*vb*), 133-*12*; 199-*28*
—d (person), 110-*28*
automatic, 21-*37*
— timekeeper, 120-*8*
automatically, 153-*19*
automation, 21-*36*
avail, — oneself of, 173-*1*
of no —, 196-*2*
available/availability, 84-*29/31*
— funds, 84-*30*
average, 148-*30*; 148-*35*
on an —, 148-*37*
await, 20-*32/39*
— further developments, 215-*12*
award, 120-*4*
make an —, 201-*24*
award (*vb*), 11-*12*; 174-*7*
away, be —, 224-*39*
do — with, 208-*2*

back, 86-*29*; 167-*35*
be —, 196-*16*
go far—, 70-*37*
back (*vb*), 142-*10*
— out, 186-28
— s.o., 163-*18*
backer, 86-*27*
background 13-*10*; 24-*15*; 70-*17*; 164-*4*
backward, 16-*29*; 196-*35*
backwards, 183-*33*; 196-*35*
bail (go — for), 40-*14*
bailiff, 120-*27*
baker, 159-*29*
— 's dozen, 87-*26*
balance, 14-*16*; 16-*30*; 30-*19*; 24-*38*;
25-*1/9*; 189-*9*; 195-*31*; 203-*6*
adverse — of trade, 25-*2*
— brought forward, 27-*25*
— due, 387-*10*
— of payments, 25-*5*
— sheet, 28-*21/34*
credit —, 203-*8*
debit —, 203-*9*
favourable — of trade, 24-*39*
on —, 215-*23*
trial —, 25-*6*
balance (*vb*) 25-*10/11*
— an account, 54-*10*
— books, 48-*10*
bale, 25-*12/13*; 31-*4/5*
ball, 28-*35*
— bearing, 28-*36*; 198-*14*
— point pen, 28-*37*
ballast, 133-*23/24*; 133-*26*
ballot, 33-*14*; 200-*35*; 224-*26*
— box, 220-*4*
ban, 178-*18*
banishment, 102-*24*
bank, 25-*16/17*; 25-*22*; 26-*4*; 26-*10/11*;
54-*27*
— book, 38-*19*
— charges, 113-*11*
— rate, 98-*22*
— holiday, 31-*16*; 131-*6*
discount —, 54-*28*
savings —, 35-*6*
bank up (*vb*), 189-*14*
bankrupt, 106-*11/14*
be declared —, 106-*15*
—'s estate, 106-*18*
discharged —, 106-*12*
go —, 79-*33*; 106-*16*
bankruptcy, 26-*5/9*; 106-*14*
— petition, 106-*20*
opening of — proceedings, 106-*19*
barber shop, 199-*18*
bargain, 185-*14*
bargain (*vb*), 142-*5*
— for account, 212-*12*
barratry, 26-*12*
barred, — by statute of limitation, 171-*10*
barrel, 26-*15*; 26-*22*; 214-*26*
barrel (*vb*), 26-*17*
barring, 200-*12/13*

book (seats) (*vb*), 138-*11*; 194-*30*
　—ed up, 33-*32*
bookbinder, 189-*8*
bookkeeper, 53-*13*
bookkeeping, 53-*7/12*; 136-*37*; 212-*3*
booklet, 137-*2*
bookmark, 202-*2*
bookpost, 25-*21*
bookshop, 134-*34*
boom, 58-*26*
boost, — an article, 148-*27*
booth (telephone), 211-*5*
　— keeper, 141-*33*
border, 57-*17*
bore (of barrel), 161-*7*
born (of), 129-*25*
borrow, 93-*24*
borrower, 93-*27*
boss, 159-*31*
　one's own —, 177-*30*
botch, 102-*30*
bottom, 26-*23*
bound, 135-*9*; 152-*13*
　— by agreement, 135-*13*
　— for, 82-*5*; 157-*41*
bounties, — on production, 173-*36*
boutique, 147-*7*
bow (vb), 164-*31*
　— to facts, 101-*10*
box, 29-*38*; 30-*1*; 101-*1*
　Post Office —, 31-*27*
boycott, 31-*26*
bracing (construction), 60-*6*
bracket, 157-*6*
　in —s, 157-*7*
brake, 114-*5*
branch, 54-*26*; 85-*27*; 207-*12/13*
branch (*vb*) out, 182-*6*
brand, 142-*39*
breach (of contract), 62-*28*; 198-*28*
　— of close, 32-*8*
　— of regulations, 125-*24*
　— of trust, 173-*2*
bread and butter, (that is his —), 114-*30*
break (*vb*), 39-*22*; 94-*29*; 198-*1*; 217-
　10; 223-*12*; 223-*14*
　— a will, 39-*23*
　— even, 113-*6*
　— into one's capital, 95-*32*
　— off, 159-*40*
　— one's oath, 157-*17*
　— one's word, 141-*11*; 157-*22*
　— open a door, 166-*21*
　— out, 73-*18*
　— the seals, 134-*14*
breakable, 39-*20*
breakage, 39-*21*
breakdown, 73-*25*; 155-*36*
breaking-in, (of motor), 197-*28*
　— off, (relations/negotiations), 198-*28*
breath, 118-*12*
breezeway, 159-*2*
brew, 31-*31/34*
bribe, 3-*34*; 204-*7*

brick-works, 32-*6*
bridge, 166-*4*
bridle, 114-*5*
bring, 166-*28*; 166-*30*
　— about, 82-*34*; 152-*22*; 208-*34*
　— about a change, 153-*40*
　— an action, 131-*43*
　— back, 182-*3*; 182-*26*
　— down (a figure), 1-*6*
　— forward, 193-*19*
　— in, 182-*20*
　— out, 75-*28/29*
　— pressure on s.o., 172-*7*
　— to a successful issue, 108-*37*
　— up to date, 131-*9*
bringing together (reconciliation), 182-*31*
brink, on the —, 30-*28*
Britain, Great —, 116-*33*
British, 61-*10*; 160-*1*
　— Isles, 121-*15*
brittle, 112-*36*
broach (*vb*), 161-*9*
broadcast, 92-*31*
broadcast (*vb*), 181-*20*
brochure, 32-*14*
brokerage, 68-*17*
brush (*vb*) aside, 88-*31*; 88-*36*
budget, 32-*31/39*; 33-*1/8*
build, 27-*13*
　— a connection, 69-*38*
　— (reserves), 186-*17*
　— up, 89-*1*
builder, 96-*14*
building, 27-*11*; 61-*1*; 121-*27*; 121-*31*;
　159-*41*; 161-*17*
　— contractor, 27-*12*
　— licence, 61-*2*
　— material, 143-*7*
　— plot/site, 27-*14*, 212-*22*
　— society, 202-*29*
　— up of reserves, 111-*16*
bulk, 143-*1*; 224-*25*
　in —, 43-*22*; 143-*2*; 224-*43*
bull, 118-*22*
　— position, 4-*1*
　— purchase/purchaser, 73-*27/28*
bulletin, 33-*9*
bullion, 135-*30*
bunch, 31-*4/5*
bundle, 31-*4/5*; 106-*31*; 134-*19*; 156-*23*
bunk (boat), 66-*19*
bunker, 42-*34*
burden, 43-*1*
　— of taxation, 109-*16*
burden (*vb*), 94-*13*; 117-*30*
bureaucracy, 33-*36*
burglary, 36-*15/17*
burn, 42-*35*
　— one's bridges, 32-*23*
bushel, 29-*36/37*
business, 7-*41/42*; 8-*8/22*; 50-*9/32*;
　68-*6*; 96-*15*; 144-*32*; 150-*13*; 152-
　25; 176-*21*
　be in —, 50-*15*

choke, 100-27
chronicle, 45-32
chronologically, 47-15
cipher, 48-17; 44-38/40
circle, 198-5
  in —s, 198-7
circular, 46-17/19
circulate, 46-27
circulation, 46-21; 213-12
  — of money, 198-12
  — of paper, 213-13
  wide —, 192-9
circumstance, 46-7 et seq.
  in/under —s, 153-2
  —s outside one's control, 110-33
cistern, 47-1
citizen, become a British —, 149-10
citizenship, 149-9
city, 46-33
civil, 47-3
  — proceedings, 175-38
  — rights, 88-6
  — servant, 110-21
  dept. of — engineering, 116-2; 166-6
claim, 69-2; 124-17; 172-29; 185-12;
    196-39; 202-9; 213-38
  contested —, 69-11
  have a — on, 69-5
  notice of —, 185-12
  prior —, 169-18
  questionable —, 61-32
claim (vb), 172-28; 197-1; 185-20; 205-
    27
  — back, 193-5
  — damages, 77-17; 158-25
  — expenses, 221-13
claimant, 185-10
clarification, 146-19
clarify, 90-9; 144-40; 165-23
clash (vb) (with), 57-26
clasp, 9-38
class, 47-5/8; 67-28; 85-27
  evening —, 67-30
  in a — by itself, 56-7
  take —es, 67-25
classification, 218-17
classified, 47-9
classify, 165-23
classroom, 199-11
clause, 17-12; 47-22 et seq.; 85-2
  arbitration —, 53-5
clean, 150-20/23
clear, 134-37; 150-21
clear (vb), 84-21; 136-1; 179-26; 195-4;
    203-4/12
  — a deficit, 195-5
  — off a mortgage, 75-26; 76-2
  — oneself of, 132-7
  — through customs, 74-12; 87-3
  — up, 188-15
  make it —, 52-37
  make oneself —, 52-38
  — up a point, 90-9
clearance, 135-22

— of goods, 74-14
— sale, 135-35; 203-3
clearing, 47-28/29
  — house, 41-33; 52-7; 135-33
  — of road, 75-25
clerk, 50-34/37; 93-10
  — of the court, 117-15
  deputy/head —, 204-25
  junior —, 10-13
clever, 112-2
client, 47-34
clipping (newspaper), 66-33
clock, 119-7
clock (vb), 165-30
  — in/on, 165-31
  — out/off, 165-32
clock-maker, 120-9
  —wise, 201-21
close, 129-26
  — of the exchange, 48-9
close (vb), 48-1/13
  — an account, 48-3
  — a meeting, 200-37
closed/closing, 48-5/7
  — case, 47-10
close-up, 164-6
closet, 163-19
closing, 107-35
  — down, 107-36
  — time, 107-37
clothes, ready made —, 56-37
club, social —, 159-34
coal, 42-31/37; 120-18
  — measure, 116-14
  — mine, 120-23
  — pit, 120-23
coast-guard, 115-23
coasting-trade, 34-7
coast-vessel, 115-23
coat, 141-12
code, 48-15 et seq.
  —d, 48-22
cognizance, 58-30; 98-16
coin, 78-18; 147-32; 162-27
  —s, 151-37
coin (vb) a word, 111-8
co-legatees, 58-19
collaborate, 56-8
collaborator, 48-39
collapse, 71-7; 76-3; 88-12
collapsible, 78-15
collateral, 49-1; 114-23
colleague, 48-39; 49-4
collect (vb), 161-12; 196-36
  — funds, 93-32
  — mail, 134-12
collecting, — agency, 25-31
collection, 93-29/30; 161-11; 174-19;
    186-22
  the last —, 134-6
  — of debts/bills, 184-17
collector (of tax), 184-21/23
colliery, 120-23
collusion (leg.), 49-7

colour, — scheme, 49-*19*
colourful, 148/*29*
colours, 159-*42*
column, 49-*9/13*
　financial —, 109-*8*
　social —, 67-*21*
combination, 49-*18*
combine (*vb*), 114-*21*; 130-*26*
　— work with pleasure, 130-*29*
combined, — deal, 135-*10*
come, 17-*4*; 178-*32*
　— alongside, 2-*35*
　— at the right moment, 165-*24*
　— back, 197-*3*
　— first, 70-*31*
　— from, 175-*35*
　— into the picture, 130-*21*
　— of age, 139-*27*
　— off, 95-*9*
　— out, 75-*28*; 156-*30*
　— to terms, 16-*17*
　— to the same thing, 107-*4*
　— true, 183-*26*
　— under, 189-*7*
　— under the provision of, 66-*22*
　— up, 171-*21*
coming, — of age, 140-*1 et seq.*
　— out, 203-*34*; 204-*1*
　— to an end, 108-*39*
comma, 223-*18*
command, 126-*1*
　a perfect — of, 167-*8*; 58-*29*
command (*vb*), 129-*3*; 171-*8*
commander, 194-*16*
comment, 55-*13*
commerce, 89-*2*
commercial, 50-*6/10*
　— firm/business, 50-*30*
　— court, 50-*31*
　— law, 48-*19*
commissary, 51-*1*
commission, 51-*5/5*; 68-*17*; 190-7
　charge —, 170-*3*
company, 202-*21*
　airline —, 51-*34/35*
　— law, 202-*22*
　financing —, 202-*26*
　form a —, 60-*26*
　holding —, 202-*25*
　investment —, 202-*27*
　joint stock —, 202-*30*
　limited —, 202-*23/24*; 13-*9*
　make a —, 51-*37*
　subsidiary —, 202-*28*
comparison, 51-*36/37*; 182-*32*
　in — with, 182-*23*
compel (*vb*), 152-*17*
compelled, 110-*34*
　be/feel — to, 150-*5*; 152-*9*
　— to, 152-*13*
compensate for (*vb*), 52-*8*; 74-*11*
compensation, 52-*5*; 124-*15 et seq.*; 192-
　12; 196-*33*; 74-*8/9*
　claim —, 24-*23*

compete (*vb*) (with), 56-*11/12*; 196-
　27
competence, 195-*19/23*; 88-*11*
　it is not within my —, 52-*13*
competency, 37-*3*; 52-*11*
competent, 52-*14*
competition, 56-*2/9*
　unfair —, 56-*10*
competitive, 52-*15*; 56-*15*
competitor, 56-*13*
complain (*vb*), 185-*19*
complaint, 117-*32*; 163-*40*; 185-*11*
complete, 113-*27*; 214-*31*; 127-*23*
complete (*vb*), 207-*31*
completed, 197-*15*
completely, 125-*12*
completion, nearing —, 224-*3*
compliance, 52-*16*
compliment, 119-*21*
　—s of the author, 119-*22*
complimentary, — clause, 111-*32*
　— ticket, 107-*23*
comply (*vb*) with, 58-*1*
compose (*vb*), 52-*26*; 111-*35*
composed of, 52-*29*
composition, 55-*19/23*
compounding, — interest, 30-*22*
compromise, 2-*22*; 216-*35*
compromise (*vb*), 16-*13*; 217-*12*
comptroller, — of the treasury, 64-*15*
compulsory, 152-*12*; 197-*22*
　— loan, 110-*34*
compute, 35-*33*
computer, 35-*31*
computor, 154-*26*
concede (*vb*), 6-*31*; 153-*6*; 186-*14*
concern, 109-*10*; 128-*13*
　no — of yours, 54-*31*
concern (*vb*), 13-*30/32*; 54-*30*; 215-*3*
　as far as I am —ed, 54-*34*
　for whom it may —, 54-*6*
　no — of yours, 54-*31*
concession, 55-*1/2*
　make a —, 55-*2*
concessionnaire, 55-*3*
conciliatory, 11-*38*
concise, — statement, 111-*29*
conclude, 55-*9*
　— an agreement, 62-*26*; 159-*16*
conclusion, 55-*14 et seq.*; 129-*26*; 196-*1*
　bring to a successful —, 143-*34*
conclusive, 55-*7*; 73-*1*; 175-*32*
concord, 219-*32*
concourse, 56-*3*
condition, 56-*18*; 100-*8*; 171-*4*
condition (*vb*), 56-*25*
conditionally, 56-*24*
conditions (terms), 177-*26*
condolence, 56-*27/28*
conduct, 143-*33*
conduct (*vb*), 116-*9*
conducting, 56-*31*
conductor (train), 44-*1*; 216-*6*
conductor (bus), 184-*22*

debtor, 72-*1*
  joint —, 72-*4*
deceit, 113-*40*
decent, 64-*16*
decide, 72-*33/34*; 195-*7*; 206-*22*; 114-*41*
  — peremptorily, 216-*33*
decimal, 72-*36*; 72-*38*
decision, 72-*35*; 73-*2*; 131-*22*; 157-*43*
decisive, 73-*1*
declaration, 73-*7*
  customs —, 73-*11*
  — of option, 193-*14*
declare, 73-*16*
  — an option, 193-*11*
decline, 188-*14*
decline (*vb*), 73-*23*; 109-*27/28*; 185-*32*;
  187-*21*
decrease, 12-*4*; 75-*37*; 187-*11*; 188-*14*
decree (leg.), 74-*3*; 129-*3*
decree nisi, 131-*23*
deduct, 74-*22*; 196-*31*; 123-*11*; 213-*19*
  — (from), 74-*23*
default, 52-*4*
  in — of, 2-*16*
default (*vb*), 74-*33*
defaulter, 160-*13*
defect, 74-*28*; 75-*4*
defective, 75-*3*
defence, 75-*9*
defend, 75-*6*; 205-*24*
defendant, 75-*5*; 124-*9*; 173-*10*
defer, 83-*36*
  — judgment, 209-*3*
  — payment, 20-*21/22*
deferred, — annuity, 83-*27*
  — payment, 89-*34*
  — share, 83-*26*
deficiency, 38-*10*; 132-*10*
deficit, 75-*13/16*
define (exactly), 169-*9*
  — powers, 77-*1*
definite, 109-*23*
definitive, 75-*17*
deflation, 75-*21*
defraud, 114-*2*
degree, 75-*34*; 165-*19*
  by —s, 75-*36*; 89-*31*
delay, without further —, 76-*6*; 190-*6*;
  196-*3*; 208-*27*
  — a decision, 73-*5*
delayed, 148-*1*
delegacy, 76-*17*
delegate, 76-*20*; 92-*28*
delegate (*vb*), 76-*21*; 80-*23*
delegation, 76-*16/17*
deletion, 183-*2*
deliberately, 127-*30*
deliberation, 76-*23*
delicate, 76-*25*
delicatessen, 42-*38*
delinquent, 77-*2*
deliver, 86-*9*; 136-*24*; 189-*24*

  — mail, 85-*10*
  — a speech, 177-*8*
deliverable, 136-*18*
delivery, 71-*24*; 136-*19*; 190-*4*
  — man, 137-*5*
  — order, 136-*21*
  awaiting —, 204-*10*
  fluent —, 71-*27*
  free —, 86-*8*; 136-*25*
  general —, 195-*30*
  letter —, 85-*13*; 105-*31*
  payable on —, 136-*27*
  special —, 104-*18*
  taking — of goods, 184-*14*
demand, 77-*7*; 150-*7*; 185-*12*; 196-*39*
  in —, 185-*1*
  on —, 171-*16*
demand (*vb*), 185-*22*; 194-*9*
demandable, 102-*23*
demonstrate, 78-*14*
demonstration, 78-*12*
  — course, 67-*29*
demonstrator, 78-*11*
demurrage (days of —), 208-*18*
  on —, 204-*10*
demurrer, 108-*35*
denial, 78-*16*
denomination, 66-*34*; 78-*24*
denunciation, 178-*17*
deny, 75-*7*
department, 31-*30*; 85-*27*; 183-*9*
  — of justice, 131-*42*; 145-*35*
  legal —, 33-*26*
  — stores, 138-*33*
departure, 157-40
dependency, 79-*2*
dependent, — persons, 43-*12*
deponent, 79-*25*
deport (*vb*), 79-*24*; 104-*23*
deportation, 79-*20*; 104-*25*
deportee, 79-*22*
deposit, 16-*26*; 40-*16/18*; 80-*2*; 179-*1*;
  222-*23*
  cash —, 80-*8*
  demand —, 80-*5*
  — book, 38-*24*
  — of minerals, 116-*12*
  luggage —, 60-*2*
  make a bank —, 80-*12*
  money —, 59-*34*; 60-*1*
  on —, 80-*11*
  pay a —, 4-*4*
deposit (*vb*), 222-*26*
  — a security, 79-*36*
  — money, 79-*29*
deposition, 79-*36*; 80-*4*
depositor, 79-*24*
depot, 80-*3*
depreciate (*vb*), 12-*2*; 80-*20*
depreciation, 23-*15/16*; 80-*19*
  — for wear and tear, 12-*4*
  — of premises, 12-*12*
  make a reserve for —, 168-*32*
depressed, 80-*22*

deprive (vb), 196-11; 213-19
— benefit, 176-32
— s.o. of his rights/shares, 72-32; 80-16
depute (vb), 80-23
deputize (vb), 190-16
deputy, 6-22; 190-13
— assistant, 207-6
derogate (vb), 80-33
derogation, 80-32
describe (vb), 81-17
description, 81-15; 201-33
deserve (to be), 84-4
design, 85-3; 177-4
finished —, 97-29
intent —, 177-17
designation, 81-15
designer, 81-30
desires, 224-21
desk, 201-8
— clerk, 184-15
pay at the —, 35-16
despatch, 79-1
despoiling, 80-14
destination, 82-3
arrive at one's —, 82-4
set out for a —, 82-7
destroy, — an edition, 163-8
detach (vb), 82-12
detail, 82-14/16
in —, 82-24; 144-10
— of account, 73-25
give —s, 82-27
detailed, 46-16; 82-25
detect (vb), 74-2
deteriorate (vb), 11-20
determination, 194-36
determine (vb), 82-33
detriment, 83-2; 169-22
detrimental, 151-28
detrimental to, 20-31; 81-29; 133-20; 169-25
develop (vb), 101-12; 220-33; 165-22
development, 83-14; 101-13; 104-27; 138-7
deviate (vb) (from), 88-37
device, 13-23
devise (vb), 55-5
devolve (vb) (upon), 124-2
diagram, 83-23; 116-37; 200-24
dial, 52-28
diamond, — like, 83-24
— cutting, 209-24
diary, 9-20; 131-11
differ (vb), 83-37
difference, 83-28/31
differential, 83-34
difficult, 76-25
— to believe, 140-9
difficulty, 77-29; 83-38
get s.o. out of —, 78-34
— in getting underway, 77-28
diminish (vb), 12-2; 74-4; 84-10; 187-12
diminution, 79-10

dining-car, 225-5
diploma, 31-36
direct, 155-1; 223-21
direction, 84-14; 124-33; 147-8; 201-19
directions (for use), 93-7; 147-9
director, 6-35; 84-12; 110-29; 168-21
film —, 183-22
managing —, 6-36; 84-13; 116-8
directory, 7-18
disadvantage, 83-2; 124-4
put at a —, 81-8
disagree, 2-33
disagreement, 83-31; 85-6
disaster, 71-7; 202-9
disburse (vb), 72-9
disbursements, 72-8
discharge, 4-16; 4-22; 134-26; 192-1
— of a debt, 12-10
discharge (vb), 82-8; 189-21; 192-5; 134-28
— ballast, 133-23
disclaim (vb), 75-8; 191-2
— responsibility, 78-22
disclaimer, 191-9
disclosure, 196-38
discontinue (vb), 208-2
discord, 85-28; 183-35; 185-31
discount, 98-18/23; 180-34; 187-11; 189-3; 193-17
to allow s.o. a —, 27-37; 30-23
— charge, 9-32
— or premium, 79-20
discover (vb), 73-34
discredit (vb), 84-15/16
discrepancy, 72-16; 83-28
discretion, 84-17; 84-19
discriminate (vb), 84-20
discriminating, 83-35
discriminatory, 83-35
discuss (vb), 71-18; 84-23
discussion, 84-22
disembarkation, 71-13
disencumber (estate), 76-2
disengage (vb), 134-31
disengaged, 134-36
disentangle (vb), 72-14
dishonest, 110-4
disinterested, 81-20
dismiss (vb), 58-12; 82-8; 135-6; 188-23; 189-21; 192-5; 197-16; 197-18
— a case, 78-3; 108-38
— an official, 197-18
disown (vb), 81-9/10; 190-34
dispatch, 79-1; 97-5; 102-36
— money, 173-37
— note, 103-2
with all possible —, 84-7
dispatch (vb), 97-9; 102-28
dispense (vb), 102-17
displacement, of, 79-14
display (of goods), 71-8; 100-1
display (vb), 104-10
displayed, 104-9

disposal, 84-*37*
  to have at one's —, 84-*34*
dispose of, 90-*23*
dispossess, 80-*1*
dispute, 61-*28/31*; 71-*15*; 136-*12*
  settle a —, 206-*23*
disregard (*vb*), 150-*12*
dissension, 85-*28*
dissent, 85-*6*
dissociate, 84-*26*
distance, 85-*7*; 216-*30*
  — covered, 157-*1*
distinct, 150-*21*
distinction, 120-*4*
distinguished, — visitor, 142-*41*
distrain, 199-*1*; 102-*4*
distrainable, 199-*3*; 126-*5*
distrainee, 72-*3*; 198-*31*
distrainer, 199-*4*
distraint, 62-*11*; 139-*19*; 198-*32*
distribute, 192-*18*
distribution, 85-*13*; 192-*19*
distributor, 85-*11*
district, 201-*13*
  postal —, 17-*11*
  — under a prefect, 169-*15*
disturb, 9-*36*
ditto, 121-*8*
divide, 74-*17*; 85-*24*; 192-*18*; 112-*35*;
  200-*27*
dividend, 85-*17*; 85-*23*
  cash —, 98-*35*
  — paid out of capital, 170-*1*
  — warrant, 66-*26*
  ex —, 66-*27*
  final —, 203-*10*
dividing, 85-*26*; 146-*33*
division, 85-*26/27*; 157-*38*
divisor, 85-*25*
divorce, 85-*29/30*
  — proceedings are taking place, 127-
  9
dock, 26-*33*; 85-*34*
  dry —, 35-*40*; 201-*1*
  floating —, 26-*39*
  tidal —, 26-*37*
  wet —, 26-*36*; 109-*32*
dock (*vb*), 27-*1/2*
docker, 85-*36*
docket (wages —), 30-*37*
document, 85-*37*; 86-*1*; 162-*29*; 111-*30*
document (*vb*) a statement, 86-*2*
dole, 11-*9*
domain, 86-*4*
domicile, 86-*6*
domicile (*vb*) a bill at bank, 86-*12*
domiciled, 86-*11*
doubt, 87-*21*
downfall, 71-*7*; 76-*3*
dowry, 4-*8*; 86-*32/34*
dozen, 87-*23*
  by the —, 87-*24*
draft, 23-*6*; 130-*15*; 140-*18*; 177-*4*;
  190-*5*; 216-*13/20*

revolving —, 91-*5*
rough —, 32-*18*
sight —, 91-*6*; 216-*18*
title —, 216-*15*
draft (*vb*), 55-*5*; 91-*21*
drafting, 187-*1*
drag, 137-*37*
  — out, 213-*29*
drain, 201-*2*
draughtsman, 81-*30*
draw, 123-*11*; 169-*28*; 213-*17/19*; 215-
  2
  — bill of exchange, 205-*7*
  — conclusions, 213-*28*
  — gun on s.o. at sight, 213-*25*
  — lots, 213-*27*
  — off, 205-*28*
  — plan, 134-*16*
  — s.o's attention to, 189-*12*
  — to an end, 213-*24*
  — up, 99-*23*; 102-*31*; 111-*35*; 187-
  5
  — up a document, 4-*40*
drawback, 87-*8*; 124-*4*
drawee, 213-*16*
drawer, 81-*30*; 204-*26*; 213-*32*
drawing, 213-*11*; 215-*24*
  — lots, 213-*15*
  — of money, 169-*26/27*
  — up, 187-*1*
  — up document, 99-*26*
dress, 211-*38*
  —making establishment, 68-*27*
  —making firm, 56-*39*
drill, 179-*24*
drive, 143-*33*
driver, 56-*30*
driving, 56-*31*
drop (*vb*), 112-*7*; 188-*14*
  — a line to, 148-*10*
  — an idea, 1-*7*; 191-*4*
  — anchor, 130-*15*; 148-*22*
  — fast, 76-*5*
  — in, 159-*12*
  — off (passenger), 79-*35*
drover, 56-*32*
drum, 26-*15*
drunk (and disorderly), 130-*4*
dry, 200-*40*
  — clean, 150-*24*
  — cleaning, 201-*3*
dubious, 11-*16*
due, 88-*18/19*
  fall —, 89-*22*; 90-*3*
  give each his —, 88-*21*
dues, 87-*29*; 187-*4*
  harbour —, 88-*8*
dummy, 140-*34*
duplicate, 88-*24*
  in —, 102-*8*
duplicate (*vb*), 166-*2*
duplicating, 194-*4*
  — machine, 88-*25*
duplication, 87-*17/18*

— fee, 126-*9*
main —, 96-*3*
entrust (*vb*), 43-*21*; 189-*24*
entrusted, 43-*16*
entry, 17-*12 et seq*; 90-*29*; 95-*36*
— form, 126-*10*
— in a register, 126-*8*
enumerate (*vb*), 78-*23*
envelope, 96-*31*; 164-*23*
in a sealed —, 164-*26*
environment, 145-*16*
envoy, 43-*17*; 92-*28*
equal, 221-*10*
other things being —, 177-*11*; 215-*18*
equal (*vb*), 91-*16*
equalize (*vb*), 91-*18*
equip, 86-*36*; 97-*37*; 148-*41*; 155-7
equipment, 11-*32*; 13-27; 97-*36*; 143-*9*
equity, 97-*39*
equivalence (of exchange), 157-*11*
equivalent, 63-22
eraser, 116-*41*
erasure, 183-2
erect, 98-*1*
errand, 77-*20*
erroneous, 107-*18*
error, 98-*3/5*; 107-*4*
— and omissions excepted, 98-7; 200-*16*
in —, 156-27
typing —, 107-*1*
escalator, 98-*13*
escape (*vb*), 101-*4*
— from, 205-*20*
essence, 99-*3*
establish (*vb*), 17-*35*; 60-*20*; 98-*1*;
99-*20*; 127-*11*
established, 99-*18*
establishment, 99-*25*; 127-*13*; 139-22
— of an award, 110-27
estate, 86-*4*
claim the —, 4-*39*
real —, 178-*4*; 221-*3*; 110-*13*; 121-
28/29; 121-*33/34*
total —, 143-*4*
esteem, 59-*28*; 99-*16*
in high —, 66-*10*
estimate, 83-*15*
annual —, 173-*18*
rough —, 13-*9*
estimate (*vb*), 101-*3*
— damages, 75-*33*
estimates, 32-*37*
estimation, 101-*2*
etcher, 117-*4*
Europe (Council of —), 59-*8*
evasion, 101-*4*
— of tax, 114-*1*
event, 153-*1*
eventful, 148-*29*
evict, 101-*11*; 104-*23*
eviction, 104-*25*
evidence, 172-*36/40*; 211-*7/10*
cumulative —, 106-*32*
documentary —, 175-*33*

evident, to be —, 195-*22*
evolution, 101-*13*
evolve, 101-*12*
exact, 101-*14*
— amount, 101-*18*
exactness, 197-*20*
examination, 56-*1*; 97-*19*; 223-*25*
cross —, 62-*10*
entrance —, 56-*4*
examine, 59-27; 126-*25*
— papers, 54-*29*
examining, 126-*9*
— board, 49-*3*
example, 202-*11*
for —, 102-*12*
exceed (*vb*) (a limit), 135-*23*
— one's power, 101-*32*
— orders, 155-*15*
exchange, 42-7
— prices, 144-22
— rate, 210-25
in — for, 196-*15*
excise, 63-*29*; 187-*23/24*
— office, 187-*23*
exclude (*vb*), 101-33
excluded, 88-*32/36*
exclusive, 101-*34*
— of, 54-*23*
— rights, 102-*1*
excuse, 102-*17*
valid —, 220-*26*
excused, 84-27
execute, — order, 102-*2*
executive, 34-*28*
executor, 102-*5*
exemplary, 102-*7*; 147-*11*
exempt, 113-*26*
— from, 102-*15/16*; 213-*1*
exempt (*vb*), 102-*17/25*
exempted, 84-*27*
exemption, 113-*30*
— from fee, 117-*2*
exert (an influence) (*vb*), 102-*18*
exhaust, 97-*26*
exhaustive, — cultivation, 103-*35*
exhibit, 64-*34*
exhibition, 104-*6*; 104-*18*; 199-*17*
world —, 104-*15*
exile, 102-*24*
exit, 129-*28*; 204-*1*
exonerate, 84-*21*; 102-*25*
exoneration, 72-*19*
exception, 101-*23*; 194-*20*
take — to, 186-*31*; 101-*27*
with the — of, 101-*24*
— to the rule, 101-*25*
exceptional, 101-*28*; 120-*14*
excerpt, 104-*37*
excess, 101-*19/30*; 208-*13/24*
— weight, 208-*9*
in —, 101-*20*
to —, 181-*34*
exchange (forward), 83-*19*
— control, 64-*3*

spot —, 83-*20*
stock —, 31-*8 et seq.*
exchange (*vb*), 161-*26*
— at par, 157-*10*
exorbitant, 120-*13*; 174-*34*
expand, 10-*3*; 104-*29*
expansion, 99-7; 102-*26*; 104-*26*
expect (*vb*), 20-*34 et seq.*
one might —, 181-*30*
expectations, contrary to all —, 62-*32*
expedient, 28-*5*
expedite, 1-*35*
expenditure, 79-*6*
expense, 43-*3*; 19-*10*; 79-*5/6*; 172-*11*
chargeable to an — account, 123-*7*
— account, 113-*18*
go to great —, 145-*3*
spare no —, 193-*30*
expenses, 113-*3 et seq.*
initial —, 99-*29*
living —, 113-*20*
sundry —, 85-*16*
travelling —, 79-*15*
working —, 103-*30*
expensive, 153-*34*
expensively, 113-*4*
experience, 103-*5*; 168-*26*
from —, 103-*9*
experience (*vb*), 103-7; 206-*34*
experienced, 103-*10*; 112-2
— in business, 198-*4*
experiment, 103-*6*
— with, 103-*11*
make an —, 103-*8*
expert, 103-*12*; 112-2; 205-*30*
expiration (of a policy), 72-*30*
expire, 103-*21*
expired, 161-*13*
explain, 90-*9*; 103-*24*; 104-*11*
explanation, 90-*10*
explanatory, 103-*22*
— note, 90-*10*
explicit, 111-*26*
explicitly, 104-*20*
exploiter, 103-*40*
exponent, 104-*7*
export, 104-2; 204-*1*
in the — business, 152-*32*
— bonus, 104-*4*
— trade, 104-*3*
export (*vb*), 104-*5*
exporter/exporting, 104-*1*
expose, — oneself to, 104-*12*
exposed to, 207-*28*
exposure (a house with a good —), 155-*2*
expound, 104-*11*
express, by — service, 223-*29*
— letters, 104-*19*
— train, 104-*17*; 182-*10*
express (*vb*), 111-*35*
— a desire to, 140-*32*
— an opinion, 92-*20*; 177-*9*
expropriate, 104-*22*
expropriation, 104-*21*

expulsion, 104-*25*
extend, 182-*6*; 191-*11*
extension, 177-*6*
external, 105-*4*
for — use only, 220-*11*
extort (from), 104-*33*
extra, 184-*24*; 208-*31*; 207 *et seq.*
extract, 104-*37*
extrajudicial, 105-*3*
extravagant, 120-*13*; 174-*34*
extrinsic, 105-*4*
eye-witness, 153-*9*; 211-*17*

fabric, 100-*25*; 213-*35*
— council, 105-*12*
fabricate (a story), 105-*16*
face, 105-*17/23*
— value, 105-*24*
facilitate, 107-*28*
facility, 105-*25*
facsimile, 105-*30*
fact, 106-*33*
positive —, 40-*40*
faction, 105-*33*
factor, 105-*32*
factory, 105-*10*; 220-*12/13*
facts, 101-*6*
fail, 1-*23*; 90-*6*; 141-7; 187-*21*
— to appear in court, 74-*33*
failing, 74-*29*; 107-*9*
failure, 74-*27*; 106-*13*; 108-*11*; 155-*36*
— of an experiment, 106-*17*
— to pay, 74-*30*
fair, 97-*38*; 110-*9*
faith, 110-*2*
have — in sth., 69-*4*
in good —, 110-*3*; 30-*15*
faithfully, yours —, 199-*22*
fake (*vb*) (a balance sheet), 36-*25*
faking, 219-*9*
fall (of market), 24-*27/37*
— in value, 80-*19 et seq.*
— of prices, 45-*34*
fall (*vb*), 214-*16*
— in/out, 190-*18*
— off, 109-*27*
— through, 1-*23*
— to s.o., 90-*2/3*
false, 107-*18*
falseness, 107-*3*
falsification, 106-*37*
falsify, 106-*40*
fame, 190-*35*
achieve —, 150-*31*
familiar, to be on — ground, 58-*31*
family concern, 96-*17*
famous, 194-*8*
fancy articles, 151-*23*
farmer, 103-*29*
farming, 10-*10*; 70-*17*
farm out (taxes), 8-*27*

flow, 100-*42*
— of goods, 90-*22*
production —, 41-*31*; 217-*31*
flower-show, 109-*29*
fluctuations, 109-*39*
fluvial, 109-*40*
fly, 23-*19*; 163-*13*
— a flag, 27-*17*
— in the face of facts, 101-*19*
flying, 149-*30*
— time, 224-*15*
flyleaf, 115-*17*
foam, 148-*25*
fob, — s.o. off, 42-*11*
fog, 32-*17*
fold, 164-*24 et seq.*
folder, 44-*9*; 79-*18*
folding, 164-*29*
folio, 155-27
food, 10-*35*
— store, 10-*37*
— stuffs, 78-*28*
foot, 162-*39*
— of the page, 26-*23*
gain a —hold, 163-*2*
forbid, 56-*16*; 128-*7*; 75-*6*
— the sale of sth., 56-*17*
forbidden, 128-*3*
forbidding, 127-*33*
force, 110-*32*; 152-*17*; 223-*6*
come into —, 96-*21*; 223-*9*
— down, 24-*37*
— on s.o., 122-*23*
forced, 110-*34*
in —, 223-*8*
forecast, 173-*13*
forecast (*vb*), 173-*19*
foreclose, 199-*1*
foreclosure, 198-*32*
foreground, in the —, 164-*5*
foreign, 100-*30*
— money order, 140-*24*
— office, 8-*12*; 100-*33*
foreigner, 100-*29*
foreman, 43-*36*; 97-*34*
works' —, 56-*34*
foresee, 173-*19*
foresight, 173-*22*
forestall, 13-*17*; 173-*4*
forfeit, 74-*6*
forfeiture, — of shares, 72-*29*
— of patent, 72-*27*
forge, 111-*5*
— a signature, 63-*6*
forger, 107-*2*
forgery, 63-*4*; 106-*35*; 107-*17*
fork (of roads), 92-*16*
form, 33-*9*; 111-*19/30*
application —, 33-*12*
entry —, 126-*10*
for —'s sake, 111-*23*
form (*vb*), 111-*28*
formal, 153-*23*
— wear, 115-*1*

formality, 111-*9*
format, 111-*12*
formation, 60-*30*; 111-*13*
formula, 111-*29*
fortnightly, 29-*14*
fortuitous, 112-*12*
fortune, 112-*14*
make a —, 106-*23*
forum, 62-*9*
forward, please —, 207-*27*
— transaction, 212-*11*
forward (*vb*), 102-*28*; 217-*16*
forwarding, 97-*5*; 102-*31*
— agent, 102-*35*; 217-*13*
— goods, 3-*25*
found (*vb*), 26-*32*; 69-*37*; 127-*11*
foundation, 69-*21*; 110-*25*
founder, 69-*20*; 110-*24*
founding, 99-*25*; 127-*13*
four-square, 99-*19*
fourth, — part, 180-*13*
fraction, 112-*34*
decimal —, 72-*36*
—al part, 112-*34*
fragile, 112-*36*
fragment, 112-*37*
—s, 72-*11*
frame/framework, 34-*27 et seq.*
franc, 113-*25*
frank (*vb*), 9-*2*; 213-*2*
franking, 9-*3*
— machine, 138-*21*
— privilege, 113-*31*
fraud, 113-*40*; 140-*12*
fraudulent, 114-*4*
free, 75-*24*; 113-*26*; 116-*42*; 134-*35*
— of, 199-*30*
— of charge, 113-*24*; 113-*34*; 116-*23/
40*
— trade area, 135-*1*
of one's own — will, 164-*19*
free (vb), 179-*26*; 102-*25*
— from, 102-*15*
— oneself, 75-*30*; 134-*29*
freedom, 134-*32*
freehold, 178-*8*
freeing, 134-*26/28*
freestone, 209-*25*
freeze, 114-*17*; 115-*37*
— a bank a/c, 29-*30*
freight, 217-*17*; 114-*8/14*
— car, 225-*2*
— charges, 36-*21*
— train, 142-*8*
— yard, 218-*19*
freighting, 9-*4*
fresh, 112-*38*
friendly, 11-*38*
fringe, on the —, 142-*25*
from, — now on, 81-*3*
fuel, 38-*9*
— oil, 143-*16*
fulcrum, 15-*9*
fulfil, 190-*19*; 200-*9*

grateful, be — to s.o., 117-*12*
gratification, 200-*6*
gratuitous, 116-*42/43*
gratuitousness, 117-*3*
gratuity, 116-*39*
grease, 116-*24/25*
Great Britain, 116-*33*
greeting, 199-*21*
grievance, 117-*32*
grocery, — trade/store, 10-*35*; 97-*17*
gross, 32-*39*; 117-*41*; 214-*31*
ground, 220-*1*; 212-*18/19*
　　adequate —s, 181-*31*
　　be on familiar —, 58-*31*
　　dumping —, 72-*21*
group, 105-*33*
　　— of stores, 138-*32*
grouping, 118-*2*
grower, 103-*29*
growth, 83-*14*; 104-*27*
grudge, 142-*6*
guarantee, 22-*17/22*; 40-*8*; 115-*10/11*
　　bank —, 40-*6*
guarantee (*vb*), 166-*36*
guaranteed, 30-*13*
guarantor, 2-*38*; 41-*13*; 86-*27*; 115-*8*
guaranty, without —, 194-*28*
guard, 115-*14/20*; 216-*6*; 221-*16*
　　— duty, 105-*34*
　　night —, 221-*17*
guard (*vb*) against, 170-*10*
guarded, well —, 115-*19*
guardian, 59-*20*; 219-*14*
　　—ship, 219-*13*
guess, 58-*16*
　　at a —, 99-*17*
　　—work, 99-*16*
guest, paying —, 161-*5*
guide, 163-*15*
guidance, 127-*14*
guild, 66-*14*
guilder, 109-*30*

haberdasher, 144-*21*
haberdashery, 44-*10/11*; 144-*20*
habit, 168-*26*
haggle, 142-*5*
haggling, 142-*4*
half, 145-*9*; 147-*22*
　　— price, 147-*23*
　　— time, 146-*32*
　　— year, 201-*16/17*
hallmark, 64-*4/10*; 165-*16*
hand, 139-*10*
　　—bill, 178-*19*
　　—made, 139-*13*
　　—out, 85-*9*
　　—picked, 218-*25*
　　—writing, 90-*29*
　　on the other —, 157-*30/33*
　　show one's —, 38-*34*
hand (*vb*), 190-*12*
　　— over, 76-*21*; 189-*24*

handing-over, 190-*4*
handle, 3-*26*; 141-*7*; 152-*33*
handler, 141-*16*
handling, 140-*36*; 141-*15*
　　— mail, 3-*25*
hang, — up (telephone), 181-*7*
happen, 17-*3*; 208-*30*
harbour, 166-*9*
　　— dues, 88-*8*
　　— station, 115-*32*; 142-*35*
　　river —, 109-*41*
heavy, 117-*35*; 153-*34*
hectare, 118-*11/32*
hecto, 118-*33*
height, 209-*19*
heir/heiress, 119-*2*
helicopter, — landing station, 118-*35*
　　— terminal, 118-*34*
help, 10-*12*
　　with the — of, 10-*15*
help (*vb*), 10-*16/17*; 18-*10*; 107-*28*;
　　205-*25*
helper, 10-*13*
herewith, 12-*30*; 46-*3/6*
heritage, 159-*30*
hide, animal —, 160-*24*
high, 118-*24*
　　— seas, 118-*24/25*, *27*; 164-*20*
　　— street, 116-*31*
　　— up, 135-*16*
　　—way, 116-*32*; 198-*20*
　　in — circles, 135-*16*
hindrance, 92-*37*
hint, take a —, 52-*35*
　　— at, 52-*36*
hire, for —, 137-*11*
　　— purchase, 221-*39*
hire (*vb*), 45-*1*; 92-*14*; 138-*10*; 95-*1*;
　　138-*8*
hiring, 137-*9*; 138-*8*
　　— of staff, 94-*32*
hit, 20-*27*
　　— upon the right plan, 130-*31*
hoard, 1-*33*; 212-*31*; 11-*28*
hoarding (advert.), 156-*3*
hogshead, 26-*22*
hold, empty the —, 36-*4*
　　— of a ship, 35-*38*
hold (*vb*), 82-*30*; 167-*6*; 211-*27*
　　— a post, 152-*29*
　　— an inquest, 95-*16*
holder, 82-*31*; 166-*37*; 167-*9*
　　— of an office, 214-*6/11*
　　— of lease, 93-*1*
holding, 107-*40*; 158-*4*; 166-*25*; 211-
　　36
holiday, 108-*1/2*; 107-*40*
　　—s, 220-*16*
　　—s with pay, 58-*7*
hollow, 69-*39*
homage, 119-*21*
home, 128-*20*
　　— country, 144-*37*
　　— Secretary, 128-*23*

— in value, 165-*1*
— price, 94-*5*; 139-*32*
— production, 3-*3*
increase (*vb*), 21-*24*; 91-*27*; 166-*30*; 187-*6*; 190-*23*
incriminate, 124-*6*
incumbent, 214-*11*
be —, 124-*2*
incur, 94-*14*
— expense, 79-*8*
indebted to, 187-*3*
indefinite, 121-*22*
indemnification, 124-*13*
indemnify, 74-*10*; 124-*14*
indemnity, 74-*8*; 124-*15*
index, 124-*25/34*
— file, 108-*14*
— of a book, 124-*26*
thumb —, 193-*2*
indicate, 3-*9*; 201-*34*
— in precise detail, 169-*9*
indication, 124-*33/34*
as an —, 124-*32*
sure —, 40-*39*
indicative, 124-*31*
indict, 124-*11*
indictment, 124-*7*
indirect, — rate of exchange, 123-*35*
individual, 158-*8*
indoors, 128-*22*
inducting, 126-*31*
induction, 126-*31*
industrial, 125-*11*
— drawing, 116-*38*
industrialist, 125-*10*
industry, 125-*8*
ineffective, 91-*10*
inefficient, 123-*15*
inexpensive, 68-*23*
inexpensively, 113-*5*
infancy, 146-*4*
infer, 55-*12*; 74-*22*
inferior, 206-*32*
inflation, 125-*14/15*
inflict, 122-*19*
— punishment, 199-*26*
influence, 168-*17*; 178-*20*; 192-*25*
gain —, 4-*7*
influential, — circles, 22-*11*
have — friends, 188-*28*
inform, 51-*27*; 67-*14/17*; 125-*20*; 157-*35*; 173-*6*; 191-*19*
information, 124-*33*; 125-*16*; 127-*14*
for your —, 108-*34*
get —, 191-*18*
inside —, 219-*16*
piece of —, 191-*15*
informed, 173-*11*
informer, 124-*29*
infraction, 125-*23*
minor —, 62-*30*
infringe, 94-*29*; 217-*10*; 223-*12*
infringement, 20-*29*; 125-*23*; 223-*11*
ingot, 26-*18*; 135-*29*

inherit, 118-*37*; 119-*1*
inheritance, 118-*36*; 207-*10*
initial (*vb*), 125-*38*; 156-*40*; 223-*22/23*
initiate, 155-*5*
— an enquiry, 175-*36*
initiative, 125-*39*
injunction, 126-*1*; 146-*22*; 185-*30*
injure (*vb*), 133-*20*; 151-*27*
injured, — party, 133-*2*
injurious, 151-*28*
injury, 20-*31*; 86-*14*; 140-*6*; 169-*22*; 214-*28*
— to a third party, 86-*16*
ink, 94-*15/18*
innovation, 151-*22*
inopportune, 126-*3*
inorganic chemistry, 145-*30*
inquire (*vb*), 95-*13/17*; 125-*18/22*; 191-*20*
— into, 84-*24*; 185-*2*
inquiries, make —, 125-*18*; 170-*17*; 191-*18*
inquiry, 60-*19*; 77-*7/8*; 95-*14*; 191-*16*; 214-*28*
— office, 7-*15*
inscribe (*vb*), 126-*12*
inscribed, 126-*15*
inscription, 126-*6*
insecure, 168-*38*
insert, 126-*16*
inside, 128-*21/22*
— out, 97-*1*
insist (*vb*), 126-*20*
insistence, 120-*18*
insolvency, 38-*10*; 126-*21*
insolvent, 126-*22*
inspect, 64-*9*; 126-*25*
inspecting, 126-*29*
inspection, 126-*29*; 223-*25*
luggage —, 223-*26*
postal —, 64-*5*
inspector, 64-*11*; 126-*27*
— in charge of a case, 95-*15*
weights and measures —, 222-*16*
installation, 127-*1*
instalment, 4-*2*; 107-*1*; 136-*20*; 211-*18*; 212-7; 222-*23*
buy on — plan, 211-*19*
by —s, 222-*24*
— selling, 221-*39*
instance, for —, 102-*12*
institution, 99-*27*; 127-*13*
instruction, 124-*33*; 127-*14*
period of —, 206-*6*
—s, 59-*35*; 147-*8*
insubordination, 126-*24*
insulate, 36-*7*
insult, 117-*1*
insurable, 18-*32*
insurance/assurance, 18-*3/5*; 19-*1/35*; 20-*1/19*
double —, 164-*38*
— policy, 62-*23*
insure, 220-*30*
integer, 150-*35*

integral, 127-*23*
intend, 54-*18*
intent, 127-*26*
  with malicious —, 127-*28*
intention, 127-*26*
  make known one's —s, 73-*17*
intentionally, 127-*30*
intercession, 163-*37*
interchange, 89-*2*; 185-*6*
interdict, 128-*4*
  issue an — against, 128-*7*
interdiction, 127-*33*
interest, 128-*13/15*; 157-*29*; 158-*4*
  allow —, 30-*25*
  bear —, 166-*33*
  common —, 51-*21*
  compound —, 52-*25*
  in their — to do so, 128-*17*
  — due/outstanding, 90-*3*
  — in arrears, 148-*2*
  vested —, 88-*5*
interested, 128-*10*
  — party, 24-*9*; 128-*9*
  not —, 81-*21*
  be — in, 128-*19*
interfere, 143-*23*
interference, 125-*32*
interim, 128-*25*
interior, 128-*20*
interlace, 95-*35*
intermediary, 128-*28*; 219-*10*
intern (*vb*), 128-*32*
interned, 128-*31*
internee, 128-*30*
interpolate, 127-*32*
interrupted, 209-*5*
interruption, 161-*18*; 209-*7*
intersect, 95-*35*
interval, 98-*28*; 159-*38*
intervention, 96-*4*
interview, 96-*30*; 128-*33*
  have an — with, 96-*28*
interview (*vb*), 129-*2*
intestate, 212-*25*
intimation, 151-*16*
intoxicated, 100-*11*
intoxication, 130-*3*
intrinsic, 129-*4*
introduce, 129-*7*; 171-*18*
  — a bill, 79-*29*
  — a new product, 132-*25*
introduction, 129-*5*; 171-*15*; 151-*15*
  letter of —, 129-*6*; 185-*32*
invalid, 121-*18*
invalidate, 129-*11*
invalidity, 129-*13*
invaluable, give — assistance, 63-*30*
invent (*vb*), 105-*16*
inventory, 129-*16*
  — of fixtures, 100-*16*
invest (*vb*), 129-*21*; 163-*31*
investigate (*vb*), 95-*17*
investigation, 60-*19*; 95-*14*; 125-*17*; 127-*15*; 184-*29/31*

conduct an —, 143-*35*
investment, 129-*22*; 166-*25*
invisible, 129-*23*
  — exports/imports, 129-*24*
invoice, 105-*35*; 106-*3/7*
invoice (*vb*), 60-*3/5*
involved, personally —, 128-*12*
IOU, 186-*12*
iron out (difficulties), 13-*20*
ironmonger, 180-*26*
irregular, 80-*24*
island, 121-*13*
isolated, 88-*34*
issue, 85-*9*; 91-*1*; 102-*6*; 129-*26*; 196-*1*
  — of magazine, 136-*20*; 151-*39*
issue (*vb*), 132-*19*; 77-*6*; 92-*23/29*
  — a warrant, 132-*23*; 140-*20*
  — a writ, 74-*3*
italicize, 130-*2*
italics, 130-*1*
item, 163-*25*; 16-*12 et seq.*
  — of an account, 82-*17*

jacket, dinner —, 202-*20*
jackpot, 117-*38*; 138-*4*
janitor, 167-*5*
jetsam, 97-*16*
jettison/jettisoning, 130-*12*
jeweller, 130-*24*
job, 93-*5*; 152-*25*; 163-*23*
  do a —, 202-*13*; 209-*18*; 106-*25*
job (*vb*), 9-*34*
jobless, 217-*29*
join, 18-*21*; 130-*25*; 196-*36*
  — in, 157-*37*
joined, 130-*32*
joining, 204-*8*
joint, 58-*17*; 125-*3*; 130-*30*; 146-*36*
  — and several, 203-*15 et seq.*
  — committee, 58-*18*
  — owner, 65-*5*
  — ownership, 65-*6*
jointly, 58-*20*
  — and severally, 58-*21*
jot down (*vb*), 151-*11*
journey, 224-*35*
  —man, 131-*17*
judge, 131-*20*; 139-*4/6*
judgement, 201-*23*
  provisional —, 179-*5*
judgeship, 139-*5*
judicial, 131-*18*
jumble, 182-*2*
junction, 130-*30*
juncture, 153-*1*
junk, 36-*19*
  piece of —, 198-*9*
  — dealer, 32-*10*
juridical, 131-*38*
jurisdiction, 52-*12*; 131-*37*; 195-*19*
jurisprudence, 131-*40*
juror, 131-*30*
jury, 131-*30/32*

leather, 70-*13*
 — goods, 142-*36*
 tooled —, 70-*14*
leatherette, 202-*8*
leave, 58-*5*; 161-*25*
 sick —, 58-*6*
 to take — of, 58-*10*
leave (*vb*), 78-*39*
 — in the lurch, 164-*1*
 — it to s.o., 190-*1*
 — out, 159-*10*
lecture, 57-*5*; 57-*8*
ledger, 116-*30*; 136-*29*; 166-*32*
leeway, 142-*28*
left, 195-*28*
 — luggage office, 59-*36*
 — overs, 195-*33*
leg, black —, 32-*9*; 117-*18*
legacy, 118-*36*; 133-*15*
legal, 131-*18/38*; 132-*28*
 by — process, 88-*16*
 — adviser, 131-*39*
 — department, 33-*26*; 61-*24*
 — redress, 192-*15*
 — tender, 147-*31*; 151-*37*
 take — action, 175-*41*
 take — advice, 24-*3*
legalities, 132-*31*
legalization, 132-*29*
legalize, 21-*34*; 32-*30*
legatee, specific residuary —, 132-*33/35*
legation, 133-*1*
legislate, 133-*2*; 137-*22*
legislation, 133-*5*
 emergency —, 101-*29*; 137-*27*
legislative, 133-*4*
legislator, 133-*3*
legislature, 133-*6*
legitimacy, 133-*14*
legitimate, 133-*9*
legitimate (*vb*), 133-*11*
lend (*vb*), 172-*31 et seq.*
lender, 172-*35*
lending, 172-*10*
 — of capital, 172-*14*
length, 67-*27*; 137-*34*
lengthening, 177-*6*
lengthwise, 137-*35*
lessee, 170-*25*
lessor, 24-*24/26*; 170-*26*
letter, 164-*22*; 133-*27*
 capital —, 133-*37*; 140-*5*
 dead —, 133-*38*
 insured —, 133-*31*
 — of allotment, 23-*26*
 — of introduction, 129-*6*; 133-*34*; 185-*32*
 — of regret, 23-*27*
 —head, 95-*34*; 133-*29*
 post a —, 133-*40*
 registered —, 133-*39*
letting, 137-*9*
level, 150-*25*; 206-*10*
level (*vb*), 13-*21*

— up, 91-*18*
levy, 169-*26*
levy (*vb*), 169-*28*
levying, 122-*24*
 — taxes, 134-*7/9*
liability, 195-*11/13*
 contingent —, 159-*24*
 tax —, 109-*18*
 unlimited —, 195-*14*
liabilities, 83-*7*; 143-*5*; 159-*23*; 221-*7*
 non-current —, 159-*25*
 — of customer, 2-*13*
liable, 195-*16*; 203-*16*
 be — for the damage, 195-*17*
 be — to duty, 153-*5*
 — for, 18-*29*
 — for tax duty, 159-*21/22*
 — to/not —, 102-*15*; 204-*15*; 208-*33*
 make s.o. —, 62-*4*
liberalism, 134-*24*
liberty, 134-*32*
 at —, 134-*35*
licence, 31-*36*; 135-*2*; 159-*26*; 161-*21*; 174-*26*
 building —, 61-*2*
 drivers —, 161-*22*
 — holder, 55-*3*
 timber —, 161-*23*
licensed, 135-*4*
 be —, 159-*28*
licensee, 135-*3*
licentiate, 135-*3*
lieu, in — of, 190-*15*
life, 149-*16*; 223-*2*
 for —, 222-*30*
 — annuity, 222-*31*
 — size, 116-*35*; 149-*19*
lift (*vb*), 134-*8*
 — an embargo, 134-*17*
lightship, 27-*7*
limit, 135-*21/22*; 212-*4*; 214-*13*
 — oneself to, 211-*29*
limitation, 171-*3*; 194-*20*
 term of —, 171-*5*
line, 31-*30*; 86-*5*; 144-*32*; 182-*7*; 201-*26*; 215-*24*; 158-*16*
 assembly —, 41-*29*
 it's not my —, 158-*19*; 183-*11*
 keep a — of stock, 211-*33*
 shipping co. —, 217-*2*
 remainder —, 201-*27*
 tear along dotted —, 82-*13*
 toe the —, 58-*2*
linen, — goods, 135-*28*
liner, 156-*21*; 217-*1*
link, 135-*11/12*; 182-*20*
 be —ed, 182-*37*
liquid, 135-*36*; 183-*21*
 — assets, 84-*30*; 136-*5*
liquidate, 135-*38*
liquidation, 135-*32*
 go into —, 135-*34*
liquidator, 135-*31*
liquidity, 136-*3*

— ratio, 75-*35*; 136-*4*
list, 136-*6*; 188-*33*; 193-*2*
  cargo —, 30-*35*
  civil —, 195-*13*
  — of applications, 136-*10*
  wine —, 38-*38*
list (*vb*), 189-*5*
literal, 201-*20*
litigation, 136-*21*
litigious, 136-*15*
litre, 136-*17*
live (*vb*), 137-*16*
  — in, 152-*30*
livelihood, 114-*29*
livestock, 28-*2/3*; 44-*12*
load, 43-*1 et seq.*
  extra —, 208-*9*
load (*vb*), 170-*16*
loading, 92-*8*
  — post, 92-*10*
loan, 93-*16*; 172-*10/18*
  compulsory —, 110-*35*
  — an overdraft, 172-*22*
  — of ten million pounds, 145-*26*
  — on stock, 93-*23*
  — society, 69-*26*
  long/short-term —, 89-*21*; 171-*21/28*
  on —, 93-*18*
  premium —, 93-*22*
loan (*vb*), 172-*31*
  apply for a —, 205-*8*
  grant a —, 59-*18*
locate, 185-*2*; 202-*17*
location, 93-*3*; 202-*12*
lodge (*vb*), — a complaint, 79-*30*; 112-*1*;
  164-*2*
lodger, 137-*6*
log book, 30-*30*; 38-*20*; 131-*12*; 136-*30*
long, 137-*30*
  — distance (telephone), 127-*31*
  — odds, 66-*8*
  — standing, 70-*29*
look, 156-*31*
  — for (new markets), 72-7
  — up, 193-*21*
loophole, 89-*16*; 102-*27*
loose, 224-*42*
  — leaf, 108-*6/10*
loot (*vb*), 163-*5/6*
lorry, 36-*20*
  — driver, 36-*23*; 198-*26*
lose (*vb*), — face, 105-*22*
  — interest, 81-*25*
loss, 79-*10*; 86-*14*; 161-*36*; 202-*9*
  at a —, 161-*27*
  dead —/total —, 162-*3/4*; 201-*5*
  heavy —, 112-*8*
  — leader, 17-*15*
  — of ground, 186-*27*
  — of rights, 72-*26*
lot, 158-*15*; 137-*41*
  drawing —s, 213-*15*
lottery, 214-*18*
  — loan, 138-*2*

lower (*vb*), 1-6; 24-*37*
  — price, 181-*4*
lubricate (*vb*), 116-*24*
lucrative, 138-*16*
luggage, 24-*14 et seq.*
  excess —, 101-*22*
  — van, 112-*18*

machine, 138-*20*
  — minder, 56-*35*
  — tool, 138-*23*
machinery, 13-*23/26*
magistracy, 139-*5*
magistrate, 139-*4*
  examining —, 127-*19*
mail, 67-*19*; 167-*28*
  by return —, 196-*17*
  — box, 39-*11*
  open the —, 67-*23*; 80-*18*
  sea —, 67-*20*
  surface —, 67-*22*
mailing, — list, 7-*17*
maintain (*vb*), 96-*22*; 139-*20*; 172-*28*;
  205-*27*
maintenance, 96-*26*
  — charges, 96-*29*
majority, 140-*1/2*
make (the/a —), 105-*7*; 142-*37*
make (*vb*), 105-*15*; 106-*21*
  — amends, 192-*17*
  — an award, 131-*27*
  — good, 68-*40*; 183-*1*
  — great strides, 99-*8*
  — known, 151-*17*
  — out, 99-*23*
  — out a cheque, 134-*22*
  — over, 217-*5/23*
  — over one's property, 84-*36*
  — the most of, 158-*2*
  — up, 105-*16*; 207-*31*
  — up for, 52-*10*
  — up for lost time, 182-*38*
maker, 105-*5*
makeshift, 102-*27*; 163-*17*
making, 105-*6*
  in the —, 111-*18*
  — over, 217-*20*
  — out (a document), 99-*26*
malicious, 127-*28*
  with — intent, 127-*28*
malversation, 140-*12*
manage, 7-*5*; 16-*16*; 17-*5*; 116-*9*; 187-*29*
  — carefully, 143-*32*
  — to cope, 204-*9*
management, 34-*32*; 84-*14*; 116-*6/11*;
  159-*37*
  board of —, 49-*28*
  joint —, 48-*35*
  new —, 42-*19*; 178-*1*
manager, 6-*35*; 44-*2/3*; 44-*5*; 84-*12*;
  116-*7*; 211-*25*
mandate, 140-*14*

manifest (*vb*), 103-*3*
mannequin, 140-*33*
manœuvre, 140-*36*
manœuvre (*vb*), 109-*9*
manœuvring, 141-*1*
manpower, 139-*15*; 153-*14*
manslaughter, 119-*19*
manufacture, 125-*8*; 141-*14*
manufacture (*vb*), 105-*15*
　— clothing, 57-*3*
manufacturer, 60-*33*; 105-*5*; 125-*10*
manufacturing, 105-*6*
map, route/road —, 38-*43*; 198-*23*
mapping, 134-*1*
margin, 142-*22 et seq.*; 214-*13*
　— of profit, 142-*26*
marine, 137-*31*; 141-*35*; 142-*32*
marital status, 47-*4*
maritime, 142-*30*
mark (*vb*), 81-*17*; 99-*12*; 142-*42*
　— down prices, 77-*24*
market, 72-*6*; 118-*14*; 142-*12*; 163-*26*
　brisk —, 12-*19*
　dull —, 142-*15*
　— gardener, 141-*20*
　— gardening, 141-*21*
　— place, 118-*14*
　— price list, 144-*22*
　— square, 38-*29*
　money —, 109-*7*
　play the —, 9-*34*
market (*vb*), 147-*34*
marketable, 141-*34*; 221-*18*
marriage, 219-*27*
　— settlement, 62-*24*; 86-*32*
mass, 143-*1/2*
　— production, 105-*9*; 176-*13*; 217-*34*
　in —es, 180-*9*
master, 37-*9*
　harbour- —, 37-*10*
match, 18-*24/25*
material, 100-*25*; 143-*9/11*; 213-*35*
　—s, 143-*8*
　raw —, 170-*6*
matter, 143-*11*; 180-*17*
　as a — of course, 153-*19*
　as —s stand, 165-*20*
　— of form, 111-*10*
matter (*vb*), 122-*6/15*
mature, 90-*3*
maturity, date of —, 89-*17*
　payable at —, 89-*20*
measure, 199-*25*
　linear —, 137-*36*
measure (*vb*), 130-*9*
measurement, 130-*8*
　—s, 95-*10*
meddle (*vb*) (with), 218-*33*
mediocre, 154-*25*; 180-*15*
medium, 148-*30*; 154-*34*; 209-*22*
meet, 193-*9*; 200-*9*
　— a bill, 120-*2*
　— a loss, 68-*40*

　— one's liabilities, 105-*21*
　— requirements, 200-*10*
　— the demand, 200-*11*
　— with, 99-*9*
meeting, 17-*30/32*; 179-*13*; 200-*36*
　call an emergency —, 220-*1*
　close the —, 200-*37*
　hold a —, 211-*31*
　open —, 200-*39*
member, be a —, 158-*22*
membership, — fee, 66-*15*
　right to —, 180-*1*
memo, 151-*7*
memorandum, 30-*32*; 148-*25/28*
memory, 143-*24*
　from —, 143-*26*
mend (*vb*), 192-*16*
mendable, 192-*10*
mending, 192-*11*
mention, 144-*3/5*; 215-*4*
　without — that, 54-*24*
mercantile, 144-*19*
mercenary, 128-*11*
merchandise, 142-*7*
merchant, 150-*15*
　—man, 141-*36*; 149-*39*
　— service, 141-*35*
　— ship, 141-*36*
merge (*vb*), 11-*24*; 114-*21*
merger, 114-*20*
mess (*vb*) (about), 218-*33*
messenger, 68-*11*; 144-*25*
Messrs, 138-*19*
metallurgy, 144-*29*
method, 147-*8*
metre, 144-*35*
metropolis, 144-*36*
mile, 145-*19*
mileage, 132-*8*
　— chart, 85-*8*
milieu, 145-*16*
mill, 105-*10*
　flour —, 146-*4*
　rolling —, 132-*16*
　saw/lumber —, 200-*26*
milliard (G.B.), 145-*20*
milliner, 147-*15*
millinery, 147-*7*
million, 145-*24/25*
millionaire, 145-*22/27*
mineral, 145-*29*
mining, 104-*36*
minister, 145-*37*
Ministry, 145-*33*
　— of Health, 200-*4*
　— of Labour, 217/*28*
minor, 145-*31*
mint, 27-*16*
mint (*vb*), 113-*39*; 147-*28/33*
minting, 113-*35*
minute, 146-*6*
　— book, 76-*24*; 187-*33/34*
minutes, 176-*1*
misappropriation, — of funds, 82-*35/37*

misbehaviour, 124-*3*
miscalculation, 35-*28*
miscarriage, — of justice, 78-*17*
miscellaneous, 113-*22*
  — expenses, 85-*16*
misconduct, 124-*3*
misdeed, 143-*17*
misdemeanour, 76-*28*; 77-*4*
mislead, 77-*4*; 98-*4*
mismanage (*vb*), 116-*10*
misprint, 107-*11*; 122-*39*
Misses, the —, 138-*29*
missed/missing, 141-*9*
mission, 146-*31*
mistake, 106-*24*; 107-*4*
  by —, 98-*3/5*; 156-*27*
mistaken, if we are not —, 98-*6*
Mister/Mr, 138-*18*
mistranslation, 215-*28*
misunderstanding, 140-*11*
misuse, 1-*30*
  — of public funds, 140-*12*
mix up, 143-*20*
mix (*vb*), 130-*26*
  be —ed up in an affair, 143-*21*
  — with, 6-*18*
mobile, 146-*38*
mock up, 116-*36*
model, 102-7; 114-*22*; 140-*33*; 141-*18*;
  147-*10/11*; 159-*32*
  latest —, 131-*23*
model (*vb*) oneself on, 102-*13*
moderate, 151-*26*
modification, 147-*12*
modify, 147-*13*; 182-*1*
monetary, 147-*25*
money, 15-*26*; 16-2; 78-*19*; 147-*27*
  — difficulties, 115-*39*
  — lender, 24-*25*; 139-*23*
  — order, 140-*18/25*
  paper —, 156-*16*; 108-*20*
  ready —, 135-*37*
monopolist, 1-*34*
monopolize, 1-*33*
monopoly, 39-*2*; 147-*35*
  government —, 147-*36*
month, 147-*16*; 147-*21*
  pay by the —, 147-*19*
monthly, 144-*1/2*; 147-*18*
  — payment, 143-*36/37*
moratorium, 147-*43*
mortgage, 69-*10*; 172-*25*; 120-*40/42*
  — charge, 8-*25*
  — deed, 120-*37*
  — lien, 174-*27*
  — loan, 120-*39*
  — registry, 33-*25*
  on —, 120-*35*
  release of —, 121-*3*
  second —, 121-*1*
mortgage (*vb*), 121-7
mortgagee, 120-*36*
mortgagor, 120-*38*
motif, 148-*14*

motion, 148-*15*
motion (leg.), 55-*14*
motive, 39-*36*; 146-*37*; 148-*13*; 195-*18*
motor, — show, 199-*20*
motto, 83-*16*; 148-*12*
mouth, 31-*6*
move, 79-*16*; 217-*5*
  — back, 142-*10*; 186-*28*
  — to, 99-*24*
moveable, 145-*6*; 146-*38*; 147-*2*
  — property, 145-*7*
movement, 67-*10*; 142-*9*; 215-*35*
multiplier, 148-*38*
municipal, 148-*39*
muslin, 148-*23*
mutation, 149-*3*
mutilate, 219-*5*
mutual, 185-*7*
  by — consent, 117-*10*

name, 78-*24*; 150-*28*
  assumed —, 150-*30*
  by —, 151-*1*
  going by the — of, 59-*5*; 150-*32*
  have a good —, 194-*7*
  mention a —, 151-*2*
name (*vb*), 144-*5*; 151-*2*
  — your terms, 56-*20*
napoleon (coin), 149-*7*
national, — debt, 179-*11*
nationality, 149-*9*
nationalize, 149-*8*
naturalize, 149-*12*
naturalized, get —, 149-*13*
nautical, — term, 149-*36*
naval, 149-*25*
navigation, 149-*31*
navvy, 140-*35*
necessary, 39-*8*; 150-*2*
  if —, 27-*40*; 89-*25*; 197-*21*
  to be —, 122-*22*
necessity, 150-*4*
  case of absolute —, 39-*9*
neckline (of dress), 94-*9*
need, 27-*38*; 219-*36*
need (*vb*), 150-7; 27-*39*
needlework, 68-*26*
negative, 150-*8*
  adopt a — attitude, 150-*9*
neglect, 150-*12*
negligible, 125-*13*
negotiable, 50-4; 125-*13*; 150-*14*
negotiate, 150-*18*; 216-*28*
negotiation, 150-*16*
  —s, 168-*9*
nest-egg, 26-*25*; 90-*16*; 132-*13*
net, 150-*29*
network, 194-*17*
news, 125-*16*; 6-*9*
  financial —, 45-*33*
newsagent, 141-*27*
newsboy, 70-*5*

newspaper(s), 131-*11*; 172-*2/3*
newstand, 21-*16*; 131-*15*
nick, 94-*8*
nip, — in the bud, 153-*11*
nominal, 150-*38*
nominate, 81-*18*
nomination, 81-*16*
non, — -delivery, 136-*23*
— -existent, 151-*32*
— -inflammable, 121-*12*
— -payment, 74-*30*
— -profit-making association, 138-*17*
— -stop flight, 98-*10*
— -stop show, 161-*20*
notaries, board of —, 41-*34*
notary, 151-*32*; 153-*26*
—'s office, 100-*39*
notch, 94-7
notch (*vb*), 48-*14*; 94-*18*
note, 151-7 *et seq.*
bank —, 29-*4*
bond/transhipment —, 4-*17*
bought —, 3-*22*; 30-*33*
consignment —, 30-*32*
credit/debit —, 30-*36*
dispatch —, 33-*15*
—book, 34-*35*; 36-*5*; 38-*17*; 143-*28*
—paper (headed), 156-*9/10*
promissory —, 28-*39*
sold —, 31-*1*
note (*vb*), 189-*5*
notice, 76-*6*; 151-*16*; 156-*20*; 168-*36*
give —, 58-*9*; 168-*37*
— board, 8-*30*
— of meeting, 23-*21*
official —, 153-*24*
receive —, 64-*36*
until further —, 79-*1*
without —, 23-*31*
notice (*vb*), 189-*11*
notification, 12-*32*; 40-*28*; 73-*9*; 106-*27/28*
notify, 125-*20*; 129-*3*; 173-*6*; 202-*4*
notion, 151-*18*
notorious, 151-*20*
novelty, 151-*22*
nowhere, — to be found, 129-*9*
nuance, 151-*24*
nugget, 32-*26*
null, 151-*32*; 129-*10*
— and void, 23-*13*; 151-*33/36*
nullify, 129-*11*
nullity, 151-*34*
number, 143-*14*; 150-*33*; 151-*38*
even/odd —, 78-*36*; 150-*36*
in round —s, 54-*14*
not in great —s, 143-*6*
number (*vb*), 54-*16*; 152-*4*
— pages, 45-*3*
numbering, 152-*3*

oath, 172-*13/15*
violate an —, 223-*15*

obedience, 204-*17*
obey (*vb*) (orders), 58-*2*
object (*vb*), 33-*40*; 152-*5/6*
— to, 186-*31*; 101-*27*
objection, 117-*32*; 124-*4*; 185-*11*
obligation, 152-7
fulfil an —, 152-*11*
— binding on all parties, 203-*19*
raise —s, 83-*40*
oblige, 152-*18*
obliged, 152-*13*
observe, 189-*11*
obsolete, 73-*20*
obstructions, 94-*10*
obtain, 176-*5*
— discharge, 188-*18*
obtainable at, 221-*30*
obverse, 105-*18*
— side, 23-*14*
obviousness, 101-*6*
occasion, 193-*32*
for the —, 46-*15*
should the — arise, 89-*25*
occupancy, 97-*8*; 152-*26*
occupant, 152-*23*
— of a post, 214-*11*
occupation, 93-*5*; 100-*8*; 158-*25*; 158-*16*; 176-*23*; 199-*32*
occupy, 152-*29*
odd, 119-*3*
— number, 122-*1*
— job man, 119-*31*
—s and ends, 32-*19*
offence, 62-*29*; 76-*28*; 77-*4*
second —, 185-*3*
serious —, 107-*13*
offender, first —, 77-*3*
offer, 153-*30*
special —, 185-*14*
offer (*vb*), 171-*17*; 177-*23*
—ed for sale, 146-*28*
off-hand, 134-*3*; 163-*41*
office, 33-*17/35*; 43-*2*; 100-*36*; 153-*17*; 166-*24*
booking —, 137-*10*
— hours, 61-*19*; 119-*12*
— of the clerk of the court, 117-*13*
officer, 153-*25*
official, 153-*23*
high —, 50-*38*
— mark, 99-*11*
— notice, 153-*24*
revenue —, 109-*14*
offprint, 213-*14*
offshore, — navigation, 137-*32*
O.H.M.S., 113-*32*
oil, 162-*9/14*
oil (*vb*), — s.o.'s palm, 116-*25*
omission, 153-*32*
omit, 159-*10*; 202-*6*
open, 155-*16*
— all year round, 155-*17*
open (*vb*), — mail, 65-*25*; 67-*23*; 80-*18*
operate, 110-*22*; 142-*17*; 153-*39*

operation, 142-*9*
—s, 205-*35*
operator, 103-*30*
  switchboard —, 206-*13*
opinion, 153-*41*
  be of contrary —, 62-*20*
  be of the —, 23-*29*
  go by s.o.'s —, 182-*30*
  legal —, 61-*18*
opportuneness, 154-*1*
opposed, — to, 154-*2*
  as — to, 154-*8*
opposite, 45-*36*; 62-*15*; 63-*14*; 105-*19*;
  185-*8*
  on the — page, 62-*31*
  — direction, 201-*22*
  take the — side, 63-*15*
opposition, 154-*4*
  considerable —, 154-*9*
  without —, 61-*30*
optician, 154-*11*
option, 45-*14/18*; 106-*9*; 154-*12*
  at the — of the buyer, 117-*7*
  market —s, 212-*13*
  — dealings, 8-*3*
optional, 106-*8*
ordeal, 97-*29*
order, 49-*30/37,39*; 154-*28*; 85-*3*; 126-
  1; 167-*8*
  in —, 111-*20*
  — book, 38-*23*; 136-*32*
  postal —, 30-*6*
orders, 59-*35*
  — in hand, 166-*26*
  standing —, 188-*4*
ordinary, 148-*301*; 154-*24*; 180-*15*
ore, 145-*28*
organ, 154-*34*
organization, 118-*3*; 154-*35*
orientation, 104-*14*; 154-*36*
origin, 155-*3*; 178-*30*
original, — draft, 146-*9*
originate, 91-*29*; 155-*5*
ounce, 153-*33*
oust, 80-*1*; 101-*11*
out of, 120-*10*; 156-*24*
  — order, 80-*24*; 220-*10*
  — print, 97-*24*
  — stock, 97-*25*
  — tune, 107-*19*
  — work, 200-*1*
out-turn report (of ship), 165-*28*
outbid, 94-*4*; 190-*24*; 208-*17*
outbuildings, 79-*4*
outcome, 1-*24*; 129-*27*; 196-*1*
outdated, 161-*13*
  — ideas, 68-*9*
outfit, 97-*36*
outfitter, 57-*4*
outflow, — of capital, 204-*5*
outgoing, 203-*34*
outlaw, 120-*15*; 137-*25*
outlet, 129-*28*
outline, 88-*30*

general —, 13-*19*
output, 34-*26/25*; 71-*24*; 190-*27*
outrage, 110-*36*
outside, 142-*25*
  — the town, 120-*12*
outstanding, 120-*14*
overboard, throw —, 30-*29*; 144-*16*
overcome (*vb*), 81-*1*; 208-*23*
overdraft, 73-*26*; 78-*37*
overdraw, 73-*26*
  —n, 73-*26*
overdue, 16-*28*; 148-*1*
overestimate (*vb*), 208-*20*
overestimated, 208-*21*
overhaul (*vb*), 144-*40*; 197-*10*
overhauling, 146-*19*; 197-*12*
overhead, 197-*10/12*
  —s, 113-*23*
overland, 224-*6*
overlapping, 186-*23*
overload (*vb*), 208-*12*
overlook (*vb*), 159-*10*
overnight, 133-*18*
overprint, 208-*8*
overprint (*vb*), 208-*11*
overproduction, 208-*26*
overrated, 203-*21*
override, 155-*13*; 159-*15*
overrule, 155-*13*; 159-*15*
overseas, 155-*14*
  — agency, 221-*29*
oversight, 153-*32*
overstock, — with, 94-*11*
overtax, 208-*22*
overtime, 119-*14*
overweight, 208-*25*
owe, 83-*21*
owing, 88-*19*; 88-*20*
  — to, 181-*32*
own (*vb*), 167-*6*
owner, 103-*30*; 159-*31*; 167-*9*; 177-*33*
  — of copyright, 82-*31*
ownership, 167-*10*; 178-*3*; 179-*19*

pace, 216-*2*
pack, 92-*3*
package, 156-*22*
  — deal, 110-*37*
package/pack (*vb*), 92-*36*
packet, make a —, 114-*35*
packing, 91-*33*
  — and shipping charges, 91-*35*; 113-*17*
  — list, 92-*2*; 136-*8*
pad, 209-*30*
pad (out) (*vb*), 100-*26*
padlock, 34-*23/24*
page, 155-*27*
page (*vb*), 155-*30*
paging, 155-*29*
paid, 199-*7*
  — off, 100-*22*
  — up capital, 134-*27*
pair (with) (*vb*), 18-*25*

palm off (*vb*), 187-*20*
pamphlet, 32-*14*; 178-*19*
panel, 156-*2*
— of teachers, etc., 136-*6*
paper, 92-*1*; 143-*25*; 162-*29*
— -backed, 32-*11*
— -clip, 219-*2*
— -mill, 156-*6*
— -trade, 156-*6*
— -work, 156-*4*
par, put on —, 91-*17*
  above/below —, 148-*36*
paragraph, 156-*29*; 156-*38*
parallel, 156-*35*
  draw a —, 156-*36/37*
parcel, 48-*36/38*; 97-*6*; 156-*22*
— out (land), 138-*6/7*
parenthesis, 157-*6*
parity, 157-*9*
parole, release on —, 157-*21*
part, 107-*1*; 136-*20*; 157-*29*; 158-*15*;
  162-*28*; 197-*31*
  in —, 158-*21/26*
  in —s, 136-*26*
  take —, 158-*7*; 157-*37*
partial, 158-*26*
partiality, 107-*29*; 169-*18*
participation, 158-*4*
particular, 158-*9*
  full —s, 82-*18*
partly, 158-*21*; 215-*21*
partner, 18-*18 et seq.*
  sleeping —, 24-*25*; 50-*1*
partnership, sleeping/limited —, 49-*41*; 50-*2*
  verbal —, 202-*31*
party, 184-*12*; 207-*17*; 157-*42*; 158-*17*
— in power, 168-*22*
— to the case, 158-*24*
pass, 66-*23*; 132-*15*
pass (*vb*), 159-*11*; 166-*29*; 166-*35*
— a law, 224-*31*
— around, 46-*29*
—ed by transmission, 83-*22*
— for press, 30-*9*
— sentence, 131-*26*
— the hat, 66-*17*
passage, 158-*31*
passer by, 159-*4*
pastry, —cook, 159-*29*
patent, 31-*36*; 32-*4*
— office, 153-*21*
— rights, 178-*9*
pathologist (of a court), 133-*8*
patronage, 107-*29*; 159-*33*; 178-*20*
pattern, 147-*10*; 148-*14*; 159-*32*
pause, 159-*38*
pave (*vb*) (the way), 212-*20*
paw (over), 218-*29*
pawn, 114-*23/27*
pawned, 94-*30*
pawning, 146-*23*
pay, 160-*5*; 199-*5*
  be in s.o.'s —, 114-*26*

pay (*vb*), 4-*24*; 72-*9*; 160-*9*; 182-*27*;
  188-*13*; 190-*32*; 196-*32*
— a call, 222-*28*
— a tax, 64-*1*
— back, 189-*19*; 160-*10*
— day, 160-*6*; 155-*32*
— in, 93-*31*; 222-*26/27*
— in hard cash, 98-*37*
— in kind, 149-*20*
— interest, 128-*18*
— off (creditors), 4-*25*; 81-*23*; 100-*20*;
  12-*5*; 135-*39*
— off an overdraft, 203-*14*
— off equipage, 58-*14*
— off mortgage, 179-*26*
— on the nail, 160-*11*
— one's respects to, 119-*23*
— one's share, 88-*22*
—the exchange and re-exchange, 184-*26*
— to the order of,
— tribute to, 119-*24*
— twice as much, 87-*19*
— with bonus, 174-*5*
payable, 89-*24*; 160-*2*
— at sight, 160-*3*
— by the tenant, 43-*4*
payee, 82-*1*
payer, 160-*12*
paying, 160-*4*
— of creditors, 81-*22*
— off, 104-*32*; 179-*25*
payment, 4-*22*; 155-*33*; 160-*7*; 172-*12*
  advance —, 22-*23/36*
  down —, 222-*25*
  make a —, 155-*34*; 188-*5*; 204-*1*; 222-*23*
  pre- —, 160-*8*
payroll, 30-*37*; 108-*8*
peak, — hours, 119-*13*
pear, 165-*34*
peculiar, 158-*9*
pecuniary, 160-*29*
pedal, soft —, 21-*7*
pedestrian, — crossing, 159-*1*
pedlar, 141-*26*
penal, 160-*35*
— laws, 137-*26*
penalization, 160-*36*
penalize, 199-*26/29*
penalty, 74-*6*; 160-*30/37*; 199-*25*; 201-*23*
  under — of, 160-*33*
pending, 204-*10*; 209-*6*
pension, 160-*42*; 196-*24*
  old age —, 161-*2*
pension off (*vb*), 146-*16*; 161-*6*; 196-*28/30*
pen-pusher, 198-*8*
per, 156-*24*
percentage, 128-*15*; 168-*8*; 177-*10*;
  209-*35*; 211-*26*
perfect, 165-*22*
perforations, 78-*30*

perform, 193-*28*
— a function, 153-*20*
performance, 193-*25*; 200-*38*
— of a duty, 102-*19*
theatre —, 188-*26*
periodical, 179-*16*
perishable, 161-*14*
perjure, 157-*15/17*
perjurer, 157-*14*
perjury, 157-*12*; 211-*9*
permanence, 161-*15*
permanent, 161-*19*
permanently, 75-*18*
permissible, 161-*24*
permission, 22-*4*; 161-*25*
without —, 125-*7*
permit, 22-*4/6*; 132-*15*; 135-*2*; 161-*21*
permitted, 161-*24*
perpetuity, 161-*27*
perquisite, 92-*34*
perseverance, 207-*16*
person/people, 158-*8*
— in question, 180-*19*
personal, 158-*9*
— allowance, 1-*9*
personally, 177-*29*
personnel, 161-*32*
persuade (*vb*), 161-*34*
pertaining, — to employers, 159-*35*
pestle, 163-*7*
petition, 162-*8*; 194-*10*
bankruptcy —, 194-*11*
file one's —, 28-*29*
— for pardon, 186-*20*
petitioner, 163-*36*
petrol, 99-*4*
petroleum, 162-*9*
pewter, 99-*31*
pharmacist, 162-*19*
'phone, wanted on the —, 77-*18*
'phone (*vb*), 66-*21*
photo, 162-*20*
photographer, 162-*23*
photostat, 162-*21/24*
phrasing, 134-*21*
pick up (*vb*), 189-*5*; 193-*21*
pickpocketing, 224-*17*
piece-work, 217-*32*
pigeonhole, 39-*11/14*
pigskin, 160-*25*
pile up (*vb*), 11-*29*
pilferage, 132-*26*
pilot, 163-*9/11*
— project, 23-*6*
pilot (*vb*), 163-*12*
pinch, at a —, 197-*21*
pinch (*vb*), 98-*14*
pipe, 219-*15*
pipe (*vb*) (oil), 36-*30*
pit, 179-*23*
— head, 38-*30*
placard, post up —, 8-*32*; 8-*34*
place, 135-*14*; 163-*26*; 202-*12*; 206-*14*
in — of, 74-*29*; 190-*15*

take the — of, 135-*20*
place (*vb*), 39-*13*; 163-*30*
— an order, 159-*17*
plaid, 90-*20*
plaintiff, 77-*19*; 163-*39*
plan, 134-*1*; 176-*35*; 177-*4*; 200-*24*
general/five-year —, 164-*3 et seq.*
plan (*vb*), 35-*35*; 54-*35/36*; 89-*1*
plank, 164-*10*
planning, 164-*12*
plant, 127-*2*; 220-*12*
plant (*vb*), 164-*14*
plantation, 164-*13*
— owner, 164-*15*
planting, 164-*13*
plastic, 164-*16*
platform, 179-*28*
platinum, 164-*17*
play, 162-*26*
play (*vb*), 130-*35*
— a trick on s.o., 131-*2*
— for high stakes, 117-*37*; 131-*1*
— the stock market, 130-*37*
plead, 163-*34*
pleading, 163-*37*
please . . ., 173-*27/30*; 224-*33*
please (*vb*), 152-*18*
pleasure, we have — etc., 23-*3*
pledge, 94-*34*
pledgee, 69-*18*
plenty, have — of, 180-*7*
plot, vacant —, 212-*23*
plug, give s.o. a —, 148-*26*
plums (coll.), 18-*3*
plunder, 163-*5/6*
pluralism, 70-*19*
plus, 164-*39*
ply, — between, 149-*29*
pocket, out of his own —, 78-*20*
pocket (*vb*), 93-*13*
point, 122-*37*; 165-*18/19*; 180-*17*
— at issue, 136-*14*
— of reference, 193-*1*
point out (*vb*), 201-*34*
— out sth. to s.o., 189-*12*
poles apart, 154-*3*
police, 165-*37*
central — station, 161-*16*
— headquarters, 169-*17*
— inspector, 126-*27*
— station, 161-*16*
—man, 166-*1*
rural —, 115-*21*
policy, take out a —, 62-*3*
insurance —, 165-*38*
pool, 34-*34*
poor, 141-*3*
popular, to be —, 224-*1*
population, — numbers, 91-*28*
port, 166-*9*
inland —, 166-*16*
home —, 166-*13*
outer —, 166-*10*
— dues/charges, 166-*12*

— of call, 166-*15*; 188-*25*
— of registry, 166-*13*
— warden, 166-*11*
— of entry, 167-*30*
sea—, 166-*14*
portable, 166-*19*
porter, 166-*37*; 167-*3/5*
portfolio, 166-*24*; 201-*30*
portion, 112-*34*; 118-*38*; 137-*38/40*;
148-*3*
position, 43-*2*; 110-*15*; 118-*7*; 163-*23*;
202-*12/13*
be in a good —, 130-*20*; 163-*33*
change the — of, 217-*24*
positive, 208-*4*; 216-*33*
positively, 75-*20*
possess (*vb*), 82-*30*; 167-*6*
possession, 167-*10*
actual —, 106-*34*
resume —, 193-*20*
— is nine points of the law, 167-*11*
possessor, 167-*9*
possible, 167-*12*
post, 110-*15*; 163-*23*; 167-*15/23*; 202-*13*
by return —, 67-*26*
find a — for s.o., 163-*32*
first —, 67-*25*
parcel —, 167-*18*
—card, 167-*17*
— free, 84-*28*
—man, 105-*32*
—mark, 32-*14*; 152-*20/21*
—master general, 167-*29*
— office, 167-*24/28*
— office box, 167-*16*
— office employee, 168-*1*
— paid, 113-*28*
post (*vb*), 166-*32*
keep s.o. —ed on, 67-*15*
— a letter, 133-*40*
postage, 9-*3*; 113-*9*; 166-*17*
— paid, 166-*18*
postal, 167-*15*
— charge, 166-*17*
— inspection, 64-*5*
— order, 30-*6*; 167-*27*
— services, 167-*20*
postdate (*vb*), 167-*21*
poster, 8-*31*; 163-*20*
poste restante, 167-*33*; 195-*29*
posting, 193-*16*
postpone, 10-*22*; 83-*36*; 189-*25*; 192-*8*;
193-*18*
—d to a later date, 219-*18*; 120-*24*
postponement, 10-*21*; 190-*6*
postscript, 168-*2*
pot, go to —, 79-*12*
pottery, 168-*5*
pound (£ or lb.), 136-*38*
one — apiece, 162-*37*
power, 106-*9*; 156-*1*; 168-*17*
have full —, 168-*20*
high —, 164-*21*
— of attorney, 140-*16*; 168-*19*

— station, 91-*26*
—s, 21-*15*
sun —, 120-*21*
practice, 47-*37*; 108-*30*; 168-*26*; 220-*5*
put in —, 168-*28*; 168-*30*
practise (*vb*), 168-*29*
— medicine, 102-*18*
pratique, 168-*29*
pray, 173-*26*
prayer, 173-*29*
precarious, 168-*38*
precaution, 173-*22*
precedent, 169-*2*
create a —, 169-*4*
without —, 169-*5*
preceding, 168-*34*; 169-*3*
precious, 169-*6*
— stones, 163-*4*
precisely, 104-*20*
predicament, 58-*25*; 202-*16*
predominate (*vb*), 172-*41*
pre-emption, 169-*12*
prefab, 169-*14*
prefabricated, 169-*13*
prefatory, — note, 103-*23*
prefectship, 169-*16*
prefecture, 169-*15*
preference, 169-*18*; 174-*14*; 187-*27*
give — to, 169-*19*
— share, 174-*16*
preferential, 169-*20*
— tariff, 169-*21*
— claim, 174-*26*
— duty, 187-*27*
prejudice, 169-*23*; 173-*8*
without —, 169-*24*
prejudiced, 173-*12*
prejudicial, 169-*25*
be — to, 169-*23*
preliminary, — examination, 127-*17*
— plan, 23-*6*
prematurely, 212-*10*
premises, 121-*27/30*; 135-*19*
premium, 79-*19*; 138-*1*; 173-*31*; 193-*17*
additional —, 173-*32*
be at a —, 173-*34*
full —, 174-*1*
exchange —, 9-*31*
— bonds, 138-*3*; 152-*10*
— hunter, 138-*14*
— to be arranged, 173-*35*
redemption —, 174-*2*
renewed —, 174-*3*
single —, 174-*4*
preparation, 84-*37*
—s, 170-*29*
prepare, 91-*21*
— goods for market, 56-*26*
prepay, 9-*2*
prepayment, 12-*13*
prerequisites, 194-*13*
prescribe (*vb*), 171-8
prescribed, 188-*8*
prescription, 171-*2/7*

presence, 171-*11*
present, 6-*11*
  at the — time, 119-*6*
present (*vb*), 171-*17*
  — a case in court, 163-*35*
  — a motion, 148-*17*
presentation, 171-*14/16*; 190-*4*
  — of a case in court, 163-*38*
preside (*vb*), 171-*27/28*
president, 171-*22*
  —s, 171-*26*
  — and his party, 207-*21*
presidential, 171-*26*
press, 172-*1/2*
  — copy, 172-*5*
  — proof, 213-*21*
  — report, 125-*19*
  —ed by, 126-*19*
pressing, 122-*3*
pressure, 62-*12*
  act on —, 62-*13*
  put/bring — on s.o., 172-7
  under the — of events, 172-*9*
presumed, 171-*29*
presumption, 171-*31*
presumptive, 171-*29*
pretence, under the — of, 68-*32*
pretension, 172-*29*
prevail (*vb*), 172-*41*
prevalent, 192-*9*
prevent (*vb*), 173-*5*
preventively, 173-*9*
previous, 168-*34*; 169-*4*
  —ly, 168-*35*; 173-*9*
price, 174-*28*
  at a —, 175-*30*
  at half —, 174-*29*
  average —, 175-*27*
  bargain —, 175-*1*
  cash —, 174-*38*
  catalogue —, 112-*6*; 175-*19/23*
  ceiling —, 175-*24*
  closing —, 68-*8*; 175-*3*
  cost —, 68-*21*; 175-*10*
  current —, 174-*37*; 175-*14*
  discount —, 175-*26*
  exorbitant —, 175-*17*
  fancy —, 175-*29*
  fixed —, 111-*4*
  for a —, 214-*5*
  full —, 112-*6*
  invoice —, 106-*6*
  issue —, 67-*42*; 175-*6*
  keenest —, 174-*36*
  list —, 67-*8*; 174-*41*
  low —, 175-*13/25*
  lowest —, 174-*33*
  maker's —, 105-*14*; 175-7
  market —, 68-*5*; 175-*15*
  manufacturing —, 175-*10*
  opening —, 68-*3/8*; 175-*2*
  pre-issue —, 175-*11*
  — cutting, 187-*11*
  purchase —, 174-*42*

retail —, 82-*21*; 175-*5*
reduced —, 181-*1*
selling —, 175-*12*
special —, 175-*8*
standing —, 175-*18*
starting —, 175-*21*
subscription —, 68-*2*
trade —, 142-*1*
upset —, 146-*18*; 175-*4*
wholesale —, 175-9/22
prices, — agreed upon, 174-*40*
  exposed —, 174-*39*
  fall in —, 174-*32*
  higher —, 118-*21*
  make up —, 8-*35*
  opening —, 170-*8*
  slashed —, 175-*28*
pricy, 44-*30*
primage, 42-*30*; 87-*38*
principal, 50-*33*
  — and interest, 37-*27*
principle, 174-9/13
  on —, 174-*13*
print, 93-*14*
print (*vb*), 213-*20*
printed, 123-*2*
  — form, 111-*34*
  — matter, 123-*1*
printer, 123-*4*
printing, 122-*37*; 123-*3*; 213-*12*
prior to, 168-*34/35*
priority, 174-*14*
  take — over, 174-*6*
private, 158-*9*; 174-*23*
  — income of . . ., 136-*39*
  — interest, 158-*11*
  — investors, 174-*24*
  —room, 158-*14*
privateer, 150-*1*
privately, 139-*11*; 141-*13*; 158-*10*
privilege, 106-*9*; 174-*26*
  tax —, 109-*20*
privy council, 174-*25*
prize, 137-*42*
  give as a —, 174-*7*
  — drawing, 138-*5*
probability, 58-*24*; 171-*31*
probable, 171-*29*
probation, 206-*6*
  period of —, 206-*6*
probate, 117-*40*
problem, 180-*17*
  this — presents no difficulties, 171-*19*
procedure, 175-*37*
proceed (*vb*), 175-*34/35*
  — from, 178-*32*
proceeding, 77-*20*
  —s, 127-*6*; 175-*37/38*
  start —s against, 125-*21*
proceeds, 176-*16*
process, 216-*5*
  — server, 103-*31*
procrastinate, 211-*21*
procuration, 176-*3*

procure, 176-*5*
produce, 78-*27*; 176-*12/18*; 190-*28*
produce (*vb*), 152-22; 176-*14*
— an alibi, 112-*24*
producer, 176-*9*
television —, 183-22
product, 176-*15/20*
production, 104-*36*; 171-*14*; 176-*11*;
105-*6*
mass —, 105-*9*; 176-*13*
productive, 176-*9/10*
profession, 176-*21*
professional, 176-*24*
professions, 176-22
profit, 27-*19 et seq.*; 114-*39*; 176-*27*;
182-*18*; 190-*26*
— sharing, 158-*6*
— taking, 174-*20*
to one's —, 22-*39*
trading —, 103-*33*
profitable, 23-*1*; 138-*16*; 176-*31*; 182-*21*
profiteer, 144-*18*
profiteer (*vb*), 176-*34*
profiteering, 144-*19*
programme, 176-*35*
progress, 32-22; 177-*2*; 176-*37*
make —, 76-*38*
progression, 3-*25*; 177-*2*
progressive, 177-*1*
prohibit (*vb*), 75-*6*; 178-*18*
prohibited, 128-*3*
— from entering an area, 128-*6*
prohibition, 75-*9*; 127-*33*; 178-*17*
prohibitive, 177-*3*
prohibitory, 177-*3*
project, 177-*4*
long term —, 118-*13*
prolongation, 177-*6*
promise, 94-*31*
promise (*vb*), 94-*34*
empty —s, 220-*21*
promissory note, 28-*39*
promote, 107-*28*
promotion, 22-*35/37*
prone, 207-*28*
pronounce, 177-*7*
proof, 60-*19*; 172-*37*; 97-*21*
galley —, 163-*21*
— by witness, 212-*28*
—reader, 65-*18*
proof-read (*vb*), 97-*22*
prop (*vb*), up, 100-*19*; 205-*26*
properties (of matter), 178-*6*
property, 24-*4/8*; 28-7/*15*; 86-*4*; 121-
28; 167-*10*; 178-*3/5*
fixed —, 221-*3*
personal —, 147-*3*
— for sale, 121-*30*
real —, 178-7
transferable —, 147-*4*
proportion, 177-*10*; 178-*12*
proportion (*vb*), 177-*15*
in — to, 178-*13/14*
proportional to, 177-*12*

proportionately, 141-*24*
— to, 178-*14*
proposal, 148-*15*; 177-*26*
propose, 177-*23*
proposition, 177-*26*
proprietor, 167-*9*
pro rata, 178-*12*
on — basis, 178-*13*
— distribution, 178-*16*
prorate (*vb*), 178-*15*
pros and cons, 62-*3*
weigh —, 162-7
proscription, 178-*17*
prosecute, 168-*12*; 175-*41*; 215-*30/32*
prosecution, no grounds for —, 151-*5*
protection, 91-*19*; 178-*20/23*; 219-13
seek —, 186-*4*
protectionism, 178-*23*
protest, 178-*24 et seq.*; 185-*11*; 200-*19*
protest (*vb*), 185-*19*
— a bill of exchange, 178-*27*
— against, 178-*25*
— one's innocence, 178-*26*
protestation, 178-*24*
prove, 99-*22*; 110-7
— an operation, 172-*38*
provide (*vb*), 112-*21*; 168-*14/15*; 148-
41; 173-*20*; 207-7
— against, 170-*11*
— for, 205-*25*
— for the needs of, 112-*22*
— work for, 152-*31*
—d by the articles of, 173-*21*
provident fund, 173-*23*
provision, 171-*4*; 173-*14*; 179-*1*
provisional, 128-*26*; 211-*20*
provisionally, 179-*6*
provisions, — of the act, 85-*4*; 171-*6*
come under the — of a law, 66-*22*
proxy, 110-*29*; 140-*16/27*; 168-*19*; 176-
3/7
P.T.O., 219-*12*
public, 179-*10*
— authorities, 168-*25*
— opinion (polling of —), 203-*33*
— opinion poll, 153-*42*
— prosecutor, 176-*8*; 145-*36*
— prosecutors' office, 157-*26*
— sale, 179-*15*
— service, 179-*12/14*
— utilities, 179-*14*
publication, 91-*1*; 158-*28*; 179-*16*
publicity, 179-*19*
publish, 156-*33*; 179-*21/22*
publishing, 179-*17*
pull, 213-*17*
— out, 196-*10*
— through, 213-22
pullman (train), 225-*3*
punch, 165-*14/17*
— line, 45-*10*
punctual, 101-*15/17*
punish, 199-*29*
punishable, 76-*27*

punishment, 160-*30*
  capital —, 160-*31*
purchase, 3-*12*
  bull —, 3-*13*
  cash —, 3-*16*
  firm —, 3-*17*
  outright —, 111-*3*
  — against sample, 3-*19*
  — book, 136-*35*
  — for settlement, 3-*15*
  — on credit, 3-*14*
  — price, 3-*24*
  — under compulsion, 104-*21*
purchaser, 4-*5*; 170-*24*
purchasing, 170-*29*
  — contract, 3-*20*
  — power, 3-*23*; 37-*4*; 168-*23*
purify, 97-*30*
purloin, 205-*19*
purpose, 110-*16*; 152-*6*; 177-*17*
  for that —, 91-*4*
purposely, 98-*17*; 200-*25*
purser, ship's —, 51-*2*
pursuance, in — of, 14-*11*
pursuit, 184-*28*
purveyor, 112-*28*
put, 144-*38*; 166-*29*
  — aside, 145-*1*; 194-*29*
  — at a disadvantage, 81-*8*
  — back, 193-*6*
  — 5% on an invoice, 139-*34*
  — in, 126-*16*
  — in at . . ., 98-*9*
  — off, 186-*28*; 189-*25*; 192-*8*
  — out of commission, 81-*6*
putting, 146-*13*
  — in, 127-*3*
  — into action, 146-*29*
  — up (of money), 146-*20*

qualification, 179-*34*
  —s, 213-*39*
qualified, 15-*11*; 81-*19*; 179-*33*; 180-*3*
qualify, 151-*26*
qualifying period, 206-*6*
quality, 11-*13*; 179-*33*; 180-*5*
quantity, 180-*6/9*
  — permitted, 214-*15*
quantum, 180-*11*
quarrel, 77-*29*
quarrying, 104-*36*
quarter, 180-*13*; 218-*27*; 212-*5*
  —ly, 218-*28*
quash, — election, 129-*11*
quay, 179-*27/29*
  alongside the —, 179-*30*
query, 180-*18*
question, 180-*23*; 197-*17*
  beg the —, 174-*12*
  raise a —, 71-*16*
  skip a —, 98-*15*
questionable, 61-*27*
  — claim, 61-*32*

questionnaire, 180-*22*
quintal, 180-*27*
quota, 61-*33/36*; 90-*21*; 180-*32*
quotation, 66-*6*
quote (*vb*), 66-*13*; 185-*23*
  — in foreign currency, 123-*26*
quoted, 66-*9*
quotient, 180-*33*
quoting, 66-*5*

rack, bottle —, 39-*6*
racket, 49-*20*; 115-*4*
radio-message, 181-*22*
radiogram, 181-*22*
radiograph, 181-*21*
radius, 183-*14*
rail, — system, 194-*18*
railcar, 22-*3*
railway, — crossing, 158-*36*
  elevated —, 7-*28*
  — station, 115-*29*
raise, 118-*21*; 134-*8*; 166-*30*
  — capital, 176-*6*
  — funds, 196-*37*
  — loan, 93-*19*
  — objections, 83-*40*
  — point of law, 55-*15*
  — price, 139-*33*
rammer, 163-*7*
ramshackle, 70-*11*
range, 18-*24*; 45-*17*; 115-*2*
rank (line), 182-*7*
  — (status), 182-*8*
rank (*vb*), 202-*14*
  — after, 174-*8*
  — before, 174-*6*
rare, 169-*6*; 67-*37*
rate, 63-*29/32*; 181-*28*; 187-*26*; 210-*7*
  et seq.
  at the — of, 181-*29*
  bank —, 210-*23*
  birth —, 210-*21*
  buying —, 67-*38*
  closing —, 67-*41*
  contango —, 68-*1*
  demand —, 67-*40*
  fix the — of, 210-*18*
  flat —, 210-*27*
  forward —, 67-*39*
  freight —, 210-*16*
  full —, 210-*8*
  hourly —, 210-*15*
  official —, 68-*7*
  printed — (postal), 210-*13*
  — of exchange (indirect), 123-*25*; 210-*25*
  subscription —, 210-*11*
  through —, 210-*27*
rateable, 122-*16*
ratepayer, 63-*23*
ratify, 119-*32*; 182-*35*
ratio, 48-*24/28*
  in direct — (to), 177-*13*

inverse — to, 177-*14*; 181-*33*
ration, 177-*10*; 181-*28*
—s, 223-*32*
rationing, 182-*36*
raw, 32-*24*; 90-*33*; 143-*12*
reach, 20-27 *et seq.*; 158-*29*
reaction, 183-*15/17*
readaptation, 183-*18*
readjust, 182-*1*
ready, be —, 165-*21*
ready-reckoner, 26-*13*
realization, 182-*23*
realize (*vb*), 183-*25/26*
reappoint (*vb*), 191-*1*
reason, 39-*36*; 148-*13*; 181-*27*
chief —, 139-*2*
every — to think, 135-*18*
for some — or other, 180-*16*
— of health, 40-*2*
sound —s, 220-*25*
reasonable, at a — hour, 119-*7*
— price, 1-*18*
reassurance, 183-*29*
reassure, 183-*30*
rebate, 98-*18*; 180-*34*; 197-*26*
rebound, 62-*35*
recall (*vb*), 182-*11*
recapitulate (*vb*), 184-*3*
recapitulation, 184-2
recapitulatory, 184-*1*
receipt, 4-*16*; 72-*19*; 180-*31*; 184-*8/11*;
186-*25*; 191-*29*
customs —, 4-*18*
— book, 35-*26*
receipt (*vb*) (a bill), 106-*2*
— an invoice, 4-*26*
receipts, 184-*16/19*
— and expenditure, 79-*9*
— and payments, 204-*3*
revenue —, 191-*31*
receivables, 53-*32*
receive (*vb*), 215-*2*
— accounts, 93-*32*
— stolen goods, 184-*5*
receiver, telephone —, 65-*13*
reception, 3-*5*; 184-*12/13*
recess, 163-*19*
recession, 186-*27*
recidivist, 185-*5*
reciprocal, 185-*7*
reciprocate, 160-*10*
reciprocity, 185-*6*
reckon (*vb*), 35-*34*; 54-*16*; 101-*3*; 208-*3*
reckoning, by dead —, 99-*17*
reclaim (land), 75-*23*
recognition, 186-*10*
in — (of), 59-*26*; 186-*11*
recognize (*vb*), 64-*19*; 133-*12*
recognized, 10-*4*
recommend (*vb*), 169-*11*; 177-*23*; 186-*2*
— a dividend, 177-*24*
recommendation, 185-*29*
reconcile, — points of view, 2-*32*
reconcilement, 14-*34/35*

reconciliation, 182-*31*
reconditioning, 190-*10*
reconsider (a decision), 197-*5*
reconstitute, 186-*15*
reconstruct (a crime), 186-*16*
record, 60-*4*; 60-*21*; 86-*31*; 187-*30*
— book, 137-*2*
for the —, 143-*27*
legal —, 39-*15*
police —, 39-*18*
record (*vb*), 53-*6*; 95-*22*; 126-*13*; 146-
10
recorded, 126-*15*
recording, 95-*18/24*
records, 15-*23*
recoup, 74-*26*; 124-*14*; 183-*1*; 187-*17*
recover (*vb*), 74-*13*; 186-*30*; 193-*21*
recoverable, 186-*21*
recovery, 189-*2*; 186-*22*; 187-*7*; 193-*30*
rectify (*vb*), 187-*8*
recuperate (*vb*), 186-*30*
red-tape, 33-*36*; 111-*11*; 156-*4*
redeem (*vb*), 12-*5*; 179-*26*; 181-*12*
— a debt, 134-*30*
— a mortgage, 75-*26*
redeemable, 12-*6*; 189-*15*
redeemed, 75-*24*
redemption, 12-*7*; 179-*25*; 181-*9*; 189-
17
accelerated —, 13-*14*
— of a loan, 12-*9*
terms of —, 12-*14*
redouble (*vb*), 187-*6*
redress (*vb*), 192-*12*
reduce (*vb*), 1-*6*; 76-*1*; 84-*10*; 181-*4*;
182-*4*; 187-*12*
— to the simplest form, 182-*5*
— tax, 82-*29*
reduced, 185-*15*; 187-*14*
— price, 181-*1*
reduction,180-*34*; 181-*3*; 187-*11*; 190-*3*
— of taxes, 75-*37*; 82-*28*
allow a —, 181-*2*
re-elect (*vb*), 191-*1*
re-establishment (of currency), 17-*29*
re-exchange, 184-*25*
refer (*vb*), 192-*7*; 199-*2*
reference, 144-*3*; 192-*3/4*
give s.o. a —, 186-*5*
refine (*vb*), 97-*30*
refinement, 184-*30*
refinery, 181-*26*
refining, 181-*25*
refloat (*vb*), 109-*35*
— a ship, 190-*33*
reform (*vb*), 17-*27/28*
refund, 189-*17*; 197-*26*
refund (*vb*), 189-*19*
refusal, 78-*16*
flat —, 39-*31*
refuse, 72-*31*; 183-*34*
refuse (*vb*), 73-*23*; 183-*32*
refusing, 181-*24*
refute (*vb*), 78-*1*

— a witness, 78-2
regard, with — to, 54-33; 96-34
register, 136-6; 187-30; 193-2
— of taxpayers, 63-24
share —, 187-32
trade —, 187-35
register (vb), 95-22; 126-13/16; 121-26
— a letter, 186-3
— a trade mark, 79-31; 80-4
registered, 70-27; 126-15; 166-27
— office, 201-31
— trade mark, 79-28; 142-40
under — cover, 164-27
registrar, 95-23; 117-16
— of mortgages, 59-21
registration, 95-18; 126-7; 121-25
— desk, 184-13
— fee, 113-21; 186-1; 126-11; 88-1
— for a letter, 185-31
— number, 143-15; 152-1
registry, 117-14
— office, 95-19
regression, 108-14
regular, 109-23; 188-8; 188-16; 214-6
regularize (vb), 188-15
regulate (vb), 188-12
regulation, 188-8 et seq.
regulations, contrary to —, 62-13
rehabilitate, 188-17
rehabilitation, 183-19
reimburse, 189-19
reimbursement, 189-17
reinstate, 188-19
reinsurance, 183-29
reinsure, 183-30/31
reinvest, 193-6
reject (vb), 178-18; 188-22
rejected, 88-32
— article, 132-14
rejects, 183-34
relapse (into crime), 185-4
relate to (vb), 54-30
related, 182-37
relation, 157-3
relationship, 188-27
business —, 182-20; 188-30
relative, 157-3/5
relays, work in —, 188-32
release, 72-20; 134-26 et seq.; 146-25
— from a promise, 75-25
release (vb), 76-29/30; 72-23; 102-25
— on bail, 134-33
— securities, 75-27
releasing, 146-25
reliable, 204-22; 208-6
— man, 119-28
— person/firm, 57-14
relief, 10-12
relieve (vb), 102-25; 188-31
relinquish, 76-15; 191-2
act of —ing, 191-9
— option, 1-7
rely on, 54-19

— on s.o., 182-30; 190-1
remainder, 189-9; 195-27/31
remaining, 195-28
remains, 72-11; 195-33
remarkable, 120-14
remarks, 177-16
reminds, that — me, 177-19
reminder, 182-12/14
remit (a punishment), 134-15
remittance, 97-7; 190-5; 186-24
remnant, 66-24/31
remote, 88-34
removal, 77-31; 79-13; 82-9; 134-5
remove (vb), 95-7; 195-4; 205-19; 217-5/22
— from a position, 82-8
removing, 208-1
remunerate (vb), 196-32
remuneration, 196-33; 92-34
remunerative, 190-22
rendering, 215-26
renew (vb), 191-11/14
renewable, 191-10
renewal, 191-13; 193-31
renounce, 78-39; 191-2
— a claim, 191-5
— a succession, 118-39
renovate, 189-10; 191-12/14
renown, 190-35
renowned, 194-8
rent, 138-15; 212-5
farm —, 107-34
ground —, 191-22
— -a-car service, 137-13
rent (vb), 138-10
rental, 137-7; 138-15; 187-4
rented, — value of a house, 220-31
renunciation, 76-14; 191-9
reopening, 191-28
repair, 16-15; 187-18; 190-8; 192-11
— shop, 192-13
in good —, 96-23
keep in good —, 115-27
be under —, 192-14
repair (vb), 145-2; 189-26; 192-16; 196-13
repairable, 192-10
repairing, 190-10; 192-11/13
repairs, 78-31
make emergency —, 78-33
tenant —, 137-8
reparation, 200-7; 192-12
repay (vb), 189-19
repayable, 189-15/16
repayment, 12-7; 189-17
repeal (vb), 1-25; 182-29
— a law, 137-19
repeat (vb), 191-11
— an offence, 185-4
repeated by, 194-1
repercussion, 62-36; 192-24
have —s, 192-25
repertory, 193-2
replace (vb), 190-16; 193-6; 207-32

267

replacement, 184-*24*; 190-*14*
reply, 193-*12*
— paid, 193-*15*
reply (*vb*), 193-*8*
report, 54-*15*; 60-*17*; 176-*1*; 182-*19*
draw upon a —, 60-*18*
official —, 51-*31*
report (*vb*), 176-*2*; 182-*28*
— on, 54-*9*
reported, it is —, 140-*30*
represent (*vb*), 193-*26/27*
representative, 140-*27*; 193-*24*
represented, as —, 81-*14*
reprieve, 208-*27*
reproduction, 65-*4*; 194-*4*
accurate —, 105-*30*
repudiate (*vb*), 81-*10*
repurchase, 181-*9*; 189-*22*
sale with option of —, 189-*23*
repurchase (*vb*), 181-*12*
reputable, 185-*27*
reputation, 194-*6*
enjoy a good —, 194-*7*
repute, 190-*35*
high —, 194-*8*
request, 173-*29*; 194-*10*
on —, 77-*13*
request (*vb*), 173-*26*; 203-*21*
require (*vb*), 150-*7*; 185-*22*
—s time, 77-*15*
required, 194-*12*
requirements, meet the — of, 28-*1*
requisite, 194-*12*
requisites, 17-*21*
office —, 112-*31*
requisition, 194-*14*
requisition (*vb*), 194-*16*
rescue, 190-*33*
research, 184-*29*
— department, 100-*38*
resell, 197-*2*
reservation, 194-*20*
—s, 137-*12*
reserve, 173-*14*; 179-*1*; 194-*19*
gold —, 194-*23*
in —, 184-*24*; 194-*21*
— for doubtful debts, 173-*17*
— fund, 173-*24*; 194-*22*
reserve (*vb*), 194-*29 et seq.*
— seats, 138-*11*
reserved, 138-*9*
reservoir, 26-*34*
reside (*vb*), 86-*13*; 152-*30*
residence, take up —, 86-*13*
resident, 194-*32*
residing, 86-*11*
residue, 189-*9*
resign (*vb*), 78-*4 et seq.*; 97-*10*
resignation, 78-*6*
tender one's —, 78-*8*
resolution, 194-*36*
pass a —, 7-*8*
resolve, 195-*7/10*; 206-*22*
resort, 186-*18*; 206-*14*

as a last —, 195-*20*
holiday —, 40-*35*
seaside —, 206-*15*
resort (*vb*) to, 186-*19*
resource, 195-*26*
resourceful, be —, 125-*40*
respect, 59-*28*
respectability, 119-*33*
respectable, 135-*27*
respects, in all —, 182-*25*
respite, 188-*24*; 208-*27*
response, 193-*12*
responsibility, 195-*11*
one's own —, 195-*15*
responsible, 43-*5*; 195-*16*; 203-*16/23*
in — quarters, 145-*17*
— for, 53-*14*; 155-*5*; 195-*12*
restock, 183-*28*
restoration, 187-*18*
— of goods, 139-*18*
restore (*vb*), 189-*4*; 186-*15*; 190-*32*
restrain, 52-*39*
restriction, 135-*21*
result, 1-*24*; 129-*27*; 196-*1*; 207-*15*
as a — of, 207-*18*
result (*vb*), 195-*24*
— in, 203-*13*
resume, 193-*22*
under —, 194-*25*
resumption, 193-*31*
retail, 50-*17*; 82-*19/23*
— dealer, 82-*20*
— store, 71-*22*
retail (*vb*), 71-*35*; 82-*26*; 221-*25*
retailer, 71-*32*; 82-*22*; 141-*31*
retailing, 71-*25*
retain (*vb*), 82-*30*; 115-*25*
retainer, 16-*26*; 119-*35*; 120-*1*
retinue, 207-*17*
retire, 196-*29*
— from business, 196-*12*
retired, 196-*27/30*
retirement, 196-*24*; 204-*1*
retiring, 203-*34/35*
retrace (*vb*) a case, 119-*17*
retract (*vb*), 74-*5*; 196-*22*
retraction, 74-*7*; 196-*20*
retraining (occupation), 183-*20*
retrench, 196-*31*
retrograde, 196-*35*
return, 150-*22*; 176-*27*; 182-*18*; 190-*26*; 192-*2*; 196-*14*; 197-*26*
in —, 186-*7*
income tax —, 73-*10*
return (*vb*), 190-*32*; 192-*6*; 197-*3*
— a bill, 63-*12*
— home, 188-*20*
— one's income, 73-*13*
— something, 182-*26*
returning (of unsold goods), 194-*3*
revamp, 189-*10*
revelation, 196-*38*
revenue, 184-*16*; 197-*6*
Inland —, 109-*11*; 184-*20*

shop, 31-*23/27*; 71-*22*; 138-*30*; 199-*16*
  ready-made —, 57-*1*
  — assistant, 221-*21*
  — soiled, 23-*10*; 75-22
shopping, go —, 3-*21*
shore, 100-*19*
short, 68-*12*
  at — notice, 76-*7*
  be — handed, 68-*14*
  be — of something, 68-*15*
  — cut, 181-*5*
  — dated, 68-*13*
  —hand, 206-*28*
  —hand writer, 206-*27*
  — lived, 133-*19*
  —/long dated, 212-*9*
  — odds, 66-*8*
shortage, 141-*2*; 182-*33*
shot, 66-*20*
show, 102-*22*; 104-*13*; 199-*17*; 200-*36*
  — of hands, 224-*29*
  on —, 104-*9*
show (*vb*), 104-*10*; 171-*17*; 203-*13*;
  211-*11*
  — loss, 3-*10*
  — to advantage, 220-*32*
  — up, 101-*8*
showing, 171-*14*
showroom, 89-*13*; 104-*16*
shunt, 10-*18*
shunting, 115-*7*; 140-*36*
shut (*vb*), out, 101-*33*
shutting, 107-*35*
shuttle, 149-*28*
side, 30-*27*; 157-*29/42*
  on both —s, 157-*32*
  — line, 152-*27*
side with (*vb*), 86-*24*; 205-*24*
siding, 92-*17*; 115-*7*
  goods' —, 224-*8*
siege, 29-*28*
sieve, 69-*43*
sift, 70-*1*
sifter, 69-*43*
sight, 146-*12*
  at —, 171-*16*
  at first—, 173-*33*
  translate at —, 155-*18*
sign, 114-*25*; 124-*34*; 142-*38*; 202-*1*
  advertisement —, 95-*27/28*
  flashing illuminated —, 185-*17/18*
sign (*vb*), 201-*36*
  — deed, 205-*6*
  — in the margin, 91-*30*
signatories, 22-*12*
signature, 201-*14 et seq.*; 204-*28*
  first —, 201-*38*; 110-*29*
  — tune, 124-*30*
signify, 151-*17*; 202-*3*
signing, 159-*6*; 204-*28*
silence, 202-*5*
silk, — fabrics, 202-*32*
  — trade, 202-*33*
  —s, 202-*32*

silver, 15-*25*; 15-*32*
simulate (*vb*) (illness), 63-*9*
sincerely, 110-*3*
  — yours, 10-*7*
  yours —, 199-*23*
single, 219-*29*
sink (*vb*), 12-*5*
site, 93-*3*; 162-*40*
situate (*vb*), 202-*17*
situation, 202-*12*
  find a — for s.o., 163-*32*
  present —, 58-*23*
  —s vacant, 93-*8*
  —s wanted, 77-*10*
size, 94-*9*; 111-*12*; 116-*34*; 122-*5*;
  177-*10*; 209-*19*
sketch, 88-*30*
skilful, 112-*2*
skin, 160-*23*
slant, 28-*4*
slapdash, 217-*33*
slip, 30-*32*; 98-*3*; 132-*26*
  pay —, 33-*11*
  paying-in —, 31-*2*; 33-*13*
  — into an envelope, 96-*33*
  — of paper, 156-*20*
slogan, 45-*10*; 83-*16*; 148-*12*; 202-*19*
slot-machine, 22-*1*; 85-*12*
slump, 145-*8*
slump (*vb*), 91-*13*
smash (financial —), 132-*9*
smattering, have a — of, 151-*19*
smelting, 114-*20*
smile, forced —, 49-*38*
smooth (*vb*) (down), 13-*21*
smuggle (*vb*), 96-*20*; 113-*41*; 114-*2*
smuggler, 114-*3*
snag, 90-*34*
snatch (*vb*), 112-*37*
soaring, 99-*7*
society, 51-*23*; 219-*25*
soften (*vb*), 21-*7*
soil, 203-*1*
  heavy —, 112-*11*
sold (out), to be — (out), 97-*25*; 141-*4*;
  221-*23*
sole, 101-*34*; 219-*29*
  be — agents for, 101-*35*
  for the — purpose of, 108-*33*
solicitation, 127-*5*
solicitor, 44-*4*; 153-*26*
  —'s office, 61-*23*; 100-*39*
solve (*vb*), 195-*6*; 216-*32*
solvency, 203-*22*
solvent, 203-*23*
sort (*vb*), 98-*30*; 149-*15*
  — out, 218-*24*
sorter, 218-*26*
sorting, 218-*16/17*
sought-after, 185-*1*
soundproof, 126-*23*
source, 178-*30*; 204-*21*
  — of energy, 120-*18*
  — of income, 204-*23*

space, 10-*20*; 39-*12*; 93-*3*; 163-*22*
space (*vb*), 98-*28/29*
spare, — part, 82-*11*; 162-*33*; 184-*27*
spare (*vb*), — no expense, 186-*29*
speak (*vb*), 157-*23*; 216-*33*
— favourably of s.o., 186-*2*
— to, 7-*22/24*
speaker, guest —, 46-*13*
specialist, 205-*30*
specie, 15-*35*; 98-*31*; 151-*37*
—s, 99-*5*; 116-*3*
specifically, 104-*20*
specification, 81-*13*; 30-*39*; 35-*1*; 31-*3*
specify, 169-*9*
speculate, 9-*34*; 205-*38*
— on a rise, 130-*38*; 206-*2*
— on a fall, 130-*36*; 206-*1*
speculation, 9-*33*; 205-*35*
speculative, 205-*33/34*
speculator, 9-*35*; 205-*31*
speech, lawyer's —, 163-*38*
speed, 34-*25/26*; 76-*6*; 84-*6*; 216-*2*; 223-*28*
maximum —, 135-*26*
— up, 1-*35*
with all possible —, 76-*9*
speedy, 102-*35*
to be —, 84-*9*
spelling, — mistake, 107-*12*
spending, without — a penny, 72-*10*
sphere, 86-*5*; 145-*16*
spike-file, 163-*16*
split (*vb*), 112-*35*
— the difference, 165-*35*
— up, 200-*27*; 206-*33*
splitting, — in two, 74-*16*
spoil, 1-*11*
spoiled, 1-*10*
to get —, 1-*12*
spoils, 33-*41*
spoliation, 163-*5*
sponsor, 49-*40*; 193-*7*
sponsored by, 21-*33*
sponsorship, 157-*28*
under the — of, 91-*20*
spot, 62-*24*; 163-*26*
on the —, 135-*19*
— check, 222-*18*
spread (*vb*), 89-*32*
— news, 46-*30*; 49-*16*
— out, 104-*29*; 192-*18*; 89-*35*
— payments, 89-*36*
spreading, 205-*37*
spurious, 13-*22*
squander, 54-*22*; 84-*5*
square, 163-*25*
stabilization, 206-*3*
stabilize, 206-*5*
staff, 34-*28*; 161-*32*
stag, 118-*22*
stag (*vb*), 118-*20*
stage, 138-*14*
stagger (of holidays), 89-*35*

staggering, 72-*16*
stagnation, 141-*22*; 145-*8*
stake, 146-*14*
be at —, 130-*22*
betting —, 95-*6*
stake (*vb*), 130-*23*; 146-*32*
stale, become —, 6-*10*
stall, 100-*1*; 206-*8*
stall (*vb*), 211-*21*
stamp, 99-*11*; 113-*36*; 117-*33*; 165-*17*
date —, 213-*3*
official —, 64-*4/10*
postage-due —, 213-*7*
postal —, 212-*38*; 213-*6*
rubber —, 213-*4*
— revenue, 213-*5*
stamp (*vb*), 9-*2*; 99-*12*; 213-*10*
stamped, 9-*1*; 213-*8*
— paper, 213-*9*
stamping, 9-*3*; 212-*37*
— of weights, 99-*10*
stand, 206-*8*
— for, 193-*27*
— in, 190-*13*; 207-*32*
— to gain, 114-*38*
standard, 206-*10*
gold —, 100-*5*
metal —, 214-*1*
— charge, 210-*35*
— of living, 150-*27*; 206-*11*
— metre, 100-*4*
— model (of car), 201-*29*
— of wages, 150-*26*; 210-*25*
— of weights, 100-*3*
standardization, 100-*6*
standardize, 100-*7*; 188-*15*; 206-*12*
standing, 202-*14*; 216-*7*
in good —, 151-*12*
staple, 9-*38*
staple (*vb*), 9-*39*
stapler, 9-*40*; 32-*13*
start, 77-*25*
start (*vb*), 95-*2*; 95-*30*
— a fashion, 129-*8*
— a fund, 204-*32*
— negotiations, 95-*31*
starve (*vb*) s.o., 223-*33*
state, 100-*8*
— -managed, 187-*25*
— of emergency, 220-*3*
state (*vb*), 95-*11*; 144-*5*
statement, 30-*32*; 95-*10*; 100-*8*; 104-*8*; 182-*19*; 188-*33*; 189-*1*
cash —, 30-*34*; 100-*1*
make a —, 73-*14*
— of account, 54-*1/8*; 105-*1*
— of affairs (bank), 26-*3*
— of analysis, 28-*22*
stating, 144-*6*
station, 167-*22*; 206-*14*
—master, 115-*30*; 43-*35*
tube —, 206-*16*
stationary, 112-*31*; 206-*20*
stationers, 156-*5*

31,
switch 168,
128,

tabulate (*vb*), 209-*15*
tag, 100-*24*
tailor, 105-*29*
taint, 210-*3*
take, 169-*28*; 170-*12/22*; 153-*7*
— a collection, 66-*17*
— an oath, 131-*33*
— away, 95-*7*
— back, 196-*10/21*; 290-*20*; 193-*20*
— down in shorthand, 206-*29*
— legal action against, 127-*25*
— necessary steps, 77-*22*
— off, 74-*24*; 196-*31*
— over (assets), 193-*23*
— on staff, etc., 92-*14*
— part in, 157-*37*; 158-*7*
— pictures, 162-*22*
— stock of, 129-*20*
— the floor, 157-*23*
— the place of, 135-*20*; 193-*26*
— up one's duty, 110-*18*
taker, 170-*25/28*
— of an option, 154-*10*
taking, 174-*18*
— back, 193-*28*
talent, 209-*27*
tall, 118-*24*
tally, 34-*33*; 130-*17*
tally (*vb*), 55-*28*; 65-*33*
tamper (*vb*) (with), 218-*29/33*
tangible (property), 65-*14*
tank, 24-*11*; 26-*34*; 47-*1/2*
tanker, 27-*4*
tap, on —, 224-*22*
tape, gummed —, 156-*11*
tape recorder, 95-*23*
tape recording, 95-*20*
target, 33-*37*
tariff, 26-*13*; 210-*9/14*
— walls, 87-*12*
tariff (*vb*), 210-*18*
tarpaulin, 24-*13*
tartan, 90-*20*
task, 209-*18*
official —, 110-*14*
taste, 11-*14*
tax, 63-*29*; 187-*4*; 210-*31*
corporation —, 122-*34*
head —, 122-*29*
income —, 122-*32*
land —, 122-*30*
non-resident —, 210-*31*
pay a —, 64-*1*
property —, 122-*30*
purchase —, 210-*33/34*
— on profits, 122-*33*
— collector, 161-*10*
— dodger, 219-*3*
—payer, 63-*23*
—payers, register of —, 63-*24*
tax (*vb*), 122-*20*; 210-*36*
taxable, 122-*16*; 210-*29*
taxation, 122-*24*; 210-*30*
taxed, 122-*17*

taxes, direct —, 63-*31*
indirect —, 63-*33*
inspector of —, 64-*14*
scheduled —, 122-*31*
to increase —, 9-*30*
tea-room, 199-*19*
team, 66-*25*; 97-*33*
teamster, 36-*23/24*
telegram, the — was worded, 55-*6*
telegraph, 210-*37*
telegraphic, 210-*38*
telephone, 210-*39/40*; 211-*3/5*
— box, 34-*2*
— call, 51-*26*; 64-*29*; 211-*4*
French —, 49-*21*
telex, 211-*6*
teller (Bank), 160-*12*
temporarily, 179-*6*
tenancy, 137-*9*
tenant, 137-*6/7*
— farmer, 144-*31*
— for life, 220-*14*
— repairs, 137-*8*
tender, 6-*24*; 153-*30*; 204-*16*
allocation to the lowest —, 6-*26*
by —, 204-*18*
illegal —, 68-*10*
legal —, 67-*9*
sale by —, 6-*28*; 222-*10*
tender (*vb*), 204-*20*
tenderer, 204-*19*
tenor, 211-*26*
tenure, 152-*26* [218-*27*
term (period of time), 140-*15*; 212-*5*;
term (expression), 212-*6*
term of payment, 76-*12*
terminal, 212-*17*
terminate (*vb*) (an agreement, etc.), 78-*25*;
212-*16*
termination, 78-*26*; 104-*31*; 135-*22*
terminus, 212-*17*
terms, 16-*10*; 177-*26*
easy —, 105-*26*
in — of, 110-*17*
technical —, 212-*14*
— of payment, 56-*19*
— of reference, 168-*24*
to be on good — with, 96-*24*
test, 97-*19*; 98-*38*; 103-*6*
— pilot, 163-*10*
test (*vb*), 103-*11*; 144-*39*; 159-*13*
testify (*vb*), 79-*33*; 211-*10*
testimonial, 21-*1*; 41-*7*
testimony, 79-*36*; 211-*7*
thanks, 189-*20*
received with —, 4-*20*
— to, 116-*20*
theatre, movie —, 199-*10*
theft, 224-*16*
theme, 148-*14*
theory, in —, 212-*30*
think (*vb*), — better of it, 183-*3*
thoroughfare, no —, 46-*24*; 128-*8*
thread, 108-*12*

transmission, 92-*31*
transmit (*vb*), 92-22; 217-*16*
transport, 43-*24*; 215-*35*; 217-*17*
  river —, 217-*18*
  road —, 198-*25*; 217-*19*
  — rate, 187-*28*
transport (*vb*), 217-22
transpose (*vb*), 217-24
trashy, 220-*35*
travel, — agency, 224-*36*
traveller, 224-*40*
  —'s cheque, 224-*37*
travelling, 79-*13*
  — allowance, 124-*20*
  — salesman, 224-*41*
treasurer, 218-*15*
  —'s office, 90-*12*
  —ship, 90-*11*
treasury, 218-*12/14*; 108-*42*
  — bill, 218-*13*
  — board, 59-*11*
  Secretary of —, 146-*2*
treatise, 216-*22*
treatment, 216-*25*
treaty, 216-*21*
  sign a —, 216-*23*
treble, 218-*30*
treble (*vb*), 218-*31*
tree, 15-*21*
  family —, 15-*22*
trend, 101-*13*; 154-*36*
  upward —, 118-*17*
trespass, 77-*4*
trespass (*vb*), 217-*10*; 223-*13*
trespasser, 217-*11*
trial, 97-*20*; 98-*38*; 103-*6*; 131-*22*; 175-
  39
  brought up for —, 131-*25*
  stand —, 218-*21*
tribunal, 218-*20*
  go before a —, 218-*21*
tribute, 119-*21*
trick, 219-*8*
tried, to be —, 175-*42*
trim, 197-*30*
  — a ship, 16-*33*
trip, 157-*1*; 216-*30*; 224-*35*; 224-*38/39*
triple, 218-*30*
triple (*vb*), 218-*31*
triplicate, 218-*32*
  in —, 102-*8*
truck-gardener/gardening, 141-*20/21*
truly, yours —, 59-*25*; 199-*23*
trust, 39-*2*; 57-*9*; 69-*1*; 108-*15/22*
  breach of —, 1-*31*; 57-*10*
  position of —, 57-*16*
  — company, 108-*21*
  — deed, 108-*16/19*
trust (*vb*), 57-*11*; 57-*13*
trustee, 59-*31*; 70-*23*; 140-27; 209-*8/9*
  — (leg.), 79-*37*; 6-*35*
  —ship, 70-22; 209-*11*; 219-*13*
trustworthy, 57-*12*; 84-*3*; 110-*5*; 208-*6*
truth, 222-22

try (*vb*), 131-*28*
  — again, 43-*13*
  — a case, 131-*29*
tube, 219-*15*
  — station, 206-*16*
tuition, — fees, 200-*34*
turn, 215-*11*
  in —, 215-*9*
turn (*vb*), 215-*11*
  — down, 73-*23*; 187-*21*; 188-22
  — out, 190-27
  — to account, 213-*30*
  — up, 171-*21*
turnover, 8-7; 44-*35*
turns, in/by —, 197-*32*
  taking —, 198-*11*
tycoon, 31-*35*
tying, — up, 121-*35*
type, 116-*3*; 206-*10*
type (*vb*), 209-*36*; 70-26
typewriter, 138-22
typing, 70-*25*
  — error, 107-7
  — mistake, 113-*38*
typist, 70-*24*
tyre, 165-*2*

ultimatum, 219-*19*
unable, 123-*15*
unalienated, 123-*14*
unanimity, 219-22
unanimous, 219-*21*
unassignable, 123-*13*
unattachable, 126-*5*
unauthorized, — official, 140-*19*
unavailable, 97-*25*; 125-*2*
unawares, 68-*16*; 143-*19*
unballast, 76-22
unbleached, 90-*33*
unbreakable, 123-*19*
uncertain, 168-*38*
unchanging, 161-*19*
unclaimed, — goods, 204-*13*
unconditionally, 56-*23*
uncovered, 73-*29*
uncut (of diamond), 32-27
undated, 70-*33*
undamaged, 124-*12*
undelivered, if — please return to sender, 85-
  14
under-age, 145-*31*
undergo (*vb*) a change, 206-*34*
underrate (*vb*), 80-*19*
undersell (*vb*), 203-*12*
undersigned, 205-*13/14*
understand (*vb*), 52-*33*; 103-*26*; 183-*25*;
  198-*33*
understudy, 100-*37*
undertake (*vb*), 18-*30/31*; 127-*24*; 170-
  15/23
undertaking, 96-*15*
underwear, 135-*28*
underwrite (of shares), 115-*13*; 205-*9*

underwriter, 13-*20*; 86-*26*; 204-*26*
underwritten, 205-*3*
undesirable, 124-*24*
undischarged (bankrupt), 72-*25*
undivided, 125-*3*; 157-*39*
unduly, 125-*7*
unemployed, 45-*28*; 45-*31*; 200-*1*; 217-
    29
unemployment, 45-*20*
    — benefit, 11-*9*; 124-*18*
    — insurance, 45-*22*
unexpected, 122-*40*
unexpectedly, 134-*3*
unfit, 100-*18*; 123-*15*
unforseen, 122-*41*
unfounded, 110-*31*; 116-*43*
ungrateful, 125-*33*
unheard, — of, 169-*5*
unhurt, 124-*12*
unify, 219-*24*
unintentionally, 127-*29*
union, 219-*25*
unit, 219-*33/34*
    work as a —, 29-*26*
unite (*vb*), 18-*21*
unity, 219-*26/32*
unknown, 127-*21*
unlawful, 76-27; 121-*16/18*
unlimited, 84-*18*; 121-22; 135-*25*
unload, 71-*14/23*
unmarketable, 129-*14*
unmatched, 78-*35*
unmortgaged, 121-*2*
unofficial, 153-*27*
unpack (*vb*), 71-*8/9*
unpaid, 122-*2*
unprecedented, 102-*14*; 169-*5*
unprotected, 15-*10*
unprovoked, — insult, 117-*1*
unqualified (leg.), 125-*35*
unquestionable, 120-*11*
unquestionably, 61-*30*
unrefined (of oil), 32-*25*
unreliable, 40-*15*; 207-*29*
unreservedly, 194-*24*
unsaleable, 129-*14*; 198-*9*
unscrupulous behaviour, 76-*26*
unseal (*vb*), 72-*15*; 81-*11/12*
unseat (*vb*) (an M.P.), 129-*12*
unsecured, 45-*5/7*; 199-*31*
    — credit, 73-*31*
unsold, 129-*15*
unstow (*vb*) (cargo), 81-*7*
unsuccessful, 1-*21*; 141-*6*
untimely, 126-*3*
untransferable, 123-*13/29*
up, 134-*2*
upset, 218-*7*
upside-down, 97-*1*
up-to-date, 146-*12*
U.P.U., 219-*28*
urge, 95-*3*
urgency, 219-*36*
urgent, 122-*3*

urgently, 127-*4*
urn, 220-*4*
usage, 88-*2*; 220-*7*
use, 146-*26*; 60-*9*; 93-*4*; 220-*6*
    make good — of, 203-*30*
use (*vb*), 84-*35*
    — a sum, 93-*11*
    — economically, 143-*32*
    — s.o., 103-*37*
    — up, 97-*26*
useless, 220-*20*
usher, 120-*26*

vacancy, 220-*15/18*
vacant, 134-*38*; 220-*17*; 222-*33*
    — seat, 223-*1*
vacuum, 222-*32*
vain, 220-*20*
valid, 188-*16*; 220-*23/24*
    make —, 21-*13*
    no longer —, 161-*13*
validate (*vb*) a passport, 221-*9*
valuable, 169-*6*; 220-*29*
    — object, 182-*34*
valuables, 220-*34*
valuation, 99-*15*; 101-2; 103-*15*
value, 220-*27*
    of no —, 220-*35*
    surrender —, 220-*36*
value (*vb*), 101-*3*; 103-*20*
valuer, 99-*14*; 103-*12*; 174-*21*
van, delivery —, 36-22
variance, at — with, 61-*29*; 83-*32*
variety, 99-*5*; 115-*2*
various, 85-*15*
vat, 24-*11*
vending, — machine, 22-*1*; 85-*12*
vendor, 141-*26*
venture, 96-*15*
verbatim, 212-*29*
verdict, 222-*14*
    return a —, 222-*15*
verification, 60-*19*
verify (*vb*), 60-*22*; 222-*19*
vest (*vb*) (property), 18-*7*
vestry, 105-*11/12*
victim, 202-*10*
vigour, 223-*6*
vindicate, 132-*6*
vineyard, 48-*4*
violate, 217-*10*; 223-*15*
violation, 223-*11*; 125-*23*
violence, use —, 224-*7*
vital, 122-*7*
vocational, 176-*24*
    — guidance, 154-*37*; 176-*26*
    — training, 111-*17*; 176-*25*
void, 129-*10*; 222-*32*
void (*vb*), 195-*8*; 194-*35*
voidable, 194-*33*
volume, 224-*24/25*
volume (cubic content), 70-*12*
volunteer, 177-*25*

window, 118-*8*
  shop/store —, 83-*13*; 223-*31*
  — -dresser, 100-*2*
  — -dressing, 100-*1*
  — -envelope, 96-*32*
wine, local —, 160-*16*
winter-sports, 206-*17*
wipe off (*vb*), 195-*5*
wipe out (*vb*), 15-*12*
wiping out, 104-*32*
wire (telegraph), 210-*37*
wire up (*vb*), 34-*6*
wish (*vb*), 127-*26*; 172-*31*; 223-*34*
  — you well, 223-*36*
wishes, 224-*21*
  against his —, 117-*9*
  last —, 224-*23*
  with best —, 223-*35*
withdraw (*vb*), 81-27; 196-*10/21*
  — from, 191-*2*; 78-*10*
withdrawal, 74-7; 81-*26*; 139-*17*; 189-
  17; 196-*23*; 196-*25*
witness, 21-*8*; 211-*12*; 110-*6*
  bear —, 166-*34*
  call to —, 211-*13*
  eye —, 211-*17*
  legal —, 79-*25*
  tamper with a —, 211-*14*
  — for the defence, 72-22; 211-*16*
  — for the prosecution, 211-*15*
wood, 29-*31/35*; 132-*12*
woodwork, 144-*11*
wool, 132-*11/12*
word, 148-*8*; 157-*18*; 212-*6*
  eat one's —s, 196-*22*
  give one's —, 157-*20*
  her own —s, 157-*24*
  in so many —s, 151-*1*
  — for —, 148-*11*; 212-*29*
word (*vb*), 134-*23*
wording, 95-*10*; 134-*21*
work, 152-*25*; 153-*12*; 209-*17*; 217-
  25/33
  be out of —, 45-*24*; 200-*1*
  manual —, 218-*1*
  more —, 208-*15*
  start — on, 42-*26*
  — by contract, 110-*40*
work (*vb*), 103-*38*; 110-*22*; 142-*17*;
  218-*6*
  — overtime, 207-*36*
  — shifts, 159-*39*; 188-*32*
  — unremittingly, 218-*9*
workable, 155-*21*
worker, 155-*24*
working, 103-*32*
  — class, 155-*26*
  — day, 131-7; 155-*22*
  — hours, 217-*27*

  — party, 97-*33*
workmanship, 105-*28*; 106-*1*; 218-*2*
works, 220-*12*; 42-*23*; 105-*10*
workshop, 20-*20*
worm (*vb*) money out of s.o., 205-*29*
worry (*vb*), 218-*7*
worsen, 9-*29*
worth, 220-27
  be —, 221-*10*
  be — one's weight in gold, 154-*22*
worthless, 151-*32*; 180-*15*; 200-*2*
worthy, 84-*2*
  be —, 84-*4*
wrap up (*vb*), 92-*36*
wrapper, 25-*18/21*
wreck (*vb*), 97-*14*
  — a ship, 90-*8*
wreckage, 72-*13*
wrecked, 90-*5*
writ, 4-*36*; 18-*5 et seq.*; 103-27; 154-27
  — server, 120-27
write (one's letters), 67-*24*
  — down, 126-*12*
  — off, 162-*1*, 162-*4*
  — out, 187-*5*
  — up, 131-*9*
writer, 119-*29*
writing, 90-*26*; 187-*1*
  in —, 90-*27/28*
  be — to s.o., 65-*26*
  — off, 12-*8/12*
  — pad, 29-*24*
wrong, 75-*28*; 86-*14*; 107-*16/18*; 140-
  6; 169-*22*; 214-*28*
  — number, 151-*40*; 181-*8*
wrong (*vb*), 133-*20*; 214-*29*
wrought-iron, 111-*7*

x-ray, 181-*21*

yachting, 149-*35*
yard, marshalling-, 115-*31*; 218-*18*
  shipbuilding-, 149-*26*
year, 12-*21/28*
  financial —, 102-*20*
  leap —, 29-*18*
  past —, 102-*21*
yield, 176-*16*; 182-*18*; 190-*28/26*; 30-
  14
  — of a stock, 210-*20*
  — to oncoming traffic, 174-*17*
yield (*vb*), 71-*34*; 164-*31*; 176-*14*; 190-
  32; 166-*28*; 182-27

zebra-crossing, 159-*1*

DESIGN HISTORY

HISTORY

a students' handbook

Edited by

HAZEL CONWAY

London and New York

First published in 1987 by
Harper Collins Academic
Second impression 1991

Reprinted in 1992, 1994, 1995, 1997, 1999
by Routledge
11 New Fetter Lane, London EC4P 4EE
29 West 35th Street, New York, NY 10001

Printed and bound in Great Britain by
Biddles Ltd, Guildford and King's Lynn

British Library Cataloguing in Publication Data
A catalogue record for this book is available from the British Library

Library of Congress Cataloguing in Publication Data
A catalogue record for this book is available from the Library of Congress

ISBN 0–415–08473–3

Contents

List of Plates

Acknowledgements

This book has grown out of many discussions which have taken place over a lengthy period and my debt to the patience of all the contributors and the support of my colleagues is considerable. In addition I would particularly like to thank the following for their encouragement, help and criticism: Mary Stewart, Anthea McCullough, Chris Mees, Victor Margolin, John Pugsley, Zara Conway.

List of Contributors

Jeremy Aynsley studied History of Art at Sussex University and became interested in the interaction between painting, graphic design and photography, especially of the Weimar period. He now teaches Art and Design History at Brighton Polytechnic and is researching German Graphic Design of the interwar period.

Hazel Conway came to design history from a background in science and technology and was a founder member of the Design History Research Group, the group which led to the setting up of the Design History Society. Her research and teaching experience of design history ranges from industrial, furniture and interior design to landscape and environmental design. Among her publications is a monograph on the furniture designer *Ernest Race* who was active in the 1940s and 1950s, and she was awarded her PhD for her study of the design and development of the municipal park in the nineteenth century. She is at present Principal Lecturer in History of Architecture and Design at Leicester Polytechnic.

John Heskett has specialized in design history since 1967, after working in town planning, publishing and secondary-school teaching. At present Head of Historical and Theoretical Studies at Ravensbourne College of Design and Communication at Chislehurst in South London, he has also lectured widely and acted as consultant for companies and governmental organizations at home and abroad. He is the author of *Industrial Design* (1980) in the World of Art Series and *Design in Germany 1870–1918* (1986) which is intended as the first of three volumes on the history of German design in the last century.

Pat Kirkham read History at Leeds University where she specialized in social and economic history as well as the history of architecture and design. Her PhD (London University) was written on furniture making in London *c* 1700–1870. Author of *William and John Linnell*, 2 vols, 1980 (with Helena Hayward), *Harry Peach: Dryad and the DIA* (1980), and numerous articles in learned and more popular journals, she has lectured widely in America and this country. At present she is working on a book on women and design and collaborating with the Geffrye Museum and London History Workshop on a study of furniture making in the East End of London. She teaches architecture and design at Leicester Polytechnic

Josephine Miller studied Embroidery and Textiles at Goldsmiths' College School of Art and subsequently was awarded an MA in the History of European Art with a special emphasis on Dress History from the Courtauld Institute of Art, London University. She is currently employed as Senior Lecturer in the History of Design at the City of Birmingham Polytechnic. She has wide-ranging experience in teaching and has worked on a series of ten programmes on Dress for Educational TV and carried out freelance picture research.

Rowan Roenisch was born in Welwyn Garden City and brought up amongst the natural beauty of Mount Park Estate (1876) and South Hill Avenue 'garden estate' Harrow on the Hill. She originally trained in Fine Art. After historical studies at the Courtauld Institute she went on to teach architectural and design history and is now Senior Lecturer at Leicester Polytechnic. More recently she has successfully completed a Postgraduate Diploma in Architectural and Building Conservation and undertaken a joint report for the Victorian Society on Church Redundancy and Re-use in Leicester. Her research interests include housing in the Soviet Union, Britain and Zimbabwe, and vernacular architecture.

Jonathan Woodham studied for the MA degree in Fine Art, mounted jointly by the University of Edinburgh and Edinburgh College of Art, which involved both practical and historical work. After studying for an MA in the History of British Romantic Art at the Courtauld Institute of Art in London, he was appointed to the staff of the North Staffordshire Polytechnic in the Potteries where he became increasingly aware of the significance of design. Since then he has researched extensively into the history of the subject, with a particular focus on British industrial design since the First World War and has written a book, *The Industrial Designer and the Public*, published by Pembridge, 1983. He is now Principal Lecturer in Design History at Brighton Polytechnic.

Introduction

This is a book about how to study design history – where to start, what sort of questions to ask and how to answer them. In recent years the possibilities of studying design history have grown enormously. It is now possible to study it at school, in colleges, polytechnics and universities and at levels which range from A level to undergraduate and postgraduate. Design history can be the main subject of a degree course, or it can be part of practical design or humanities courses, yet until now there has been no book which offers guidance to students on how to study it or how to approach the subject. The aim of this book is to provide an introduction to the study of design history which can be used by students in colleges, polytechnics and universities. No matter whether your main subject is a two- or three-dimensional design course, or whether you are studying design history as a main subject, this book will provide a clear introduction to it, and teachers of design history at A level will find that it provides a wealth of information on the topic. Studying is traditionally associated with educational establishments, but being a student is not only a matter of attending courses, it is much more concerned with attitude of mind and a spirit of inquiry. So this book also aims to help to make the study of design history more accessible to those with an interest in the subject, whether or not they are involved in formal education.

Design history is a large subject and the chapter headings of the book indicate broad areas of it. However such sub-divisions are in many ways artificial as I suggest in the first chapter, 'Design History Basics'. 'Design History Basics' introduces the basic tools necessary to any historical study and discusses some of the general problems and issues that may be encountered. Each of the following chapters on dress and textiles, ceramics, furniture, interiors, industrial design and graphics indicates the scope of the subject in terms of its breadth, chronology and the links between the various subject areas. Case studies illustrate some of the possible approaches to each area and the types of problem and pitfalls to look out for. In addition some indication is given on how historians have approached particular areas in the past. As the subject of environmental design and the literature on it is so large, a rather different approach has been adopted in this chapter. The emphasis there is primarily concerned with the question of project work on various aspects of twentieth-century issues, and indications are given of a variety of potential topics.

At the end of each chapter there are notes to the references and quotations that appear and a Further Reading list for each chapter is given at the end of the book. These are an important supplement to each chapter since they enable readers to build on the introductory material in the chapters, and so pursue particular interests in more detail. Although some readers may be interested primarily in one or two of these areas, many points of interest may well appear in other chapters. The index which lists all the main topics provides access to relevant material in other chapters. Also at the end of the book is a glossary which can be referred to whenever (q.v.) or (qq.v) follows a name or term in the text. This is followed by a list of useful addresses or organizations which relate in a variety of ways to the study of design history.

1

Design History Basics

HAZEL CONWAY

There are examples of design and opportunities for studying design history all around us, yet when our surroundings are very familiar, as our houses and streets are, we tend to take them for granted. We cease to see them, or even to think that there is anything much of interest in them. Wherever we are design affects us all, both directly and indirectly, consciously and subconsciously. At home the lighting, carpets, curtains, wallpaper and furniture all contribute to the interior design of a room. Every period has its own ways of arranging furniture, and today is no exception. Not long ago the main focus of a living-room would have been the fireplace, but this is not necessarily so today. Outside, the design of the front gardens, the variety of colours of the front doors, the textures of the bricks, contribute to the environment, as do the shops, the traffic and the open spaces. Of course not all the features that go towards creating our environment were consciously designed, some occurred by accident, or neglect, or by juxtaposition. One of the most obvious examples of design in our society, intended to attract our attention wherever we find ourselves, is that of advertisements. In the street, in the shops, reading the papers or magazines, or watching television, advertisement designers hope to have a direct effect on us, and this we recognize. Their indirect effects are, however, much more subtle and not nearly so easy to recognize, yet our perception of ourselves, our surroundings and our society are affected by them.

At home among familiar furniture you know from experience which chairs are comfortable, but how closely do you ever look at any particular one? If you are asked to describe one chair exactly from memory, could you do so, and where would you begin? When you note – almost without thinking about it because it is so obvious – that

3

the form taken by a dining chair is different from that of an easy chair for relaxing in, you are beginning to identify how form is related to use, and this is one aspect of design analysis. If you visit a museum and see a collection of dining chairs from a period covering a century or more you will again note differences in the forms the chairs take, even though they all have a similar use. If you ask yourselves the reasons for these differences then you will again be involved in design analysis.

All the examples of design that you see around have their histories, but the development of the study of design history is very recent and it is only in the last decade that a range of degree courses has been introduced in which it forms a major element. Those who are involved in the practice of design history, whether they are in museums, in teaching, research or elsewhere, have clear but differing ideas about what it is, but outside this group few people have any real understanding of the subject or how it can be studied. Common misconceptions include the idea that design history is primarily about aesthetics and collecting rare and beautiful objects, or about fashion, or historic periods and the styles of design associated with particular periods. What makes it even more complex is that there are elements of truth in all these views, and these will be explored. Another confusion lies in the interpretation of the word 'design'. When we talk about the design of a lamp, for example, we may be concerned with the mental processes and the drawings and models that eventually result in that particular lamp; we may be concerned with the production process, the form and material of the lamp and how it is used; we could also be concerned with how the lamp was marketed, advertised, packaged and sold. Design history can be concerned with any or all of these aspects.

Another area of confusion concerns the scope of design history as a subject and its relationship to other histories. It was largely as a result of these and other confusions that the idea for this book came about.

Although many historical examples are included in this introduction to design history, it is not intended to be a concise history of the subject. The aim is to show how to study the subject by looking at a number of different areas, and illustrating a variety of approaches by means of case studies. The approaches and skills needed to study advertising design, say, differ from those needed to study shoe or aircraft design, and in practice design historians tend to specialize, as do designers. It is for this reason that this book divides design history into a number of areas which reflect those specializations. Dress and textiles, ceramics, furniture, interior design, industrial design, graphics, and environmental design are the titles of the chapters and in general the designers working in these areas have their particular professional institutions and publications. The exception to this is environmental design. Environmental design can include architecture, town planning, landscape design and civil engineering and each of these areas has their own professional institutions and publications.

Although this division of design history into various areas reflects the professional structure of practising designers, it is in many ways arbitrary for there are many links between the areas both in terms of theory and practice. The practical link between furniture and interior design is an obvious example, and the presence of graphic design in the environment, whether in the form of advertising, or street or shop signs, is another.

Stylistic influences such as that of Neo-Classicism (q.v.) affected architecture as well as dress design, ceramics, silver, furniture and interiors. In addition important theories affected a broad spectrum of design, as well as architecture. For example de Stijl (q.v.) philosophy, which developed in Holland from 1917 on, embraced painting, architecture, furniture and interior design, town planning/environmental design and graphics. The work of many designers ranges across a spectrum of design: William Kent's (q.v.) work included architecture, landscape, furniture and interior design while William Morris (q.v.) worked in textiles, stained glass and book design, and his theories embraced the whole basis of society. The various chapter headings of this book should not therefore be taken to imply rigid boundaries, for these do not exist. This means that readers with a particular interest in, say, industrial design or furniture should not restrict themselves to reading only those chapters for there may well be useful material elsewhere.

The reasons for studying design history are similar in many ways to those for any historical study. They relate to our need to understand the present, and are based on the belief that such an understanding is impossible without a knowledge of the past. Studies of the past enable us to understand where we have come from, and something of the complex choices and decisions that have led to where we are today. Without that perspective our understanding is limited. We become prisoners of the present, unable to forsee alternatives, or recognize our own possibilities of choice. When, for example, newspapers talk of 'Victorian values', they imply an era when thrift, self-reliance, and hard work were the norm. That view of the Victorian period conveniently ignores the appalling living conditions, high mortality rate, and excessive hours of work, often in dangerous conditions, in order to make a particular point about society today, in comparison with that of a hundred years or so ago. Newspapers are not in the business of historical accuracy, they are in the business of selling papers and ideas, but unless we as readers have some historical understanding, we are likely to accept uncritically the viewpoint being projected. An understanding of history is part of the process of exercising control over our own lives, whether as individuals, groups or societies. The objects that are the main focus of studies in design history, the forms that they take and the ways in which they were produced and used, are the material result of complex changes and choices. Studies of how our material culture evolved, its meaning and influence, can give us a larger perspective of our past. The core of the discipline of design history concerns the search to understand particular designs in the context of the period in which they were produced, and the enjoyment of the subject lies in the intellectual and emotional stimulus that this provides. There are however many factors which can inhibit that understanding.

Subjective and Objective Responses

Design history, like any other history, is not solely concerned with the accumulation of facts. It is concerned with understanding and finding explanations of the past by evaluating, selecting and ordering data, as E. H. Carr discusses so clearly in *What is History?* (1961). Everyone has his or her own preferences and prejudices, and our own likes and dislikes can come between us and our historical studies. We all know from personal experience that we like some designs for particular reasons, and not others. This is a subjective reaction that everyone experiences, but you must be careful not to draw historical conclusions from your own likes and dislikes, or to argue that because you do not like a design it is therefore not important historically. Although the qualitative analysis of design and your imaginative response to it may be one of the reasons encouraging you to study the subject in the first place, there is a great difference between such design appreciation and the study of design history. In talking about your reactions to familiar and to unfamiliar surroundings I implied that looking carefully is one important aspect of an interest in design and in design history. Designing if it is to move beyond theory into practice means putting

Figure 1.1   Cast-iron seat, Richmond Park, *c.* 1870

ideas into form. These may be two-dimensional or three-dimensional, and they could be drawings or sketches or they could result in a finished object such as a chair. Form is thus a very important part of design and hence of design history. However opinions concerning the beauty of particular forms have varied widely in the past and although some of the major philosophers have tried to evolve satisfactory criteria in order to identify clearly what is beautiful and what is not, opinions on it remain subjective.

You can look at the design of this cast iron garden seat (Fig. 1.1) with its highly ornamental foliage design in terms of the material it is made of and the processes of production, but if you look at the ornamentation, how are you to talk about it in a way that has any historical validity? Attitudes towards such design have altered and continue to do so, and a subjective analysis in terms of today's criteria, that is, whether you like it or not, would tell you more about today's criteria than it would about this particular design. To attempt to understand this seat design and why those particular forms were used you would need to know what the Victorians at that time thought of ornament, and what they meant by the 'correct use of ornament'. You would also need to understand

7

the criteria affecting design and read the works of those who were influential in defining those criteria, like John Ruskin, A. W. N. Pugin, Henry Cole and William Morris (qq.v.). Design history implies trying to understand an object in the context of the period in which it was produced. Criticism of good and bad design in any period cannot be approached from the basis of your own individual likes and dislikes, but must come from an understanding of the theories and philosophies prevailing at the time. It is in this area that many of the older books on the subject can prove confusing, for they take the standpoint of, say, the Modern Movement (q.v.) of the 1920s and 1930s, and evaluate everything from that basis, with obvious distortions arising. This is one of the reasons why the following chapters try to provide guidance on the books available.

The Problem of Survival

Most of us have vivid memories of our home, which go back to early childhood, but how much remains of that furniture or furnishings some ten, twenty or more years later? Wear and tear, changing family requirements, moving house and successive schemes of decoration will all have left their mark and much will have changed or disappeared. It might be possible to build up a partial picture of the past from photographs, or bills from shops that supplied furniture, or from firms that undertook to redecorate, or from diaries or letters. For most of us such documentary evidence would have been destroyed long since and it would be a very rare family that had a written record or a photographic survey made of all the rooms in their home. Herein lie many of the historian's problems. You may be thrilled to discover the grandfather clock which had been handed down through several generations of the family, but is it more significant historically than the everyday articles that each generation takes for granted, uses, and then throws away? A variety of objects survive from the past and you need to be cautious in your interpretation of them. You need to ask why some have survived and others have not. You need to consider strength and durability as well as real and assumed values, and sentimental attachment, when attempting to assess the historical value of such evidence.

If we look at any period of history our picture of it derives from many sources, the literature, paintings, buildings and artefacts that have survived and that have been collected. For many people it is the museum's picture of the past that is one of the most readily accessible sources, and until very recently the main emphasis of many museum collections was on the rare and exotic, and objects which were commonplace did not appear. This was partly a question of what had survived from the past, for the things that were in everyday use got worn out, broken and were thrown away, while the precious and expensive were looked after carefully and survived. Many museums were set up in the nineteenth century and were based on the collections of private individuals with their emphasis on curiosities from strange lands, and precious items. There was no incentive to collect the commonplace. Recently an enormous interest has developed in the commonplace, and the balance is being redressed, but if you are studying the artefacts of today or yesterday you need to be very aware of the type of image you are likely to receive unless you are very careful. Two books on this topic that I have found both stimulating and provocative are Donald Horne, *The Great Museum* (1984), and Patrick Wright, *On Living in an Old Country, The National Past in Contemporary Britain* (1985). Both books explore, in their very different ways, the question of images of the past, the variety of distortions that can arise, and the reasons for them.

The Heroic Approach

Exhibitions, books, magazine articles and some museum collections tend to emphasize the heroic approach to design history. That is to say they concentrate on the rare and expensive and the major works of major designers in any period: Adam, Wedgwood, Aalto, Dior (qq.v.). The work of these people was very important and I am certainly not trying to deny this. Part of the historian's task is that of evaluating and determining what is significant and what is not, and this in turn relates to what is history and the approaches that can be taken. In general historical studies we no longer concentrate solely on kings and queens and battles and conquests. Similarly in design history it is important to recognize that there is more to it than the study of key figures and key objects. The design of goods that most people live with is important. Indeed it was the feeling that design was part of everyday life and used, that it was an activity with a social and material context, rather than something isolated, to be put in a museum, that attracted many of us to its study in the first place.

Today opinions on the beauty and on the financial value of particular objects are inextricably linked. Newspapers report extraordinary sums reached in auctions for the work of a particular designer; the emphasis of collectors and of museums on the rare or the expensive object, and lavishly illustrated books, encourage the belief that it is only such items that are of importance or of any interest and that the main criterion for such importance and interest is the market value. This attitude in turn tends to encourage us to devalue our own surroundings, for logic indicates that they cannot be important if they are not worth much. Yet the surroundings of each individual are very important and design history recognizes this in focusing studies on those surroundings as well as on the rare, the valuable and the beautiful.

Often it is very difficult to find out about the 'anonymous' design in any period. For recent periods of the last sixty or so years, the techniques of oral history, recording the memories of those who were there and experienced working in a particular factory, or using a particular design, have made a significant contribution to areas that were previously 'hidden from history'. Obviously there are limitations to how far back in time you can reach by this method and there are real challenges in disentangling what is 'remembered' and what actually took place. Examples of the application of oral history techniques are given in the chapters on ceramics, furniture and environmental design. Feminist history has also made a significant contribution to rescuing women designers previously 'hidden from history'. In the chapter on furniture the author indicates how feminist history has influenced the study of furniture, and this approach is applicable to other areas of design history.

Sources

In the study of design history you will be involved in a process of finding out, questioning and interpretation. In order to gain a full picture of the topic that you are studying you may be involved with a wide range of source material ranging from the object itself, or drawings, to books and documents such as letters, bills or diaries. This material is divided into two main areas: primary sources and secondary sources. In general primary sources are sources contemporary with the period that is being studied, while secondary sources are interpretations of a period by later historians and writers. The deciding factor is the context in which the material is being studied and there are no rigid boundaries between the two. This book, for example, would, according to the above definition, qualify as a secondary source, but if the topic of research was concerned with the way design history is perceived, or the way it is taught today, then this book could qualify in that context as a primary source. The initial way in which to familiarize yourself with a subject is by means of secondary sources.

SECONDARY SOURCES
These can include general histories, articles in magazines and journals, monographs and picture books. In any study using secondary sources you need to be aware of the stance taken by the authors towards their material, for authors as much as anyone else respond to and reflect the criteria and prejudices of the time they are living in, and this in turn affects their interpretation of the material they are writing about. The author's viewpoint is thus important in itself for it is another factor which can help you to build up your understanding of a period, particularly if a book was written at a time when a great argument was raging about a particular topic. What you need to be careful of is how you weigh and evaluate secondary sources. It is useful to start by asking who wrote a particular text, and when it was first published. The date of publication can provide an indication of the author's viewpoint, and the context in which the study was undertaken. You should also look at the primary evidence that the book is based on. Here the bibliography and footnotes will give some indication, but if these are absent, or few in number, then you will have to rely on a critical examination of the text and its conclusions. When you have read a number of secondary sources relating to a particular topic, the areas where there is confusion or contradiction will become evident.

Bibliographies, dictionaries and directories can prove useful sources of information on a new topic. There are a number of bibliographies which include references to design history and A. J. Coulson, *A Bibliography of Design in Britain, 1851–1970* (1979), is one of the most important of them. Despite its title this includes references to design in Europe, Japan, the USA and the USSR and also refers readers to journals and to other bibliographies, indexes and abstracts. It does not include environmental design. This bibliography is divided into three main areas: fostering design, which includes official organizations, international exhibitions, museums and collections; design and designers; and areas of design activity such as those included in this

11

book. In addition there is a table of important dates which provides an overview of the period covered, and a subject index which enables the reader to use the book efficiently.

For references covering the period since 1970 *Design and Applied Arts Index*, produced by Design Documentation, Gurnleys, Burwash, E. Sussex, is available in many Polytechnic and College Libraries. This also excludes environmental design. This topic is however included in Ruth H. Kamen, *British and Irish Architectural History: a Bibliography and Guide to Sources of Information* (1981). This includes much information of interest to students of design history and the chronological span is from prehistory to this century.

Dictionaries and directories can provide quick access to information on design and designers, but they naturally tend to reinforce the heroic view of design history. In areas of design popular with collectors, such as ceramics or silver, there are numerous dictionaries. Among the most comprehensive is H. Honour and J. Fleming, *The Penguin Dictionary of Decorative Arts* (1977). Since it covers that area of design indicated in its title, industrial design is not included. It was hoped that this gap would be filled by Simon Jervis, *The Penguin Dictionary of Design and Designers* (1985), but this was not to prove the case. Few industrial designers or indeed twentieth-century designers found their way into that dictionary, although it does include a wealth of information on the decorative aspects of design since *c.* 1450.

One of the most comprehensive directories of designers active in all areas of design this century is Ann Lee Morgan, *Contemporary Designers* (1984), which gives biographical information on 600 designers, some of which is unavailable elsewhere. Each entry includes bibliographic details, but these are not always reliable. The most irritating aspect of the directory is the omission of a subject index. All the entries are in alphabetical order, but there is no way of picking out car designers from ceramic or graphic designers other than by going through all the entries systematically.

PRIMARY SOURCES
Once a preliminary study using secondary sources has been made, it is important to try and locate the primary material. This primary material includes the artefact itself, plans, drawings, models, sketches, contemporary paintings, photographs, and statements by the designer and by contemporary design critics, theorists and users of that design. The

secondary sources can often help in the detective work needed to track down the location of this primary material. For reasons of copyright most publications list the museum, individual, industry, or shop which allowed them to take and publish a particular picture in the first place. The picture credits at the back of the book are thus a valuable source of information on where to find particular artefacts or drawings. Often one particular centre specializes in collecting the work of a particular designer such as the Charles Rennie Mackintosh collection in Glasgow, or a particular material such as pottery at Stoke-on-Trent. Any serious secondary source would list where such collections are to be found, and guidance on this is also given in the various chapters of this book. Backing up studies based on secondary sources with a study of primary sources is most important, for it is the only way you can really find out what a design was like originally. Each of the chapters gives guidance on how to do this.

One of the advantages design history has over other areas of historical study is that in questions of doubt the actual physical object or drawing can be referred to if it still exists, and this will enable you to answer certain questions about the design. For example although illustrations may be accompanied by measurements, you still may have no clear idea of, say, the thickness of a ceramic jug, or the depth of carving on the leg of a chair. Furthermore colour illustrations may not always be entirely faithful to the original, and texture is notoriously difficult to reproduce. The importance of first-hand experience of the subject you wish to study cannot be over-emphasized, for it will enable you to see how a piece of machinery or a chair was constructed, and you will be able to see for yourself the workmanship, and the colour, form and texture of the materials used. The advantages of studying something that you can really handle are apparent, but clearly the local museum or stately home are not going to be happy to allow everyone to handle their displays and indeed items would deteriorate rapidly if this were allowed. Most museums do however have study collections which are accessible to serious students.

Local libraries often have collections relating to local history, and local Record Offices, though daunting at first sight, usually have information leaflets describing how to use them. Societies such as the Civic Trust, the Victorian Society, the Thirties Society, the Industrial Archaeological Society and very many more will arrange visits to places which are perhaps not generally open to the public. In the following chapters reference is also made to the main specialist collections where particular examples of design can be seen. Only a few of these can be referred to but there are a number of handbooks and directories covering this area. For example, *The Libraries, Museums and Art Galleries Yearbook, 1978–9* (1981) and The Museums Association, *Museums Yearbook*, which is published annually. At the end of the book is a list of useful addresses. Many of these organizations issue their own publications, arrange visits, hold conferences and generally provide opportunities for extending first-hand experience of the wide range of design history introduced in the following chapters.

2

The Study of Dress and Textiles

JOSEPHINE MILLER

The study of historic dress can present a formidable and baffling variety of problems which may well provide an obstacle to the unwary. Everybody wears clothes which are normally selected and purchased by their owners, and yet, when challenged, most people are unable to provide a rational explanation for wearing particular outfits on a given day. Indeed, one student questionnaire produced the unlikely response that the majority chose their clothing on the basis of what they could find that was clean!

Certainly, there can be no doubt that dress provides, and has provided, an endless source of fascination. There is an unwritten 'language' of dress that is easy to recognize yet so difficult to define. To what extent are we what we wear? Many people will confess that they make preliminary judgements concerning a person's place in society or personality based solely on a silent scrutiny of dress. Indeed, the so-called psychology of dress has produced a platform of debate which has resulted, perhaps, in a top-heavy proportion of literature on this topic at the expense of other aspects of costume history.

This is a multi-faceted subject and in some ways can be seen to relate to almost every area of design and many aspects of the fine arts. It needs to be placed firmly within a cultural context, against a background of technological and industrial change, literary and aesthetic ideas. In the post-industrial period, the marketing and retail outlets, together with developments in advertising and publishing techniques, have brought a new set of considerations with them. Moreover, the study of dress and its production cannot be separated from women's history. For example, whilst it would be a wild exaggeration to state that women actually died from the immediate effects of wearing extremely tight-fitting garments in the 1870s and 1880s, no one can deny the concern of the medical professions about this practice. They gave considerable support and weight to the arguments of the dress reformers in the 1880s and 1890s.

Both female and male dress have reinforced traditional gender roles which are being challenged at present. Why should it be acceptable currently for women to wear trousers, but not for men to don skirts, at least not often?

In this chapter, I intend to cast further light on the variety and scope of dress and textiles and indicate the wide range of knowledge of related subjects which are beneficial to its study. The reasons for, and mechanisms of, change are considered together with an investigation of some of the visual and written sources which can be encountered. It is useful to know something about the strategies concerning museum display of dress and the purposes for which texts on costume history have been written in the past.

The Study of Dress

It is useful to be able to differentiate between fashion and dress. Not all dress is fashionable, but may rather symbolize occupation or allegiance to a peer group. Of course, fashions are not confined to clothes. There are many who cast a disapproving eye over what they may consider as superficial vagaries or whims on the part of the fashionably dressed person, but they forget that there are also fashions in styles of painting, architecture, music, indeed every aspect of the arts. I am sure that no single theory can explain why a group of people collectively adopt a given style in clothes, only to drop it in favour of another one long before those garments are worn out. Indeed, it is generally believed that changes of style are far from haphazard, but systematic and deliberate.[1]

Until the middle of the nineteenth century in Western Europe, changes tended to take place relatively slowly, with modification building on modification, until a noticeable shift in the total shape of a garment took place. As a broad generalization, this kind of change was accomplished over ten or so years. However, after the middle of the nineteenth century, the pace of change quickened and was fortified by the new breed of dressmaker/designer for the wealthy, the couturier. The proliferation of fashion journals at this time, with the minutest nuance of change being recorded, meant that ideas could rapidly be disseminated. In this century, the pace of change has quickened to the extent that a fashionable Mod might have been tempted to change style every two days. But why are fashionable people compelled to change their styles so rapidly?

As I have already indicated, many writers have addressed themselves at length to this problem.[2] The ideas expressed by Thorsten Veblen are still given some credence.[3] He put forward an argument based on the notion of conspicuous consumption, whereby people display their wealth and power through the clothes they buy: 'Elegant dress serves its purpose of elegance not only in that it is expensive, but also because it is the insignia of leisure. It not only shows that the wearer is able to consume a relatively large value, but it argues at the same time that he consumes without producing.'[4] In his opinion, those people aspiring to power attempt to 'ape' their betters, who, feeling their status threatened, consequently adopt fashions that are unfunctional and involve the use of expensive materials and labour. For instance, the adoption of the crinoline on the part of working-class women in the 1860s was met with much censure by the middle and upper classes. The wide skirts produced by the cage crinoline were prone to being caught up in factory machinery or carriage wheels, with unfortunate results. Interestingly, it was also feared that unmarried girls could successfully conceal pregnancies beneath the voluminous cage, leading to a subsequent rise in illegitimacy. By the 1850s, very fashionable women were in the habit of changing their clothes many times a day, perhaps as many as seven times. The etiquette established at the court of the Empress Eugénie in France was partially responsible for this, but a woman needed a very extensive wardrobe in order to fulfil her social obligations, and thus access to a substantial income.

An alternative view to Veblen's is that we choose clothes to express ourselves and present an acceptable image to society. The 'correct' garments, immaculately clean and well-fitting, the use of cosmetics and carefully coiffured hair can all act as a shield or mask, or intensify the expression of personality. Moral judgements have often been made concerning dress, although the law is vague on the subject. Uniform can effectively suppress personal expression in dress in favour of allegiance to a group. Of course, we need to be initiated into the

17

meaning of these garments. When we need to summon the help of a nurse there must be no confusion of identity.

Today, many people are in a position to choose the image which they wish to present, either individually or collectively, and to the chagrin of some designers and manufacturers this may well not be high fashion. In Britain, it has recently become quite acceptable to wear track suits and sports shoes in the high street as well as the sports ground. Casual and informal styles have taken precedence and many manufacturers have responded rapidly to this demand. Perhaps the universal adoption of these clothes can reveal certain aspects of our society. They show allegiance to the values inherent in the recent aerobics craze – fitness, youth, vitality, agility. Moreover, these garments can be reasonably priced and, therefore, accessible to the unwaged. The transference of items of clothing from one 'station in life' to another is certainly not new. In eighteenth-century England, the country gentleman's informal frock coat, with its turned-down collar, was adopted in highly fashionable urban circles and subsequently viewed by supporters of the French Revolution as a symbol of freedom. Many young people's 'street fashions' today have rejected the dictates of the fashion industry, so that rather than people slavishly following fashion, the fashion industry has been following people. A very simple example of this was the short lived adoption of 'punk' styles by the designer, Zandra Rhodes.[5]

FASHION CHANGES
But when did fashionable change begin and where does the mechanism for that change lie? Opinion is much divided on the subject, but it does seem that the desire for such change is noticeable first of all in Western society where there was a growing middle-class and merchant community, coupled with a shifting, sometimes restless population. This is usually considered to be at the beginning of the fourteenth century. In societies where there was a fixed hierarchy according to class divisions and religious convictions, this kind of fashionable change has not existed. The Indians and Japanese, for instance, were quite content to wear the same styles with only minor modifications for centuries. National costume in Europe was worn by rural or peasant communities and conformed to traditional, fixed standards.

In the West, until the influence brought by industrialization and the consequent proliferation of the consuming middle classes, the leaders of fashion were the ruling families of Europe, with the French court taking the lead. Competition to vie with them in excellence of dress led to a kind of 'Square dance, with the lower ranks following the higher ranks, and the higher ranks sidestepping this by adopting new fashions'. [6]

To be well dressed was a very serious matter and the clients were served by a small army of private tailors, dressmakers, milliners, etc. In the eighteenth and early nineteenth centuries, dressmaking was largely a female concern. Decisions on style were made on a private basis between the dressmaker and the customer until the advent of the influence of Charles Frederick Worth in Paris in the middle of the nineteenth century. [7] After this time, the status of the dressmaker was elevated to that of a designer who soon possessed sufficient power to dictate certain styles to clients. Since the Second World War this influence has in general been gradually eroded and people from all walks of life are now exercising more personal choice in their style of dress.

We have seen the emergence of the cult groups, mods, rockers, skinheads, punks, who express group affinity through common styles of dress. In order to understand these styles we need to examine the aims and beliefs of each group, and to absorb the messages contained in the current pop idiom, its music and literature. Some of the garments have been combined deliberately to effect a display of menace or aggression. Why should this be so? What are people protesting or aggressive about? In the study of dress it is very important to gain a considerable knowledge of the background to the society which is being examined in order to reach an understanding of the garments which are being worn at a given time.

PROBLEMS OF IDENTIFICATION

One of the problems encountered in studying this subject is the scarcity of surviving specimens of dress dating from before the beginning of the seventeenth century. Some British museums possess a few items from the sixteenth century, such as shirts, chemises, ruffles, lace and accessories. [8] The Victoria and Albert Museum possesses a complete suit, alleged to have belonged to King James I, which is generally believed to be the oldest suit of clothes on display in Britain. Therefore, in the absence of sufficient examples of extant items before the beginning of the seventeenth century, graphic evidence forms one of the most important sources from which to draw information. One means of acquiring information is by comparing representations of dress in well-authenticated, dated works of art in order to build up a knowledge of the normal patterns of dress at a given moment. This is particularly useful in the study of high fashion for both men and women from the beginning of the fourteenth century until the beginning of the twentieth.[9]

This method can also be employed for the study of earlier periods, so long as the identification of the source used for evidence is correct. Indeed, the study of Greek and Roman sculpture can be useful. There are large numbers of representations of dress on Greek vase painting where a surprising variety of types of garment were depicted. Those with a knowledge of pattern cutting may be interested in unravelling the intricacies of construction from such sculptures. The Greeks did not dress in glorified sheets as I was once reliably informed.

Having established a framework of normality, deviation from the norm can then be ascertained. This method, however, can be riddled with problems and subtleties. For instance, in the case of portraits, in order to reach a satisfactory conclusion, the student has to take into account the social status of the sitter and his/her age (since the older we become, the more we tend to cling to the styles of our youth). Does the sitter reside in a centre of fashion or in some provincial society where there is a time lag in taste or a refusal to adopt the dress of the metropolis? Is the person represented a foreigner? What is the attitude of the painter towards the representation of dress and is he painting from life? This detective work should not be confined to portraiture, but spills over into religious representation and reconstruction of historical themes, where the painter may be striving to recreate the fashions of the time he depicts, sometimes with hilarious results. In many cases, the painter unconsciously dresses his figures in thinly disguised contemporary clothes, with modern faces and hairstyles. It is also believed by some dress historians that nudes in sculpture or painting reflect the ideal fashionable body shape of the time. Of course, it is always possible that a painting might have been substantially altered, 'restored', or, horror of horrors, be a downright forgery. Painters who are trying to pass off their work as someone else's usually experience a great deal of trouble in representing the correct garments and display serious errors in accuracy. Fastenings may be misunderstood, or construction and seam lines inappropriate, simply because unless the garments are part of an artist's everyday experience, he is unable to recreate them on canvas.[10]

Unless the student possesses a sound knowledge of background

Figure 2.1 Thomas Gainsborough, *Blue Boy*, 1770.

Figure 2.2 Joseph Wright of Derby, *Susanna Hope, c.* 1760.

history in the study of dress, many pitfalls will be encountered when using painting as evidence. These can be well demonstrated by selecting examples from the dress of eighteenth-century England. It has been demonstrated that between the 1730s and 1780s many sitters are not depicted in high fashion.[11] This is a rich and sophisticated area of research but it is well worth noting simply that there was a long-standing interest in representing people in at least three variations on standard dress. One of these concerned interpretations of the dress of the 1630s, under the influence of Van Dyck and Rubens. For instance, everybody can recognize Gainsborough's *Blue Boy*, painted *c.* 1770 (Fig. 2.1), but he is not dressed in high fashion. The falling band collar, shoulder 'wings', plumed hat and rosettes on the knee and shoes are reminiscent of the dress depicted by these seventeenth-century painters. Similarly, in representations of female dress, when one compares the garments seen in Joseph Wright of Derby's *Susanna Hope*, painted *c.* 1760 (Fig. 2.2) with Rubens *Hélène Fourment* (Fig. 2.3) there are strong similarities between the style of hats and their position on the head, with sleeves which reach almost to the wrist, and with the use of diaphanous fabric. Had Susanna Hope been wearing fashionable dress she would have looked substantially different, much more like Gainsborough's *Mary, Countess Howe*, painted in the early

Figure 2.3   Peter Paul Rubens, *Hélène Fourment, c.* 1630.

1760s (Fig. 2.4). Her chip hat would not have been positioned at a rakish angle, but perched neatly and squarely on the top of her head. Her sleeves would have reached to the elbow, descending from which there would have been a cascade of extravagant lace ruffles. She would not have worn an asymmetrically arranged display of pearls.

In order to gain a thorough understanding of the reasons behind this admiration for the seventeenth century, it is necessary to study painting, literature and philosophy. Descriptions of actual costume can be found in diaries, letters and newspapers of the time. To confuse matters still further, there are two other alternatives to high fashion

Figure 2.4   Thomas Gainsborough, *Mary, Countess Howe, c.* 1765.

which were acceptable at this time: pastoral dress and 'classical' styles. Some fashionable women tried to capture a spirit of rural innocence by adopting an elegant interpretation of the dresses of shepherdesses and milkmaids. These provided useful themes for the Masquerade, because the costume was relatively simple to devise and, therefore, cheap, although it had very little to do with the dress of the actual poor. The straw hat was the most important item to be elevated in social status, together with the use of an apron for everyday wear and the addition of a neckerchief. The most notorious figure to disregard convention and habitually dress in rustic style was the Duchess of Queensberry. Although protected by wealth and status, her contemporaries were baffled by her refusal to conform. Her response to being banned from Court for wearing an apron was to rip it off in public and stamp on it, but before long it was an accepted part of high fashion.

The use of the so called 'classical' gown, employed particularly in the work of Joshua Reynolds, is the third alternative form of dress. His desire to return to a classical ideal, as stated in his *Discourses*, was expressed in the representation of figures in wrapping gowns, sometimes displaying Turkish overtones. There was some concern that the status of a portrait might be demoted to that of a fashion plate by the adoption of fashionable dress, and this was Reynolds' method of remedying this situation. It is very rewarding to be able to identify the meaning behind the adoption of certain garments, to see how certain items, initially used to signify particular ideas, became absorbed into everyday wear.

I have cited these examples from the eighteenth century in order to demonstrate how easy it is to be misled by purely visual sources. There was such a variety of styles which were acceptable at the same time for very specific reasons. The visual evidence must be backed up by extensive use of documentary sources for supporting material. Diaries, wills, letters, journals, household accounts and bills are all useful. As far as novels and diaries are concerned, these often contain some observation on what was regarded as proper or improper at a given moment in history. It is a good idea to compare a number of examples of the same type of dress. Is it possible to find different artists' representations of a particular fashion? Do they also appear in engraving, drawing, sculpture or, after the mid-nineteenth century, in photography? Is it possible to match these with surviving examples?

APPROACHES TO THE STUDY OF DRESS
In this section, I have deliberately chosen examples from published sources, in order that you may have the opportunity to study them in depth. For the nineteenth and twentieth centuries it is possible to add to the range of evidence with trade catalogues, paper patterns, fashion journals and videos. Dress represented in films can also enrich the scope of research. The comparative method of utilizing a balanced combination of visual and written sources would apply to earlier periods in history, although there are clearly difficulties inherent in approaching project work when original texts are in ancient or foreign languages. In these cases, I would recommend that a short period of time or a narrowly defined theme should be tackled. After all published sources have been exhausted and analysed, it is worth making the effort to locate visual examples of your subject and study them at first hand.

For instance, if you are studying dress worn during the Italian Renaissance, first consult published works on the subject. Then select your special area of interest. Perhaps it would be interesting to investigate the garments worn by one ruling family in one city state. What representations can be found in painting? What descriptions of their clothes existed in wardrobe accounts, letters, diaries? What kind of textiles do they appear to be made from? How many layers of clothing are worn in a single outfit and how were they constructed? Is there any correspondence in shape between men's and women's clothes?

Of course, there are many alternatives to the chronological, stylistic approach. Specific themes can be selected and studied in depth. It is wise to tackle a small aspect of a subject and pose interesting questions about it, rather than taking on 'shoes' or 'wedding dresses through the ages' which tend to be too broad in scope and become over-generalized in content. The investigation of ceremonial dress and uniforms is fascinating. Vestigial elements of high fashion from a former time can often be found lingering in ceremonial dress. Why should the fashionable hanging sleeve of the fifteenth century still be seen in today's academic gown, for example? When did uniforms start and what do they mean? How are members of society conditioned to respond to them? Where is the dividing line between official and unofficial uniform? It could be argued that the male business suit could be interpreted as a uniform. Could the financial advice of a (male) bank manager be trusted if he was wearing, say, jeans, lurex boots and earrings?

Occupational and working-class dress is also a rewarding subject, but detailed research into these topics is still in its infancy. What did servants and farm labourers wear? How did they obtain and afford clothes? What relationship was there between working-class dress and high fashion? Sadly, there are few surviving examples of the clothing of the poor as they were so often passed on to others or simply worn out, but there is certainly sufficient visual and documentary published evidence to reward this study from the eighteenth to twentieth centuries. [12] Recently, there has been increased interest in production methods in the clothing industry. What influence did the introduction of the sewing machine have on design and production? Under what conditions did seamstresses work? How did the retail trades expand? What were the significant inventions in new fabrics and dyes? Although Mackintosh patented his waterproof fabric in 1823, it was not until the 1870s that waterproof clothing was worn by women whilst out walking. Why was this?

It can be appreciated that this subject is truly multi-faceted. It can be likened to a giant jigsaw, which admittedly can be quite difficult to piece together. The variety of approaches which can be employed are as diverse as the subject, and no single one is categorically correct. In the past, most writers on the subject tended to concentrate on broad, general histories of high fashion or somewhat repetitive investigations into the psychology of the subject. There are still so many avenues to explore and it is this which makes it exciting.

Sources

The major, and most widely used, source of information for the study of dress comes from the study of books on the subject. These vary so considerably in their intentions that it seems useful to consider a little the history of costume history. As I have previously indicated, unlike the well established pedigree of written material on art-historical matters, literature on this subject is relatively scant. Many of the early books on costume were largely pictorial and were hardly more than scrapbooks, containing ill-conceived engravings copied from paintings. Others contained examples of dress chosen from exotic parts of the world. One such example, *A Collection of the Dresses of Different Nations both Ancient and Modern* by Thomas Jefferys, published in 1757 and 1772, although serious in intention provided those who attended the Masquerade with amusing inspiration for fancy dress. [13]

The emphasis of interest shifted with the contribution of Joseph Strutt[14] whose concern for historical accuracy is evident in *A Complete View of the Dress and Habits of the People of England* (1796–7). This is the work of an antiquarian, and his work should be reviewed in that context. His contribution was followed by that of J. R. Planché and F. W. Fairholt who fed the popular-history painters of the nineteenth century with information on historical costume which could be translated immediately into painting. It would seem that Planché was skilled at promoting his ideas and became known as an arbitrator on matters of historical dress.[15] Fairholt began to publish in 1846, using contemporary line drawings which, in their interpretations, inevitably distorted the originals. His work provided important fodder for the history painter, but also represented an important example of increased awareness of costume history, however subjective and emotive in its leanings. Fashion periodicals began to publish articles, some carefully researched, on costume history, and these were intended to reach a wide audience. High fashion in much of the nineteenth century was rife with historical references and the growth of publications on this subject helped to consolidate the historical elements in fashion.

The third most influential writer in the nineteenth century was Camille Bonnard, whose work, *Costume Historique* (1829–30), was eagerly sought by members of the Pre-Raphaelite Brotherhood. It is known that Ford Madox Brown, J. E. Millais, and D. G. Rossetti used this book for costume reference to perfect detail in history painting. The Pre-Raphaelites' concern for accuracy led to an unfortunate problem when working from costume books in that the illustrations showed only one viewpoint of a garment which no longer existed and so the painter was forced to recreate this aspect in his painting as he had no idea what the other sides of the costume looked like! Hence Millais' *Isabella* is similar to the drawing of Beatrice D'Este by Paul Mercuri in Bonnard's book.[16]

Interests in historical costume broadened with the establishment of the Aesthetic Movement and Rational Dress Society in the 1870s and 1880s. Supporters of these movements were anxious to draw on the vagaries in previous fashions in order to promote their own ideas of reform. Two such writers were Mrs Haweis and Luke Limner.[17] In some instances, examples of past fashions were cited as displaying good taste. Indeed the fourteenth-century style of dress was admired by Mrs Haweis who drew her inspiration not from original examples but from the work of Fairholt.[18] *Aglaia*, the journal of the Rational

Dress Society, promoted a return to Grecian styles which conformed to their notions of function and beauty.

Eighteenth and nineteenth century literature on dress was aimed at specific markets and it is most important to view them in context in order to comprehend their significance. In this century, other factors have been stressed. One of the most influential writers has been J. C. Flugel who wrote *The Psychology of Clothes* and whose ideas have penetrated the work of many other writers including James Laver, Rudofsky and Geoffrey Squire.[19] In my view psychological considerations of dress are best left to the psychologists. The student should be wary of books which combine factual history with psychological interpretation and learn to distinguish between the two. Examples of this can be found in some of James Laver's work. His oft quoted dictum 'bad money, no corsets', is a case in point. His view was that in periods of recession, women threw modesty to the winds together with their corsets, resulting in promiscuity. This author is also well known for his theory of the 'shifting erogenous zone' which needs no explanation here. He also promoted the theory of the *Zeitgeist*, the 'spirit of the age', to attempt to explain concurrent emergence of a given unified style in many branches of the arts.

Such viewpoints should be treated with caution and analysed with care. They have been counterbalanced by the work of C. Willett and Phyllis Cunnington. Although these authors cover too wide a field, their work is meticulous and reliable, more suitable for reference than reading from cover to cover.

Both Norah Waugh and Janet Arnold have made a substantial contribution in their analyses of surviving garments.[20] They were among the first writers to grapple with the prodigious task of describing and dissecting actual garments – a task from which many people will shrink. Stella Mary Newton and her graduates from the Courtauld Institute of Art are currently publishing and working on very detailed texts. It is being realized increasingly that the subject should be approached in a detailed and scholarly manner. Many newly published texts are relying on primary source material and combine bona fide visual evidence with supporting detailed documentation.[21] The contribution of women's studies, placing the subject in a wide cultural context, is also proving most valuable. The pioneering work of Roszika Parker with *The Subversive Stitch* (1984) is a case in point.

If I have dwelt at some length on this topic, it is because I have found in the past that many students have not realized the subjective nature of so much of the literature on this subject. As I have demonstrated, a great number of secondary sources were produced for a particular purpose and it is vital that each work should be analysed and its context assessed.

Museums and their Use

Unlike many areas of the decorative arts, garments have rarely been considered suitable objects for systematic collecting. Dresses which have survived have frequently been 'best' ones, perhaps worn at court or for special occasions. Many accessories or items of underwear are extant simply because they are alleged to have been worn by famous or notorious owners. Indeed, much of that which survives has been locked away and forgotten for years, or turned into fancy dress.

The common practice of 'handing down' garments from the upper to the servant classes or from elder to younger members of the family has meant that many clothes have worn out, or been altered to suit changing fashions. Often trimmings, lace and buttons have found their way to new garments. During the last few years there has been a lively trade in the second-hand clothes market, and this has led to the wide dispersal of clothes.

Of course, it is obvious that clothes are extremely fragile and need to be stored under special conditions in order to preserve them. Both natural and artificial light and pollution from the atmosphere rapidly contribute to decay. Many items have suffered from the well-intentioned but amateur attempts to clean them: a William Morris (q.v.) wall-hanging was apparently once cleaned with a proprietory brand of carpet cleaner. Many collectors in the past have been reluctant to purchase items which may rapidly fall apart under their noses and cause a great deal of bother in storage and cleaning, and it is only recently that sales of historic costumes and textiles have become popular with the major auction houses. Incidentally, although certainly a by-product of their purpose, such sales can provide an opportunity for viewing and carefully examining garments.

So it can be seen that clothing does not usually survive in sufficient quantities in order to provide a constant over-view of the dress from most periods, and this state of affairs is reflected in museum collections of dress, of which there are over 120 in this country. [22] Many establishments possess small collections and in order to display them may be forced by circumstance to place garments together which originate from different times or social classes. Such a situation, although inevitable, may cause confusion on a first visit, particularly if the items are displayed in a single 'room-setting' display. I would, therefore, advise students to read with care the museum labels accompanying garments.

Bearing these points in mind, it is also important, when looking at the displays, to ascertain whether the outfits are complete and original. Are the accessories absolutely contemporary with the dresses? Have items which have been worn at different times of day or for different occasions been muddled up? At certain times, particularly in the nineteenth century, fashionable women were obliged to change their clothes on many occasions throughout the day. It is sometimes very difficult for us to recognize precisely the original function of items.

It must also be remembered that many outfits have survived in a very incomplete form. Ann Buck in *Dress in Eighteenth Century England* (1979) points out that the important undergarments, the stays, hoops and petticoat, would rarely survive with a dress and so it is essential to ascertain whether the correct understructure has been recreated on the museum dummy. The basic dress of a fashionable Englishwoman for much of the eighteenth century would consist of the following: a chemise, stays, petticoat, dress with robings and facings split vertically from the waist to the hem to reveal the petticoat, the 'V'-shaped stomacher pinned to the front of the bodice, lace ruffles, perhaps a lace apron, kerchief and a cap on the head and shoes and stockings. It would be virtually unheard of for all of these to survive as a piece, so I would advise all readers to inspect the individual components of items in order to ascertain the extent to which they are original or recreated. Garments may well have been altered, especially those from the eighteenth century. Styles in silk changed more rapidly than the shape of dresses, but the fabrics were expensive and highly prized, so it is common to see a dress which is of a later date than the fabric. If it is possible to examine the garment closely, look out for signs of former creases or tell-tale pin pricks indicating older seam lines. Are the linings, threads or any fastenings of the same date as the dress? Is there any sign that trimming has been removed? Has any stitching been carried out on a sewing machine? This is not so silly as it sounds as machine stitchery may give away the fact that the dress has been altered for fancy dress or theatrical purposes. Many of these comments would also apply to other periods in history, particularly those moments in the nineteenth century when dresses were composed of separate parts or required a large number of accessories. This would be particularly true of fashionable dress in the 1870s and 1880s.

There can be no substitute for examining surviving specimens of dress when studying this subject. It is often possible to view examples of a study area on show in a museum, but sometimes the student will need to examine examples from the reserve collection. In most museums, only a tiny proportion of the collection is on show at once and the bulk of it is stored away. [23] Having made an appointment to view a reserve collection, it is important to bear in mind that the visit will be of short duration and it is as well to arrive armed with the right questions and correct equipment for noting information and ideas. When inspecting surviving items, museum staff are particularly allergic to those that carry pen and inks, paint and water, sharp implements, food, drink, large, bulky bags and poachers' pockets or dirty hands. I do realize that all this is painfully self-evident, but I have to admit that on certain occasions I have forgotten to bring with me such important items as a pencil with which to make notes, a tape measure or a magnifying glass. Most museums will allow photography, but they prefer to supply their own, approved, lighting and copy stands.

The Study of Textiles

The history of textiles is linked indissolubly with their techniques and methods of production. Moreover, in many parts of the world, the success of the national economy has, in the past, rested partly on the extent to which the textile industry has been flourishing. Wool and cotton have been very important in England; the silk industry in Italy, notably that of Venice and Florence, was highly developed and, indeed, was in a state of decline by the end of the sixteenth century. These trades offered a major source of employment and potential for profit that were considered so vital that Venetian ambassadors abroad, for example, were instructed to report back to the Doge and Senate on the state of the textile industry in the host country. It was potentially disastrous for the supply of raw materials to be cut off, and therefore some countries went to great lengths to secure their own supplies of raw silk. King James I, taking no heed of the vagaries of the English climate, tried – but failed – to establish sericulture in England.

There exists already a strong body of literature on some aspects of this subject. Tapestries and rugs were long ago collectors' items and have been well documented but this is certainly not the case with furnishing and dress fabrics. The difficulties of describing actual designs with words, combined with often doubtful pedigrees and attribution, have led to an abundance of over generalized picture books which often cover a very long time span. On the other hand, the links with economic, technological and social history have been well established, and due to the work of certain pioneers in the field such as K. Ponting, A. P. Wadsworth and J. L. Mann, a great deal of research has been undertaken in these areas. [24]

ANALYSIS OF DESIGNS

It is in the analysis of actual designs, their sources and uses that research has lagged behind. Even if pattern books survive, and this is rare before the eighteenth century, the researcher is unlikely to establish the identity of the designer, or glean many clues about the sources of inspirations for designs. It would often be useful to know how much of a particular design was produced, how long it was in fashion, how much it cost, over how wide an area it was distributed. Work of this kind is painstaking and laborious and the business records which may provide such information are surprisingly rare. I have worked on European textiles and their design from 1580–1630, and in order to establish some kind of chronological change in pattern and design during this period, I resorted to matching textiles with those represented in well authenticated, dated paintings. Using this method, I was able to establish a surprising number of varieties in pattern, but this was, of course, only a first step. One cannot necessarily say that a design was new and in the height of fashion simply by virtue of the fact that it appears in a dated work of art. Observations need to be backed up with written contemporary documentation. However, inventories, wills and diaries may give tantalizingly short-hand descriptions of textiles. I was dismayed to find contemporary stuffs described merely as 'sprigg'd' or 'branched'. However, even in the absence of detailed recorded material, it is possible to arrive at some useful conclusions, although it is wise to express these in a guarded manner.

When searching for sources of inspiration in eighteenth-century silk design it would be profitable to investigate connections between botanical drawings, herbals and textile design. A fine collection of the textile designs of Anna Maria Garthwaite[25] is housed in the Print Room of the Victoria and Albert Museum. After comparing these with botanical drawings it would be a good idea to contrast them with surviving examples of silk from the Spitalfields industry and then consult the work of Nathalie Rothstein on the subject.[26] Following these investigations, a visit to the Spitalfields silk collection at the Bethnal Green Museum would be beneficial. Here surviving specimens of dress made of such silk are displayed.

This is only one example of the many approaches to textile history. The most obvious way to begin is to examine carefully the samples of textiles under review. If it is possible to examine a sample which is free of a frame or glass case, the use of a good magnifying glass can be most helpful. Some of the questions which might be asked are: of what materials are the fibres made? How is the fabric constructed? If it is a woven textile, what kind of weave is being employed? How is the pattern made? Is the textile a fragment of a whole piece? If so, of what? Does the repeat of the pattern survive? What is the scale and nature of this repeat? Are the dyes derived from chemical or vegetable sources? These are technical questions which are beyond the scope of this chapter, but it is certainly vital to have some tuition on these matters, ideally together with a practical demonstration of weaving. It should be possible to identify many fabrics.

Following a physical examination of the fabric, the next stage is to establish whether it is a significant example of the work of a particular culture, represents an important technical innovation or is important in the oeuvre of a designer.

SOCIAL CONTEXT

In certain regions and historic periods, textile designs have contained significant religious symbolism, much of which may be lost on another religion or culture. The richness of associational meaning contained within fabrics from, say, the Islamic World, from Peruvian textiles, from European peasant designs, cannot be realized to the full without a thorough understanding of religious beliefs and cultural background. The structure of society, its organization in social terms, is also important in the study of the character of textiles. It would, for instance, be particularly relevant in an assessment of certain textiles in peasant communities. The beliefs and superstitions of these people literally coloured their work with symbolism. It would also be possible to ascertain, from the kinds of fabrics used and patterns employed, the extent to which fashionable or foreign elements crept in at certain moments. The status of members of these communities was also signified by the type of textiles and dress which was worn. The clues lie in 'cracking the codes' that were used. Sometimes this is not so easy as it may sound, particularly if the answers lie in an untranslated Romanian text. It is axiomatic to stress the importance of a sound knowledge of technical developments and their influence on textiles. Today we happily cut out garments on the bias, use curved seam lines, insert 'V' shaped gores. In short, we waste quite a proportion of the material which comes off the loom. Our fabrics are usually machine-produced on a massive scale and relatively cheap.

However, a close inspection of many of the garments worn by other cultures reveals a very different attitude. For instance, the Japanese kimono is composed of rectangles of various proportions, sewn together and then dismantled for laundering. European peasant costumes were also constructed from rectangles of cloth, some sewn into 'T'-shaped garments and gathered at the neck, wrist or perhaps the waist. The Indian sari is made from six yards of material, straight from the loom. The common factor behind all these is that the clothes are made from fabric which has not been cut, or cut as little as possible. In these societies, cloth is so precious, the labour of producing it so great, that none can be spared.

After coming to grips with factors such as these, it might seem easier to investigate the work of specific textile designers. Individual designers are, and have been, linked with business concerns, and it is regrettable that few business archives are in existence and that it can be difficult to gain access to them. The excellent work which has already been published on William Morris could have been enriched still further if complete records of his firm had been extant. In spite of these difficulties, there are many aspects of a designer's work which can provide fruitful areas of research. You might investigate a designer's work in terms of inventiveness, sources of inspiration, development of ideas and themes, colour palette. There are retail outlets' individual clients' price ranges to consider. The materials employed and methods of production can add further insights. Perhaps it may be possible to relate written theory to artistic practice. How does the designer relate to the work of his/her contemporaries and how was this work considered by them? Many of these questions may be aimed rather obviously at William Morris, who has been singled out for much attention, but there are many other designers who could withstand such investigation. It would be fruitful to study the textile work of Morris's contemporaries, C. F. A.

Voysey, Talbert, Mackmurdo, Baillie Scott, Lewis F. Day (qq.v.), amongst others.

In the twentieth century, individual designers did tend to become swallowed up under the names of the large firms, such as Edinburgh Weavers or Sandersons, for instance, where significant shifts in taste tended to lean towards corporate identity.

The field of textile history ranges in scope from the self-conscious effort of individual designers to the untrained symbolic work of countless people who have built their designs on traditional values. Progress in industrial methods, economic change, shifts in the structure of society all play a vital role in the understanding of textiles. So vast is this subject's range that it is worthwhile not to be over ambitious, at least when beginning. Select a small and manageable subject and analyse it as carefully as possible from the points of view which I have indicated.

Notes

1 Polhemus, T., and Proctor, L. (1978), *Fashion and Anti-Fashion* (London: Thames & Hudson).
2 These views are succinctly summed up by Bell, Q. (1976), *On Human Finery* (New York: Schocken).
3 For a fuller description of his ideas, see 'Society Today' in *New Society*, 2 February 1984.
4 Veblen, T. (1912), *Theory of the Leisure Class* (New York: Macmillan).
5 Rhodes, Z., and Knight, A. (1984), *The Art of Zandra Rhodes* (London: Jonathan Cape), pp. 177–9.
6 'Society Today', op. cit.
7 De Marly, D. (1980), *The History of Haute Couture, 1850–1950* (London: Batsford).
8 See Arnold, J. (1973), *Handbook of Costume* (London: Macmillan), for a complete list of holdings in British museums.
9 Ibid. Janet Arnold considers this subject in depth and provides a useful select list of artists whose work may be of use in the study of costume.
10 De Marly, M. (1970), 'Georges de la Tour: a note on the Metropolitan Fortune Teller', *Burlington Magazine*, vol. cxii, no. 807, p. 388.
11 Ribeiro, A. (1984), *The Dress Worn at Masquerades in England, 1730–1790, and its Relation to Fancy Dress in Portraiture* (New York: Garland). Harris, J., and Cherry, D. (1982), 'Eighteenth century portraiture and the Seventeenth century past: Gainsborough and Van Dyck', *Art History*, vol. 5, no. 3.
12 Baines, B. (1981), *Fashion Revivals from the Elizabethan Age to the Present Day* (London: Batsford).

13   Fox, C., and Ribeiro, A. (1983), *Catalogue for Masquerade Exhibition* (London: Museum of London), p. 8.

14   Baines, op. cit., p. 123.

15   Ibid. Barbara Baines provides a thorough account of this subject, pp. 123–5.

16   Newton, S. M. (1974), *Health, Art and Reason* (London: Murray), p. 28.

17   Haweis, H. R. (1878), *The Art of Dress* (London: Chatto & Windus); Haweis, H. R. (1878), *The Art of Beauty* (London: Chatto & Windus). Limner, L. (1874), *Madre Nature Versus the Moloch of Fashion* (London: Chatto & Windus).

18   Baines, op. cit., p. 133.

19   In her article 'Fashions in fashion history', *Times Literary Supplement*, 21 March, 1975, Stella Mary Newton summed up Flugel's work and ideas.

20   Arnold, J. (1973), *Patterns of Fashion* (London: Macmillan); Waugh, N. (1968), *The Cut of Women's Clothes, 1600–1930* (London: Faber).

21   The series *A Visual History of Costume*, published by Batsford, is a typical example.

22   Cumming, V. (1976), 'The group for costume and textiles staff in musuems', *Museums Journal*, vol. 75, no. 4, pp. 173–5.

23   Both Janet Arnold and Valerie Cumming, op. cit., offer sound advice on how to approach museum staff and arrange a museum visit.

24   Ponting, founder of the journal *Textile History*; Wadsworth, A. P., and Mann, J. L. (1931), *The Cotton Trade and Industrial Lancashire, 1600–1780* (Manchester: Manchester University Press) is considered the definitive work on manufacturing and printing in Lancashire.

25   Anna Maria Garthwaite was an important designer of silks for the Spitalfields silk industry between the 1730s and 1750s.

26   Rothstein, N. (1961), 'The silk industry in London, 1702–1766', MA thesis, University of London.

3

Ceramic History

JONATHAN WOODHAM

The Scope of the Subject

For many people the study of ceramic history conjures up images of products associated with well-known firms such as Wedgwood, Royal Worcester, Spode, Doulton, Sèvres or Meissen. Generally located within the field of what is termed the Decorative Arts, research and publication in ceramic history has, until comparatively recently, been dominated by museum curators, collectors and connoisseurs, antique dealers and motivated amateurs. Museums themselves have been traditionally concerned with the development of collections of ceramic artefacts which embody high aesthetic quality and represent the output of distinguished designers and celebrated factories. Enshrined behind. glass in museum cases these exhibits take on the status of art, for they are removed from their original context as objects of practical use or decorative significance in a given historical period. It is, however, very much the understanding and awareness of context that is an essential tool for the prospective student of ceramic history, as it is with any other branch of design history.

Ceramics, in its many and various forms, has played a vital role in society, from the invention of the potter's wheel in the fourth millennium BC to the use of ceramic tiles on the American Space Shuttle. Its history embraces many areas other than those which spring immediately to mind: equipment for the aerospace, chemical, electrical, engineering, pharmaceutical, telephone, textile, transport and other industries; bricks, terracotta chimney pots and roof tiles for the building industry; architectural and sculptural ceramics. Tiles have also adorned a wide variety of public buildings and private dwellings, from town halls, railway stations, churches, Victorian (Fig 3.1) and Edwardian

Figure 3.1 *Agriculture and Horticulture,* tile panels from St Mungo Vintners, Glasgow (building now destroyed), designed by J. H. McLennan.

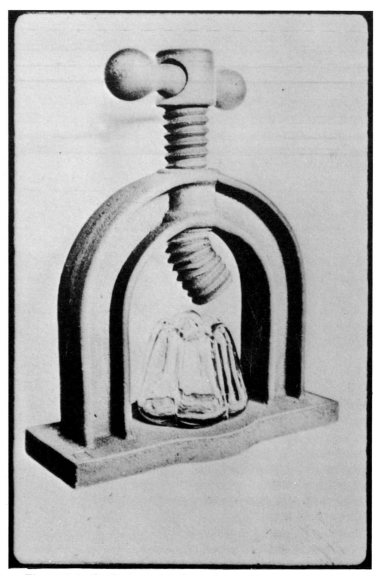

Figure 3.2 D. Cookson, *Jelly Press.*

public houses or even fish and chip shops, to floors, walls and fireplaces in everyday housing. Other aspects relate to home life and include ornaments, tableware, ceramic cooker hobs as well as sanitaryware for the bathroom. The fine arts encompass work which involves ceramics, as in sculpture by Gauguin, Matisse and Picasso, and the medium has also been imaginatively explored by studio potters and artist–craftsmen. (Fig 3.2).

In common with other branches of design history there are several fields of academic study, research and publication which illuminate and inform the study of ceramic history. The ability to make links with other disciplines is particularly relevant since most ceramic history published to date has centred on the work of well-known designers, manufacturers or particular types of ceramic ware. Parallels have often been seen in the fine and other decorative arts but other branches of cultural, social, economic and technological history, as well as archaeology and industrial archaeology, have an equally, if not more, important role to play in ceramic history.

Approaches to Study

STYLISTIC ANALYSIS: USES AND LIMITATIONS
The ability to recognize particular stylistic characteristics in terms of the shape, colour, material, or decoration of an object is an important means of locating it within the context of a specific historical period, movement or country of origin. When confronted with a piece of ceramic, either as an item in a museum case or as a photographic plate in a book, it is generally in splendid isolation from its former life as a dining plate, storage jar or chimney ornament. It is useful to develop the ability to make stylistic connections with other fields of artistic endeavour wherever possible, such as the fine and decorative arts – especially glass and silverware with which the study of ceramics is often linked. Such interconnections can be demonstrated in most historical periods, for example between black- and red-figure vase painters and sculptural practice in sixth- and fifth-century BC Greece; between birth, marriage and other commemorative ceramic ware and contemporary artistic developments in Early Renaissance Italy; and, much more emphatically, between most arts in the Rococo, Neo-Classical, Art Nouveau or Art Deco (qq.v.) eras. The Victoria and Albert Museum exhibition catalogue *Rococo Art and Design in*

Hogarth's England, (1984) is a very useful vehicle for examining the ways in which such stylistic interrelationships flourish.

Stylistic influence can be transmitted in a number of ways. One of the most potent is the medium of engraving which could, conveniently, cheaply and in detail, convey pictorial motifs and decorations from one patron to another, from one producer to another. For instance, engravings of the Italian Commedia dell'Arte influenced the form of figurines produced at Meissen and Nymphenburg in the early eighteenth century; publications of books and plates illustrating classical remains infused Europe with the Neo-Classical spirit in the later eighteenth century; and material of a much more overtly popular nature, culled from magazines and other similar sources, influenced the design and decoration of Victorian mass-produced chimney ornaments.

There are often particular reasons which bring about close stylistic links between one design medium and another. For example, similarities between ceramic and silverware design in late-seventeenth- and early-eighteenth-century France were at least partially due to edicts which caused the nobility to send their silver to be melted down in the interests of the national economy. Since ceramics widely replaced silver on the table and elsewhere it was perhaps inevitable that it should conform to the same stylistic inclinations. Nonetheless it must be stressed that stylistic analysis on its own has its limitations within the context of the history of material culture. For instance, the fact that Wedgwood-produced Jasper and Black Basalt (qq.v.) wares have become almost synonymous with the term Neo-Classicism (q.v.)' (as seen in the Wedgwood advertisement from the *Observer Colour Supplement* in Fig. 3.3) is not in itself particularly revealing. It is only through a careful examination of the wider patterns of taste and patronage that you can begin to understand *why* the various decorative arts in fashionable society of the late eighteenth century assumed similar guise. Many patrons of the arts made the Grand Tour of Europe, paying particular regard to the remains of Classical antiquity in Rome, Naples and other Italian cultural centres. Interest had been stimulated by a number of factors, including the decline of artistic patronage in Italy, with the resulting influx of Italian artists and craftsmen into northern Europe, the opening to the public of the Capitoline Museum in 1734 and the publication of numerous illustrations of recent archaeological discoveries and other classical remains. There was also a strong philosophical and aesthetic interest in the Antique which gained force in the middle of the century. In order,

Figure 3.3   Wedgwood advertisement.

therefore, to have some insight into the reasons which led to the adoption of particular styles it is necessary to look beyond the narrow confines of their outward appearance. In this particular case it would prove useful to read H. Honour, *Neo-Classicism* (1977), to inform yourself of the possible wider dimensions of the subject. It was no accident that the factory built by Wedgwood in 1769 should have been named after Etruria, the ancient Roman state, nor that it should have produced so-called Etruscan ware. Nor was it by chance that Josiah Wedgwood should have commissioned John Flaxman, one of the leading Neo-Classical artists of the day, to produce designs which catered for the taste of fashionable society. A. Kelly, in her book *Decorative Wedgwood in Architecture and Furniture*, (1965), examines Wedgwood production within the context of late-eighteenth-century fashion and shows the ways in which ceramics were incorporated into work in other design fields.

THE TOOLS OF ATTRIBUTION: USES AND PROBLEMS

An important weapon in the ceramic historian's armoury is a sound knowledge of techniques, thus enabling distinctions to be made between various types of pottery, whether earthenware, stoneware, 'hard' or 'soft-paste' porcelain or whatever. E. Rosenthal's *Pottery and Ceramics: From Common Brick to Fine China* (1949) covers many broad issues in which facets of ceramic work are discussed together with explanations of materials, processes and clays. Knowledge of materials, combined with the ability to differentiate between various glazes and other means and types of decoration, will help to give some clear indications of period, provenance and, in some cases, designer. Another means of establishing the artist, manufacturer or date of a piece of ceramics is through the correct identification of the marks made on pieces to indicate their origin, a practice which became widespread in Europe in the eighteenth century. J. P. Cushion and W. B. Honey, *Handbook of Pottery Marks* (1965), gives a fairly full coverage of the field in Britain, Europe and the East, arranged by country and with a helpful introduction. G. A. Godden, *Encyclopaedia of British Pottery and Porcelain Marks* (1979), is useful for products in this country. Marks can denote some aspect of organization within a factory or even, in some instances, be used by retailers of ceramic goods. Nonetheless, reliance on marks alone for the identification of particular pieces is fraught with difficulties, especially in the case of apparently collectable, and thus valuable, items where marks have been altered in order to increase interest and monetary value. Decoration can also be altered or elaborated upon. The problem of fakes and reproductions is also problematic. As collecting developed so the field expanded: Samson of Paris, a firm founded in 1845, reproduced Chinese, Meissen, Sèvres and English porcelain, making life very difficult for the collector. The field of Chinese ceramics presents other difficulties since potters often paid homage to the work of earlier periods that they admired by including reign marks of emperors associated with such work. A deep knowledge and experience of ceramic styles and techniques is perhaps the most accurate means of identification, but even those supposedly well-versed in the field are capable of some fairly spectacular errors. A noted recent example of this was the identification and sale of a number of 'Bernard Leach' pots at a leading auction house, items which, it later transpired, were made by an inmate of one of Her Majesty's prisons.

Ceramics and Society:
Social History

As has been mentioned earlier, much of the writing on the history of ceramics has focused on various categories of ceramics or the artists, factories and families that produced them rather than on those who actually used the products. The study of social history can tell us about the ways in which various levels of society lived and worked, their tastes and habits and the ways in which they looked upon, and used, ceramic products. For example, although the eighteenth-century desire to emulate Oriental porcelain stimulated production at Meissen and elsewhere in Europe, a knowledge of social history helps to explain its wider adoption and fashionable aspect. In part, the spread of porcelain manufacture also clearly related to contemporary drawing-room culture and the emergent popularity of tea, coffee and chocolate drinking for which porcelain was particularly well-suited. A more recent example which illustrates a similar correspondence between social patterns and ceramic production is the development and adoption of oven-to-tableware in the 1950s and 1960s. This was bound up in the more practical and relaxed attitudes of the period to food preparation and presentation, as well as the changes in house-planning which led to the move towards kitchen–dining and dining–living rooms.

Social history can also tell us about the conditions and organization of factory life, as well as the different status and pay of various jobs within the industry. Pottery conditions are by no means conducive to healthy living, with exposure to high temperatures from firing, lead poisoning from glazing, or sillicosis, and other respiratory diseases from dust. This is not a subject likely to be dwelt on at great length in the histories of factories still in operation for obvious reasons. Something of the attempts to campaign for better working conditions can be seen in F. Burchill and R. Ross, *A History of the Potters' Union* (1977). Social history can also inform us about the reasons for the widespread use and poor payment of women in the industry, and the differentiation between middle-class employment in decorating and designing and working-class involvement in more health-hazardous jobs such as dipping and transferring. Oral history is an important means of helping to build up a picture of twentieth-century working conditions and practices. The organizers of an exhibition of painted decorative ware produced at Gray's Pottery between the founding of the factory in 1907 and its closure in 1961, mounted in the City Museum and Art Gallery,

Figure 3.4   Paintresses at Gray's Pottery, Mayer Street, Hanley, Stoke-on-Trent in 1929.

Stoke on Trent in 1982, were eager to document factory life as far as possible (Fig. 3.4). Most of the detail and information about working conditions in the factory only came to light after an appeal on local radio: trained paintresses, polishers, designers, office-workers, despatch staff and others all helped to build up a fairly complex picture of life in Gray's Pottery since the First World War.

Economic and Business History and the Study of Ceramics

Economic history is another branch of study which can lend many insights into the organization of the ceramic industry, both in terms of business strategy and the marketing and retailing of the end product. To use Josiah Wedgwood as an example once more, a knowledge of economic history can help to explain why he was such an entrepreneurial success in the early years of the Industrial Revolution. He was quick to realize the importance of improved factory organization, and the 'division of labour' as described by Adam Smith in *The Wealth of Nations* in 1776, in order to bring about more efficient (and thus profitable) modes of ceramic production. The manufacturing process was subdivided into various distinct stages such as turning, moulding, pressing and decorating and was carried out by employees working in each area. These factors, together with greater mechanization, made larger-scale production at Wedgwood's Etruria factory easier. It then became important for him to develop new markets for his wares, both in this country and abroad. The development of transportation systems during the Industrial Revolution was a key factor in reaching out to these new markets, enabling the economic supply of raw materials to, and despatch of wares from, the factory. Wedgwood was himself intimately involved in the transport revolution and helped in the promotion of the Grand Trunk (Trent and Mersey) Canal which passed his Etruria factory, providing links with the Mersey, the Midlands and London. Production, marketing and transport are factors important in any period in relation to quantity-produced ceramics. It is important to establish how products were actually sold, how they were priced and what type of customer bought them. It is through a reading of social and economic history that you can gain some insights into this area.

Traditional town markets, fairs, travelling potters, pedlars and travelling salesmen are all part of the history of the marketing of ceramics. In the eighteenth century purchases by the upper reaches of society were often made in the fashionable shops of London or Paris, venues and meeting places for elegant society. During this period many major manufacturers opened warehouses and showrooms to increase their markets: Josiah Wedgwood opened showrooms in London, since Stoke-on-Trent was by no means a mecca for fashionable society, unlike Worcester which was able to open shops and showrooms in support of its pottery industry. Another method which Wedgwood used to stimulate sales was through the circulation of catalogues advertising his products, issued in several languages. Indeed, trade catalogues and advertising material are extremely useful as ways of estimating what goods were available at any given period, often listing prices and helping to define more precisely the nature of the consumer market. Business history, a closely related discipline, can also be useful in many of these contexts. Industrial archives, such as the Wedgwood archive at Keele University, provide valuable sources of information on the workings of the pottery industry. There are, however, some problems which relate to archive work since there are often conflicts between accessibility and conservation, as well as issues affecting confidential and possibly damaging material. Royal Doulton Tableware Ltd has one of the largest industrial and design archives stemming from the nineteenth century, although only Minton entered the Doulton Group with any archives of significance, with all aspects of the family business intact. As a result, it is possible to gain a real insight into the running of an important nineteenth-century industry. In terms of the ways in which design work was used, the Minton archive includes some 20,000 drawings which range from the everyday products of factory hacks to the more inspired designs of distinguished figures in the history of nineteenth-century design in Britain, such as A. W. Pugin or Christopher Dresser (qq.v.).

The History of Technology

The history of technology is important in any study of ceramic production, especially since the Industrial Revolution. The mechanization of many aspects of eighteenth-century pottery production, including the grinding of flint and the mixing of pigments and clays, helped the change from a small-scale, conservative and regionally-oriented industry to a comparatively large-scale productive concern. Improved clay technology, methods of moulding, turning and throwing, combined with new possibilities of decorating on a large scale brought about by the invention of transfer-printing in Liverpool in the early 1750s, were also factors in this respect. The nineteenth century witnessed further changes including the mechanization of tile making, improvements in kiln design and firing, and the widespread adoption of steam-powered machinery, itself to be superseded by electricity.

Archaeology and Industrial Archaeology

Archaeology has had an important bearing on our knowledge of the pottery of ancient civilizations, such as the Minoan, Greek, Roman or Chinese, as well as casting light on the ways in which it was used, made and marketed. For the medieval period, when most pottery was of a thoroughly practical nature and was thus discarded once it had been broken, archaeological evidence is also particularly enlightening. In terms of our more recent past, since the days of the early Industrial Revolution, the field of industrial archaeology has provided many insights into ceramic production, processes and factory organization. Through analysis of the surviving physical evidence much can be learnt of the history of the pottery industry, and research, publication and general interest in the field of industrial archaeology has developed considerably since the 1950s when the term began to be used. Useful general introductions to the field are K. Hudson, *Industrial Archaeology* (1963), and R. A. Buchanan, *Industrial Archaeology in Britain* (1972). A. Burton, *Remains of a Revolution* (1975), has a chapter devoted to the Potteries and some memorable photographs by C. Coote.

The value of industrial archaeology can be illustrated by the research carried out at the Caughley porcelain works in Shropshire in the early 1960s. The factory, which had been established in 1754 and closed for economic reasons sixty years later, was to make way for open-cast clayworking in 1964. Before the site was destroyed new evidence was unearthed which made it clear that a far wider range of types and patterns had been produced at the factory than had previously been supposed. Not only were pieces of French and Chinese porcelain discovered, indicating the types of models used in the factory, but also pieces of Caughley-produced gilded ware which established that such work was executed outside London at that time.

Over the past twenty years a great deal of similar research has been carried out in the Ironbridge Gorge and Coalbrookdale in Shropshire, 'the cradle of the Industrial Revolution', culminating in the setting up of the Ironbridge Gorge Museum Trust in 1968. As well as an important library and large repositories of material relating to various local industries, there are also archives and trade catalogues relating to the clay industry and the important Jackfield tile and Coalport china factories. Not many miles away, in the Potteries in North Staffordshire, is an important museum of the industrial past. Situated in Longton, Stoke-on-Trent, the Gladstone Pottery is a nineteenth-century potbank arranged around the sequence of operations in pottery manufacture reflecting the 'division of labour', much in its mid-nineteenth-century form. Nearby at Cheddleton is a working survivor of the many flint mills which once populated the North Staffordshire industrial landscape and provided materials widely used in ceramic manufacture. It is in projects such as these that industrial archaeology is so helpful in providing a more complete picture of the past.

Wider Dimensions of the Subject

The history of ceramics has of course exerted a wider influence on our lives than the types of collectable and aesthetically pleasing products around which this introduction to the subject has so far centred. For example, one area in which ceramic production has had an important bearing is that of public health and hygiene. This is a complex facet of the history of the subject since, in order to understand the complete picture fully, you need to have an awareness of the social, environmental, technological, economic and legislative implications, as well as the historical significance of cleanliness and hygiene in the home. One direct consequence of industrialization and urban growth in the nineteenth century was a decline in standards of health, hygiene and sanitation in many European towns and cities. The ceramics industry helped to ameliorate the position through the mass-production of stoneware water and sewerage pipes. Doulton and Watts, for example, concentrated on this area of production at their Lambeth factory from 1845 onwards and were exporting wares from the late nineteenth century until the outbreak of the Second World War. The closely related field of sanitaryware – baths, basins, water closets (such as the Dolphin model, Fig. 3.5) and other related products – came of age in late nineteenth-century Europe and the United States. The industry, whether in the production of ewers and basins which were to be found on the washstand in the nineteenth-century home or in terms of developments in sanitary technology, played a central role in the quest for domestic cleanliness, health and hygiene.

The bathroom, involving as it does ceramic basins, bidets, shower trays, lavatory pans and, although far less frequently in this age of plastics technology, porcelain-enamelled baths, provides a useful case study in ceramic history. For example, it is important to realize that in the nineteenth century bathrooms were largely the preserve of the wealthy, although they became more widely spread among the middle classes by the early years of this century. Even by 1919 only about 10 per cent of all households in Britain boasted a plumbed-in bath. Although legislation in that year stipulated that all new houses should

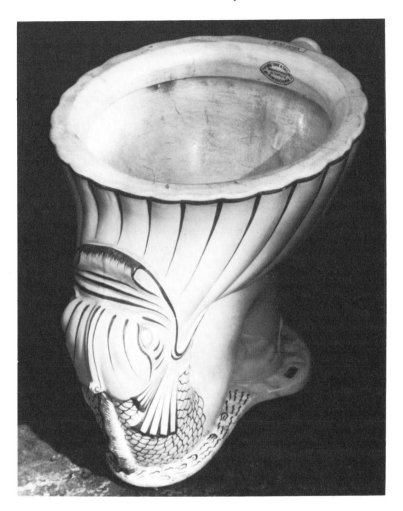

Figure 3.5 The Dolphin Water Closet.

have a bath installed and, in addition, the 1924 Housing Act required that all new council houses should have separate bathrooms, overall provision did not change as dramatically as one might suppose. The 1951 Census revealed that over one-third of houses in Britain were still without a bath. Dorothy Bradell, an important British writer on design matters in the interwar period, made an interesting observation in *The Book of the Modern Home*, published in 1939. She saw the provision of bathrooms for the working man as problematic since they did not normally contain washbasins. Water heating was quite expensive, thus making the taking of a bath a comparative luxury and ensuring that the kitchen sink retained its place as the principal family washing place. However, attitudes to installing bathrooms were not only affected by economic or legislative considerations. At one time the mere possession of a bathroom was a sign of social status, but in the interwar period there were other signs of status that envious neighbours or relatives might detect in its equipment or features. The increasing square-footage of wall-tiling and splashbacks reflected wider concerns than the merely hygienic – the higher they reached up the walls the greater the social status and desirability.

Associative and psychological values can also affect the use of sanitaryware, as in the case of the bidet which was, until comparatively recently, not widely accepted as a normal part of the bathroom's equipment in either Britain or the United States. This was at least partially due to a misunderstanding about its function, thought to be an essentially feminine preserve, coupled with misguided associations with illicit sex which stemmed from the First World War years when many American and British servicemen first encountered the bidet in France. Such associations became emotionally charged and hindered the widespread introduction of a practical aid to personal cleanliness for both males and females. A useful book for exploring a wide range of ideas relating to sanitaryware design is A. Kira, *The Bathroom Book* (1979). Attention is paid to many important aspects: possible philosophical, psychological, religious and social considerations, as well as ergonomic, anthropometric and physiological factors. Also useful is S. Giedion, *Mechanization Takes Command* (revised edition 1969), where the field is covered in Part 7, 'The Mechanization of the Bath'. On a much more factual level, but easily readable and enjoyable, is L. Wright, *Clean and Decent* (1960), especially the later chapters.

Further Reading Suggestions

We have seen that ceramic history is wide-ranging in its scope, geographical spread and chronological span and correspondingly there is a vast array of diverse books and articles on the subject. *World Ceramics* (1968) edited by R. Charleston is a well-illustrated introduction with a bibliography, covering many aspects of Eastern and Western ceramic history, with material on Pre-Colombian, Oceanic and African work as well as a brief modern section. G. Savage and H. Newman, *Illustrated Dictionary of Ceramics* (1974), which looks at the subject from antiquity to the present is also useful as an introduction although it does not have a bibliography. It is important to understand the role of technological development, whether in terms of the invention of the potter's wheel or the impact of automation in modern production processes. For such information reference should be made to *A History of Technology*, Vols 1–5 edited by C. Singer, E. J. Holmyard and A. R. Hall (1954–8) and Vol. 6 edited by T. Williams (1978).

The Concise Encyclopaedia of English Pottery and Porcelain (1968) by W. Mankowitz and R. G. Haggar, in which factories, techniques, decoration and materials are all considered, has a rather more direct focus. It contains a useful bibliography as well as appendices with details of museum collections in Britain and the United States. Similarly comprehensive is R. G. Haggar's earlier *Concise Encyclopaedia of Continental Pottery and Porcelain* (1960).

A knowledge of Oriental ceramics is important to the ceramic historian since they have had a considerable impact on production and decoration in the West. The literature is extensive and the following titles are useful introductions to the field: W. B. Honey, *The Ceramic Art of China and Other Countries of the Far East* (1945), B. Gray, *Early Chinese Pottery and Porcelain* (1953), S. Jenyns, *Later Chinese Porcelain* (1951), *Japanese Porcelain* (1973), and *Japanese Pottery* (1971). The work of other cultures may be seen in A. Lane, *Early Islamic Pottery: Mesopotamia, Egypt and Persia* (1947), and *Later Islamic Pottery* (1971). R. M. Cook, *Greek Painted Pottery* (1966), includes some aspects of the broad economic and historical context.

For the medieval period B. Rackham's brief *Medieval English Pottery* (1972) is useful. Covering a rather later period is the same author's *Italian Majolica* (1963), which provides a succinct account of the origins and techniques important for the spread of European tin-glazed pottery. A. Lane, *French Faience* (1949), covers the field in a factual manner, from its Italian majolica-inspired beginnings through to its eighteenth-century decline. European porcelain is well-covered by the literature as in H. Morley-Fletcher, *Meissen* (1971), B. Watney, *English Blue and White Porcelain in the 18th Century* (1973) or A. Lane, *Italian Porcelain* (1954). An interesting adjunct to several of these books is R. E. A. Drey, *Apothecary Jars: Pharmaceutical Pottery and Porcelain in Europe and the East 1150–1850* (1978).

Much writing about post-Industrial-Revolution ceramics has concentrated on the output of individual factories but has not always taken up in any real detail the wider social and economic implications of production in relation to the consumer, marketing or retailing. By way of contrast B. Hillier, *Pottery and Porcelain 1700–1914* (1968), is essential and absorbing reading. This covers the subject from Rococo to Art Nouveau (qq. v.) in England, Europe and North America, within a cultural and social historical context. Emphasis is placed on the social status of the potter, folk pottery, marketing, reproductions and fakes, together with a good bibliography. One brief company-oriented history which gives an enjoyable and well-illustrated introduction to a wide range of possibilities inherent in the subject is P. Atterbury and L. Irvine, *The Doulton Story* (1979), produced for an exhibition held at the Victoria and Albert Museum. It covers the concerns of a major firm from its early days to the present, including material on studio pottery, artists and decorators, sanitary and industrial production, architectural and sculptural ceramics, and commemorative and advertising wares. Some of these areas are yet to be satisfactorily covered in depth by ceramic historians. The more traditional approach to factory-oriented history is reflected in literature such as G. A. Godden, *Coalport and Coalbrookdale Porcelain* (1970), or L. Whiter, *Spode: A History of the Family Factory and Wares* (1970). Another example of this introverted approach, although very informative and useful in its own terms, can be seen in H. Sandon, *Royal Worcester Porcelain from 1862 to the Present Day* (1975), which gives considerable detail on factory changes, product developments, and on individual painters, paintresses, decorators and modellers.

Nineteenth-century British ceramic history is well-covered in G. A. Godden, *British Pottery* (1970), which surveys the subject from the Victorian era until about 1930, and discusses the production of British porcelain factories, focusing on particular artists. A useful piece on the decorative arts is H. Wakefield's chapter on 'Pottery, Porcelain and Glass' in R. Edwards and L. Ramsey, *The Early Victorian Period 1830–1860* (1958). On a more everyday level P. D. G. Pugh, *Staffordshire Portrait Figures and Allied Objects of the Victorian Era* (1970), provides a well-illustrated account of the sources used for the figure compositions, with material on factories and production. W. S. Bristowe, *Victorian China Fairings* (1964), lends another perspective to the period.

But there are other aspects of ceramic production of the time which relate both to architecture and interior design as can be seen in J. Bernard, *Victorian Ceramic Tiles* (1972). Although he concentrates mainly on British developments there is also material on North America, together with a discussion of makers, production methods and costs. The material ranges from goods produced labour-intensively under the influence of the Arts and Crafts Movement (q.v.) to industrial wares. Many applications which relate to interior design can be explored in M. Girouard, *Victorian Pubs* (1978), which sets the subject within a social context. The possible range of interior and architectural examples are sketched in by P. Atterbury and L. Irvine in *The Doulton Story* (1979), to which reference has already been made. Further related material is to be found in D. Hamilton, *Architectural Ceramics* (1978), and books devoted to architectural history, especially of the Victorian, Edwardian or Art Deco (q.v.) periods.

The importance of crafts in the development of studio pottery is undeniable and an outline background can be gleaned from E. Lucie-Smith, *The Story of Craft: the Craftsman's Role in Society* (1981), which discusses the general role of crafts from antiquity to the present. There were positive reactions against the mass-produced designs of the late nineteenth century, articulated by William Morris (q.v.), John Ruskin (q.v.) and others. These were reflected in the work produced in the Arts and Crafts/Aesthetic Movement (q.v.) vein. Two useful introductions which include many aspects of ceramic production are G. Naylor, *The Arts and Crafts Movement* (1971), and E. Aslin, *The Aesthetic Movement* (1969). The period witnessed the growth of many art potteries which are charted in M. Haslam, *English Art Pottery 1865–1915* (1975), and, in terms of individual artists, in books such as the same author's *The Martin Brothers, Potters* (1978), or W. Gaunt and M. Clayton-Stamm, *William de Morgan* (1971).

Certain strands of the Arts and Crafts Movement's retreat from nineteenth-century commercialism and mass-production modes continued through into this century and the Orient provided important sources of inspiration. For example, Bernard Leach brought the Japanese potter Shoji Hamada to Britain and set up his studio pottery in St Ives. C. Hogben, *The Art of Bernard Leach* (1975), and Leach's own *A Potter's Book* (revised edition 1976), provide useful insights into this outlook. G. Beard considers a wide range of British twentieth-century developments in Britain, the United States and Scandinavia in *Modern Ceramics* (1969), a useful introduction to the area, as is T. Birks, *The Art of the Modern Potter* (1976). P. Lane, in *Studio Ceramics* (1983), includes a very useful list of where to see studio ceramics together with a concise bibliography and periodicals guide. The American dimensions of the subject are discussed in R. S. Donhauser, *History of American Ceramics: the Studio Potter* (1978).

During the twentieth century there has been a number of notable examples of craftsmen working in industry, particularly in Scandinavia. Wilhelm Kage joined the Gustavsberg China Factory in 1917 and combined the role of producing artistic stoneware alongside mass-produced tableware, kitchenware and sanitaryware, all with great style and panache. A similar relationship can be seen in Finland in the interwar period in Kurt Ekholm's work at the Arabia factory. The continuation of this interplay between art and industry can be seen in *Design in Sweden* (1977), edited by L. Lindkvist, with a chapter on ceramics in the context of other design media and practices.

There has been comparatively little penetrating and substantive writing about twentieth-century industrial ceramics. The bulk is to be found in writings within the broader context of industrial design which is gradually emerging as the pivotal area of the history of design since the Industrial Revolution, an aspect of design discussed in Chapter 6. Useful material is also to be found in magazine articles, conference papers or exhibition catalogues. The British Industries Fair, international exhibitions, exhibitions to promote design, such as those of the 1930s, the Britain Can Make It and Festival of Britain exhibitions, all provide interesting material.

Museums and Other Opportunities to see Ceramic Work

It is clearly important to visit as many museums, collections and galleries where ceramic work is shown as possible, as well as to look closely at monuments and buildings which include ceramic work on their exteriors or in their interiors. Such buildings are to be found in almost any town more than fifty years old, whether in Victorian or Edwardian public houses, public lavatories, or even Art Deco cinema buildings. More recently, the decorative schemes for many London Underground stations and other similar work in the public arena provide examples. There are an increasing number of museums of local and social history where ordinary ceramic objects can be seen in their everyday settings, in marked contrast to the glasscase syndrome which pervades many provincial and metropolitan collections. The latter cover all kinds and periods of ceramics, ranging from the magnificent holdings of Eastern and Western wares at the British Museum to the rather idiosyncratic Willet Collection of pottery and porcelain, illustrating popular British History, at Brighton Museum. British and European ceramics can be seen in profusion at the Victoria and Albert Museum in London. There are also many specialist collections such as the Percival David Foundation of Chinese Art, which has an important collection of oriental ceramics, or the Wellcome Institute for the History of Medicine, both in London, and many others. There are also factory museums such as the Wedgwood Museum at Barlaston, near Stoke-on-Trent, where you can see pottery being made and decorated (but in rather ersatz and un-factory-like surroundings), as well as Wedgwood ceramics and related paintings and pattern books of various periods since the company was founded. Rather different in scope is the Gladstone Pottery Museum at Longton, Stoke-on-Trent, mentioned earlier, where you can get a real (but sanitized and safe) 'feel' of a nineteenth-century pottery, and which has an interesting display of all types of ceramics including a splendid collection of sanitaryware, often with ornate decorations.

You should also bear in mind the many country houses which have rich collections of ceramics, often displayed in period, or context, and providing another range of experience, and the number of museums in Britain which have important ceramic collections, particularly those in towns with a pottery past such as Stoke-on-Trent where the City Art Gallery and Museum boasts a particularly fine collection. Reference has already been made to Mankowitz and Haggar, *The Concise Encyclopaedia of English Pottery and Porcelain* (1968), which lists all the principal British collections, and P. Lane, *Studio Ceramics* (1983), which provides extensive coverage of showplaces for studio pottery.

4

Furniture History

PAT KIRKHAM

Furniture history is simply one aspect of history and, within that broad spectrum, forms part of the growing subject of design history. There is a variety of approaches to furniture history which, in chronological terms, extends from the earliest pieces made to the present day: it therefore includes ancient willow chairs as well as mass-produced plastic seating for football stadiums. It covers the furniture made for all sectors of society from the humble beds and tables of Russian serfs to the elaborate marquetry cabinets imported by their Empress Catherine. The geographical spread of the subject is world-wide although most published works in English concentrate on Europe and the USA. They also focus mainly on the period from the Renaissance onwards, in the tradition of European art historical studies.

Furniture history covers the whole range of domestic furniture, as well as furniture made for use outside the home. In the past the latter included furniture for religious orders, fortresses, palaces, parliaments and theatres. Today it includes airports, hotels, cafés, offices, hospitals, lecture rooms and sports arenas. This aspect of the trade is known as the 'contract market' where orders can amount to hundreds or thousands of items of furniture rather than small individual commissions for a single chair or bedroom suite.

Approaches to Furniture History

Furniture history relates to several other discrete academic disciplines (and sub-sections thereof), particularly history and art history. At present furniture history has gained more from the parent discipline of history than from the more recently constituted design history. A qualitative shift in recent furniture studies came with the involvement of a group of British university-trained historians from about 1960 onwards. They applied to furniture history the rigours of historical research and method as well as the preoccupations of historians and transformed a subject which had hitherto been dominated by museum curators, collectors and antique dealers. At the same time, furniture history was also influenced by the more scholarly approach apparent in a great deal of art historical writing. This led to more serious studies of furniture styles as well as of individual designs and designers. It is to the credit of the museum profession that those within its ranks concerned with furniture responded positively to these changes with the result that museums in Britain, on the Continent and in the USA now have a much more serious approach to research than they did twenty years ago. This, coupled with a lively approach to the display of objects, means that there are excellent opportunities for seeing furniture of the past, accurately labelled and well presented to the public.

The founding of the Furniture History Society in England in 1964 grew out of a determination to win for furniture history the academic respectability enjoyed by architectural history, which by then had established itself as a serious offshoot of art history. Its journal is now internationally acclaimed and that academic respectability has been won. Two other societies dealing with furniture history, The Scottish Furniture History Society and the Regional Furniture History Society, have recently been formed. Although a great deal of research remains to be undertaken and new approaches developed, furniture history today is one of the most academically strong areas within the umbrella of 'design history'.

'History' and 'Furniture History'

Within furniture studies, historians have raised questions concerning patronage; the use of furniture; workshop organization; the division of labour; the relationship between craft, design and entrepreneurial functions; exports and imports; the impact of the 'Industrial Revolution'; market growth; working conditions; bankruptcy rates and the apprenticeship system. In *Furniture 700–1700* (1969) Eric Mercer examined the function of furniture in society, for instance, while

Lindsay Boynton exploded the myth of the eighteenth century as 'the Age of Elegance' in an account of life in the age of the bed-bug.[1]

Furniture history is part of social and cultural history because furniture is an expression of the material culture in which it was designed, made, commissioned, marketed, purchased and used. The furniture used by different groups of people signifies a great deal about the different ways they live or lived and about the images people create around themselves. As with most history, the surviving evidence is largely weighted towards the upper echelons of society who kept records and bought the most expensive pieces of furniture. For those students who want to know more about the furniture used by the vast majority of the population at any given time, however, a host of material survives including inventories, legal records, guild records, newspapers, novels, photographs and archaeological evidence.

Furniture history is also part of economic history in that furniture making can be studied in the same way as, say, the textile trade or the steel industry. The business and financial organization of furniture making, from small workshop to large factory, is part of business history, an expanding sub-section of historical study. The history of technology tends to be a specialist field within history yet it is important for furniture historians to understand not only the techniques involved in different production processes but also the nature and qualities of the materials used. Wood is the material most associated with furniture making, even today when a vast range of modern materials is available to designers and manufacturers. Nevertheless, furniture has been made from a wide variety of materials from papier mâché to plastics and from cast iron to cane, as well as upholstered in a wide range of fabrics from Genoa velvet to lycra and from hide to rexine. Whatever the material, questions such as its availability, strength, durability and cost as well as the craft skills required to work it need to be asked.

The precise relationship of technology to production is vitally important. It must never be assumed that certain techniques were widely used in production simply because they had been invented or were known to entrepreneurs. For instance, the availability of cheap labour which was sufficiently skilled and speedy to meet quality and production targets slowed down the introduction of machinery to furniture making in Britain in the nineteenth century. Even at the top end of the market, where labour was less cheap, only those machines which could be in more or less continuous use and thus proved cheaper than hand work tempted employers to lay out the large amounts of

Figure 4.1 Black, red and gold japanned bed and two of a set of armchairs from bedroom suite made for the 4th Duke of Beaufort, 1752–4, designed by John Linnell, and made by the Linnell firm, London. Here shown in the Chinese bedroom, Badminton House, Gloucestershire, before the sale of the furniture in 1921. The bed is now in the Victoria and Albert Museum, London, as is a design for the chairs by John Linnell. For many years the bed was wrongly attributed to Thomas Chippendale.

Detail: gilt dragons carved in wood. This shows the expertise of the most skilled carvers in London in the mid-eighteenth century who were known as 'wood sculptors'.

capital necessary to purchase the machines in the first place. The use of carving machinery proved economic at the New Palace of Westminster in the 1840s when huge amounts of repeat patterns were used in the woodwork. Even so, all the finishing of the carved work had to be done by hand. By contrast, such machines did not prove economic when it came to producing individual cabinets or tables.[2] Furthermore, furniture historians have revealed that certain products or materials hailed as new or revolutionary in one period were used, or at least invented, earlier. Water beds, for instance, were hailed as a great novelty in the 1960s and 1970s yet patents for water and air beds date back to the years of the Napoleonic Wars when doctors and others sought to increase the comfort offered to invalids by using a newly invented rubberized material.[3]

Knowledge of who did what in the production process at a particular point in time is vital to an understanding of how furniture is or was made, particularly in periods when an extensive division of labour operated. The famous 'Badminton' bed (Fig. 4.1), for instance, was not made by one person but by a bed joiner, a japanner, a carver, a gilder and an upholsterer. A wide variety of crafts have been involved in furniture making, including carpenters, turners, cabinet makers, chair makers, and basket makers besides those already mentioned. Here the work of the furniture historian draws on that of historians interested in particular crafts or the guild system, which from the middle ages to the eighteenth century offered some form of protection to craft workers in various parts of Europe.

The question of who did what also relates to the crucial relationship between design and execution. To continue with the same example, the 'Badminton' bed was not *made* by John Linnell who *designed* it *c.*1752–3. Linnell was one of the first full-time professional furniture designers to emerge from the ranks of the English craft. As such, he marks an important stage in the split between designer and craft worker in furniture making. Linnell, however, had been craft trained and had a thorough understanding of the various production processes carried out in the workshops whereas many designers working after him did not.

The history of the working people who made the furniture of the past fills an important gap in labour and trade union history which has tended to concentrate on more militant or well-documented groups of workers such as miners, mill girls and engineers. It is in this area of furniture history that oral history has been used most but interviews with designers, directors, workers, managers and sales representatives as well as consumers have all added to our knowledge of how and why furniture is or was designed and made. It is of vital importance that recollections of people with first-hand knowledge is recorded. I personally find video and tape recording to be interesting and rewarding methods of documentation which anyone can undertake. If you know someone involved with furniture design, production, management or retailing, at any level, do not hesitate to record their reminiscences. Whilst remembering that memories can fail and that one person's interpretation of events may not always tally with another, their experiences provide a unique type of evidence which can not be extracted from documents.

Whilst oral history has proved a useful tool for furniture historians, most have ignored the new feminist history. A great deal of furniture is still described as 'feminine' if it is light, delicately made or elegant in form, while bold, massive or muscular forms of decoration are often described as 'masculine'. This use of sexist terminology may be frowned upon by feminists but its use is widespread. Indeed, it is an interesting exercise to take any standard work and see how many examples of its use one can find. But a feminist analysis involves more than ridding the subject of sexist terminology and assumptions. Art historians have retrieved many women artists from obscurity and design historians are beginning to do the same for women designers. [4] It is important to give known women furniture designers such as Eileen Gray and Ray Hille (qq.v.) their due credit and when, like Ray Eames and Alison Smithson (qq.v.), they worked with their husbands, to assess accurately the contributions of each partner to the collaborative effort.

It has to be acknowledged, however, that in the period *c.* 1700–1980 there have been relatively few women furniture designers or makers in an area dominated by men at all levels. This may even be the case for furniture making in earlier periods about which we know relatively little. Nevertheless, a feminist analysis is necessary to explain the *exclusion* of women from furniture making and design at certain times in history. This can be done by asking different questions of existing data as well as searching out new evidence and examining it all in terms of women's role in society at that time. It is not surprising to learn, for instance, that the main area in which women were employed in furniture making in the eighteenth and nineteenth centuries was upholstery, and even then they were restricted to sewing – a traditional domestic craft taught to women in the home as one of the skills essential to looking after a family. Furthermore, the role of women as consumers is an important but neglected factor in furniture history, as is the types of interiors created by women.

The Impact of 'Design History' on Twentieth-Century Furniture Studies

To date, the emphasis within design history on the years *c.* 1860 to the present has tended to discourage study of earlier periods. Whilst by no means a healthy trend, it has, ironically, helped those within furniture studies who wished to break out of the chronological barrier marked by the years *c.* 1820–40. Museum collections stopped at this period, which was taken to mark the end of 'Georgian' furniture and the date after which objects were no longer 'antiques'. Today several museum collections continue up to the very recent past. Ever quick to spot a growing market, the antique trade has also extended its boundaries. Furniture designed by the 'great' names of the twentieth-century design world is much in demand in the leading auction houses today. The current wave of nostalgic revivalism is producing a keen interest in furniture and interiors of the post-1945 period and 'antiques' now date back to at least the 1960s. This has its benefits for the student of furniture in that, rather than simply being discarded on rubbish heaps or relegated to attics, furniture made after the Second World War is appearing in antique/junk shops at a greater rate than ever before.

A great deal of design history concentrates on well-known designers, and furniture history is no exception. Yet an emphasis on 'classic' or seminal pieces and a concentration on a 'great name' approach to history leaves out the bulk of furniture which remains anonymous. Even a great deal of that designed in avant-garde or fashionable styles in high quality materials by expert craft workers has no recorded maker or designer. For less fashionable pieces which have, by and large, not interested dealers, collectors or museums, there is usually even less documentary evidence. Nevertheless there are a few studies, particularly of country furniture, which deal with such items.[5] Welsh vernacular furniture forms part of the activities of the Regional Furniture Study Group which also emphasizes the importance of 'common' everyday furniture. This is a type of furniture too long 'hidden from history' which is only slowly being rediscovered.

The strength of design history in twentieth-century studies has produced useful monographs on individual furniture designers but no new methodological approach has as yet emerged. There are interesting new developments which borrow from cultural studies, particularly semiotics, and emphasize the social as well as the aesthetic aspect of design, but it remains to be seen how these will affect furniture history.

'Art History', Stylistic Analysis and Attribution

The stylistic analysis of furniture according to movements such as Baroque, Neo-Classicism or the Modern Movement (qq.v.) is rooted in traditional art historical concerns out of which both architectural and furniture history grew and which, indeed, influenced the development of design history. The prime concern of many furniture historians remains the appreciation of visual form. The stylistic antecedents of a particular piece of furniture or decoration are assiduously chased and charted in the manner of traditional art history. A great deal of emphasis is placed on authenticity and the attribution of work to particular designers within a generalized framework of style. There is nothing wrong with this approach *per se*. It is an absolutely necessary first step but, in isolation, can lead only to a partial understanding of the subject.

There have been too many wrong assumptions in the past about who designed particular pieces of furniture for anyone to feel confident in attributing a piece without sound documentary evidence. It is when that evidence is not available that attributions have to be made on stylistic grounds. Some attributions are carefully and convincingly argued while others seem to be conjured out of thin air. The introduction to Christopher Gilbert, *The Life and Work of Thomas Chippendale* (1978), reveals just how much furniture has been attributed to one single individual. Some of the attributions were pure flights of fancy while others were based on a chair or cabinet bearing only the slightest resemblance to a design in Chippendale's (q.v.) well-known pattern book. It was not until more work was done on other eighteenth-century designers as well as Chippendale himself that a more balanced picture was achieved. If wrong attributions can happen with the leading names in English furniture, just imagine how ill-founded are many others. It is particularly important to read any book written before about 1960 (and

Figure 4.2 Two armchairs from Ham House. On the right is a 1670s armchair which was re-covered in the early nineteenth century. On the left is a similar armchair made in 1813 but upholstered with eighteenth-century material. These examples reveal some of the problems of authentification and emphasize the need to be precise and accurate about every part of a piece of furniture when identifying it.

quite a few after that date) with great care. Whenever a piece is attributed to any designer, always check to see exactly what evidence is given. Attributions can be based on a multiplicity of factors including signed designs; resemblance to other designs; surviving bills; family records such as account books, diaries or inventories; labels which some firms attached to pieces; or location in a building which has other pieces of furniture by the same designer. Just how difficult attribution can be is shown in Fig 4.2 which shows similar armchairs of different dates, one from the 1670s, the other made in 1813. The earlier chair is covered in a nineteenth-century fabric while the later one is covered in an eighteenth-century fabric. The correct attribution of both frame and upholstery is necessary in each case, as is the detection of the original and the copy.

Fakes and Reproductions

Authenticity is crucial to collectors and dealers as well as scholars and a great deal of time and effort has been spent in the past on establishing whether or not a piece is genuine, a fake, a reproduction, or a piece which includes a few genuine parts, such as one leg out of a whole chair. A fake is a piece of furniture which is wholly or partly new but made to look old and passed off as such. A reproduction is one which is reproduced, often using modern woods and techniques, in the style and materials of a past period without pretending to be old when it is sold to the customer. Some process of ageing, such as battering with a bag of nails or adding subtle ink stains, may be used on reproduction pieces but they are not used primarily for purposes of pretence but rather to better evoke the past.

Reproductions are not a contemporary phenomenon: they were common in the nineteenth century and some of the best firms made them. The London firm of Edwards & Roberts was famous for its high-quality reproductions of English and French eighteenth-century styles and it is often only their label that has stopped the most experienced historian or dealer from making a faulty attribution.[6] A great deal of reproduction furniture was made in the 1920s and 1930s and, of course, it is still popular today. The 'antique' trade, which developed in the Wardour Street area of London in the early nineteenth century, involved the use of genuine parts of medieval, Elizabethan and Jacobean (q.v.) furniture. These were often fragments of carved work, used to give 'new' pieces a look of authenticity.

The whole area of faking and reproduction is a specialist one. A useful introduction is Herbert Cescinsky, *The Gentle Art of Faking Furniture* (first published in 1931; revised edition 1969). However, there is no substitute for looking and learning. Auction houses are good places to look at furniture because one can pick up a chair and look underneath or pull out a drawer and see if new fittings have been added. Otherwise one has to learn from objects in museums and from illustrations.

Furniture in Interiors

Within a design history divided into discrete areas of study, furniture history most closely relates to and overlaps into the history of interior design (see Chapter 5). Fascinating advances in our understanding of how furniture looked and functioned in an interior have recently come about by furniture historians broadening their horizons and grappling with problems previously considered outside the boundaries of their subject. In *Seventeenth-Century Interior Decoration in England, France and Holland* (1978), Peter Thornton argues for the accurate recreation of historical interiors utilizing the conventions of room arrangement current at the time the interior was designed. This involves the formal placing of chairs and other items of furniture around the walls of seventeenth- and eighteenth-century rooms, a practice which has been adopted at Ham House and Osterley Park House, both of which are in the charge of the Department of Furniture and Interior Design at the Victoria and Albert Museum.

This new approach to room arrangement has also been adopted at certain National Trust houses with the result that the public are currrently seeing furniture set out in formal arrangements to which they are unaccustomed and to which they sometimes object. When visiting a house, or museum where furniture is set out in room settings, always look to see if furniture is formally arranged around the walls in an eighteenth-century room in a historically accurate manner or picturesquely clustered around the fireplace in the 'cosy' manner loved by later generations. No matter how odd the stark impression of rearranged rooms might be to the uninitiated visitor, they are more historically accurate and also reveal much more of the design features of individual pieces of furniture as well as the rooms as a whole.

Architect/Furniture Designers

Architectural history and furniture history are linked at an obvious level by the fact that certain architects also designed furniture; indeed some, such as Charles Eames and Ernest Gimson, (qq.v.) spent more time designing furniture than they ever did designing buildings. It needs to be remembered, however, that architects who designed complete interiors, including every item of furniture, in the manner of C. R. Mackintosh (q.v.) were rare. Unless there is clear documentary evidence, it should never be assumed that the architect of a building designed its furniture.

Jill Lever, *Architects' Designs for Furniture* (1982), covers designs from the eighteenth century to the 1960s in the collection of the Royal

Institute of British Architects, the library of which is a good starting point for research on British architects who designed furniture. Another general book is Marc Emery, *Furniture By Architects* (1983), which covers 500 so-called 'International Masterpieces of Twentieth Century Design'. Although architect-designed furniture is usually discussed in monographs, reflecting a 'high art' approach to 'great' designers, some authors locate their particular subjects within wider contexts. The furniture of Robert Adam, C. R. Mackintosh (qq.v.) and others is covered in specialist studies.[7] That designed by Frank Lloyd Wright (q.v.) still awaits a separate study although his furniture is included in D. A. Hanks, *The Decorative Designs of Frank Lloyd Wright* (1979). The work of Charles and Ray Eames (qq.v.) also cries out for a comprehensive study.[8]

Furniture as Industrial Design

Furniture history also relates to the study of industrial design (see Chapter 6) in that furniture historians concern themselves with the industrial world and its products. If industrial design implies a study of objects designed for and made by industrial processes, then some furniture clearly forms part of that study. The work of certain designers such as Robin Day (q.v.) who developed polypropylene furniture for mass-production clearly falls into this category (Fig. 4.3). Any discussion of industrial design raises the question of how far machines simply added power to speed up hand production. Does industrial design in furniture begin with hand tools or with the extensive use of wood cutting and shaping machinery in the twentieth century? A further fascinating question is how far craft skills are still necessary in the world of industrial production. Fred Scott (q.v.), whose machine produced Supporto chair won a Design Council award in 1982, used as many craft skills in the making of the jigs, from which were made the extremely expensive moulds for mass-production (about £120,000), as he did when he worked as a cabinet maker producing furniture by hand. Robin Day also makes the prototypes for his furniture by hand.

Not all contemporary furniture designers fall into the category of industrial designers. The current craft revival enables many designer/ craftworkers to make a living outside the world of factory production. Edward Barnsley, who has worked solidly in the Arts and Crafts tradition of his father and Ernest Gimson (qq.v.), now trains apprentice

Figure 4.3   The 'Poly' chair. *Left*: Polypropylene stacking chair with metal legs designed by Robin Day, 1963, for the manufacturers Hille. *Right*: armchair version with single stem base. The seat consists of a single moulded shell stamped out from dies and mass-produced all over the world. Day had refused to design a single shell chair in glass reinforced plastic (GRP) because he felt that the design by Charles and Ray Eames made by Hermann Miller in America was the best design solution possible for a single stacking chair in that material. When the tougher and cheaper polypropylene was invented, however, both Day and Hille took up the challenge of producing a cheap (it retailed at about £3) mass-produced chair. (Courtesy of Hille.)

furniture makers as does John Makepeace (q.v.), whose school and workshops at Parnham have played a major part in raising the status of hand-crafted furniture.

Upholstery and Metalwork

Neither historians of furniture, textiles nor interior design have paid much attention to the 'soft' side of furniture making, i.e. the upholstery of furniture and the provision of curtains and cushions. Peter Thornton is unusual amongst furniture historians in that he combines a

Figure 4.4 Chamber of Isabel of Bavaria, Queen of France, from an early fifteenth century miniature in the British Museum. This room shows the importance of textiles in the furnishing of a medieval interior. The walls are hung with textiles, the bed is lavishly upholstered and the Queen sits on a couch bed receiving her guests. The illustration also indicates the way in which a certain group of women, including the Queen of France, used a particular interior at a particular date.

knowledge of textiles with that of wood furniture. Most large museums divide their departments by types of product and materials into furniture (largely wood), textiles, glass, ceramics, etc. Design students specialize in similar areas and specialist research tends to stay within these parameters. This has meant that although upholstery is an important part of many pieces of furniture it has largely been ignored by furniture and textiles historians alike. Yet upholstery can play an essential role in providing comfort to a chair or beauty to a bed and, before the mid-eighteenth century, was often the most expensive part of a piece of furniture (See Fig. 4.4). Upholstery can be decorative in terms of colour, pattern or both and can dominate the form of certain pieces such as modern foam seating. Those wishing to study textiles,

Figure 4.5 Cane and tubular steel furniture made by Dryad, Leicester, *c.* 1933. The designer is not known. It was probably the manager of the cane section of the firm or one of the craft workers. The cantilever chairs borrow a feature then popular with Modern Movement architects and designers. Cane, viewed thirty years earlier as a 'new' material by avant-garde designers, had lost its novelty by the late 1920s. The avant-garde took to tubular steel with the same enthusiasm it had earlier shown to cane. These pieces show both materials used together but other steel furniture was upholstered in different materials, including canvas and leather. The cane is hand-woven and the single shell of the chair seats is similar to that of the polypropylene chair in Fig. 4.3 in that it shapes round the human form. Furthermore, both cane and polypropylene have some resilience which adds to the comfort of the chairs. (Courtesy of Dryad.)

their use in upholstery and their role in the furnishing of an interior will find Karin Walton, *The Golden Age of English Furniture Upholstery, 1660–1840* (1973), a useful starting point.

Furniture history also relates to the history of metalwork but the overlap between the two areas is sadly neglected. A small amount of furniture has been made from metal: some solid silver pieces were made in Europe in the seventeenth century, cast-iron furniture enjoyed a brief vogue in the mid-nineteenth century and tubular steel was the darling of the Modernists (q. v.) in the late 1920s and early 1930s. (Fig. 4.5). Gold leaf has been used to decorate furniture since Egyptian times (Fig. 4.6). A great deal of gilding, in both gold and silver, was

Figure 4.6 Chair from Tomb of Tutankhamun, Egypt, *c.* 1350 BC, discovered in 1922. Gold and silver overlaid on wood and inlaid with coloured glass, faience, lapis lazuli and translucent calcite. (Original in Cairo Museum.)

done in Europe in the eighteenth century and is popular in the Gulf States today. Metal furniture fittings are often both functional and decorative but only the more elaborate tend to be discussed by furniture historians. One of the few design historians who has specialized in metalwork is Nicholas Goodison, whose book *Ormolu: the Work of Matthew Boulton* (1974) deals with furniture, door fittings, clocks and other items.

Barometers and Clocks

Goodison's *English Barometers 1680–1860* (1968) indicates his interest in other 'marginal' areas of design history which, if they fit in anywhere, are often included within furniture history. The history of clocks and barometers falls uneasily between technological histories and histories of furniture making. Edward Joy, *The Country Life Book of Clocks* (1967), which covers the medieval period to about 1900, looks at both technical and stylistic developments and is a useful starting place for any student interested in clocks.

The Study of Actual Objects

Language presents no barriers for those who prefer to study furniture by looking rather than reading. Museums, antique shops, junk shops, workshops and auction houses of the world are there to be visited. Auction houses and antique/junk shops present a unique way of looking at furniture because one is allowed to handle it. Looking underneath a table may reveal a trade label or even a craft worker's name, while pulling out a drawer might reveal poor construction, an unusual type of wood or the replacement of handles.

Museums present furniture in a variety of ways. For instance, the Victoria and Albert Museum, which has the largest collection of high-quality furniture in Britain, mostly displays its furniture in galleries arranged chronologically by country or continent. This has the advantage of indicating and partly explaining changes in materials, style and construction over a period of time. Furniture is normally shown in isolation from other objects which have their own galleries. In the planning of a new twentieth-century gallery at the V and A, however, it was felt that it would be educationally and visually stimulating to bring together furniture, ceramics, glass, textiles and other objects. Indeed, the new gallery is known as the gallery of British Art and Design 1900–1960.

The Museum of Modern Art, New York, has a history of encouraging contemporary design as well as collecting it. Most other national museums are now making greater efforts to collect and display twentieth-century objects, despite decades of neglect. Other ways of seeing twentieth-century furniture is at small company museums such as that run by Gordon Russell Ltd, Broadway, Gloucestershire, and *in situ* at places such at Gatwick Airport or the Barbican Arts Centre as well as in the homes of friends and relations.

Most provincial museums have furniture collections, much of it displayed in country or town houses in their care. Some have specialist collections such as the splendid Ernest Gimson collection at Leicester and the broader collection of Arts and Crafts furniture at Cheltenham. Leeds has an excellent collection of eighteenth-century furniture at Temple Newsam House and of nineteenth-century furniture at Lotherton Hall, and is enterprisingly pioneering the collection of Utility furniture as well as vernacular furniture. Welsh furniture is best seen at St Fagan's, Cardiff. French furniture can best be studied in Britain at the Wallace Collection, London, the Lady Lever Art Gallery, Port Sunlight, and the Bethnall Green Museum, London. For those who wish to study American furniture in Britain, the American Museum at Bath is the best place to start. Country house collections provide another way of viewing furniture. Ones not to be missed are Knole, Kent (for the seventeenth century), Osterley Park House, Syon House and Kedleston Hall (for the eighteenth century) and Wightwick Manor, near Wolverhampton (for the work of Morris & Co. in the late nineteenth century).

If chronological displays of furniture set out in isolation from other objects represent one polarity of furniture display, then full room settings, complete with window curtains and candelabra, represent the other. These can vary from the very humble to the very grand. The state rooms of country houses open to the public are usually set out in full room settings, as indeed are the family bedrooms and, on occasions, the servants' rooms. Less grand room settings can be seen at the Geffrye Museum, London, which has assembled a 1930s suburban living room, the fireplace, door, picture rail, light switch and power point of which came from a house built *c.* 1937 in Woodford, Essex. Various furnished rooms depicting working-class domestic life in a pit village at different periods have been recreated in colliery houses transported to Beamish, North of England Open Air Museum, Co. Durham.

Room settings are the main method of furniture display at the Henry Du Pont Museum, in Winterthur, Delaware, USA, which is one of the main centres for furniture studies in North America. In an effort to achieve authenticity, rooms are lit only by daylight or the equivalent of contemporary candle power. This makes it difficult to view the furniture in any detail on a dull winter's day but it does impress on the visitor what it must have been like to live in those rooms. The cultural shock of viewing furniture against lighting contemporary to the period of the room setting is great and shows how ill-conceived are so many of our conceptions of the past. By contrast with Winterthur, the J. Paul Getty Museum, Malibu, California, displays some of its collection of

French eighteenth-century furniture in semi-room settings, i.e. it places console tables, commodes, mirrors, chairs and other items in their correct position in a room, using contemporary panelling and other objects such as sconces and tripods where possible, but it does not pretend that the totality presented is in any way an authentic individual room of the past. Both of these collections appear traditional in their approach when contrasted to the stark bare white walls and strong spotlight illumination used at the Garvan Collection, Yale, which has pioneered new methods of displaying furniture in the last dozen years. There, chairs are hung on walls so that visitors can view the underneath. Others are shown next to an identical or similar one which has been dismembered in order to show how all the various parts fit together. Other ideas include showing chairs of similar date and material but from different parts of America in order to emphasize regional variations in construction and decoration, or showing chairs of the same date and design but made in different materials. Another way is to juxtapose a chair of 1700 with a chair of 1970 to make points by way of comparison.

The points of comparison depend on the items selected but even the most cursory comparisons between the Egyptian chair (Fig. 4.6) and the chair designed by Robin Day and made by Hille (Fig. 4.3) highlights the lack of decoration in the modern chair. The comparison further reveals a piece made for mass production and meant to serve many purposes as opposed to one made for a specific reason. In one the materials are chosen for cheapness and durability, in the other the use of expensive materials was a fundamental part of its design. The designer and firm which produced the later chair is known while we know little about the person or persons who designed and made the Egyptian chair. Both use colour but only one employs surface decoration. In the Egyptian chair there is religious symbolism while the polypropylene chair has none. Yet both chairs are so well known that they themselves have come, each in their own way, to encapsulate and symbolize the cultures from which they sprang.

Conclusion

Several different strands of study, including history, art history and architectural history, have all affected the development of furniture studies in recent years. The development has not been a narrow and linear one but overlaps and strays into new areas. Furniture history has managed to retain all that is best in the tradition of detailed stylistic analysis while absorbing new approaches to the study of furniture and its interior settings. The Furniture History Society has encouraged young scholars and broken down the sense of isolation felt by students of all ages who were formerly working in splendid isolation, be it in Leeds, Liverpool, Budapest or Vienna. Collaborative teaching, writing, conferences and exhibitions have helped to bring together social historians, economic historians, business historians and experts in stylistic analysis and room arrangement, as well as those involved with the making and conservation of furniture. Much remains to be done but the forging of links and the acknowledgement of new areas of study account for the present strengths of furniture history.

The breadth of subject range and diversity of approach make furniture history an interesting and exciting field of study. Although the number of publications mentioned might seem formidable, it should be remembered that there are still major designers, let alone lesser ones, awaiting their historian – to say nothing of types of furniture such as wheelchairs, garden seating, pianofortes or kitchen furniture. Even with major design institutions such as the Bauhaus or the Design and Industries Association (qq.v.) there is still a great deal to be learned and reappraised, so do not be put off by the fact that certain topics appear to have been 'done'. There are many other exciting topics of research which need to be unearthed. I hope that interest in some of the topics raised in this chapter will lead future scholars to study, say, ancient Roman willow furniture, women furniture designers, Saudi Arabian furniture and interiors of the 1980s, or working-class 'parlour' furniture of the twentieth century.

The ways we view and study furniture influence our opinions of it and we should always try and understand the setting in which furniture is viewed. The ideas pioneered at Yale arose because the collection forms part of a teaching institution. Furthermore, the collection on display is well supplemented by study collections open to students. The Victoria and Albert Museum now has a furniture study collection. Such developments augur well for furniture studies as does the formation of a new Museum of Design in London founded by Sir Terence Conran. Furniture will only be one of the many different designed objects shown and studied there but that is how it should be. Furniture can not be studied in any satisfactory way in isolation and recent developments suggest that increasingly furniture history will be seen within broader contexts.

Suggestions for Further Reading

This guide aims to help those students wishing to delve further into furniture history. It also indicates the variety of approaches adopted by furniture historians as well as some of the strengths and weaknesses of particular publications. Please note that many key books have already been mentioned in the text or notes, and will not be repeated.

BIBLIOGRAPHIES AND DICTIONARIES
Helena Hayward (ed.), *World Furniture* (1965) and *The History of Furniture*, with an introduction by Sir Francis Watson (1976), both provide useful bibliographies. Anthony J. Coulson, *A Bibliography of Design in Britain 1851–1970* (1979), has ten pages on furniture while the comprehensive bibliography published most years in *Furniture History* covers all major articles and books published on furniture history in the previous year, thus providing an easy way of keeping in touch with the latest publications.

John Gloag, *A Short Dictionary of Furniture* (1969), is probably more useful for students than the larger detailed dictionaries.[9] It includes over 2,600 entries, covering names and terms used in Britain and the USA – from 'Acanthus Foot' to 'Zebrawood'. Twenty-eight pages are devoted to a chart indicating types of furniture, materials, techniques and styles for different periods from the tenth century to the present. *A Short Dictionary* also includes a brief list of British and American designers. Sir Ambrose Heal, *The London Furniture Makers From The Restoration To The Victorian Era 1660–1840* (1953), has only recently been superseded by the mammoth compilation sponsored by the Furniture History Society, *Dictionary of English Furniture Makers 1660–1840* (1986). The latter covers all the leading furniture makers of those years as well as thousands of lesser known and hitherto unknown ones.

GENERAL SURVEYS
World Furniture and *The History of Furniture* (both already mentioned) provide introductory surveys. The former, with over 300 pages and hundreds of illustrations, is based largely on stylistic analysis. Furniture is studied as 'art', although some attempt is made to relate it to its background. It is useful to new students of furniture because it covers Ancient Egypt, Greece and Rome, as well as Byzantine, early medieval and Gothic furniture before moving on to the Renaissance and the

seventeenth, eighteenth and nineteenth centuries. The strengths of the book lie in the latter four periods, each of which are divided by country. Those wishing to study pre-Renaissance furniture must go to other studies. *World Furniture* gives only twelve pages to the furniture of the Middle and Far East while 'Primitive Furniture' (mainly African) is only given two pages. The twentieth century is also somewhat cursorily dealt with, although it is more thoroughly covered in *The History of Furniture*. The latter is divided into major stylistic movements – Renaissance, Baroque, Rococo, Neo-Classicism, nine-teenth-century revivalism, the Arts and Crafts Movement and Art Deco. Like *World Furniture*, it has a glossary which helps the beginner to understand specialist terms such as cabriole leg or tallboy. Some of the explanations are accompanied by line drawings for further clarity. Any student wishing to know the major collections of furniture in Europe, the USA and the USSR should consult this book.

PRE-RENAISSANCE FURNITURE

For those who wish to read about furniture in more detail the pre-Renaissance periods present most difficulty. Hollis S. Baker, *Furniture in The Ancient World, Origins and Evolution 3100–475 BC* (1966), introduces Egypt, the Near East and the Aegean. Extremely well illustrated, its colour plates will whet anyone's interest in the products of these cultures. There is no good general book on Roman furniture in English. For those interested in archaeology and British history Joan Liversidge's *Furniture in Roman Britain* (1955) indicates how the archaeologist's evidence is essential to the furniture historian for periods where a great deal of evidence has to be dug out of the ground. For the medieval period, Mercer's book, already mentioned, is a good broad survey while Penelope Eames, *Medieval Furniture* (1977), has transformed our understanding of medieval furniture and set new standards for the use of contemporary and extant furniture records.

Oriental furniture provides a fascinating area of study. The best known books include Gustav Ecke, *Chinese Domestic Furniture*, (published in Peking in 1963 but written in 1944 by a European living in China)[10] and G. N. Kates, *Chinese Household Furniture* (1962). American collections of Chinese furniture are covered in R. H. Ellsworth's comprehensive *Chinese Furniture* (1971) which also has an annotated bibliography. There is little written on the furniture of other Far Eastern countries but students could begin with R. Clarke,

Japanese Antique Furniture (1983), E. and M. Pai Wright, *Korean Furniture: Elegance and Tradition* (1985).

C. 1600–1840

By contrast, European and North American furniture of the period 1660–1840 is well served with publications. They cannot all be listed but include Pierre Verlet, *French Royal Furniture* (1963); F. J. B. Watson, *Louis XVI Furniture* (1960); Hans Huth, *Roentgen Furniture* (1974); Charles Montgomery, *American Furniture: The Federal Period* (1967); Ian M. Quimby (ed.), *American Furniture and Its Makers* (1979); Helena Hayward, *Thomas Johnson and the English Rococo* (1964) and the Faber and Studio Vista series on English furniture makers and designers.[11] The dictionaries of furniture makers by Heal and the Furniture History Society, discussed above, also devote themselves to the period 1660–1840.

C. 1840 TO THE PRESENT

Edward Joy, *English Furniture 1800–1851* (1977) covers the years to 1851 in depth, examining the structure of the industry and the use of new materials and techniques as well as stylistic developments. British furniture of the Victorian period as a whole is covered in Elizabeth Aslin, *Nineteenth Century English Furniture* (1962); R. W. Symonds and B. Whineray, *Victorian Furniture* (1962); and Simon Jervis, *Victorian Furniture* (1968). The period 1850–1915 is somewhat sketchily covered in Pauline Agius, *British Furniture 1850–1915* (1978), which has a useful bibliography covering contemporary pattern books, trade catalogues and books of instruction.

Alistair Duncan, *Art Nouveau Furniture* (1982), introduces a topic which fascinates many and takes the story of furniture into the twentieth century. This is also done in J. L. Fairbanks and E. B. Bates, *American Furniture, 1620 to the Present* (1981). Two books by Philippe Garner focus on the twentieth century itself. *Twentieth Century Furniture* (1980) contains over 400 illustrations and surveys the decades up to the 1980s; its companion, *The Contemporary Decorative Arts* (1980), covers the period 1940 to the present and includes a chapter on furniture and interior design.

Despite the great interest shown in 'modern' furniture of the late nineteenth and twentieth century, it is not as well researched as students might imagine. Although there are publications on Ettore Sottsass and the Memphis group, particularly P. Sparke, *Ettore*

Sottsass Jnr (1981) and B. Radice, *Memphis*, (1985), other Italian postwar designers still warrant research. Indeed, many of the best-known furniture designers, makers, and entrepreneurs of this century, let alone lesser known figures in earlier periods, have not yet been the subject of sustained analytical study. Robin Day, Joe Colombo, Vico Magistretti and Terence Conran are amongst those awaiting definitive studies.

DESIGNS

Nearly all the books mentioned so far concern themselves with design in one way or another. A few books, however, concentrate exclusively on furniture designs. Simon Jervis, *Printed Furniture Designs Before 1650* (1974), provides an excellent introduction and has the distinction of a European focus. Later years are covered by Peter Ward-Jackson, *English Furniture Designs of the Eighteenth Century* (1959), John Harris, *Regency Furniture Designs from Contemporary Source Books 1803–1826* (1961), and Edward Joy, *Pictorial Dictionary of British 19th Century Furniture Design* (1977), but these are restricted to Britain, and largely to England.

The designs reproduced in these books, together with the reprints of the better known pattern books now available, give students easy access to first-hand evidence. There is always something to be learned from examining a collection of original furniture designs, be it in the realization that they resemble the work of another designer or that they concentrate on one or two particular types of furniture.

As with other areas of furniture history, the eighteenth and early nineteenth century is well served. There are reprints of the pattern books of the famous trio – Chippendale, Hepplewhite and Sheraton.[12] The very selection of books reprinted tells us a great deal about furniture studies at the time of publication. While Christopher Gilbert's work has borne out Chippendale's abilities as a designer and Sheraton is known to have been one of the first people trained in the furniture trade to try and make a living as a professional designer, Hepplewhite's standing as a 'great name' in the history of furniture design has to be challenged. It is based on nothing except the fact that his name was associated with a book of designs published two years after his death by his widow. Sheraton pointed out that the Hepplewhite designs were mediocre and old fashioned and so they are. Yet the very fact that a pattern book survived led historians to ignore this and to assume that its author had been influential and famous in his day. The recent discovery that Hepplewhite bound an apprentice at a very low rate confirms Sheraton's evidence that Hepplewhite was by no means in the forefront of his trade. By now, however, 'Hepplewhite' is firmly established in the popular imagination as a 'great' English furniture designer and maker. This example of how the head of a small and insignificant firm in late-eighteenth-century London came to be claimed as a 'hero' of design history is a salutary one. In periods where less research has been done and less evidence is available, the risk of gross distortion of the facts is all too great.

Collections of designs only form one aspect of the study of a designer but when, as in the case of A. W. N. Pugin's *Gothic Furniture* (1835), reprinted 1972, they are published together with designs by the same person in other media, useful cross-referencing can take place. Questions can be asked such as how sensitive the designer was to the materials used or how far he or she was trying to impose a predetermined aesthetic irrespective of the materials and the techniques involved in working them.

FURNITURE TYPES

Some historians approach furniture history from an interest in one particular type of furniture such as writing desks or tables, and many books divide furniture into separate categories. Edward Joy's pictorial survey of nineteenth-century furniture designs, for instance, is divided into bedroom furniture; cabinets; chairs; chests; couches; desks; hall stands; mantelpieces; mirrors; screens; shelves; sideboards; tables; and miscellaneous.

Ecclesiastical furniture made for churches or other religious institutions covers a wide range of items from pews to pulpits and from lecterns to fonts. There are several studies devoted to this area. A comprehensive survey is Cox and Harvey, *English Church Furniture* (first published in 1907 but reprinted in 1973). The best up-to-date account is Gerald Randall, *Church Furnishing and Decoration in England and Wales* (1980). It has excellent photographs of church furniture, mostly in original settings, and covers the medieval period to the present day. Randall divides furniture into types such as congregational seating, chests and eucharistic furniture and shows the development of particular pieces over a period of several hundred years. Visual comparisons between, say, the lectern at King's College Chapel, Cambridge (c.1515) and that at either St Mary the Virgin, Wigginhall, Norfolk (1518) or St Andrew, Co. Durham (designed by

Ernest Gimson *c.* 1907) prove most rewarding. By and large, the study of domestic and ecclesiastical furniture are two distinct aspects of furniture history: those who write about the former rarely mention the latter unless they are discussing the Gothic style, either in its original or revised forms. A splendid exception to the domestic/religious division is the furniture of the Shakers, an American religious sect, whose furniture reflected its faith so clearly that it is difficult to write about Shaker furniture without considering their religious beliefs: [see, for example, E. D. and Faith Andrews, *Religion in Wood* (1966)].

The chair is the favourite type selected for specialist study by twentieth-century writers. Recent publications on the chair include *Modern Chairs 1918–1970* (1970). This is the catalogue of an exhibition of that name presented by the Whitechapel Art Gallery in association with *The Observer* which featured 'classic' modern chairs. This approach represents the chair as 'high art' and also indicates the 'antiques' of tomorrow. *A Century of Chair Design*, by Frank Russell, Phillippe Garner and John Read (1980), deals with a longer period and includes Arts and Crafts, Art Nouveau and Art Deco styles but still clings to the 'great names' approach to design history. The section on the Modern Movement adopts the same approach as the Whitechapel catalogue, stating that the 'Wassily' chair, designed by Marcel Breuer in 1925, used on the cover of the book, has become a 'classic of modern design'.

An antidote to the 'classics' approach comes in a book which, ironically, still feels obliged to 'sell' the object of the study by claiming it to be a 'classic'. It is Ivan Sparkes, *The Windsor Chair, An Illustrated History of a Classic English Chair* (1975). Apart from the indication in the sub-title of the pressure on publishers and historians to pander to the collectors' market, Sparkes' work is refreshing in that he draws on his knowledge of chair making, workshop organization and the popularity of the type outside England to bring breadth to his subject. Furthermore, it indicates museums with collections of either Windsor chairs, relevant tools, or photographic records. An example of just how specialized the study of chairs can be is illustrated by the large literature on Windsor chairs alone.

Other fascinating books on chairs include Nanna and Jørgen Ditzel, *Danish Chairs* (1954), which concentrates on the upsurge in design in Denmark in the previous twenty years, and Patricia Kane's well-documented *300 Years of American Seating* (1976). Broader studies of chairs include Edward Joy, *Chairs* (1967), which covers English chairs from Roman Britain to the 1960s, and John Gloag, *The Englishman's Chair* (1964), which attempts a social history of seat furniture from the ancient world to the modern period.

MATERIALS AND TECHNIQUES

As far as materials and technology is concerned, historians such as Edward Joy who take such factors into account have already been mentioned. Otherwise one is left with specialist studies on materials or technology. The most useful include F. Lewis Hinckley, *Directory of the Historic Cabinet Woods* (1960), which has a short but useful bibliography should one wish to delve further. D. N. Buttrey, (ed.), *Plastics in the Furniture Industry* (1964), aids an understanding of more modern materials, as does Dennis Young's publications on upholstery, *Sitting in Comfort* (1952) and *Upholstery With Latex Foam* (1957). Tools are covered in R. A. Salaman, *Dictionary of Tools Used in the Woodworking and Allied Trades c.1700–1970* (1975), and W. L. Goodman, *The History of Woodworking Tools* (1962). However, it is Charles F. Hummel who has provided a model for further research: his *With Hammer in Hand. The Dominy Craftsmen of East Hampton, New York* (1968) combines a detailed study of the tools used by the craft workers with their living and working conditions and the products they produced. Chairs and parts of chairs are illustrated together with the tools used to make them in this unique study.

CATALOGUES OF COLLECTIONS

Nearly every major collection of furniture has its own printed catalogue. These range from the large and lavishly illustrated to the two- or three-page introductory leaflet. Exemplary catalogues of collections are Geoffrey de Bellaigue's two volumes on furniture and gilt bronzes in *The James A. De Rothschild Collection at Waddesdon Manor* (1974) and Christopher Gilbert's *Furniture at Temple Newsam House and Lotherton Hall* (1978). For those just embarking on the study of furniture history such catalogues not only provide detailed information about individual pieces of furniture but they also give a picture of the collections as a whole. As yet the history of the collecting of furniture is largely unwritten. When this fascinating area of cultural history is studied in detail, catalogues of furniture collections will be of great importance as will biographies of individuals who collected the furniture.

Notes

1 L. O. J. Boynton, 'The bed bug and the "Age of Elegance"', *Furniture History*, 1965, vol. 1, pp. 15–31.

2 E. T. Joy, 'Wood-working and carving machinery', *Antique Collecting*, September 1978, pp. 42–5.

3 This information came from a study of patent applications held at the Patent Office, Chancery Lane, London. The newly-invented rubberized material achieved lasting fame when it was used for one of the most important garments in the history of design, the mackintosh.

4 See A. Callen, *Angel in the Studio: Women in the Arts and Crafts Movement* (1979); R. Parker and G. Pollock, *Old Mistresses: Women, Art and Ideology* (1981); Isabelle Anscombe, *A Woman's Touch. Women in Design from 1860 to the Present Day* (1984); and R. Parker, *The Subversive Stitch – Embroidery and the Making of the Feminine* (1984).

5 Jane Toller, *Country Furniture* (1973); Marjorie Filbee, *Dictionary of Country Furniture* (1977); and the catalogues to two influential exhibitions at Leeds, *Town and Country Furniture* (1972), and *Back-Stairs Furniture* (1977).

6 E. T. Joy, 'Victorian revivals of 18th century furniture', *Antique Finder*, October 1975, pp. 12–15.

7 See Eileen Harris, *The Furniture of Robert Adam* (1963); Mary Comino, *Gimson and the Barnsleys* (1980); Roger Billcliffe, *Charles Rennie Mackintosh – The Complete Furniture, Furniture Drawings and Interior Design* (1986) and *Mackintosh Furniture* (1984); Randell L. Makinson, *Greene & Greene. Furniture and Related Designs* (1979); Riccardo Dalisi, *Gaudi Furniture* (1980); D. Baroni and G. Thomas, *Rietveld Furniture* (1978); Renato De Fusco, *Le Corbusier, Designer: Furniture, 1929* (1977); C. Wilk, *Marcel Breuer, Furniture and Interiors* (1981); W. Blaser, *Mies van der Rohe Furniture and Interiors* (1982).

8 See A. Drexler, *Charles Eames Furniture From the Designer Collection, The Museum of Modern Art, New York* (1973).

9 See Ralph Edwards and Percy Macquoid, *The Dictionary of English Furniture Makers* 3 vols (revised edition 1954) and Ralph Edwards, *The Shorter Dictionary of English Furniture* (1974).

10 See Tuttle reprint of 1963 edition (1970).

11 The Faber series, edited by Peter Thornton, includes R. Fastnedge, *Sheraton Furniture* (1962); S. Grandjean, *Empire Furniture 1800–1813* (1966); C. Musgrave, *Regency Furniture 1800–1830* (1970); as well as E. Aslin, *Nineteenth Century English Furniture* (1962). The Studio Vista series comprises C. Gilbert's work on *Chippendale* (2 vols) and H. Hayward and P. Kirkham, *William and John Linnell, Eighteenth Century London Furniture Makers*, 2 vols (1980).

12 Hepplewhite's designs of 1794 were reprinted in London in 1965 with a preface by Ralph Edwards. There is a paperback reprint of the 3rd edition of Thomas Chippendale's *The Gentleman & Cabinet-Maker's Director*, (1762), New York, 1966. Also published in America in 1980 by Praeger were reprints of Thomas Sheraton, *The Cabinet-Maker and Upholsterer's Drawing Book* (1793) and *The Cabinet Dictionary*, 2 vols (1803).

5

Interior Design

ROWAN ROENISCH and HAZEL CONWAY

In Broussa in Asia Minor, at the Green Mosque, you enter by a little doorway of normal human height; a quite small vestibule produces in you the necessary change of scale so that you may appreciate, as against the dimensions of the street and the spot you come from, the dimensions with which it is intended to impress you. Then you feel the noble size of the Mosque and your eyes can take its measure. You are in a great white marble space filled with light. Beyond you can see a second similar space of the same dimensions, but in half-light and raised on several steps (repetition in a minor key); on each side a still smaller space in subdued light; turning round, you have two very small spaces in shade. From full light to shade, a rhythm. Tiny doors and enormous bays. You are captured, you have lost the sense of the common scale. You are enthralled by a sensorial rhythm (light and volume) and by an able use of scale and measure, into a world of its own which tells you what it set out to tell you. [1]

Thus Le Corbusier described his response on entering the Green Mosque. To him the most important features were the changes in scale, the light and shade and the rhythm produced by them. Perhaps a summer tourist would also add the change in temperature and quiet inside, in contrast with the bustle in the street outside. Whether we go into a mosque, or our own home, a car, or a cinema, it is the change in light and the change in scale that generally have the most immediate effect upon us. The height of the ceiling, the proximity of the walls, the colours and the types of surfaces, the lighting, whether it is artificial or natural, all affect our reactions to interior space in very complex ways.

Interior design, as its name implies, is design that is inside, but the question then is, inside what? The obvious answer would seem to be inside architecture or building and therefore the range of interior design would extend as widely as they do. It would include domestic interiors such as flats, houses, palaces, castles; public interiors such as churches, railway stations, airports, pubs and cinemas; and industrial and commercial interiors such as factories and shops, but not perhaps monuments, tombs, caravans or potting sheds. Yet even here exceptions should surely be made for the Egyptian pyramids had very complex interiors designed for a well-defined purpose, and although the Statue of Liberty is a monument, there is a lift inside and visitors can travel to the top for a splendid view. Caravan interiors are certainly designed, while the interior of the average potting shed is almost certainly not.

Interior design is a very broad subject and it also has a very long history as the example of the Egyptian pyramids indicates. Indeed interior design predates architecture for people lived in sheltered environments long before they built houses or developed architecture. Caves are certainly interiors and paleolithic people used them to live in. This meant not only the basic functions such as eating and sleeping, but also far more complex functions in which the images delineated on the walls played their part.

Interior design embraces most of the design areas covered in this book, and numerous people such as architects, engineers, builders, joiners, plasterers, textile designers, fine artists and furniture designers have played a part in the development of particular interiors. Perhaps this is one reason why it is one of the least developed subjects within the young discipline of design history, for it relates to so many different areas.

Architecture and Interiors

A further factor which has perhaps inhibited the development of interior design as a separate area of study, concerns its relationship to architecture. There are many who would argue that interior design is so much part of architecture that it would not be logical to try to separate them, but there are no rigid rules in this and the emphasis in the end will depend on what is being studied and the sort of questions that are being asked.

In the case of church and religious architecture of any period, including the more modern churches of the twentieth century, the interiors are not usually discussed as a separate entity, but are seen as an inseparable part of the whole building. These interiors therefore form part of the wealth of literature on religious architecture, even if church architecture and the services performed within are undergoing major reform. William Butterfield's (q.v.) church of All Saints, Margaret Street, in London (1849–59), was the first church to incorporate the facilities deemed appropriate by one of the major reform movements of the Anglican church in the late 1840s, the Ecclesiologists. Although the vivid interior with its varied marbles and tiles are discussed in Paul Thompson, *William Butterfield* (1971), they are seen as part of the whole building. It would however be possible to see how changes in church services over a period were reflected in the organization of the interior, without necessarily looking at the whole external fabric of the building.

Auguste Perret (q.v.) was a pioneer in developing reinforced concrete and the church of Nôtre Dame du Raincy (1922–3), in Paris was one of the first to be built in that material. The way in which Perret used concrete for the shell of the building and in the interior is discussed in Peter Collins, *Concrete, The Vision of a New Architecture* (1959). Here again the interior is seen as part of the whole building. If however we were concerned with the question of the structural and decorative use of concrete for interiors, and how it appeared with different types of lighting, or in different situations, then the interior of that church could be one example that was selected for study.

The link between interior design and architecture is a close and important one, and a study of architecture, or even the shell of a building, can provide useful evidence about the interior. In some interiors structural expertise was fully exploited to provide sufficient space. The domes and vaults of ancient Roman baths, the iron and glass structures of the nineteenth-century railway sheds, exhibition halls or shopping galleries, the 1930s airship hangars or cinemas are examples of this. In each of these buildings it was the technical properties of the available materials that largely determined the shape and character of the interior. Some of these interiors such as the Roman baths or the cinemas of the 1930s were lavishly decorated, whereas others were not. To understand why Paddington Station, London, designed by I. K. Brunel and Digby Wyatt (qq.v.) in 1850 was decorated in the way it was, and the connections between it and the interior of Joseph Paxton's Crystal Palace (qq.v.), London, built in 1851, would involve an investigation into the problems of using iron in architecture in the mid-nineteenth century and what influential critics such as John Ruskin (q.v.) thought about the correct use of that material.

Often the shell of a building is all that remains of, say, the working environments, or the cottages of ordinary people such as those working on the land or in the textile or iron industry in the mid-eighteenth century or earlier. In order to build up a fuller picture of what those vernacular interiors were like, and the experience of living and working within them, evidence must be gleaned from other sources. W. M. Barley, *The House and the Home* (1963), shows how it is possible to do this.

A study of particular features of the shell of a building such as windows can provide useful insights into the problems of interior design, and some of the social and economic factors of the time. In the Middle Ages in Western Europe glass was expensive and hence the prerogative of the wealthy or the church. Most openings were unglazed and the value of admitting light and allowing smoke from the open fire to escape had to be weighed against the draughts, the weather and the escape of heat. These factors affected the location, design and size of windows as well as the organization of activities within.

With the introduction of picturesque (q.v.) taste in the late eighteenth and early nineteenth centuries, some domestic windows began to be positioned so that a good view could be seen from inside rather than according to principles of classical symmetry. In that instance the development of a new attitude towards the landscape and architecture in turn affected interior design. The relationship of interiors to architecture becomes even more complicated today when old buildings are rehabilitated. In order to provide a satisfactory environment for a new use, false ceilings, partitions, and intermediate floors are sometimes introduced. Whether it would be possible to study such interiors without examining the rest of the building would depend on the scope and approach of the investigation. Insight into the many varied problems involved in rehabilitation can be found in S. Cantacuzino, *New Uses for Old Buildings* (1975).

The Manchester Exchange Theatre (Fig. 5.1) is an example of an interior within an interior. It would be possible to study the theatre without examining the mid-nineteenth-century Royal Exchange building at all. But the rationale of the theatre design depended on it being within another building which sheltered it and provided subsidiary services such as off-stage effects, box office, cloakrooms and eating and drinking facilities. Furthermore, the theatre is not just an interior design, it too has an exterior which would have to be examined to see how the structure frames the theatre with its raked seats and stage.

section
(scale 1 :600)

key
8, stores
11, cafe/bar
18, restaurant

18
11
8

Figure 5.1 Manchester Exchange Theatre, Levitt Bernstein Associates, 1976: section.

Domestic Interiors

Although the relationship of architecture to interior design is very important, in general the research and publications on interior design have not reflected the breadth of those on architecture. Until recently the main emphasis of books has concentrated on domestic interiors particularly those of the aristocracy and the wealthy. As with any other history this was partly owing to the fact that it was those interiors that have been valued and have survived. Because of the problem of survival, periods earlier than the Middle Ages have tended to be ignored.

Architectural histories are nevertheless an important initial source for studies in interior design. D. L. Smith, *How to Find Out in Architecture and Building* (1967) is an annotated bibliography surveying building and architectural literature as a whole, and the architectural volumes of the Pelican History of Art Series are also of great value.

Nicholas Pevsner, *A History of Building Types* (1976), which discusses the historical development of buildings of different functions is of particular help to those who wish to break from stylistic surveys. R. Brunskill, *The Traditional Buildings of Britain* (1981), and Bernard Rudofsky, *The Prodigious Builders* (1977), are useful introductions to the field of vernacular architecture, whilst J. M. Richards, *The Functional Tradition in Early Industrial Buildings* (1958), surveys early industrial buildings.

In the area of general histories directed specifically at interior design Sherill Whiton, *Interior Design and Decoration* (1974), and the entry on interior design in the McGraw-Hill *Encyclopedia of World Art* (1958), give a more balanced overview of the subject in terms of chronology and types of interior. Alastair Service, *Edwardian Interiors* (1982), is a recent example of a study which also offers a glimpse 'inside the homes of the poor and the average' as well as the wealthy.

Many histories reflect the background and specialism of the author. For example George Savage, *A Concise History of Interior Decoration* (1966), reveals his great knowledge of antiques. In contrast, Mario Praz, in *An Illustrated History of Interior Decoration* (1964), bases his survey on some 400 paintings, engravings and drawings contemporary with the interiors which they illustrate. He focuses on the design of each scheme, trying to analyse the approach of the artist or draughtsman, and links each interior to the history of taste in a range of periods from Pompeii to Art Nouveau. Peter Thornton, *Seventeenth-Century Interior Decoration in England, France and Holland* (1978), takes a briefer period and again only the homes of the wealthy. This study is based on his own and his colleagues' long experience of conservation and restoration in the Department of Furniture and Interiors at the Victoria and Albert Museum. The processes of restoration and conservation led to wide-ranging questions being asked about decoration and life among the landed classes in that period. Social and political history, careful study of numerous other surviving houses, furniture and fittings, contemporary illustrations, inventories and documents have been brought together and form a rounded picture of how those interiors were created and used.

One of the most important sources are architects', designers' and craftsmen's technical manuals and pattern books. Even prior to the printing press manuscripts of this kind are known to have existed for the use of a master craftsman or mason's lodge. Well-known examples are *De Architectura* by Vitruvius (q.v.) the first-century BC Roman architect and engineer, and the album of Villard de Honnecourt (preserved in the Bibliothèque Nationale, Paris), a French master mason active between 1220 and 1235. Since the Renaissance such works have been published for the general use of craftsmen and designers, and pattern books in particular have played a great part in influencing fashions and spreading ideas. An early-nineteenth-century example is Thomas Hope (q.v.), *Household Furniture and Interior Decoration* (1807), which illustrates the interiors of his own house in Duchess Street, London. Its aim was to provide examples for manufacturers of the period whose design he found wanting.

Since at least the nineteenth century, a prolific literature has emerged, advising at first the middle classes but latterly the working class, on household management and how to decorate their houses. Books such as Charles L. Eastlake, *Hints on Household Taste in Furniture, Upholstery and other Details* (1868), aimed to suggest some fixed principles of taste for the popular guidance of those who were not accustomed to hear such principles defined. Although not a blueprint of how English middle-class domestic interiors of the second half of the nineteenth century actually looked, it and popular books like it can often help to confirm or suggest the possible character and arrangement of particular types of interior, where similar taste is in evidence. Books on household management which describe how wooden floors might best be cleaned, or how to prepare a guest bedroom, may indicate some of the incidentals of interior design such as the quality of finish of a floor surface or the range of items included in a room.

The relationship between each individual interior and the next may be the product of careful design in the architectural plan, as well as in the effects created by furnishing and fittings within. At Syon House, near London, Robert Adam (q.v.) in 1762 worked within the quadrangular plan of a Jacobean house, and created a variety of contrasting geometrically-shaped rooms, each based on a classical prototype (Fig. 5.2). His intention was to entice and vary the experience of the visitors, very much in the way that Le Corbusier reacted to the changing scale and experience of the mosque in the opening quotation. There was a domed hall or Pantheon (q.v.) at the centre and around this was a basilica-shaped (q.v.) entrance hall with an apse (q.v.) at one end (Fig. 5.3). This had ante rooms at either end, one oval and the other a rectangle, made to appear as a square, by a dividing screen of free-standing columns. Adjoining this latter room was a long dining room with an apse at either end. To understand the significance of the

Figure 5.2 Syon House, near London, Robert Adam, begun 1762: plan.

interiors at Syon House it is important to see how the various spaces led one to the other, and how particular effects were achieved, and also to appreciate the development of Neo-Classicism (q. v.) in Britain in the mid-eighteenth century which affected all the arts, including interior design.

Although much interior design history concentrates on domestic interiors, it is surprising how selective most such histories are. Domestic structures such as castles and palaces may house whole communities under one roof with a variety of interior spaces; vernacular buildings such as cottages, prior to industrialization, provided living and sleeping space, workplace, storage facilities and sometimes even housed the livestock. However, most studies of domestic interiors

Figure 5.3 Syon House, near London, Robert Adam, begun 1762: entrance hall.

concentrate on the reception rooms, such as the dining room or lounge. As for relating their design to types and patterns of usage, to size and composition of families, for the differing needs of men, women, children, the elderly or the handicapped – this awaits detailed study, although feminist history has made a promising start as in D. Hayden, *The Grand Domestic Revolution: A History of Feminist Designs for American Homes, Neighbourhoods and Cities* (1981); and Matrix, *Making Space, Women and the Man-Made Environment* (1984).

Terminology

The study of interiors is further complicated by the changing use of areas associated with particular words. For example, a hall today can be either a large room for sports, entertainments, or big gatherings of people, or a sizeable lobby just inside the door of a dwelling, usually containing the staircase. In the late Middle Ages a hall was the main central living space of a house and contained the fire. By the eighteenth century the hall was the term applied to the ceremonial entrance to a house. When British Arts and Crafts Movement (q.v.) architects such as Baillie Scott (q.v.) looked back to medieval precedents, to apply to domestic housing in the late nineteenth century, the term began again to be applied to what had become a central living space.[2]

The term 'bedroom' has not always been used in England. A great chamber or solar in the medieval house was used as the main bedroom and as a private bed-sitting room for the family. By the mid-seventeenth century the development of a second room in a two-roomed dwelling was known as a chamber in the South of England. Towards the North it was called the parlour but in both cases the room was a room for sleeping in.[3] So in order to be sure that the name of a particular room and its use are clear, it is important to recognize how terms are used in particular periods and in different parts of a country.

In other parts of the world, concepts such as that of 'home' will be determined by a wholly different culture and climate. In areas of Africa, the hot, sunny weather and the need to provide accommodation for a kinship group rather than a Western nuclear family, may mean that the home consists of a series of individual huts for sleeping, cooking and storage, alongside designated exterior space for social activities, washing, food preparation and for drying utensils. Thus part of what we may take for granted as interior design may, in hot climates, consist of exterior design. Moreover, it may be difficult to find parallels else-where for the range of functions assigned to particular huts. In Zimbabwe, for example, the cooking huts of the Shona people also contain a bench or place of worship, as well as accommodating sleeping children and babies.

Similarly, particular phrases, if they are to be understood, must be related to the context in which they were used. In the early twentieth century Le Corbusier (q.v.) planned the rooms of his houses and apartments like ship interiors, with spacious living areas and compact utilities such as kitchen, bathroom and bedrooms. He attempted to suit the plan to what he saw as a new efficient life style. His often quoted, but often misunderstood phrase: 'The house is a machine for living in'[4] seemed to many people to sum up the ideas of the avant-garde architects and designers of the 1920s. At face value it suggests that a house is a machine whose function is to provide the basic necessities of life, in the same way as a car, or aeroplane functions as a mode of transport. To understand what Le Corbusier meant we would need to study the context in which this phrase was used by him in *Vers Une Architecture* (1923), and look at some of his house designs of the period. We would find from this that Le Corbusier wanted his houses to look and be manufactured like machines. However he was not con-cerned with any machines, only with those that were relatively new and appealed to his aesthetic sensibilities through their use of new mater-ials and their undecorated, geometrical and clean cut forms. So the quotation takes on a fuller meaning which relates to Le Corbusier's aesthetics and preferences regarding methods of production and materials. Many of the books on the Modern Movement (q.v.) of which Le Corbusier was a key figure, tended to label Modern Movement architecture and design as 'functional' (q.v.), and Le Corbusier's phrase seemed to support that view. A closer look at the movement as a whole reveals the role of aesthetic considerations, but to understand why that term became so widely adopted, we would need to look at how a small minority of avant-garde architects and designers tried to establish a new style, against the fierce opposition of traditionally-minded patrons and industry in the late 1920s.

Current disenchantment with the legacy of the Modern Movement suggests that the avant-garde have created more problems with their interiors than they solved. The economics of heating large, open-plan living rooms, with great expanses of glazing; the practicalities of using one space which has to cater for television, friends, homework, record players, whilst the mother is isolated in the small kitchen, have yet to be adequately solved. The open-plan living room was the Modern Movement version of the medieval hall, but the activities each had to cater for were very different.

Kitchen Design

Interior design is about space used by people, so it concerns questions of access and use. This applies to all types of interior whether they be domestic or for work, recreation or transport for they all concern the interaction between people and their environment, and this is a two-way process. If we take one area, such as that of the domestic kitchen, it is possible to see how social attitudes, developing technology and many other factors are reflected in the interior design. In large medieval houses in England the kitchen was a separate building from the house, because of the danger of fire and the scale of the catering. Food was stored in a separate pantry, ale in the buttery, milk, butter and cheese in the dairy. In humbler homes cooking took place outside, or on a fire in what was then called the hall.

By the nineteenth century sculleries were used for laundry, and cooking took place in the kitchen. The servants might eat in the kitchen, but not their employers. In working-class nineteenth-century housing water was obtained from outside the house, but cooking, laundry and bathing took place in the kitchen which was also the living room in many cases. Indeed until the early twentieth century the bath was often in the working-class kitchen. Today we cook, store food, do our laundry and often eat in the kitchen.

The unravelling of the processes which have led to the changing design and uses of the kitchen is a complex task in which many factors need to be considered. The introduction of 'clean' sources of power such as gas and electricity gave rise to a whole new range of domestic appliances from gas cookers, to electric kettles, refrigerators and washing machines. The application of science to the design of the kitchen had its roots in mid-nineteenth-century studies of the organization of domestic work, intended to minimize the effort and time needed to walk between the four main areas of storage, food preparation, cooking and cleaning up.[5] Other factors of significance concern changes in social patterns, smaller families, and changes in attitude towards health and hygiene.

Since the Second World War women have formed an increasing proportion of the workforce outside the home. This has led to the demand for a more even distribution of household tasks and the need for a more efficient arena within which they could be undertaken. The growth of the domestic appliance industry could be seen as part of that change. For the middle classes another factor concerned the decline in servants and the impact this had on the design of household equipment.

But a kitchen is not just a place in which food is prepared, it is part of 'home', a sanctuary from the pressures of the workplace, and the outside world. As well as being a sanctuary from outside pressures, the home is also the focus of outside influences, for commercial pressures affect our ideas of what our homes should be like. The visions presented in glossy advertisements and the commercial pressures to consume various products influence our ideas, but against these commercial pressures, most must settle for what they can afford. Thus the kitchen or any other area of the house can illustrate the tension between illusion and reality, and a comparison between an actual kitchen, say, and contemporary kitchen advertising will reveal some of these tensions.

Interiors for Recreation

We have concentrated so far on domestic interiors because so much of the studies on interior design concentrate on that area. The lack of literature makes it much more difficult to study commercial and industrial interiors or those associated with recreation or transport. In the area of buildings for recreation, these usually fall into a number of categories of fairly obvious building types and theatres, cinemas, public houses have all attracted their historians.[6] The development of buildings to house large numbers of people was often a matter of new technology, and confronting a particular problem: early film was highly inflammable, for example, so the question of isolating the projection box in the cinema, was given a high priority.

One of the most interesting aspects of study in this area concerns the question of the changing pattern of recreational activity in the past 200 years. The shift from cinema-going to bingo, the development of the disco and the arts centre, are areas that remain largely uncharted. Current magazines ranging from *The Face* to *Architectural Review* or *Blueprint* can prove a rich source of information on interiors in these areas.

Figure 5.4   Interior of original central London railway car, 1900.

Transport

Another major area of interior design is associated with transport. Liners, aeroplanes, trains, cars and buses, even a space capsule, have designed interiors though in the latter case they are more the province of the electronics engineer and industrial designer. Just by looking at the interior of, say, a Central London railway car, (Fig. 5.4) it is possible to deduce what type of traffic it was catering for and the comfort that passengers could experience on their journey. The seats have a solid wooden frame with the back and seat of punched plywood and the armrests are covered in what appears to be a form of leather. Plywood seats are very hard and uncomfortable for a long journey. There are movable straps suspended from rails on either side of the ceiling arch, and a wide floor space in front of the longitudinal seats, from which one could conclude that the railway line also catered for standing passengers and was probably part of the short-haul commuter service of the period. There is very little space for luggage, just a narrow rack on either side immediately over the window, which would confirm this deduction. The main windows are fixed, the top sections can be opened or closed for ventilation. Lights at regular intervals in the central aisle would provide adequate general lighting, but would probably be insufficient to allow passengers to read in any comfort. The floor is probably of wood, and ribbed to provide a non-slip surface when wet. The central and side panels of the ceiling are painted a light colour to give an impression of space, and perhaps what strikes one most, in contrast to today's public transport, there are no posters or any form of advertising.

All of this information can be deduced from this photograph, but to do a proper study of the interior design of this car you would need to know more about the transport networks of the period, the pricing system, the frequency of the trains, the number and type of passengers they were intended to carry, the policy of this particular railway company and how it compared with competing companies.

Some useful and vivid accounts of transport interiors can be gained from journal articles or case studies of individual means of transport: for example B. Greenhill and A. Giffard, *Travelling by Sea in the Nineteenth Century: Interior Design in Victorian Passenger Ships* (1972); Paul Skilleter, *Morris Minor: The World's Supreme Small Car* (1981); and C. H. Ward-Jackson and D. E. Harvey, *The English Gypsy Caravan* (1972).

This area of interior design also includes the design of airports and railway concourses. Here one of the main problems is to enable a large number of people to find their way quickly and calmly to one among many possible destinations. Information display plays an important role. Among the first of the transport organizations to consider the relationship between passenger comfort at all stages of travel, and the interior design of stations, rolling stock and buses, was the London Passenger Transport Board in the 1920s and 1930s. The role of Frank Pick in commissioning Charles Holden (q.v.) to design stations has been recorded in a number of publications.[7]

Commercial and Industrial Interiors

This area of interior design is closely linked to the history of technology, architecture and social, political and economic history. Imagine a high-rise office block with chimneys, stairs, oil lamps, and no telephones. Think of the inconvenience of delivering messages up and down twenty floors, not to mention the potential fire-hazards. We take it for granted that individual offices in such a skyscraper do not have a fireplace as the focal point of the room, that the environment is controlled by central heating and even air conditioning, that a lift provides easy access to each floor and that electric lights offer a bright, clean and safe means of illuminating the whole building. The development of the architectural form in this case was dependent on suitable technology to control and make practicable the resulting interior. Indeed a large percentage of the cost of many modern buildings is in heating, lighting, plumbing and other systems.

However, to study the development of commercial interiors only in terms of developing technology would provide little insight into other interesting and significant areas. For example the positioning of various offices and the existence of various dining rooms used by different sections of staff can provide useful insights into the question of hierarchy and the role of women in the workforce.

The development of the department store in the latter part of the nineteenth century, and the changes in marketing and consumption that accompanied it, forms another whole area of interior design. Some of the literature in this area focuses on the history of particular stores, and their interiors are seen as part of their development.[8] Certain stores such as Liberty performed an important role in promoting avant-garde design, indeed Samuel Bing is credited with inventing the term Art Nouveau (q.v.) for this was the name of his shop in Paris which sold the work of Gallé (q.v.) and many others around the turn of the century.[9] The demise of the corner shop and the development of supermarkets and hypermarkets is another aspect of a rich topic which has so far been researched only fragmentarily.

Factories are another important area. To study the development of the cotton-spinning factory in the late eighteenth century say, would involve questions about the types of machinery used, the hours of work and conditions, the problems of lighting and the fire hazards. Many histories of the development of the factories in this period do not however take such a comprehensive view. Jennifer Tann, *The Development of the Factory* (1970), for example, concentrates on the development of building technology, rather than looking at the working conditions. A similar approach is often adopted for recent factories. Norman Foster's Inmos Factory in Newport, Gwent, was designed to provide the ultraclean environment necessary for the production of micro-chip technology. Articles in the architectural press provide details of the space frame and large open floor spaces but it is often very difficult to obtain more detailed information.

A History of Technology, vols. 1–5, edited by C. Singer *et al.* (1954–8) and vol. 6, edited by T. I. Williams (1978), are helpful in charting general technological changes over the centuries, some developments of which may be relevant to interior design. Rayner Banham, *The Architecture of the Well-Tempered Environment* (1969) offers a pioneering attempt to discuss the role of mechanical services (air conditioning, lifts, telephones, central heating, lighting) in the interior environment of twentieth-century buildings, and books such as Robert F. Wilson, *Colour in Industry Today* (1960), offer guidelines on the practical and psychological impact of light and colour in institutional and work environments.

Architectural and interior design periodicals may feature plans and useful articles, and from time to time various architectural and design organizations may organize visits. If published information is not available it is often very difficult to get access to other sources because of industrial and commercial secrecy, and a general concern with security. Even the use of a camera can lead the keen student into trouble, as the editor of this book found out when she was about to take photographs of examples of design at an English airport. The notice 'No photography' was politely but firmly pointed out to her! Banks and other enterprises can assume that photography is a prelude to criminal activity, so it is wise to secure permission in advance and to carry the letter giving that permission with you.

Extant Interiors

There is no substitute for direct access to, and experience of, surviving interiors. The first-hand feel of their space, light and form cannot be reproduced, even by film or television. N. Pevsner's *Buildings of England* (1951–) series is helpful for locating important historical buildings of all types, although the aim of these guides was not to identify surviving interiors. Although the shells of interiors regularly survive this has often been at the expense of the interior which has been altered to cater for new needs. Far fewer intact interiors survive than buildings or shells.

Surviving interiors generally consist of an isolated room or space, or a suite of rooms in a single building. It is rare to have the opportunity of studying a range of interiors in one building, or a cross section of different types of interior design belonging to one historical period and geographical location. Hence the high value placed on the *in situ* architectural and design remains from the volcanic eruption of AD 79 at Pompeii in Italy. This offers a unique chance to experience and compare the interiors of a wide range of contemporary building types in a very ancient, but ordinary, relatively prosperous Italian town. Public buildings, upper-class mansions and one- and two-roomed dwellings and workshops of artisans survived.

Since most extant interiors will not be intact, you will often need the advice of archaeologists, conservationists and other experts to deduce the significance and help interpret what survives. A question such as 'Who designed the interior?' doesn't always have a straightforward answer. It may be simple: the furniture maker, the interior designer, the architect. But in other cases the answer will be quite complicated. Was the interior even consciously designed? How much was it, like most people's homes, a product of alterations and accumulations of items over a period of time? Was everything introduced and designed all at one time specifically with this interior scheme in mind? How many features and fittings were selected from items already available on the market and whence do they derive? Are they all contemporary products from the same place, by the same hand, a large department store or a small craftworkshop? Who then designed what, when, where and for what purpose? It may prove to be quite a complex task to unravel the respective contributions of client, architect, designer, craftsman, manufacturers and users who may have been consulted, or perhaps have altered, the interior to suit their needs. Often, then, an interior design is the product of a number of people – at one extreme they may have worked closely as a team, at the other independently, some even unconsciously, organizing, designing and selecting items for an interior.

Contemporary fashions and taste in design may not necessarily be reflected in a scheme of interior design. Several factors may be responsible for an interior designed at one date, having decor and fittings in tune with fashions of an earlier period. For example the type of commission, the finances available and factors such as the age, class, position and the personality of the client can each affect the style of the interior design. Thus you shouldn't be surprised to find a French bank interior of 1900 designed in a conservative style, while the home of a cultured patron of the same date was decorated in the then fashionable Art Nouveau (q.v.) style. Moreover, you shouldn't assume that every feature in a room will be of the same date; items from earlier periods may have been retained for reasons of practicality, sentiment, taste or economy.

Linley Sambourne House, 18 Stafford Terrace, London W8, which is now a museum open to the public, was a middle-class terraced house of the mid-nineteenth century with an exterior in one style, the interior in another. The house was part of a terrace erected by Joseph Gordon Davis, a speculative builder, between 1868 and 1874, and was Italianate in style. On completion, Linley Sambourne, a cartoonist for *Punch* moved in. He chose to decorate the interior, over successive years, in 'artistic' taste, employing William Morris wallpapers, stained glass, blue and white china. This reflected another, more novel strand of contemporary fashion. Many extant interiors survive only as single rooms and the Linley Sambourne Museum is rare in providing largely intact a full range of domestic interiors.

Conservation

A distinction needs to be made between day-to-day alterations and redecoration, which are the result of wear and tear, changing needs, individual taste and fashion, and alterations which have resulted from a desire to preserve, and even enhance the character of an old interior which was considered historically important. Attitudes towards the practice of conserving historic buildings and interiors have differed from period to period and this is a subject in its own right. During the early part of the nineteenth century, some restorers considered it acceptable to take away or demolish perfectly sound and/or practical fittings and parts of medieval buildings which had been added in intervening centuries, such as a sixteenth-century screen or transept in a twelfth-century church. These were replaced by similar features, made in the nineteenth century but copying the same twelfth-century style of the main body of the church. Products of great skill and perhaps historic importance were often destroyed because they happened to have been designed in a later style or one considered unfashionable by the nineteenth-century restorers. Today such practices would, in general, be unthinkable, but it is important to be familiar with the changing pattern of approaches towards historically significant designs in order to understand the reasons for alterations. A useful book on the subject is J. Fawcett (ed.), *The Future of the Past: Attitudes to Conservation 1147–1974* (1976).

Even if the original decor and fittings survive, age leads to accumulations of dust and dirt; the fading and alteration of colours in paint, fabric dyes and wallpapers; chipping of paints, plasterwork and finishes; carpets and fabrics becoming threadbare or bald. Moreover, changing customs lead to new patterns of room usage which affect the arrangement of furniture and moveable objects. If an historic interior is open to the public the owner or custodian will often rearrange furniture to enable easy access, with an eye to the comfort or convenience of themselves or visitors. Moreover, they may also install more modern and efficient heating or lighting. The strict fire regulations of today may also lead to historically-inappropriate additions such as fire doors and stairs, and the problem of limited budgets may lead to the replacement of decayed parts, such as floors, with materials and methods of construction not conforming to the original. Furthermore, concern for the preservation of textiles, pictures, even wallpaper, may result in the introduction of exceedingly low levels of light quite out of keeping with the original design and its usage.

Some exemplary research has been carried out recently which has transformed our knowledge about original country-house room arrangements. An example of such work is P. K. Thornton and M. F. Tomlin, *The Furnishing and Decoration of Ham House* (1980). Peter Thornton argues that historical interiors should use the conventions of room arrangement current at the time the interior was designed. In seventeenth- and eighteenth-century rooms this involves placing the chairs and other items of furniture around the walls. This practice has been adopted at Ham House and Osterley Park House, both of which were in the charge of Peter Thornton when he was Keeper of the then Department of Furniture and Woodwork at the Victoria and Albert Museum, and at certain National Trust houses (see Ch. 4).

Reconstructions

The reconstruction in the Hunterian Gallery, Glasgow, of Charles Rennie Mackintosh's (q.v.) home at 78 Southpark Avenue (where he and his wife Margaret Macdonald (q.v.) lived between 1906 and 1914, finally selling it in 1919) is a mixture of actual interior fittings used by

Figure 5.5   Dining room, 78 Southpark Avenue, Glasgow, C. R. Mackintosh and M. Macdonald.

the couple, replicas of known pieces and reconstructions based on partial evidence and guesswork. It is significant that only one of the bedrooms, the dining room and the upstairs studio-cum-lounge have been reconstructed.

In the dining room (Fig. 5.5) only a small fragment of the wallpaper which had an irregular trellis pattern survived. The trellis was designed to fill the various wall spaces between items of furniture located against the wall but there were no drawings, descriptions or even photographs contemporary with the original scheme to show exactly how it was used. The reconstruction of the particular pattern of the wallpaper and the layout of the furniture could only be a rough approximation. Two of the high-backed chairs are reproductions made by an Italian firm and the plush cream pile carpet used in the lounge and studio, whilst perhaps practical for modern visitors, is not intended to reproduce the original floor covering which may have been stencilled canvas nailed to the floors. Many of the knick-knacks scattered around the rooms are not original, but merely give a flavour of the interests and tastes of Charles and Margaret.

In studying extant interiors, it is important then to ask how they have changed over the years and why, and also to identify the many ways in which our own conceptions about interior design differ from those of patrons, designers or occupants of the interior.

Period Interiors

Most historic houses, museums and buildings open to the public contain 'period' interiors rather than completely original interiors with all their furnishings and decorations surviving intact. Often these only contain a few items of primary source material, or the primary material may not be consistent with what was originally in a specific interior. Owners of historic buildings who wish to open them to the public have to face the dilemma of having incomplete schemes because elements have been damaged beyond repair, sold or disposed. They often do this by seeking 'sympathetic' replacements. In similar vein, some museums try to construct synthetic interiors utilizing pieces of furniture or elements of decoration already in their collections. Their intention is to give a general idea of how such pieces of design might have looked in an ensemble, or to give a 'flavour' of a particular period and class of interior.

'Period interiors' should not be confused with intact interiors or precise reconstructions of historic interiors. However much care has been taken in the selection of items it is important to recognize that such interiors are artificial and based on interpretations of the appearance of typical interiors of that class and period. The taste of client or designer; the available finances for the commission; the geographical location of the scheme; the orientation of the room to the natural source of light and within the plan of a building; the precise dimensions and shape of rooms or 'shell'; the character of the work by different craftsmen and manufacturers: these are some of the major factors which can subtly or substantially affect the final form and atmosphere. Thus 'period rooms' can only offer general guidelines concerning a particular type of interior at a given time.

Exhibitions and Catalogues

There are many exhibitions which mount reconstructions or tableaux of interior designs. For example there were large national and international displays such as the Exposizione Internazionale d'Arte Decorativa Moderna, Turin, 1902, and the Exposition Internationale des Arts Décoratifs et Industriels Modernes, Paris, 1925. The Musée des Arts Décoratifs, Paris, has selections of materials both from this latter exhibition and the earlier Exposition Universelle 1900, Paris. The Interior Design International (the International Contract Furnishing and Interior Design Exhibition) has been held annually in London since 1964, as has the Daily Mail Ideal Home Exhibition which was first held in London in 1910. The catalogues, reports and accounts of such events in books, journals and newspapers often provide vivid and useful information.

Apart from their permanent collections, larger galleries and museums from time to time mount exhibitions of particular types of interior. Two examples were 'Victorian Church Art', Victoria and Albert Museum (1971), which was devoted to the decorative arts in British churches in the nineteenth century, and 'Frescoes from Florence', Hayward Gallery (1969), which exhibited examples of painted wall decorations of the fifteenth and sixteenth centuries. Other types of exhibition attempt to capture the general character of design in a period, rather than actual interiors, for example 'Vienna in the Age of Schubert: The Biedermeier Interior 1815–1848', Victoria and Albert Museum (1979) which included ensembles of furniture and artefacts, as well as prints and pictures of interiors. It is also well worth looking out for exhibitions at smaller commercial galleries such as Fischer Fine Art, London, which specializes mainly in the fine arts of the late nineteenth and early twentieth centuries but occasionally holds exhibitions such as 'The Wiener Werkstätte and their Associates 1902–32' (1982), or the Fine Art Society, Edinburgh, Glasgow and London, which hold exhibitions of nineteenth- and twentieth-century decorative arts, including hangings and carpets.

Much of the design on display in the museums and exhibitions discussed so far reflects a concern with post-medieval, European, middle- and upper-class taste. To help to balance the picture visit industrial, vernacular or folk museums, such as The Downland Open Air Museum, Singleton, West Sussex, and St Fagan's Museum, Cardiff, which specialize in vernacular architecture, and Blists Hill Open Air Museum, Coalbrookdale, Shropshire, which has reconstructions of late-nineteenth-century industrial, commercial and domestic structures. Also visit the non-European art and design galleries at the Victoria and Albert Museum and the pre-medieval artefacts and ethnographical collections at the British Museum, but remember they are not intended as a representative sample of artefacts of the chosen cultures, but are the products of accidents of preservation and reflect the taste of European curators, connoisseurs, collectors and adventurers.

Notes

1 Le Corbusier (1970 edn), *Towards A New Architecture*, pp. 167–9.
2 This development began to take place slightly earlier in the United States.
3 Barley, W. M. (1963), *The House and the Home*, pp. 25–6.
4 Le Corbusier, (1970 edn), *Towards A New Architecture*, p. 10.
5 Beecher, C. E. and Beecher Stowe, H. (1869), *The American Woman's Home*.
6 Glasstone, V. (1975), *Victorian and Edwardian Theatres*; Sharp, D. (1969), *The Picture Palace and Other Buildings for the Movies*; Girouard, M. (1975), *Victorian Pubs*.
7 Barman, C. (1979), *The Man Who Built London Transport*; Middleton, G., 'Charles Holden and his London underground stations', *Architectural Association Quarterly*, 1976, vol. 8, pp. 28–39. Pick, F., 'The meaning and purpose of design', *The Listener*, April 1933, pp. 640–54, reprinted in *Documents*, Open University Course Unit A305, 1975 (Milton Keynes: Open University).
8 Adburghan, A. (1975), *Liberty's: A Biography of a Shop*.
9 Mourey, G., 'The house of Art Nouveau Bing', *The Studio* 1900, vol. 20, pp. 164–80.

6

Industrial Design

JOHN HESKETT

Industrial design is concerned with the vast array of goods manufactured by serial- or mass-production methods. The profession of industrial designer emerged in the twentieth century and can be seen as a feature of the division of labour and specialization characteristic of large-scale modern industry. Before this specialism developed the function of design in industry was less well-defined and was performed by a variety of people, from major artists to anonymous workers. These more obscure and distant circumstances present particular problems and challenges.

Modern practice for industrial designers generally falls into two broad categories, when s/he is either a direct employee of an organization and designing exclusively for it, or an independent consultant commissioned to design for a variety of clients. Examples of the first category are the design groups employed by all major motor-vehicle manufacturers, or by the giants of electrical goods manufacturers, such as the Dutch company Philips or Matsushita Electric of Japan. Such teams are responsible for translating the possibilities of scientific and technological invention into products that are appropriate and appealing to the buying public. Their success or failure can profoundly influence the performance of a company. Consultants perform a similar function but for a variety of clients and product types. Kenneth Grange of the consultancy Pentagram has been responsible for a range of work of as diverse a nature and scale as the front-end and cab of British Rail's High-Speed 125 train, kitchen appliances for Kenwood and disposable razors for Wilkinson's Sword.[1]

Whatever the mode of employment, or type of product under consideration, the task of modern industrial designers is to produce a plan and specification of a form or mechanism for large-scale

110

production. An essential feature of their work is the separation of concept from manufacture or realization.

The Significance of Industrial Design in Modern Society

A key characteristic of industrial design is therefore the manufacturing context for which designs are created. Unlike design for ceramics, glass or textiles, it is not confined to one material, nor, as in furniture or interior design, to a particular category of artefact or environment. It can frequently overlap with other areas of design, indeed, practitioners have claimed its range of concerns extends from 'a lipstick to a steamship' or from 'a match to a city'. Such breadth can be problematic. The sheer extent and diversity of the innumerable products of industry is itself confusing. To illustrate this, consider some details of your own daily life. To simplify the illustration, concentrate on one area: the kitchen as working space and the preparation of food as a main activity. Basic fittings will include storage spaces and containers for food and equipment, with a table or cupboard-top surface at which to work. To prepare food, there will be hand-implements such as knives, spoons, ladles, vegetable-peelers and spatulas, for use with basins, jugs and cutting boards, and mechanical appliances such as a hand-whisk or powered mixer/beater. Vessels for cooking will include saucepans, frying-pans, baking-tins and casserole dishes, of varying shapes, materials and sizes. For cooking there will be a stove, using gas, electricity or solid fuel, possibly supplemented by appliances such as a toaster or electric kettle.

An examination of any other area of domestic life will reveal a similar diversity. Neither is such a consideration limited to the home environment. To go anywhere beyond immediate walking distance of where you live will require access to a form of transport, of a personal kind, perhaps; bicycle, moped, motor-cycle or car; or maybe public forms: bus, tram, underground or train. Whilst out you may wait at a bus-shelter, stop at a traffic light, or make a call from a telephone box. Whatever your destination, school, work, public buildings or sites for sport and recreation, there will again be a remarkable variety of objects to facilitate particular activities. All will have been conceived to serve a certain purpose and embody a particular set of values.

It would be possible to continue in similar vein and compile a lengthy catalogue. The examples given above are just the tip of a very large iceberg, but they do illustrate the degree to which our environment, in all its details, is composed of industrial products. They are so numerous and ubiquitous as to be frequently taken for granted. Yet they form the material framework of our existence, enabling it to function, not only in practical or utilitarian terms, but also in ways that give pleasure, meaning and significance to our lives. The public outcry in Britain in 1984, when British Telecom announced the replacement of the traditional red telephone booth by a bland modern design, ignored the undoubted efficiency of the latter and was essentially a lament for the loss of a familiar image, that communicated a strong sense of identity. Industrial products are therefore elements of our material culture, tangible expressions of individual and social values. This means objects cannot be studied simply in terms of visual characteristics and qualities, or as ends in themselves. Instead, visual analysis needs to be supplemented by questions exploring wider reaches of meaning.

What Does the Study of Industrial Design Involve?

Basically, questions on the nature and role of industrial design point in two directions. The first concerns how artefacts come into existence: who designed what, when, how, where and why? This is obviously vital in establishing a basis of fact and understanding about the activity of design, though it is susceptible to differing interpretations and emphases, stemming from the variable meaning of the word 'design' itself. This can be illustrated by a seemingly nonsensical sentence: 'Design means designers design designs by means of designs.' The noun 'designers' refers to individuals or groups engaged in the activity, whose background, talent and achievement needs to be described and understood. The verb 'to design' describes an action or process, implying a development or sequence of thought and practice through which industrial designers create and evolve a concept for later production. The sentence also contains three usages of 'design' as a noun. The first word describes the total activity in an all-embracing and undifferentiated sense, as in: 'Design is an essential ingredient in successful industrial performance.' The final word refers to a concept or plan, the end result of the design process, e.g. 'The completed design was ready for production.' As used following the verb, however, 'design' describes the realized object after the process of production, e. g. 'Like all great designs, the Mini became the symbol of an entire generation.'

The second major direction of questioning explores the application of an object: who is it intended to be used for, who uses it, for what purposes, with what effect and what meaning. Widely differing conclusions can be drawn from these two channels of inquiry, since the meaning intended for an object by its designer may not be the same as the meaning of an object in use. The context may alter, and with it the manner in which an object is utilized or perceived.

An example indicating how these different approaches can combine in the history of industrial design is the German car, the Volkswagen, popularly known as the 'Beetle', which became the best-selling vehicle of all time, with over 20 million being produced. The character and career of its designer, the Austrian engineer Ferdinand Porsche, are obviously important and, in particular, the ideas and influences leading him to the conception of a small car with a rear-mounted air-cooled engine which he developed by the early 1930s. Attempts to have such a car manufactured commercially failed, but in 1936 he was commissioned by Adolf Hitler to produce an inexpensive 'People's Car' by mass-production methods similar to those earlier used by Henry Ford in the USA. This shift from the possibility of commercial to state-supported production in itself altered the significance of the concept. The intention was to manufacture a vehicle available to broad sections of the population previously unable to afford a car, as a means of securing support for the regime and diverting attention from its less savoury aspects. The detailed design process of how Porsche fulfilled a very tight brief on cost and performance to create the most enduring example of 1930s streamlined style is itself fascinating, and after models and plans had been approved by Hitler the first prototypes were demonstrated in 1938. The various stages of design as process, concept and object can all be identified in its development to this date.

The significance of the Volkswagen, however, does not end there. The car was promoted as an achievement of the Nazi regime but remained an unfulfilled promise. Few were produced before the outbreak of war, when the concept was adapted for a military vehicle. As such it was given an incredibly rigorous testing, from the snows of Russia to the sands of North Africa. After Germany's defeat, a new company was formed to commence commercial production of the original 'Beetle'. It became an astonishing success, a sound, reliable and inexpensive vehicle, capable of coping with rugged conditions. Even more remarkable was the way it became a cult object, particularly in the USA, where it became the star feature of the 'Herbie' series of films produced by the Walt Disney organization.

It was, in so many ways, an astonishing process: from being the symbol of the Third Reich, known pompously as the 'Strength-through-Joy' car, to the fun object of the 1950s. Its form and construction, though modified and improved in detail, remained unaltered, and its functional qualities, though refined, were also unchanged. Yet its meaning and significance had totally changed.

Of course, not all objects have such extensive a public impact or as dramatic a history as the Volkswagen. Many have more private and intimate significance, the importance of which was apparent to the American novelist Henry James. In his novels he used a technique of precisely detailed descriptions of the objects and interiors surrounding his main characters, which expressed their nature, as a means of increasing readers' awareness of their personalities. The importance of this ambience was summed up by him in the evocative phrase, 'the empire of "things" ',[2] a term entirely appropriate to the role of industrial products in modern life.

The Scope of Industrial Design History

The scope of the history of industrial design, is obviously closely linked to the development of industrialization, and much depends on how that term is interpreted. It is most commonly associated with the introduction of mechanization, mainly steam-power, and large-scale manufacturing and commercial organization, which gathered momentum from the late eighteenth century, the period of the Industrial Revolution. Indeed, research on industrial design has overwhelmingly concentrated on Western Europe and North America since that revolution.

Industrialization has transformed virtually every aspect of material existence. Machines have been devised not only to produce age-old categories of artefacts, such as ceramics and furniture, but also to create new objects and other machines for use in daily life, from aircraft and cars, to refrigerators and vacuum cleaners. With mechanization values changed from an emphasis on tradition, the conservation of tested models which ensured survival, to an emphasis on innovation, of new ideas in a condition of superfluity. The new scale of production hinged on duplicating predetermined forms and, in the division of labour which developed, the role of industrial designer emerged as the creator and specifier of that form. The transition from predominantly agricultural/craft cultures to ones based on industrialization, with all the consequences for technique, form, organization and social significance, will therefore continue to be the main focus of attention in any history of industrial design.

There is, however, a strong case for extending the range of research further back in time and over a greater geographical area than is generally the case at present. This requires a distinction to be drawn between industrialization and steam- or electrically-powered mechanization. The two are often regarded as synonymous, but are not necessarily so.

If industrialization is defined in terms of organizational structure instead of sources of power, a different perspective becomes possible. Productive capacity on a scale beyond individual capacities, and based on specialization of tasks and division of labour, need not involve large-scale mechanization, but can be based on hand techniques. There is evidence, for example, of forty-five distinct pottery forms in Egypt in the Archaic Period, *c.* 3000 BC, being found in such profusion in excavations that an archeologist, W. B. Emery, writes of their 'mass-production'.[3] Archaeological research provides a wealth of information on the classification of forms and their identification in relation to place and time. There is a potential role for design historians not only to draw on such research, but also to contribute to it with studies of forms related to materials and processes, and analyses of the functions they performed.

The pottery and stoneware vessels of civilizations such as those of Archaic Egypt were precise solutions to particular functional and cultural requirements which emerged from centuries of craft adaptation. In this shadowy process of evolution it is generally impossible to identify individual figures or groups to whom specific forms can be attributed. This has given rise to a concept that has come to play an important role in histories of industrial design. Anonymous forms of this type are generally considered to be part of a vernacular or folk tradition. By this is meant those implements and artefacts which, over an extended period of time, have established basic forms appropriate to their function and cannot be fundamentally improved: for example, the shapes of tools such as spades, hoes, axes and saws, and domestic items such as jugs and ladles. Some may be specific to particular cultures, others may be more widespread. An example universally used as a cutting instrument, is scissors. Exactly when, where or how this solution to the problem of cleanly cutting material evolved is unknown, though it is believed to have been in the Bronze Age. Certainly, they were widespread over 2000 years ago as far afield as Ancient Rome and China. But whatever detailed variations have subsequently appeared, and they are innumerable, the fundamental configuration remains unaltered. The vernacular tradition is thus an important source of design concepts and forms, often known as type-forms, which have become firmly established due to their appropriateness and widely adapted to industrial mass-production. In principle, there is little difference of form in relation to function of modern scissors to those evolved long ago, despite the very different production techniques used.

The concept of the vernacular tradition can be romanticized in mystical terms as an expression of the soul of an age or people. Such treatments gloss over the fact that we simply do not know, and often have no conceivable way of knowing, what particular individuals, events or processes contributed to the evolution of a form. Neither is this kind of approach restricted to studies of the distant past; for example, writing of American design in the early nineteenth century, Arthur Pulos asserts: 'In the young and virile democracy it was thought that everyone was, or may have been, a contributor to the evolution of a product . . . It would seem that anonymity was then, and continues to be, part of the burden that designers must bear for their role in democratic utilitarian design.'[4] Anonymity is equated with democracy, but what this really means is that not enough research has been done or inadequate material is available for us to know what really took place.

Whatever the limitations and misuse of the concept of the vernacular tradition, it does have a positive side. It provides a useful corrective, in its acknowledgment of collective effort, to a one-sided emphasis on individualism and an important means of demonstrating the essential continuity of many design forms through time. The idea of continuity, however, needs complementing by an awareness of the forces producing change within a culture, of the contrasts existing between different cultural traditions and the extent of exchange between them.

Considered in terms of cultural awareness, the history of industrial design is afflicted with the academic equivalent of tunnel vision, an inability to focus other than in a very restricted range. The prevailing emphasis on recent events in an exceedingly limited number of countries has neglected trends that, even in the twentieth century, have had a profound impact in global terms. An example is the rise to economic power and the influence of designs from the countries of the Western Pacific arc, Japan in particular. Equally neglected are those countries under communist systems of government, or Third World countries, where differing economic and social structures have led to differences in design theory and practice. If this limited outlook is true of the present, it is even more marked in studies of the past.

Once again, however, a corpus of work from various disciplines exists which can give important leads to a wider understanding, such as Romila Thapar's history of her native India. She describes how, in the period *c.* AD 200–300, political and economic events combined to produce an expansion of trade:

With the increasing demand for particular commodities and the consequent necessity to raise their output, some guilds began to employ hired labour and slaves ... Leading guilds were those of the potters, metalworkers, and carpenters. Their size can be gauged from the fact that even at an earlier period one wealthy potter named Saddalaputta had owned five hundred potter's workshops. In addition, he had organized his own distribution and owned a large number of boats which took the pottery from the workshops to the various ports on the Ganges.[5]

That raises many intriguing questions. Some relate to the effect increased trade and larger scale organization had on methods of production and the forms manufactured for expanded markets. Such research could be a valuable contribution to knowledge of the role of design for handicraft industry in one of the world's most diverse cultures, where continuities from the past provide distinctive challenges and problems for modern Indian industrial designers. It could also enable valuable comparisons with developments in other countries to be made. Perhaps even more significant, however, is the point Romila Thapar makes about the role of Indian traders as middlemen between East and West, based on a long association with Graeco-Roman civilization and their trading ventures into South-East Asia, which she succinctly sums up in the statement: 'Exchange of merchandise led inevitably to an exchange of ideas.'[6] It is a statement valid for all periods of history and has considerable, if yet inadequately explored, relevance to the development of industry and the design of its products.

From Craft Industry to Mechanized Industry

Under the more stable social and economic conditions of earlier ages, with slower processes of change and growth, craftsmen were not basically concerned with innovation, in terms of entirely new artefacts, but with handing on and adapting the skills and forms developed by previous generations. However, in Europe, under the more dynamic economic conditions of the fifteenth century onwards with the growth of competition, innovation became a vital ingredient of success and gradually the craft tradition of maintaining established standards came under increasing threat. In the early stages of this process, innovation might not necessarily mean the development of new forms, but rather some eye-catching or fashionable feature of decoration or treatment of material, but nevertheless it was recognized as a valuable instrument in attracting the attention of potential customers. Yet again, the influence of this important transitional phase and the role of design for larger scale production has been comparatively neglected.

The long-term effect of increased trade and competition was funda-mental, however, largely due to the interest in technological invention which drew upon new scientific knowledge and offered means of producing goods faster, in greater quantities, and at lower prices. By the mid-eighteenth century this process reached a cumulative take-off point into the Industrial Revolution. When industrialization gathered momentum the consciousness of those societies experiencing it changed profoundly. By the mid-nineteenth century, Britain was a predominantly urban country, the human environment increasingly man-made, its systems increasingly detached from nature, and inno-vation seemingly an indissoluble element of progress and economic success.

The nineteenth century was a complex age and there are problems in presenting particular aspects of it as 'typical'. Nevertheless, there are some that are of particular relevance to the Victorians' view of what was significant for design. Firstly, their attitude to history. As an academic subject, history was not a nineteenth-century invention, but few ages have shown such intense interest in it. Perhaps the scale and pace of change being experienced made them conscious of the process of change through time. Whatever the reason, historical research rapidly grew to give a much more detailed view of the past and provided an expanded repertoire of stylistic sources. Secondly, there was an attitude towards the design of objects that evaluated their quality in terms of decorative rather than structural features. Thirdly, the importance of religion cannot be underestimated. It provided a unifying world-view which helped to temper and absorb the impact of change and made it possible to imbue any aspect of life with moral significance. The element of decoration requires closer examination because it clearly lay at the heart of what was then considered important in questions of design. The reasons were varied. The emphasis in many industries of the period was in producing goods of an essentially traditional nature, in quantities and at prices accessible to a larger market. Their criteria and standards were derived from an age when elaborate form, costly materials and intricate decoration were symbols of wealth, for only the richest members of society could afford the products of highly skilled craftsmen. The new mechanical processes, however, were capable of replicating not only the fine decorative patterns of traditional forms and techniques, but also of simulating the qualities of rare materials. For many manufacturers, decoration could make an object look more expensive than it really was. From the consumer's point of view, ostentatious display could symbolize wealth, or at least its appearance, an important consideration in an age when the financial system depended upon creditworthiness, the ability to borrow money. It was thus important to keep up appearances, and this frequently became synonymous with ostentatious display.

An interesting feature of the discussion of decoration in the nineteenth century is that few voices were raised against it. On the contrary, it was generally accepted as necessary or desirable and the main thrust of argument centred on the appropriateness of the style of decoration to an object and its function. Consequently, if one wishes to understand the objects of that period, they must be understood in the light of contemporary preoccupations with what was appropriate decorative style, and indeed some historical accounts reveal a similar preoccupation. For example, Simon Jervis, *High Victorian Design* (1974), a volume based on an exhibition of the same title, is divided into chapters which discuss the nature and characteristics of various styles of that time.

Whilst decorative motifs derived from historical research, and travellers' collections were frequently used by entrepreneurs interested only in fashionable novelty, some scholars and practitioners sought a unified style as an expression of national identity in the contemporary world. Henry Cole (q.v.), a leading figure in organizing the 1851 Great Exhibition, argued for the establishment of principles governing ornamentation that could be reconciled to machine production, looking to nature for inspiration. In 1849 he founded *The Journal of Design*, a periodical to publicize these ideas, which gives a valuable insight into Victorian design for industry.[7] However, Cole has been generally overshadowed by John Ruskin and William Morris (qq.v.), who shared his love of nature and also advocated it as the source of ornament, but as part of a powerful moral indictment of conditions to which life and labour were subjected in the new industrial cities. They regarded industrial workers as depersonalized adjuncts to machines, deprived of skill and creativity in their work, and robbed of an essential element of their humanity. As a remedy they put forward a philosophy proposing a recreation of the values of the Middle Ages, of a harmonious society, close to nature, the works of man being dignified by the skills and creativity of craftsmanship. It was a nostalgic and idealized vision of the past, in which joy in work was manifested in the virtuosity of skilled, artistic ornament. The views of Ruskin and Morris have received most prominence in historical accounts of nineteenth-century design, with their anti-industrial bias generally unquestioned. Whatever the power or validity of their analysis, one needs to know the extent of their influence, to whom their ideals appealed and why, and also why there were no effective counter-arguments. Or if the latter did exist, why they have been neglected in design histories of the period.

Some Problems of Interpretation

Nineteenth century industrialization generated new methods of production and new materials which created new skills or enabled old ones to be adapted. For example, the new machines of industry and transport created the many skills of mechanical engineering, whilst the older skills of coachbuilding were adapted to the production of railway carriages, and later of motor vehicles. In all the new large-scale industries, the task of designing models for production was developed in a variety of ways. Sometimes well-known artists were commissioned to provide designs, in a manner foreshadowing today's consultancies, such as John Flaxman's work for Wedgwood (q.v.), or Christopher Dresser's (q.v.) designs for various metalworking companies. Sometimes those responsible for designs were engineers, as in the manufacture of locomotives and industrial machinery, or modellers and pattern-makers, for example in textiles and furniture production, in a manner anticipating modern in-house designers.

Decoration and the revitalization of craft-work were thus vital focal points of critical attitudes in the nineteenth century, not only towards design, but also for an extensive range of reaction against industry and contemporary society. There were, however, other developments of at least equal importance for the subsequent evolution of industrial design which require recognition. The bias of interpretation resulting from an emphasis on one aspect or another of the past can shape, and even distort, our understanding of the present. For example, in 1979 Fiona McCarthy organized an exhibition in Sheffield under the title 'Home Spun to High-Speed', which depicted the development of modern British industrial design as stemming from the Arts and Crafts tradition.[8] In part this is true, but by omitting the contribution of, for example, the very strong tradition of locomotive engineering and design to the evolution of the high-speed train, it shapes an understanding of present-day practice, emphasizing the crafts, that may not be appropriate for current needs. In terms of history, such approaches lead to an emphasis on William Morris, one of the most important progenitors of the Arts and Crafts Movement, whilst ignoring William Morris, later Lord Nuffield, whose small cars of the 1920s and 1930s were important for British design, and of profound social significance.

The problem of interpretation of the past is further complicated by a powerful strand of theory and practice in design stemming from Europe in the early twentieth century, in which groups of avant-garde architects and artists sought to come to terms with the nature of industrial society. In movements such as de Stijl in Holland, Constructivism in the Soviet Union, the New Objectivity in Germany, and Purism (qq. v.) in France, talented individuals and groups developed ideas and forms that had in common an attempt to unite aesthetic concerns with the concepts and processes of technology, and so create a framework of values for a new society.

Common to all these groups was a complete rejection of decoration as an emblem of past decadence. In its place structure and function were stressed as a symbol of moral and social renewal. Contemporary historians and critics who shared this viewpoint interpreted the past in a way that was essentially an attempt to find justification for it. Typical was the work of Herbert Read, whose book *Art and Industry* (1934) did much to propagate the ideas of the Modern Movement (qq. v.), as it became collectively known in Britain. Its opening lines declare: 'The aim of this book may be stated quite briefly. For more than a hundred years an attempt has been made to impose on the products of machinery aesthetic values which are not only irrelevant, but generally costly and harmful to efficiency.'[9] In such a manner was the central preoccupation of the previous century dismissed. What Read did was to emphasize those aspects of past design which were utilitarian and functional as precursors of what he advocated for his own time. According to his thesis, the role of a designer was to adapt 'the laws of symmetry and proportion to the functional form of the object that is being made'.[10] Depending on the extent to which this is successfully achieved, a designer is an abstract artist. Machine art is thus equated with the abstract formal concepts of the Modern Movement. In so far as Read deals with history, it is completely subordinate to the polemics of his book.

A considerable body of work on the history of industrial design advocates similar ideals, focusing on the institutions that formulated them, most notably the Bauhaus (q.v.), the famous German school established in 1919. Nicholas Pevsner, *Pioneers of Modern Design*, first published in 1936 but subsequently revised, was probably the most widely influential book on design history ever published. It postulates the Bauhaus as the apogee of a line of development leading from nineteenth-century Britain to Germany in the 1920s. The book goes no further than the Bauhaus, indeed it can hardly do so since it is both a historical justification and assertion of the primacy of the ideas of the Modern Movement.

The ideas, practices and work emanating from this tradition have been profoundly influential, shaping the patterns of design education in many countries, and visible in the work of many modern designers, such as Hans Gugelot and Dieter Rams for Braun, the German electrical products company.[11] The emphasis on simple, geometric form as epitomizing contemporary industrial culture has, however, been frequently elevated to an article of faith, and the histories based on its advocacy have a common flaw. This is that they ignore, dismiss or even deride a range of other tendencies, values and approaches which coexisted with the ideals they advocated. Even Pevsner, one of the most scholarly writers in this tradition who did so much to emphasize the importance of industrial design in modern life, commented in 1937: 'When I say that 90 per cent of British industrial art is devoid of any aesthetic merit, I am not exaggerating.'[12] The basis of that sweeping judgement was fundamentally a question of whether designs conformed to the aesthetic canons of the Modern Movement (q.v.) and the appearance of so-called Functionalism (q.v.).

Concurrently with the development of that movement, however, were other tendencies that had considerable influence on designs for industry and on public taste. The fashion for stepped and saw-toothed geometrical forms and colourful, jewel-like decoration of the interwar years, subsequently given the collective label of Art Deco (q.v.), was a powerful influence in much commercial production. From a very different source, scientific research into the problems of movement through the elements of air and water and techniques of wind-tunnel testing led to the emergence of streamlined style, drawing on the forms of airships and submarines for a variety of utilitarian and decorative forms.

In addition to concepts of style considered appropriate to industrial products, there were also many other developments which profoundly affected the structure of industry, its methods and form of production, and thus the practice of industrial design. The methods of mass-production introduced by Henry Ford for the manufacture of his 'Model T' car in the USA involved new concepts of the standardization and integration of the production line that were adopted across the world. New materials such as plastics and light metals, new power sources such as the small electric motor, and new processes of stamping, moulding and welding enabled the design and mass-production of a spectrum of products in the interwar years, such as cars, radios and domestic appliances, that fundamentally altered the material basis of everyday life. As the size of businesses and the scale of their markets increased, with competition becoming more intense, so the visual form of products became an important element of advertising and market strategy. Artists, architects, engineers and model-makers continued to undertake the function of design in many companies, but in the late 1920s in the USA a body of specialists emerged who established industrial design as a discrete profession, bringing its activity a new status and recognition. Governments too began in this period to show a greater awareness of the economic role and propaganda possibilities of industrial design, often forming bodies to encourage its development, with, for example in Britain, the Council of Art and Industry being established in 1932, followed by the Council for Industrial Design in 1944.

Even when the above factors and developments are taken into

consideration, there still remains a sector of industrial production which does not conform to any canons of style, taste, 'good design' or technical quality and to which the standards of professional industrial design are alien. They may frequently be dominant in particular market categories. Such forms may be in a variety of revivalist styles that have little to do with utility, such as Tudor- or Georgian-style electric fires with imitation coal-effect. They may express a taste for materials and forms that become fashionable, such as 'farmhouse-style' pine kitchen furniture, or exploit commercial imagery, such as Mickey Mouse telephones. Little attention has been given to such products, and their sources are frequently obscure, often overseas, and difficult to trace. They represent an area of choice and often aspiration in terms of popular culture which often sharply contrasts with the more clearly defined standards and norms of high culture as it has been adapted to industrial design.

At any point in history, therefore, one is faced with a plurality of tendencies and ideas affecting the nature and role of design for industrial production, in its widest sense, and its social impact. The task of a historian of industrial design, I believe, is to investigate and communicate an understanding of that diversity. Opinions, arguments and interpretations on what is significant will inevitably vary and, indeed, are necessary to give vitality to debate, but this need not mean using history as justification for a partial viewpoint, as has often been the case, reducing it to the level of propaganda for a particular tendency.

Sources for the History of Industrial Design

If the scope of the history of industrial design is exceedingly broad, so too is the range of materials and sources relevant to its study, though at present the potential of these has yet to be fully tapped. Only one thing can be stated in this respect with any certainty: as with all other aspects of design, the central focus of any study must be the designed object. There can therefore be no substitute for seeing and actually experiencing the artefacts or mechanisms that are the subjects of any investigation, or the sketches, drawings, models and documentation tracing the evolution of a design. Although this experience is crucial, however, it is not enough in itself, for there are limitations to what can be learnt from an artefact or its preliminary documentation. To concentrate on that alone would be to indulge in a form of connoisseurship. Rather, the artefact should be a point of departure into, and a point of return from, a wider range of investigation. This may involve business structures, professional and industrial organization, economic and political policy, social influence and impact, which should enlarge and enhance understanding of the design process and designed artefacts. To emphasize the latter as an autonomous activity is to ignore the element of social formation and effect in industrial design. Conversely, however, to reduce human creativity simply to an expression of social or material factors is to diminish this essential feature of our humanity. If industrial design is a crucial element in material culture, our concern must therefore be with its place in everyday life, with the interactions of creativity in society.

The problems of study in this area are compounded by the fact that there is no single institution where a general overview of industrial design history is available, so it is necessary to draw on a variety of sources. Industrial museums, such as Ironbridge and Beamish, give good insights into manufacturing processes with examples of products, as do museums of technology such as those at Manchester and Birmingham. In addition, local museums frequently have extensive collections of local products, such as cutlery in Sheffield or glassware at St Helens or Stourbridge. There are also specialist collections, such as the Bakelite Museum at Blackheath and a fine cross-section of electrical appliances at the Milne Museum in Tonbridge. One initiative by a local museum of great interest is a collection of mass-produced appliances and artefacts, such as radios, vacuum cleaners and kitchen equipment dating from the early part of the century, at Calderdale in Yorkshire. Advertisements were placed in the local press appealing for contributions and a valuable collection has been assembled, some of which is occasionally shown in exhibitions at the Piece Hall Museum, Halifax.

Transport is a field which is well covered and accessible. The National Railway Museum at York is amongst the finest of its kind, whilst the National Motor Museum at Beaulieu has built up a magnificent collection sited in delightful surroundings. London Transport has its own historical collection at Covent Garden in London and British Leyland have a fine museum of their products at Castle Donington. The list could be endless and there are specialist publications that give detailed accounts of transport collections across the country, such as *Historical Transport,* published annually by the Transport Trust.

Two of the greatest national collections in Britain lie across the road from one another in London: the Science Museum and the Victoria and Albert Museum. The division between them in terms of their exhibits is perhaps symbolic of the gulf that exists still between technological and aesthetic values in Britain. There is sometimes an overlap between the objects exhibited by each museum, though each will have its own emphasis. Wedgwood pottery may be shown at the Science Museum, but in the context of an exhibition on the scientific research of Josiah Wedgwood. Radios have been exhibited at the V and A, but with technical developments being subordinate to aesthetic considerations. All the above are collections of objects without any discussion of the wider aspects of design. Indeed, there is a real problem in the traditional approach to exhibiting objects in isolation with little more than identifying captions that requires reassessment if industrial design is ever to be depicted adequately in exhibitions.

Whilst artefacts are, I believe, the focus of studies in industrial design, there are distinct limitations to the information they can in themselves provide. A detailed analysis of forms, in an attempt to understand why a particular shape has evolved, or how it fulfils its function, or how materials and techniques have contributed to the end result, will all provoke more questions than an object can provide answers. It is at this point that investigation of design as object leads into an investigation of design as process and concept. A documented example is the catalogue of the Boilerhouse exhibition, *The Car Programme,* which focused on the planning and design of the Ford Sierra.[13]

On a limited level, the study of process can be confined to individual designers and the characteristics of their designs, an approach that can easily romanticize designers as 'star' figures. This can be assiduously cultivated by designers themselves. The French designer Raymond Loewy who carved a very successful career in America in the 1930s showed himself a master in the cult of personality, projecting his name and image at every opportunity. At one point, however, he had offices in New York, Chicago, Los Angeles, London and Sao Paulo in Brazil with a staff of hundreds. It is unlikely that more than a small proportion of the designs submitted under his name were actually created by him. The design process, especially in a modern context, generally involves a considerable number of people and specialisms other than design.

Although no one pattern of organization can be described as typical, many industrial designers will have colleagues or access to specialist advice in such areas as graphics and packaging, ergonomics, market research and analysis, various branches of engineering and materials science. Support staff may include research assistants, secretarial and administrative staff, visualizers and technical illustrators, modellers in clay and other materials and, increasingly, operators of computer-aided design equipment and programmes. The interaction between all these skills obviously varies with the nature of the organization and project as, similarly, does the manner in which a project is developed. It will probably go through the stages of initial contact and briefing, investigation and definition of the problem, preparation of preliminary solutions, leading to decisions on and specification of a final solution.

Research into the detailed structure and dynamics of design teams and how they have functioned in various situations is relatively sparse. One programme has recently been based at the Institute of Advanced Studies at Manchester Polytechnic, where research has been carried out into case studies of design projects from initiation to completion, with the on-going results intended to be used as the basis of an archive. [14] Business archives of particular companies may also yield important information on the role of design, with design management research contributing to knowledge of recent structures and projects.

Even on that scale of investigation, only a restricted understanding of the design process in a modern industrial setting is possible, for it must be remembered that individual designers or design teams have to reconcile many, and often competing, factors which may constrain their freedom of choice or action. This should not imply a limitation on their creativity, however, since it is when working within conflicting demands that creativity is really challenged. The kind of consideration designers need to take into account include the state of materials science and production technology; the size, capacity and policies of the organization for which they are working; the role assigned to design within the organization and its relationships with other sectors such as production and marketing. On a wider plane, there can be policies and influences affecting design work directly or indirectly, such as the specific nature of a particular country or market; the role of bodies promoting design, such as the Design Council with its centres in London, Cardiff and Glasgow and advisory services to industry; or the policies of governments. These latter can be specific, as with the 1836 Royal Commission on Art and Manufacture, or the more recent 'Design for Profit' campaign introduced in 1983, or they may be indirect, in terms of the basic economic and political decisions which set the framework for industrial and commercial activity. Many of these areas will necessitate coming to terms with material and problems in related subjects, such as the histories of technology, economics, politics and society – indeed the historian of industrial design requires an interdisciplinary competence. In this sense it parallels a widely quoted definition of a designer: 'A jack of all trades and master of one.'

Whilst it is easy to advocate what should be done, the dearth of primary documentation on the areas discussed above creates major problems for research into industrial design history, though also providing a considerable challenge. In the USA, the Singer company recently donated archival material to the Smithsonian Institute in Washington DC, which documents a century of evolution of sewing-machines. In Britain it is difficult to cite any comparable industrial documentation. However, the Art and Design Archive of the National Art Library is building a collection of individual, group and company papers and documents relating to major exhibitions. The publications and documentation of bodies such as the Design and Industries Association and the Design Council are accessible but also need cataloguing. There is no equivalent in Britain of the Werkbund Archiv and Bauhaus Archiv, both in Berlin, dedicated to scholarship in relation to particular institutions. Sources such as the Public Record Office, for government documentation, and the Patents Office, for details of legally registered designs, offer huge potential as yet barely touched. A further primary source is the memory of living designers, using the techniques of oral history. Though reminiscences may not always be factually accurate, they are capable of giving a living insight in vivid detail of the human relationships and reactions in a given situation. The situation therefore is that whilst design as object is relatively easy to research, design as process or concept and the broader aspects of the subject are less well-served, though there is undoubtedly a wealth of material to be explored and a growing number of facilities.

A recent initiative of enormous potential for the study of industrial design is the Boilerhouse Project, funded by the Conran Foundation. Since 1982 it has organized a series of exhibitions, partly historical, partly thematic, sometimes with associated seminars and conferences. It is moving to a new purpose-built site at Butler's Wharf, near Tower Bridge, and the plan is for a permanent collection of artefacts, with space for temporary exhibitions, and a library and archive with study facilities. Whilst the Boilerhouse Project has not entirely succeeded in overcoming the limitations of prevailing concepts of exhibitions, the new premises could provide the kind of flexible and wide-ranging facilities to stimulate a wholly new approach to the study of industrial design, particularly if its collection of archival material is given priority and substantially developed.

In the provision of secondary works, the pattern of coverage remains uneven, not only in terms of subject but also of treatment and approach. The diversity of approaches possible in industrial design history, and some of the achievements and pitfalls associated with them, are evident in the readily available books on the subject.

In the category of books that give a general introduction to the subject are Ann Ferebee, *A History of Design from the Victorian Era to the Present* (1970), a lightweight account which gives a pictorial overview of the last century and contains some examples of industrial developments, and my own *Industrial Design* (1980), which attempts a general historical overview of the history of this area of practice. Edward Lucie-Smith, *A History of Industrial Design* (1983), is beautifully illustrated, but the text shows little understanding of the subject beyond aesthetic concerns. Stephen Bayley, *In Good Shape* (1979), is a useful compendium of twentieth-century documents on industrial design with a selection of case studies of particular works.

Reference was made earlier to the strand of published work based on the tenets of the Modern Movement and, in particular, Pevsner, *Pioneers of Modern Design* (1960). Another work informed by the same spirit and similarly of seminal importance in establishing the study of industrial design as a serious branch of scholarship was Siegfried Giedion, *Mechanization takes Command* (1948). This examines the evolution of concepts of mechanization and their realization in industrial products and although eccentric in some respects is packed with fascinating examples.

These two works and the standpoint they represent have inspired many others in similar vein, such as Herwin Schaeffer, *The Roots of Modern Design* (1970), and Kurt Rowland, *A History of the Modern Movement* (1973), both of which advocate so-called functional design, although from a standpoint which does not argue a case, but rather assumes its unquestioning acceptance. Of all aspects of the Modern Movement and, indeed, of design history as a whole, the Bauhaus has been covered most prolifically. This is a testament to the power of its ideas, though its influence on industrial design is often exaggerated to the level of an exclusive claim. H. M. Wingler, *The Bauhaus* (1969), is a massive, profusely-illustrated collection of documents that provokes as many questions as it answers. Although individual documents can be considered primary sources, their selection and presentation emphasize the international role of the institution and neglect the context in which it existed. Frank Whitford, *Bauhaus* (1984), is a general survey emphasizing artistic aspects, but for a more thorough treatment of design, Gillian Naylor, *The Bauhaus Reassessed* (1985), is to be preferred.

Whilst the Modern Movement was important in the context of relating concepts of avant-garde art to industry, the wider context of design in Germany has been comparatively neglected. My own *Design in Germany 1870–1918* (1986), gives a general account of the period before the First World War. Two scholarly works that go some way to redressing the balance are Joan Campbell, *The German Werkbund* (1978), which is concerned more with the theory of design for industry than its practice, and *Industriekultur: Peter Behrens and the AEG* (1984) by Tilman Buddensieg and Henning Rogge, a most thorough account of one of the forerunners of German industrial design.

On developments in the USA, a number of publications have appeared providing a much broader understanding of developments there. Arthur Pulos, *The American Design Ethic* (1983), is a large, profusely-illustrated volume of sometimes dubious methodology in its bias to the myths of American history, though many interesting features of design do survive this treatment. Donald Bush's well-illustrated *The Streamlined Decade* (1975) is a readable if generalized account of the 1930s, but the most scholarly contribution on American design yet to appear is Jeffrey Meikle, *Twentieth Century Limited* (1979), a detailed account of the development of design and streamlining in the interwar years. Many consultant practitioners prominent in America have written autobiographies, though some smack of self-advertisement, especially Raymond Loewy's. One of the best is *Designing for People* (1955), by Henry Dreyfuss, which gives fascinating and often wryly humorous insights into his work for many leading American corporations. In-house design in the USA has been less extensively covered, though Stephen Bayley, *Harley Earl and the Dream Machine* (1983), is an excellent account of the career of General Motors' design chief, drawing extensively on company archives.

On developments in Britain there are few works that give an adequate overview. Fiona McCarthy, *A History of British Design*

(1979), is a concise, readable book, but of limited scope, focusing essentially on tendencies leading to, and associated with, the Design Council. A similar point of view characterizes Michael Farr, *Design in British Industry – a Mid-Century Survey* (1955), which is an extensive review of what constituted 'good design' according to the Design Council. Noel Carrington, *Industrial Design in Britain* (1976), is a misleading title, being more of a personal account of the Design and Industries Association between the wars.

The influence of technology and materials on design is as yet inadequately researched, but Sylvia Katz, *Plastics Design and Materials* (1978), is a well-illustrated introduction. *Tubular Steel Furniture* (1979), edited by Tim Benton and Barbie Campbell-Cole, is a collection of articles on the title subject. Several of the texts for the course on 'History of Architecture and Design' formerly presented by the Open University are useful in this context, such as A. Forty and G. Newman, *British Design* (1975), which includes a good account of electrification in the home between the wars.

Many works exist on the development of specific products, though they are often for enthusiasts and lack detailed information on design. Brian Haresnape, *Railway Design Since 1830* (1968), is a useful survey, as is Jonathan Hill, *The Cat's Whisker: 50 Years of Wireless Design* (1978). Despite limitations of approach, it is often possible to glean much information from the host of books on such subjects as cars, household gadgets and tools.

There is a growing body of work on individual designers and consultant groups. In the former category is a Design Council series, of which three studies have so far been published, including Penny Sparke, *Ettore Sottsass Jnr* (1982), on the remarkable if eccentric Italian designer. Two works from the Pentagram Design Partnership, *Pentagram* (1972), and P. Gorb (ed.) *Living by Design* (1978), and John and Avril Blake's book on the Design Research Unit, *The Practical Idealists* (1969), give an insight into the work of particular consultancies, whilst Penny Sparke, *Consultant Design* (1983), is a review of this particular form of design organization.

Little work exists on the role of government or the responses of the public. Whilst the title of Jonathan Woodham, *The Industrial Designer and the Public* (1983), might refer explicitly to the latter, it is in fact better on the former.

Two recent works reveal the poles of treatment apparent in books on this subject. Deyan Sudjic, *Cult Objects* (1985), is a review of 'classic' designs which have achieved unique recognition, though mainly in design circles. In stark contrast, Adrian Forty, *Objects of Desire* (1985), argues that designs manifest social concepts and values, and cannot be considered solely as expressions of personality. Penny Sparke, *An Introduction to Design and Culture in the Twentieth Century* (1986), concentrates on the design of consumer products and also argues that design must be placed in its economic, social and technological context.

Two observations are necessary to conclude this brief review of published books. First, the coverage of industrial design is characterized by large gaps, though these can be filled to some extent by a wide range of catalogues, pamphlets and journal articles on a variety of subjects. Second, there is a considerable amount of work on industrial design in the process of publication, which makes any general survey in constant need of updating. It seems highly likely that the current interest in the evolution of industrial design will extend the range of readily available information and current interpretation far beyond its present limitations.

Notes

1 See the exhibition catalogue (1983), *Kenneth Grange at the Boilerhouse,* The Boilerhouse Project.
2 From James' novel *The Ambassador,* quoted in Douglas, M. and Baron Isherwood (1980), *The World of Goods* (Harmondsworth: Penguin), p. 6.
3 See Chapter 9, 'Industry', for the section on pottery in Emery, W. B. (1961), *Archaic Egypt* (Harmondsworth: Penguin), pp. 206–14.
4 Pulos, A. J. (1983), *American Design Ethic: A History of Industrial Design,* (Cambridge, Mass.: MIT Press), p. 100.
5 Thapar, Romila (1966), *A History of India,* Vol. 1 (Harmondsworth: Penguin), pp. 109–10.
6 Thapar, op. cit., p. 118.
7 *The Journal of Design,* of which six volumes were published 1849–51.
8 Sheffield City Art Galleries, exhibition catalogue (1979), *From Home Spun to High Speed: A Century of British Design 1880–1980.*
9 Read, Herbert (1934), *Art and Industry* (London: Faber), p. 6.
10 Read, op. cit., p. 49.
11 On the work of these two designers see *Die Neue Sammlung,* Munich, Exhibition Catalogue, 'System – Design Bahnbrecher: Hans Gugelot 1920–1965, 1984; and Burkhardt, F. and Franksen, J. (eds) (1980), *Design: Dieter Rams* (Berlin: Gerhardt Verlag).
12 Pevsner, N. (1937), *Industrial Art in England* (Cambridge: Cambridge University Press), p. 12.

13 The Boilerhouse Project (1983), *The Car Programme: 52 months to Job One or How they Designed the Ford Sierra.*

14 For an account of some of the work and methods adopted as part of this project see Alexander, Mary, 'Creative marketing and innovative consumer product design – some case studies', *Design Studies*, vol. 1, January 1985.

7

Graphic Design

JEREMY AYNSLEY

We live in a world in which we are kept informed by a mass-media. Newspapers, television, radio and advertising all help to keep us in touch with worldwide events, while at the same time they influence or form our attitudes. In other societies direct human contact still operates as a way of communication, although because of the power and appeal of industrialized communication, these constitute a diminishing proportion of the world. Inevitably, mass-communications involve many specialized activities. Journalists, writers, illustrators or photographers supply the media with information, while technicians, engineers and printers specialize in the most effective ways of transmitting those ideas. Somewhere, very often at an intermediate stage, there are people who are responsible for coding information and ideas, using patterns, styles and sequences that are at once conventional enough to be understood, but also sufficiently novel to attract our attention. It is at this intermediate stage that what we call graphic design happens.

It would seem sensible, if our world is made up of so much that has passed through the hands of the graphic designer, or been under the graphic designer's direction, that we should learn to understand its workings. This would help us to assess the quality of the design, and to test its effectiveness. A study of graphic design might also prevent us from becoming too passive or 'brainwashed', to use a popular word. As early as the 1920s, the writers Aldous Huxley, Bertrand Russell and F. R. Leavis, suggested that schoolchildren should be taught how to 'read' advertisements, in order to defend themselves against their persuasion.[1]

In this chapter, I shall outline what a history of graphic design can involve. Of the stages outlined above, most design historians have

134

concentrated on the second, that is, when the designer makes decisions which determine the visual aspect of the object, such as which typeface to use, or what sort of composition to employ. While I agree that analysis of particular images is important and will form a basis on which to develop an understanding of design principles and theory, the design only becomes part of a process if we ask questions about the other two stages. In other words, visual analysis is not sufficient as history. We also need to ask whose ideas were being conveyed by this design and for what context it was intended.

The Term 'Graphic Design'

As Raymond Williams has pointed out in his book *Keywords* (1976) words have their own histories and their use and meaning change with time. The term graphic design is no exception and we should first consider what it means. Graphic design has existed for a very long time, even if only relatively recently have these words been used to denote the activity. For example, we know that the Romans used advertising and that since pictographs on cave walls dating from *c*.15,00–10,000 BC there have been attempts at visual language.[2]

Other areas of design such as ceramics and textiles can be defined by their materials, but for graphic design there has been no cohesive factor about its medium since the invention of film. The suggestion that items with words and images printed by ink, registering on a surface form a distinct category, is still accepted by the Victoria and Albert Museum in London as a way of guiding its collection in the Department of Prints and Drawings. This department could be considered the major 'graphics' collection in the United Kingdom. Such a definition by medium can only be partial now that photography, audio-visual and filmic work are significant areas for graphic training and activity. Before the Second World War, graphic design was most often called 'commercial art'. The word 'commercial' as a prefix distinguished art for reproduction from 'fine' art, a distinction you may still hear today. Underlying this distinction was often the different training for these activities, the fine artist training at a school of art, the commercial artist very often training as an apprentice with a printer during the day, and at technical school at night.

Illustration and typography had long and interesting histories of their own, but in the nineteenth century these had been combined, in many

135

instances prompted by the changing function of word and image within an industrialized society. The poster, combining word and image as a visual form, as well as mass-circulation magazines, newspapers and books, all required new kinds of organization and 'design' for print. An introduction to these changes is given in F. Klingender, *Art and the Industrial Revolution* (1972), and William M. Ivins, Jr, *Prints and Visual Communication* (1969). After 1945 graphic design courses evolved in art colleges, technical colleges and polytechnics, and the trained designers moved into the steadily expanding field of publication design, advertising and television, as well as corporate design for trade and industry. At its broadest, graphic design, and consequently its history, came to cover anything from the design of a bus ticket to sign systems for motorways, the packaging of cigarettes to the typographical organization of dictionaries, the design of the lead-in to nightly television news to art-directing a magazine. Recently, the term 'visual communication' has been adopted as one which allows film-based media to be subsumed under its heading. When we come to people, we still tend to define them as either 'illustrators' or 'graphic designers', even when the person does both. For instance, the well-known American illustrator, Milton Glaser (q.v.) not only illustrates books and art-directs magazines, he also recently turned to work on the corporate design of a chain of foodstores in the United States.[3]

If we take communication as the characteristic of graphic design, then we should be aware that it is a social rather than a technical category. This means that advertising and book design, although carried out for different purposes and occupying distinct places within the economy, have something in common. Remaining at this very broad level, we can also say that graphic design is a *medium* for transferring an object or an idea. On the one hand, it is the medium by which you choose one type of product rather than another, and has a very clear purpose in material culture. On the other hand, it is often the material substance by which we reach ideas. For example, a book is important for the ideas assembled in its argument or narrative. We can be persuaded to like the ideas more because of their appearance and organization on the page, and in this way the designer, typographer, printer and publisher affect our understanding, but at some stage we dissociate a book's *form* from its *meaning*. It is this characteristic which makes graphic design so ambiguous in its status, but also so interesting. It is what distinguishes the design of a timetable, which I would place firmly within graphic design, and the design of wallpaper, which I would not, even though their materials, ink and paper, can sometimes be the same. An enjoyable way to define your position, if you are interested in the ambivalent status which graphic design holds as both transmitter and substance of the idea, would be to read Marshall McLuhan's work. In his book *The Gutenberg Galaxy* (1962), McLuhan discussed the relationship technology has with the potential content, and suggested that in advertising the two were in danger of becoming confused, a view he put succinctly in the phrase 'the medium is the message'.[4]

Range of Material

Clearly a tremendous amount of accessible material exists for the study of graphic design, but I would like to distinguish now between kinds of material available. It is also important to comment here on those historical periods which have already been well interpreted, with easily-found primary and secondary sources, and those periods which have still to be charted.

The scope of graphic design history is given in surveys, such as J. Müller-Brockmann, *A History of Visual Communications* (1971), and Philip Meggs, *A History of Graphic Design* (1983). These are useful reference books, from which you can quickly find out who designed something and when. The limitations of such books, which are ambitious in scope, charting graphic art from Stone Age man to contemporary design, is that they produce a sequence of stylistic and technical change, linking designed objects with other designed objects. An assumption underlying this kind of history is that design has an autonomy. This encourages the view that designers only refer to previous design, whereas the real environment and public for design is in nearly all cases much broader than this.

Different periods have been researched to different stages, according to the sorts of questions they offer historians. For example, the Victorian era has proved popular, partly because the graphic art of that time was so central to the developing consumer society. Changes in the demand for a medium such as the newspaper or the poster were encouraged by the proliferation in printing developments and enormous growth in the types of design produced. This raises the question of the relationship design has to economic and social change and how design participates in that change.

Other periods which are well documented include the interwar years in Britain and the First and Second World Wars. Arriving in Britain in the interwar period, Modernism (q.v.) produced a wealth of designers' writings, giving explanations and definitions of theories and principles. In graphic design Modernism can be identified by stylistic simplicity, a flatness of form, a taste for asymmetrical composition and the reduction of elements to a minimum. I would guard against the view, which you will find quite often expressed, that the success of the design depends on its approximation to the Modernist ideal. This ideal arose as a result of particular debates within design at a certain time, and the values held cannot be transposed across changing functions and contexts of design, in spite of a wish for graphic and stylistic homogeneity. A useful anthology of designers' and architects' writing from the period, which includes some specifically on graphic design, is T. and C. Benton and D. Sharp, *Form and Function. A Sourcebook for the History of Architecture and Design 1890–1930* (1975).

The enforced emigration of many exponents of Modernism in the 1930s in graphic design, from Germany to Switzerland, Britain and the United States, and their impact on the indigenous design traditions in these countries, has been the subject of considerable investigation. In the patronage by certain British companies, such as Shell Mex and BP and the London Transport Passenger Board, in advertising agencies such as Crawfords or Highams, in commissions from government and other institutional bodies, such as the Empire Marketing Board and the GPO Film Unit, the impact of Modernism was felt (Fig. 7.1). Also effective techniques of persuasion were necessary to mobilize a population at war under state control. During both world wars, graphic techniques were developed which were to prove formative for subsequent design in peacetime. Other similar moments of social and political change are also interesting to examine, when often a prescribed set of demands operated. This can be said, for example, about the National Socialists' use of film in Germany between 1933 and 1945,[5] the recent tradition of poster design in Poland,[6] or the political graphics of May 1968 in Paris.[7]

By contrast, the postwar period in graphic design has been relatively uncharted so far. This means that there are fewer secondary sources to approach. By contrast the proliferation of designers' writings continues throughout this period, and these form a good basis. Another

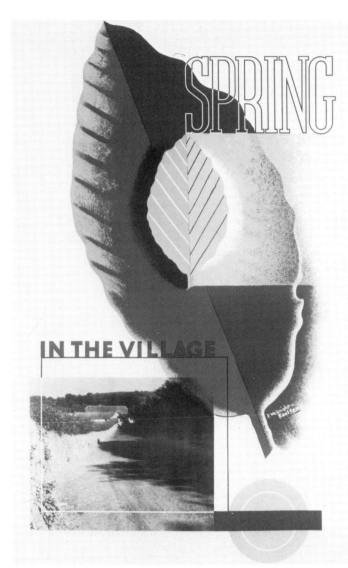

Figure 7.1   E. McKnight Kauffer's (1890–1946) poster for London Transport, *Spring in the Village*, 1936, shows how by the mid–1930s Modernist poster design was a possible solution to promote travel. This example acknowledged Cubism in the arrangement of lettering and shadow, and also Constructivism in the use of the photograph and its 'frame'. You might go on to ask why such a design was considered suitable in 1936, and what the alternatives might have been.

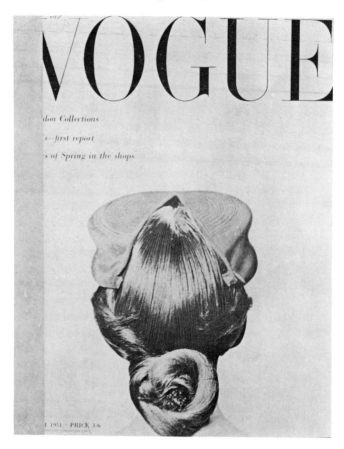

Figure 7.2   Cover to the British edition of *Vogue*, March 1951. Questions might concern the use of a photograph on the cover, the layout design, the content of the magazine, its readership or its production.

advantage of working on a postwar subject is that most libraries will stock magazines and periodicals which can provide invaluable primary material. For example, by looking at a run of *Vogue* magazine, from 1945 to 1965, you could make notes about many different aspects of the magazine (Fig. 7.2). One obvious approach would be to trace the content of the magazine, to consider how the subjects of articles change and to evaluate the pattern of editorial work. You might then contrast this pattern with the kinds of advertising which went alongside it, to find how complementary or otherwise both aspects of the content were. If you were pursuing this subject, a next step would be to place your observations against a reading on the position of women as a workforce and as consumers during the period in Britain. It might interest you, instead, to concentrate on the graphic style of the magazine. During this time in Britain, the American approach to magazine design infiltrated, whereby an 'art director' was responsible for commissioning and coordinating the different activities which go towards layout.[8] An analysis of the changing style in layout, typography and photographic and line illustrations, leading to a comment on the pattern of their use in magazines, can be made. Most magazines list their staff on the frontispiece and you should decide whether to trace an individual's work, or whether it would be more interesting to ask thematic questions. Increasingly during this period, illustrators and photographers were acknowledged next to their work, which makes a search and identification easier. This also raises the significant point about the developing recognition of design and artwork by the public and industry.[9]

History of Art and History of Graphic Design

The notion of a separate discipline called the history of graphic design has its advantages and disadvantages. The history of art has developed a language and methodologies, now taught in schools, colleges and universities, which are often useful for a vocabulary to define characteristics of design. It is possible to transfer labels such as Constructivist and Art Nouveau (qq. v.) and apply them to graphic design, and to realize that the graphic work of these movements was a central and integrated part of them. More significantly, perhaps, art and design can share a vocabulary because they are received by the same senses, and involve our visual sensibility.

Where a distinction enters is concerning the idea of uniqueness. As the German critic, Walter Benjamin, noticed in a series of important essays in the 1930s, whereas it is possible to speak of the unique object in painting and sculpture, this is not the case for design.[10] Although both objects of study, a painting and a poster, can be analysed in visual terms alone, the fact that the poster was made with reproduction specifically in mind should alter our approach to it.

Especially since the rise of Modernism, painting and sculpture have taken on areas of perception and experience which are extremely specialized and can depend on a public which is familiar with the ideas in the work. There is a complex apparatus which supports art, including aesthetic criteria, patronage, market value and the discourse of criticism, books and histories. [11] This is what is known as high culture. The intention of the graphic designer, on the other hand, is most often to render a message widely accessible with a systematic and public language. Whereas the art historian may address the subject of intention, and speak in terms of an artist's reaction as manifested in a unique object (although this is by no means all the art historian should do), the design historian, even when considering the object in its making, has to think in terms of a system, a group of people, and a process of manufacture. Although I have suggested that interpretative books will be less available for this recent period by contrast with earlier ones, this does not count them out entirely. To trace relevant books, as well as articles, you should use the art and design bibliographies. Articles from the design press are a major source of information and critical reviews and bibliographies usually list these by theme as well as by name. I include those most useful for graphic design at the end of this chapter.

Graphic Design Beyond Capitalism

Most of this chapter concerns approaches to design in the Western world, which has capitalism as its particular form of economic organization. Clearly graphic design exists in non-capitalist countries, as also in non-Western cultures. There has been considerable interest in the Soviet culture which followed the 1917 revolution, especially in the years of artistic experiment between 1917 and *c.*1928, known as 'Constructivism' (q.v.). Forms of graphic communication played a tremendously significant part in the literacy campaigns during the revolution and posters were a central part of agitational propaganda. An artistic language which was not associated with the realism of Tsarist Russia, but was dependent on Parisian avant-garde ideas in painting, was preferred for a while. A detailed analysis of Constructivism, including a chapter on the events in publication and graphic design, is given in C. Lodder, *Russian Constructivism* (1983), while for an anthology of manifestoes and artists' and designers' writings, I would recommend S. Bann (ed.), *The Tradition of Constructivism* (1974). The material is rich in questions concerning the place and form of mass-communications within a communist society. Many of these issues were formative for the debates which took place in the 1930s in Britain and the United States. By studying how a system operated under a different economic organization, we can often distance and objectify our approach from the one with which we are familiar.

In the past, an interest in non-Western cultures has frequently started from an ethnocentric point of view. That is, other cultures are placed in relation to the West, and to their disadvantage. Too often the West was considered to be the dominant and more sophisticated culture, and used for establishing a set of comparisons by which other cultures were judged in a one-way relationship. This ideology informed artists and designers, who turned to oriental and tribal art and products to reinvigorate their work, finding attractive what they could not understand. Edward Said analyses the changes within this process in *Orientalism: Western Conceptions of the Orient* (1978).

The example of Japanese prints is illuminating with respect to graphic design. Japan's impact on the West was substantial once trade routes had been reopened after almost 200 years of isolation, in 1854.[12] In European capitals during the 1860s, a fashion for collecting Japanese artefacts for interiors was followed by painters, designers and architects adopting Japanese motifs and compositional devices and applying Japanese techniques. For graphic artists, Japanese woodblock prints were very different from the tradition of the European woodcut and the more recent wood-engraving. Their asymmetrical compositions, the unusual changes in scale in the depicted subjects, their concentration on silhouette, organic line and flattened patterns, were all borrowed. Painters such as van Gogh and Gauguin started to integrate the effect of the woodcut in their paintings, other artists, including Manet, Toulouse-Lautrec and Vuillard, imitated woodblock effects in lithography, while Munch learnt how to cut woodblocks in the Japanese manner. For the historian of graphic design, there are many questions to be asked about the interaction between *fin-de-siècle* France and Japan. They might concern distinctions between what was borrowed directly and what was adapted stylistically and technically from Japanese prints. The contrasting markets for prints and their functions might be compared. For example, the print in France was partly developed as a commercial medium for advertising in the form of the poster, but also limited editions of lithographs and etchings were issued for private consumption. How does this compare with Japan? Were the Japanese woodcuts in Japan considered as art, or as a form of communication, or were these distinctions not made at that time? To proceed, you would need to read about Japanese society, the patterns of work and leisure and find out what were the dominant moral and cultural attitudes. How the woodcut participated in forming these attitudes might be your focus. Whether you are considering Japanese or British graphic works, or the product of any other culture or period, it is always important that you recognize that your own background and attitudes will play their part in the sorts of questions that you ask.

Case Studies

I shall now give examples of three objects which have been chosen previously for design historical interpretation, in order to demonstrate which questions can be asked about graphic design.

TYPOGRAPHIC DESIGN: EL LISSITZKY, PELIKAN PROSPECTUS (1924), FOR BÜRO BEDARF (OFFICE EQUIPMENT)

The basic structures of communication had been established by the turn of the century, as department stores, stations, magazines, newspapers and all varieties of literature testified. The next stage was for many artists and designers to address this area, in the awareness that mass-reproduction needed aesthetic as well as technological criteria to govern it. Many of the principal theories underlying graphic communication were projected for the first time in the years following the First World War. In Holland, Germany and the Soviet Union especially, many design theories were formulated. [13] After several years of avant-garde activity an embryonic language of abstraction could be said to have developed, which could be applied to design and architecture. In graphic design, this formal preparation was matched by technical advances, with improvements in photogravure printing for the reproduction of photography, followed by developments in colour printing and the sophistication of 16mm film techniques. El Lissitzky (1890–1941) had been trained as an engineer in Darmstadt prior to the war, and was conversant in debates concerning the role of the designer in the newly-formed communist society of the Soviet Union. When approaching El Lissitzky, you will find that there have been exhibitions

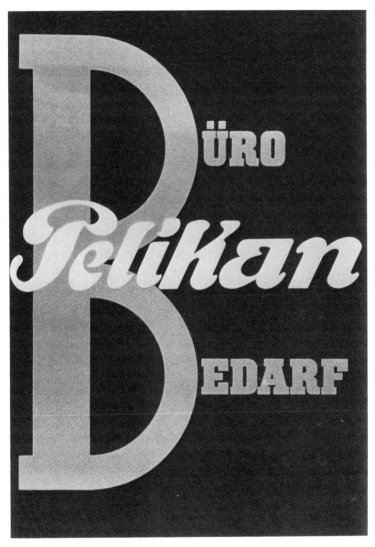

Figure 7.3 El Lissitzky's (1890–1941) cover for the prospectus for the stationery and office equipment company Pelikan, designed in 1924.

devoted to him, and the definitive monograph by his wife, Sophie Lissitzky-Kuppers, *El Lissitzky – Life, Letters, Texts* (1980 edn), assembles his writings and letters. Similarly, there is much written on debates within Constructivism, the movement in which El Lissitzky's later work is placed. By pursuing these sources you find his statement on typography of 1923, one year before the Pelikan prospectus. Here, El Lissitzky wrote of the importance of designing according to the visual quality of letters: 'optics instead of phonetics' was the phrase he used.[14] The way in which the whole page (Fig. 7.3) was used actively, with no sense of distinction between a foreground and background, and a concrete recognition of the weight of lettering was something he had developed from his abstract paintings and lithographs of earlier years, before moving to typographic design. Stylistically, we could connect this approach with de Stijl (q.v.) as well as with individual typographers such as Jan Tschichold and Herbert Bayer (qq.v.), who were also working on sans-serif typefaces based on geometry and simplification of form.[15]

We would be able to go a long way in talking about the work stylistically, and could also comment on how it fits into the sequence of El Lissitzky's other designs. We could assume that this was bread-and-butter work, done when recovering from an illness while resident in Germany, by reading between the lines of the biography.

However from secondary sources there is apparently a limit to the kind of questions we can ask of an object, and because of this only a certain kind of history results. El Lissitzky is attributed as the 'designer', but we know little of the further circumstances of its production. For example, who did he work alongside, was there a design department or a publicity department at Pelikan, at that time? The monograph approach prevents other examples of Pelikan publicity from being shown in a book devoted to El Lissitzky. By cross reference we can find that Herbert Spencer, *Pioneers of Modern Typography* (1984 edn), illustrates examples of work by Kurt Schwitters for Pelikan, incorporating the same distinctive logo. El Lissitzky mentioned ideas about 'mobile and plastic advertising' also planned for the company.[16] Does this mean that someone at Pelikan was an enlightened patron of advanced design?

Our sources apparently produce material that make this design an isolated object. For although on earlier pages of the book we are shown posters also designed by El Lissitzky for Pelikan, we know very little about how they related to one another. Where were they intended to be used? Was El Lissitzky's choice of technique and colour expensive? The bronze on the lettering of 'Büro Bedarf' presumably was.

These types of questions are not restricted to this particular example, but can be applied to many of the reproductions of graphic work that you will encounter in the literature of graphic design. Quite often a piece of graphic design was destined for a specific context and had a currency which is subsequently lost. The original piece of design would be of a different size and texture and its general quality would most probably be unlike that of the clean page of a book. In order to find answers to this work by El Lissitzky, the researcher would need to find out whether Pelikan Inks have an archive. If not, then a search for references to the design in contemporary graphics journals would be useful. This example is a difficult one, as further research might require a reading knowledge of German and possibly Russian. I have chosen it as an example because it is a popular subject with students, and also because Constructivist design is a well-used reference within Post-Modern design (q. v.). It would be appropriate now to outline the sort of questions which might be asked about a piece of graphic design. Before embarking on research, you could approach your example with such considerations as: Why was it designed? What is its technique? How should I characterize its style? Does the design imply that a set of principles or a design theory has been applied? In what context was it shown originally? Where am I seeing it now?

APPROACHING BOOK DESIGN:
PENGUIN EDITION OF NABOKOV, *LAUGHTER IN THE DARK* (1963)
To understand the process of graphic design means more than simply placing a known designer in relation to his or her work. Once you leave the monograph approach behind, the sources of a history are diverse. The example of a paperback publishing company may help to show this (Fig. 7.4).

The book illustrated is one that I happened to have on my shelf, and this shows how accessible the primary objects of graphic design history frequently are. On the cover is given the book's title, the names of author and publisher, as well as the price. On the spine is a number – this is the company's number for the book and in more recent editions would be the ISBN (International Standard Book Number) – referring to the position of this title in the overall list. What is called the 'history' of the book is given on the verso of the frontispiece. Here we learn that the book was printed by Richard Clay of Bungay, and that it is set in

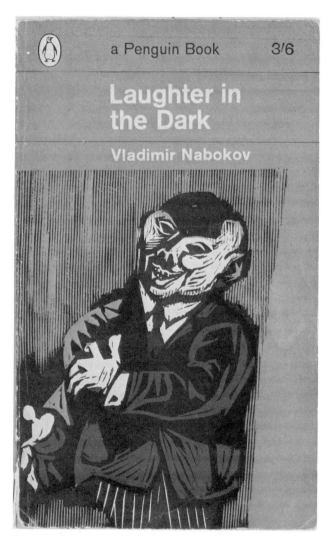

Figure 7.4 Cover for the Penguin Books edition of Vladimir Nabokov, *Laughter in the Dark*, 1963. The grid layout was the house-style, overseen by the Penguin design department, which in this case incorporated an illustration by Morton Dimonstein.

Monotype Garamond typeface. The novel, we are told here, was first published in 1933, under the title *Kamera Obskura*, in Paris, and the author translated it for publication in 1938 in the United States. Prior to Penguin's paperback edition, the hardback house Weidenfeld & Nicolson had published it in 1961 for distribution in the United Kingdom. We can analyse the cover, its colour, typography and layout. Familiar with other paperbacks, we know that this book is of conventional size and format, that there is a house-style to which this volume conforms. Comment on the use of illustration, an engraving which is acknowledged on the inside cover to be by Morton Dimonstein, can also be made at this stage. Depicting a masked man, it is evocative rather than descriptive, a style of drawing that derives from the visual tradition of *Expressionism* (q.v.). In the end pages, details of other books from the Penguin list are given, which might be useful for comparison. Finally, information concerning copyright is given, explaining that the book was for sale in Australia, but not in the USA or Canada.

At this stage the empirical or obvious evidence is exhausted. The next step is to pursue questions which take this object into the context of publication design in 1963, questions which assess how effective the design was and how it can be related to design issues of that period, to consider the design, printing and marketing of paperback books.

To answer why the book looks as it does, a general sense of early 1960s design is important. By referring to surveys of graphic design and to the contemporary graphics press, especially *Graphis* and *Typographica* (first and second series), you can find comparative examples and also quite quickly find that Penguin Books occupied a place among seriously-considered design. Penguin has published its own history at different stages of its development, but apart from these publications you now need to move to secondary sources.[17]

Concerning the design of the book, you can consider the interior and exterior. The text was printed in a Monotype face. To read about the Monotype Corporation and how it made examples of historical typefaces available, at a time of hot-metal setting, refer to the writings of Stanley Morison.[18] Histories of printing and design are readily accessible in S. H. Steinberg, *Five Hundred Years of Printing* (1979 edn), and John Lewis, *The Twentieth Century Book*, (1984 edn), and one step is to place the typographic design of the book in a tradition. Again, if you are interested in the history of technology, you can investigate the technical considerations of paperback printing, those to do with paper, inks, size and binding. Cover design is the most controversial area of paperback design, and one that the historian needs to address. It is by the cover that the book is introduced to the public and the famous phrase, 'never judge a book by its cover' implies the potential conflict which might arise. In our example, the question of pictorial covers on a series which had become established and famous with typographical covers was a much-debated issue in the company and among the book-buying public. You need to ask who was responsible for the conception of the design. To speak of the 'designer' of the cover, we need to distinguish between the person responsible for the grid and house-style of the book, and the illustrator or designer commissioned to provide the visual panel on the book. More difficult questions, but equally interesting ones, concern the cultural significance of such a design. What did it mean to put a commissioned illustration on a book cover, and what messages did it give? How did the illustration relate to the title? How did it help to sell the book, and to whom? Here questions of class and gender, age and interest can be raised. By this time in Britain, active marketing with front-forward display and self-service shops had changed patterns of book-buying, and Penguin Books were concerned to give a strong corporate identity in this competitive climate. To research the impact of this marketing change, you need to refer to trade journals, such as *The Bookseller* and *Publisher's Weekly*, rather than the design press. However, to assess the corporate solution made by the art director, Germano Facetti, for Penguin, you could refer to the design magazines of the period, to compare other publishers' design solutions and packaging. This need not be restricted to British examples, and an interesting comparison is with the French and German companies, Livres de Poche and Gallimard, or DTV and Sührkamp.

To stray too far into editorial questions would take you into the social history of literature. Nevertheless, in order to assess whether the design was effective, you would need to understand the changes in editorial patterns. A familiarity with the subject of the books would also help. Why, for instance, should Nabokov be published in 1963? Was it at the first opportunity given, or did it reflect a positive campaign to introduce recent European and American writing? You may not be able to answer this directly, but to establish a sense of readership patterns you could refer to social histories of the period. One approach would be to relate publishing to changes in British society, the education system, the place of television and radio and changing patterns in leisure. Richard Hoggart, *The Uses of Literacy* (1957), is an analysis of working-class life which attempts a broad cultural survey, giving invaluable background to the study of design of this period. I would also recommend Raymond Williams, *Communications* (1962), as a book which organizes highly complex material about changes in the media in a useful way. Also at this introductory stage I would recommend Christopher Booker, *The Neophiliacs: A Study of the Revolution in English Life in the Fifties and Sixties* (1969), as a social history running parallel to Penguin Books' development.

Certain material or answers prove inaccessible during the process of historical investigation. You may find that the articles and books that you read do not provide information that you are looking for, or that the questions you think are important are not raised in the sources. This in itself is significant, if also frustrating. Occasionally your question may be inappropriate, but more often you may be pursuing a line of inquiry which connects things in new ways, for which the answers are not readily available.

With the example of the Penguin paperback book, I hope it becomes clear that graphic design history requires reference to many different fields. However the material which is the object of study is an important and accessible part of daily experience. A good visual analysis of an object, using the specific vocabulary that you will learn from other writers on design, is essential. To do this, it is a good idea to develop the habit of noticing the credits to designers at the end of television programmes, to check whether illustrators' or photographers' names are credited in magazines. Similarly, by looking carefully at the layout of the next book or magazine you read, consider: What was the role of the designer, typographer or illustrator? Can I place it in a stylistic category and, if not, how would it be best described? Are there any particularly noticeable features of the typography? By accumulating such references and training your eye, an approach to the history of graphic design can only be enhanced.

ANALYSIS OF A MAGAZINE:
THE SUNDAY TIMES COLOUR SUPPLEMENT
The choice of magazine can reflect your own interests, and possibly the other areas of design you are studying. If you need some general ideas about the process of magazine layout, Jan A. White, *Magazine Design* (1982), is useful. [19] Most publication design is arranged according to a grid, which means that standardized and conforming column widths are applied throughout, and when illustrations are included,

they are worked in as single, double or triple column widths, and so on.

Perhaps the most accessible kind of magazine for a first analysis is one of the Sunday supplements. The first of these in Britain, the *Sunday Times* colour supplement, was introduced in February 1962, and in spite of uncertainty about its potential in drawing advertisers, the magazine quickly became the model for many free supplements published by weekend and daily newspapers.

The supplement can be looked at as a designed product, in the way I have already suggested with the example of *Vogue* above. It also raises moral and political issues. In 1971, the writer and critic John Berger pointed out the impact of magazine advertising on the editorial content of a publication in his influential book, *Ways of Seeing*.[20] At the time, East Pakistani refugees were fleeing Bangla Desh in the midst of civil war. Berger criticized the juxtaposition of a picture of refugees by the photojournalist Don McCullin with an advertisement for a bath oil. Consumerism and values of domestic comfort seemed badly out of place, but the two were connected, because advertising subsidized the publication, and because the position of the refugees was defined so acutely by this juxtaposition. Since *Ways of Seeing* was published, courses in Cultural Studies have extended this interest in the relationship of the media with political and ideological structures. For example, the Glasgow Media Group has studied television news programmes.[21] The Group's suggestion, an underlying principle of a sociological approach, is that language cannot be objective. In verbal language, factors such as the amount of time spent on the different sides of the debate, the adjectives used to describe news events and the tone of the newsreader's voice all construct an 'interested' point of view. The Group provides analysis and statistics to support this view.

An example of this approach applied to an historical study is Stuart Hall, *The Social Eye of Picture Post* (1972). Hall examined the position of the illustrated weekly magazine, *Picture Post*, which had begun in 1938 and continued during the Second World War. He was concerned to place *Picture Post* in the range of political options available to journalists and photographers during the war, and to evaluate the usual assumption that *Picture Post* represented a left-of-centre position. To do this, Hall analysed the 'construction' of messages through photographic and textual narrative. He concluded that the war had the impact of changing the subjects covered by the magazine: instead of the pressing social concerns of housing, education and a probing approach, the language and sequences of photographs went towards resolving problems and providing a positive vision of a Britain worth fighting for. If you are interested in ways to extend analysis to such questions of ideology and meaning, I would recommend this essay as a possible starting point.

Hall's essay is an early example of a historical analysis which is theorized. In this case he used Soviet and French theory about narrative construction. Since the early 1970s reference to texts which can clarify methods of approach has become more frequent, particularly in histories which attempt to explain the *meaning* of an object as well as its *production*.

Advertising

My final comments are on approaches to advertising design. Instead of a case study of one example, it is more useful to remain at the general level of methods of analysis, as the system is so large, and often similar approaches can be applied, with discrimination, to different examples.

Advertising is one of the most abundant forms of visual communication, occurring in diverse contexts, on street hoardings, in film and television, as well as in newspapers and magazines and collectively known as 'press advertisements'. Appropriately for such a vast system, there are many methods of approach and analysis to be taken by the commentator or historian. These can be broadly categorized into three types. First, there are the insiders' stories, explaining the intentions and techniques of particular campaigns, as well as tales of their success or failure. For an amusing early account, I would recommend E. S. Turner, *The Shocking History of Advertising* (1965), and for a more recent account, *Ogilvy on Advertising* (1983). The promotion of products, whether as a brand name or as a type, is another way insiders' stories about advertising are related. An interesting version of the former is B. Sibley, *The Book of Guinness Advertising* (1985), whereas M. Frostick, *Advertising and the Motorcar* (1970), compares advertising campaigns for different brands of the same product. Especially in the United States, there has been a tradition of publishing tributes to successful campaigns, or selecting examples from a company's work, as in L. Dobrow, *When Advertising Tried Harder* (1984), which traces the highly successful work of Doyle, Dane, Bernbach. From such a source, a mixture of empirical evidence and private anecdote can be gained, but I would recommend that you assess critically any evaluation of the design's success.

The second category of writing on advertising is that which addresses the moral issues of consumer culture. Vance Packard, *The Hidden Persuaders* (1957), was an exposé of advertising techniques in the United States, which condemned the use of market research and 'mass psychoanalysis to guide campaigns of persuasion'.[22] Packard's approach was new at the time, and formative for subsequent cultural criticism, especially as his attack was based on a knowledge of advertising in the United States, where it was at its most sophisticated. For an analysis of British traditions in advertising and the special part played by the promises in the slogans and advertising copylines, Raymond Williams' essay, 'Advertising, the magic system', is instructive.[23] His point of view is an example of a moral, left-wing indictment of advertising. He argues that the structures of advertising turn people from 'users' to 'consumers', and that the practice of finding words and images to persuade someone to believe that their lives will be transformed 'if they do this' is dishonest and hides real needs behind a language of magic.

Thirdly, for the historian or designer, a system of analysis that provides a specialist language that can be applied to a diverse set of examples from advertising has its appeal. Such an approach is offered by 'semiology'. This can be defined as 'the science of signs'. The term semiology derives from the work of the linguist Ferdinand de Saussure, who worked in Paris before 1914, and its possible applications are taken up by advertising agencies and universities alike, although by no means all agencies consider de Saussure or practise semiotics. De Saussure, *A Course in General Linguistics* (1974), was concerned to study the way language produces meaning, and his work can be placed broadly in a tradition of linguistic philosophy. He distinguished between what an object is and how it is depicted linguistically or visually. For example, we know the difference between a picture of a cow, the word 'cow' and the animal in the field, but accept the conventions by which we call that animal (and all other animals in the species) 'cow'. De Saussure suggested that the word 'cow' be called a 'sign': it is used to label an object. For the purposes of analysis, the sign is broken down to the 'signified', which is the meaning of the object, and the 'signifier', which is the object itself. In the case of the cow, it becomes a particular cow by the process of signification; colour, texture, size and associative values are added to the animal, to make it a real cow with qualities that we can refer to, whether they are ' holy', 'frightening' or 'brown'. De Saussure believed that in daily experience we do not distinguish between the signifier and signified, but he also argued that it was at this abstract level of signification that so much of our knowledge and meaning is given to representation.

Advertising is not referred to in De Saussure's work, but it is an appropriate area for such analysis, because it depends on an immediate and efficient system of references, which can be understood by a wide audience. More than anyone else, the French sociologist Roland Barthes extended the application of semiology to visual language. During the modern period, art historians have developed ways of studying past paintings by iconography and iconology, suggesting meanings for depicted figures and subjects which are no longer readily apparent or available to the contemporary viewer. Semiology provided a similar method of looking at contemporary images from popular culture, which depended on an equally elaborate system as painting. In the compilation of his short essays, *Mythologies* (1973), Barthes tested his opinion that a viewer reads associative meanings into advertisements and other photographic imagery. Among subjects he discussed were the face of Greta Garbo, the new Citroën (the DS 19), and cooking articles from *Elle* magazine. For Barthes, popular visual images were made up of signs, often understood unconsciously by the public. He applied the idea from social anthropology, that as long as a system is consistent, it need not be logical or relate to a real world; instead it can develop what he called a mythical structure. In advertising, this meant that the possible contradictions of life are avoided by constructing an ideal world. Barthes explained his theory in the essays, 'The photographic message' and 'The rhetoric of the image', which are in the anthology, *Image Music Text* (1977). For a commentary on semiology, I would recommend T. Hawkes, *Structuralism and Semiotics* (1979).

In the case of advertising, values can be given to consumer objects, status can be given to film actors and properties given to consumer durables, which are fictional. For example, a woman in a cosmetic advertisement is presented as having 'perfect' skin. (Fig. 7.5) If we read the caption we are given information which persuades us, giving an explanation of how she has achieved it, with references to science as well as a promise of transformation. Barthes' approach would be to consider the language of the copy for the hidden associative values in the writing. Semiology would also suggest that we could 'decode' the

Figure 7.5 An advertisement for Lancôme, from *Vogue* magazine, November, 1986. A semiological analysis might question the use of words or the interaction of word and image.

photograph here, black and white, clinical, and with light used as an active element in the composition, to reinforce the authority of the text. Although we may agree that the idea of pure skin is physiologically impossible, as we look at the advertisement we make the imaginative leap to believe that by using that product our skin could be similar.

Judith Williamson, *Decoding Advertisements* (1978), is an example of this approach applied to a range of commonplace press advertisements. Like Barthes', her language is specific and theoretical, using recent French philosophical ideas. If you are interested in extending this approach to advertising in which a narrative is implied, Erwing Goffmann, *Gender Advertisements* (1979), shows how advertising uses the language of the theatre to suggest relationships between the sexes which can be understood at a glance.

As you might have guessed from the use of the word 'structure' in explaining Barthes' work, he was one of the first generation of Structuralist thinkers. The semiological approach to an object should be distinguished from the historical. Barthes assumed the existence of the image or object he is interested in. Instead of asking how has this object been *made*, and considering the range of possible determinants and conditions which surrounded its making, the semiologist asks how this object *gives* meaning. In this case the *consumption* of design is the focus. The designer is no different from a member of the public, and is not the 'author' of the work, with a privileged understanding of its entirety. The emphasis tends to be on the contemporary reading – Barthes does not ask whether it was different to look at the same image at other times, a question that should interest the historian.

As a way of analysing graphic imagery, there is much that can be learnt from such sources. When you read them, you should test whether they are guilty of 'reading in' meaning which might not have been present at the time of the making or the original reception of the advertisement. The advantage of the semiological approach for a history of graphic design is that it takes the subject from the particular to the general, to place single images within a system of representation, a process which in turn questions cultural values.

Graphic design is a rich and complex subject and the possible approaches to the study of its history reflect that richness and complexity. In this chapter I have indicated some possible approaches to its study with examples of book, poster and advertising design. The semiological approach to advertising design can provide rewarding insights although initially it may seem rather daunting. It is however a technique that is being applied to an increasing range of two- and three-dimensional designs, particularly under the influence of Post-Modernism.

Suggestions for Further Reading

A general reading list for this chapter is given at the end of the book. Below are some suggestions for more specialized reading.

BIBLIOGRAPHIES
Research can often be started by using one of the many design bibliographies. These give the sources for articles and books published, usually arranged according to themes as well as named artists and designers. Those most useful for the history of graphic design include:
Bland, D. (1955), *A Bibliography of Book Illustration* (Cambridge: Cambridge University Press).
Herdeg, W. (1983), *Who's Who in Graphic Art* (Dubendorf: De Clivo Press). This is international in its range.
Nevett, T. (1982), *Advertising in Britain: A History* (London: Heinemann) A bibliography is given on pp. 218–25.
Thompson, J. W. Ltd, (1972), *Advertising: An Annotated Bibliography* (London: National Book League).
Williamson, E. 'Advertising', in Inge, M. T. (1980), *Handbook of American Popular Culture* (Westport, Conn.: Greenwood). This is an extremely useful introductory chapter, part history, part historiography, strong on material in the United States and with an extensive reading list on pp. 21–9.

THE GRAPHIC DESIGN PRESS
Another way to retrieve information is to watch the graphic design press. Sources for contemporary graphics, which give not only an idea of current visual styles but also the issues of style, technologies and design patronage, include:

Baseline – International Typographics Magazine (intermittent), *Campaign*, 1968– (weekly), *Creative Review*, 1980– (monthly), *Design*, 1949– (monthly), *Design and Art Direction*, 1982– (monthly), *Designer*, 1945– (monthly), *Illustrators*, 1977– (monthly), *Typographica*, 1972– (intermittent).

For design in the United States, I would recommend:
Art Direction, 1949– (monthly), *Communication Arts*, 1959– (bi-monthly), *Print*, 1940– (bi-monthly) and *Upper and Lower Case*, 1974– (quarterly).

Finally, the tradition of graphic design in Switzerland has produced two significant journals, *Graphis*, 1944– (bi-monthly) and *Typographische Monatsblätter* (*TM*), 1882– (bi-monthly). Many of these publications also produce annual selections of work, which provide a range of a year's design. It is important to remember that these are not representative surveys, but instead reflect the priorities and tastes of a selection committee.

GRAPHIC DESIGN THEORY AND PRACTICE
Although contemporary practice is accessible, in the form of the journals recommended above, past examples of graphic design were often carried out by methods and techniques not in use today. The list below suggests a range of theories, which were central to the development of graphic design:

Cooper, A. (1938), *Making a Poster* (London: The Studio Ltd). A useful account from the time when the poster was a major form of public display.
Crane, W. (1898), *The Bases of Design* (London: G. Bell). An early attempt to find a basic vocabulary of form, indicative of a way of thinking to be applied continually in the twentieth century.
Curwen, H. (1937, second edn 1947) *Processes of Graphic Reproduction in Printing* (London: Faber). A very useful account of the main processes and, in itself, an interesting example of book design.
Frutiger, A (1980), *Type Sign Symbol* (Zürich: Éditions ABC). An approach to design from one of the major exponents of Swiss-style graphic design, working in Britain in the post-1945 period.
Games, A. (1960), *Over My Shoulder* (London: Studio), How a designer works, described by a British designer who witnessed the growth and professionalization of graphic design in the 1950s.
Gorb, P. (ed.) (1978), *Living by Design: Pentagram* (London: Lund Humphries). Gives examples of the work of Pentagram, an association of architects, designers and interior designers, who have been instrumental in applying a broad, multi-media approach to design solutions in recent years.
Hurlburt, A. (1977), *Layout: The Design of the Printed Page* (New

York: Watson Guptill) Useful for recent attitudes to publication design.

Lewis, J. (1956), *A Handbook of Type and Illustration* (London: Faber) A good review of type and printing technology before the advent of film-setting.

Moholy-Nagy, L. (1969), *Painting Photography Film* (London: Lund Humphries) An essential reference for understanding debates on visual communication in the twenties. It was originally published as a Bauhaus book in 1925.

Rand, P. (1967), *Thought on Design* (New York: Reinhold) By one of the New York school of graphic designers, receptive to European Modernism, who worked in the entire range of advertising and communication design.

Simon O. (second edn 1963). *Introduction to Typography* (London: Faber). The author worked with the Curwen Press, one of Britain's most important printing presses in the first half of this century.

Tschichold, J. (1967), *Asymmetric Typography* (New York: Reinhold). Outlines the principles of the New Typography, originally formulated between 1924 and 1935.

Notes

1 As quoted in Williams, Raymond (1979), 'Advertising, the magic system', in *Problems in Materialism and Culture* (London: Verso), p. 181.

2 For such early examples of visual language, see Müller-Brockmann, J. (1971), *A History of Visual Communications*.

3 Milton Glaser resists being labelled, as the article in *Design and Art Direction*, 12 July 1985, showed. For Glaser's earlier work, see (1973), *Milton Glaser Designer* (London: Secker & Warburg).

4 For a commentary on McLuhan's ideas, see Miller, J. (1971), *McLuhan* (London: Fontana).

5 See Petley, J. (1979), *Capital and Culture: German Cinema, 1933–45* (London: British Film Institute), and Welch, D. (ed.), (1983), *Nazi Propaganda* (London: Barnes and Noble)

6 For the work of Polish poster design there are several magazine articles, but fewer books in English. The range of visual styles can be seen in *Das Polnische Plakat von 1892 bis Heute* (The Polish Poster from 1892 until Today) (Berlin: Hochschule der Künste), 1980. Barnicoat, J. (1972), *A Concise History of Posters* (London: Thames & Hudson), outlines the general tradition of poster design.

7 See Atelier Populaire, (1969), *Posters from the Revolution, Paris, May 1968* (London: Dobson).

8 See Schneider, William H., 'What is an art director?' in *Art Director's Eighteenth Annual* (1939) (New York: Longmans Green).

9   For an introduction to *Vogue*, see Packer, W. (1980), *The Art of Vogue Covers, 1909–1940* (London: Octopus).

10 Walter Benjamin, member of the Frankfurt School of Social Research, was most interested in photography as it changed the status of the art object. See his essays, 'The work of art in the age of mechanical reproduction', in *Understanding Brecht*, ed. S. Mitchell, (1977) (London: New Left Books) and 'The author as producer', in *Illuminations*, ed. H. Arendt (1973) (London: Fontana). For a commentary on Benjamin and other members of the Frankfurt School see Anderson, P. (1979), *Considerations on Western Marxism* (London: Verso) and Wolff, J. (1985), *The Social Production of Art* (London: Macmillan).

11 Pointon, M. (revised edn 1986), *History of Art: A Students' Handbook* (London: Allen & Unwin).

12 See Whitford, F. (1977), *Japanese Prints and Western Painters* (London: Studio Vista). For the French prints affected by the Japanese prints refer to the British Museum catalogue (1978), *From Manet to Toulouse-Lautrec, French Lithographs 1860–1900* (London: British Museum Publications), and for Japanese prints see (1980), *Japanese Prints: 300 Years of Albums and Books* (London: British Museum Publications).

13 For an introduction to the period, see Banham, Reyner (1960), *Theory and Design in the First Machine Age* (London: Architectural Press).

14 Lissitzky-Kuppers, S. (revised edn 1980), *El Lissitzky – Life, Letters, Texts* (London: Thames & Hudson), p. 359.

15 For this work, see Spencer, H. (revised edn 1984), *Pioneers of Modern Typography* and (1985), *Bauhaus Typographie* (Düsseldorf: Edition Marzona).

16 Lissitzky-Kuppers, S., op. cit., p. 57.

17 See Williams, W. E. (1956), *The Penguin Story* (Harmondsworth: Penguin), and (1985) *Fifty Penguin Years* (Harmondsworth: Penguin).

18 Morison, Stanley (1973), *A Tally of Types* (Cambridge: Cambridge University Press), and (1963), *The Typographic Book, 1450–1935* (London: Benn).

19 Also extremely useful, Evans, Harold (1973) *Editing and Design, Books I–V* (London: Heinemann), considers the stages of newspaper production. Volume IV is on *Picture Editing* and Volume V is on *Newspaper Design*.

20 Berger, John (1972), *Ways of Seeing* (London: BBC and Penguin Books), was also produced as a BBC television series in that year.

21 Glasgow Media Group (1976), *Bad News* (London: Routledge & Kegan Paul). This was followed (1980) by *More Bad News* (London: Routledge & Kegan Paul) and (1982) *Really Bad News* (London: Writers and Readers Press).

22 Packard, Vance (1961), *The Hidden Persuaders* (Harmondsworth: Penguin), p. 11.

23 Williams, R., op. cit., p. 2.

8

Environmental Design

HAZEL CONWAY

Environmental design concerns the total environment and how it is used, and it can include architecture, town planning, urban geography, urban conservation, transport and civil engineering, technology, landscape gardening and agriculture, as well as social, economic and political history. If environmental design and its history are subsumed under the titles of numerous other disciplines, should we then leave it at that, or is there a case for studying it in its own right? One of the reasons why I think that the subject deserves discussion in a handbook such as this is that it is, as its name implies, all around us, and affects us all in many different and complex ways. Although the history of environmental design can include all the areas listed above, it is significantly different from the history of, say, town planning or architecture. Indeed in the context of the urban environment, it would almost be true to say that the subject is concerned with all those aspects of the environment that have not been claimed by the town planners, or the architects, as well as those that have.

Recently increasing attention has been focused on environmental design by the mass-media as well as by official bodies. The issues have included threats to sites of special scientific interest (SSSIs), the general state of the city, however that is defined, high-rise housing, and the role of Modern and Post-Modern (q.v.) architecture in important city locations. These issues are all important and complex and it is only when more people become aware of what is happening, and from an informed basis make their voices heard, that positive action will become not only possible but inevitable. So the reasons for including this topic relate to its importance and the recognition of that importance by students who are working in a variety of disciplines including design and design history. Often because of the way in which courses are structured the only way in which students could develop that interest was in their final year, with its opportunities for personal research projects. In the main the focus of these projects has been on developments in the twentieth century and especially in the period following the Second World War. This chapter is therefore intended to provide guidance for those who are concerned with environmental issues and would like to pursue that interest by means of project work. It is not intended to be an introduction to all the disciplines which could be included in the subject of environmental design.

Environmental design is concerned with human beings and their institutions, and how these affect their surroundings. Chronologically, therefore, it could be said to date from the time of the earliest settlements. I cannot hope to do justice to all aspects of such a vast topic so I have chosen to concentrate on the nineteenth and twentieth centuries, the period of industrialization and urbanization, in which urban expansion with all its attendant problems accelerated.

The Countryside

Generally environmental design falls into two broad and overlapping areas, that of the town and that of the countryside. Studies of the effects of human activity on the countryside have a long history which ranges from the remains of prehistory and the industrial archaeology of abandoned mines, to the effects of Enclosure Acts, or the results of changing patterns of transport, or agriculture. One of the most vivid examples this century of the action of particular agricultural techniques on the landscape was the creation of the dust bowl in the middle and western states of America in the 1930s. The effects on share-croppers who could no longer eke out an existence was vividly recorded in the photographs sponsored by the Farm Security Administration and in John Steinbeck's novel *The Grapes of Wrath* (1939).[1]

My eyes were first opened to the history hitherto hidden in the English countryside by W. G. Hoskins, *The Making of the English Landscape* (1970). Hoskins analysed and identified some of the factors that had contributed to the creation of the landscape as we knew it at that date. He was concerned with ancient footpaths, Roman roads, patterns of medieval field systems, the creation of hedgerows and their subsequent destruction as agricultural machinery and the increased sizes of agricultural holdings created their own demands. He was concerned with the siting of villages and the disposition of key buildings such as churches and he showed how it was possible by looking at a range of elements to 'read' the landscape, and deduce from their presence or absence that certain changes had taken place. His book provides an excellent introduction to the historical dimension of the environmental design of the English countryside. However as his emphasis was on the past he tended to give less weight to recent developments, and although he showed the reader how to deduce evidence of change it was beyond the scope of the book to go into detail about the reasons for particular changes.

Reading the history of the landscape from the visual evidence that remains is one of the many approaches that can be brought to studies of environmental design. Another approach concerns the development of a new way of 'seeing' the landscape in aesthetic terms, which developed in the latter part of the eighteenth century. The landscapes created by Lancelot (Capability) Brown (q.v.) with their rolling contours and 'natural' lakes, rivers and groups of trees are still, in many people's view, regarded as typical of the English landscape. They seem to have evolved naturally, whereas they were in fact largely artificial. The ways in which we read the countryside today are still very much influenced by the practitioners, theorists and critics of landscape gardening of the late-eighteenth and early-nineteenth centuries. The development of the picturesque (q.v.) way of reading the landscape is vividly described by Christopher Hussey in *The Picturesque* (1927) while David Watkin in *The English Vision, The Picturesque in Architecture, Landscape and Garden Design* (1982) argues that picturesque values of reading landscapes and townscapes are still in evidence today.

The question that I want to consider is the relationship between landscape design and environmental design. Can they be seen as one and the same thing or are there different approaches to the study of the environmental design of the countryside? In general most of the literature on landscape design in any period has concentrated on the major works of designers such as Capability Brown, or Humphry Repton (q.v.), or the landscapes associated with particular country houses. The emphasis has been on the particular features of the design, its significance in the context of the period in which it was created and its relationship to the buildings in the landscape.[2] Yet between the mid-eighteenth and mid-nineteenth centuries the majority of landscapes that were laid out were part of estates that comprised not only the designed landscape but also farms, forests and rivers. The

Enclosure Acts ensured that many of these estates expanded rapidly in this period. How the whole enterprise worked in terms of the financial organization and the lives of workers on the estate as a whole is rarely investigated and there is a great need for the equivalent of Mark Girouard's *Life in the English Country House* (1978)[3] which would cover life outside the country house. Environmental design in this context would look not only at the landscape itself but also at those that worked on the estate, conditions of work and the housing provided, and the farm buildings and sheds for machinery – the total environment, in other words, including the footpaths and roads and also waste disposal. Aspects of this have been the subject of specific research, but the picture tends to be a fragmentary one.[4]

As the nineteenth century progressed the urban population expanded and attitudes towards the countryside began to change. As towns grew so concern began to be expressed about the need for access to the open air for the urban dweller, particularly the poorest sections of the community, since the others had resources of both time and money to make journeys outside the towns. The enclosure of commons and wasteland had meant that the traditional areas for recreation were no longer available:

> The law locks up the man or woman
> Who steals the goose from off the Common
> But lets the greater robber loose
> That steals the Common from the goose.[5]

One solution to the problem was to develop municipal parks in the major industrial towns. With the development of railway excursions more people could visit the seaside and the country. The countryside provided a recreational amenity to the urban dweller, but was itself under threat from continued urban expansion. The setting up of the National Trust in 1895 to preserve areas of outstanding natural beauty was one outcome of these changing attitudes to it. Our attitude towards the countryside today is very much part of that legacy, yet as Nan Fairbrother, in *New Lives, New Landscapes* (1970), described so clearly, the designation of areas of outstanding natural beauty encourages a front-parlour attitude. Those areas are cherished and excellently maintained, but the rest is not. Gravel pits, refuse dumps and the outskirts of towns need not necessarily be the eyesores that they all too often are.

The conflict between the countryside as an amenity for recreation, and as a resource for 'agri-business' is illustrated clearly by the example of footpaths. To those who like to walk, the Ordnance Survey maps can in principle provide a guide to days of walking along the numerous footpaths that are marked. The farmer has other priorities and even though in theory one could walk around a field whose footpath has been ploughed up, often it is not possible to do so in practice. The threats to the diminishing resources of the countryside under such proposed developments as the Okehampton bypass, sited to go over Dartmoor, and the development of greenfield industrial sites and new housing estates, while ample derelict space remains within our cities, indicate the need for concern and action. Environmental design is about conflicting needs and how they are resolved. Case studies provide a useful way of alerting a greater number of people to the implications of proposed developments, and detailed historical studies of small areas, particularly those on the outskirts of towns, can provide evidence of what has happened in the recent past and why.

The problem facing anyone who would like to undertake research in such topics is the vastness of the subject and the great volumes of literature covering various aspects of it. Often a more direct route into some of the important local or national issues can be obtained through the publications of the many organizations actively concerned with the countryside. An additional advantage is that local branches of such organizations as the National Trust, the Civic Trust or the Council for the Protection of Rural England exist in many parts of the country. The most comprehensive directory to such organizations is *The Environmental Directory: National and Regional Organisations of Interest to those Concerned with Amenity and the Environment* (1981), published by the Civic Trust.

The Urban Environment

Britain is an urban industrialized country and around 85 per cent of the population live in urban areas. This directly affects our attitude to the environments of the town and of the country for they tend to be experienced in very different ways. Towns are where we live, and the country is what we see when we travel. As we travel across the country the scale of the landscape that we experience is inevitably larger than the one that we live in, although of course we do stop in the country and experience small areas of it in a closer relationship to ourselves. We experience the urban environment by walking, standing and sitting still, so urban views are measured in terms of hundreds of metres, and the spaces that we inhabit are the restricted settings of streets, gardens, squares or spaces between buildings. We move around cities by public and private transport, but the speeds at which we do so tend, by virtue of traffic congestion, to be low unless we are on motorways which pass through cities. When motorways slice through the urban environment, as they do in cities such as Birmingham, then the scale of the landscape for high speed is brought into the city: the view for motorists may be interesting but the time the journey takes is more important. For the people living in the city the intrusion of a motorway destroys the small-scale, self-contained aspect of city life that forms one of the pleasures of the urban environment, and divides the city into areas that are accessible only with difficulty. So reactions to the motorway will depend very much on whether we are motorists who use them, or pedestrians who want to cross the road, or whether we live in property alongside it and are concerned with the effects of lead pollution on our children.

Cities are complex places in which there are many conflicting needs, and studies of the urban environment should reflect that complexity and conflict. Many people who look at our urban environment today see it largely in negative terms, with arid city centres and traffic-free or transportless precincts, the depressing look of weathered concrete, inner-city deprivation and slums, badly designed high-rise housing estates, increasing vandalism and unsafe streets. The tendency has been to blame town planners and architects for this state of affairs. Finding scapegoats however does not usually result in increasing our understanding of how things came to be the way they are, or what can be done to improve them. In order to understand how our cities have developed into the forms that they take today the history of town planning and of architecture needs to be studied alongside the history of central and local government intervention into these areas, together with the role of local developers. All city developments in any period are concerned with land and its value and with who will benefit from increases in that value.

The literature analysing townscapes is vast and ideas concerning the subject have changed in the past and are continuing to do so. An important contribution to the debate on townscapes in the 1960s was made by Gordon Cullen, *Townscape* (1961), while today the theories on urban space of Robert Krier (q.v.) and his urban schemes for such cities as West Berlin form part of the Post-Modern (q.v.) debate on the urban environment.

A useful introductory study to the urban environment, which seeks to analyse it in terms of townscapes that 'work' and those that do not is Gerald Burke, *Townscapes* (1976). After identifying the general components of townscapes the author analyses medieval, Renaissance, Victorian, Edwardian and twentieth-century elements. These he does not treat as isolated features, but as part of particular environments in which street furniture such as lights, parking meters, traffic signs and telephone boxes have a place. Another significant element is that of texture of materials, whether they be roofing or building materials, or the tarmac, paving or cobbles used on the roads and pavements. Rooflines, fenestration (pattern of windows), chimneys and television aerials all contribute to the townscape. Burke makes his own architectural preferences clear, but these should not be allowed to obscure the insights that he provides into some of the problems of analysing the urban environment. The second part of the book provides a very broad introduction to such issues as conservation, rehabilitation, development and design control. The main emphasis of this book is on the visual forms of the townscape. In order to understand how our environment works we need to understand not only how these forms developed, but how people of all ages, incomes and abilities interact with those forms, and how our lives are limited or enhanced by them.

In many areas of design the solution reached will depend upon the objectives that were identified. The urban environment has been the target of many objectives, some of them clearly stated but many of them not clearly stated. City planning objectives in the past have included defence or the maintenance of food supplies, or symbolic reasons such as showing the power of the king, or the church, or other bodies. By the middle of the nineteenth century town planning in Britain was beginning to be recognized as a necessary function of central and local government and two main goals were identified – improving public health and, later, improving public transport. The improvement of working-class housing was seen as a goal by certain philanthropists, but it was not until the end of the century that this was recognized as a goal by central or local government. If the objectives are not too many their effectiveness can be related to how they were put into practice.

At the turn of the century one of the most significant contributions to planning thought was the Garden City invented by Ebenezer Howard (q.v.).[6] Howard's goals included social justice, health, efficiency and contact with nature, and to achieve those objectives the Garden City was zoned so that the public buildings and the main shops were at the centre and the industrial area was on the periphery. In between lay the residential area with generous gardens. By studying Letchworth we can see how these goals were put into practice. The Garden City was a new development in the countryside, quite distinct from existing cities, which combined the best features of living in the country and the city. It was very influential nationally and internationally, and was an example of dispersal planning. It was not intended to solve 'the problem' of cities as Howard made quite clear, for if garden cities were widely adopted then their effect would be the destruction of existing large unplanned cities. 'These crowded cities have done their work', they were 'crowded, ill-ventilated, unplanned, unwieldy, unhealthy cities – ulcers on the very face of our beautiful island'.[7]

Howard's ideas were taken up and applied in a variety of forms. One of these was the development of co-partnership housing schemes such as the Brentham Estate in Ealing, or the Humberstone Garden Suburb in Leicester. Some of the original occupiers still live on these estates and they therefore can provide an opportunity for oral history. Howard's ideas involved decentralizing cities and thinning them out into towns. The ideal was suburban privacy and the implication for town planning was that the presence of many people should be minimized; commerce, industry and residential areas should be segregated and the planned community self-contained and resistant to change, so every detail should be controlled by the planners from the start. The influence of some of Howard's ideas could be seen in the development of garden suburbs and in low density housing schemes such as the LCC cottage estates of the interwar period. The building of New Towns in the 1950s and 1960s as a response to the problems of major cities such as London, Liverpool or Glasgow can also be seen as partly due to the influence of the Garden City Movement.

Sense of Place

From our personal experience of cities we know that there are areas that we like and those that we do not. We like areas that have 'character', however that is defined, and we tend not to like those that appear to be monotonous or uncared for. When Gertrude Stein visited the new town of Oakland in California she was asked how she liked it there. When she replied that there was no there, there, she encapsulated feelings shared by many of us when visiting certain new developments.

One of the qualities that we like in towns is that associated with the sense of place, that is, the qualities that give a place its character. These qualities may be associated with the use of particular materials in a particular way, that are found only in certain regions: the decorated exterior plasterwork of Essex cottages, for example, or the graded flints of Norfolk. They may have to do with history and the development of an area over a particular period so that the buildings and street patterns share features in common.[8] Such a historic legacy is different from that which results from the presence of isolated buildings of historic and architectural significance. Sense of place may be to do with the scale and harmony of the buildings and their relationship to each other and to the open spaces.

We can recognize the presence or absence of sense of place no matter what part of the urban environment we are concerned with, whether it be the town centre, industrial or residential districts, or areas of mixed use. The importance of the need to preserve areas of architectural and historic interest was recognized in 1967 when the Civic Amenities Act was passed. This Act encouraged local authorities to define such areas in the hope that this would help to preserve them from redevelopment. Conservation areas have been designated in many of our cities, but the question of the type of alteration or development that is allowed within them is a very complex one. The alteration of windows, the addition of artificial stone cladding, or the alteration of roof lines can seriously affect the appearance of an area and yet these are generally permitted developments. If they occur too frequently then the reasons for designating the area as a conservation area may be completely undermined. Essex has produced a design guide for residential areas.[9] However the design features appropriate to Essex will not necessarily be appropriate to any other part of the country since many of the features that contribute to the sense of place are associated with local materials and local techniques of craftsmanship.

The designation of conservation areas, the question of permitted development and the role of amenity societies such as the Georgian Group and the Victorian Society in trying to preserve particular urban environments has contributed to the growing public awareness of the need for vigilance. When developments are proposed which affect well-known major monuments or areas, then the question becomes one of public debate. One recent example of such public debate was the proposed extention to the National Gallery in Trafalgar Square, London, which earned the opprobrium of Prince Charles. The 'monstrous carbuncle' has become a useful journalist's phrase for disparaging Modern or Post-Modern architecture. Another recent example concerned Mansion House Square in the City of London. Peter Palumbo had, over previous decades, acquired a considerable proportion of the buildings in the area of the Mansion House. These he proposed to demolish and in their stead build a tower block, designed by Mies van der Rohe some twenty-five years earlier, which would face a wide open piazza (q.v.). Much of the public debate on the issue was polarized in terms of the reactionaries, or conservationists, who wished to retain the old Mansion House district because, it was implied, they were against all new development, and the 'Modernists' who were looking to the future. The new technologies, it was argued, were essential to the businesses of the future, and needed to be housed in new buildings (even though this particular new building design was about twenty-five years old). But the real issues were concerned not with modernists versus conservationists, or with the future versus the past, but with the scale of the streets and buildings in that area of the City, and the effect of a point block (q.v.) and open piazza (q.v.) on the remaining buildings.

In the 1960s and 1970s the proposed development of Covent Garden and of the Barbican area of London were frequent topics of public debate, as are London's docklands, the Liverpool docks and many other developments today. Today's developments will form the urban environment of tomorrow and they illustrate the problem of establishing new uses for old areas and pose questions regarding how much of the old should be preserved. If a new development entails pedestrianization should the surfaces of the streets, pavements and kerbs be retained, for example? If an old development provided accommodation that was cheap to live and work in, what will happen to those people and ventures in the new development? This in turn is not only a question of the urban qualities of the old areas, it is also a question of the range of activities that are viable in old areas and not in new.

A comparison between the plans proposed, the issues raised in public debate and how the final plans have affected a particular area can provide very instructive topics for research, particularly if they are backed up by research into how the development has affected those who lived and worked in the area.

Post-War Planning

For many people the absence of sense of place and character in the urban environment is associated with a general disenchantment with Modern Movement architecture and principles of town planning. The period from the 1950s to the 1970s was the era of clean-sweep planning in which our city centres were redeveloped, slums cleared, and people rehoused in high-rise estates. The main influences on ideas in that period were the town planning ideas of Le Corbusier (q.v.) and CIAM (Congrès Internationaux d'Architecture Moderne) (q.v.). Like Howard, Le Corbusier made his attitude towards existing cities clear: 'The centres of our towns are in a state of mortal sickness, their boundaries are gnawed as though by vermin.'[10] In 1922 Le Corbusier exhibited his plans for a Contemporary City for Three Million. During the following decade he refined his ideas and in 1933 published his plans for the Radiant City, which was also to have a population of 3 million, and this provided the most potent image of Modern Movement town planning principles. The Radiant City would be dense (400 people per acre, 1,000 per hectare), pedestrians and vehicles would be segregated, apartments would be built on pilotis (q.v.) and the ground under the buildings as well as roof spaces would be given over to pedestrian activities. Apartment blocks would form unbroken ribbons of housing and each block would house about 2,700 people who would all use a single entrance. In each block there would be communal domestic services, nurseries and kindergartens, but there would be no commercial premises. Most of the city's streets would be inside the apartment blocks (the *rues interieurs*) and each floor would be served by lifts. There would be large areas of open space for recreation and the city would be zoned with the business centre, the housing and the industrial districts linked by rail and motorways (Fig. 8.1).

At the Congrès Internationaux d'Architecture Moderne (CIAM) held in 1933 the methodology for dealing with town planning problems was further elaborated and 111 propositions were established. These principles were intended to guide architects and town planners in dealing with all the problems of twentieth-century town planning, and from them Le Corbusier wrote his Charte d'Athènes which established

Figure 8.1 The Radiant City, showing ribbon blocks of apartments with parks, sports grounds and schools between them.

a hierarchical arrangement of problem categories: dwellings, recreation, work, transportation, historic buildings:[11] 'My object was not to overcome the existing state of things, but by constructing a theoretically water-tight formula to arrive at the fundamental principles of town planning.'[12]

The opportunity for applying these principles to the problems of Britain's towns came in the aftermath of the Second World War. Areas of blitz (bomb damage) and blight (worn out and obsolete housing and buildings) were identified. Another problem that was identified was the need for replanning road systems to cope with the increasing traffic volumes, and at the same time provide adequate access to city centres. The old unplanned environment was to be replaced by the planned, efficient city in which the hierarchy of activities identified by Le Corbusier would be segregated and the architects and town planners would take complete responsibility for deciding what the new urban environment would be like. Most of our major cities are testaments to the clean-sweep planning that resulted.

In the mid-1960s practically the only voice to criticize the effects of applying those principles was Jane Jacobs who recognized that what both the Garden City Movement and Le Corbusier had in common was their rejection of unplanned, disorganized existing cities. Their ideas were directed towards undermining existing cities, yet those ideas were being applied to solve city problems. In *The Death and Life of Great American Cities* (1965) she looked at the results of applying such techniques as zoning and segregation of activities and argued that what made cities interesting places to be in, was their diversity and variety. Zoning meant that the city was divided into specialized areas – residential, business, cultural – and these areas were only alive when there were people about, at particular times. For the rest of the day or night there were so few people about that they became potentially hazardous areas, for the use of streets and public and semi-public areas is of direct relevance to the question of safety. If a district supports a wide variety of activities then different people will go out at different times for different purposes and the area will be a lively one and a safe one to be in. Jane Jacobs then went on to analyse the functions of the street, for if the streets are interesting then the city is interesting. Streets are used for carrying traffic, pedestrians and maintaining safety, for in cities streets are full of strangers. To handle strangers safely there must be a clear demarkation between public and private space, a function that was clearly performed by small front gardens to houses; there must be eyes upon the street, therefore buildings must not turn their blank sides towards the street; there must be a number of pedestrians to add their eyes and to give the people living and working in the buildings lining the street something to look at, since no one likes looking out on an empty space. Since you cannot make people use streets that they do not want to use, or watch those that they do not find interesting to watch, streets must contain facilities which will encourage those activities. Shops, bars and restaurants that are in use day, evening and night will encourage use, particularly if they are so spaced that the users will walk past the things that they are not interested in to get to those that they are. People like watching people doing things such as eating or shopping, or being around, and the more a street is used the more strangers it can accommodate safely. It is very instructive to look at the results of clean-sweep planning, in particular city centres such as Birmingham or Coventry, in order to see how Modern Movement criteria of town planning were put into effect. The question of liveliness, diversity and safety in the streets at various times of the day or night can then be related to the presence or absence of particular facilities.

One of the most comprehensive introductions to the complexities of post-war planning and the resulting effects on the urban environment is *Remaking Cities* (1980) by Alison Ravetz. The first section of this book examines the roots of twentieth-century town planning and looks at the planning machinery that evolved during the 1940s. Alison Ravetz argues that it was this planning machinery that led 'inevitably' to a style of planning that was applied during the 1950s, 1960s and 1970s. The second section of the book looks at the development of the segregated city in terms of land values, the role of the developer, the social costs of developments, transport policies, the city centre and housing. At the same time that a new style of city planning was being put into practice the technology of building was undergoing major changes. Industrialized building systems meant that factory-produced units could be assembled on site. In the third section the development of the built environment is analysed in terms of its changing technology, the changing roles of the architectural and town planning professions nationally and internationally, and how these changes affected people's experience of the environment. The last section of the book takes the theme of cities in crisis and looks at alternatives to development in both the capitalist and communist urban societies, and the possibilities of radical alternatives. The strength of this particular study is that it confronts the complexity of the urban environment by approaching it from many different points of view. This multi-faceted approach provides insight at the same time as it illustrates the contradictions.

Housing

The state of our city centres, the problem of traffic and pollution in towns are all important aspects of the problems of urban design, but for those that believe that every human being has a right to adequate food and adequate shelter the most important problem of them all is that of housing. Housing is an enormous topic whose chronological span goes back almost to prehistory. Types of housing can range from nomadic structures to the development of shanty towns in South America and South Africa, from cottages to high-rise housing. Approaches to the study of housing reflect this variety since social history, political and economic history as well as architectural history are all involved. Because of the large scale of the topic I shall only attempt to look at some aspects of housing in Britain this century. I have already referred to such cooperative ventures as that at Brentham as potential topics for research.

The period immediately following the First World War saw the Government's decision to build 'homes for heroes'. The role of the Government, and the reasons why these houses were built where and when they were, is investigated by Mark Swenarton in *Homes for Heroes* (1981). This was a short-lived period of central government intervention and although local authority housing was built in the interwar period, the role of the private speculative developer was much more important in terms of the volume of housing built. Alan Jackson in *Semi-detached London* (1973) shows how railway and housing developments around London went hand in hand and resulted in clearly distinct areas of 'ideal homes' and districts of working-class housing. Another book relating to this topic is the idiosyncratic *Dunroamin. The Suburban Semi and its Enemies* (1981) by P. Oliver, I. Davis and I. Bentley. This is a mixture of pseudo-psychology and architectural history which leads to some very curious conclusions. While the writing can carry some readers along, the approach cannot be recommended. The whole subject of interwar housing is a rich one to research since many of the housing estates are still in existence.

Local newspapers of the period can provide a useful source of information on the progress of building these estates and the advertising and selling of individual houses. If there were debates in the local council about these developments then they were often recorded in the local newspapers, whereas official local government minutes only recorded the final decisions. Public record offices may have plans of various stages of development and local builders may still have archives from this period. In addition there are a few people still living in the houses that they bought in this period and they may be willing to volunteer information on the running of these houses, or relationships with neighbours, or why particular features were chosen.

The period after World War Two saw the application of clean-sweep planning to slums and the building of high-rise council housing estates. Much has been written about the design failures of high-rise housing estates both in environmental terms and in terms of the technology of the actual buildings. Blowing up such estates has become an accepted 'solution' to such problems, for they are increasingly seen as the slums of today. Less has been written about the success of such high-rise housing as the privately-owned flats of the Barbican, London.

One of the most significant contributions to the debate on the relationship between safety and urban design was Oscar Newman, *Defensible Space, People and Design in the Violent City* (1972). Newman related crime statistics to the design of particular New York public-housing projects (similar to British council housing estates). He claimed that the design of certain spaces promoted crime and he identified three factors which did so: lack of surveillance, anonymity and the presence of alternative escape routes. If people did not know their neighbours, then they could not distinguish between those who had a right to be in a building and those who did not: lifts, halls, corridors were places where anyone could lurk. Newman argued that it was possible to correct some of these defects by design measures, and from case studies carried out by his team he showed how alterations to the design could enable residents to keep an eye on their own environments, and then establish their own and their neighbours' right to be there, but not that of strangers. Newman's work struck a chord of recognition for it seemed to show the importance of territoriality already established in the animal kingdom. Others however felt that to place such importance on design measures meant that socio-economic factors were being under-emphasized.

Alice Coleman, *Utopia on Trial* (1985), which reports the findings of five years' research on design disadvantagement in housing in Britain was inspired by Oscar Newman's work. Alice Coleman's team at the Land Use Research Unit, London, studied the relationship between design and layout on modern problem estates. The research covered over 4,000 blocks containing over 100,000 dwellings. Design features such as number of dwellings per block, number of dwellings per entrance, number of storeys, entrance and circulation characteristics and features of the grounds, were mapped in detail and tested to see which of them were associated with such lapses in civilized behaviour as: litter dropping, graffiti, vandalism, pollution by urine and excrement; and family breakdown leading to children being placed in care. She did not claim that design was the only factor in the promotion or prevention of social breakdown, but that it did have an effect. Her recommendations listed specific design modifications and ended with the suggestion of phasing out the Department of the Environment's Housing Development Directorate and returning housing initiatives to the free market. Not a very encouraging solution for the increasing numbers of people who are unable to participate in the free market for reasons not of their own making, such as unemployment, old age, youth, disablement or any of the other host of reasons that helped to awaken government awareness of the need to provide adequate housing for all in the first place.

Housing is part of the 'man-made' environment and an interesting contribution to the debate is *Making Space. Women and the Man-Made Environment* (1984) by Matrix, who are a group of feminist designers and include teachers, researchers, mothers, a journalist, a housing manager and architects. Their aim is to help architects (usually male) to understand how the environment is dictated by men without reference to women, and to show their understanding as women of their relationship to the built environment.

Post-Modernism

One of the general criticisms of the urban environment whether it be the city centre, industrial estates, or housing estates has been the anonymity of the buildings and their surroundings. The development of Post-Modern architecture is of direct relevance here since one of the aims of certain Post-Modern architects is to reintroduce the qualities of sense of place and ornamentation to architecture. The literature on the subject of Post-Modernism (q.v.) is vast and a considerable proportion of it comes from the pen of Charles Jencks who almost seems to have invented it. The term itself is not particularly helpful since it means after modernism (i.e. after the Modern Movement) and does not differentiate between the many different trends which are occurring in architecture today.

One of these trends is concerned with the reintroduction of ornament in architecture. Modern Movement architecture dispensed with ornament and the Post-Modernists argue that by so doing people became alienated because they could not relate to the language of the Modern Movement. The reintroduction of ornament takes many forms, one of which is the development of 'free-style' classicism. Often the rationale behind the use of particular forms of decoration associated very loosely with classicism relate to local uses of classical forms, so Terry Farrell's (q.v.) Clifton Nurseries (1981) in Covent Garden, London makes reference to Inigo Jones (q.v.), while Ricardo Bofill and the Taller d'Arquitectura's Les Arcades du Lac (1975–81), at Saint Quentin-en-Yvelines near Paris, makes reference to nearby Versailles. The intention behind some of the developments of free-style classicism is the reintroduction of architecture that people can relate to, and local references are used in order to create a sense of place. But the question of how architecture communicates and whether free-style classicism or any other form of Post-Modernism communicates more effectively than Modern Movement architecture, or that of any other period, has not been answered satisfactorily.

Another aspect of Post-Modernism concerns the breaking down of barriers between the professional town planners and architects and their clients, the people who will live in or use their buildings. Ralph Erskine's Byker Wall (1969–80) in Newcastle can be seen as an example of participatory planning. Community architecture is another area of lively debate. Community architecture is certainly not the invention of Post-Modernism although certain writings give that impression and questions concerning the role of the architect, the community and the market-place can only be investigated satisfactorily by means of case studies. Post-Modernism in its many forms is an important part of urban design for it is challenging many of the conventional ideas about the role of architects and town planners, and about the sort of environment we want to create in our cities in the future. Since this is an area in which changes are taking place very rapidly current architectural journals tend to be the best way of keeping in touch with the latest developments. Charles Jencks and William Chaitkin, *Current Architecture* (1982), provides a broad international survey with useful biographies of architects and Charles Jencks, *Modern Movements in Architecture* (1985 edn), has a postscript on the topic.

The ways in which Post-Modern architecture plunders the past needs to be set in the context of attitudes towards history, and the relationship between the economics of house ownership or prestige office building, and styles of architecture.[13] Current attitudes towards preservation and conservation would superficially seem to have little in common with Post-Modernism's use of columns, capitals and pediments, until we start thinking about how much the past is part of our urban environment, particularly in Britain and Europe. If we think about Post-Modernism in the context of the commercialization of that architectural heritage then we should not be surprised that so much of the architecture that goes under the name of Post-Modernism is

architecturally and emotionally rather thin. This however takes us into
the arena of defining what is architecture. Our cities need to grow and
change to provide environments in which we can all live positive and
active lives to the best of our abilities. New forms of architecture and
new forms of environment are part of that process. How this will be
achieved is part of the challenge of urban design.

Notes

1 Steinbeck, J. (1939), *The Grapes of Wrath* (London: Heinemann).
2 Woodbridge, K. (1970), *Landscape and Antiquity: Aspects of English
  Landscape at Stourhead, 1718–1838* (Oxford: Clarendon).
3 Girouard, M. (1978), *Life in the English Country House: a Social and
  Architectural History* (New Haven, Conn.: Yale University Press).
4 Robinson, J. M., 'Model farm buildings of the Age of Improvement',
  Architectural History, 1976, Vol. 19, pp. 17–31.
5 Cheney, E. (1901), *Industrial and Social History of England* (New York:
  Macmillan), p. 221.
6 Howard, E. (1902, reprinted 1963), *Garden Cities of Tomorrow*, first
  published 1898 as *Tomorrow a Peaceful Path to Real Reform*.
7 Ibid., p. 145.
8 Clifton-Taylor, A., *The Pattern of English Building* (1972).
9 Smales, L. M. and Goodey, B. (1985), *The Essex Design Guide for
  Residential Areas*.
10 Le Corbusier, *The City of Tomorrow and its Planning* (1947 edn), p. 110.
11 Le Corbusier, 'Guiding principles of town planning', *Urbanism*, in
   Conrads, U. (1970), *Programmes and Manifestoes in Twentieth Century
   Architecture*.
12 Le Corbusier, *The City of Tomorrow and its Planning*, p. 172.
13 Wright, P. (1985), *On Living in an Old Country: The National Past in
   Contemporary Britain*.

Further Reading

Chapter 1

Brink, A. (ed.) (1981), *The Libraries, Museums and Art Galleries Yearbook 1978–1979* (Cambridge: James Clark)

Carr, E. H. (1961), *What is History?* (London: Macmillan)

Coulson, A. J. (1979), *A Bibliography of Design in Britain, 1851–1970* (London: Design Council)

Honour, H. and Fleming, J. (1977), *The Penguin Dictionary of Decorative Arts* (Harmondsworth: Penguin)

Horne, Donald (1984), *The Great Museum: The Re-presentation of History* (London: Pluto)

Jervis, S. (1984), *The Penguin Dictionary of Design and Designers* (Harmondsworth: Penguin)

Kamen, R. H. (1981), *British and Irish Architectural History: a Bibliography and Guide to Sources of Information* (London: Architectural Press)

Morgan, A. L. (1984), *Contemporary Designers* (London: Macmillan)

Museums Association, *Museums Yearbook* (London: Museums Association)

Wright, P. (1985), *On Living in an Old Country: The National Past in Contemporary Britain* (London: Verso)

Chapter 2

Ashelford, J. (1983), *A Visual History of Costume: The Sixteenth Century* (London: Batsford).

Byrde, P. (1985), *A Visual History of Costume: The Twentieth Century* (London: Batsford).

Cumming, V. (1983), *A Visual History of Costume: The Seventeenth Century* (London: Batsford).

Cunnington, C. W. and P. and Beard, C. (1976), *A Dictionary of English Costume* (London: A. & C. Black).

Foster, V. (1984), *A Visual History of Costume: The Nineteenth Century* (London: Batsford).

Lurie, A. (1981) *The Language of Clothes* (London: Heinemann).

Parry L. (1983), *William Morris Textiles* (London: Weidenfeld & Nicolson).

Parker, R. (1984), *The Subversive Stitch – Embroidery and the Making of the Feminine* (London: Women's Press).

Ribeiro, A. (1984), *Dress in Eighteenth Century Europe, 1715–1789*, (London: Batsford).

Scott, M. (1980), *Late Gothic Europe, 1400–1500* (London: Mills & Boon, History of Dress Series).

Scott, M. (1986), *A Visual History of Costume: The Fourteenth and Fifteenth Centuries* (London: Batsford).

Wilson, E. (1985), *Adorned in Dreams, Fashion and Modernity* (London: Virago).

Chapter 3

Aslin, E. (1969), *The Aesthetic Movement* (London: Elek).

Atterbury, P. and Irvine, L. (1979), *The Doulton Story* (Stoke on Trent: Royal Doulton Tableware).

Beard, G. (1969), *Modern Ceramics* (London: Studio Vista).

Bernard, J. (1972), *Victorian Ceramic Tiles* (London: Studio Vista).

Birks, T. (1976), *The Art of the Modern Potter* (London: Country Life).

Bristow, W. S. (1964), *Victorian China Fairings* (London: A. & C. Black).

Buchanan, R. A. (1972), *Industrial Archaeology in Britain* (Harmondsworth: Allan Lane).

Burchill, F. and Ross, R. (1977), *A History of the Potters' Union* (Stoke-on-Trent: Ceramic and Allied Trades Union).

Burton, A. (1975), *Remains of a Revolution* (London: Deutsch).

Charleston, R. (1968), *World Ceramics* (Feltham: Hamlyn).

Cook, R. M. (1966), *Greek Painted Pottery* (London: Methuen).

Cushion, J. P. and Honey, W. B. (1965), *Handbook of Pottery Marks* (London: Faber).

Donhauser, R. S. (1978), *History of American Ceramics: the Studio Potter* (Dubugue, Iowa: Kendall/Hunt).

Drey, R. E. A. (1978), *Apothecary Jars: Pharmaceutical Pottery and Porcelain in Europe and the East 1150–1850* (London: Faber).

Edwards, R. and Ramsey, L. (1958), *The Early Victorian Period* (London: Connoisseur Period Guide).

Gaunt, W. and Clayton-Stamm, M. (1971), *William de Morgan* (London: Studio Vista).

Giedion, S. (1969), *Mechanization Takes Command* (New York: Norton).

Girouard, M. (1978), *Victorian Pubs* (London: Studio Vista).

Godden, G. A. (1968), *Encyclopaedia of British Pottery and Porcelain Marks* (London: Barrie & Jenkins).

Godden, G. A. (1970), *British Pottery* (London: Barrie & Jenkins).

Godden, G. A. (1970), *Coalport and Coalbrookdale Porcelain* (London: Barrie & Jenkins).

Gray, B. (1953), *Early Chinese Pottery and Porcelain* (London: Faber).

Haggar, R. G. (1960), *Concise Encyclopaedia of Continental Pottery and Porcelain* (London: Deutsch).

Hamilton, D. (1978), *Architectural Ceramics* (London: Thames & Hudson).

Hogben, C. (1978), *The Art of Bernard Leach* (London: Faber).

Hannah, F. (1986), *Ceramics* (London: Bell & Hyman).

Haslam, M. (1975), *English Art Pottery 1865–1915* (Woodbridge: Antique Collectors' Club).

Further Reading

Haslam, M. (1978), *The Martin Brothers, Potters* (London: Richard Dennis).

Hillier, B. (1968), *Pottery and Porcelain 1700–1914* (London: Weidenfeld & Nicolson).

Honey, W. B. (1945), *The Ceramic Art of China and Other Countries of the Far East* (London: Faber).

Honour, H. (1977), *Neo-Classicism* (Harmondsworth: Penguin).

Hudson, K. (1963), *Industrial Archaeology* (London: John Baker).

Jenyns, S. (1951), *Later Chinese Porcelain* (London: Faber).

Jenyns, S. (1971), *Japanese Pottery* (London: Faber).

Jenyns, S. (1973), *Japanese Porcelain* (London: Faber).

Kelly, A. (1965), *Decorative Wedgwood in Architecture and Furniture* (London: Country Life).

Kira, A. (1979), *The Bathroom Book* (Harmondsworth: Penguin).

Lane, A. (1947), *Early Islamic Pottery: Mesopotamia, Egypt and Persia* (London: Faber).

Lane, A. (1949), *French Faience* (London: Faber).

Lane, A. (1954), *Italian Porcelain* (London: Faber).

Lane, A. (1971), *Later Islamic Pottery* (London: Faber).

Lane, P. (1983), *Studio Ceramics* (London: Collins).

Leach, B. (1976), *A Potter's Book*, revised edition (London: Faber).

Lindkvist, L. (1977), *Design in Sweden* (Stockholm: The Swedish Institute).

Lucie-Smith, E. (1981), *The Story of Craft: the Craftsman's Role in Society* (London: Phaidon).

Mankowitz, W. and Haggar, R. G. (1957), *The Concise Encyclopaedia of English Pottery and Porcelain* (London: Deutsch).

Morley-Fletcher, H. (1971), *Meissen* (London: Barrie & Jenkins).

Naylor, G. (1971), *The Arts and Crafts Movement* (London: Studio Vista).

Pugh, P. D. G. (1970), *Staffordshire Portrait Figures and Allied Objects of the Victorian Era* (London: Barrie & Jenkins).

Rackham, B. (1963), *Italian Majolica* (London: Faber).

Rackham, B. (1972), *Medieval English Pottery* (London: Faber).

Rosenthal, E. (1949), *Pottery and Ceramics: From Common Brick to Fine China* (Harmondsworth: Penguin).

Sandon, H. (1975), *Royal Worcester Porcelain from 1862 to the Present Day* (London: Barrie & Jenkins).

Savage, G. and Newman, H. (1974), *Illustrated Dictionary of Ceramics* (London: Thames & Hudson).

Singer, C., Holmyard, E. J. and Hall, A. R. (eds) (1954–1958), *A History of Technology*, Vols 1–5 (Oxford: Clarendon).

Victoria and Albert Museum (1984), *Rococo Art and Design in Hogarth's England* (London: Trefoil).

Watney, B. (1973), *English Blue and White Porcelain of the 18th Century* (London: Faber).

Whiter, L. (1970), *Spode: A History of the Family Factory and Wares* (London: Barrie & Jenkins).

Williams, T. (1978), *A History of Technology*, Vol. 6 (Oxford: Clarendon).

Wright, L. (1960), *Clean and Decent* (London: Routledge & Kegan Paul).

Chapter 4

Agius, P. (1978), *British Furniture 1850–1915* (Woodbridge: Antique Collectors' Club).

Andrews, E. D. and Faith (1966), *Religion in Wood* (Bloomfield, Ind.: Indiana University Press).

Anscombe, I. (1984), *A Woman's Touch. Women in Design from 1860 to the Present Day* (London: Virago).

Aslin, E. (1962), *Nineteenth Century English Furniture* (London: Faber).

Baker, H. (1966), *Furniture in the Ancient World, Origins and Evolution 3100–475 BC* (London: The Connoisseur).

Baroni, D. and Thomas, G. (1978), *Rietveld Furniture* (London: Academy Editions).

Beard, G. and Gilbert, C. (eds) (1986), *Dictionary of English Furniture Makers* (Leeds: Furniture History Society).

Bellaigue G. de, (1974), *The James A. De Rothschild Collection at Waddesdon Manor*, 2 vols (Fribourg: Office du Livre).

Billcliffe, R. (1986), *Charles Rennie Mackintosh – The Complete Furniture Drawings and Interior Design*, (London: Murray).

Billcliffe, R. (1984), *Mackintosh Furniture* (Cambridge: Lutterworth).

Blaser, W. (1982), *Mies van der Rohe Furniture and Interiors* (London: Academy Editions).

Buttrey, D. N. (ed.) (1964), *Plastics in the Furniture Industry* (London: Macdonald).

Callen, A. (1979), *Angel in the Studio: Women in the Arts and Crafts Movement* (London: Astragal).

Cesinsky, H. (1969), *The Gentle Art of Faking Furniture* (London: Chapman & Hall).

Chippendale, T. (1966 reprint), *The Gentleman and Cabinet-Maker's Director* (New York: Dover).

Clarke, R. (1983), *Japanese Antique Furniture* (New York: Weatherhill).

Comino, M. (1980), *Gimson and the Barnsleys* (London: Evans).

Cox, J. C. and Harvey, A. (1973 reprint), *English Church Furniture* (Wakefield: E. P. Publishing).

Dalisi, R. (1976), *Gaudi Furniture* (Milan and New York: Academy Editions).

Ditzel, N. and J. (1954), *Danish Chairs* (Copenhagen: Høst & Søns).

Drexler, A. (1973), *Charles Eames Furniture From the Designer Collection, The Museum of Modern Art, New York* (New York: MOMA).

Duncan, A. (1982), *Art Nouveau Furniture* (London: Thames & Hudson).

Eames, P. (1977), *Medieval Furniture* (London: Furniture History Society).

Ecke, G. (1970 reprint), *Chinese Domestic Furniture* (Rutland, Vermont and Tokyo: Tuttle).

Edwards, R. and Macquoid, P. (1954), *The Dictionary of English Furniture Makers*, 3 vols (London: Country Life).

Edwards, R. (1974), *The Shorter Dictionary of English Furniture* (London: Country Life).

Ellsworth, R. H. (1971), *Chinese Furniture* (New York: Collins).

Emery, M. (1983), *Furniture by Architects* (New York: Abrams).

Fairbanks, J. L. and Bates, E. B (1981), *American Furniture, 1620 to the Present*, (London: Orbis).

Fastnedge, R. (1962), *Sheraton Furniture*, (London: Faber).

Filbee, Marjorie, (1977), *Dictionary of Country Furniture* (London: The Connoisseur).

Fusco, Renato de, (1981), *Le Corbusier, Designer: Furniture, 1929* (London: Architectural Press).

Garner, P. (1980), *Twentieth Century Furniture* (London: Phaidon).

Garner, P. (1980), *The Contemporary Decorative Arts* (London: Phaidon).

Gilbert, C. (1978), *Furniture at Temple Newsam House and Lotherton Hall* (Bradford and London: National Art Collections Fund and Leeds Art Collections Fund).

Gilbert, C. (1978), *The Life and Work of Thomas Chippendale*, 2 vols (London: Studio Vista).

Gloag, J. (1964), *The Englishman's Chair* (London: Allen & Unwin).

Gloag, J. (1969), *A Short Dictionary of Furniture* (London: Allen & Unwin).

Goodison, N. (1974), *Ormolu: the Work of Matthew Boulton* (London: Phaidon).

Goodison, N. (1968), *English Barometers 1680–1860* (Woodbridge: Antique Collectors' Club).

Goodman, W. L. (1964), *The History of Woodworking Tools* (London: Bell).

Grandjean, S. (1966), *Empire Furniture 1800–1813* (London: Faber).

Hanks, D. (1979), *The Decorative Designs of Frank Lloyd Wright* (London: Studio Vista).

Harris, E. (1963), *The Furniture of Robert Adam* (London: Tiranti).

Harris, J. (1961), *Regency Furniture Designs from Contemporary Source Books 1803–1826* (London: Tiranti).

Hayward, H. (ed.) (1965), *World Furniture* (London: Hamlyn).

Hayward, H. (1964), *Thomas Johnson and the English Rococo* (London: Tiranti).

Hayward, H. and Kirkham, P. (1980), *William and John Linnell, Eighteenth Century London Furniture Makers*, 2 vols (London: Studio Vista).

Heal, Sir A. (1953), *The London Furniture Makers From the Restoration to the Victorian Era 1660–1840* (London: Batsford).

Hinckley, F. L. (1960), *Directory of the Historic Cabinet Woods* (New York: Crown).

Hummel, C. F. (1968), *With Hammer in Hand. The Dominy Craftsmen of East Hampton, New York* (Charlottesville: University Press of Virginia).

Huth, H. (1974), *Roentgen Furniture* (London: Sotheby Parke Bernet).

Jervis, S. (1974), *Printed Furniture Designs Before 1650* (Leeds: Maney for The Furniture History Society).

Jervis, S. (1962), *Victorian Furniture* (London: Ward Lock).

Joy, E. T. (1967), *Chairs* (London: Country Life).

Joy, E. T. (1967), *The Country Life Book of Clocks* (London: Country Life).

Joy, E. T. (1977), *Pictorial Dictionary of British 19th Century Furniture Design* (Woodbridge: Antique Collectors' Club).

Joy, E. T. (1977), *English Furniture 1800–1851* (London: Sotheby Parke Bernet).

Kane, P. (1976), *300 Years of American Seating* (Boston: New York Graphical Society).

Kates, G. N. (1962), *Chinese Household Furniture* (New York: Dover).

Leeds City Art Galleries (1972 catalogue), *Town and Country Furniture* (Leeds: City Art Galleries).

Leeds City Art Galleries (1977 catalogue), *Back-Stairs Furniture* (Leeds: Leeds City Art Galleries).

Lever, J. (1982), *Architects' Designs for Furniture* (London: Trefoil).

Liversidge, J. (1955), *Furniture in Roman Britain* (London: Tiranti).

Makinson, R. L. (1979), *Greene & Greene. Furniture and Related Designs* (Salt Lake City, Utah: Peregrine Smith).

Mercer, E. (1969), *Furniture 700–1700* (London: Weidenfeld & Nicolson).

Montgomery, C. (1967), *American Furniture. The Federal Period* (London: Thames & Hudson).

Musgrave, C. (1970), *Regency Furniture* (London: Faber).

Parker, R. (1984), *The Subversive Stitch – Embroidery and the Making of the Feminine* (London: Women's Press).

Parker, R. and Pollock, G. (1981), *Old Mistresses, Women, Art and Ideology* (London: Routledge & Kegan Paul).

Pugin, A. W. N. (1972 reprint), *Gothic Furniture* (London: Gregg International).

Quimby, I. (ed.) (1979), *American Furniture and Its Makers* (Chicago: University of Chicago Press).

Radice, B. (1985), *Memphis* (London: Thames & Hudson).

Randall, G. (1980), *Church Furnishing and Decoration in England and Wales* (London: Batsford).

Russell, F., Garner, P. and Read, J. (1980), *A Century of Chair Design* (London: Academy).

Salaman, R. A. (1975), *Dictionary of Tools Used in the Woodworking and Allied Trades c.1700–1970* (London: Allen & Unwin).

Sheraton, T. (1980 reprint) *The Cabinet-Maker and Upholsterer's Drawing Book* (New York: Praeger).

Sheraton, T. (1980 reprint), *The Cabinet Dictionary* (New York: Praeger).

Sparke, P. (1981), *Ettore Sottsass Jnr* (London: Design Council).

Sparkes, I. (1975), *The Windsor Chair* (Bourne End: Spur).

Symonds, R. W. and Whineray, B. (1962), *Victorian Furniture* (London: Country Life).

Thornton, P. (1978), *Seventeenth-Century Interior Decoration in England, France and Holland* (New Haven, Conn.: Yale University Press).

Toller, J. (1973), *Country Furniture* (Newton Abbott: David & Charles).

Verlet, P. (1963), *French Royal Furniture* (London: Barrie & Rockliff).

Walton, K. (1973), *The Golden Age of English Furniture Upholstery, 1660–1840* (Leeds: Leeds City Art Galleries).

Ward-Jackson, P. (1959), *English Furniture Designs of the Eighteenth Century* (London: HMSO).

Watson, F. J. B. (1960), *Louis XVI Furniture* (London: Tiranti).

Watson, F. J. B. (ed.) (1976), *The History of Furniture* (London: Orbis).

Wilk, C. (1981), *Marcel Breuer, Furniture and Interiors* (London: Architectural Press).

Wright, E. and Pai, M. (1985), *Korean Furniture: Elegance and Tradition* (New York: Kodansha).

Young, D. (1952), *Sitting in Comfort* (London: British Rubber Development Board).

Young, D. (1957), *Upholstery With Latex Foam* (London: British Rubber Development Board).

Chapter 5

Adburgham, A. (1975), *Liberty's: A Biography of a Shop* (London: Allen & Unwin).

Banham, R. (1969), *The Architecture of the Well-Tempered Environment* (London: Architectural Press).

Barley, M. W. (1971), *The House and the Home* (London: Studio Vista).

Barman, C. (1979) *The Man Who Built London Transport* (Newton Abbot: David & Charles).

Beecher, C. E. and Beecher Stowe, H. (1869), *The American Woman's Home* (New York: Thames & Hudson).

Brunskill, R. W. (1981), *The Traditional Buildings of Britain* (London: Gollancz).

Cantacuzino, S. (1975), *New Uses for Old Buildings* (London: Architectural Press).

Collins, P. (1959), *Concrete: The Vision of a New Architecture* (London: Faber).

Eastlake, C. L. (1868, reprinted 1969), *Hints on Household Taste in Furniture, Upholstery and Other Details* (London: Constable).

Encyclopedia of World Art (1951–68) (London and New York: McGraw-Hill).

Fawcett, J. (ed.) (1976), *The Future of the Past: Attitudes to Conservation 1147–1974* (London: Thames & Hudson).

Fischer Fine Art (1982), *The Wiener Werkstätte and their Associates 1902–1932* (London: Fischer Fine Art).

Girouard, M. (1975), *Victorian Pubs* (London: Studio Vista).

Glasstone, V. (1975), *Victorian and Edwardian Theatres* (London: Thames & Hudson).

Greenhill, B. and Giffard, A. (1972), *Travelling by Sea in the Nineteenth Century: Interior Design in Victorian Passenger Ships* (London: A. & C. Black).

Hayden, D. (1981), *The Grand Domestic Revolution: A History of Feminist Designs for American Homes, Neighbourhoods and Cities* (Cambridge, Mass.: MIT Press).

Hayward Gallery (1969), *Frescoes from Florence* (London: Arts Council).

Hope, T. (1807, reprinted 1971), *Household Furniture and Interior Decoration* (London: Constable).

Le Corbusier, (1923) *Vers Une Architecture* (Paris: G. Cres); translated 1927 by Etchells, F. (1974 edn) *Towards a New Architecture* (London: Architectural Press).

Mackintosh, I. and Sell, M. (eds) (1982), *Curtains!!! or New Life for Old Theatres* (Eastbourne: Offord).

Matrix (1984), *Making Space: Women and the Man-made Environment* (London: Pluto).

Pevsner, N. (1951–), *Buildings of England* (Harmondsworth: Penguin).

Pevsner, N. (1976), *A History of Building Types* (London: Thames & Hudson).

Pick, F. 'The meaning and purpose of design', *The Listener*, April, 1933, pp. 640–54. Reprinted in *Documents*, Open University Course Unit A305, 1975 (Milton Keynes: Open University)

Praz, M. (1964), *An Illustrated History of Interior Decoration: from Pompeii to Art Nouveau* (London: Thames & Hudson).

Richards, J. M. (1958), *The Functional Tradition in Early Industrial Buildings* (London: Architectural Press).

Rudofsky, B. (1977), *The Prodigious Builders* (London: Secker & Warburg).

Savage, G. (1966), *A Concise History of Interior Decoration* (London: Thames & Hudson).

Service, A. (1982), *Edwardian Interiors: Inside the Homes of the Poor, the Average and the Wealthy* (London: Barrie & Jenkins).

Sharp, D. (1969), *The Picture Palace and Other Buildings for the Movies* (London: Hugh Evelyn).

Singer, C., Holmyard, E. J., Hall, A. R. and T. I. Williams (eds) (1954–8), *A History of Technology*, 5 vols (Oxford: Clarendon).

Skilleter, P. (1981), *Morris Minor: The World's Supreme Small Car*, (London: Osprey).

Smith, D. L. (1967), *How to Find Out in Architecture and Building* (Oxford: Pergamon).

Tann, J. (1970), *The Development of the Factory* (London: Cornmarket Press).

Thompson, P. (1971), *William Butterfield* (Cambridge, Mass.: MIT Press).

Thornton, P. (1978), *Seventeenth Century Interior Decoration in England, France and Holland* (New Haven, Conn.: Yale University Press).

Thornton, P. K. and Tomlin, M. F. (1980), *The Furnishing and Decoration of Ham House* (London: Furniture History Society).

Victoria and Albert Museum (1971), *Victorian Church Art* (London: HMSO).

Victoria and Albert Museum (1979), *Vienna in the Age of Schubert: The Biedermeier Interior, 1815–1848* (London: Elron Press).

Ward-Jackson, C. H. and Harvey, D. E. (1972), *The English Gypsy Caravan* (Newton Abbot: David & Charles).

Whiton, S. (1974), *Interior Design and Decoration* (Philadelphia: Lippincott).

Williams, T. I. (ed.) (1978), *A History of Technology*, vol. 6 (Oxford: Clarendon).

Wilson, R. F. (1960), *Colour in Industry Today* (London: Allen & Unwin).

Chapter 6

Bayley, S. (1979), *In Good Shape: Style in Industrial Products 1900–1960* (London: Design Council).

Bayley, S. (1983), *Harley Earl and the Dream Machine* (London: Knopf).

Benton, T. and Campbell-Cole, B. (1979), *Tubular Steel Furniture* (London: Art Book Co.).

Further Reading

Blake, J. and A. (1969), *The Practical Idealists* (London: Lund Humphries).

Buddensieg, T. and Rogge, H. (1984), *Industriekultur: Peter Behrens and the AEG 1907–1914*, translated by I. B. Whyte (Cambridge, Mass.: MIT Press).

Bush, D. J. (1975), *The Streamlined Decade* (New York: Braziller).

Campbell, J. (1978), *The German Werkbund* (Princeton, NJ: Princeton University Press).

Carrington, N. (1976), *Industrial Design in Britain* (London: Allen & Unwin).

Dreyfuss, H. (1955), *Designing for People* (New York: Simon & Schuster).

Farr, M. (1955), *Design in British Industry – a Mid-Century Survey* (Cambridge: Cambridge University Press).

Ferebee, A. (1970), *A History of Design from the Victorian Era to the Present* (New York: Van Nostrand Reinhold).

Forty, A. (1985), *Objects of Desire* (London: Thames & Hudson).

Forty, A. and Newman, G. (1975), *British Design* (Milton Keynes: Open University).

Giedion, S. (1948), *Mechanization Takes Command: A Contribution to Anonymous History* (New York: Norton).

Gorb, P. (ed.) (1978), *Living By Design* (London: Lund Humphries).

Haresnape, B. (1968), *Railway Design Since 1830* (London: Allen & Unwin).

Heskett, J. (1986), *Design in Germany 1870–1918* (London: Trefoil).

Heskett, J. (1980), *Industrial Design* (London: Thames & Hudson).

Hill, J. (1978), *The Cat's Whisker: 50 Years of Wireless Design* (London: Oresko).

Jervis, S. (1974), *High Victorian Design* (Ottawa: National Gallery of Canada).

Katz, S. (1978), *Plastics Design and Materials* (London: Studio Vista).

Loewy, R. (1951), *Never Leave Well Enough Alone* (New York: Simon & Schuster).

Lucie-Smith, E. (1983), *A History of Industrial Design* (Oxford: Phaidon).

McCarthy, F. (1979), *A History of British Design* (London: Allen & Unwin).

Meikle, J. (1979), *Twentieth Century Limited: Industrial Design in America 1925–1939* (Philadelphia: Temple University Press).

Naylor, G. (1985), *The Bauhaus Reassessed: Sources and Design Theory* (London: Herbert).

Pentagram Design Partnership (1972), *Pentagram* (London: Lund Humphries).

Pevsner, N. (1960), *Pioneers of Modern Design* (Harmondsworth: Penguin). First published as *Pioneers of the Modern Movement* in 1936.

Pulos, A. (1983), *The American Design Ethic* (Cambridge, Mass.: MIT Press).

Read, H. (1934), *Art and Industry* (London: Faber & Faber).

Rowland, K. (1973), *A History of the Modern Movement* (New York: Van Nostrand Reinhold).

Schaeffer, H. (1970), *The Roots of Modern Design* (London: Studio Vista).

Sparke, P. (1983), *Consultant Design: The History of the Designer in Industry* (London: Pembridge).

Sparke, P. (1982), *Ettore Sotsass Jnr* (London: Design Council).

Sparke, P. (1986), *An Introduction to Design and Culture in the Twentieth Century* (London: Allen & Unwin).

Sudjic, D. (1985), *Cult Objects* (London: Paladin).

Whitford, F. (1984), *Bauhaus* (London: Thames & Hudson).

Wingler, H. M. (1969), *The Bauhaus – Weimar, Dessau, Berlin, Chicago* (Cambridge, Mass.: MIT Press).

Woodham, J. (1983), *The Industrial Designer and the Public* (London: Pembridge).

Chapter 7

Bann, S. (ed.) (1974), *The Tradition of Constructivism* (London: Thames & Hudson).

Barthes, R. (1977), *Image Music Text*, ed. Heath, S. (London: Fontana).

Barthes, R. (1973), *Mythologies* (London: Paladin).

Benton, C. and T., and Sharpe, D. (1975), *Form and Function. A Sourcebook for the History of Architecture and Design 1890–1930* (London: Crosby Lockwood Staples).

Booker, C. (1969), *The Neophiliacs: A Study of the Revolution in English Life in the Fifties and Sixties* (London: Fontana).

Dobrow, L. (1984), *When Advertising Tried Harder* (New York: Friendly Press).

Frostick, M. (1970), *Advertising and the Motor Car* (London: Lund Humphries).

Goffmann, E. (1979), *Gender Advertisements* (London: Macmillan).

Hall S. (1972), *The Social Eye of Picture Post, Working Papers in Cultural Studies*, no. 2 (Birmingham: University of Birmingham), pp. 71–120.

Hawkes, T. (1979), *Structuralism and Semiotics* (London: Methuen).

Hoggart, R. (1957), *The Uses of Literacy* (London: Chatto & Windus).

Ivins, W. Jr (1969), *Prints and Visual Communication* (Cambridge, Mass.: MIT Press).

Klingender, F. (1972), *Art and the Industrial Revolution* (London: Paladin).

Lewis, J. (revised edn 1984), *The Twentieth Century Book* (London: Herbert Press).

Lissitzky-Kuppers, S. (revised edn 1980), *El Lissitzky – Life, Letters, Texts* (London: Thames & Hudson).

Lodder, C. (1983), *Russian Constructivism* (New Haven, Conn.: Yale University Press).

McLuhan, M. (1962), *The Gutenberg Galaxy* (London: Routledge & Kegan Paul).

Meggs, P. (1983), *A History of Graphic Design* (Harmondsworth: Allen Lane).

Müller-Brockmann, J. (1971), *A History of Visual Communications* (London: Tiranti).

Myers, K. (1986), *Understains: The Sense and Seduction of Advertising* (London: Comedia).

Ogilvy, D. (1983), *Ogilvy on Advertising* (London: Pan).

Packard, V. (1957), *The Hidden Persuaders* (London: Longmans Green).

Rand, P. (1986), *A Designer's Art* (New Haven, Conn.: Yale University Press).

Said, E. (1978), *Orientalism: Western Conceptions of the Orient* (London: Routledge & Kegan Paul).

Saussure, F. de (1974), *A Course in General Linguistics* (London: Fontana).

Sibley, B. (1985), *The Book of Guinness Advertising* (London: Guinness Books).

Spencer, H. (revised edn 1984), *Pioneers of Modern Typography* (London: Lund Humphries).

Steinberg, S. H. (reprinted 1979), *Five Hundred Years of Printing* (Harmondsworth: Penguin).

Turner, E. S. (1965), *The Shocking History of Advertising* (Harmondsworth: Penguin).

White, J. (1982), *Magazine Design* (Epping: Bowker).

Williams, R. (1962), *Communications* (Harmondsworth: Penguin).

Williams, R. (1976), *Keywords* (London: Fontana).

Williamson, J. (1978), *Decoding Advertisements* (London: Marion Boyars).

Williamson, J. (1985), *Consuming Passions: The Dynamics of Popular Culture* (London: Marion Boyars).

Chapter 8

Burke, G. (1976), *Townscapes* (Harmondsworth: Penguin).

Civic Trust (1981), *Environmental Directory: National and Regional Organisations of Interest to those concerned with Amenity and the Environment* (London: The Trust).

Clifton-Taylor, A. (1972), *The Pattern of English Building* (London: Faber).

Coleman, Alice (1985), *Utopia on Trial: Vision and Reality in Planned Housing* (London: Hilary Shipman).

Conrads, U. (1970), *Programmes and Manifestoes in Twentieth Century Architecture* (London: Lund Humphries).

Cullen, G. (1961), *Townscape* (London: Architectural Press).

Curtis, W. (1982), *Modern Architecture since 1900* (Oxford: Phaidon).

Department of Education and Science (1981), *Environmental Education* (London: HMSO).

Fairbrother, N. (1972), *New Lives, New Landscapes* (Harmondsworth: Penguin).

Glen, M. H. (ed.) (1976), *Town Trails and Urban Walks*, 2nd edn (London: British Tourist Authority).

Goodey, B. (ed.) (1981), *East Anglia's Built Environment as an Educational Resource* (London: RIBA).

Halliday, J. (ed.) (1973), *City Centre Redevelopment: A Study of British City Centre Planning and Case Studies of Five English City Centres* (London: Charles Knight).

Hoskins, W. G. (1977 edn), *The Making of the English Landscape* (London: Hodder & Stoughton).

Howard, E. (1963 edn), *Garden Cities of Tomorrow* (London: Faber).

Hussey, C. (1967 edn), *The Picturesque: Studies in a Point of View* (London: Cass).

Jackson, Alan (1973), *Semi-detached London: Suburban Life and Transport 1900–1939* (London: Allen & Unwin).

Jacobs, Jane (1965 edn), *The Death and Life of Great American Cities* (London: Penguin).

Jencks, C. (1985 edn), *Modern Movements in Architecture* (London: Penguin).
Jencks, C. and Chaitkin, W. (1982), *Current Architecture* (London: Academy Editions).
Krier, R. (1979), *Urban Space* (London: Academy Editions).
Le Corbusier, (1947 edn), *The City of Tomorrow and its Planning* (London: Architectural Press).
Le Corbusier (1964), *The Radiant City* (London: Faber), first published in 1933, as *La Ville Radieuse*.
Lowenthal, D. (1985), *The Past is a Foreign Country* (Cambridge: Cambridge University Press).
Matrix (1984), *Making Space, Women and the Man-made Environment* (London: Pluto).
Newman, Oscar (1973), *Defensible Space, People and Design in the Violent City* (London: Architectural Press).
Oliver, P., Davis, I. and Bentley, I. (1981), *Dunroamin. The Suburban Semi and its Enemies* (London: Barrie & Jenkins).
Open University (1973), *Planning and the City*, DT 201 Block 7: Unit 27, *The Optimum Size*; Unit 28, *Urban Renewal*; Unit 29, *Planning Residential Areas* (Milton Keynes: Open University).
Ravetz, Alison (1980), *Remaking Cities: Contradictions of the Recent Urban Environment* (London: Croom Helm).
Smales, L. M. and Goodey, B. (1985), *The Essex Design Guide for Residential Areas*, Bibliography A1426 (Monticello, Ill.: Vance).
Swenarton, Mark (1981), *Homes for Heroes: The Politics and Architecture of Early State Housing in Britain* (London: Heinemann).
Watkin, D. (1982), *The English Vision, The Picturesque in Architecture, Landscape and Garden Design* (London: Murray).
Wright, P. (1985), *On Living in an Old Country: The National Past in Contemporary Britain* (London: Verso).

Useful Names and Addresses

Britain

Advertising Association, 15 Wilton Road, London SW1V 1NJ.
Library and information centre.

Arkwright Society, c/o Tawney House, Matlock, Derbyshire.
Presentation of Arkwright's buildings in Cromford and the preservation of buildings and machinery of industrial archeological and historic interest.

Arts Council of Great Britain, 105 Piccadilly, London W1V 0AU.

Scottish Arts Council, 19 Charlotte Square, Edinburgh EH2 4DF.

Welsh Arts Council, 9 Museum Place, Cardiff CF1 3NX.
Will supply information about forthcoming exhibitions.

Association of Art Historians, 18 Fitzwarren Gardens, London N1G 3TP
Publishes a bulletin and quarterly journal and organizes an annual conference, held outside London in alternate years.

Association of Illustrators, 1 Colville Place, London W1P 1HN.
Gallery, newsletter and advice to illustrators.

Association of Industrial Archaeology, Ironbridge Gorge Museum, Telford, Salop TF8 7AW.
To promote the study of industrial archaeology and improve and encourage standards of recording, research and conservation.

Association for the Protection of Rural Scotland, 20 Falkland Avenue, Newton Mears, Renfrewshire G77 5DR.
Similar aims to those of The Council for the Protection of Rural England.

British Numismatic Society, 63 West Way, Edgware, Middlesex HA8 9LA.
Monthly meetings held at which papers are presented on new discoveries and the results of recent research. Covers British coinage and that of territories formerly subject to the British Crown.

British Theatre Association, 9 Fitzroy Square, London W1P 6AE.
Mainly concerned to develop the art of theatre, but the library also has documentation on theatre buildings and interiors.

Brunel Society, Mrs M. Williams, Hon. Secretary, Brunel Technical College, Ashley Down, Bristol BS7 9BU.
Formed to promote research into and study the lives of I. K. and Sir M. I. Brunel. Lecture programmes, visits, newsletter published occasionally.

Business Archives Council, 185 Tower Bridge Road, London SE1 2UF.
Encourages the preservation and efficient organization of business records. Maintains a library of business histories and has regional branches. *Business Archives* is published annually.

Charles Rennie Mackintosh Society, Patricia Douglas, Director, Queens Cross, 870 Garscube Road, Glasgow G20 7EL.
Conserves Mackintosh's buildings and artefacts and promotes interest in him via visits, lectures and study tours.

Chartered Society of Designers, 29 Bedford Square, London WC1 3EG
Formerly, Society of Industrial Artists and Designers. Professional organization for practising designers in all areas of design.

Cinema Theatre Association, 123b Central Road, Worcester Park, Surrey KT4 8DA.
Voluntary association to promote studies in history, architecture and equipment associated with film. Publishes a bulletin six times a year and maintains an archive. Organizes visits and occasional lectures.

Civic Trust, 17 Carlton House Terrace, London SW1 5AW.
Encourages the protection and improvement of the environment by means of films, conferences, reports and projects. Provides information on local amenity societies nationally.

Civic Trust for the North West, 65 Oxford Street, Manchester M27 2UX.

Civic Trust for the North East, 34–5 Saddler Street, Durham DH1 3HL.

Scottish Civic Trust, 24 George Square, Glasgow, G2 1EF.

Civic Trust Wales, Welcome House, Llandaff, Cardiff CF5 2YZ.

Commemorative Collectors Society, 25 Farndale Close, off Wilsthorpe Road, Long Eaton, Notts NG10 3PA.
Represents the interests of commemorative collectors internationally, arranges meetings and exhibitions and publishes a quarterly journal.

Costume Society, 63 Salisbury Road, Liverpool.
Promotes interest and research in costume.

Council for the Protection of Rural England, 4 Hobart Place, London SW1W 0HY.
To improve, preserve and protect the countryside and its amenities.

Council for the Protection of Rural Wales, 14 Broad Street, Welshpool, Powys SY21 7SD.

Crafts Council, 8 Waterloo Place, London SW1Y 4AT.
Set up to promote the work of craftspersons in Britain. Maintains an index of individuals active in a variety of crafts. Has a large slide collection and organizes exhibitions.

Decorative Arts Society, c/o The Keeper of Decorative Arts, The Royal Pavilion Art Gallery and Museums, Brighton BN1 1UE
Promotes research and general interest in the decorative arts of the period 1850 to the present, by means of lectures, visits and its annual journal. The quarterly newsletter also lists forthcoming sales of decorative arts at the major auction houses.

Design Council, 28 Haymarket, London SW1Y 4SU.
Promotes the improvement of British design via awards, publications and exhibitions. Slide library makes slides available for loan and there is a range of slide packs for sale.

Design History Society, 22 Hickman Close, Fulmer Road, London E16 3TA.
Formed to promote research and provide a forum for the interchange of ideas on design history. Conferences, study days and visits are organized regularly and details are carried in the quarterly newsletter. Annual Conference papers have been published by the Design Council.

Design and Industries Association, c/o 17 Lawn Crescent, Kew Gardens, Surrey TW9 3NR.
Voluntary independent pressure group with a number of regional groups set up to improve design standards. Publishes a yearbook and newsletters; study tours, conferences.
Design Research Society, 24 Kensington Gore, London, SW7 2EX.
Promotes contact between people concerned with research into design, its nature, products and role in society. Organizes meetings, international conferences and publishes a quarterly journal *Design Studies*.
Designers and Art Directors Association, 12 Carlton House Terrace, London SW1Y 5AH.
Annual exhibition and publications.
Ephemera Society, 12 Fitzroy Square, London W1P 5HQ.
Provides a forum for interchange of ideas.
Friends of Fashion, Museum of London, The Costume Department, London Wall, London EC2Y 5HN.
Focuses on studies in that collection, but also concerned with the broader implications of the subject.
Furniture History Society, c/o Department of Furniture and Interior Design, Victoria and Albert Museum, London SW7 2RL.
Founded to increase the knowledge of furniture and to promote its preservation and its records. *Furniture History* is published annually and the society arranges visits, courses and an annual conference.
Garden History Society, 12 Charlbury Road, Oxford OX2 6UT.
To bring together those who are interested in all aspects of the subject: horticulture, forestry, landscape design.
Georgian Group, 2 Chester Street, London SW1X 7BB.
Mainly concerned with the preservation and conservation of eighteenth-century and early-nineteenth-century buildings. Visits organized in the summer.
Glass Association, Broadfield House Glass Museum, Barrett Lane, Kingswinford, West Midlands DY6 9QA.
Promotes understanding of historical and contemporary glass and glassmaking methods. *The Glass Cone* is published quarterly and a scholarly journal every two years.
Historic Churches Preservation Trust, Fulham Palace Road, London SW6 6EA.
Information and register of churches of historic interest.
Historic House Association, 38 Ebury Street, London SW1W 0LU.
Information on houses in private ownership which are open to the public.
History of Advertising Trust, Unit 2.02, Butlers Wharf Business Centre, 45 Curlew Street, London SE1 2UD.
Holds archives of the Advertising Association, the Advertising Standards Authority and a number of companies. Charges for access to archives.
National Art Library, Victoria and Albert Museum, South Kensington, SW7 2RL.
Large collection of design source books.

National Association of Decorative and Fine Arts Societies, 38 Ebury Street, London SW1W 0LU.
Promotes interest in the decorative arts nationally through lectures and visits.
National Association for Design Education, 'Kirby Hill', Plawsworth, Chester-le-Street, Co. Durham DH2 3LD.
An interdisciplinary group with members from across the whole breadth of design activities found in the school curriculum.
National Monuments Record, Fortress House, 25 Saville Row, London W1X 1AB.
National Society for Education in Art and Design, 7a High Street, Corsham, Wilts, SN13 0ES.
Concerned with art and design within the school curriculum.
National Trust, 42 Queen Anne's Gate, London SW1H 9AS.
National Trust for Scotland, 5 Charlotte Square, Edinburgh EH2 4DU.
Details obtainable at all National Trust properties.
Newcomen Society, Executive Secretary, Science Museum, London SW7 2DD.
To promote study of the history of engineering and technology.
Piers Information Bureau, 38 Holte Road, Atherstone, Warwicks CV9 1HN.
To promote contact among those active in this field. Concentrates on the nineteenth century. Bulletin published quarterly.
Planning History Group, Department of Civil Engineering, University of Salford, Salford M5 4WT.
Main emphasis on late-nineteenth- and twentieth-century planning internationally. *Planning History Bulletin* published three times a year; conferences and seminars. Publishes *Planning Perspectives*.
Plastics Historical Society, 11 Hobart Place, London SW1W 0HL.
To promote the study of all aspects of plastics history. Bulletin published two or three times a year gives details of meetings. Open free to individuals and groups.
Railway and Canal Historical Society, 20 Neston Drive, Chester CH2 2HR.
To investigate and record details. Local groups organize lectures, visits and tours.
Railway Heritage Trust, Melley House, 65 Clarendon Road, Watford WD1 1DP.
Assists in negotiations over British Rail property and administers grants for buildings in the listed category. Independent of British Rail and the Government.
Royal Academy of Arts, Piccadilly, London W1V 0DS.
To help practising artists and art historians with their inquiries.
Royal Society of Arts, 8 John Adam Street, London WC2N 6EZ.
To promote the advancement of science in connection with the arts and to act as a liaison between the practical arts and the sciences.
Royal Institute for British Architects, 66 Portland Place, London W1N 4AD.
The Institute includes a library with an excellent catalogue of books and articles on architecture and design. The RIBA drawings collection is housed at Portman Square.
Save Britain's Heritage, 3 Park Square West, London NW1 4LJ.
Conservation pressure group to awaken concern about the destruction of historic buildings.

Scottish Tramway Museum Society, PO Box 78, Glasgow G3 6ER.
Formed to preserve selected tramcars and publish historical information on tramway fleets. Details of monthly meetings, slide and film nights, and visits are published in the Newsletter and *Scottish Transport*, which is produced regularly, is free to members.

Society of Architectural Historians of Great Britain, Room 208, Chesham House, 30 Warwick Street, London W1R 6AB.
Maintains a register of research, organizes an annual conference, study tours and an annual public lecture. *Architectural History* is published annually.

Society of Designer Craftmen, 24 Rivington Street, London EC2A 3DU.
Formerly the Arts and Crafts Exhibition Society, it represents the interests of people working in the crafts in Britain. Details of conferences, exhibitions and lectures published in the quarterly newsletter.

Society of Industrial Artists and Designers
See Chartered Society of Designers.

Society of Typographic Designers, Dunstable College, Kingsway, Dunstable, Beds LU6 4HG.
Professional organization to safeguard and help those working in this field.

Terracotta Association, Drayton House, 30 Gordon Square, London WC1H 0AU.
Information and advice on restoring terracotta- and faience-clad buildings.

Textile Society, David Graysmith, Related Studies Department, Wolverhampton Polytechnic, Wolverhampton WV1 1DT.
Promotes research in the history and conservation of textiles.

Thirties Society, 3 Park Square West, London NW1 4LJ.
Founded as a pressure group to draw attention to the qualities of 1920s and 1930s buildings and interiors and to preserve and conserve them.

Tools and Trades History Society, Winston Grange, Stowmarket, Suffolk.
To increase interest in pre-industrial tools and technology and to foster pride in craftmanship. Meetings, exhibitions, newsletter and journal.

Twentieth Century Ceramics Society, 100d Clapham Common Northside, London SW4 9SQ.
Formed to bring together historians, collectors, potters, dealers and auctioneers. Organizes meetings, visits and private views and publishes a newsletter.

Victorian Society, 1 Priory Gardens, Bedford Park, London W4 1TT.
Concerned with the preservation and conservation of nineteenth- and early-twentieth-century buildings, and the effects of planning legislation and proposed planning on towns and cities. Groups in many parts of the country which organize visits and lectures on all aspects of Victorian architecture, art and design.

Vernacular Architecture Group, 18 Portland Place, Leamington Spa, Warwicks CV32 5EU.
To promote study of lesser traditional buildings.

Wallpaper History Society, Victoria and Albert Museum, London SW7 2RL.
To encourage research, provide information on wallpaper production, consumption and design and foster awareness of the importance of preserving period decorations. Newsletter, visits, tours of design studios and manufacturers archives.

World Ship Society, 35 Wickham Way, Haywards Heath, Sussex RH16 1UJ.
Encourages research and organizes nautical activities in most of the major
cities. Details are published in *Marine News* published monthly.

AUSTRALIA
Industrial Design Council of Australia, 114 William Street, Melbourne, Victoria
3000.
New South Wales Design Centre, 50 Margaret Street, Sydney 2000.
Queensland Design Centre, Central Railway Plaza, 315 Edward Street,
Brisbane 4000.
Victoria Design Centre, 37 Little Collins Street, Melbourne 3000.

AUSTRIA
Bund Österreichischer Gebrauchsgraphiker, Hollgasse 6, 1050 Wien.
Professional association for graphic designers.
Bund Österreichischer Innenarchitekten, Penzingerstrasse 23, A 1140 Wien 14.
Professional organization for interior designers.
Osterreichisches Institut für Formgebung, Salesianergasse 1, A 1030 Wien.
Association for companies involved in industrial design.

BELGIUM
Design Centre, 51 Galerie Ravenstein, 1000 Brussels.
Project Industrieel Erfgoed, c/o Begijnhof 39, B 3800, Sint Truiden.
Centre for the study and conservation of the industrial heritage.
Union des Designers de Belgique, Hall du Palais des Beaux Arts, 61 Ravenstein,
1000 Brussels.
Professional organization for graphic and interior designers.
Union Professionnelle des Industrial Designers de Belgique, 2 rue de la
Régence, 1000 Brussels.
Vlaamse Vereniging voor Industriële Archeologie, PO Box 30, Maria Hendrika-
plein, B 9000 Ghent 12.
Flemish association for industrial archeology.

BULGARIA
Central Institute of Industrial Design, 34 Totleben, Sofia.

CANADA
Association of Canadian Industrial Designers, c/o School of Industrial Design,
Carleton University, Ottawa K1S 5B6.
National Design Council, Department of Industry, Trade and Commerce, 300
Sparks Street, Ottawa, Ontario, K1A OH5.

CZECHOSLOVAKIA
Biennale Brno, Moravaska Galerie, Husova 14 CS6626, Brno 2.
Poster archive of Brno Biennale competitions.

DENMARK
Dansk Designrad, Nyhavn 39, DK 1051, Copenhagen.
Danish Design Council.

Useful Names and Addresses

Dansk Kunsthåndvaerker Råd, Ameliegade 15, DK 1256, Copenhagen.
Council for Arts and Crafts.

FINLAND
Oy Finnish Design Centre AB, Kasarmikatu 19, SF 00130 Helsinki 13.
Suomen Taideteollisuusyhdistys, Unioninkatu 30, SF 00100 Helsinki 10.
Finnish society of crafts and design.

FRANCE
Bibliothèque Forney, Hôtel des Achevêques de Sens, 1 Rue du Figuier, Paris
75004.
Design, visual communication. Books, periodicals, photographs and slides.
Bibliothèque du Musée des Arts Decoratifs, 107 Rue de Rivoli, Paris 75001.
Graphic arts and product design.
Centre de Création Industrielle, Centre Georges Pompidou, Paris 75191.
Documentation and resources covering design, architecture and town
planning; exhibitions, conferences.
Centre de Récherche sur la Culture Technique, 69 bis rue Charles Laffitte,
92200 Neuilly.
Conferences, exhibitions. Publishes *Technique et Culture*.

GERMAN DEMOCRATIC REPUBLIC
Amt für Industriel Formgestaltung, Breitestrasse 11, 102 Berlin.
Promotional organization. Publishes *Form und Zweck*.

GERMAN FEDERAL REPUBLIC
Bauhaus Archiv, Museum für Gestaltung, Klingelhöferstrasse 13–14, D 1000
Berlin 30.
Books and documents on the Bauhaus and on art, architecture and design
since 1850.
Deutscher Werkbund, Alexandra Weg 26, Ernst Ludwig Haus, 61 Darmstadt.
Publishes *Werk und Zeit*.
Die Neue Sammlung Staatliches Museum für Angewandte Kunst, Prinzregent-
strasse-3, 8 Munich 22.
Collection of posters.
Internationales Design Zentrum, Ansbacherstrasse 8–14, D 1000, Berlin 30.
Visual communication and product design.
Rat fuï Formgebung, Eugen-Bracht Weg 6, 61 Darmstadt.
Gives quality awards for design; publishes *Design Report*.
Werkbund-Archiv, Schlossstrasse 1, 1 Berlin 19.
Documentation of the Werkbund and on the history of design and mass
culture.

HONG KONG
Industrial Design Council, Eldex Industry Building 12/F, 21A Ma Tau Wei
Road, Hung Hom, Hong Kong.

HUNGARY
Hungarian Council of Industrial Design, Martinelli Ter 8, 1052 Budapest.

INDIA
Industrial Design Centre, Indian Institute of Technology, Powai, Bombay 400 076.
National Institute of Design, Paldi, Ahmedabad 380 007.

IRELAND
Crafts Council of Ireland Ltd, Thomas Prior House, Merrion Road, Balls-bridge, Dublin 4.
Kilkenny Design Workshops Ltd, Kilkenny.
Government agency for promoting design.

ISRAEL
Israel Design Centre, 51 Petach-Tikvah Road, Tel-Aviv.

ITALY
Archeologia Industriale, Via Rossellini 8, 20100 Milan.
Association for industrial archeology.
Associazione per il Disegno Industriale, Via Montenapoleone 18, 20121 Milan.
Professional organization for industrial designers.

JAPAN
The CoCoMAS Committee, 5–5–6 Bancho, Chiyoda-Ku, Tokyo 102.
Visual communication and corporate identity.
Japan Craft Design Association, 21–13 Sendagaya 1–Chome, Shibuya-ku, Tokyo 151.
Japan Industrial Designers Association, PO Box 198, Trade Centre 105.
Osaka Design Centre, Senba Centre Building, 2–2 Senba-Chuo, Higashi-Ku, Osaka.

MEXICO
Design Centre, Rio Churubusco 353, Mexico 13.

NETHERLANDS
Beroepsvereniging van Nederlandse Interierarchitekten, Keizergracht 321, Postbus 19610, 1000 G P Amsterdam.
Interior designers' organization.
Gafisch Vormgevers Nederland, Nieuwe Keizergracht 58, 1018 DT Amsterdam.
Graphic designers' organization.
Kring Industrielle Ontwerpers, Keizergracht 321, Amsterdam.
Industrial designers' organization.

NEW ZEALAND
New Zealand Industrial Design Council, 70 Ghuznee Street, Wellington.

NORWAY
Norsk Design Centrum, Drammensveien 40, Oslo 2.
Norwegian Council of Industrial Design, Uranienborg un 2, Oslo 2.

PAKISTAN
Pakistan Council of Industrial Design, 52 G 2 Pechs, Karachi 29.

POLAND
Central Office of Design for Light Industries, ul Swietojerska 5/7, 00 236 Warsaw.

RUMANIA
Centrul Romän de Design, 169 Calea Floreasca, S 2 Bucharest 7000.
Rumanian Design Centre.

SPAIN
Asociación de Diseñadores Profesionales, Apartado de Correo 12174, Barcelona.
Professional association for designers.
Instituto Promoción Industrial, Poeta Queral 15, Valencia 2.
Covers design, architecture and town planning. Publishes *Diseño Comunicación*.

SWEDEN
Ekoteket, Tjärhovsgatan 44, S 11629 Stockholm.
Centre of environmental movement in Sweden.
Föreningen Svensk Form, PO Box 7404, S 103 91 Stockholm.
Swedish society of industrial design; publishes *Form* monthly.

SWITZERLAND
Arbeitsgemeinschaft Schweizer Grafiker, Chorgasse 18, 8001 Zürich.
Association of graphic designers.
Verband Schweizer Industrial Designers, Weinbergstrasse 11, 8001 Zürich.
Association of industrial designers.

UNITED STATES
American Institute of Graphic Arts, 1059 3rd Ave, New York, NY 10021.
American Society of Interior Designers, 730 Fifth Avenue, New York, NY 10019.
Boston Museum of Fine Arts, 479 Huntington Avenue, Boston, Mass. 02115.
Original art and correspondence on or about Hermann Zapf, Jan Tschichold and others.
Busch-Reisinger Museum, 29 Kirkland Street, Cambridge, Mass. 02138.
Bauhaus archive.
Center for Design, 227 Forest Avenue, Palo Alto, Calif. 94301.
Aims to promote public awareness of design and supports design projects such as design for the disabled.
Chicago Historical Society, Clark Street at North Avenue, Chicago, Ill. 60614.
Exhibits and archives related to design and architecture in Chicago.
Cooper-Hewitt Museum, 2 East 91 Street, New York, NY 10028.
The design branch of the Smithsonian Institute. Donald Deskey Archives, Henry Dreyfus Archives, Ladislav Sutnar Archives.
Cooper Union Art School, Cooper Square, New York, NY 10003.

Slide archives of posters by members of the Alliance Graphique Internationale.

Cranbrook Academy of Design, Box 801, Bloomfield Hills, Md 48013.
Library of books relating to graphic design and designers.

Design History Forum, c/o Professor Herbert Gottfried, College of Design, Iowa State University, Ames, Iowa 50011.
An association of people, mostly academics, interested in design history.

Design Management Institute, 621 Huntington Avenue, Boston, Mass. 02115.

Institute for Environmental Action, 81 Leonard Street, New York, NY 10013.

ITC Center, 2 Hammarskjøld Plaza, Third Floor, New York, NY 10017.
Graphic design exhibitions.

Rosenbach Museum and Library, 2010 Delancey Place, Philadelphia, Pa 19103.
Maurice Sendak drawings and related ephemera. The library has a collection of drawings by eighteenth- and nineteenth-century illustrators.

Society of Typographic Arts, 233 East Ontario Street, Suite 201, Chicago, Ill. 60611.

University of Illinois at Chicago, Manuscript Collection, Box 4348, Chicago, Ill. 60680.
Archive on the Institute of Design and Moholy-Nagy.

University of Texas, Humanities Research Center, PO Box 7219, Austin, Tex. 78712.
The Harry Ransom Center, Archives of Norman Bel Geddes.

Upper and Lower case International Typeface Corp., 2 Hammarskjøld Plaza, New York, NY 10017.
An archive of correspondence and interviews with graphic designers including Saul Bass, Bill Goldin, Herb Lubalin and Paul Rand.

USSR

Vsesojuzny Naučno Isledovatelski Institut Techničeskoj Estetiki, VNIITE, Moscow 129223.
Research Institute of industrial design with affiliated branches in other cities.

YUGOSLAVIA

Dizajn Centar, Zmaj Jovina 13, Belgrade.
Yugoslav Design Centre.

Glossary

AALTO, Alvar (1898–1976)
Finnish architect and designer. In design Aalto made major contributions to the development of plywood furniture.

ADAM, Robert (1728–92)
Architect, interior and furniture designer. Among his most famous interiors are Syon House, 1760–9, and Osterley Park, 1761–80, both near London.

Aesthetic Movement
A movement focused mainly on London and Oxford c.1860–80, which offered an alternative lifestyle summed up in the phrase 'Art for Art's sake'. Aesthetic forms were drawn from the medieval and from Japan.

Apse
A semicircular or polygonal projection found in basilican buildings and in the east ends of churches.

Art Deco
A term coined from the Paris Exposition des Arts Décoratifs held in 1925, it embraced architecture and design. The stylistic influences on Art Deco ranged from Expressionism to Egyptian and the Modern Movement.

Art Nouveau
Decorative style often associated with whiplash curves and plant forms, popular throughout Europe between c.1890 and 1910. Known as Jugendstil (literally 'youth style') in Germany, and in Italy as Stile Liberty after the Regent Street store in London.

Arts and Crafts Movement
Largely influenced by the ideas and ideals of Ruskin and Morris the movement sought to revitalize the arts of architecture and design. It was influential not only in Britain, but also in the USA and in Europe.

BAILLIE SCOTT, M. H. (1865–1945)
Architect and designer closely associated with the Arts and Crafts Movement, who worked in England, Russia, the USA and Europe.

Baroque
Originated in Italy and spread in seventeenth century to Europe generally. It embraced architecture and design.

BARNSLEY, Edward (1865–1926) see GIMSON, Ernest.

BARNSLEY, Sidney (1863–1926), see GIMSON, Ernest.

Basilica
A Roman public building with double colonnades inside and an apse at one end.

Bauhaus (1919–33)
School of art, architecture and design set up in Weimar by Walter Gropius. Later moved to Dessau, then Berlin where it was closed down by the Nazis. Of enormous importance to the development of avant-garde movements not only because of the work undertaken by Bauhaus

members, but also because of the way its ideas and activities were publicized.

BAYER, Herbert (1900–)
Born in Austria, Bayer developed his typography at the Bauhaus and emigrated to the USA in 1938. His work covers architecture, interior, product and graphic design.

Black Basaltes
Fine hard-grained black stoneware perfected by Wedgwood and used for vases, busts and other wares.

BOFILL, Ricardo (1939–)
Spanish architect, founded Taller de Arquitectura in Barcelona, in 1960. Completed buildings include Le Téâtre and Palace of Abraxes, Marne-la-Vallée, and Les Arcades du Lac, Saint Quentin-en-Yvelines, near Paris. These exploit the language of classical architecture very freely.

BREUER, Marcel (1902–81)
Student and teacher at the Bauhaus where he designed a series of chairs reflecting the various phases of development at the school. These included chairs of tubular steel. Practised as an architect and designer in England and the USA.

BROWN, Lancelot (1716–83)
Nicknamed 'Capability'. Architect and landscape gardener who worked with the natural materials of trees, water and grass, rather than with architectural elements, to produce his landscapes.

BRUNEL, Isambard Kingdom (1806–59)
Trained as an engineer and designed bridges, iron ships and the Great Western Railway from Paddington Station, in London, to Bristol.

BUTTERFIELD, William (1814–1900)
Architect of great importance to the Gothic Revival. Mainly involved with ecclesiastical buildings, schools and colleges.

CIAM
Congrès Internationaux d'Architecture Moderne set up in 1928 aimed at a revolution in housing and town planning. Drew up its findings in the *Athens Charter* (1933). These were published by Le Corbusier in *The Radiant City* (1933).

CHIPPENDALE, Thomas (1718–79)
One of the best-known English furniture names and author of *The Gentleman and Cabinet Maker's Director*, first published in 1754.

Classicism
The principles of Greek and Roman architecture and design.

COLE, Henry (1808–82)
Founder of Summerly's Art Manufacturers in 1847, and of the *Journal of Design*. Closely involved in the 1851 Great Exhibition and an influential critic of design through his work and writings.

COLOMBO, Joe (1930–71)
Italian architect, designer and artist, his innovative furniture and interiors of the 1960s received wide acclaim.

CONRAN, Sir Terence (1931–)
Designer and entrepreneur who has aimed to improve design in Britain

through retailing in the Habitat shops and by sponsoring, through the Conran Foundation, the Boilerhouse Project.

Constructivism
A movement embracing architecture and all the arts in the Soviet Union in the period following the 1917 revolution. It sought to redefine the relationship between society, architecture, art and design.

Crystal Palace, See Paxton, Joseph.

DAY, Lewis F. (1845–1910)
English designer involved in a wide range of design for industry and also associated with the Arts and Crafts Movement.

DAY, Robin (1915–)
Furniture and interior designer one of whose best-known contributions was the development of the polypropylene chair, available in a wide variety of forms for indoor and outdoor use.

Decorative Arts
An umbrella term which can include design in ceramic, silver, glass as well as furniture or jewellery. Generally associated with small scale objects.

De Stijl
Title of a magazine and a movement initiated by Theo van Doesburg in Holland in 1917. The red/blue chair (1917) and the Schröder House (1924) designed by Gerrit Reitveld are among the best-known examples of de Stijl principles translated into three dimensions.

Design and Industries Association
Organization set up in 1915 to promote awareness of design among British manufacturers. Inspired by the work of the Deutsche Werkbund.

DIOR, Christian (1905–57)
French fashion designer who introduced the New Look in 1947.

DRESSER, Christopher (1834–1904)
Writer and designer of glass, ceramics, wallpaper, textiles, furniture and metal work. His metalwork designs for Hukon and Heath, Elkington and others in the 1870s and 1880s were based on clear geometric forms.

EAMES, Charles and Ray
American architects, designers and experimental film-makers whose plywood furniture and designs of the 1950s and 1960s were accorded international acclaim. Ray and Charles married in 1941 and work attributed solely to Charles was often the result of their partnership.

Etruscan Ware
Etruscan pottery dates from *c*.700 BC to *c*.100 BC. Eighteenth-century Etruscan ware featured classical motifs and colour schemes mainly of black, terracotta and white which were derived from Greek pottery vases, assumed at that date to be Etruscan.

Expressionism
A movement involving literature and many of the arts. In architecture and design expressionism occurred predominantly in Germany and Holland *c*.1911–23. It had spiritual, Utopian, aesthetic and socialist implications.

FARRELL, Terry (1938–)
Early work 1965–80 in partnership with Nicholas T. Grimshaw. Since 1980 Farrell has contributed to Post-Modernism in Britain with such buildings as

the Clifton Nurseries, Covent Garden, and TV AM Building at Camden Lock with its finials of eggs in eggcups.

Functionalism

A philosophy of design with roots in Greek philosophy [see E. R. de Zurco (1957), *Origins of Functionalist Theory* (New York: Columbia U.P.)]. Often associated today with the Modern Movement and the Machine Aesthetic.

GALLÉ, Emile (1846–1904)

French glassmaker, founder of the Nancy School and a leading exponent of Art Nouveau.

Garden City

See HOWARD, Ebenezer

GIMSON, Ernest (1864–1919)

Trained as an architect but became best known for his furniture design. In 1895 he set up a workshop in the Cotswolds with Edward and Sidney Barnsley.

GLASER, Milton, (1929–)

American graphic designer, founder of Push Pin Studios (1954), much influenced by Picasso in the development of graphic images.

GRAY, Eileen (1878–1976)

Irish architect and furniture designer who worked in Paris. Her furniture ranged from lacquered pieces to the use of tubular metal and steel rod.

HILLE, Ray

Born in Russia, came to Britain and worked in the First World War as a VAD she joined her father's company S. Hille & Co. as a furniture designer subsequently becoming Managing Director and Chair.

HOLDEN, Charles (1875–1960)

Architect who designed more than thirty stations for the London Passenger Transport Board and introduced certain aspects of the Modern Movement in them.

HOPE, Thomas (1769–1831)

Merchant, patron and author of *Household Furniture and Interior Decoration* (1807), a catalogue and guidebook to his London mansion, with its Egyptian, Roman and Greek room settings.

HOWARD, Ebenezer (1850–1928)

'Inventor' of the Garden City. The first garden city to be built was Letchworth, started in 1903 and designed by B. Parker and R. Unwin.

Jacobean

Early seventeenth century, of the period of King James I and VI.

Jasper Ware

A slightly translucent stoneware perfected by Wedgwood in 1775. Fine grained and hard, it could be stained, the most famous colour being Wedgwood blue.

JONES, Inigo (1573–1652)

Architect and stage designer who introduced the classical style to England from Italy. Among his important buildings are the Queen's House, Greenwich, the Banqueting House, Whitehall and the first London square at Covent Garden.

KENT, William (1645–1748)
Architect, painter, furniture designer and landscape gardener. Contributed to the development of informality in garden design at Chiswick House, London and elsewhere.

KRIER, Robert (1838–)
An important theorist of Post-Modernism and the urban environment, he has produced urban schemes for Vienna, Stuttgart, and Berlin. The Ritterstrasse Housing Scheme in West Berlin (1978–80) illustrates his theories of social housing. He is Professor of Architecture at Vienna Technical University with a practice in Vienna.

LE CORBUSIER, Charles Édouard (Jeanneret) (1887–1966)
One of the most influential of twentieth-century architects, designers and town planners, by virtue not only of his work, but also his writings.

LEACH, Bernard (1887–1979)
English studio potter who founded the Leach pottery at St Ives, Cornwall, and developed pottery forms based on both Eastern and Western traditions.

LOEWY, Raymond (1893–1986)
Flamboyant industrial designer whose office has been much involved in transport design. These include the Greyhound bus and Skylab.

MACDONALD, Margaret (1865–1933)
Trained at the Glasgow School of Art, worked as a designer, embroideress and metalworker and married C. R. Mackintosh in 1900. The attribution of her work thereafter is illustrative of the difficulties posed by husband-and-wife teams.

Machine Aesthetic
Advocated by many exponents of the Modern Movement, the machine aesthetic embraced references to transport and machinery and associated simple geometric forms with ease of mass production.

MACKINTOSH, Charles Rennie (1868–1928)
Architect and designer mainly associated with Glasgow. Designed many buildings including the Glasgow School of Art (1896) and with his wife Margaret Macdonald was involved in graphic, interior and furniture design.

McKNIGHT KAUFER, Edward (1890–1954)
American stage, graphic/textile designer who worked in England 1914–40 where he made his name as a poster designer.

MACMURDO, A. H. (1851–1942)
Architect and designer and founder, in 1882, of the Century Guild which was inspired by Ruskin and Morris.

MAGISTRETTI, Vico (1920–)
Italian architect and designer who has continually experimented with new forms and materials in seating and lighting.

MAJORELLE, Louis (1859–1926)
French cabinet maker and leading exponent of Art Nouveau furniture which was made in Nancy.

MAKEPEACE, John (1939–)
Furniture craftsman. Set up the Parnham School in Dorset, England, to promote and encourage craftsmanship in wood.

MEMPHIS, See Sotsass Jr, Ettore.

MIES VAN DER ROHE, Ludwig (1886–1969)

Active as an architect in Germany until 1938, when he moved to the USA. 'Less is more', one of his many aphorisms, sums up his quest to simplify his architectural language.

Modern Movement

An umbrella term for a number of avant-garde movements in architecture, art and design which occurred in Europe and the USSR in the early twentieth century. Colloquially, and incorrectly, the term is often limited to avant-garde architecture built in Germany and by Le Corbusier in the 1920s.

Modernism

See Modern Movement

MOHOLY-NAGY, Laszlo (1895–1946)

Joined the Bauhaus in 1922 and in the 1930s moved to London and then to USA where he established the New Bauhaus. This subsequently became the Chicago Institute of Design. His work included graphics, photography, painting, film and metalwork.

MORRIS, William (1834–96)

Of major influence on all areas of architecture and design from his writings and lectures, as well as his own work, and that of his firm, Morris, Marshall & Co. (later Morris & Co.).

Neo-Classicism

New Classicism, the revival of the principles of Greek and Roman architecture and design.

New Objectivity

A term associated with early-twentieth-century avant-garde movements in Europe and the USSR that were searching for a new language in architecture and design that had no historic precedent.

Pantheon

Major Roman religious building *c.*AD100–25 whose dome was an engineering feat of the time.

PAXTON, Joseph (1801–65)

Gardener, architect and designer of the iron and glass Crystal Palace (1851) for the first international exhibition ever to be held.

PERRET, Auguste (1874–1954)

French architect associated with bold experiments in the use of concrete.

Piazza

An open space, usually surrounded by buildings.

PICK, Frank (1878–1941)

Commercial manager of the London Passenger Transport Board, responsible for reorganizing its corporate identity through new station and interior design, and graphics.

Picturesque

A landscape or building which looked as if it has come out of a painting, particularly paintings in the style of Claude or Poussin. *C.*1790 it was defined as an aesthetic quality, between the sublime and the beautiful. In both landscape gardening and architecture picturesque qualities implied variety and diversity in forms and materials.

Glossary

Pilotis
Pillars, or stanchions. French term for the vertical supporting member of a building.

Point Block
A high-rise, commercial, industrial or residential building almost square, cruciform, or circular in cross-section, as compared with slab-blocks (rectangular in cross-section) or ribbon blocks (continuous blocks).

Post-Modernism
An umbrella term for architecture and design which show characteristics *not* espoused by the Modern Movement. Can include any kind of ornament and revived styles such as classicism, or neo-vernacular.

PUGIN, A.W.N. (1812–52)
Architect, designer and writer of enormous influence to the Gothic Revival, and to the development of an ethical approach to architecture and design.

Purism
A form of abstraction invented by Le Corbusier and A. Ozenfant and influential in the development of Le Corbusier's architectural language in the 1920s.

REPTON, Humphry (1752–1818)
Writer, theorist and practitioner of landscape gardening of the generation after Brown. Through his writings his ideas continued to be influential until well after the mid-nineteenth century.

Rococo
The last phase of the Baroque, the Rococo was a new form of decoration initiated in France, which was light, asymmetrical and abstract.

RUSKIN, John (1819–1900)
Writer, theorist and critic of enormous influence on nineteenth-century art, architecture and design.

SCOTT, Fred (1942–)
Trained as a cabinet maker and visited Scandinavia on a travelling scholarship. He joined Hille International as a freelance designer in 1969.

Shakers
A Christian sect founded in the late-eighteenth century in England and USA. American Shaker furniture reflected the sect's ideals in its simple forms and good craftsmanship.

SMITHSON, Alison (1928–) and **Peter** (1923–)
The partnership of Alison and Peter Smithson has been active in the field of architecture, design and writing since the 1950s when their school at Hunstanton, Norfolk (1954) caused considerable controversy.

SOTSASS, Ettore Jnr (1917–)
Architect, designer, writer, worked as an industrial designer for Olivetti since late 1950s. In 1981 Memphis, founded by Sotsass and others sought to challenge ideas and criteria relating to design.

TALBERT, B. J. (1838–81)
Scottish architect and designer influential for his wallpaper, furniture and metalwork designs.

Transept
The arms on either side of the crossing in a cruciform church.

TSCHICHOLD, Jan (1902–74)
Swiss typographer, lettering and book designer whose new typography, developed in the 1920s and 1930s, was very influential.

VITRUVIUS POLLIO, Marcus (active 46–39 BC)
Roman architect and writer of a ten-volume treatise on architecture, *De Architectura*. As the only complete Roman treatise to survive, this was very influential from the early Renaissance onwards.

VOYSEY, C. F. A. (1857–1941)
Architect and designer influenced generally by William Morris and Arthur Macmurdo. Voysey designed the furniture, metalwork and details of his country houses. He also designed wallpapers and textiles.

WEDGWOOD, Josiah (1730–95)
One of the most successful English potters and entrepreneurs whose influence was international.

WRIGHT, Frank Lloyd (1860–1959)
Internationally acclaimed American architect whose work spanned sixty years and ranged from the prairie houses in Chicago to the Imperial Hotel, Tokyo (1924), successfully designed to withstand earthquakes, and the Guggenheim Museum, New York (completed 1960), with its spiral ramp.

WYATT, Matthew Digby (1820–77)
Architect and architectural journalist involved in the circle of Henry Cole and in work on the 1851 Great Exhibition.

Index

Index

215

Index

The Confidence Book

Building

trust

in the

language

classroom

**Paul Davis
and Mario Rinvolucri**

Pilgrims

Longman

Longman Group UK Limited,
Longman House, Burnt Mill, Harlow,
Essex CM20 2JE, England
and Associated Companies throughout the world.

© Longman Group UK Limited 1990

This book is produced in association
with Pilgrims Language Courses Limited
of Canterbury, England.

First published 1990
Fourth impression 1995

Set in Linotron 10/12pt Cheltenham

Produced by Longman Singapore Publishers Pte Ltd
Printed in Singapore

British Library Cataloguing in Publication Data
Davis, Paul *1952-*
   The confidence book: Building trust in the language
   classroom – (Pilgrims Longman teachers resource
   books)
   1. Non-English speaking students.
   Curriculum subjects: English language. Teaching
   I. Title II. Rinvolucri, Mario III. Series
   428.2407

ISBN 0582 03766 2

Acknowledgements
We are grateful to the following for permission to
reproduce copyright material;

Cambridge University Press & University of Cambridge
Local Examination Syndicate for extracts from the
examination paper *First Certificate in English, Paper 1
Reading Comprehension* 14.6.88, morning; International
Universities Press, Inc for an extract from *Children Tell
Stories* by E G Pitcher & E Prelinger (1969); the author,
Leon Leszek Szkutnik for extracts from *Thinking in
English* (Panstwowe Wydawhictwo Nauhowe, 1986).

We are grateful to Stuart Oglethorpe for permission to
reproduce the photograph of Paul Davis on page iv.

Illustrations
Cover illustrated by Michael Sheehy